Mercedes-Benz 230, 250 and 280 Owners Workshop Manual

by J H Haynes
Member of the Guild of Motoring Writers
and P G Strasman
MISTC

Models covered
UK
　250 Saloon and Coupe. 2496 cc
　280 Saloon, Coupe and Roadster. 2778 cc
USA
　230 Sedan. 139 cu in (2292 cc)
　250 Sedan and Coupe. 152 cu in (2496 cc)
　280 Sedan, Coupe and Roadster. 170 cu in (2778 cc)

Series 108, 111, 113 and 114 carburettor and fuel injection models with six cylinder sohc engine

ISBN 978 0 85733 614 9

Haynes Group Limited
Haynes North America, Inc

www.haynes.com

Acknowledgements

Special thanks are due to Mercedes-Benz NA Inc., for the supply of technical information and certain illustrations.

Castrol Limited supplied the lubrication data and the Champion Sparking Plug Company supplied the photographs of various spark plug conditions. The bodywork repair photographs used in this manual were provided by Lloyds Industries Limited who supply 'Turtle Wax', 'Dupli-color Holts', and other Holts range products.

Lastly, thanks are due to all those people at Sparkford who helped in the production of this manual. Particularly Brian Horsfall who undertook the mechanical work, Leon Martindale (Member of Master Photographers) and Les Brazier who shared the photographic work, John Rose who edited the text and Stanley Randolph for planning the layout of each page.

About this manual

Its aims

The aim of this book is to help you get the best value from your car. It can do so in two ways. First it can help you decide what work must be done (even should you choose to get it done by a garage), the routine maintenance and the diagnosis and course of action when random faults occur. It is hoped that you will also use the second and fuller purpose by tackling the work yourself. This can give you the satisfaction of doing the job yourself. On the simpler jobs it may even be quicker than booking the car into a garage and going there twice, to leave and collect it. Perhaps most important, much money can be saved by avoiding the costs a garage must charge to cover their labour and overheads.

The book has drawings and descriptions to show the function of the various components so that their layout can be understood. Then the tasks are described and photographed in a step-by-step sequence so that even a novice can cope with complicated work. Such a person is the very one to buy a car needing repair yet be unable to afford garage costs.

The jobs are described assuming only normal spanners are available, and not special tools, but a reasonable outfit of tools will be a worthwhile investment. Many special workshop tools produced by the makers merely speed the work, and in these cases guidance is given as to how to do the job without them. On a very few occasions the special tool is essential to prevent damage to components, then its use is described. Though it might be possible to borrow the tool, such work may have to be entrusted to the official agent.

To reduce labour costs a garage will often give a cheaper repair by fitting a reconditioned assembly. The home mechanic can be helped by this book to diagnose the fault and make a repair using only a minor spare part.

The manufacturer's official workshop manuals are written for their trained staff, and so assume special knowledge; detail is left out. This book is written for the owner, and so goes into detail.

Using this manual

The book is divided into twelve Chapters. Each Chapter is divided into numbered Sections which are headed in **bold type** between horizontal lines. Each Section consists of serially numbered paragraphs.

There are two types of illustration: (1) Figures which are numbered according to Chapter and sequence of occurrence in that Chapter. (2) Photographs which have a reference number on their caption. All photographs apply to the Chapter in which they occur so that the reference figure pinpoints the pertinent Section and paragraph number.

Procedures, once described in the text, are not normally repeated. If it is necessary to refer to another Chapter the reference will be given in Chapter number and Section number. Cross references given without use of the word 'Chapter' apply to Sections and/or paragraphs in the same Chapter.

When the left or right side of the car is mentioned it is as if looking forward from the rear of the car.

Whilst every care is taken to ensure that the information in this manual is correct no liability can be accepted by the authors or publishers for loss, damage or injury caused by any errors in, or omissions from, the information given.

Contents

In addition each Chapter contains, where applicable: specifications, general description and fault diagnosis.

Use of English

As this book has been written in England, it uses the appropriate English component names, phrases, and spelling. Some of these differ from those used in America. Normally, these cause no difficulty, but to make sure, a glossary is printed below. In ordering spare parts remember the parts list may use some of these words:

English	American	English	American
Accelerator	Gas pedal	Locks	Latches
Aerial	Antenna	Methylated spirit	Denatured alcohol
Anti-roll bar	Stabiliser or sway bar	Motorway	Freeway, turnpike etc
Big-end bearing	Rod bearing	Number plate	License plate
Bonnet (engine cover)	Hood	Paraffin	Kerosene
Boot (luggage compartment)	Trunk	Petrol	Gasoline (gas)
Bulkhead	Firewall	Petrol tank	Gas tank
Bush	Bushing	'Pinking'	'Pinging'
Cam follower or tappet	Valve lifter or tappet	Prise (force apart)	Pry
Carburettor	Carburetor	Propeller shaft	Driveshaft
Catch	Latch	Quarterlight	Quarter window
Choke/venturi	Barrel	Retread	Recap
Circlip	Snap-ring	Reverse	Back-up
Clearance	Lash	Rocker cover	Valve cover
Crownwheel	Ring gear (of differential)	Saloon	Sedan
Damper	Shock absorber, shock	Seized	Frozen
Disc (brake)	Rotor/disk	Sidelight	Parking light
Distance piece	Spacer	Silencer	Muffler
Drop arm	Pitman arm	Sill panel (beneath doors)	Rocker panel
Drop head coupe	Convertible	Small end, little end	Piston pin or wrist pin
Dynamo	Generator (DC)	Spanner	Wrench
Earth (electrical)	Ground	Split cotter (for valve spring cap)	Lock (for valve spring retainer)
Engineer's blue	Prussian blue	Split pin	Cotter pin
Estate car	Station wagon	Steering arm	Spindle arm
Exhaust manifold	Header	Sump	Oil pan
Fault finding/diagnosis	Troubleshooting	Swarf	Metal chips or debris
Float chamber	Float bowl	Tab washer	Tang or lock
Free-play	Lash	Tappet	Valve lifter
Freewheel	Coast	Thrust bearing	Throw-out bearing
Gearbox	Transmission	Top gear	High
Gearchange	Shift	Torch	Flashlight
Grub screw	Setscrew, Allen screw	Trackrod (of steering)	Tie-rod (or connecting rod)
Gudgeon pin	Piston pin or wrist pin	Trailing shoe (of brake)	Secondary shoe
Halfshaft	Axleshaft	Transmission	Whole drive line
Handbrake	Parking brake	Tyre	Tire
Hood	Soft top	Van	Panel wagon/van
Hot spot	Heat riser	Vice	Vise
Indicator	Turn signal	Wheel nut	Lug nut
Interior light	Dome lamp	Windscreen	Windshield
Layshaft (of gearbox)	Countershaft	Wing/mudguard	Fender
Leading shoe (of brake)	Primary shoe		

Introduction to the Mercedes-Benz

The range of cars covered by this manual differs widely in body style but mechanically the cars are very similar. All power units are of the six cylinder in-line single overhead camshaft type with either carburettors or a fuel injection system.

The Mercedes-Benz is undoubtedly rugged and carefully constructed with attention to detail and safety aspects.

Due to its very size, the car may seem complicated but it is quite conventional and should not present the home mechanic with any problems, provided he possesses adequate lifting and jacking equipment and realises that most major operations will take longer than would be the case with a smaller and less sophisticated vehicle.

General Dimensions

Model	Wheel Base	Overall Length	Overall Width	Kerb Weight +
230 Saloon 250 Saloon 250 Coupe	108.3 in (2750 mm)	184.4 in (4685 mm)	69.7 in (1770 mm)	*2944 lb (1335 kg) **3000 lb (1360 kg)
* 230 Saloon with M180 engine 2965 lb (1345 kg) ** 250 Saloon with fuel injection 3045 lb (1380 kg)				
250 SL 280 SL	94.5 in (2400 mm)	168.7 in (4285 mm)	69.3 in (1760 mm)	2999 lb (1360 kg)
280 Saloons	108.3 in (2750 mm)	192.9 in (4900 mm)	71.3 in (1810 mm)	with carburettor 3220 lb (1460 kg) with fuel injection 3270 lb (1483 kg)

+These weights must only be regarded as asguide. The kerb weight may vary according to the type of transmission used, whether air conditioning is fitted and the emission control system - consult your particular vehicle sticker.

Capacities

	Imperial Measure	U.S. Measure	Metric Measure
Engine			
Sump	9.7 pints	11.5 pints	5.5 litres
Filter	0.9 pints	1.0 pints	0.5 litres
Cooler	0.9 pints	1.0 pints	0.5 litres
Total	11.5 pints	13.5 pints	6.5 litres
Cooling system			
230/8 models	19.0 pints	23.0 pints	10.8 litres
250 models	17.4 pints	20.9 pints	9.9 litres
280 models	18.8 pints	22.6 pints	10.7 litres
*Fuel tank			
Except 250C and 280 Series	14.3 gal	17.25 gal	65.0 litres
250C and 280 Series	18.0 gal	21.5 gal	82.0 litres
Certain models have a reserve of 2.64 Imp gal (3.1 US gal, 12.0 litres)			
Manual transmission			
Type G72	3.2 pints	3.8 pints	1.4 litres
Type G76/18	5.1 pints	6.1 pints	1.6 litres
Type G76/27 (4 speed)	5.3 pints	6.3 pints	1.8 litres
(5 speed)	7.5 pints	9.0 pints	2.5 litres
ZF S520	3.5 pints	4.2 pints	1.1 litres
Automatic transmission			
Routine drain and refill with change of filter	6.6 pints	7.9 pints	3.75 litres
Filling new unit from dry	9.5 pints	11.4 pints	5.3 litres
Rear axle			
With enclosed axle shafts	4.4 pints	5.3 pints	2.5 litres
With open axle shafts	2.0 pints	2.4 pints	1.15 litres
Steering			
Manual	0.5 pints	0.6 pints	0.3 litres
Power (including reservoir)	2.5 pints	3.0 pints	1.4 litres

The Mercedes-Benz 280SL Roadster used as the project car for this manual

Buying spare parts
and vehicle identification numbers

Buying spare parts

Replacement parts are available from many sources, which generally fall into one of two categories – authorized dealer parts departments and independent retail auto parts stores. Our advice concerning these parts is as follows:

Retail auto parts stores: Good auto parts stores will stock frequently needed components which wear out relatively fast, such as clutch components, exhaust systems, brake parts, tune-up parts, etc. These stores often supply new or reconditioned parts on an exchange basis, which can save a considerable amount of money. Discount auto parts stores are often very good places to buy materials and parts needed for general vehicle maintenance such as oil, grease, filters, spark plugs, belts, touch-up paint, bulbs, etc. They also usually sell tools and general accessories, have convenient hours, charge lower prices and can often be found not far from home.

Authorized dealer parts department: This is the best source for parts which are unique to the vehicle and not generally available elsewhere (such as major engine parts, transmission parts, trim pieces, etc.).

Warranty information: If the vehicle is still covered under warranty, be sure that any replacement parts purchased – regardless of the source – do not invalidate the warranty!

To be sure of obtaining the correct parts, have engine and chassis numbers available and, if possible, take the old parts along for positive identification.

Vehicle identification numbers

Modifications are a continuing and unpublicized process in vehicle manufacture quite apart from major model changes. Spare parts manuals and lists are compiled upon a numerical basis, the individual vehicle number being essential to correct identification of the component required.

The *vehicle identification plate* is fixed to the engine compartment rear firewall and includes the vehicle number. This number is repeated on the top of the instrument panel just inside the windshield on North American vehicles (photo).

The *engine number* is stamped into the cylinder block on a machined surface just below the spark plugs. On North American vehicles, a sticker or decal may be affixed to the door edge or body pillar giving additional information on tune-up and dimensional and weight details (photo).

Vehicle identification plate

Engine number

Tools and working facilities

Introduction

The nuts and bolts used in the models covered by this manual are to Metric specification generally but a few components are secured by AF fixings.

A very large number of socket-headed screws are used and it is essential that a good set of Metric Allen keys is available before working on the car.

A selection of good tools is a fundamental requirement for anyone contemplating the maintenance and repair of a motor vehicle. For the owner who does not possess any, their purchase will prove a considerable expense, offsetting some of the savings made by doing-it-yourself. However, provided that the tools purchased meet the relevant national safety standards and are of good quality, they will last for many years and prove an extremely worthwhile investment.

To help the average owner to decide which tools are needed to carry out the various tasks detailed in this manual, we have compiled three lists of tools under the following headings: *Maintenance and minor repair, Repair and overhaul* and *Special*. The newcomer to practical mechanics should start off with the *Maintenance and minor repair tool kit* and confine himself to the simpler jobs around the vehicle. Then, as his confidence and experience grows, he can undertake more difficult tasks, buying extra tools as, and when, they are needed. In this way a *Maintenance and minor repair tool kit* can be built up into a *Repair and overhaul tool kit* over a considerable period of time without any major cash outlays. The experienced do-it-yourselfer will have a tool kit good enough for most repairs and overhaul procedures, and will add tools from the *Special* category when he feels the expense is justified by the amount of use to which these tools will be put.

It is obviously not possible to cover the subject of tools fully here. For those who wish to learn more about tools and their use there is a book entitled *How to Choose and Use Car Tools* available from the publishers of this manual.

Maintenance and minor repair tool kit

The tools given in this list should be considered as a minimum requirement if routine maintenance, servicing and minor repair operations are to be undertaken. We recommend the purchase of combination spanners (ring one end, open-ended the other); although more expensive than open-ended ones, they do give the advantages of both types of spanner.

> *Combination spanners - 6, 7, 8, 9, 10, 11 and 12 mm*
> *Adjustable spanner - 9 inch*
> *Engine sump/gearbox/rear axle drain plug key (where applicable)*
> *Spark plug spanner (with rubber insert)*
> *Spark plug gap adjustment tool*
> *Set of feeler gauges*
> *Brake adjuster spanner (where applicable)*
> *Brake bleed nipple spanner*
> *Screwdriver - 4 in. long x ¼ in. dia. (flat blade)*
> *Screwdriver - 4 in. long x ¼ in. dia. (cross blade)*
> *Combination pliers - 6 inch*
> *Hacksaw, junior*
> *Tyre pump*
> *Tyre pressure gauge*
> *Grease gun (where applicable)*
> *Oil can*
> *Fine emery cloth (1 sheet)*
> *Wire brush (small)*
> *Funnel (medium size)*

Repair and overhaul tool kit

These tools are virtually essential for anyone undertaking any major repairs to a motor vehicle, and are additional to those given in the *Maintenance and minor repair* list. Included in this list is a comprehensive set of sockets. Although these are expensive they will be found invaluable as they are so versatile - particularly if various drives are included in the set. We recommend the ½ in square-drive type, as this can be used with most proprietary torque wrenches. If you cannot afford a socket set, even bought piecemeal, then inexpensive tubular box spanners are a useful alternative.

The tools in this list will occasionally need to be supplemented by tools from the *Special list*.

> *Sockets (or box spanners) to cover range in previous list*
> *Reversible ratchet drive (for use with sockets)*
> *Extension piece, 10 inch (for use with sockets)*
> *Universal joint (for use with sockets)*
> *Torque wrench (for use with sockets)*
> *'Mole' wrench - 8 inch*
> *Ball pein hammer*
> *Soft-faced hammer, plastic or rubber*
> *Screwdriver - 6 in. long x 5/16 in. dia. (flat blade)*
> *Screwdriver - 2 in. long x 5/16 in. square (flat blade)*
> *Screwdriver - 1½ in. long x ¼ in. dia. (cross blade)*
> *Screwdriver - 3 in. long x 1/8 in. dia. (electricians)*
> *Pliers - electricians side cutters*
> *Pliers - needle noses*
> *Pliers - circlip (internal and external)*
> *Cold chisel - ½ inch*
> *Scriber (this can be made by grinding the end of a broken hacksaw blade)*
> *Scraper (this can be made by flattening and sharpening one end of a piece of copper pipe)*
> *Centre punch*
> *Pin punch*
> *Hacksaw*
> *Valve grinding tool*
> *Steel rule/straight edge*
> *Allen keys*
> *Selection of files*
> *Wire brush (large)*
> *Axle stands*
> *Jack (strong scissor or hydraulic type)*

Special tools

The tools in this list are those which are not used regularly, are expensive to buy, or which need to be used in accordance with their manufacturer's instructions. Unless relatively difficult mechanical jobs are undertaken frequently, it will not be economic to buy many of these tools. Where this is the case, you could consider clubbing together with friends (or motorists club) to make a joint purchase, or borrowing the tools against a deposit from a local garage or tool hire specialist.

The following list contains only those tools and instruments freely available to the public, and not those special tools produced by the vehicle manufacturer specifically for its dealer network. You will find occasional references to these manufacturer's special tools in the text of this manual. Generally, an alternative method of doing the job without the vehicle manufacturer's special tool is given. However, sometimes, there is no alternative to using them. Where this is the case and the relevant tool cannot be bought or borrowed you will have to entrust the work to a franchised garage.

> Valve spring compressor
> Piston ring compressor
> Balljoint separator
> Universal hub/bearing puller
> Impact screwdriver
> Micrometer and/or vernier gauge
> Carburettor flow balancing device (where applicable)
> Dial gauge
> Stroboscopic timing light
> Dwell angle meter/tachometer
> Universal electrical multi-meter
> Cylinder compression gauge
> Lifting tackle
> Trolley jack
> Light with extension lead

Last, but not least, always keep a supply of old newspapers and clean, lint-free rags available, and try to keep any working area as clean as possible.

Buying tools

For practically all tools, a tool factor is the best source since he will have a very comprehensive range compared with the average garage or accessory shop. Having said that, accessory shops often offer excellent quality tools at discount prices, so it pays to shop around.

There are plenty of good tools around at reasonable prices, but always aim to purchase items which meet the relevant national safety standards. If in doubt, ask the proprietor or manager of the shop for advice before making a purchase.

Care and maintenance of tools

Having purchased a reasonable tool kit, it is necessary to keep the tools in a clean and serviceable condition. After use, always wipe off any dirt, grease and metal particles using a clean, dry cloth, before putting the tools away. Never leave them lying around after they have been used. A simple tool rack on the garage or workshop wall, for items such as screwdrivers and pliers, is a good idea. Store all normal spanners and sockets in a metal box. Any measuring instruments, gauges, meters, etc., must be carefully stored where they cannot be damaged or become rusty.

Take a little care when the tools are used. Hammer heads inevitably become marked and screwdrivers lose the keen edge on their blades from time-to-time. A little timely attention with emery cloth or a file will soon restore items like this to a good serviceable finish.

Use of tools

Throughout this book various phrases describing techniques are used, such as:

'Drive out the bearing'
'Undo the flange bolts evenly and diagonally'

When two parts are held together by a number of bolts round their edges, these must be tightened to draw the parts down together flat. They must be slackened evenly to prevent the component warping. Initially the bolts should be put in finger-tight only. Then they should be tightened gradually, at first only a turn each; and diagonally, doing the one opposite that tightened first, then one to a side, followed by another opposite that, and so on. The second time each bolt is tightened, only half a turn should be given. The third time round, only quarter of a turn is given each, and this is kept up till tight. The reverse sequence is used to slacken them.

If any part has to be 'driven', such as a ball bearing out of its housing, without a proper press, it can be done with a hammer provided a few rules for use of a hammer are remembered. Always keep the component being driven straight so it will not jam. Shield whatever is being hit from damage by the hammer. Soft headed hammers are available. A drift can be used, or if the item being hit is soft, use wood. Aluminium is very easily damaged. Steel is a bit better. Hard steel, such as a bearing race, is very strong. Something threaded at the end must be protected by fitting a nut. But do not hammer the nut: the threads will tear.

If levering items with makeshift arrangement, such as screwdrivers, irretrievable damage can be done. Be sure the lever rests either on something that does not matter, or put in padding. Burrs can be filed off afterwards. But indentations are there for good, and can cause leaks.

When holding something in a vice, the jaws must go on a part that is strong. If the indentation from the jaw teeth will matter, then lead or fibre protectors must be used. Hollow sections are liable to be crushed.

Nuts that will not undo will sometimes move if the spanner handle is extended with another. But only extend a ring spanner, not an open jaw one. A hammer blow either to the spanner, or the bolt, may jump it out of its contact: the bolt locally welds itself in place. In extreme cases the nut will undo if driven off with drift and hammer. When reassembling such bolts, tighten them normally, not by the method needed to undo them.

For pressing things, such as a sleeve bearing into its housing, a vice, or an electric drill stand, make good presses. Pressing tools to hold each component can be arranged by using such things as socket spanners, or short lengths of steel water pipe. Long bolts with washers can be used to draw things into place rather than pressing them.

There are often several ways of doing something. If stuck, stop and think. Special tools can readily be made out of odd bits of scrap. Accordingly, at the same time as building up a tool kit, collect useful bits of steel.

Normally all nuts or bolts have some locking arrangement. The most common is a spring washer. There are tab washers that are bent up. Castellated nuts have split pins. Self-locking nuts have special crowns that resist shaking loose. Self-locking nuts should not be reused, as the self-locking action is weakened as soon as they have been loosened at all. Tab washers should only be reused when they can be bent over in a new place. If you find a nut without any locking arrangement, check what it is meant to have.

Working facilities

Not to be forgotten when discussing tools, is the workshop itself. If anything more than routine maintenance is to be carried out, some form of suitable working area becomes essential.

It is appreciated that many an owner mechanic is forced by circumstances to remove an engine or similar item, without the benefit of a garage or workshop. Having done this, any repairs should always be done under the cover of a roof.

Wherever possible, any dismantling should be done on a clean flat workbench or table at a suitable working height.

Any workbench needs a vice: one with a jaw opening of 4 in (100 mm) is suitable for most jobs. As mentioned previously, some clean dry storage space is also required for tools, as well as the lubricants, cleaning fluids, touch-up paints and so on which soon become necessary.

Another item which may be required, and which has a much more general usage, is an electric drill with a chuck capacity of at least 5/16 in (8 mm). This together with a good range of twist drills, is virtually essential for fitting accessories such as wing mirrors and reversing lights.

Spanner jaw gap comparison table

Jaw gap (in.)	Spanner size
0.250	¼ in. AF
0.275	7 mm AF
0.312	5/16 in. AF
0.315	8 mm AF
0.340	11/32 in. AF; 1/8 in. Whitworth
0.354	9 mm AF
0.375	3/8 in. AF
0.393	10 mm AF
0.433	11 mm AF
0.437	7/16 in. AF
0.445	3/16 in. Whitworth; ¼ in. BSF
0.472	12 mm AF
0.500	½ in. AF
0.512	13 mm AF
0.525	¼ in. Whitworth; 5/16 in. BSF
0.551	14 mm AF
0.562	9/16 in. AF
0.590	15 mm AF
0.600	5/16 in. Whitworth; 3/8 in. BSF
0.625	5/8 in. AF
0.629	16 mm AF

Jaw gap (in.)	Spanner size	Jaw gap (in.)	Spanner size
0.669	17 mm AF	1.259	32 mm AF
0.687	11/16 in. AF	1.300	¾ in. Whitworth; 7/8 in. BSF
0.708	18 mm AF	1.312	1 5/16 in. AF
0.710	3/8 in. Whitworth; 7/16 in. BSF	1.390	13/16 in. Whitworth; 15/16 in. BSF
0.748	19 mm AF	1.417	36 mm AF
0.750	¾ in. AF	1.437	1 7/16 in. AF
0.812	13/16 in. AF	1.480	7/8 in. Whitworth; 1 in. BSF
0.820	7/16 in. Whitworth; ½ in. BSF	1.500	1 ½ in. AF
0.866	22 mm AF	1.574	40 mm AF; 15/16 in. Whitworth
0.875	7/8 in. AF	1.614	41 mm AF
0.920	½ in. Whitworth; 9/16 in. BSF	1.625	1 5/8 in. AF
0.937	15/16 in. AF	1.670	1 in. Whitworth; 1 1/8 in. BSF
0.944	24 mm AF	1.687	1 11/16 in. AF
1.000	1 in. AF	1.811	46 mm AF
1.010	9/16 in. Whitworth; 5/8 in. BSF	1.812	1 13/16 in. AF
1.023	26 mm AF	1.860	1 1/8 in. Whitworth; 1 ¼ in. BSF
1.062	1 1/16 in. AF; 27 mm AF	1.875	1 7/8 in. AF
1.100	5/8 in. Whitworth; 11/16 in. BSF	1.968	50 mm AF
1.125	1 1/8 in. AF	2.000	2 in. AF
1.181	30 mm AF	2.050	1 ¼ in. Whitworth; 1 3/8 in. BSF
1.200	11/16 in. Whitworth; ¾ in. BSF	2.165	55 mm AF
1.250	1 ¼ in. AF	2.362	60 mm AF

Routine maintenance

Maintenance is essential for ensuring safety and desirable for the purpose of getting the best in terms of performance and economy from the car. Over the years the need for periodic lubrication - oiling, greasing and so on - has been drastically reduced if not totally eliminated. This has unfortunately tended to lead some owners to think that because no such action is required the items either no longer exist or will last for ever. This is a serious delusion. It follows therefore that the largest initial element of maintenance is visual examination. This may lead to repairs or renewals.

Every 250 miles (400 km) or weekly

Check tyre pressures and inflate if necessary.
Check and top-up engine oil (photo).
Check and top-up battery electrolyte level.
Check and top-up windscreen washer fluid level.
Check and top-up coolant level.
Check operation of all lights.

After first 500 miles (800 km) after major engine overhaul

Check torque of cylinder head bolts.
Adjust valve clearances.
Check tightness of all other bolts and nuts which were disturbed at overhaul.
Change engine oil and filter.
Adjust engine idling speed.

Every 3,000 miles (4,800 km)

Lubricate suspension linkage (photos).
Check fluid level in brake and clutch hydraulic reservoirs and top-up if necessary.
Check oil bath type air cleaner (if fitted) oil level and top-up.

Every 6,000 miles (9,600 km)

Change engine oil and renew filter.
Check carburettor adjustment or fuel injection system.
Check emission control system.
Check and adjust drivebelt tension.
Clean and re-gap spark plugs.
Clean, adjust or renew contact breaker points in distributor.
Check ignition timing.
Check and top-up manual gearbox or automatic transmission fluid level (photo).
Check for wear in steering linkage joints and condition of flexible dust excluders.
Check and top-up power steering fluid level (photo).
Check clutch pedal free movement and adjust if necessary.
Check wear in brake disc pads.
Inspect brake hydraulic system hoses and pipes for leakage, corrosion or deterioration.
Lubricate door hinges and controls.
Renew fuel line filter.
Clean dirt from rear axle casing breather (left-hand axle tube - enclosed type axleshafts).
Inspect tyres for tread wear, damage and remove any embedded flints.
Clean flame trap and moisture separator (crankcase ventilation system).

Topping up engine oil

Greasing front suspension (king pin type stub axle)

Greasing front suspension (king pin stub axle)

Greasing front suspension (king pin stub axle)

Greasing front suspension (king pin stub axle)

Checking auto transmission fluid level

Topping up power steering fluid level

Renew spark plugs.
Top-up manual steering box oil level.
Change manual transmission fluid.
Check rear axle lubricant level.
Clean, repack with fresh grease and adjust, front wheel bearings.
Lubricate distributor (shaft felt pad up to 1970 only).
Adjust parking brake shoes.
Have front wheel alignment and steering angles checked.
Have headlight beams aligned.

Every 30,000 miles (48,000 km)

Check operation of shock absorbers.
Renew automatic transmission fluid and filter.
Check parking brake shoe linings.
Renew air cleaner element.
Change rear axle (differential) oil.

Annually

Renew coolant antifreeze mixture.

Every two years

Bleed both brake hydraulic circuits and refill with fresh fluid.
Renew windscreen wiper blade rubber inserts.
Renew the brake servo unit air filter.

Every 12,000 miles (19,300 km)

Clean air cleaner element by tapping or with compressed air.

Jacking and towing

1   **The jack supplied in the car tool kit** should be used only for emergency roadwheel changing in the event of a flat tyre.
2   Apply the handbrake fully and, if possible, chock the opposite roadwheels.
3   Prise off the hub cap and release but do not remove, the wheel bolts.
4   Insert the jack into the hole provided in the bodysill and raise the car until the roadwheel is clear of the ground (Fig. 1).
5   Unscrew and remove the wheel bolts and remove the roadwheel.
6   Fit the spare wheel onto the hub and insert the bolts finger tight. If a centring bolt is provided in the tool kit, this can be used to align the bolt holes (Fig. 2).
7   Lower the car to the ground, remove the jack and fully tighten the roadwheel bolts. Refit the hub cap.

8   When carrying out repairs and maintenance, use a hydraulic or screw jack, preferably of the trolley type. The jack should be located under the front crossmember to raise the front wheels, using a wooden block as an insulator to prevent damage to the crossmember.
9   To raise the rear of the car, place the jack under the differential housing (open axleshafts) or under the axle casings on the enclosed type axleshaft rear axle. Never jack up under the rear suspension link arms.
10 The bodysill jacking points may be used to raise either side of the car, provided there is no chance of the jack slipping off them.
11 Always supplement the jack with axle stands when working under the car.
12 When being towed, if the car is equipped with automatic transmission then the towing speed must be restricted to 30 mph (50 kmh)

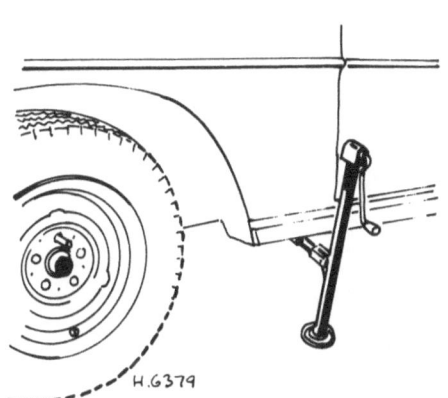

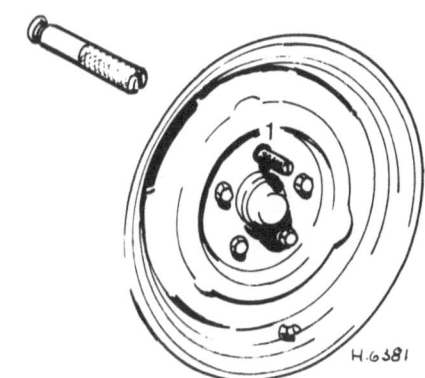

Fig. 1. Raising the car with the jack supplied with the tool kit

Fig. 2. Roadwheel alignment tool   1 Tool in position

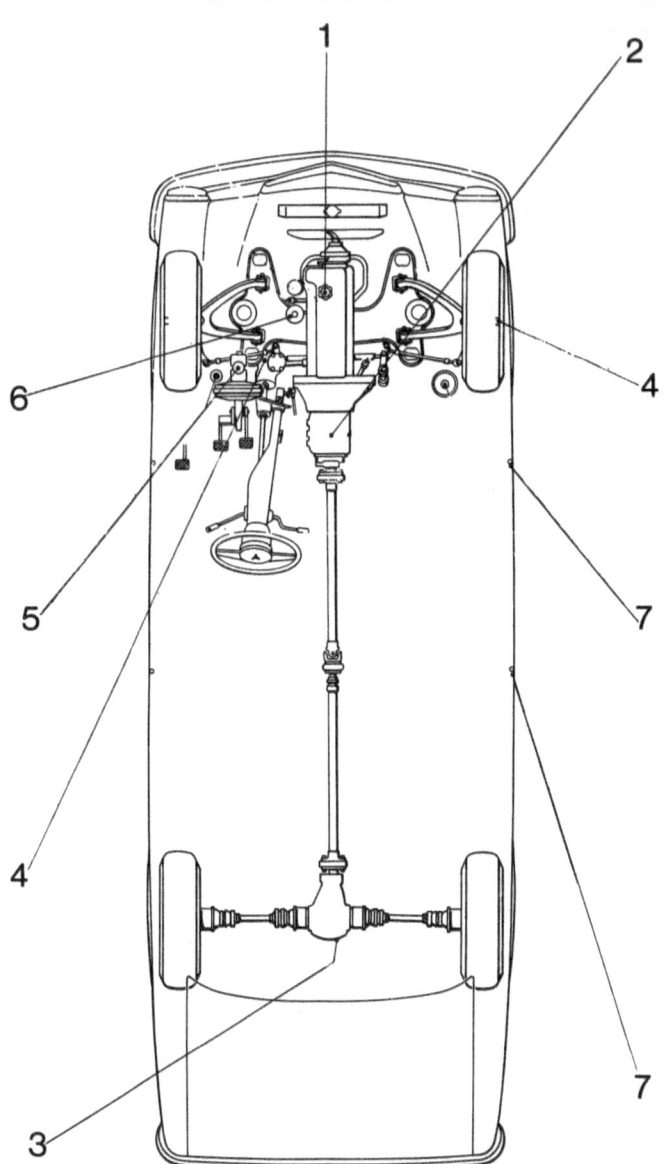

Typical lubrication
diagram for 230 and 250 models

Component												Lubricant
Engine (1)	...	...	...	...	...	...	...	...	...	...	...	Castrol GTX
Gearbox (2)												
Manual	...	...	...	...	...	...	...	...	...	...	...	Castrol TQ
Automatic	...	...	...	...	...	...	...	...	...	...	...	Castrol TQ
Rear axle (3)	...	...	...	...	...	...	...	...	...	...	...	Castrol Hypoy B
Front wheel bearings (4)		...	...	...	...	...	...	...	...	...	...	Castrol LM Grease
Brake and clutch systems (5)	...	...	...	...	...	...	...	...	...	...	...	Castrol Girling Universal Brake and Clutch Fluid
Power steering (6)		...	...	...	...	...	...	...	...	...	...	Castrol TQ
Door hinges etc (7)		...	...	...	...	...	...	...	...	...	...	Castrol LM Grease

The above are general recommendations only. Different territories require different lubricants. If in doubt consult your nearest Mercedes-Benz dealer or the Driver's Handbook supplied with the car.

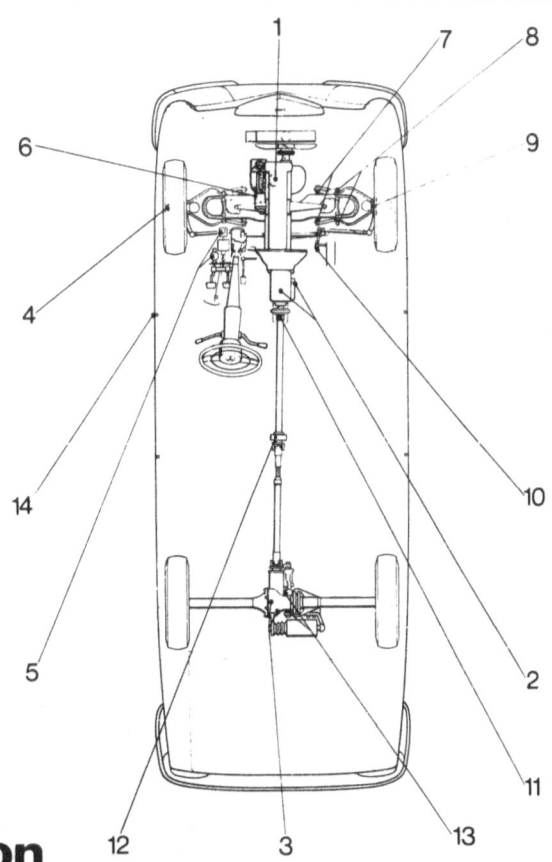

Typical lubrication diagram for 280 models

Component												Lubricant
Engine (1)	...	...	...	...	...	...	...	...	...	...	...	Castrol GTX
Gearbox (2)												
Manual	...	...	...	...	...	...	...	...	...	...	...	Castrol TQ
Automatic	...	...	...	...	...	...	...	...	...	...	...	Castrol TQ
Rear axle (3)	...	...	...	...	...	...	...	...	...	...	...	Castrol Hypoy B
Front wheel bearings (4)	...	...	...	...	...	...	...	...	...	...	Castrol LM Grease
Brake and clutch systems (5)	...	...	...	...	...	...	...	...	...	Castrol Girling Universal Brake and Clutch Fluid
Fuel injection pump (6)	...	...	...	...	...	...	...	...	...	...	Castrol GTX

The grease nipple positions are as follows:

Component												Lubricant
Lower wishbone (7)	...	...	...	...	...	...	...	...	...	...	Castrol LM Grease
Upper wishbone (8)	...	...	...	...	...	...	...	...	...	...	Castrol LM Grease
Steering knuckle (9)	...	...	...	...	...	...	...	...	...	...	Castrol LM Grease
Intermediate steering lever (10)	...	...	...	...	...	...	...	...	...	Castrol LM Grease
Front universal joint (11)	...	...	...	...	...	...	...	...	...	Castrol LM Grease
Centre universal joint (12) (unless maintenance free)	...	...	...	...	...	...	...	...	...	Castrol LM Grease
Rear axle (13)	...	...	...	...	...	...	...	...	...	...	Castrol LM Grease
Door hinge (14)	...	...	...	...	...	...	...	...	...	...	Castrol LM Grease

The above are general recommendations only. Different territories require different lubricants. If in doubt consult your nearest Mercedes-Benz dealer or the Driver's Handbook supplied with the car.

Chapter 1 Engine

Contents

Specifications

Engine ... ... Six cylinder in-line, single overhead camshaft

Application

Type	Car model
M180	230/8
M114	250/8
	250 SE
	250 SL
	250 CE
M130V	250/8
	250 C
	280 S/8
M130	280 SL
M130E	280 SE/8
	280 SEL/8
	280 SL/8

Engine data

		Engine type	
	M180	M114	M130
Bore	3.22 in (81.75 mm)	3.23 in (82.0 mm)	3.41 in (86.5 mm)
Stroke	2.87 in (72.8 mm)	3.10 in (78.8 mm)	3.10 in (78.8 mm)
Capacity	139.6 cu in (2292 cc)	152.4 cu in (2496 cc)	169.5 cu in (2778 cc)
Firing order	1 - 5 - 3 - 6 - 2 - 4	1 - 5 - 3 - 6 - 2 - 4	1 - 5 - 3 - 6 - 2 - 4
Compression ratio	9 : 1	9 : 1	9 : 1 (280 S/8 and 280 SEL/8 9.5 : 1)

Engine output

Maximum brake horsepower (hp & rev/min)

230/8	135/5600		
250SE - 250SL - 250CE - 250/8 ...	—		
250/8 - 250C - 250S/8 - 280S/8 ...		146/5600	
280SL - 280SE/8 - 280SEL/8 -			157/5400
280SL/8			180/5750

Maximum torque
(lb/ft @ rev/min)

Model				
230/8		145/3800		
250SE - 250SL - 250CE - 250/8 ...			161/3800	
250/8 - 250C - 250S/8 - 280S/8 ...				181/3100
280SL - 280SE/8 - 280SEL/8				
280SL/8				193/4500

Note: All the following manufacturing tolerances and dimensions are to metric sizes.

Crankshaft and main bearings

Number of main bearings	7 except M180 engine which has 4
Main journal diameter	59.955 to 59.965 mm
Main bearing running clearance	0.045 to 0.065 mm
Crankshaft end float	0.100 to 0.240 mm
Crankpin diameter	47.955 to 47.965 mm
Big-end bearing running clearance	0.035 to 0.055 mm
Connecting rod side float	0.110 to 0.260 mm

Connecting rods

Big-end internal diameter	51.600 to 51.619 mm
Small end internal diameter	28.000 to 28.021 mm
Connecting rod length (between centres)	124.95 to 125.05 mm
Maximum weight difference between rods	5.0g

Cylinder block and pistons

Standard bore (M180 engine)	81.750 to 81.772 mm
(M114 engine)	82.000 to 82.022 mm
(M130 engine)	86.500 to 86.522 mm
Piston to sidewall clearance	0.020 to 0.030 mm
Gudgeon pin diameter	25.000 to 24.995 mm
Gudgeon pin clearance in piston	0.012 to 0.023 mm
Maximum weight difference between pistons	4.0g
Piston ring end gap (compression)	0.30 to 0.45 mm
(oil control)	0.25 to 0.40 mm
Piston ring groove clearance (compression)	0.05 to 0.08 mm
(oil control)	0.03 to 0.06 mm

Valves

Seat angle	45°±15'
Valve stem diameter (inlet)	8.955 to 8.970 mm
(exhaust)	10.918 to 10.940 mm
Valve spring free length (inner)	45.0 mm
(outer)	49.0 mm
Valve clearance (cold)	
Inlet	0.003 in (0.08 mm)
Exhaust	0.007 in (0.18 mm)

Valve timing

Model	*Camshaft code	INLET VALVE Opens BTDC	Closes ABDC	EXHAUST VALVE Opens BBDC	Closes ATDC
230/8	...				
250/8	... 0835				
250 CE	...	11°	47°	48°	16°
250 C	...				
280 S/8	...				
280 SE/8	... 04 or 08				
280 SEL/8	...				
280 SL	... 09	12°	56°	53°	21°
280 SL8	...				
280 SL8 (exhaust emission)	... 01 or 05	16°	46°	53°	15°

Model	*Camshaft code	Opens BTDC	Closes ATDC	Opens BTDC	Closes ATDC
250 SE	...	11°	53°	47°	21°
250 SL	...				

* Stamped on end face of camshaft.

Engine oil capacity

Sump	9.7 Imp. pts, 11.5 US pts, 5.5 litres
Filter	0.9 Imp. pt, 1.0 US pt, 0.5 litre
Cooler	0.9 Imp. pt, 1.0 US pt, 0.5 litre
Total	11.5 Imp. pts, 13.5 US pts, 6.5 litres

Torque wrench settings

	lb f ft	Nm
230 Series cars		
Cylinder head bolts (cold)	58	80
(hot)	65	90
Rocker ball pivots	72	100
Connecting rod big-end cap bolts	44	61
Main bearing cap bolts	58	80
Flywheel (or driveplate) bolts	50	69
Sump bolts	6	8
Spark plugs	25	35
Oil filter centre bolt	30	41
Oil cooler drain plug	18	25
Camshaft sprocket bolt	58	80
Fuel injection pipe unions	25	35
Crankshaft pulley bolt	150	207
Crankshaft damper socket screws	25	35
Engine rear plate bolts	36	50
Oil pump mounting bolts	36	50
Chain tensioner plug	42	58
Sump drain plug	30	41
Clutch or torque converter housing to engine	36	50
Driveplate to torque converter bolts	25	35
250 Series cars		
As 230 Series except for the following differences:		
Flywheel (or driveplate) bolts	72	100
280 Series cars		
As 230 Series except for the following differences:		
Cylinder head bolts (cold)	72	100
(hot)	80	111
Main bearing cap bolts	65	90
Flywheel bolts	28	39
Sump bolts	8	11

1 General description

The engine is of six cylinder in-line type with a single overhead camshaft.

The cylinder block is of cast-iron construction while the cylinder head and the crankshaft bottom housing are aluminium.

The crankshaft is supported in seven main bearings, with the exception of type M180 which has four.

At the front end of the crankshaft, a sprocket drives the timing chain which in turn is connected to the overhead camshaft and to an auxiliary shaft.

This auxiliary shaft drives the oil pump, distributor shafts and also the rev. counter cable on those engines which are so equipped.

An externally mounted, disposable element type oil filter is mounted on the left-hand side of the cylinder block.

The crankshaft pulley is used to drive various belts for the alternator, power steering pump, water pump, air conditioning compressor and other ancillaries according to the particular specification of the car.

The intake and exhaust manifolds are mounted on the right-hand side of the car and the pre-engaged type starter motor is located below them.

2 Major operations possible with the engine in the car

1 The following operations can be carried out without removing the engine from the car.

a) *Removal and refitment of cylinder head/camshaft assembly.*
b) *Removal of ancillary components including: Alternator, (Chapter 10). Oil filter, (Section 13, this Chapter), Fuel filter, (Chapter 3), Starter motor, (Chapter 10), Fuel injector pump assembly, (Chapter 3), Steering pump, (Chapter 11), Distributor, (Chapter 4), Thermostat housing, (Chapter 2), Intake manifold and carburettors, (Chapter 3), Exhaust manifold, (Chapter 3), Air cleaner, (Chapter 3).*

2 If the cooling system is drained and the radiator removed, then the following components can be removed:
Fan/coupling
Crankshaft pulley/damper and front oil seal.
Water pump main housing (after damper removal).
Distributor driveshaft.
Distributor housing.

3 If the engine oil is drained and the sump cover plate removed, the oil pump can be withdrawn.

4 It is possible to renew the timing chain if the following operations are strictly adhered to.

5 Set the engine so that No. 1 piston is at TDC on its compression stroke.

6 Remove the rocker cover and chain tensioner.

7 Grind off the ends of two adjacent link pins from the original endless type of timing chain.

8 Separate the ends of the chain but keep the chain in engagement with the camshaft and crankshaft sprockets and the tensioner and idler sprockets.

9 Using a connecting link, attach a new chain to the end of the old one and then rotate the crankshaft (by means of a 28 mm socket applied to the pulley bolt) in the normal direction of rotation until the new chain is drawn round the crankshaft sprocket (Fig. 1.2).

10 Continue turning the crankshaft until No. 1 piston is again at TDC on compression.

11 Remove the old chain and keep upward tension on the two ends of the new chain to keep it in engagement with the teeth of the crankshaft sprocket.

12 Reconnect the ends of the new chain using a connecting link which has its closed end pointing in the direction of rotation (photo).

13 Check the timing as described in Section 33.

3 Engine - methods of removal

1 Provided a heavy duty hoist is available, it is probably easier to

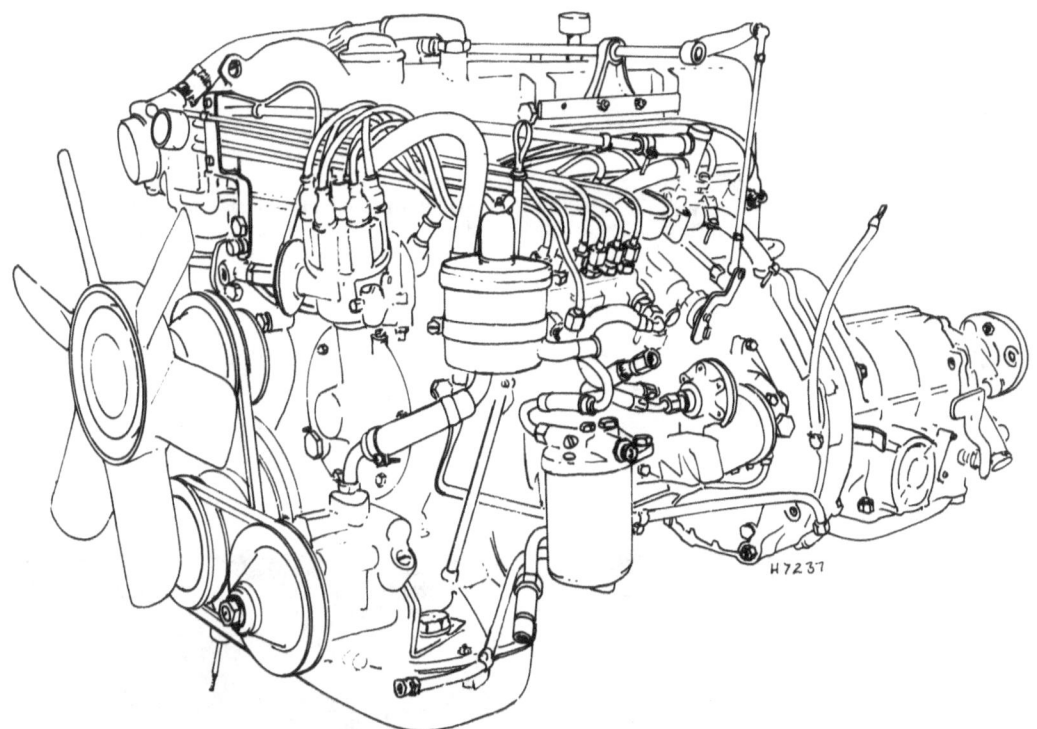

Fig. 1.1. 280 Series engine with automatic transmission and fuel injection system

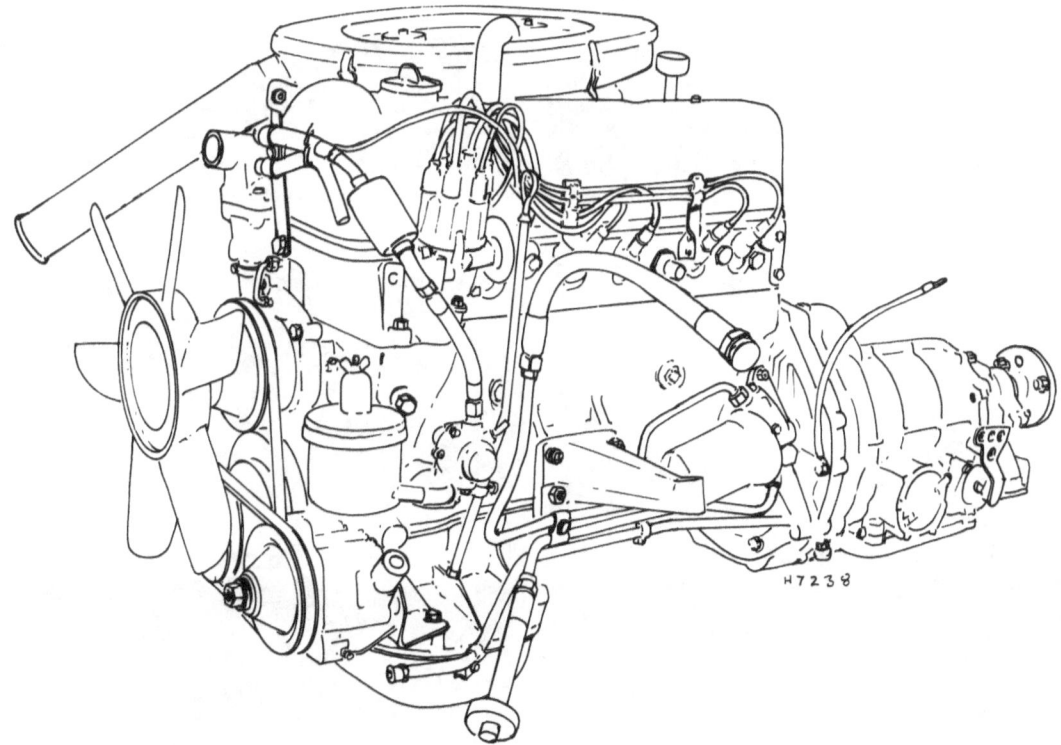

Fig. 1.1A. Typical carburettor type engine. Note variation in distributor mounting.

remove the engine and transmission together as one unit.

2   However, in view of the overall weight of such a heavy engine and transmission, it is recommended that if only light duty lifting equipment is available, that the engine is removed separately leaving the transmission in position in the car.

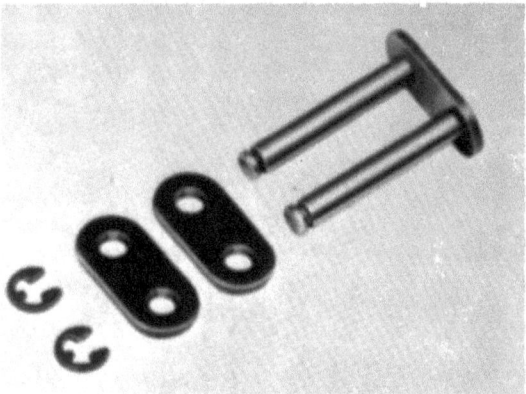

Fig. 1.2. Timing chain connecting link (Sec. 2)

4   Engine - removal, leaving automatic transmission in car

1   Open the bonnet to its fullest extent and mark the position of the hinge plates on the under lid surface.

2   With the help of an assistant, unscrew the hinge bolts from the bonnet lid. Take care that the torsion rod which acts as a prop does not fly up and damage the paintwork as the hinges are released.

3   Drain the cooling system by unscrewing the drain plug at the base of the radiator and the large hexagon plug on the right-hand side of the cylinder block.

4   Drain the oil cooler which is located at the left-hand side of the radiator. To do this, unscrew the plug at its base and then disconnect the two hoses from it (photos).

5   Disconnect the automatic transmission fluid cooler lines from the base of the radiator.

6   Disconnect the radiator hoses and battery leads. **Warning:** If the car is equipped with air conditioning, on no account disconnect any part of the system, particularly the hoses from the condenser which is mounted ahead of the radiator. The compressor may be unbolted and moved aside as far as the flexibility of its connecting hoses will allow. If your operations are still impeded by the components of the air conditioning system, then have the system discharged by your Mercedes dealer or a professional refrigeration engineer.

7   Remove the air cleaner assembly complete from the right-hand

2.12 Timing chain connecting link

4.4A Base of engine oil cooler and radiator

4.4B Top hose connection to engine oil cooler

4.14 Heater hose connection at rear bulkhead

front cover of the engine compartment. This will give access to the radiator mounting bolts on that side.

8 Remove the radiator mounting bolts and lift the radiator from the engine compartment.

9 Remove the fan assembly. To do this, unscrew the small bolts which are located in the slotted flange at its rear.

10 Withdraw the pulley from the front of the water pump after having first slipped off the driving belt.

11 Disconnect the HT leads from the spark plugs, unclip the distributor cap and then remove the cap and leads together.

12 Disconnect the rev. counter drive cable (if fitted) by unscrewing its collar from just to the rear of the distributor.

13 Remove the windscreen washer bottle from the engine compartment, also the battery from its tray.

14 Disconnect the heater pipes from the left-hand side of the engine block and from the right-hand side of the engine compartment rear bulkhead (photo).

15 Before disconnecting any more electrical leads, prepare to mark them with a piece of tape and to identify them so that they can be reconnected to their original positions.

16 Disconnect the leads from the two thermal switches located on the water housing on the left-hand side of the cylinder block. On some engines a capillary tube type coolant gauge is fitted. Unscrew this from the cylinder head.

17 Disconnect the oil pressure gauge pipe from the top of the oil filter on the left-hand side of the engine.

18 Disconnect the earth strap from the left-hand upper edge of the torque converter housing.

On carburettor type engines
19 Disconnect the fuel flow and return lines from the filter.
20 Disconnect the leads from the automatic choke.
21 Disconnect the exhaust downpipes from the exhaust manifolds.
22 Disconnect the vacuum hoses from the carburettor diaphragm units.

On fuel injection type engines
23 Disconnect and securely plug the flow and return pipes from the fuel pressure relief valve which is located on the left-hand side of the engine.
24 Unscrew and remove the fuel filter canister from the left-hand side of the engine.
25 Working on the right-hand side of the engine, disconnect the switch housing from the extreme front of the intake manifold.
26 Disconnect the electrical lead from the centre of the outside edge of the intake manifold.
27 Unbolt the constant speed (anti-stall) solenoid from the central inner branch of the intake manifold.
28 Disconnect the fume extraction hose and the coolant hose from the front end of the intake housing.
29 Disconnect the vacuum hose which runs between the distributor and the intake manifold.
30 Disconnect the securing clips and withdraw the intake manifold shield towards the front of the engine.

On all types of engine
31 Unbolt and remove the alternator.
32 Disconnect the heater hose from the rear of the radiator bottom hose connector nozzle on the cylinder block.
33 Disconnect the (automatic transmission) vacuum pipe at the banjo type connecting union at the rear of the intake manifold.
34 Disconnect the brake servo vacuum pipe from the rear of the intake manifold.
35 Disconnect the electrical leads from the terminals of the starter solenoid. Small grub screws are used here but the leads cannot be mixed up as the terminal holes are of different sizes.
36 Disconnect the accelerator linkage. To do this, unbolt the transverse rod from the rocker cover and the intake manifold on fuel injection engines and disconnect the rod balljoints on carburettor type engines.
37 *On fuel injection type engines,* disconnect the exhaust downpipes, pull them downwards out of the manifold sockets. Unbolt the manifolds and withdraw them an inch or two from the engine. The intake manifold can now be lifted off its studs, followed by the exhaust manifold.
38 *On carburettor type engines,* unbolt and remove the manifold assembly complete with carburettors.

39 Disconnect the flexible fluid pipes from the top of the steering box. Plug the box and the pipes.
40 Detach the coolant pipe which runs across the rear of the engine block.
41 The remaining operations are carried out from underneath the car. Either place the car over an inspection pit or on ramps.
42 Unbolt and remove the cover plate from the lower front face of the torque converter housing.
43 The three pairs of bolts which secure the driveplate to the torque converter must now be unscrewed. First mark the relative position of the torque converter to the driveplate and starter ring gear using quick drying paint.
44 Now bring each pair of bolts into view by turning the crankshaft pulley bolt with a 28 mm socket wrench and extension. Unscrew the bolts.
45 Unscrew the small terminal block from the left-hand side of the torque converter housing.
46 Disconnect the fluid cooler pipes from their unions on the transmission.
47 Unscrew and remove the bolts which secure the torque converter housing to the engine. The lower ones are readily accessible but the upper ones can only be reached by using a socket wrench on a universally-jointed extension some two feet in length and inserted through the propeller shaft centre bearing aperture in the floor pan.
48 The starter motor upper socket screw must be removed to enable the starter to be withdrawn. To do this, cut a section from an Allen key to fit the socket screw and then insert it into the screw. Again using the universally-jointed long extension, and a 10 mm socket wrench applied to the Allen key, unscrew the socket screw.
49 Unbolt and remove the starter front bracket and withdraw the starter motor.
50 Attach a hoist and slings or chains securely to the engine and take its weight.
51 Place a jack and block of wood as an insulator under the transmission oil pan and support its weight.
52 Release the engine front mountings by unscrewing the centre bolts.
53 Pull the engine forward and upwards from the engine compartment. The help of an assistant will be required for this work, to manoeuvre the engine round obstacles and also to keep the torque converter pressed fully rearwards to prevent it falling out of the transmission as the engine is withdrawn (photos).
54 A retaining bar should be bolted to the front face of the converter housing while the engine is removed, to prevent the converter being displaced.

5 Engine - removal, leaving manual transmission in car

1 The operations are as described in the preceding Section up to and including paragraph 40, then continue as follows.
2 The remaining operations are carried out from underneath the car. Either place the car over an inspection pit or on ramps.
3 Unscrew and remove the bolts which secure the clutch bellhousing to the engine. These can be unscrewed as described in paragraph 47 of the preceding Section.
4 Remove the starter motor as described in paragraphs 48 and 49 of the preceding Section.
5 Attach a hoist and slings or chains securely to the engine and take its weight.
6 Support the transmission on a jack and then release the engine front mountings by unscrewing the centre bolts.
7 Pull the engine forward and incline upwards at a slight angle until the gearbox input shaft disengages from the clutch driven plate and then lift the engine out of the car.

6 Engine - removal, complete with automatic transmission

1 Repeat the operations described in paragraphs 1 to 40 of Section 4.
2 Disconnect the control cable at the bracket on the engine compartment rear bulkhead.
3 Working under the car, disconnect the speedometer cable from the transmission.
4 Disconnect the fluid filler tube and vacuum pipe from the right-hand side of the transmission. These are joined together and should be

4.53A Removing engine leaving automatic transmission in car

4.53B Hoisting engine from car

6.15A View of left-hand side of engine/auto transmission during removal

6.15B View of right-hand side of engine/auto-transmission during removal

Fig. 1.3. Rear mounting detail (Sec. 7)

1 Crossmember   2 Flexible mounting   3 Exhaust bracket

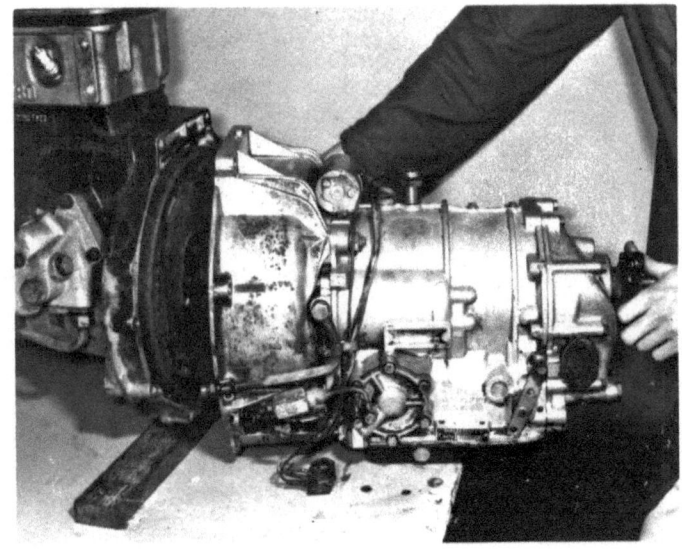

8.3 Separating auto transmission from engine

removed as an assembly.

5 Disconnect the leads from the multi-terminal block on the left-hand side of the transmission. The terminal holes are of different sizes so that the connecting leads cannot be mixed up.

6 Support the weight of the transmission on a jack and a block of wood used as an insulator.

7 Remove the shield from above the exhaust pipes at the side of the transmission. Phillips screws are used for this.

8 Remove the large centre bolt from the transmission mounting plate.

9 Unbolt the mounting plate from the body floor pan, or cross-member from the bodyframe according to type.

10 Unbolt the rear mounting from the rear face of the transmission.

11 Disconnect the propeller shaft front rubber coupling by unbolting it from the transmission output flange. Push the shaft upwards and lock it with a block of wood.

12 Disconnect the speed selector control rod from the lever on the left-hand side of the transmission.

13 Disconnect the downshift cable from the transmission.

14 Take the weight of the engine on a suitable hoist and disconnect the engine mountings.

15 Lower the jack under the transmission and simultaneously raise the hoist. The engine/transmission can then be removed from the engine compartment at a steeply inclined angle (photos).

7 Engine - removal, complete with manual transmission

1 Repeat the operations described in paragraphs 1 to 40 of Section 4.

2 Disconnect the gearshift control according to type (see Chapter 6).

3 Unbolt the clutch slave cylinder from the clutch bellhousing and tie it up out of the way; there is no need to disconnect the hydraulic line.

4 Disconnect the speedometer cable from the transmission.

5 Disconnect the leads from the reversing lamp switch.

6 Disconnect the exhaust pipe support bracket from the rear of the transmission.

7 Disconnect the propeller shaft front flexible coupling by extracting the bolts which secure it to the transmission output flange. Push the shaft upwards and lock it with a block of wood.

8 Support the weight of the transmission on a jack and unbolt and remove the rear mounting and crossmember.

9 Support the weight of the engine on a hoist and disconnect the engine mountings (Fig. 1.3).

10 By simultaneously lowering the transmission jack and raising the engine hoist, remove the complete engine/transmission at a steeply inclined angle from the engine compartment.

8 Engine - separation from automatic transmission

1 Where the engine and automatic transmission have been removed together, disconnect the driveplate from the torque converter as described in paragraphs 42 to 44 of Section 4.

2 Unscrew and remove the bolts which secure the torque converter housing to the engine.

3 Withdraw the transmission in a straight line from the engine. Retain the torque converter rearwards in the transmission by bolting a retaining bar to one of the torque converter housing bolts (photo).

9 Engine - separation from manual transmission

1 Where the engine and manual transmission have been removed together, unscrew and remove the bolts which secure the clutch bellhousing to the engine.

2 Withdraw the transmission in a straight line, supporting its weight so that it does not hang upon the input shaft while the latter is still engaged in the splined hub of the clutch driven plate.

10 Preparation for dismantling the engine

1 With the engine removed, clean away external dirt using paraffin and a brush or a water soluble grease solvent. If the latter is used, take care not to let water from the rinsing jet enter the carburettor or fuel injection equipment or any open ports or apertures. Cover them with plastic bags or adhesive tape beforehand.

2 Gather together an adequate range of spanners and sockets. On earlier models, the nuts and bolts are a mixture of metric and AF sizes. On later cars they are to metric dimensions only.

3 An essential requirement is a comprehensive set of metric Allen keys due to the large number of socket screws which are used on these engines.

4 Rags, paper towelling and a number of tins or small boxes in which to keep small nuts and bolts and other components will be found very useful.

5 If a really substantial bench is available, strip the engine on it; failing this, the engine will have to be dismantled on the floor.

11 Cylinder head and camshaft - removal and dismantling

1 If the engine is in the car, carry out the following preliminary operations:

Drain the cooling system.
Disconnect the battery.
Disconnect the radiator hoses.
Disconnect the air cleaner.
Disconnect the spark plug leads and distributor cap on fuel injection engines. Remove the distributor complete on carburettor type engines.
Disconnect the fuel flow and return pipes (carburettor).
Disconnect the automatic choke leads (carburettor).
Disconnect all connections from the intake manifold (fuel injection).
Disconnect vacuum hose from the distributor.
Disconnect the brake servo vacuum hose from the intake manifold.
Disconnect the accelerator linkage.
Disconnect the exhaust downpipes.

2 *On cars equipped with fuel injection,* disconnect the fuel injection pipes which run between the injection pump and the individual cylinders. Unscrew the union nuts to do this. Unbolt the throttle linkage support bracket from the left-hand side of the cylinder head.

3 Remove the rocker cover by unscrewing the centre bolts (Fig. 1.4).

4 Remove the thermostat housing.

5 Unscrew the large chain tensioner nut which is located just below the thermostat housing. Withdraw the nut and internal coil spring.

6 From the front upper edge of the cylinder head remove the chain tensioner sprocket bolt. Screw in a suitable bolt into the sprocket shaft and extract the shaft and the sprocket.

7 Unscrew and remove the two socket headed screws and remove the chain guide.

8 Unscrew and remove the camshaft sprocket bolt and tap the sprocket gently forward from its Woodruff key. Remove the sprocket, support the chain upwards.

9 Unscrew and remove the two socket screws which are located inside the front edge of the chain aperture at the forward end of the cylinder head (photos).

10 Unscrew and remove the two socket screws which are located just behind the distributor. These screws also secure the front end of the cylinder head.

11 Release the power steering fluid reservoir and push it to one side.

12 From the front face of the cylinder block, unscrew the banjo type of pipe unions from each end of the coolant by-pass tube.

13 From the left-hand side of the cylinder head, unbolt and remove the coolant temperature switch housing.

14 Unscrew and remove the cylinder head bolts. These are of socket-headed type and a section of Allen key should be used in conjunction with a 10 mm socket wrench to remove them. Some of the cylinder head bolts are longer than others, and these longer ones also retain the camshaft pedestals.

15 Unscrew the socket screw which retains the front end of the oil pipe to the rocker cover support.

16 Remove the cylinder head, camshaft and rocker assembly from the cylinder block. With assistance, the cylinder head can be lifted away complete with the manifolds. Support the timing chain in an upward direction using a piece of wire hooked to it, but of course allowing it to pass through the aperture in the cylinder head.

17 The cylinder head can now be completely dismantled in the following way:

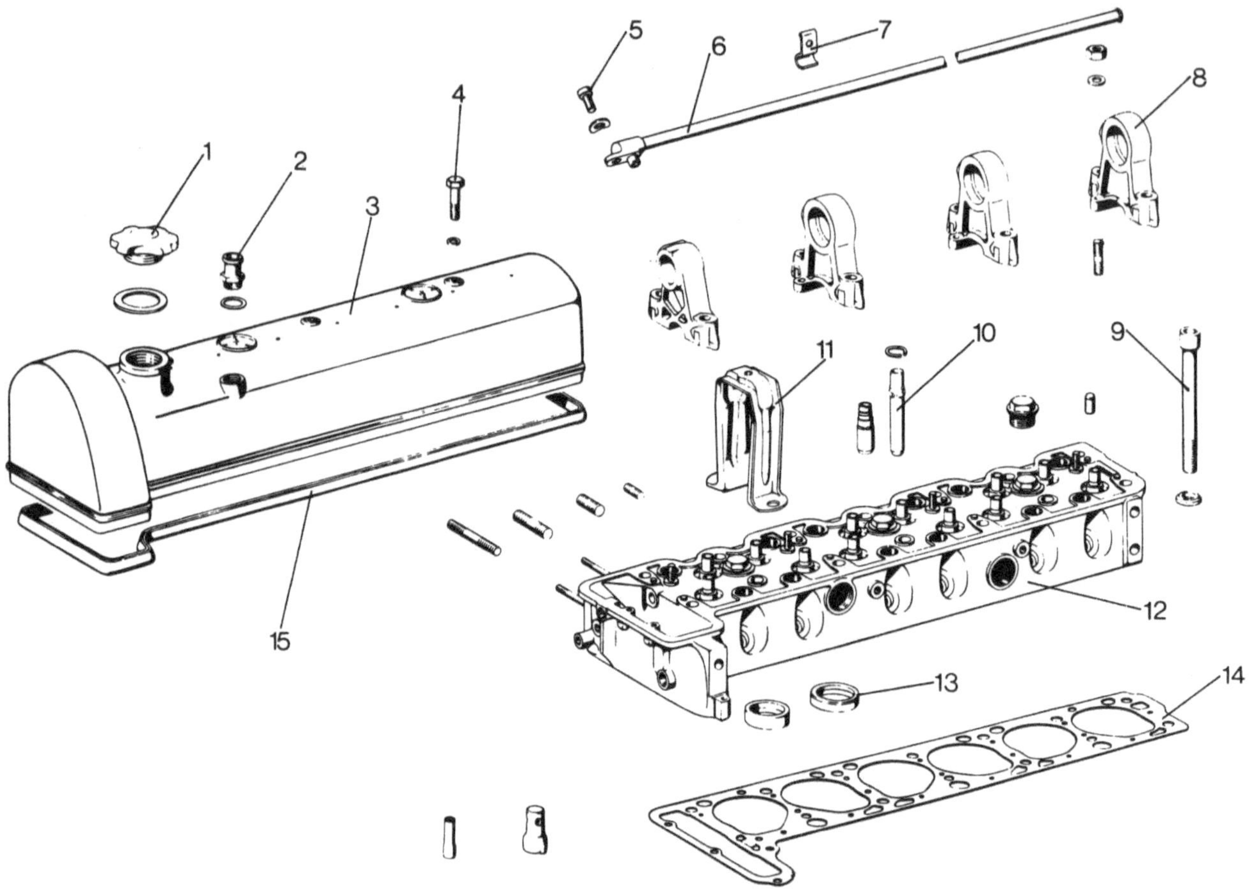

Fig. 1.4. Cylinder head components (Sec. 11)

1	Oil filler cap	6	Oil pipe	11	Rocker cover support
2	Connector	7	Support clip	12	Cylinder head
3	Rocker cover	8	Camshaft pedestal	13	Valve seat
4	Rocker cover bolt	9	Cylinder head bolt	14	Cylinder head gasket
5	Oil pipe securing screw	10	Valve guide	15	Rocker cover gasket

11.9A Socket screws inside timing chain aperture

11.9B Socket screws to rear of timing chain aperture

18 Detach the spring tension clamps from the end of each rocker arm.
19 Using a suitable lever, positioned between the underside of the camshaft and the surface of a valve spring retainer, compress the valve spring so that the rocker arm and the thrust block can be removed. Repeat this operation on the remaining rocker arms. The camshaft will have to be rotated from time to time to position the lowest profile of the cams above the rocker arms. Keep the rocker arms in their original sequence.
20 With all the rocker arms removed, the camshaft can now be withdrawn from the bearing pedestals.
21 Unless absolutely essential, do not unbolt and remove the pedestals as any disturbance may upset their alignment.
22 To remove a valve from the cylinder head, compress the valve springs. A tool can easily be made up to do this, similar to the one shown in the photograph which will engage under the ball stud. Lever the spring downwards and have an aperture in the tool through which the split retaining collets of the valve can be extracted (photos).
23 Having extracted the split collets, release the compressor slowly and remove the retainer, valve springs (inner and outer) lower spring seat and valve stem oil seal. Finally withdraw the valve from its guide. When compressing the valve springs, it will be found that the valve has a tendency to project into the combustion chamber of the cylinder head. To overcome this, place a small wooden block under the head of the valve while the cylinder head is flat on the bench.
24 Drop the valve out of its guide and extract it from the combustion chamber.
25 It is essential that the valves are kept in their original sequence of fitting unless they are so badly worn that they are to be renewed. If they are to be kept and used again, place them in a sheet of card or a box with sub-divisions and numbered from 1 to 12 corresponding with the position of the valves in the head (No. 1 is nearest the front of the cylinder head).
26 If the timing chain idler sprocket is to be removed from the cylinder head, unscrew the plug from the end of the idler shaft, insert a suitable bolt and use this to pull out the shaft. Detach the sprocket.

12 Engine - complete dismantling

1 The operations described in paragraphs 1 to 12 of this Section can be carried out without removing the engine from the car provided the cooling system is first drained and the radiator removed.
2 Remove the power steering fluid reservoir.
3 *On fuel injection engines,* unbolt and remove the distributor, then remove the distributor drive housing.
4 Unscrew the auxiliary shaft nut and remove the distributor drive gear. Extract the Woodruff key which retains the auxiliary shaft sprocket.
5 Extract the lockbolt and unscrew the rev. counter and oil pump drive gear.

6 Carefully tap out the auxiliary shaft towards the rear and then remove the auxiliary shaft sprocket.
7 *On carburettor type engines* the distributor will already have been removed in order to withdraw the cylinder head. Now unbolt the fuel pump from the side of the engine and withdraw its rocker arm or rod from the cam on the oil pump driveshaft.
8 Withdraw the distributor driveshaft and then the auxiliary shaft and its lockbolt from the engine and detach the sprocket from the timing chain.
9 Unbolt and remove the steering pump and pipework. To remove the pump, first unbolt the pump pulley and remove it, unbolt and lift the pump from its mounting cradle and then unbolt and remove the cradle.
10 Unbolt and remove the alternator bracket.
11 Unbolt and remove the crankshaft pulley/damper bolt. Lock the starter ring gear with a cold chisel or a piece of flat steel bar bent to shape, to prevent the crankshaft turning.
12 To remove the damper assembly, first extract the circle of socket-headed screws and withdraw the pressed steel pulley. Mark the position of the damper in relation to the crankshaft mounting hub and then tap the damper from the hub. The mounting hub is prevented from rotating on the crankshaft by two solid dowels which act as keys. Use a suitable two or three legged puller to extract the hub from the front end of the crankshaft. Once the mounting hub is removed unbolt and withdraw the water pump (Fig. 1.5) (photos).
13 *On cars equipped with fuel injection,* unbolt and remove the fuel injection pump.
14 Unbolt and remove the left-hand engine mounting (on fuel injection engines, the mounting will come away complete with the fuel pressure regulator). Always mark the upper surface of the engine mounting struts before removal as it is possible to refit them upside down.
15 Turn the engine on its side or turn it completely upside down.
16 Unbolt and remove the flywheel securing bolts (driveplate on cars fitted with automatic transmission). This component is positively located by a dowel and cannot therefore be refitted incorrectly.
17 Remove the engine rear plate.
18 The small sump cover plate need only be unbolted and removed to gain access to the oil pump if the engine is still in the car, otherwise unbolt and remove the complete crankshaft housing/sump assembly (Fig. 1.6).
19 Unbolt and remove the oil pump.
20 The big-end bearing caps are unmarked and they should therefore be centre punched or identified with quick drying paint starting with No. 1 at the front of the engine. Note that the shell bearing cut-outs in the caps are towards the left-hand side of the engine.
21 Unscrew the big-end nuts, remove the caps and push each piston/connecting rod assembly from its cylinder bore. If the bearing shells are to be used again, keep them together with their respective caps or connecting rods, do not mix them up (Fig. 1.7).
22 Mark each of the seven (four on M180 engine) main bearing caps

11.22A Valve spring compressing tool made from 1 inch box section

11.22B Compressing a valve spring

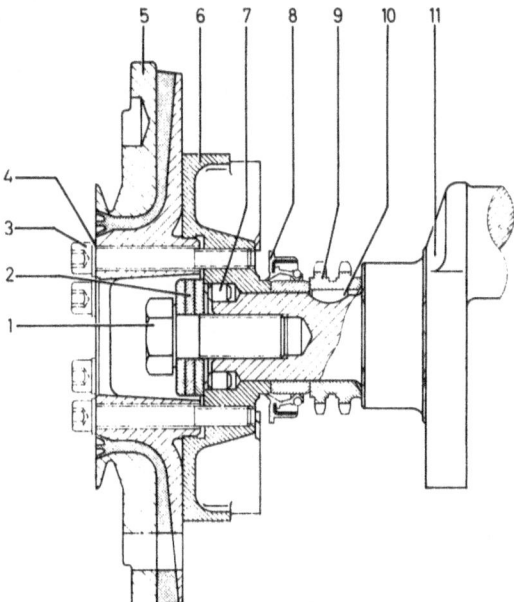

Fig. 1.5. Sectional view of crankshaft pulley and damper (front pulley
for power steering pump or air conditioning not shown (Sec. 12)

1 Retaining bolt	8 Oil seal
2 Conical spring washers	9 Sprocket for timing chain
3 Socket headed bolt	10 Woodruff key
4 Washer	11 Crankshaft
5 Vibration damper	
6 Mounting hub	
7 Set pin	

12.12A Removing crankshaft pulley

12.12B Withdrawing crankshaft damper mounting hub

using a centre punch or quick-drying paint. Make sure that one side of
the crankcase is also marked with matching numbers to ensure that
the caps are refitted the correct way round.
23 Unscrew the main bearing cap bolts and remove the caps by
carefully tapping them away from the crankcase web. Do not try to
tap the caps sideways as they are located on dowels. Note that the
crankshaft end-float thrust washers are flanged to the bearing shells of
the third main journal counting from the front of the engine on all
except M180. On M180 engines the thrust flanges are located on the
second main journal from the front.
24 From the front face of the engine, unscrew the plug followed by
the oil pressure relief valve so that the timing chain can be released.
Extract the chain idler sprocket and shaft by screwing a bolt into the
centre of the shaft. The oil pressure relief valve is designed so that
when it blows off, the oil released lubricates the chain (Fig. 1.8).
25 Lift the crankshaft complete with timing chain from the crankcase.
26 The chain slippers can be removed if they are worn, after withdrawing the retaining bolts. These can be extracted, after first having
screwed in a small bolt into their tapped centres.

---

13 Engine lubrication system, filter and cooler

1 The oil pump is mounted within the crankcase and is driven from
the auxiliary shaft which in turn is driven by the timing chain.
2 Engine oil is drawn from the sump through the intake filter screen
by the oil pump, then pressurised and forced from the top of the oil
filter housing to the oil cooler which is mounted beside the radiator.
3 Having been cooled by the air flow generated by the forward motion
of the car, the oil then returns to the oil filter, passes through the filter
element and is distributed to all the engine bearing surfaces (Fig. 1.9).
4 Overflow and by-pass valves are fitted as a precaution against a
clogged element or flow resistance in the oil cooler during very low
outside temperatures.
5 The main oil pressure relief valve is screwed into the front face of
the cylinder block. On some models a second pressure relief valve is
located in the base of the oil pump. As this is very similar to the
cylinder block valve, it is identified by the figure 12. Do not interchange these valves.

6 At engine oil and filter changes, always drain the oil cooler by
unscrewing the drain plug at its base. Refit the plug and tighten to a
torque wrench setting of 18 lb f ft (25 Nm).
7 Always drain the engine oil hot and then renew the oil filter
element in the following way.
8 Unscrew the centre bolt from the base of the filter body, **do not
unscrew the upper bolt** (1) (Fig. 1.9) which is sealed in position.
9 Withdraw the filter body, catch any ejected oil, tip out the filter
element and discard it.
10 Clean out the filter body, insert the new filter element and fit the
new sealing ring supplied, having picked out the old one from its
groove with a sharp-pointed instrument.
11 Hold the filter body squarely and tightly against the base and then
tighten the centre bolt to the specified torque wrench setting.
12 Start the engine; the oil pressure gauge will register after a few
seconds delay while the oil filter body fills with oil.
13 Switch off, and top up the engine oil level to make up for the oil
taken up by the new filter element and empty filter body.

---

14 Engine - examination and renovation - general

   With the engine stripped down and all parts thoroughly cleaned, it
is now time to examine everything for wear. The following items should
be checked and where necessary renewed or renovated as described in
the following Sections.

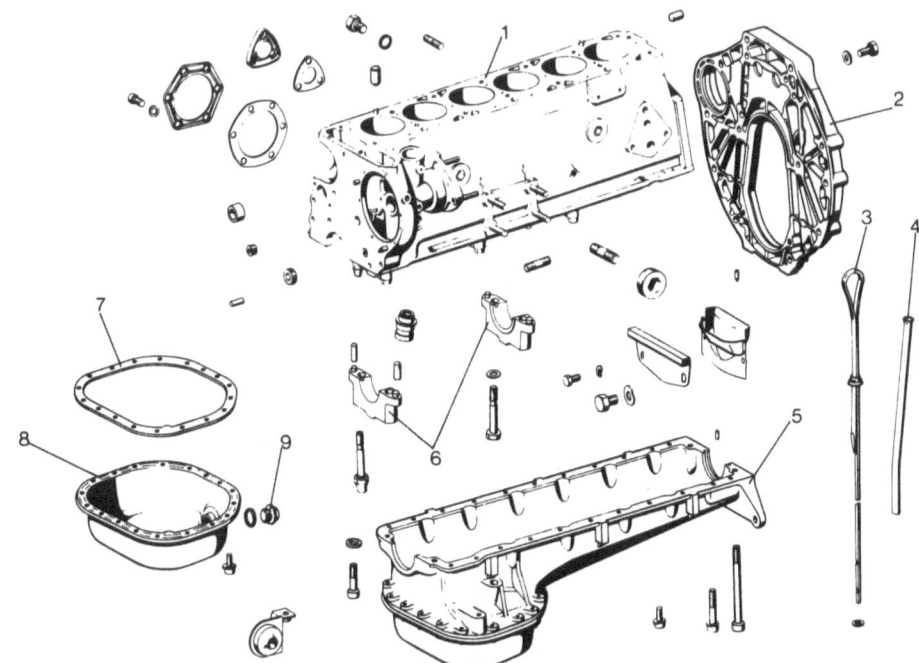

Fig. 1.6. Crankcase and sump components (Sec. 12)

1	Crankcase	4	Dipstick guide tube	7	Gasket
2	Rear plate	5	Crankshaft housing	8	Sump
3	Dipstick	6	Bearing caps	9	Oil drain plug

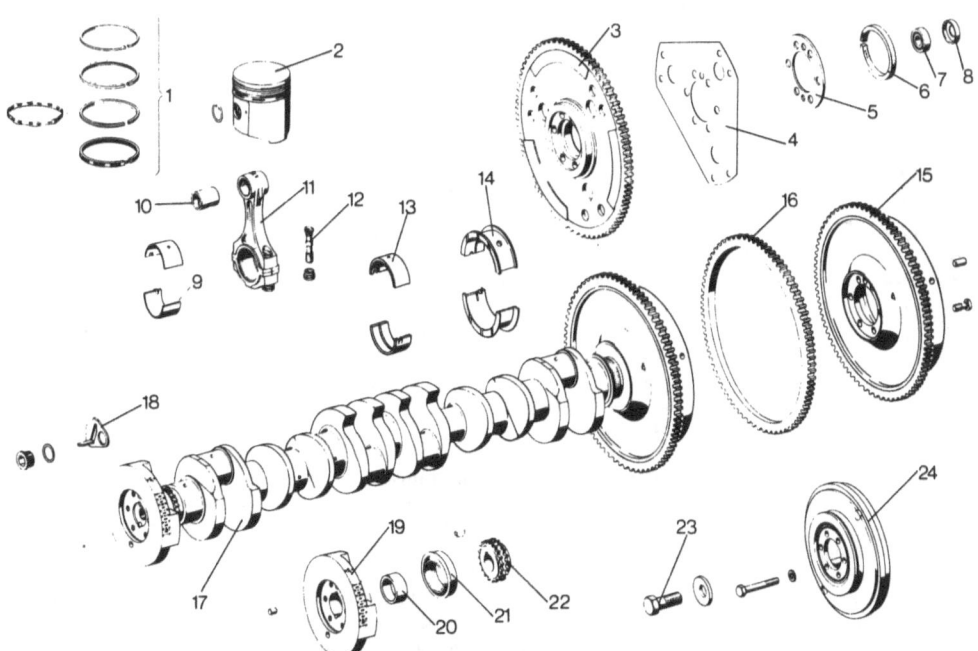

Fig. 1.7. Engine internal components (M180 engine has single link chain and sprockets) (Sec. 12)

1	Piston rings	10	Connecting rod small end bush	17	Crankshaft
2	Piston	11	Connecting rod	18	Timing pointer
3	Starter ring gear plate (auto. transmission)	12	Big-end bolt	19	Crankshaft balancing disc
4	Flexible (shear) plate - auto. transmission	13	Main bearing shells	20	Oil seal
		14	Main bearing shells with thrust flanges	21	Oil seal
5	Backing plate	15	Flywheel (manual transmission) complete with starter ring gear	22	Sprocket
6	Ring			23	Damper centre bolt
7	Spigot bearing	16	Starter ring gear	24	Damper assembly
8	Cap				
9	Big-end bearing shells				

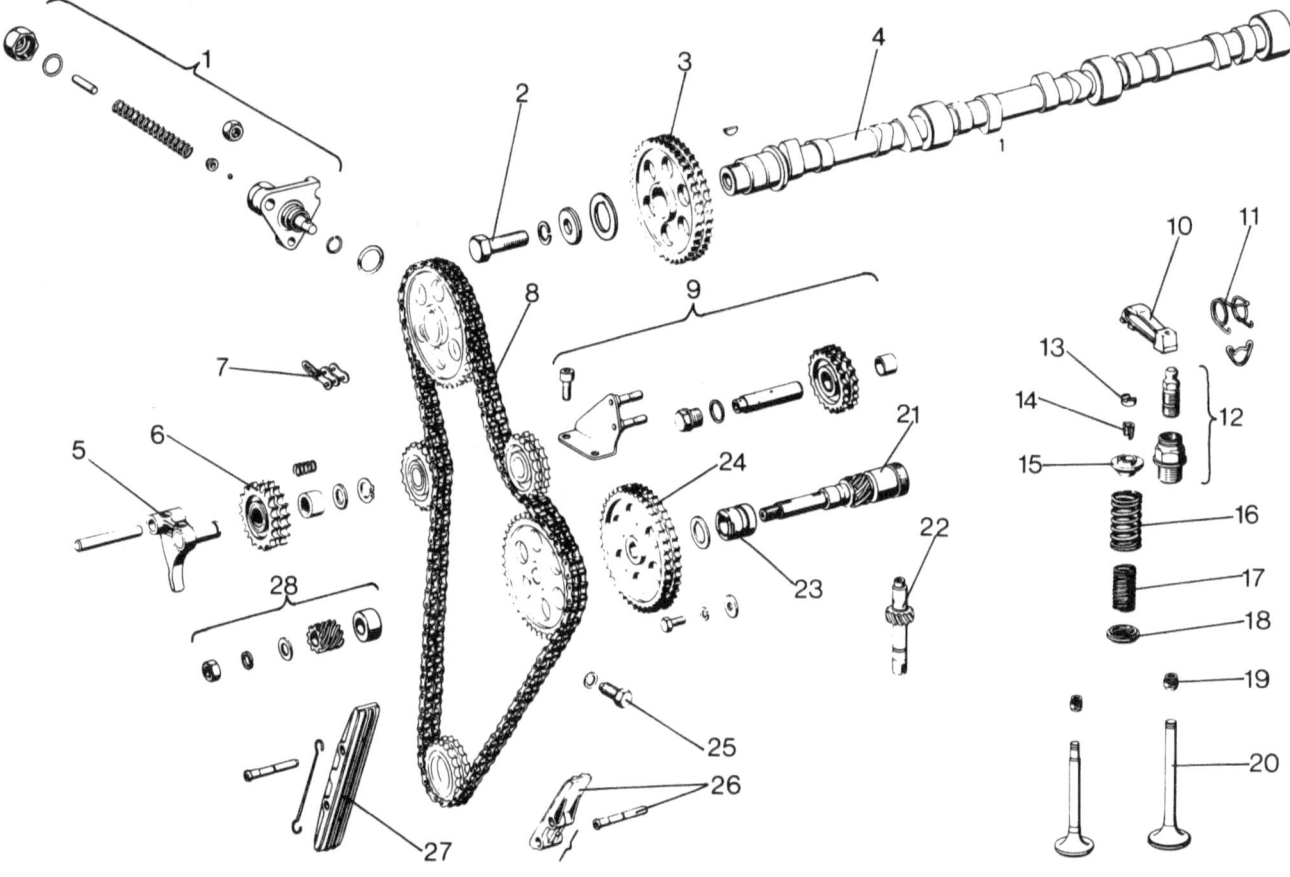

Fig. 1.8. Camshaft and associated components (Sec. 12)

1	Chain tensioner	9	Idler sprocket	16	Outer valve spring	23	Bearing
2	Camshaft sprocket bolt	10	Rocker arm	17	Inner valve spring	24	Auxiliary shaft sprocket
3	Sprocket	11	Clamp spring	18	Spring cover seat	25	Stop bolt
4	Camshaft	12	Ball pivot	19	Valve stem oil seal	26	Chain slipper
5	Tensioner sprocket pivot	13	Thrust piece	20	Valve	27	Chain slipper
6	Tensioner sprocket	14	Split collets	21	Auxiliary shaft	28	Oil pump drive gear on
7	Chain link (where fitted)	15	Valve spring retainer	22	Oil pump drive shaft		auxiliary shaft
8	Timing chain						

15 Crankshaft and main bearings - examination and renovation

1   Examine the crankpin and journal surfaces for signs of scoring or
scratches. Check the ovality of the crankpins at several different
positions using a micrometer. If more than 0.0004 in (0.01 mm) out of
round, the crankshaft will have to be reground. Check the journals in
the same manner.
2   If it is necessary to regrind the crankshaft and to fit new bearings,
your Mercedes-Benz dealer will decide how much to grind off and he
will supply new oversize shell bearings to suit. Details of regrinding
tolerances and bearings are given in the Specifications.
3   The crankshaft end-float should be checked after temporarily fitting
the crankshaft, the bearing shells and main bearing caps and tightening
the main bearing cap bolts to the specified torque wrench setting.
Alternatively push and pull the crankshaft using a long screwdriver as a
lever and check the gap between the main bearing thrust washer flange
and the crankshaft web. This should be between 0.004 and 0.007 in
(0.100 and 0.175 mm).
4   If the end-float is outside the specified tolerance, renew the main
bearing shells. It is recommended that the bearing shells are always
renewed at the time of a major engine overhaul, even if they appear to
be in good condition. If the crankshaft has been checked and found to
be fit for further service without regrinding, make sure that any new
bearing shells are identical to those being discarded, either standard or
undersize.
5   Check the clutch input shaft ball bearing in the centre of the

crankshaft rear flange. If it is noisy when rotated with the fingers or
obviously worn, renew it.

16 Connecting rods and bearings - examination and renovation

1   Big-end bearing failure is indicated by a knocking from within the
crankcase and a slight drop in oil pressure.
2   Examine the big-end bearing surfaces for pitting and scoring. Renew
the shells where necessary with ones of exactly similar size to the
originals. Where the crankshaft has been reground, the correct undersize big-end shell bearings will be supplied by the repairer.
3   Check each connecting rod for bending or twisting.
4   Fit each connecting rod to its crankpin on the crankshaft, complete
with bearing shells, and tighten the cap bolts to the specified torque
wrench setting. Now check the side float which should be between
0.004 and 0.010 in (0.110 and 0.260 mm). Excessive side float will
mean that new connecting rods must be fitted.
5   The piston may be removed from the connecting rod after extracting the circlip from each end of the gudgeon pin and pressing the pin
from the connecting rod small end. The pistons should not be warmed
as the gudgeon pins are a floating fit in them.
6   Renew the small end bush and gudgeon pin as necessary. The piston
gudgeon pin and connecting rods are colour coded and any new
components should maintain this coding. The weight deviation between
any one of the six connecting rods must not exceed 5.0 g.

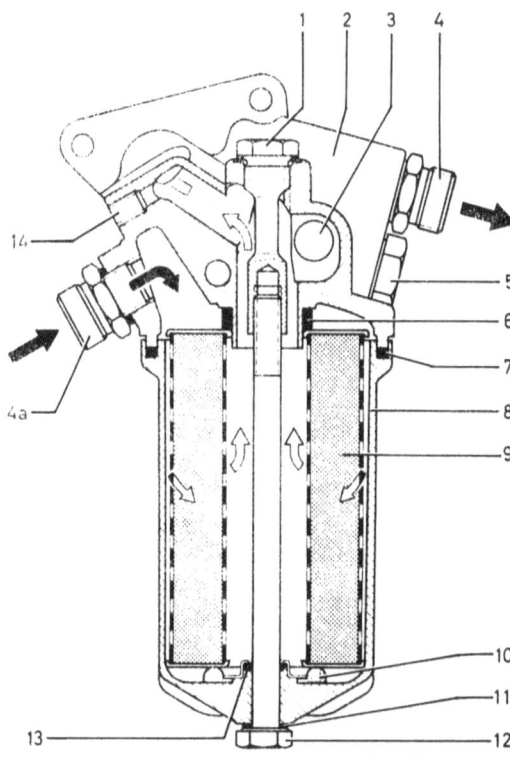

Fig. 1.9. Sectional view of engine oil filter (Sec. 13)

1 Upper bolt	8 Bowl
2 Base	9 Filter element
3 Pressure relief oil duct	10 Sealing ring
4 Outlet union	11 Seal
4A Inlet union	12 Centre bolt
5 Oil cooler	13 Seal
6 Sealing ring	14 Oil pressure gauge connection
7 Bowl sealing	

17 Cylinder bores - examination and renovation

1   The cylinder bores must be examined for taper, ovality, scoring and scratches. Start by carefully examining the top of the cylinder bores. If they are at all worn, a very slight ridge will be found on the thrust side. This marks the top of the piston ring travel. The owner will have a good indication of the bore wear prior to dismantling the engine, or removing the cylinder head. Excessive oil consumption accompanied by blue smoke from the exhaust is a sure sign of worn cylinder bores and piston rings.

2   Measure the bore diameter just under the ridge with a micrometer and compare it with the diameter at the bottom of the bore, which is not subject to wear. If the difference between the two measurements is more than 0.0008 in (0.02 mm) then it will be necessary to fit special pistons and rings or to have the cylinders rebored and fit oversize pistons. If no micrometer is available remove the rings from a piston and place the piston in each bore in turn about ¾ in (19.05 mm) below the top of the bore. If a 0.0012 in (0.03 mm) feeler gauge slid between the piston and cylinder wall requires less than a pull of between 2.2 and 5.5 lbs (1.0 and 2.5 kg) to withdraw it, using a spring balance, then remedial action must be taken.

3   Oversize pistons are available and these are machined to provide the correct running clearance in the new oversize bores. The weight deviation between any one of the six pistons must not exceed 4.0 g.

4   If the bores are slightly worn but not so badly worn as to justify reboring them, then special oil control rings and pistons can be fitted which will restore compression and stop the engine burning oil. Several

different types are available and the manufacturer's instructions concerning their fitting must be followed closely.

5   If new pistons or rings are being fitted and the bores have not been reground, it is essential to slightly roughen the hard glaze on the sides of the bores with fine glass paper so the new piston rings will have a chance to bed in properly.

18 Pistons and piston rings - examination and renovation

1   If the original pistons are to be refitted, carefully remove the piston rings by opening each of them in turn, just enough to enable them to ride over the lands of the piston body.

2   In order to prevent the lower rings dropping into an empty groove higher up the piston as they are removed, it is helpful to use two or three narrow strips of tin or old feeler blades inserted behind the ring at equidistant points and then to employ a twisting motion to slide the ring from the piston.

3   Clean the grooves and rings free from carbon, taking care not to scratch the aluminium surfaces of the pistons.

4   If new rings are to be fitted, then order the top compression ring to be stepped to prevent it impinging on the 'wear ring' which will almost certainly have been formed at the top of the cylinder bore.

5   Before fitting the rings to the pistons, push each ring in turn down to the bottom of its respective cylinder bore (use an inverted piston to do this so that the ring is kept square in its bore) and then measure the ring end gap. The gap for all rings should be between 0.0024 and 0.0036 in (0.060 and 0.092 mm). If the gap is incorrect, carefully grind the end of the ring.

6   Each ring should now be tested in its respective groove for side clearance. Using a feeler gauge, the clearances should be checked against those given in the Specifications. Where the side clearance is excessive, renew the piston as it will be the groove (width) that is worn.

7   Where necessary a new piston ring which is slightly tight in its groove may be rubbed down holding it perfectly squarely on an oil-stone or a sheet of fine emery cloth laid on a piece of plate glass. Excessive tightness can only be rectified by having the grooves machined out.

19 Camshaft and timing components - examination and renovation

1   Check the camshaft journals for scoring and then measure them at several different points to detect taper or out of round. Use a micrometer to do this.

2   Inspect the bearing surfaces in the pedestals for grooving or scoring.

3   Where any of the foregoing conditions are evident, renew the camshaft and pedestals.

4   Any wear in the camshaft lobes or gears can only be rectified by renewal of the camshaft.

5   Examine the camshaft sprocket, crankshaft sprocket, auxiliary shaft sprocket and distributor drive gear for wear or damage and renew as necessary.

6   Wash the timing chain in paraffin and examine it for wear. Support the chain at both ends so that the rollers are vertical. A worn chain will take on a deeply bowed appearance while an unworn one will dip only slightly at its centre point.

7   Check the chain tensioner for wear, also the chain guides and renew if necessary.

20 Flywheel (or driveplate - auto. trans.) - examination and renovation

1   Any scoring or tiny cracks (caused by overheating) which are visible on the clutch contact surface of the flywheel on manual gearbox cars can be removed by surface grinding provided the dimensions shown in the illustration are complied with (Fig. 1.10).

2   If the starter ring gear is worn, remove it either by drilling and splitting with a cold chisel or by heating it quickly and tapping it from the flywheel.

3   Heat the new ring gear to 392°F (200°C) until it is a light straw colour in appearance and drop it onto the flywheel making sure that the lead-in chamfer on the teeth is nearer the engine side.

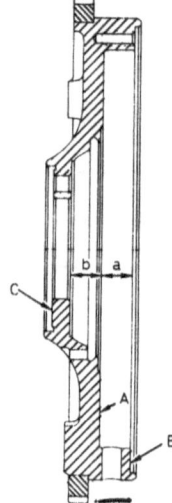

**Fig. 1.10. Flywheel re-finishing diagram
(Sec. 20)**

A *Clutch friction lining contact surface*
B *Pressure plate cover mounting flange*
C *Flywheel to crankshaft mounting face.*
a *19.4 to 19.5 mm*
b *not less than 17.5 mm*

21 Oil pump - overhaul

1 The oil pump can be dismantled and the backlash between the gears and also the end-float checked using feeler blades and a straight edge (photo).
2 If the clearances prove excessive or there have been previous indications of low oil pressure (although the general condition of the engine was known to be satisfactory) it is recommended that a new oil pump is fitted rather than fit individual new components including a new secondary oil pressure relief valve (where fitted).
3 Check that the oil pump pick up pipe filter mesh is unbroken.
4 When reassembling the oil pump cover, do not fully tighten the securing bolts until the pump spindle has been rotated to check for smoothness. As no cover positioning dowels are used, it may be necessary to tap the cover gently in order to centralise it and to prevent any undue side pressure on the pump gears.

22 Crankshaft front oil seal - renewal

1 It is possible to renew this oil seal with the engine in the car, if the radiator is first removed, the drivebelts released and the power steering pump moved to one side and the radiator fan removed.
2 Unbolt the pulley from the front of the crankshaft.
3 Remove the damper and mounting hub, using a suitable extractor (see Fig. 1.5), for the latter.
4 Prise out the defective seal and tap in the new one using a suitable socket or piece of tubing. A flange is moulded onto the seal to prevent it going in too far (photo).

23 Crankshaft rear oil seal - renewal

1 This oil seal can only be renewed with the engine removed from the car and completely dismantled. Refer to Section 28, paragraph 3.

24 Cylinder head - decarbonising and examination

1 With the cylinder head removed, use a blunt scraper to remove all trace of carbon and deposits from the combustion spaces and ports. A wire brush in an electric drill will speed up the carbon removal operation. Scrape the cylinder head free from scale or old pieces of gasket or jointing compound. Clean the cylinder head by washing it in paraffin and take particular care to pull a piece of rag through the ports and cylinder head bolt holes. Any dirt remaining in these recesses may well drop onto the gasket or cylinder block mating surface as the cylinder head is lowered into position and could lead to a gasket leak after reassembly is complete.
2 With the cylinder head clean, check for distortion if a history of coolant leakage has been apparent. Carry out this test using a straight edge and feeler gauges or a piece of plate glass. If the surface shows any warping in excess of 0.039 in (0.1015 mm) then the cylinder head will have to be resurfaced which is a job for a specialist engineering company.
3 Clean the pistons and top of the cylinder bores. If the pistons are still in the block then it is essential that great care is taken to ensure that no carbon gets into the cylinder bores as this could scratch the cylinder walls or cause damage to the piston and rings. To ensure this does not happen, first turn the crankshaft so that the end two pistons are at the top of their bores. Stuff rag into the other bores or seal them off with paper and masking tape to prevent particles of carbon entering the cooling system and damaging the water pump.
4 Rotate the crankshaft and repeat the carbon removal operations on the remaining pistons and cylinder bores.
5 Thoroughly clean all particles of carbon from the bores and then inject a little light oil round the edges of the pistons to lubricate the piston rings.

21.1 Oil pump dismantled

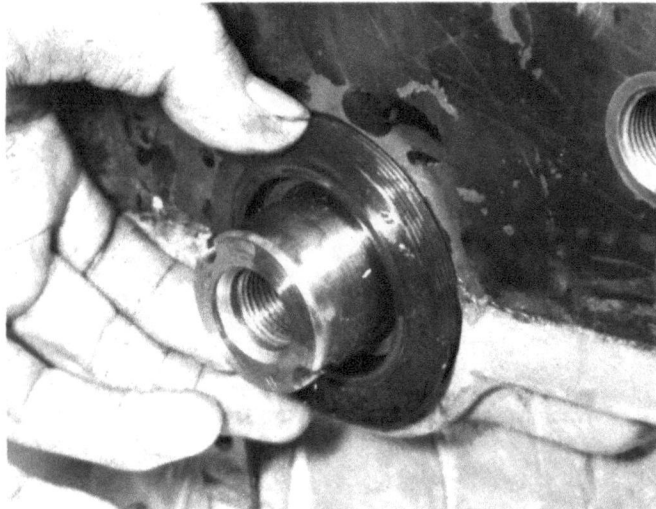

22.4 Crankshaft front oil seal

25 Cylinder block - examination and renovation

1 Examine the crankcase and cylinder block for cracks especially around the bolt holes and between the cylinders.
2 Probe waterways and oil galleries to ensure that they are not

blocked.

3 Check the security of all the small cover plates on the side of the crankcase and cylinder block. Where any of the gaskets are suspect or leakage is evident, extract the cover plate socket screws, and remove the plate.

4 Clean the plate and mating surface of the crankcase, fit a new gasket and insert and retighten the screws.

26 Cylinder head and valves - servicing

1 With the cylinder head dismantled as described in Section 11 examine the heads of the valves for pitting and burning, especially the exhaust valves.

2 The valve seats should be examined at the same time. If the pitting on the valve and seat is very slight, the marks can be removed by grinding the valves and seats together using first coarse and then fine valve grinding paste.

3 Where the valve seats are badly pitted, it will be necessary to re-cut them to give a finished seat angle of $45^\circ\pm15'$. Unless you have the correct valve cutting equipment, it is best to leave this to the local dealer. Normally it is the valves that are too badly worn or burned away and have to be renewed and then ground into their seats. Fitting of new valve seats should be left to your dealer.

4 Valve grinding is carried out as follows. Smear a trace of coarse carborundum paste on the seat face and apply a suction grinder tool to the valve head. With a semi-rotary motion, grind the valve head to its seat, lifting the valve occasionally to redistribute the grinding paste. When a dull matt, even surface finish is produced on both the valve seat and the valve, wipe off the paste and repeat the process with fine carborundum paste, lifting and turning the valve to distribute the paste as before. A light spring placed under the valve head will greatly ease this operation. When a smooth unbroken ring of light grey matt finish is produced, on both valve and valve seat faces, the grinding operation is completed.

5 Scrape away all carbon from the valve head and the valve stem. Carefully clean away every trace of grinding compound, taking great care to leave none in the ports or in the valve guides. Clean the valves and valve seats with a paraffin soaked rag then with a dry rag, and finally, if an air line is available, blow the valves, valve guides and valve ports clean.

6 To test for wear in a valve guide, insert a new unworn valve and check to see whether it rocks from side to side.

7 If it does, the guide must be driven out of the cylinder head using a suitable mandrel.

8 Always fit an oversize guide (+ 0.012 mm) in order to maintain the interference fit of the guide in the head.

9 Before fitting the guide, heat the cylinder head to between 176 and 194°F (80 and 90°C) and cool the guide in liquid air or dry ice if possible. Drive in the guide until the circlip is tight against the upper surface of the cylinder head (Fig. 1.11).

27 Engine - preparation for reassembly

1 To ensure maximum life with reliability from a rebuilt engine, not only must everything be correctly assembled but all components must be spotlessly clean and the correct spring or plain washers used where originally located. Always lubricate bearing and working surfaces with clean engine oil during reassembly of engine parts.

2 Before reassembly commences, renew any bolts or studs the threads of which are damaged or corroded.

3 As well as your normal tool kit, gather together clean rags, oil can, a torque wrench and a complete (overhaul) set of gaskets and oil seals.

4 The fitting sequence recommended is as follows:

Crankshaft and main bearings.
Piston/connecting rod assemblies.
Oil pump.
Sump/crankshaft housing.
Engine rear plate.
Flywheel (driveplate - automatic transmission)
Crankshaft pulley/damper assembly.
Auxiliary shaft, distributor, oil pump drive gear.
Distributor drive housing.
Cylinder head/camshaft, rocker cover.

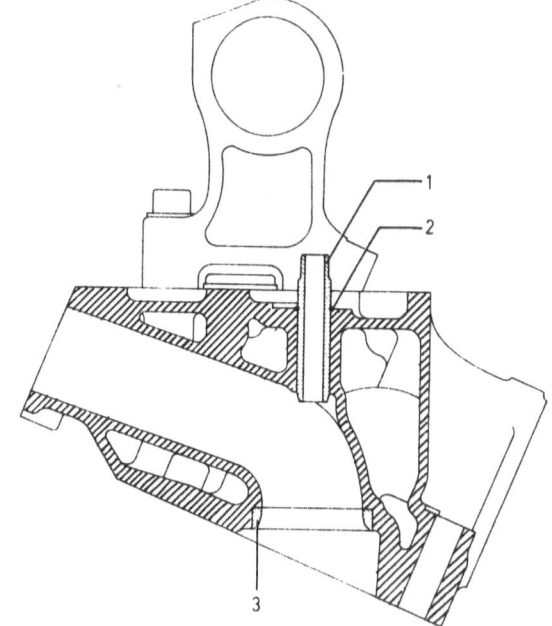

Fig. 1.11. Valve guide installation diagram (Sec. 26)

1 Valve guide   *2 Circlip*   *3 Valve seat*

28 Engine reassembly - crankshaft and connecting rods

1 With the crankcase inverted, locate the main bearing shells in their crankcase recesses noting that on all engines except M180, the No. 4 bearing shell is plain without an oil groove but with an oil hole and that the shells with the thrust flanges are located in No. 3 web counting from the front of the engine. On M180 type engines, the thrust washers are located on No. 2 web in the crankcase (photos).

2 If new shells are being fitted, it does not matter into which recess they are fitted but if the original ones are being used again, make sure that they are returned to their original recesses (photo).

3 Press new sealing strips into the grooves at the rear of the crankcase and the crankshaft housing. Use a handle of a hammer to press the strip into position, making sure that it is positively engaged on the anti-rotation spike in the crankcase groove. Put the sealing strips so that they both project at their ends, above the metal mating surfaces by about 0.024 in (0.6 mm) (Figs. 1.12, 1.13 and 1.14).

4 Oil the main bearing shells in the crankcase liberally and then lower the crankshaft, *complete with timing chain* into the crankcase. If a split type timing chain is being fitted, join the ends together with a piece of wire (photo).

5 Fit the bearing shells to the main bearing caps and fit the caps in their numbered sequence. The caps have locating dowels of different diameters so that they can only be fitted one way round. Remember No. 3 cap from the front of the engine carries the bearing shells with the thrust flanges on all engines except M180. On M180 engines No. 2 cap carries the thrust flanges (photo).

6 Screw in the bolts and tighten to the specified torque. Remember that the right-hand bolt on the front cap retains the oil pump (photo).

7 Check the crankshaft for smooth rotation.

8 If the timing chain slippers were removed, refit them.

9 If the oil pressure relief valve was removed from the front face of the engine, now is the time to refit it together with its plug.

10 Turn the engine on its side and prepare to fit the piston/connecting rods. Check that the piston is correctly assembled to No. 1 connecting rod and that the gudgeon pin circlips are securely engaged in their grooves (photos).

11 Fit the piston rings by reversing the removal operations described in Section 18. The compression rings can be fitted either way up but the oil control ring is stepped on its lower face. Set the piston ring end gaps at equidistant points of a circle to prevent end gap alignment and consequent gas blow-by.

12 Oil the piston rings liberally and fit a piston ring clamp. Compress the rings into their grooves.

13 Fit a new bearing shell to the connecting rod big-end and then

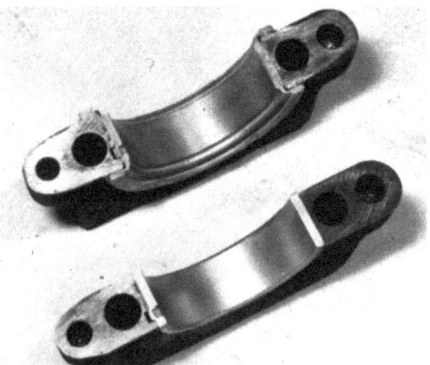

28.1A No. 3 (top) and No. 4 main bearing caps and shells (not M180)

28.1B Main bearing shells fitted to crankcase

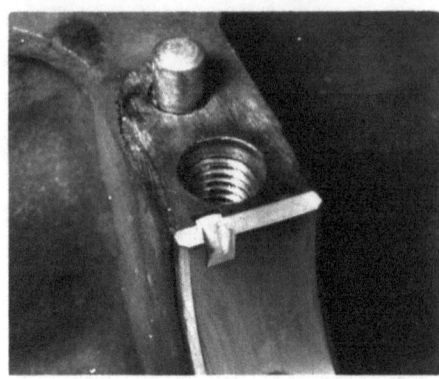

28.2 Main bearing shell locating tab and cap positioning dowel

28.3 Crankcase rear sealing strip (supplied in one piece for cutting)

Fig. 1.12. Pressing in new crankshaft rear oil sealing strip (Sec. 28)

Fig. 1.13. Crankshaft rear oil sealing strip anti-rotational spike (Sec. 28)

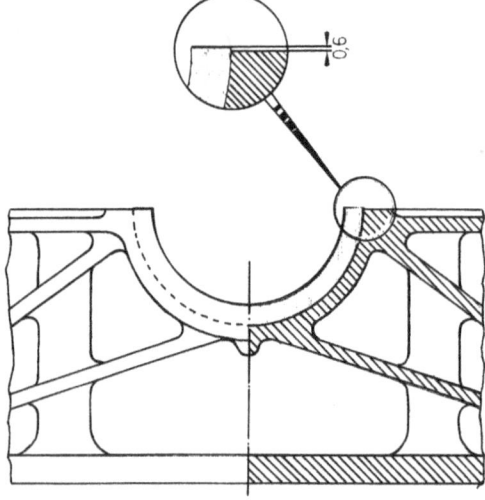

Fig. 1.14. Crankshaft rear oil sealing strip installed showing projection of end (Sec. 28)

lower the connecting rod into the cylinder bore so that the base of the piston compressor rests squarely on the top of the block (photo).

14 Check that the front facing mark on the piston crown is towards the front of the engine (photo).

15 Apply the end of the wooden handle of a hammer to the centre of the piston crown and then give a sharp blow to the hammer head to drive the piston assembly into the cylinder. As this happens, the piston ring clamp will be released (photo).

16 Pull the connecting rod down and engage it with the crankpins (previously oiled) on the crankshaft. Turn the crankshaft as necessary to facilitate this and to enable the big-end cap, complete with bearing shell, to be fitted. Make sure that the cap is fitted the correct way round and then fit the nuts and tighten them to the specified torque wrench setting (photos).

17 Repeat the foregoing operations on the five remaining piston/connecting rod assemblies, making sure that the crankpins are well

28.4 Crankshaft installed complete with timing chain

28.5 Main bearing cap bolts at front end (oil pump not fitted in interests of clarity)

28.6 Tightening a main bearing cap bolt

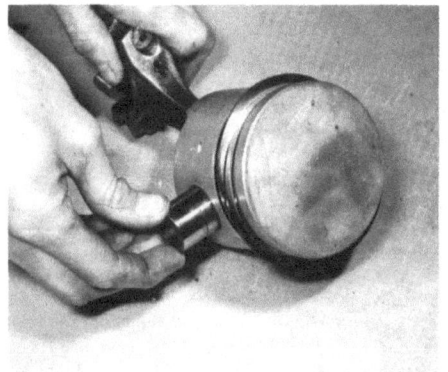

28.10A Fitting a gudgeon pin

28.10B Piston rings and gudgeon pin circlip installed

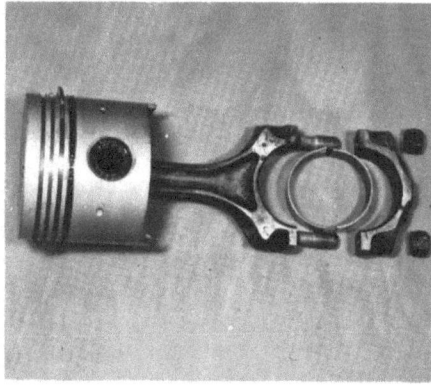

28.10C Piston/connecting rod components

28.13 Piston ring compressor in position

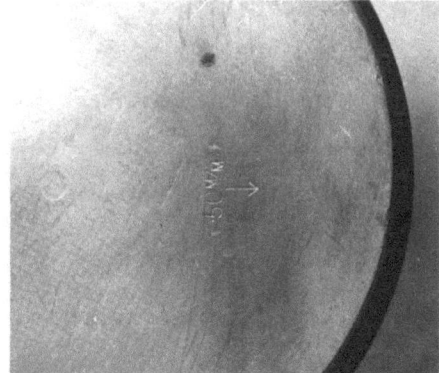

28.14 Piston crown marks

28.15 Installing piston into cylinder bore

28.16A Fitting a big-end cap

28.16B Tightening a big-end cap

29.1A Installing oil pump

lubricated and that the assemblies are fitted in the correct numbered sequence with the piston crown marks facing the front of the engine.

29 Engine reassembly - oil pump and sump

1   Fit the oil pump into the crankcase, noting that one of the retaining bolts also acts as the front right-hand bolt for No. 1 main bearing cap. **Note: It is imperative that the retaining bolts are fitted so that their nuts are located at the filter intake end as shown, otherwise the ends of the bolts will foul the big-end connecting rods (photos).**
2   Refit the small sump cover plate using a new gasket (photo).
3   Refit the crankshaft housing complete with new rear sealing strip (see Section 28). Make sure that the metal to metal surfaces are quite clean and apply jointing compound to both surfaces (photo).
4   Tighten the socket headed screws evenly and in diagonally opposite sequence.

30 Engine reassembly - rear plate and flywheel

1   Fit the rear plate to the rear of the engine but only screw in the bolts finger tight (photo).
2   The crankshaft should now be rotated so that the crankshaft rear flange can be checked for out-of-true in relation to the machined recess at the periphery of the rear plate. This operation is not absolutely essential unless the rear plate has been dropped or mishandled, in which case, the mating of the engine and transmission could prove difficult because of misalignment.
3   The crankshaft damper bolt can be temporarily refitted as a means of rotating the crankshaft and a dial gauge or small block and feeler blades used to check the run-out which should not exceed 0.002 in (0.05 mm). Give the rear plate light blows as necessary to correct and to even out the run-out at all points round the flange.
4   When adjustment is correct, fully tighten the retaining bolts to the specified torque wrench setting.
5   Engage the flywheel or drive plate with the dowel on the crankshaft rear flange, insert new bolts (the original ones stretch in service) and tighten to the specified torque wrench setting (photo).
6   Refit the water pump housing to the front of the engine.

31 Engine reassembly - crankshaft damper, auxiliary shaft and allied components

1   Refit the oil pressure relief valve (if removed) to the front of the engine and screw on the cap. Bolt on the ignition timing pointer (photos).
2   Make sure that No. 1 piston is at TDC and then fit the damper mounting hub to the front end of the crankshaft. Make sure that the ignition timing scales are at the top. Before screwing in the hub retaining bolt, make sure that the conical spring washers are not all facing the same way otherwise their locking characteristic will be non-effective (photo).
3   Now fit the auxiliary shaft and sprocket. To do this on fuel

injection type engines, smear the shaft with oil and then push it through the thrust washer and sprocket (thinner boss of sprocket towards rear of the engine). The sprocket will be held in position during this operation with the chain engaged with its teeth. Fit the Woodruff key and push the shaft through the sprocket (photos).
4   Fit the spacer to the front of the auxiliary shaft (photo).
5   Fit the second Woodruff key and push the distributor drive gear onto the auxiliary shaft (photo).
6   Fit the washer, spring, second washer and nut to the auxiliary shaft.
7   From above, tap in the revolution counter/oil pump drive gear so that it meshes with the gear on the auxiliary shaft. Screw in the lock bolt (photos).
8   Using a new gasket, bolt on the distributor drive housing (photo).
9   *On carburettor type engines,* fitting the auxiliary shaft is similar to that just described except that no rev. counter gear is used and the shaft design differs by having no rear coupling or seals for connection to the fuel injection pump.

32 Engine reassembly - cylinder head and camshaft

1   Reassemble the valves to the cylinder head, making sure that they are in their correct sequence and located in the seats into which they have been ground (photo).
2   Using the valve spring compressor tool, reassemble the oil seal, the valve spring seat, the valve springs, the retainer and the split collets to the first valve. The tighter coils of the outer valve spring should be next to the cylinder head (photos).
3   Follow with the other valves and when they are all assembled into the cylinder head, tap the end of each valve stem with a hammer and a block of hardwood to settle the components. If the timing chain idler sprocket was removed, now is the time to refit it and its shaft into the cylinder head. Screw on the cover cap (photo).
4   Set the crankshaft damper scale TDC mark opposite to the pointer on the front face of the engine.
5   Locate a new gasket on the top of the cylinder block and then lower the cylinder head into position, making sure that the timing chain is pulled through the aperture at the front of the cylinder head. Support the chain in an upward direction using a hooked piece of wire (photos).
6   Insert those cylinder head bolts, complete with their washers, into all the holes with the exception of those where the rocker cover support arches are also mounted. Note that the longer bolts pass through the holes in the camshaft bearing pedestals.
7   Tighten the bolts progressively in stages to the specified torque wrench setting. Do not overlook the small bolts at the front of the cylinder head - two inside and two outside the timing chain aperture (photo).
8   Always tighten the cylinder head bolts at the centre first and then work outwards to the front and rear of the engine in diagonally opposite sequence (Fig. 1.15).
9   Fit the camshaft by passing it carefully through the (previously oiled) bearings (photo).
10 Fit the rocker cover support arches and screw in the remaining cylinder head bolts.
11 Refit the oil pipe to the rocker cover supports (photo).

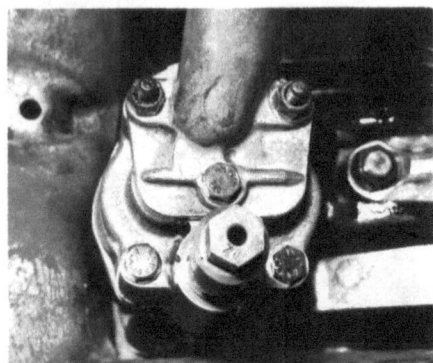
29.1B Position of oil pump nuts and bolts

29.2 Fitting sump cover plate and gasket

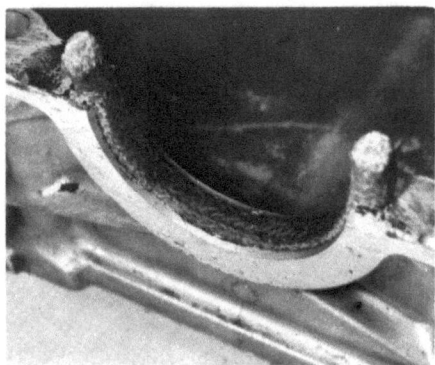
29.3 Crankshaft housing rear sealing strip (not yet trimmed)

30.1 Fitting engine rear plate

30.5 Fitting driveplate assembly (automatic transmission)

31.1A Fitting oil pressure relief valve

31.1B Oil pressure relief valve

31.1C Ignition timing pointer

31.2 Crankshaft damper mounting hub installed

31.3A Installing auxiliary shaft

31.3B Fitting thrust washer to front of auxiliary shaft

31.3C Fitting chain sprocket to auxiliary shaft

31.4 Fitting spacer to front of auxiliary shaft

31.5 Fitting distributor drive gear to front of auxiliary shaft

31.7A Fitting rev counter/oil pump drive

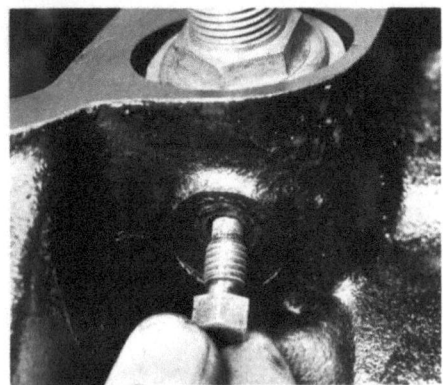
31.7B Fitting lock bolt to rev counter/oil pump drive

31.8 Fitting distributor drive housing and gasket

32.1 Installing a valve to cylinder head

32.2A Valve stem lower oil seal

32.2B Valve stem upper oil seal

32.2C Fitting double valve springs

32.2D Fitting valve spring retainer

32.2E Installing split collets through aperture in special valve spring compressor tool

32.3 Timing chain idler sprocket in cylinder head

32.5A New cylinder head gasket installed

32.5B Timing chain supported for cylinder head installation

32.7 Tightening a cylinder head bolt

33 Engine reassembly - timing chain and tensioner

1   Check that the crankshaft damper TDC mark is still opposite the pointer on the front face of the engine (No. 1 piston at TDC on compression).

2   Pull the chain upwards so that it is engaged and runs taut between the crankshaft sprocket and the auxiliary shaft sprocket.

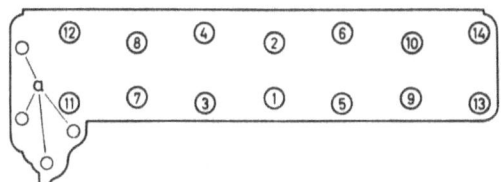

Fig. 1.15. Cylinder head bolt tightening sequence diagram (Sec. 32)

3   Turn the camshaft so that when the camshaft sprocket is fitted, the marks on the rear of the sprocket thrust washer and the No. 1 camshaft bearing pedestal will be in alignment (photo).

4   Refit the chain tensioner sprocket and its shaft positioning the coil spring so that it will force the sprocket forward (photos).

5   Engage the camshaft sprocket within the loop of the timing chain, then fit the thrust washer and the sprocket onto the camshaft flange. In order to be able to push the sprocket complete with chain onto the camshaft flange, the camshaft will have to be pushed slightly backwards. Once the sprocket is partially engaged on its Woodruff key, push the camshaft fully forward again. Make sure that the timing chain is kept taut between the teeth of the auxiliary shaft sprocket and the camshaft sprocket. Screw in the camshaft sprocket bolt complete with spring and plain washers (photos).

6   Refit the chain guide by screwing in the two socket-headed screws (photo).

7   Refit the chain tensioner assembly complete with the coil spring and large cap nut (photos).

8   Throughout these operations, do not let the chain jump off the

32.9 Installing the crankshaft

32.11 Oil feed pipe and rocker cover supports

33.3 Camshaft sprocket thrust washer and pedestal alignment marks

33.4A Chain tensioner sprocket and shaft being installed

33.4B Chain tensioner sprocket showing coil spring

33.5A Camshaft sprocket installed

33.5B Camshaft sprocket bolt and washers

33.6 Timing chain guide

33.7A Fitting timing chain tensioner

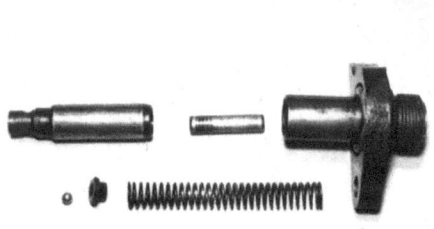

33.7B Timing chain tensioner assembly

33.9 Coolant by-pass tube

33.11 Fitting a rocker arm thrust piece

33.12 Fitting a rocker arm

33.14 Rocker clamp spring attachment

34.4 Adjusting a valve clearance

camshaft sprocket teeth or its timed position will be altered.
9   To the front of the engine head and block reconnect the coolant by-pass tube (two banjo unions) (photo).
10 Valve timing can become inaccurate when the timing chain becomes worn or stretches. Checking the valve timing is too complicated for the home mechanic and requires the use of special gauges. It is best therefore to let your Mercedes-Benz dealer do this work. In order to avoid having to renew the timing chain as a means of rectifying valve timing, offset Woodruff keys are supplied for use with the camshaft sprocket. If the key is fitted with the offset to the right in the normal direction of chain rotation, the valve opening will be advanced. If the offset is to the left then the valve opening will be retarded. Offset keys are available in the following sizes:

Offset	Crankshaft correction
2° (0.7 mm)	4°
3° 20′ (0.9 mm)	$6\frac{1}{2}^o$
4° (1.1 mm)	8°
5° (1.3 mm)	10°

If the inlet valve opening is advanced too much there is a possibility of the valve head damaging the piston crown.
11 The rocker arms, thrust pieces and spring clamps should now be fitted. To engage the rocker arms on their ball studs, first turn the crankshaft so that all the pistons are a little way down the bores. Observe this through the plug holes or by inserting a length of wire into the plug holes. This setting of the position of the pistons will avoid any possibility of the valve heads hitting the piston crowns (photo).
12 Now lever each valve downwards, using a large screwdriver or similar tool to compress the valve springs (photo).
13 Rotate the crankshaft as and when necessary to bring the lowest cam profile into its correct position over each rocker arm.
14 Fit the rocker arm and thrust piece and spring clamp to each valve position in turn (photo).
15 Adjust the valve clearances after all the rocker arms and thrust pieces have been refitted, as described in the next Section.

34 Valve clearances - checking and adjusting

1   The valve clearances should always be checked with the engine cold.
2   Remove the spark plugs and the rocker cover.
3   Turn the crankshaft by means of the pulley bolt until the long profile of the camshaft lobe nearest the front of the engine is pointing upward (cam base circle of camshaft next to rocker arm).
4   Now insert a feeler blade *between the cam lobe and the rocker arm*. The clearance should be as specified in the Specifications Section, indicated by the feeler blade being a stiff sliding fit. If it is not, adjust the clearance by turning the ball pin. The ball pin has stiff threads and is self-locking. Where it is found that moving the ball pin still does not provide enough clearance between the camshaft lobe and the rocker arm then an alternative thickness thrust piece should be obtained and fitted. These thrust pieces are available in several different thicknesses (Fig. 1.16) (photo).
5   When the first (exhaust) valve has been checked, continue with the next valve and so on. If the firing order of the engine (1 - 5 - 3 - 6 - 2 - 4) is followed it will avoid excessive rotation of the crankshaft.
6   Remember that the inlet and exhaust valve clearances are different so identify the valve carefully before checking its clearance (Fig. 1.17).
7   Refit the spark plugs and rocker cover.

35 Engine - final reassembly before refitting

1   Refit the fuel injection pump as described in Chapter 3.
2   Reconnect the fuel injection pipes (photos).
3   Refit the engine mounting struts (with the pressure regulator valve on the fuel injection engine). Make sure that the struts are fitted the correct way up (photo).
4   Refit the distributor as described in Chapter 4.
5   Fit the water pump impeller into the water pump main housing.
6   Refit the coolant temperature switch housing to the left-hand side of the cylinder head (fuel injection engines) or screw in the temperature sender capillary unit (carburettor engines) (photos).

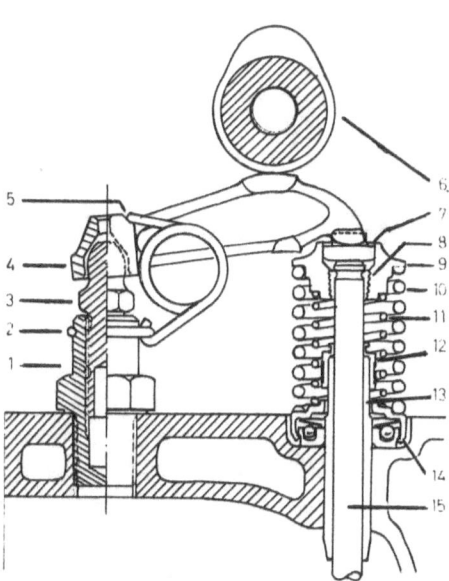

Fig. 1.16. Valve clearance checking diagram (Sec. 34)

1   Adjuster mounting bolt
2   Spring ring
3   Ball pivot adjuster
4   Rocker arm
5   Clamp spring
6   Camshaft
7   Thrust piece
8   Split collet
9   Spring retainer
10 Outer valve spring
11 Inner valve spring
12 Valve stem oil seal
13 Valve guide
14 Valve spring lower seat
15 Valve

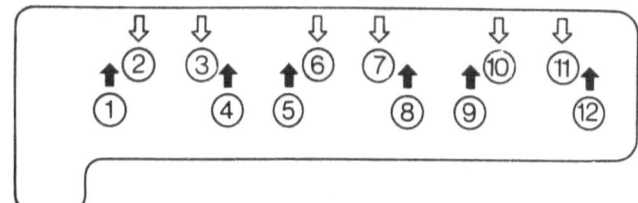

Fig. 1.17. Location of valves (Sec. 34)   ⇧ Inlet

Inlet   2 - 3 - 6 - 7 - 10 - 11
Exhaust   1 - 4 - 5 - 8 - 9 - 12   ⬆ Exhaust

7 Refit the power steering pump bracket (photo).
8 Fit the steering pump (photo).
9 Fit the damper and pulley to the crankshaft mounting hub.
10 Fit the power steering fluid reservoir. **Note: It is very important that the lower mounting bolt for the reservoir is the correct one. If a bolt longer than the original is used, it could foul the timing chain (photo).**
11 Refit the alternator mounting bracket (photo).
12 Refit the thermostat housing.
13 Fit the thermostat, a new gasket and the thermostat housing cover (photo).
14 Connect the oil feed pipe between the rear of the fuel injection pump and the hole which is located just below the power steering fluid reservoir lower mounting bolt (photos).
15 Refit the oil filter base to the left-hand side of the crankcase (photo).
16 Connect the pipes for the engine oil cooler to the engine connecting unions.
17 *On fuel injection engines,* refit the throttle linkage support bracket to the left-hand side of the cylinder head.
18 *On carburettor type engines,* refit the fuel pump to the left-hand side of the crankcase.
19 Fit the engine as described in the next Section (photo).

35.2A Reconnecting fuel injection pipes to pump

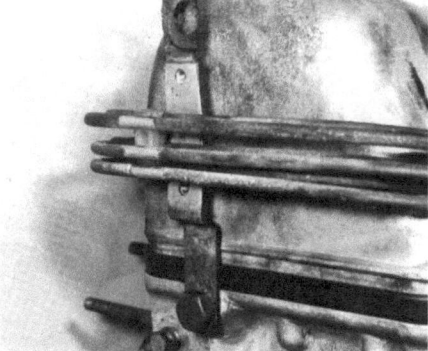

35.2B Routing of fuel injection pipes at front of rocker cover

35.3 Marking on right-hand engine mounting strut

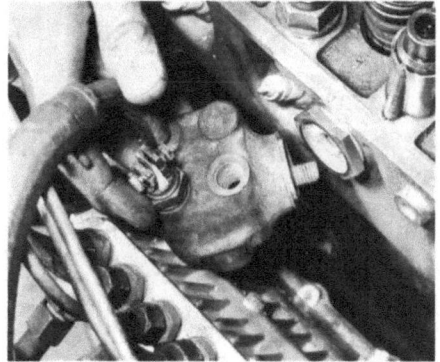

35.6A Fitting coolant temperature switch housing

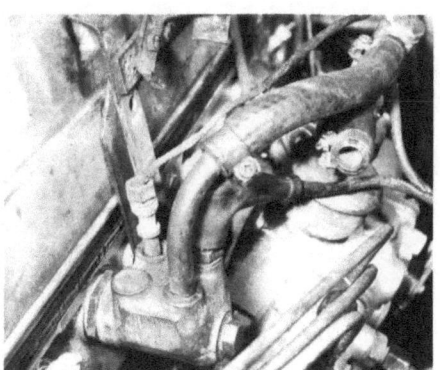

35.6B Coolant switch housing connections

35.7 Power steering pump bracket

35.8 Power steering pump installed

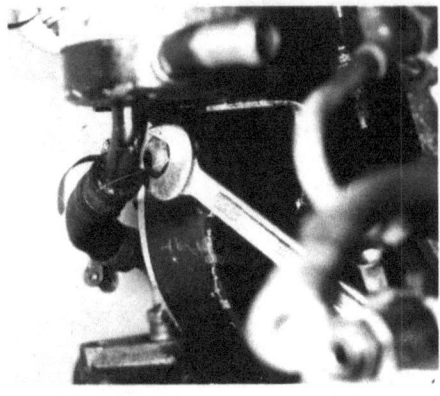

35.10 Power steering pump reservoir lower mounting bolt

35.11 Alternator mounting bracket

35.13 Thermostat housing

35.14A Oil feed pipe connection to fuel injection pump

35.14B Oil feed pipe connection (fuel in injection pump) on crankcase

35.15 Fitting oil filter base

35.19 Fuel injection engine ready for installation

36.11A Pipe arrangement on left-hand side of fuel injection engine

36.11B Power steering fluid lines (engines front lower left)

36.11C Power steering fluid lines (engine front lower right)

36.11D Power steering fluid lines on right-hand side of engine

36 Engine - refitment

1 Refitment is a reversal of the removal method described in Sections 4, 5, 6 or 7 according to which was chosen.

2 If the engine is to be connected to a manual transmission before refitting, refer to Chapter 5 and centralise the clutch driven plate.

Automatic transmission

3 Using the hoist and the help of one or two assistants, lower the engine into the car. Connect it to the automatic transmission making sure that the torque converter is fully to the rear once the temporary retaining clip is removed. The jack under the transmission can be used to raise or lower the unit to improve alignment of the engine and transmission.

Manual gearbox

4 With a manual gearbox, the engine will have to be moved further forward to be able to engage the gearbox input shaft in the splined hub of the clutch driven plate and the gearbox should be raised at its front end at a more steeply inclined angle than the automatic transmission unit.

5 Screw in the engine mounting securing bolts.

6 Refit the starter motor.

7 Using the socket wrench with a long extension, insert the bellhousing to engine bolts.

8 Fit the starter motor front bracket.

9 *On automatic transmission cars,* reconnect the fluid cooler pipes to the transmission and reconnect the torque converter to the driveplate by turning the crankshaft as required to be able to insert the bolts.

10 *On fuel injection engined cars,* locate the metal coolant pipe which runs behind the engine cylinder block and will eventually connect with the underside of the intake manifold.

11 Reconnect the power steering flexible fluid pipes between the power steering pump and the top of the steering box (photos).

12 *On carburettor engined cars,* the manifold assembly can now be refitted complete with carburettors.

13 *On fuel injection type engines,* fit the exhaust manifold using a new gasket so that the downpipes are loosely engaged in the manifold outlet sockets. Pull the exhaust manifolds an inch or two from the cylinder head and refit the intake manifold (photos).

14 Bolt up the manifolds securely also the exhaust downpipe connections.

15 Reconnect the accelerator linkage.

16 Reconnect the leads to the starter solenoid terminals.

17 *On cars with automatic transmission,* connect the vacuum pipe to the rear of the intake manifold by means of the banjo union.

18 Reconnect the brake servo pipe.

19 Reconnect the heater hose to the water pump connection near the radiator hose connection.

20 Refit the alternator and adjustment link.

21 *On cars with fuel injection engines,* make the following reconnections:

Refit the intake manifold heat shield.

Connect the vacuum hose between the distributor and the intake manifold (throttle housing).

Connect the fume extraction hose to the front end of the throttle valve housing.

Connect the coolant hose to the front end of the throttle valve housing.

Bolt on the constant speed (anti-stall) solenoid to the inner branch of the intake manifold.

Reconnect the electrical leads to the outer edge of the intake manifold (throttle valve housing).

Refit the switch housing to the extreme front of the throttle valve housing.

Fit a new element to the fuel filter and fit it to the left-hand side of the crankcase.

Connect the fuel flow and return pipes to the pressure relief valve attached to the engine mounting strut on the left-hand side of the engine.

22 *On cars with carburettor type engines,* make the following reconnections:

Connect the vacuum hoses to the carburettor diaphragm units.

Connect the lead to the automatic choke.

Connect the fuel flow and return lines to the fuel filter.

23 Reconnect the earthing strap which runs between the bellhousing top left-hand bolt and the engine compartment rear bulkhead (photo).

24 Reconnect the oil pressure gauge pipe to the top of the oil filter (photo).

25 Fit a new oil filter element and screw the filter bowl into position using the long centre bolt from the bottom of the bowl.

26 Reconnect the leads to the coolant thermal switches located on the housing on the left-hand side of the cylinder block.

27 Reconnect the heater pipe to the left-hand side of the cylinder block.

28 Refit the windscreen washer reservoir.

29 Reconnect the rev. counter drive cable (if fitted) by inserting the squared inner cable into its recess and then tightening the knurled collar. Make sure that the inner cable is pushed fully up into the outer cable conduit. Failure to do this before reconnecting to the engine can sometimes cause failure of the rev. counter to indicate any reading on the gauge itself (photo).

30 Reconnect the distributor cap and HT leads to the spark plugs.

31 Fit the pulley to the front of the water pump.

32 Fit the fan assembly.

33 Fit the two drivebelts to their pulleys and adjust their tension by moving the position of the alternator and the power steering pump. The tension of a drivebelt is correct when the deflection at the centre point of the longest run of the belt is ½ in (12.7 mm) under finger pressure (photos).

34 Refit and reconnect the radiator.

35 Reconnect the engine oil cooler pipes to the oil cooler.

36 *On cars with automatic transmission,* reconnect the transmission fluid cooler pipes to the base of the radiator.

37 Refit the air cleaner assembly, using a new filter element.

38 Refill the cooling system.

39 Refill the engine with oil.

40 Check the oil level in the transmission.

41 Reconnect the battery.

42 With the help of an assistant, refit the bonnet lid.

43 Make a final check for loose connections, tools left in the engine compartment etc.

36.11E Pipe connections on power steering box

36.13A Manifold gasket in position

36.13B Exhaust manifolds being fitted

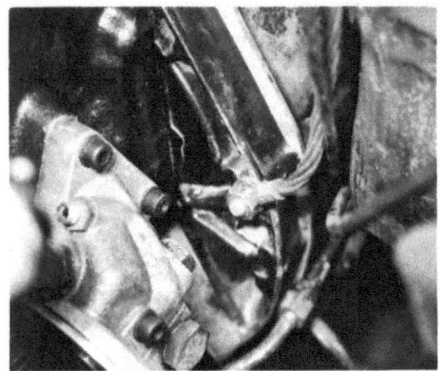

36.23 Engine to bodyframe earthing strap

36.24 Oil pressure gauge connection to oil filter body

36.29 Revolution counter cable connection

36.33A Fitting a drivebelt

36.33B Power steering pump adjuster for drivebelt tension

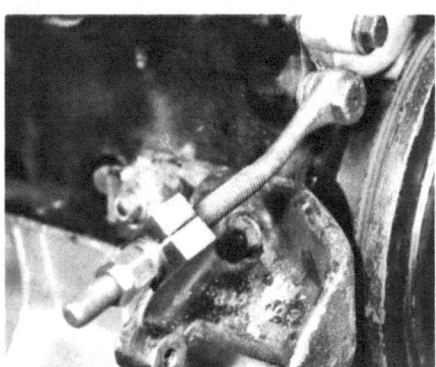

36.33C Alternator drivebelt tension adjuster

44 On cars with manual transmission check the clutch pedal free movement (see Chapter 5).

---

37 Engine - initial start up after major overhaul

1 Set the engine idle speed rather higher than that specified in order to offset the stiffness of new internal components.
2 Start the engine and immediately check the oil pressure and look for oil or coolant leaks.
3 At the earliest opportunity, check the carburettor or fuel injection settings, the ignition timing and emission control system operation.

4 If a large number of new internal components have been fitted to the engine, restrict speeds as for a new engine for the first few hundred miles.
5 At the end of the first 1000 miles (1600 km) operation, change the engine oil and filter, check the torque of the cylinder head bolts and the valve clearances. To check the cylinder head bolts, unscrew the first bolt one quarter of a turn and then tighten it to the specified torque wrench setting. Repeat with all the other bolts but only unscrew them one at a time so that there is never more than one bolt loose at once.
6 Bleed the power steering system as described in Chapter 11.
7 Have the air conditioning system re-charged if this was discharged before overhaul began.

38 Fault diagnosis

Symptom	Reason/s
Engine will not turn over when starter switch is operated	Flat battery.
	Bad battery connections.
	Bad connections at solenoid switch and/or starter motor.
	Starter motor jammed.
	Defective solenoid.
	Starter motor defective.
Engine turns over normally but fails to start	No spark at plugs.
	No fuel reaching engine.
	Too much fuel reaching the engine (flooding).
Engine starts but runs unevenly and misfires	Ignition and/or fuel system faults.
	Incorrect valve clearances.
	Burnt out valves.
	Worn out piston rings.
	Worn timing chain.
Lack of power	Ignition and/or fuel system faults.
	Incorrect valve clearances.
	Burnt out valves.
	Worn out piston rings.
	Worn timing chain.
Excessive oil consumption	Oil leaks from crankshaft rear oil seal, timing cover gasket and oil seal, rocker cover gasket, oil filter gasket, sump gasket, sump plug washer.
	Worn piston rings or cylinder bores resulting in oil being burnt by engine.
	Worn valve guides and/or defective valve stem seals.
Excessive mechanical noise from engine	Wrong valve clearances.
	Worn crankshaft bearings.
	Worn cylinders (piston slap).
	Slack or worn timing chain and sprockets.
Poor idling	Leak in inlet manifold gasket.
	Perforated or leaking PCV connecting pipe.
	Perforated or leaking brake servo pipe.

Note: When investigating starting and uneven running faults, do not be tempted into snap diagnosis. Start from the beginning of the check procedure and follow it through. It will take less time in the long run. Poor performance from an engine in terms of power and economy is not normally diagnosed quickly. In any event, the ignition and fuel systems must be checked first before assuming any further investigation needs to be made.

In addition to the foregoing, reference should also be made to the fault finding chart for emission control equipment which is to be found at the end of Chapter 3. Such a fault can have an immediate effect upon engine performance.

Chapter 2 Cooling system

Contents

Specifications

System type	Pressurised, thermo-syphon with water pump assistance
Radiator cap type	No. 100
Thermostat type and marking	Wax pellet 87°C
Capacities	
230/8 models	19 Imp pts (23 US pts/10.8 litres)
250 models	17.4 Imp pts (20.9 US pts/9.9 litres)
280 models	18.8 Imp pts (22.6 US pts/10.7 litres)

1 General description

The cooling system comprises the radiator, top and bottom water hoses, water pump, cylinder head and block water jackets, radiator cap with pressure relief valve and flow and return heater hoses. The thermostat is located in a housing at the front of the cylinder head. The principle of the system is that cold water in the bottom of the radiator circulates upwards through the lower radiator hose to the water pump, where the pump impeller pushes the water round the cylinder block and head through the various cast-in passages to cool the cylinder bores, combustion surfaces and valve seats. When sufficient heat has been absorbed by the cooling water, and the engine has reached an efficient working temperature, the water moves from the cylinder head past the now open thermostat into the top radiator hose and into the radiator header tank.

The water then travels down the radiator tubes where it is rapidly cooled by the in-rush of air, when the vehicle is in forward motion. A multi-bladed fan, mounted on the water pump pulley, assists this cooling action. The water, now cooled, reaches the bottom of the radiator and the cycle is repeated.

When the engine is cold, the thermostat remains closed until the coolant reaches a pre-determined temperature (see Specifications). This assists rapid warming-up.

An electrosensitive capsule located in the cylinder head measures the water temperature.

All late models have an expansion tank located remotely from the radiator. When the system is hot and pressurised, excess coolant is expelled into the reservoir tank and when the engine cools down, the space left by the contraction of the coolant in the radiator is filled by liquid flowing from the expansion tank. The necessary valves to permit this two way flow are incorporated in the radiator cap. Under normal circumstances, no topping up of the cooling system is required.

The cooling system also provides the heat for the car interior heater.

On vehicles equipped with automatic transmission, the transmission fluid is circulated through a cooler built into the base of the radiator.

On cars equipped with air conditioning systems, a condenser is placed ahead of the radiator and is bolted in conjunction with it.

The radiator cooling fan is of the fluid coupling type and is a sealed unit. This device permits the fan to slip when the engine speed reaches a pre-determined level and the ram effect of the air passing through the fan blades caused by the forward motion of the car is sufficient to dissipate the heat being generated by the engine. On fuel injection models, the coolant is used for pre-heating purposes at the air intake housing and also at the fuel injection pump.

2 Cooling system - topping up

1 When carrying out the regular weekly check on the coolant level on cars without an expansion tank, preferably have the engine cold. If it is hot, cover the cap with a cloth and release the cap slowly until any steam pressure has been released before completely removing it.
2 With a cold engine, the coolant level should be up to the indicator inside the filler neck (Fig. 2.1).
3 With a hot engine, the level should be ½ in (12.7 mm) above the indicator.
4 On cars with an expansion tank, keep the level up to the marker within the tank in the same way as described for the radiator in the

Fig. 2.1. Radiator filler neck indicator mark (Sec. 2)

preceding paragraph (photo).
5   Where excessive topping up is required, check for leaks anywhere in the system and rectify.

3   Cooling system - draining

1   Remove the radiator cap or the cap from the expansion tank as applicable.
2   Set the heater control levers to 'HOT'.
3   Unscrew and remove the drain plug at the base of the radiator and also the one on the side of the cylinder block. Catch the coolant in a suitable container if it is fit for further use (photo).
4   Disconnect the heater hose from the cylinder head; lower its end as far as possible; this will drain the heating system.
5   If there is any reluctance for the coolant to flow from the drain plugs, probe them with a piece of wire.

4   Cooling system - flushing

1   The radiator and waterways in the engine after some time may become restricted or even blocked with scale or sediment which reduces the efficiency of the cooling system. When this condition occurs or the coolant appears rusty or dark in colour the system should be flushed. In severe cases reverse flushing may be required as described later.
2   Place the heater controls to the 'HOT' position and unscrew fully the radiator and cylinder block drain taps.
3   Remove the radiator filler cap and place a hose in the filler neck. Allow water to run through the system until it appears free from impurities.
4   In severe cases of contamination of the coolant or in the system, reverse flush by first removing the radiator cap and disconnecting the lower radiator hose at the radiator connection end and remove the radiator as described in Section 8.
5   Invert the radiator and insert the hose in the bottom outlet pipe. Continue flushing until clear water comes from the radiator top tank.
7   To flush the engine water jackets, remove the thermostat as described later in this Chapter and place a hose in the thermostat location until clear water runs from the water pump inlet. Cleaning by the use of chemical compounds is not recommended.

5   Cooling system - filling

1   Set the heater controls to 'HOT'.
2   Pour in the coolant slowly until it reaches the bottom of the radiator filler neck.
3   Start the engine and let it run for a few minutes varying the speed

level.
4   Let the engine resume idling and top up the radiator.
5   On cars fitted with an expansion tank, fill the tank to the correct level mark with an antifreeze mixture made up in the same proportions as that used for the cooling system.
6   Refit the radiator cap and expansion tank cap.

6   Antifreeze mixture

1   The cooling system should be filled with antifreeze solution in early autumn. The heater matrix and radiator bottom tank are particularly prone to freezing if antifreeze is not used in air temperatures below freezing. Modern antifreeze solutions of good quality will also prevent corrosion and rusting and they may be left in the system to advantage all year round, draining and refilling with fresh solution each year.
2   Before adding antifreeze to the system, check all hose connections and check the tightness of the cylinder head bolts as such solutions are searching. The cooling system should be drained and refilled with clean water as previously explained, before adding antifreeze.
3   The quantity of antifreeze which should be used for various levels of protection is given in the table below, expressed as a percentage of the system capacity.

Antifreeze volume	Protection to	Safe pump circulation
25%	$-26^{o}C$ $(-15^{o}F)$	$-12^{o}C$ $(10^{o}F)$
30%	$-33^{o}C$ $(-28^{o}F)$	$-16^{o}C$ $(3^{o}F)$
35%	$-39^{o}C$ $(-38^{o}F)$	$-20^{o}C$ $(-4^{o}F)$

4   Where the cooling system contains an antifreeze solution any topping-up should be done with a solution made up in similar proportions to the original in order to avoid dilution.

7   Thermostat - removal, testing and refitting

1   Partially drain the cooling system.
2   Unbolt the cover from the thermostat housing and lift it, still attached to the radiator hose, to one side.
3   Extract the thermostat (photo).
4   To test the thermostat, suspend it in a container of water and heat the water until the thermostat opens. By inserting a thermometer into the water, check the opening temperature of the thermostat and if this varies considerably from the figure stamped on it, fit a new one. Always renew the thermostat if it is stuck open or if one of incorrect rating (see Specifications) has been fitted by a previous owner. The fitting of a thermostat of incorrect rating will cause either overheating or cool running of the engine, slow warm up and an inefficient car interior heater.

2.4 Cooling system reservoir (280 S/L)

3.3 Radiator drain plug and auto transmission fluid cooler pipe connections

7.3 Thermostat and sealing ring

5   Refitting is a reversal of removal, but use new gaskets and seals. Make sure that the small ball valve (5) is located at the highest point on those engines where the thermostat housing is inclined at an angle (Figs. 2.2 and 2.3).

8   Radiator - removal, inspection and refitting

1   Unscrew the radiator drain plug and drain the coolant into a suitable container. Retain the coolant if it contains antifreeze mixture. There is no need to drain the cylinder block when removing the radiator.
2   Disconnect the radiator upper and lower hoses (photos).
3   Disconnect the engine oil cooler which is attached to the side of the radiator and move it to one side. It may be easier to drain the oil cooler, disconnect the oil lines from it and to remove the radiator complete with cooler for later separation. This largely depends upon whether the oil cooler is also to be cleaned or renewed at the same time.
4   Unbolt the radiator and lift it carefully from the engine compartment. Take care not to allow coolant to spill on the paintwork of the car.
5   *On cars equipped with automatic transmission* the inlet and outlet pipes which connect with the fluid cooler at the base of the radiator must also be disconnected.
6   Inspect the radiator for leaks; if evident it is recommended that the repair is left to a specialist or the radiator is exchanged for a reconditioned one.
7   Whenever the radiator is removed, take the opportunity of brushing all flies and accumulated dirt from the radiator fins or applying air from a tyre air compressor in the reverse direction to normal airflow.
8   The radiator pressure cap should be tested by a service station and if it leaks or its spring has weakened, it must be renewed with one of specified pressure rating (Fig. 2.4).
9   Refitting the radiator is a reversal of removal. Refill the cooling system as described in Section 5 (Fig. 2.5).

9   Water pump - removal and refitting

1   Drain the cooling system (see Section 3).
2   Remove the radiator (see Section 8).
3   Remove the fan/coupling assembly by unscrewing the small bolts which secure the slotted flange at the rear of the coupling unit (photo).
4   Slacken the water pump drivebelt and remove the belt and pulley from the front of the water pump (photo).
5   Unbolt and remove the impeller section of the water pump from the main pump housing (photo).
6   If for any reason, the main housing must be removed from the front face of the engine then the crankshaft damper must first be

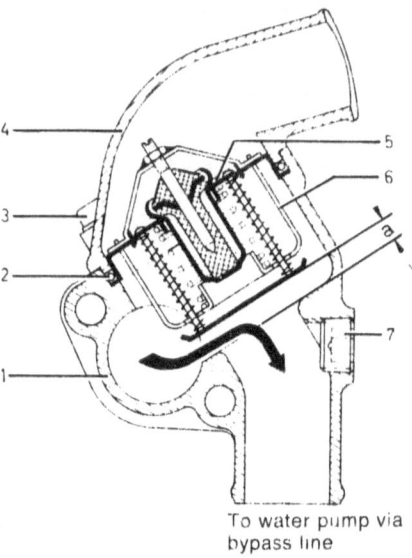

To water pump via bypass line

Fig. 2.2. Diagrammatic view showing thermostat main valve closed, by-pass valve open. Stroke 'a' = 6 mm at between 74 - 78°C (Sec. 7)

1 Thermostat housing	5 Ball valve
2 Sealing ring	6 Thermostat
3 Cover bolt	7 Plug
4 Thermostat cover	

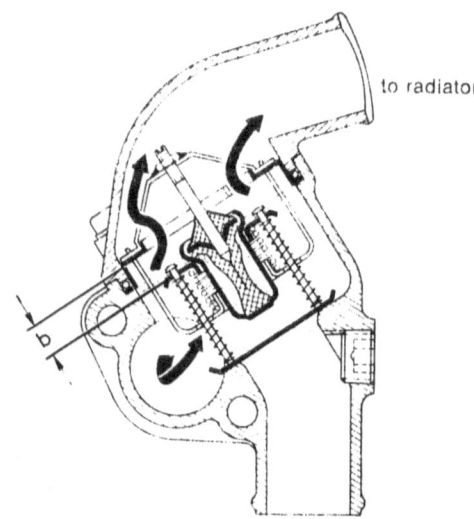

to radiator

Fig. 2.3. Diagrammatic view showing thermostat main valve open, by-pass valve closed. Stroke 'b' =8 mm at between 91 and 94°C. (Sec. 7)

withdrawn and the coolant hose disconnected (photo).
7   Refitting is a reversal of removal but use a new flange gasket and tension the drivebelt.

10 Water pump - overhaul

1   When a fault occurs in the water pump it is recommended that a new unit is fitted. However, if only a water leak is evident from the pump, the seal may be renewed. If the water pump bearings become worn then these can only be renewed as an assembled unit complete with new pump shaft.
2   Using a suitable claw type extractor draw the impeller from the shaft of the pump. Prise out the ring seal (4) and counter ring (5) complete with its 'O' ring (Fig. 2.7).

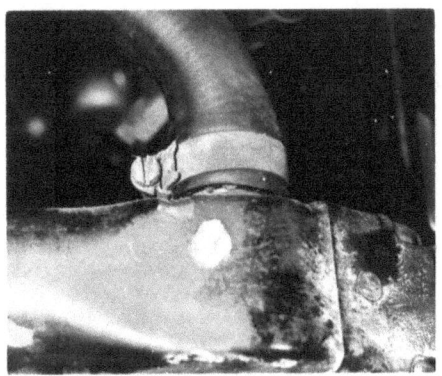

8.2A Radiator upper hose

8.2B Hose connecting expansion tank to radiator

8.2C Radiator hose connection to water pump main housing

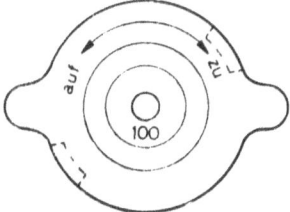

Fig. 2.4. Radiator pressure cap marking (Sec. 8)

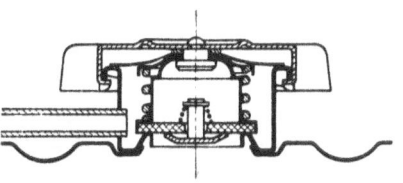

Fig. 2.5. Sectional view of radiator pressure cap (Sec. 8)

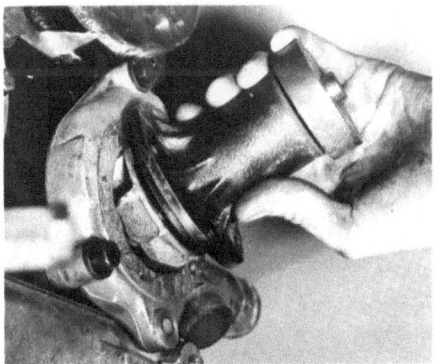

9.3 Unbolting fan from water pump pulley hub

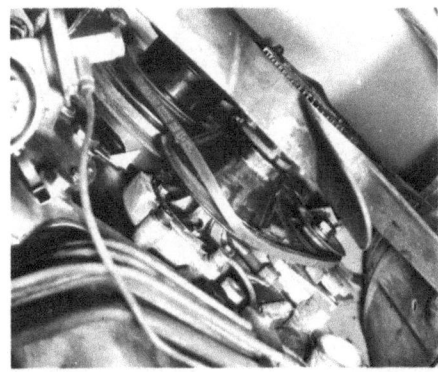

9.4 Prising off fan drivebelt

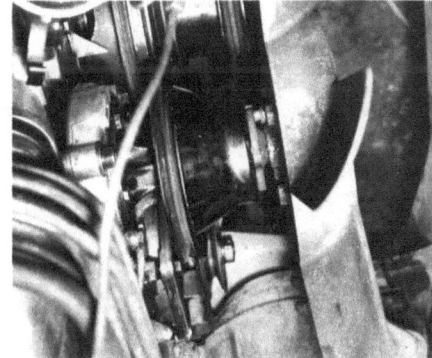

9.5 Withdrawing water pump impeller

9.6 Water pump main housing

3   *On earlier type pumps,* and pumps used where an air conditioning system is fitted, the bearing locating circlips should now be extracted and the bearings and shaft removed.

4   *On later type pumps,* no bearing locking rings are fitted but the bearing/shaft assembly is an interference fit in the water pump body and should be pressed out so that it emerges from the impeller end.

5   Press the new shaft/bearing assembly into the water pump housing, inserting it from the impeller end and exerting all pressure on the bearing outer track only, with a piece of suitable tubing.

6   Make sure that the bearing when in the fitted position is flush with the end of the water pump housing at the fan end.

7   Remove the fan mounting hub from the old shaft. To do this, heat the hub to a temperature of about 437°F (225°C) - bright yellow in colour and tap the old shaft out of it.

8   Maintain the temperature of the fan hub and press it onto the front end of the new shaft. Make sure that the rear end of the shaft is well supported during this operation so that there is no chance of the bearing position in the water pump housing being disturbed. Check the fitted position of the hub is in accordance with the diagram.

9   Let the fan hub cool naturally without quenching.

10 Renew the 'O' ring seal and refit the counter ring (5) (Fig. 2.7).

11 Press the new sliding seal (4) into the water pump housing.

12 Support the front end of the water pump shaft and press the impeller into position on the rear end of the shaft. Check that the impeller fitted position is in accordance with the appropriate diagram (Fig. 2.7 or 2.8).

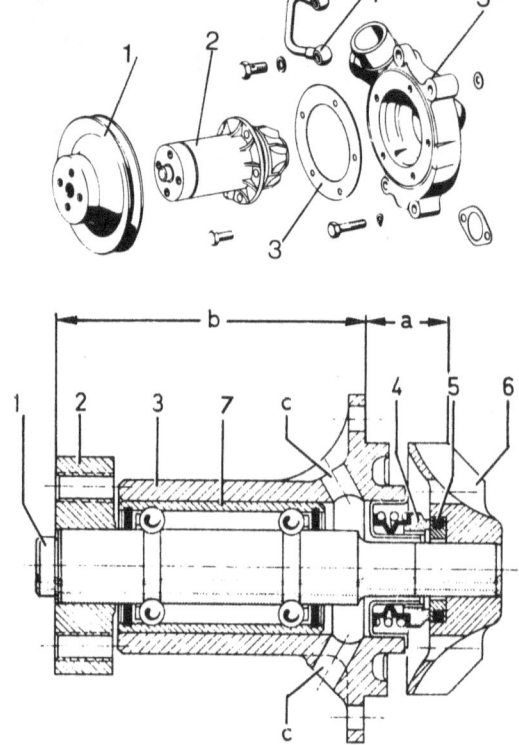

Fig. 2.6 Exploded view of typical water pump (Sec. 10)

1 Fan pulley
2 Bearing/shaft/impeller assembly
3 Gasket
4 Chain tensioner oil feed pipe
5 Water pump housing

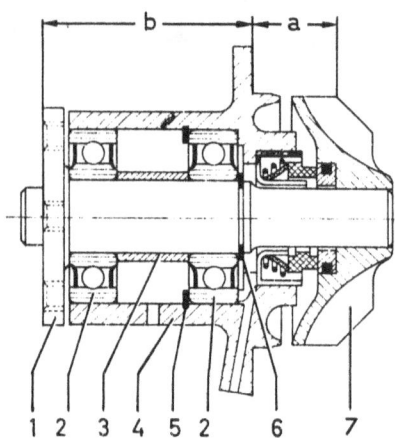

Fig. 2.7. Sectional view of water pump/bearing/impeller assembly on
engine without air compressor pump for air conditioner (Sec. 10)

1 Shaft	5 Counter ring with O-ring
2 Fan mounting hub	6 Impeller
3 Water pump body	7 Bearing assembly
4 Sliding ring seal	

a 22.8 to 23.2 mm   b 89.0 to 89.4 mm   c Vent holes

Fig. 2.8. Sectional view of water pump used where engine is fitted
with air compressor for air conditioner (Sec. 10)

1 Fan mounting hub	5 Circlip
2 Bearings	6 Circlip
3 Spacer	7 Impeller
4 Body	

a 22.8 to 23.2 mm   b 60.35 to 62.25 mm

11 Water temperature transmitter and gauge

1 An obviously incorrect reading on the water temperature gauge may
be due to lack of coolant, broken drivebelt to the fan or a radiator
which has become clogged with flies or leaves. A thermostat which has
seized shut will cause overheating.

2 Having checked out these possibilities, now inspect the security of
the leads to the transmitter and to the rear of the gauge on the instrument panel.

3 Testing of either of these components is not really within the scope
of the home mechanic and the only satisfactory check is to substitute
new components.

4 Before the transmitter can be removed, drain the cooling system.

5 Access to the water temperature gauge is obtained as described in
Chapter 10.

6 On earlier cars, a capillary tube/bulb type coolant temperature
gauge is used. The bulb section can be unscrewed from the cylinder
head but the complete unit is sealed and can only be renewed by
withdrawing the gauge complete with tube and bulb as described
in Chapter 10.

12 Fault diagnosis - Cooling system

Symptom	Reason/s
Overheating	Insufficient water in cooling system. Fan belt slipping (accompanied by a shrieking noise on rapid engine acceleration) Radiator core blocked or radiator grille restricted. Bottom water hose collapsed, impeding flow. Thermostat not opening properly. Ignition advance and retard incorrectly set (accompanied by loss of power, and perhaps, misfiring). Fuel system incorrectly adjusted (mixture too weak). Exhaust system partially blocked. Oil level in sump too low. Blown cylinder head gasket (water/steam being forced down the radiator overflow pipe under pressure) Engine not yet run-in. Brakes binding.
Cool running	Thermostat jammed open. Wrong temperature thermostat fitted allowing premature opening of valve. Thermostat missing.
Loss of cooling water	Loose clips on water hoses. Top, bottom, or by-pass water hoses perished and leaking. Radiator core leaking. Thermostat gasket leaking. Radiator cylinder head gasket (pressure in system forcing water/steam down overflow pipe). Cylinder wall or head cracked.

Chapter 3 Carburation;
fuel, exhaust and emission control systems

Contents

Specifications

System type ...	Rear mounted fuel tank with mechanical or electric fuel pump according to whether model equipped with carburettors or fuel injection

Fuel tank
Capacity (except 250C and 280 Series) ...	14.3 Imp gals, (17.25 US gals, 65.0 litres)
*250C and 280 Series ...	18 Imp gals, (21.5 US gals, 82.0 litres)

Certain models have a reserve of 2.64 Imp gals (3.1 US gals, 12.0 litres)

Fuel pump
Type
Carburettor engines ...	Lever or push-rod mechanical, engine mounted
Pressure ...	2 to 3 lb/in^2 (0.1406 to 0.2109 kg/cm^2)
Fuel injection engines ...	Electrical mounted adjacent to fuel tank
Pressure ...	19 lb/in^2 (1.3358 kg/cm^2)

Fuel system application

Car model	Year	Engine	Carburettors	Fuel injection	*CO level %	*Idle speed (rpm) Manual	Automatic in 'N'
230/8 Sedan	1968 - 69	M180	Two Zenith 35/40 INAT	—	1.5 to 2.5	750 - 800	800 - 850
250/8 Sedan	1968 - 70		Two Zenith 35/40 INAT	—	1 to 1.5 for 1968 - 69	800 - 900	650 - 700
250 SE Saloon	1968 - 70	M114	—	Bosch mechanical fuel injection	1.5 to 3.5 thereafter	750 - 800	750 - 800
250 SL Coupe	1968 - 70		—			750 - 800	750 - 800
250 CE fixed head coupe	1968 - 70		—			800 - 900	800 - 900
250/8 Sedan	1971 - 72			—	1.0 to 1.5	800 - 900	800 - 900
250C Coupe	1970 - 72	M130V	Two Zenith 35/40 INAT	—	1.0 to 1.5	800 - 900	800 - 900
280 S/8 Sedan	1968 - 71			—	2 to 3.5	800 - 900	800 - 900
280 SL Coupe	1968 - 71	M130	—			750 - 800	750 - 800
280 SE/8 Sedan	1968 - 72		—			750 - 800	750 - 800
280 SE/8 Coupe	1968 - 72	M130E	—	Bosch mechanical fuel injection	3 to 4.5 for 1968 - 69 1.5 to 3.5 thereafter	750 - 800	750
280 SEL/8 Sedan	1968 - 71		—			750 - 800	750
280 SL/8 Roadster	1968 - 71		—			750 - 800	750

*Consult also vehicle sticker

**Carburettor calibration data

	Stage 1	Stage 2
Venturi	24	28
Main jet (up to 1970)	115	125
Main jet (1970 on with temperature switch in cylinder head)	120 plus air correction jet 100	120
Air correction jet	90	110
Mixing tube	4S	4N
Idling speed fuel jet	45	—
Transition fuel jet	—	80
Idling speed air hole	1.3 mm dia.	—
Transition air hole	—	1.0
Accelerator pump fuel volume per stroke	0.7 to 1.0 cc	—
Injection nozzle	0.5	—
Fuel inlet needle valve	2.0	2.0
Float weight	8.5g	8.5g
Float adjustment (see text)	0.827 to 0.906 in (21.0 to 23.0 mm)	
Fuel inlet needle valve gasket (thickness)	0.039 in (1.0 mm)	
By-pass holes	0.8 - 1.0 - 0.8 mm dia.	
Choke gap adjustment (except North America)	0.094 in (2.4 mm)	
(North America)	0.087 in (2.2 mm)	
Fast idle speed (except North America)	2400 to 2600 rpm	
(North America)	2500 to 2700 rpm	

**There are small variations between the calibration of carburettors used on the various engines in the range. When ordering spare parts, verify by reference to parts list at your dealer.

Torque wrench settings

	lb f ft	Nm
Fuel injection valves to cylinder head	25	35
Fuel injection pressure valve (Stage 1)	29	40
(Stage 2)	25	35
Carburettor mounting nuts	15	21

1 General description

The fuel system differs according to the model and reference should be made to the application list in the Specifications to check whether a particular car has a carburettor or a fuel injection system.

The carburettors are of the dual barrel type while the fuel injection system is a mechanical type driven from the engine auxiliary shaft.

A rear mounted fuel tank is used on all models, but those with carburettors have a mechanical fuel pump driven by the engine, while an electric pump is mounted near the fuel tank on cars equipped with a fuel injection system.

An emission control system is fitted to all models but its complexity varies with the year of production and operating territory as described in later Sections of this Chapter.

2 Air cleaner (paper element type) - servicing

1   Various types of air cleaner are used according to engine model and fuel system (Figs. 3.1, 3.2 and 3.3).
2   Periodically it is a good plan to release the air cleaner cover toggle clips, move the cover to one side and extract the filter element (photos).
3   Tap the element on a hard surface to dislodge any adhering dirt and

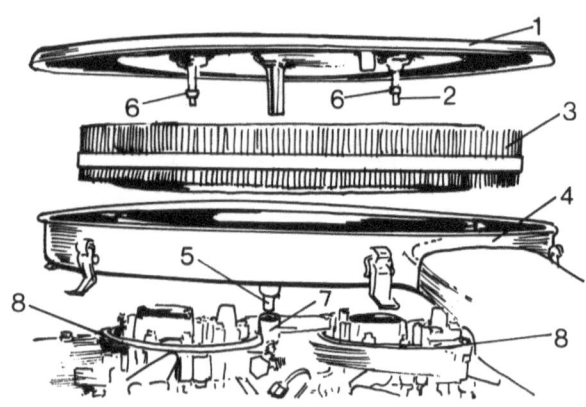

Fig. 3.1. Air cleaner used in conjunction with carburettor type fuel system (Sec. 2)

1 Cover	5 Moisture separator
2 Securing screws	6 Nut
3 Filter element	7 Rubber sleeve
4 Base	8 Rubber ring

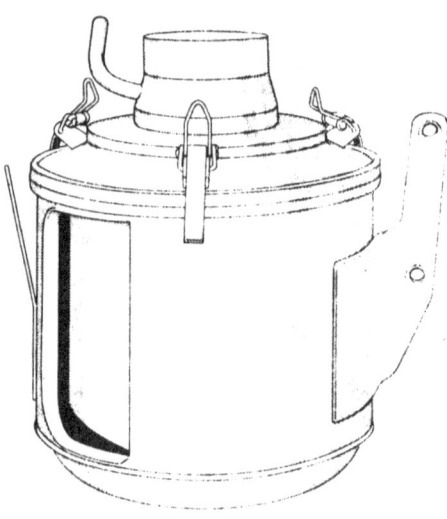

Fig. 3.2. One type of air cleaner fitted in conjunction with fuel injection system, without air intake spout (Sec. 2)

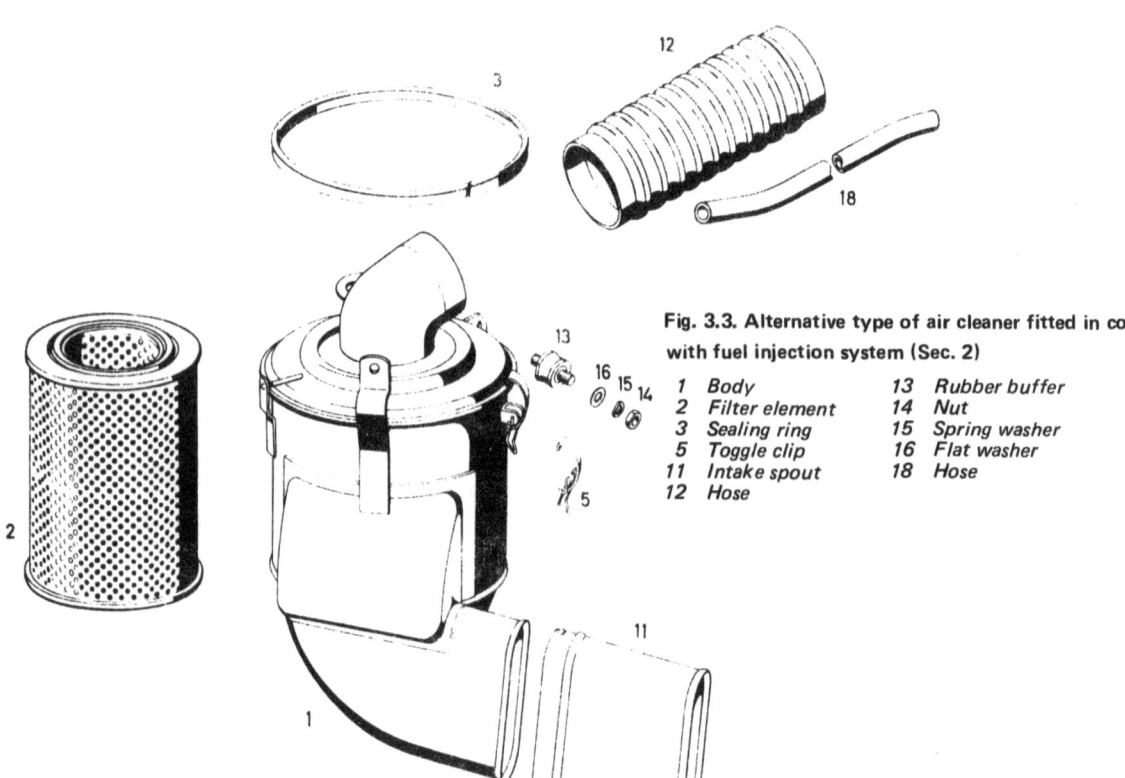

Fig. 3.3. Alternative type of air cleaner fitted in conjunction with fuel injection system (Sec. 2)

1 Body	13 Rubber buffer
2 Filter element	14 Nut
3 Sealing ring	15 Spring washer
5 Toggle clip	16 Flat washer
11 Intake spout	18 Hose
12 Hose	

2.2A Removing air cleaner lid

2.2B Air cleaner element

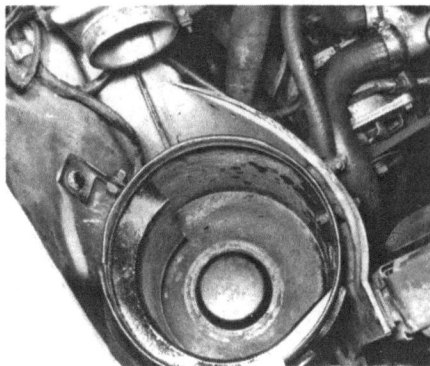

2.4 View of air cleaner body

dust particles or apply compressed air to the inside surface of the element - driving any dirt outwards.

4   Wipe out the air cleaner body and lid and refit the element and cover clips (photo).

5   At the specified intervals, discard the filter element and fit a new one. Always make sure that any rubber sealing rings are in good condition and are correctly positioned.

6   The air cleaner body can be removed by disconnecting any intake ducts and hoses and then unscrewing the mounting brackets or both according to type.

7   Where strict emission control regulations are in force, the air cleaner fitted in conjunction with carburettor engines incorporates an activated carbon ring. The purpose of this device is to absorb the fuel vapour from the float chambers once the engine is switched off. When the engine is re-started, the vapour is then drawn out of the ring and burned during the normal engine combustion cycle (Fig. 3.4).

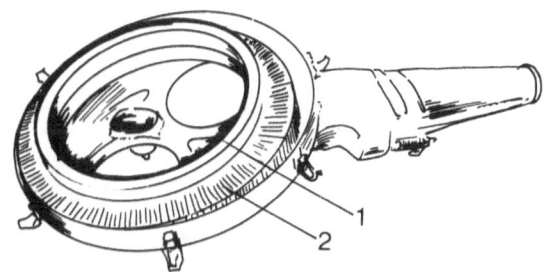

Fig. 3.4. Type of air cleaner used in conjunction with emission control systems (Sec. 2)

1   Carbon ring   2   Filter element

3   Air cleaner (oil bath type) - servicing

1   This type of air cleaner is fitted to models destined for operation in particularly dusty conditions.

2   Check the oil level in the cleaner at the intervals specified in the Routine Maintenance Section. Do this with the car on level ground with the engine having been switched off for at least five minutes. The oil level should be maintained between the two arrows embossed on the casing.

3   At the specified intervals or whenever the oil in the air cleaner appears thick and sludgy, it should be renewed. To do this, first remove the air cleaner cover and extract the filter mesh.

4   Drain the oil from the lower casing.

5   Wash the lower casing, the cover and the filter mesh in paraffin and blow dry. Do not use water soluble solvent to clean the filter mesh as the rinsing water will rust the filter mesh and steel wool inside.

6   Pour in fresh engine oil to the upper arrow level mark, insert the filter and fit the lid.

4   Air intake pre-heater - description, removal and refitting

1   On certain carburettor type engines, a thermostatically controlled pre-heater is installed in the air intake of the air cleaner. Its purpose is to regulate the volume of air by a flap valve drawn from two sources, cold air or hot air. Hot air comes around the exhaust manifold. The air is mixed in pre-determined proportions for optimum engine performance (Fig. 3.5).

2   For test purposes the following conditions apply:

Cars built up to 1970

Flap valve fully open to admit warm air up to 59°F (15°C).
Flap valve fully closed to warm air above 82°F (28°C).

Cars built after 1970

Flap valve fully open to admit warm air up to 41°F (5°C).
Flap valve fully closed to warm air above 82°F (28°C).

3   If on inspection, the flap valve does not operate according to the

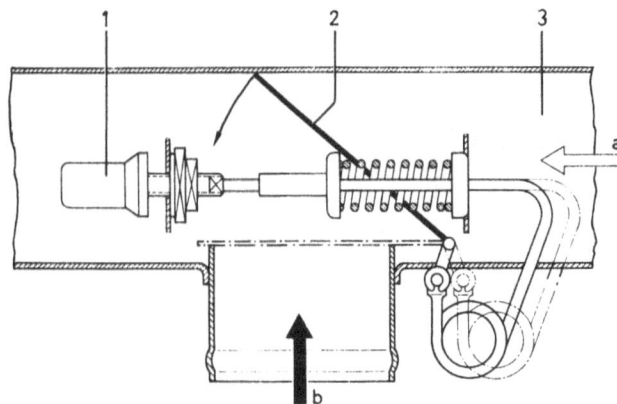

Fig. 3.5. Air cleaner pre-heater (Mann and Hummel) (Sec. 4)

a   Fresh air   1   Thermostat
b   Warm air   2   Warm air flap
                                              3   Air cleaner intake spout

specification, then the thermostat must be removed and a new one fitted.

One of two different types of thermostat may be encountered, either a Mann and Hummel or a Knecht.

4   *To remove the Mann and Hummel type,* pull off the locking ring (7) and pull the actuating lever (6) from the flap valve shaft (8) (Fig. 3.6).

5   Pull the actuating lever forward against the pressure of the spring (5) until the guide sleeve (4) moves out of the actuating pin of the thermostat.

6   Push the actuating lever rearwards and disconnect it from the fastening eye of the intake spout.

7   Unscrew the hexagon nut (3), remove the air cleaner lid and

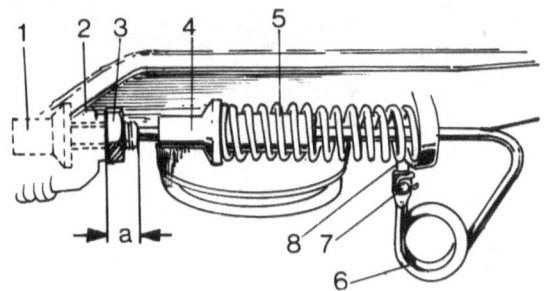

Fig. 3.6. Air cleaner pre-heater adjustment diagram (Mann and Hummel) (Sec. 4)

1 Thermostat	5 Spring
2 Plastic nut	6 Actuating lever
3 Steel nut	7 Snap-ring
4 Guide sleeve	8 Flap valve shaft

(a) = 0.32 to 0.35 in (8.0 to 9.0 mm)

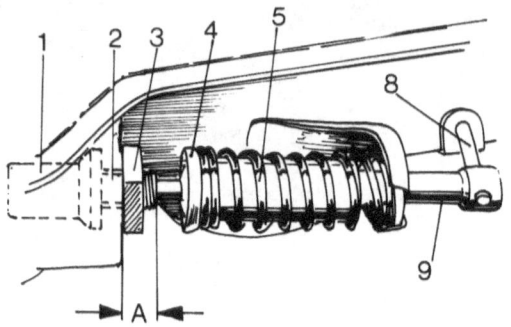

Fig. 3.7. Air cleaner pre-heater adjustment diagram (Knecht type) (Sec. 4)

1 Thermostat	5 Spring
2 Plastic nut	8 Cranked warm air flap valve
3 Steel nut	shaft
4 Guide sleeve	9 Actuating bolt

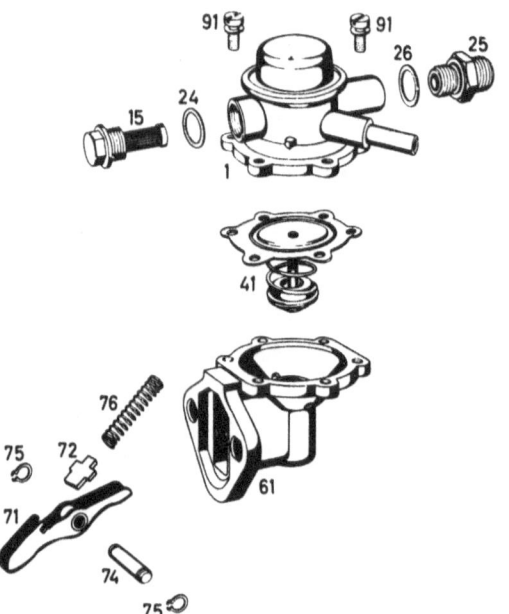

Fig. 3.8. Exploded view of rocker arm (lever) type mechanical fuel pump (Sec. 5)

1 Upper body	71 Rocker arm
15 Filter	72 Spring anchor
24 Sealing washer	74 Pivot pin
25 Union	75 Circlip
26 Sealing washer	76 Spring
41 Diaphragm	91 Screw
61 Lower body	

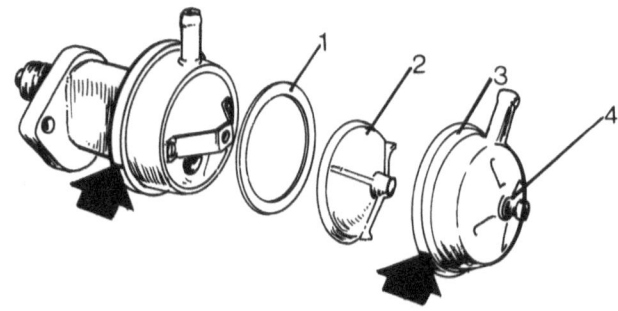

Fig. 3.9. Pushrod type mechanical fuel pump (Sec. 5)

1 Rubber sealing ring	3 Cover
2 Filter	4 Aluminium sealing washer

Take care not to twist the plastic fastening nut (2) or to force it out.

13 Refitting is a reversal of removal but the new thermostat should be screwed into the plastic fastening nut from the inside and then adjusted to give a stroke (a) of between 0.28 and 0.32 in (7.0 and 8.0 mm).

5 Fuel pump (mechanical type) - description and servicing

1   The fuel pump which is fitted to the carburettor engines may be one of two types. One type is actuated by a rocker arm while the alternative type is actuated by a short pushrod in contact with an eccentric cam on the oil pump driveshaft (Figs. 3.8 and 3.9).

2   The rocker arm or lever type pump can be fully dismantled, while the pushrod type is a sealed pump which, although its filter gauze can be cleaned, cannot be dismantled and in the event of wear occurring or a fault developing, it must be renewed complete.

3   At the specified intervals, remove the fuel filter screen from the pump, wash any dirt from it in clean fuel and refit. Make sure that any sealing washers or gaskets are in good order.

4   To remove the filter from the lever type pump, simply unscrew the filter plug from the side of the pump body.

5   To remove the filter from the pushrod type pump, extract the cover screw, withdraw the cover, gasket and filter.

6   Refitting is a reversal of removal, do not overtighten the cover screw on the pushrod type pump.

7   To test the operation of a fuel pump, disconnect the fuel supply pipe from the carburettor. Place the open end of the pipe in a container and then disconnect the LT lead from the negative terminal of the ignition coil to prevent the engine firing when the starter is actuated.

unscrew the thermostat (1). Take care not to twist the plastic fastening nut (2).

8   Refitting is a reversal of removal but the new thermostat must be screwed into the plastic nut (2) from the inside and adjusted to provide the actuating lever with a stroke of between 0.32 and 0.35 in (8.0 and 9.0 mm).

9   *To remove the Knecht type,* compress the spring (5) and force the actuating pin (9) from the warm air flap shaft (8) and out of the eye of the air intake spout (Fig. 3.7).

10 Remove the actuating pin and guide sleeve (4) from the thermostat.

11 Unscrew the nut (3).

12 Remove the air cleaner lid and unscrew the thermostat (1) from the inside of the air intake.

8   Have an assistant turn the ignition key to 'START', when, as the engine spins, several well defined spurts of fuel should be seen to be ejected into the container from the open end of the pipe.

9   If no fuel is ejected and fuel is known to be in the tank, the pump must be removed and either overhauled or renewed as described in the following Sections.

6   Fuel pump (mechanical) - removal and refitting

1   Disconnect the fuel inlet and outlet pipes at the pump unions. Plug the open ends of the pipes to prevent the entry of dirt.

2   Unscrew the pump mounting nuts and withdraw the pump from the engine crankcase. Note the number and thickness of the gaskets and insulator used at the mating flanges. They must be renewed or refitted exactly as originally fitted.

3   Refitting is a reversal of removal.

7   Fuel pump (mechanical lever type) - overhaul

1   Remove the pump as described in the preceding Section and clean away external dirt.

2   Scribe a mark across the edges of the upper and lower pump body mating flanges so that they can be refitted in the same relative position on reassembly.

3   Unscrew and remove the screws which secure the upper and lower pump body flanges together and then separate the body sections.

4   Examine the upper body, particularly the valves, for wear or damage. If the valves are worn, renew the upper body complete.

5   If the diaphragm is split or perforated, it must be dismantled. To do this, extract the small circlip from one end of the rocker arm pivot pin. Push out the pivot pin and extract the rocker arm spring and spring support. As the rocker arm is withdrawn, the diaphragm pushrod will be disengaged.

6   Reassembly is a reversal of dismantling. Make sure that the lower end of the diaphragm pushrod engages correctly with the end of the rocker arm as the latter is pushed into the lower body of the pump.

8   Fuel pump (electric) - description, removal and refitting

1   The fuel pump fitted in conjunction with a fuel injection system is of the electrically-operated type and it is mounted adjacent to the left-hand side of the rear mounted fuel tank. It is partially obscured by a protective shield. With an electric pump, if the tank has run dry, at least four gallons of fuel must be poured in before the pump will re-start (photo).

2   Earlier cars were fitted with a pump of a large design while later cars are equipped with a more compact pump incorporating a bypass system which prevents vapour lock in the fuel system (Figs. 3.10 and 3.11).

3   To remove the fuel pump, disconnect the battery and then disconnect the leads from the pump positive and negative terminals.

4   Disconnect the fuel lines from the pump and then unbolt and remove the mounting bolts and the pump.

5   It is very important that the leads are reconnected to the correct terminals otherwise the pump will run in reverse and fail to deliver fuel. If the cable colour code has been obliterated make sure that the cables are identified before removing them from their terminals.

6   The positive terminal has a red plastic plate and the negative terminal has a brown plastic plate.

7   Refitting is a reversal of removal. The smaller type of pump can be fitted in place of the larger one provided an adaptor plate is obtained at the time of purchase and the following modifications are also made (Fig. 3.12).

8   Cut the fuel return hose in two at a point about 6 in (152 mm) from the fuel tank. Insert a tee piece. Connect a hose between the pump bypass connection and the tee piece. Make sure that the fuel suction line does not sag; shorten if necessary (Fig. 3.13).

9   Finally, unscrew the pressure regulating valve on the injection pump (see photo) and check whether it incorporates a gas hole or not. If necessary, replace the valve with one not having a hole (photo).

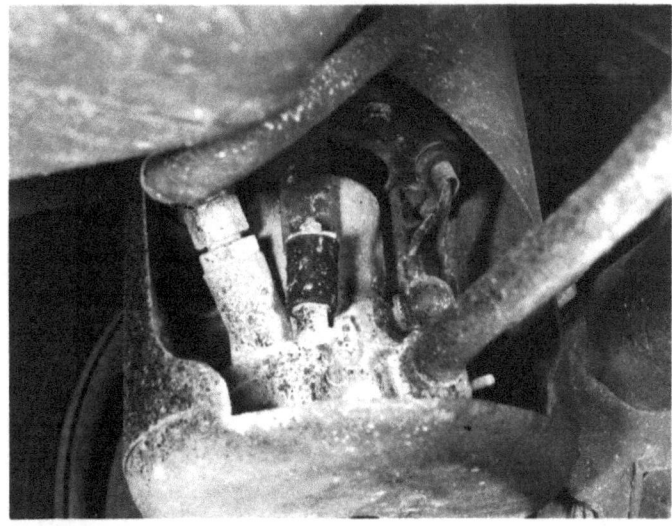

8.1 Electric fuel pump (fuel injection)

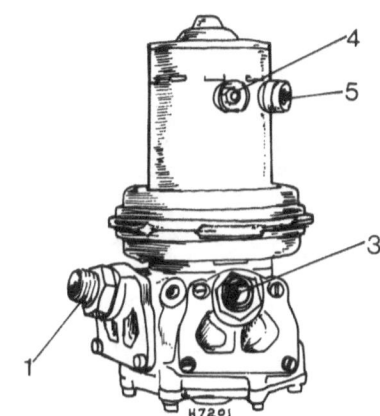

Fig. 3.10. Large design of electric fuel pump used with fuel injection engines (Sec. 8)

1 Fuel outlet	4 Positive terminal
3 Fuel inlet	5 Negative terminal

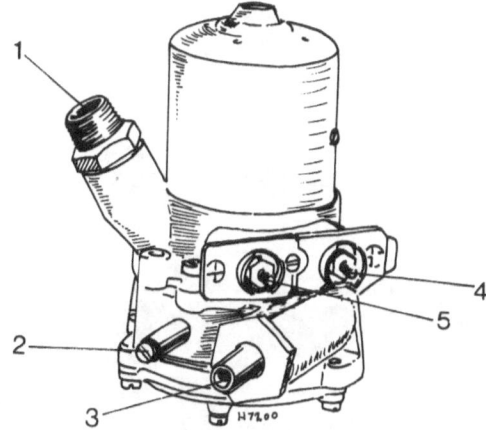

Fig. 3.11. Smaller type of electric fuel pump used with fuel injection engine (Sec. 8)

1 Fuel outlet	4 Positive terminal
2 By-pass connection	5 Negative terminal
3 Fuel inlet	

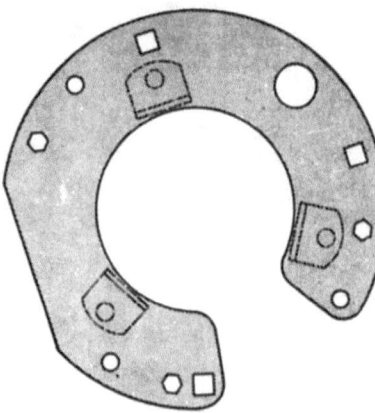

Fig. 3.12. Adaptor plate for substitution of smaller electric fuel pump.
Use square shaped holes for cars covered by this manual (Sec. 8)

Fig. 3.13. Smaller type electric fuel pump mounted in position (Sec. 8)

1   Fuel outlet line   6   Mounting bracket
2   Fuel by-pass line   7   Vibration damper
3   Fuel inlet line   8   Adaptor plate

8.9 Pressure regulating valve

9 Fuel line filter (fuel injection) - servicing

1   A large fine mesh filter is fitted on the left-hand side of the engine
if the car is equipped with a fuel injection system (photo).
2   At the specified intervals (see 'Routine Maintenance') the filter
element should be renewed as described in the following paragraphs.
If the fuel being used is impure then the filter should be renewed
more frequently.
3   Unscrew the bolt (1) from the top of the filter (2) and draw the
filter bowl downwards (Figs. 3.14 and 3.15).

9.1 Location of fuel line filter (fuel injection)

Fig. 3.14. Top view of fuel line filter (fuel injection system) (Sec. 9)

1   Centre bolt   2   Filter top

Fig. 3.15. View from bottom of fuel line filter (fuel injection system)
(Sec. 9)

4 Pour away the old fuel from the bowl and discard the filter element.
5 Clean out the bowl and fit a new element.
6 Refit the bowl and tighten the securing bolt. Start the engine and check for leaks. Renew the bowl sealing ring whenever it appears compressed or deteriorated.

10 Fuel tank (standard type) and fuel level sender unit - removal, repair and refitting

1 The standard type fuel tank is slung below the luggage compartment floor at the rear of the car.
2 Drain the fuel from the tank into a suitable container. Do this either by unscrewing the drain plug or by syphoning (photo).
3 Disconnect the fuel lines from the tank.
4 Remove the cover from the floor of the luggage boot to expose the fuel level unit connections.
5 Disconnect the lead (1) (Fig. 3.16).
6 If only the fuel level unit is to be removed, the retaining nuts can now be unscrewed and the unit withdrawn together with the sealing ring.
7 If the fuel tank is to be removed complete, the sender unit can remain in position until later, although of course, the lead must be disconnected.
8 Unbolt the tank and remove it from the car.
9 If the tank is leaking, a temporary repair can be made with fibreglass or a proprietary patch but more permanent repairs should be left to the professionals.
10 **Never be tempted to weld or solder a tank yourself**. Even experts will steam or boil out an empty fuel tank for several hours before bringing heat near it!
11 Refitting is a reversal of removal but make sure that the sender unit sealing ring is in good order.
12 The fuel level sender unit operates in the following way. When the fuel level falls, the sliding contact (1) on the float (2) increases the resistance and in consequence the voltage drops and the needle on the fuel contents gauge falls back. As the fuel level continues to drop, the reserve warning contact (5) will close and the reserve warning light will come on. The system is energized when the ignition is switched on (Fig. 3.17).
13 Any fault in the fuel level indicating system will necessitate renewal of the sender unit or gauge or both but before taking this action, check the security of the connecting leads and the circuit fuse (No. 5).

11 Fuel evaporative control type tank - description and removal

1 In order to reduce the discharge of fuel vapour from the tank directly to atmosphere, a compensating tank is fitted within the luggage boot of later cars.
2 The compensating tank is connected by two pipes, one to the fuel filler and the other to the outside air.
3 If the main fuel tank is completely filled, fuel is forced into the lines (2) and rises into the compensating tank. As the fuel level in the main tank falls and one of two lines becomes empty, fuel flows back to the main tank while fuel vapour escapes to atmosphere through line (3) (Fig. 3.18).
4 On North American vehicles, the discharge of fuel vapour to atmosphere is not permitted at all. In consequence a larger compensating tank is fitted, with a valve system, which directs the vapour

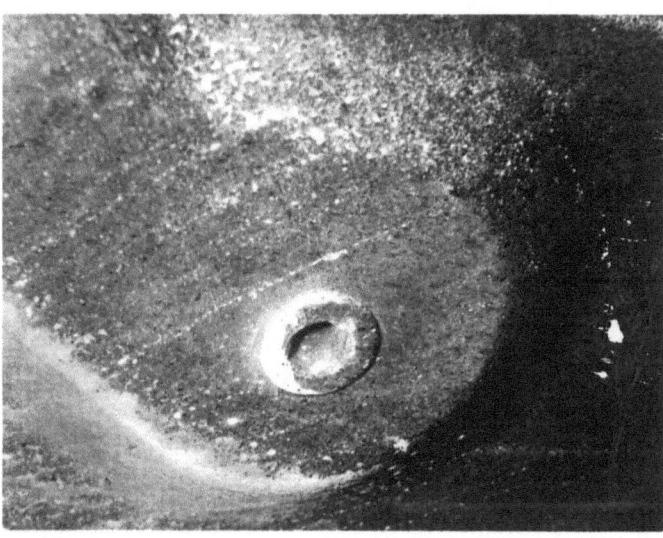

10.2 Fuel tank drain plug

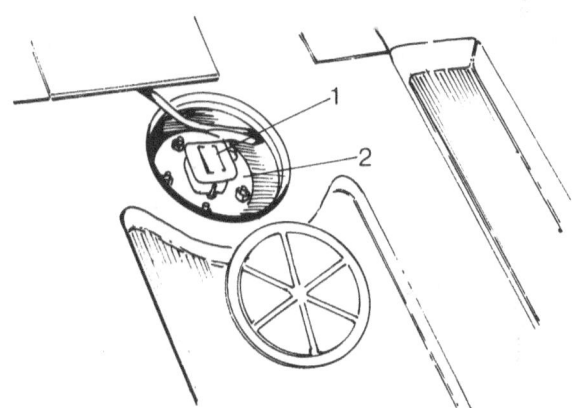

Fig. 3.16. Fuel contents sender unit (Sec. 10)

1 Plug connector   2 Sender unit

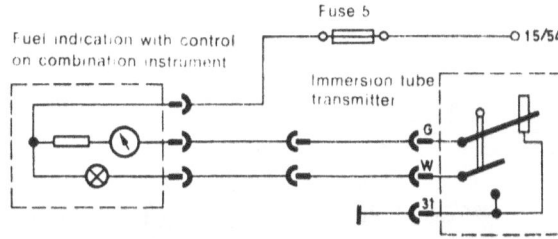

Fig. 3.17. Diagrammatic view of fuel contents sender unit (Sec. 10)

1 Sliding contact   3 Contact plate   5 Reserve warning contact
2 Float   4 Guide rod

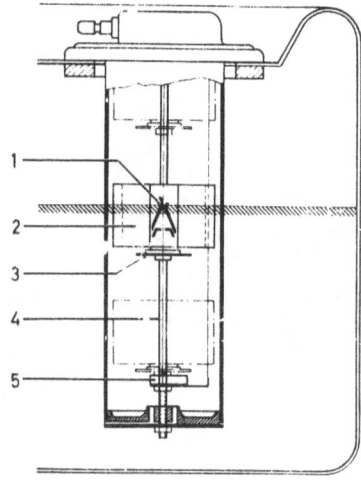

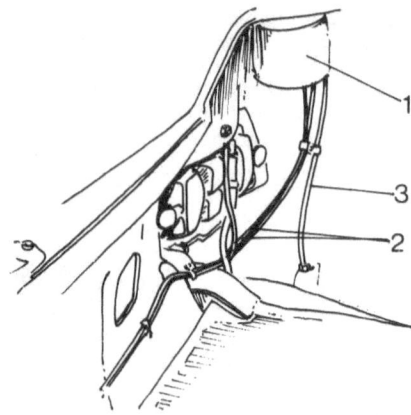

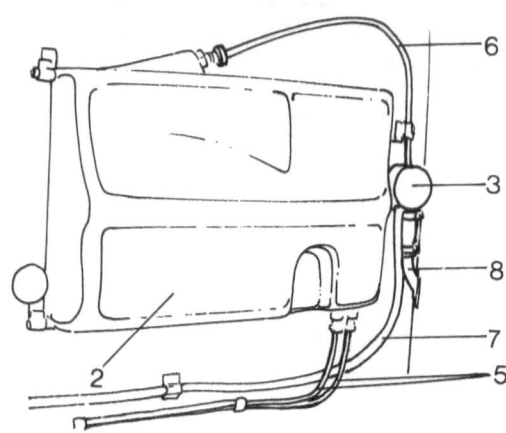

Fig. 3.18. Luggage boot components of the fuel evaporative control type fuel tank (Sec. 11)

1 Compensating tank
2 Lines to fuel filler
3 Pipe to atmosphere

Fig. 3.19. Luggage boot components of the fuel evaporative control type tank used on North American vehicles (Sec. 11)

2 Compensating tank
3 Valve system
5 Flow and return line
6 Vent line
7 Vent to atmosphere
8 Vent to crankcase

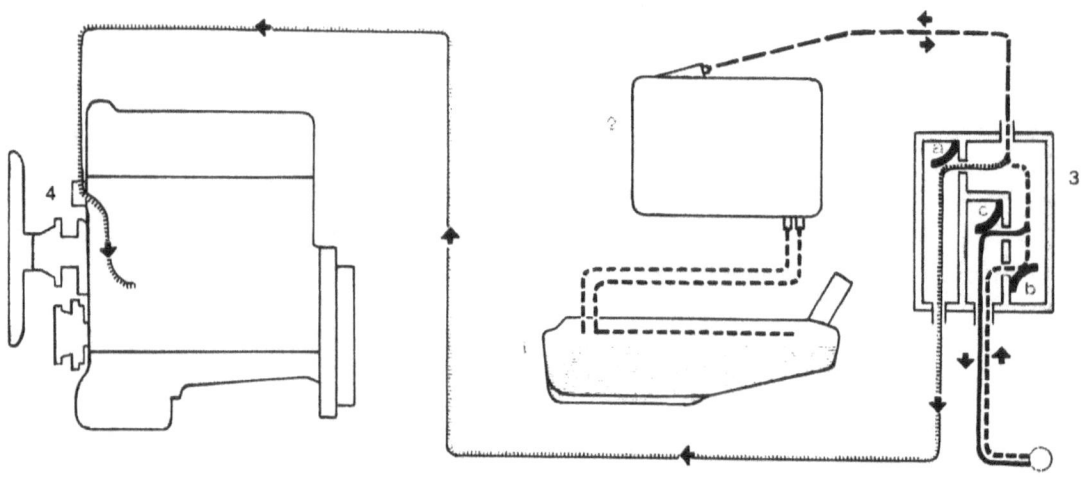

Fig. 3.20. Layout of fuel evaporative control type fuel tank used on North American vehicles (Sec. 11)

1 Fuel tank
a Venting air inlet valve
2 Compensating tank
b Venting air outlet valve
3 Valve system
c Pressure relief valve
4 Crankcase connection

12.1A Accelerator linkage (left-hand side) on fuel injection engine

12.1B Accelerator linkage (right-hand side) on fuel injection engine

12.1C Accelorator linkage cross-shaft (fuel injection engine)

back to the engine where it is burned during the normal combustion process. This vapour is drawn into the engine crankcase through an inlet on the timing chain housing and then by means of the crankcase ventilation system (see Section 34) it is drawn into the engine combustion chambers (Figs. 3.19 and 3.20).

5 Removal of the fuel tank on these later cars is similar to that described in Section 10 except that the additional pipes and hoses must be disconnected first.

12 Accelerator linkage (carburettor engines) - description and adjustment

1 The control mechanism on both carburettor and fuel injection type engines is by means of ball jointed control rods (photos).

2 The control rods can be disconnected from the ball pins on the levers simply by prising them off.

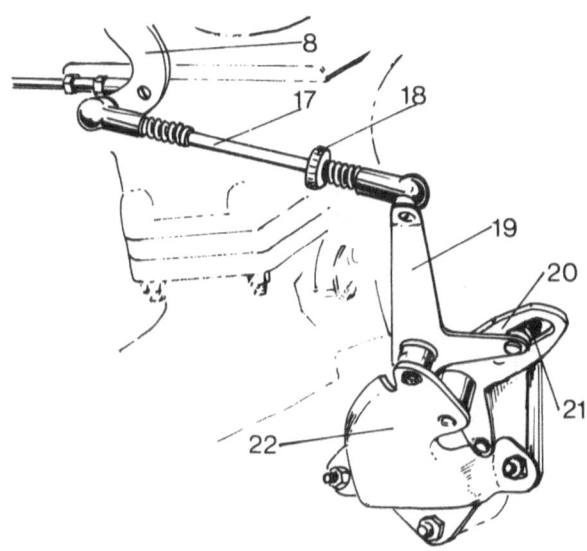

Fig. 3.21. Throttle linkage (carburettors and manual transmission) (Sec. 12)

8	Lever	20	Slotted lever
17	Control rod	21	Roller
18	Adjusting nut	22	Bearing support bracket
19	Bellcrank		

3 *On cars with manual transmission and carburettors*, adjust the control rod (17) such that the roller (21) within the slotted lever contacts the end of the slot when the actuating lever is fully moved without any tendency to twist or override (Fig. 3.21).

4 *On cars with automatic transmission*, disengage the pull rod (23) from the adjustment lever (15) and push the rod right back as far as it will go. Slacken the clamping bolts (16) at the intermediate lever (14) and then rotate the adjustment lever (15) until the ball socket of the pull rod (23) can be fitted directly to the ball pin on the adjustment lever without any tendency to misalign. Tighten the clamping bolts (16) (Fig. 3.22).

5 Now start the engine and with it idling, adjust the control rod (17) at its ball joint end to permit the control rod (disconnected and pulled fully forward) to be fitted directly to the ball pin on the actuating lever without any tendency to misalign. When carrying out this adjustment, ensure that the actuating lever is in contact with the idle speed stop screw.

6 Have an assistant fully depress the accelerator pedal (engine switched off) and check that the Stage 1 or primary throttle valve lever contacts the carburettor body. If it does not, adjust the regulating shaft (6) after having first released the hexagon bolt (7) on the engine compartment rear bulkhead (Fig. 3.23).

7 In addition to the foregoing adjustments to the accelerator linkage, also refer to the various tuning adjustments described in Sections 15 to 19.

13 Regulating linkage (fuel injection system) - adjustment

1 Disconnect the rod (6) by prising its ball socket from the ball stud on the regulating lever (Fig. 3.24).

2 Now check all the ball joints and swivels of the linkage for wear or distortion, renew components as necessary.

3 When inspecting the lever (9) do not necessarily expect it to return to the idling position. It will revert to idling sometimes only when the starter motor is actuated.

4 Disconnect the regulating rod (4) from the venturi control unit and check that the throttle valve in the unit is closing without binding. When the throttle valve lever (1) is tightly pressed against the idling speed stop screw (3), the throttle valve should just be felt to grip slightly but not to bind. Adjust if necessary using the stop screw (Fig. 3.25).

5 Locate the ball head on the regulating shaft by means of the centring bolt (11) (Fig. 3.26). If no centring bolt is fitted, adjust the length of the regulating rod (8) to 9.2 in (233.0 mm) measured between the balljoint centres (see Fig. 3.24).

6 Repeat this last adjustment on regulating rod (4) shown in Fig. 3.24, but make quite sure that the throttle valve lever rests against the idling speed stop.

7 Now slowly actuate the regulating shaft from the central regulating

Fig. 3.22. Throttle linkage (carburettors, and automatic transmission) (Sec. 12)

14	Intermediate lever	22	Bearing support bracket
15	Adjustment lever	23	Transmission pull rod
16	Clamp bolts	24	Regulating shaft pull rod
17	Control rod		

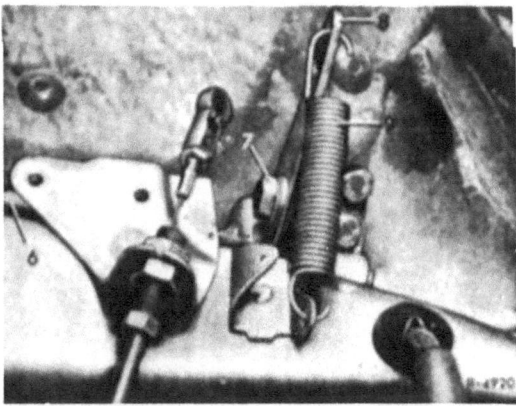

Fig. 3.23. Regulating shaft attachment at engine compartment rear bulkhead (carburettors and automatic transmission) (Sec. 12)

6	Regulating shaft	8	Lever
7	Hexagon bolt	9	Return spring

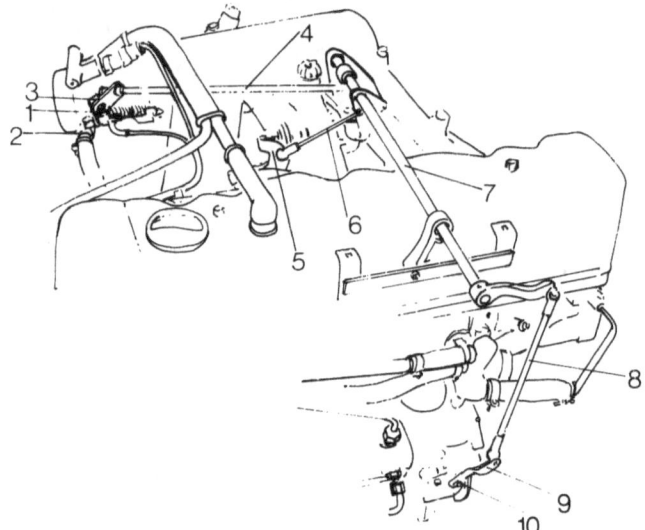

Fig. 3.24. Regulating linkage (fuel injection engines)
(Sec. 13)

1   Throttle valve lever
2   Full load stop
3   Idling speed stop screw
4   Regulating rod
5   Regulating lever
6   Regulating rod
7   Regulating shaft
8   Regulating rod
9   Adjusting lever
10 Idling speed and full load stop

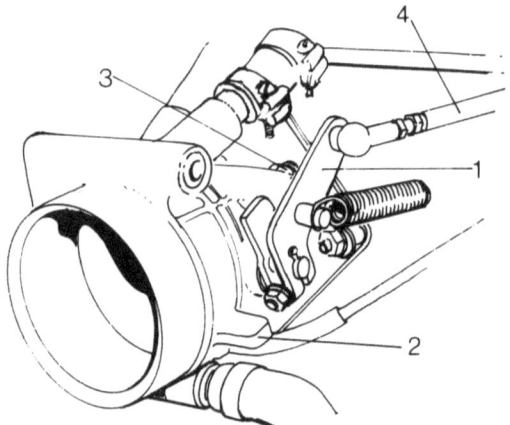

Fig. 3.25. Venturi control unit (fuel injection) (Sec. 13)

1   Throttle valve lever   3   Idling speed stop screw
2   Stop   4   Regulating rod

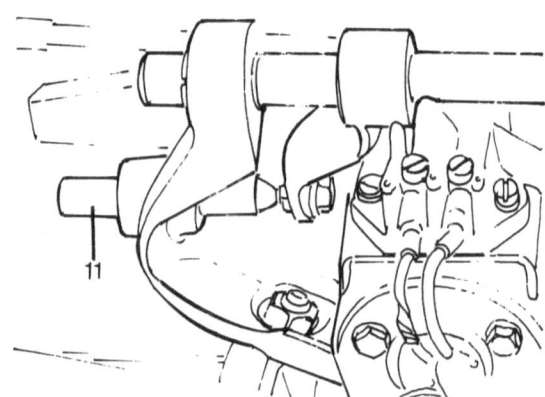

Fig. 3.26. Regulating shaft centring bolt (11) (fuel injection) (Sec. 13)

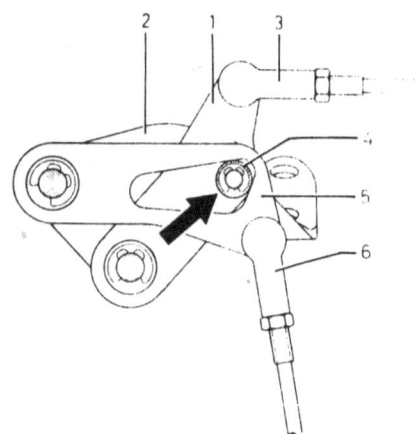

Fig. 3.27. Progressive type regulating linkage (fuel injection) (Sec. 13)

1   Lever   3   Pull rod   5   Cam lever
2   Holder   4   Roller   6   Rod

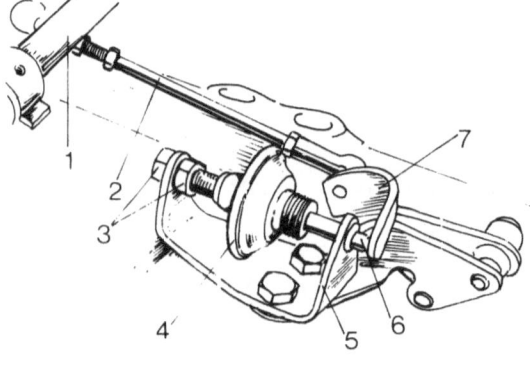

Fig. 3.28. Throttle closing damper (fuel injection)

1   Regulating shaft   5   Mounting plate
2   Thrust rod   6   Pin
3   Adjusting nut   7   Lever
4   Vacuum capsule

lever on the shaft and check whether the adjusting lever on the injection pump and the throttle valve lever are lifted simultaneously. If necessary adjust the rod (4), see Fig. 3.24, which is located between the venturi control unit and the regulating shaft, in such a way to achieve it.

8   Check whether the idling speed and full load stop on the venturi control unit and on the injection pump, are in the equivalent position at idling. The throttle valve and injection pump adjusting levers should rest simultaneously against the stops in the full load position. The throttle valve lever on the venturi control unit should have at least 0.04 in (1.0 mm) play. Do not move the idling speed and full load stop on the injection pump.

9   On engines fitted with progressive regulating linkage, the regulating rod (3) should be adjusted to permit the roller (4) to rest against the end of the slot in the cam lever (5) without any tendency to exert tension on the end of the slot (Fig. 3.27).

10 On engines equipped with a throttle closing damper, move the regulating shaft (1) very slowly until the lever (7) is just lifting from the pin (6) of the damper. Measure the stroke of the damper which should be between 0.16 and 0.20 in (4.0 and 5.0 mm). Adjust if necessary with the damper lock nuts (Fig. 3.28).

11 On cars with automatic transmission, disconnect the control thrust rod (17) on the guide lever (16). Disconnect the pull rod (15) and adjust its effective length so that in its extended state it can be connected to the ball stud on the guide lever without any tendency to misalign (Fig. 3.29).

12 Push the control rod (17) back to the idling position and adjust its effective length so that it can be connected to the ball stud on the guide lever without any tendency to misalign.

13 Have an assistant fully depress the accelerator pedal to its stop. Check that the adjusting lever on the fuel injection pump is against its full load stop. If it is not, adjust by means of the shaft (6)(Fig. 3.23) on the engine compartment rear bulkhead. Loosen the bolt (7) before adjusting.

14 In addition to the foregoing adjustments, refer also to Sections 24, 25, 26 and 27.

14 Carburettors - description

1   Twin carburettors are used and these are of the Zenith dual barrel multi-stage type (Fig. 3.30 and 3.31).

2   The carburettors have an electrically-heated automatic choke.

3   The carburettors fitted to the various model cars vary slightly in detail and specification, also between the design of the front and rear units but the information given in this Chapter applies to all versions unless otherwise stated.

4   The principle of operation of the two throttle valves should be understood. The primary or stage 1 throttle valve is opened mechanically by means of the throttle control linkage while the secondary or stage 2 throttle valve is opened by vacuum only after the primary throttle valve is fully open.

5   A vacuum regulator (throttle closure damper) is fitted to control the final closure of the throttle valve plate as an aid to reducing exhaust emission hydrocarbons.

6   The automatic choke housing incorporates a small vacuum diaphragm unit.

15 Carburettor tuning - automatic choke adjustment

1   On cars built up until 1970 both front and rear automatic choke mechanisms were electrically heated without reference to the temperature of the engine coolant.

2   On these cars remove the air cleaner assembly, switch on the ignition and observe whether the choke valve plates in both carburettors are fully open after a few minutes.

3   On later cars, this action will cause only the front carburettor valve plate to open. The rear carburettor choke mechanism is controlled by two thermostatic switches screwed into the cylinder head and block and the engine will have to be run until the coolant reaches the pre-set temperature level before the valve plate is seen to open fully. The effect of the thermostatic switches is to complete the choke bimetallic coil heating circuit and in consequence to open the choke valve plate but only when the coolant temperature reaches

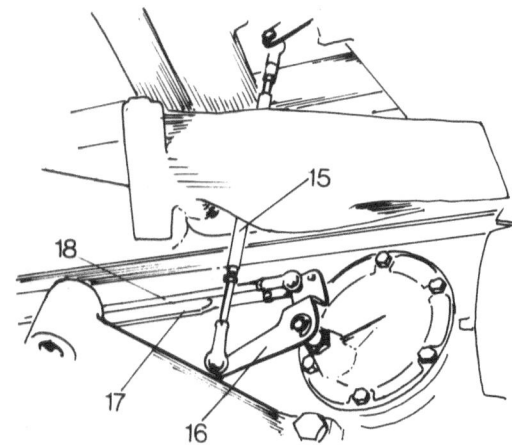

Fig. 3.29. Linkage support bracket on engine crankcase (fuel injection)

15 Pull rod   17 Push rod (Auto. transmission)
16 Lever   18 Regulating shaft pull rod

either 149°F (65°C) monitored by the cylinder head switch or 131°F (55°C) by the cylinder block switch (Fig. 3.32).

4   Having verified the operation of the choke valve plates, check that the marks on the automatic choke housing and cover are in alignment. If necessary, release the cover screws and turn it as required (Fig. 3.33).

5   The choke valve plate should now be adjusted. To do this have the engine cold or warm but not hot. Start the engine and open the throttle slightly. Insert a screwdriver between the automatic choke housing (1) (Fig. 3.34) on one of the carburettors and the throttle lever (2) and push the transmission arm (5) up to the stop that can be felt at the diaphragm rod (5) (Fig. 3.35). Release the throttle control linkage.

6   Switch off the engine and let the engine cool completely before attempting the next stage of the checking and adjustment procedure.

7   Once the engine is cool, measure the gap between the edge of the choke valve plate and the carburettor wall. Use a twist drill of appropriate diameter to make this check. On all cars except North American versions, the gap should be 0.094 in (2.4 mm) and on North American cars, 0.087 in (2.2 mm). Where necessary, adjust the gap with screw (5) which is located on the diaphragm unit cover (Fig. 3.36).

8   Repeat the foregoing operations on the other carburettor.

9   The cold start fast idle speed should now be checked.

10 Have the engine at its normal operating temperature and the idling speed correctly set as described in Section 16 (connect a tachometer to the engine in accordance with the maker's instructions if a revolution counter is not fitted as standard).

11 With the engine switched off, slightly lift the throttle control linkage. Refer to Fig. 3.34 and on one carburettor insert a screwdriver between the automatic choke housing (1) and the throttle lever (2) and push the transmission arm (5). Release the throttle control linkage and remove the screwdriver when the adjustment screw (3) should be resting on the top notch of the fast idle cam (4) shown in Fig. 3.35.

12 Start the engine which should run at a fast idle speed of between 2400 and 2600 rev/min for all cars except North American, and for North American (with emission control) between 2500 and 2700 rev/min. The following points should be noted when carrying out this check on North American vehicles:
(i) Disconnect the distributor vacuum hose from the front carburettor.
(ii) Adjust the fast idle on the front carburettor only.

13 Where the fast idle speed is incorrect, switch off the engine and turn the adjustment screw (3) (Fig. 3.37). This adjustment screw is visible and accessible through the aperture in the choke housing once the throttle linkage is fully opened. Turning the screw clockwise will increase the fast idle speed.

16 Carburettor tuning - idle speed adjustment

1   Before carrying out this work, make sure that the ignition system is correctly adjusted and timed.

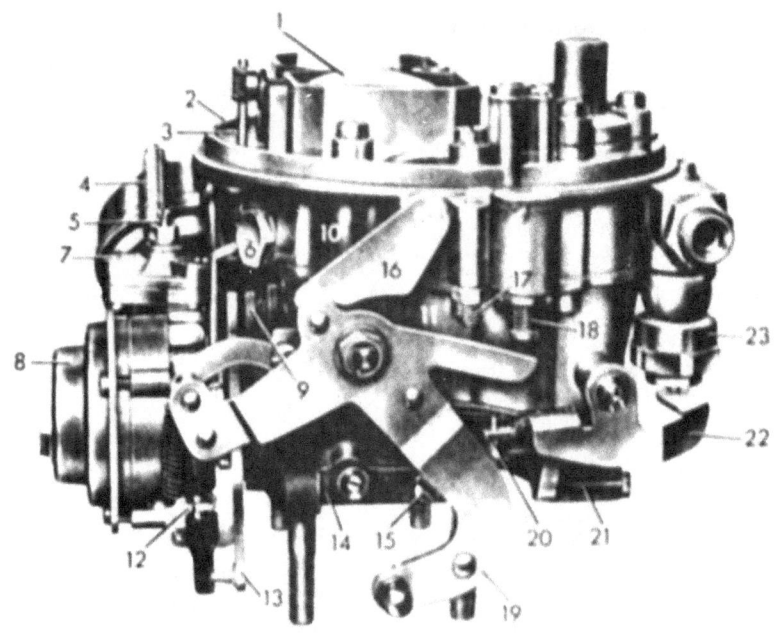

Fig. 3.30. Front carburettor (Sec. 14)

1	Choke valve plate	7	Starter diaphragm unit	13	Primary throttle lever	19	Actuating lever
2	Cover	8	Automatic choke housing	14	Throttle valve housing	20	Adjusting screw
3	Connecting rod		cover	15	Idle speed mixture screw	21	Fuel cut off solenoid
4	Secondary throttle vacuum	9	Secondary throttle lever	16	Accelerator pump lever		valve (N. America)
	diaphragm unit	10	Jet block	17	Idle speed stop	22	Actuating lever
5	Adjusting screw	11	Float housing	18	Float chamber vent valve	23	Fuel return valve
6	Lockbolt	12	Idle speed adjusting screw				

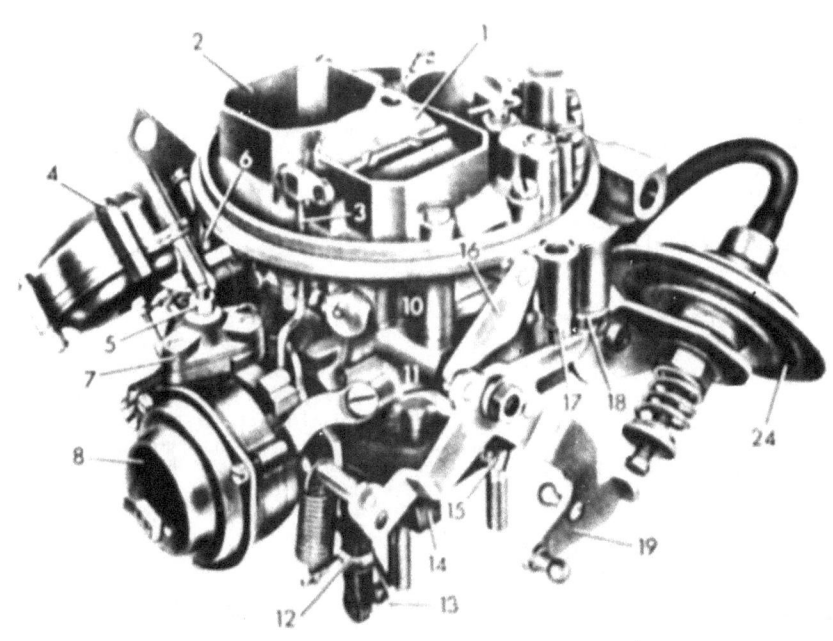

Fig. 3.31. Rear carburettor (Sec. 14) See key to Fig. 3.30.

24 Vacuum regulator (throttle closing damper)

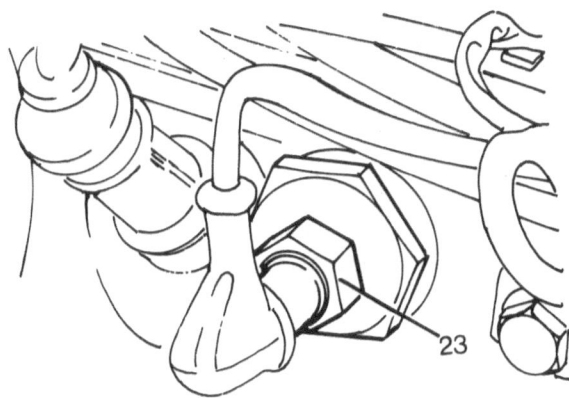

Fig. 3.32. Cylinder block coolant temperature switch for automatic choke (23) (N. America 1971 on) (Sec. 15)

Fig. 3.35. Automatic choke mechanism (cover removed) (Sec. 15)

1 Follower arm
2 Stop lever
3 Adjustment screw
4 Fast idle cam
5 Diaphragm rod stop
6 Return spring

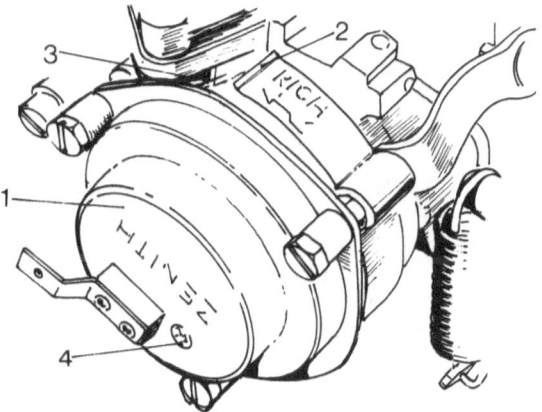

Fig. 3.33. Automatic choke assembly (1) showing alignment marks (2 and 3) housing cover (4)   (Sec. 15)

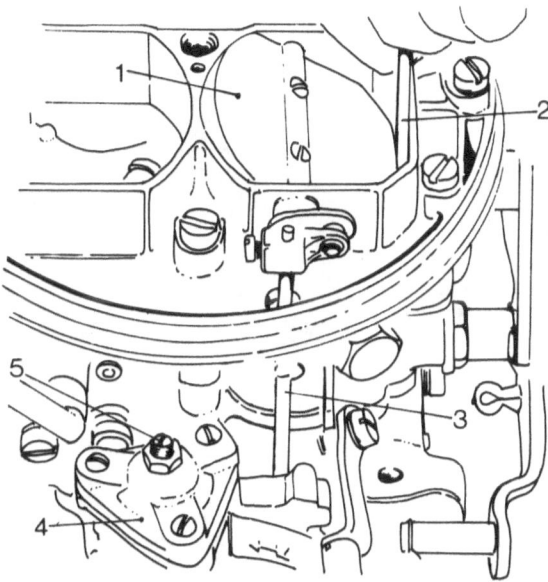

Fig. 3.36. Measuring carburettor choke valve plate gap (Sec. 15)

1 Choke valve plate
2 Twist drill (gauge)
3 Link rod
4 Diaphragm valve
5 Adjusting screw and locknut

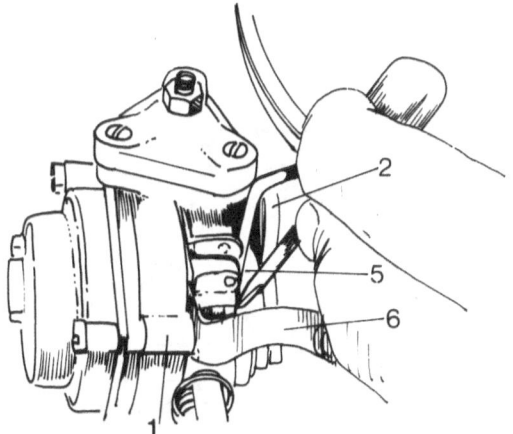

Fig. 3.34. Adjusting automatic choke (Sec. 15)

1 Automatic choke housing
2 Throttle lever
5 Transmission arm
6 Choke housing bracket

Fig. 3.37. Fast idle screw (3) on front carburettor (Sec. 15)

2   A carburettor balancing device (air flow meter) and an exhaust gas analyser will be required to achieve optimum setting of the twin carburettor fittings, also a tachometer if a revolution counter is not already fitted to the car.

3   Run the engine to normal operating temperature.

4   Remove the air cleaner.

5   On North American versions, fitted with emission control, disconnect the lead from the coolant thermostat in the thermostat housing.

6   Disengage the link rod (12) which runs between the two carburettors, also disconnect the control rod (17) by prising its ball socket from the ball stud (Fig. 3.38).

7   Check that the two actuating levers (8) contact the idle speed stop (4). Back off the adjusting screw (6).

8   With the engine running, turn the idle speed screws (1) equally until the engine speed is between 800 and 900 rpm. A balancing

device (flow meter) will be needed to synchronize the carburettors. Fit it in accordance with the maker's instructions. Most flow meters are placed on each carburettor in turn while the idle speed screw is adjusted to give an equivalent air intake volume for each carburettor (indicated on the meter) and at the same time achieving the specified overall engine idling speed.

9   An exhaust gas analyser should now be connected in accordance with the maker's instructions.

10 With the engine idling, turn each of the mixture adjustment screws until the appropriate CO value is obtained:

Other than North America (up to 1970)		3.5 to 4.5% CO
	(1970 on)	*2.0 to 3.5% CO
North America		*1.0 to 1.5% CO

*Incorporate emission control systems

11 On later cars, the mixture control screws have limiter caps fitted

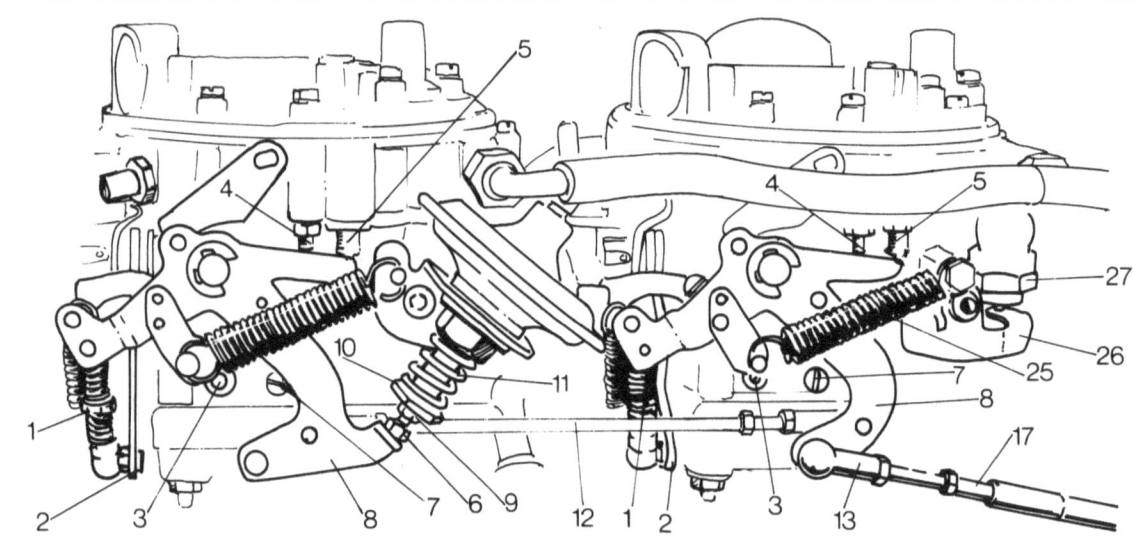

Fig. 3.38. View of twin carburettor assembly (Sec. 16)

1	Idle speed adjusting screw	6	Throttle damper adjusting screw	10	Adjusting nut	17	Control rod
2	Throttle valve arm			11	Spring	25	Fuel return valve adjusting screw
3	Test connection plug	7	Idle mixture screw	12	Link rod		
4	Idle speed stop screw	8	Actuating lever	13	Balljoint socket	26	Fuel return valve lever
5	Float housing vent valve	9	Locknut				

Fig. 3.39. Carburettor vacuum regulator (throttle closing damper) (Sec. 17)

4	Idle speed stop screw	9	Locknut
5	Float housing vent valve	10	Adjusting nut
6	Adjusting screw	11	Spring
8	Actuating lever		

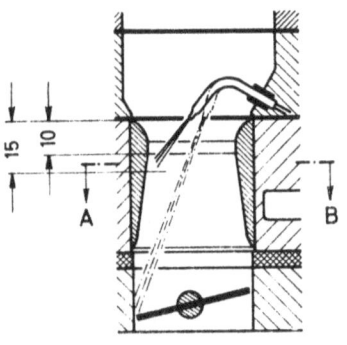

Section A - B

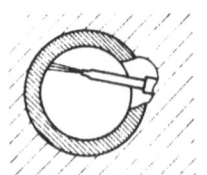

Fig. 3.40. Fuel nozzle spray pattern and alignment diagram (Sec. 18)

to them to restrict their travel from the factory preset positions. Before adjusting carburettors fitted with this type of screw, turn them fully clockwise to their stops.

12 On cars not equipped with emission control, the use of a device such as a 'Colortune' is an acceptable alternative to an exhaust gas analyser when adjusting the mixture.

13 Once the mixture (CO level) has been adjusted, re-check the idling speed and carburettor synchronization.

17 Carburettor tuning - vacuum regulator adjustment

1 Run the engine to its normal operating temperature and make sure that the idling speed is correct. Fit a tachometer to the engine if one is not already fitted.

2 Switch off the engine and back off the adjustment screw (6) until the valve (5) is raised approximately 0.039 in (1.0 mm). Before carrying out this adjustment always release the locknut and at the same time prevent the diaphragm unit from twisting (Fig. 3.39).

3 Start the engine and adjust the spring (11) by means of the nut (10) to obtain a clearance of 0.039 in (1.0 mm) between the end of the screw (6) and the actuating lever (8).

18 Carburettor tuning - accelerator pump checking

1 Remove the air cleaner.

2 Slowly operate the accelerator pump lever and observe whether a well-defined spurt of fuel is ejected from the ejection nozzle within the carburettor air intake. If not, the accelerator pump components must be dismantled and renewed or obstructions cleared, as described in Section 22.

3 The fuel spray pattern must be as shown in the diagram, if it is not, it is permissible to carefully bend the nozzle (Fig. 3.40).

4 On cars with manual transmission, the fuel jet may be changed to be directed at the throttle valve plate gap where increased acceleration is desired.

19 Carburettor tuning - fuel return valve adjustment

1 Check the engine speed on the rev counter (or fit a tachometer if a rev counter is not already fitted) and then observe that at a speed of 2,000 rpm the fuel return valve (27) is completely closed. If necessary, adjust the actuating lever (26) by means of the screw (25) (Fig. 3.41).

2 Recheck the operation at the specified engine speed.

20 Carburettor tuning - float chamber vent valves adjustment

1 These valves are normally set in production and should not be altered. However, where they have been renewed or tampered with, carry out the following operations.

2 Turn the actuating lever (8) while the engine is hot and the choke valve plate is open, to a position where the vent valve cannot be raised any further (Fig. 3.42).

3 Now measure the gap between the end of the stop screw (4) and the lever (8). Use a twist drill or rod 0.091 in (2.3 mm) diameter for this.

4 Adjust the gap if necessary by means of screw (4) which is accessible after removing the cover from it.

21 Carburettor - removal and refitting

1 Remove the air cleaner.

2 Disconnect the lead from the terminal on the automatic choke housing.

3 Disconnect the fuel lines from the carburettor.

4 Disconnect the throttle linkage.

5 Unscrew and remove the carburettor flange mounting nuts and remove the carburettor from the intake manifold.

6 Note carefully the order of the gaskets and plate insulators (Fig. 3.43).

7 Refitting is a reversal of removal, but always use new insulators and

Fig. 3.41. Carburettor fuel return valve adjustment (Sec. 19)

4 Idle speed stop screw	26 Fuel return valve actuating
5 Float housing vent valve	lever
8 Throttle valve actuating lever	27 Fuel return valve
25 Fuel return valve adjusting	28 Cap
screw	

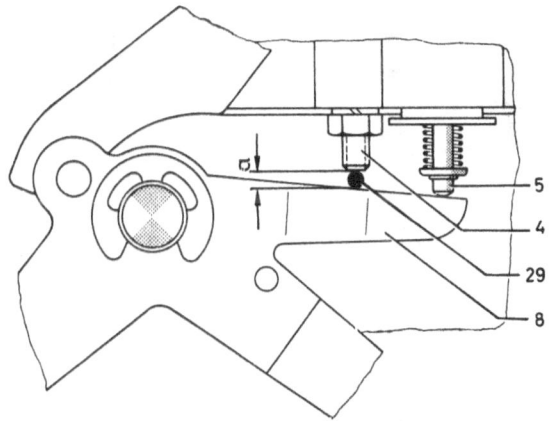

Fig. 3.42. Float chamber vent valve adjustment diagram (Sec. 20)

4 Adjusting screw	8 Actuating lever
5 Vent valve	29 Gauge
a = 0.091 in (2.3 mm)	

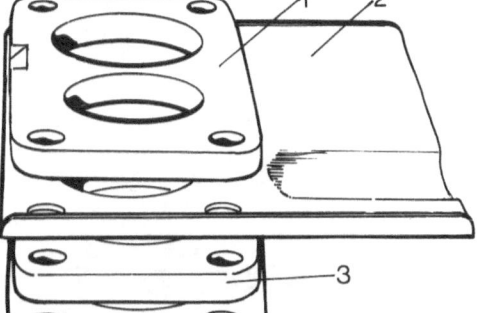

Fig. 3.43. Carburettor mounting components (Sec. 21)

1 Insulating plates	3 Insulating plates
2 Shield	4 Intake manifold

Fig. 3.44. Method of access to automatic choke control rod (Sec. 22)
Sealing cap (75)   Carburettor cover (113)

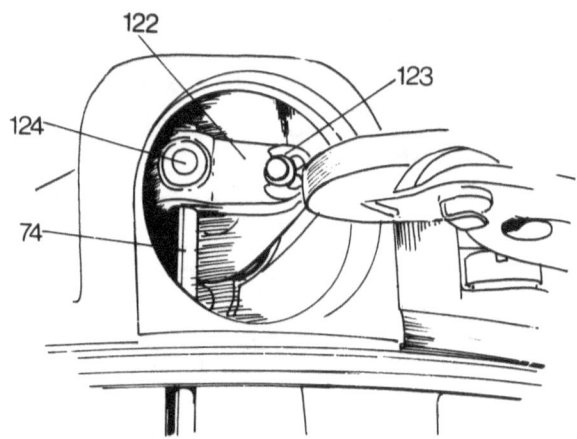

Fig. 3.45. Sealing cap removed from carburettor cover to expose
(Sec. 22)

74   Connecting rod   123 'E' clip
122 Crank arm   124 Socket headed screw

Fig. 3.46. Alternative method of attaching automatic choke control
rod to crank arm (Sec. 22)

122 Arm   124a Pinch screw

Fig. 3.47. Removing carburettor top cover (Sec. 22)

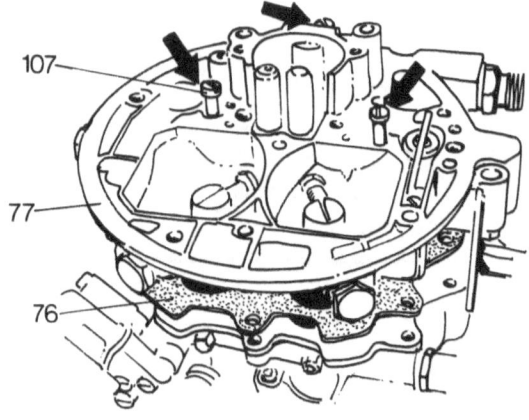

Fig. 3.48. Jet block securing screws (Sec. 22)

76 Gasket   107 Securing screws
77 Jet block

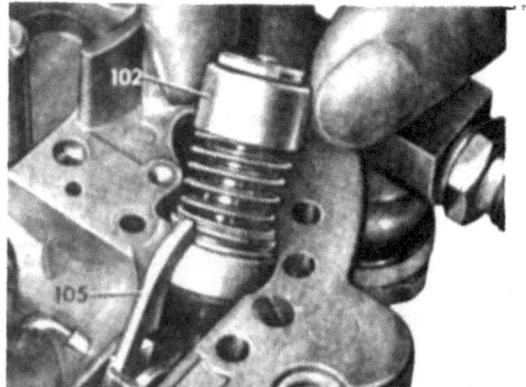

Fig. 3.49. Removing accelerator pump piston from jet block (Sec. 22)

102 Accelerator pump   105 Arm

gaskets to ensure a perfect seal.

8   Repeat all the foregoing operations on the second carburettor if it is to be removed.

22 Carburettor - overhaul

1   The carburettor should not be dismantled unless a fault has developed or wear has taken place to internal components. After a very high mileage it will probably be found more economical to renew the complete carburettor rather than to purchase many individual components.

2   Remove the carburettor as described in the preceding Section and clean away external dirt.

3   The carburettor comprises four main components:

   (i) The carburettor cover.
   (ii) The jet block.
   (iii) The float housing, and
   (iv) The throttle valve housing.

   Once the appropriate main section has been dismantled, restrict further dismantling to that and do not dismantle the other major assemblies needlessly.

4   Prise off the closure cap seal (75) to give access to the automatic choke control rod (Fig. 3.44).

5   Prise off the 'E' clip (123) and disconnect the choke rod (74). On earlier types of carburettor, the choke connecting rod is released after extracting the pinch screw (124a) (Figs. 3.45 and 3.46).

6   Unscrew and remove the nine screws which retain the cover to the carburettor jet block. Note that the centre screw is countersunk in the tapped hole into which the air cleaner mounting pillar is screwed and this pillar will have to be unscrewed first.

7   Prise the cover off, using one or two screwdrivers carefully inserted at the flange joint (Fig. 3.47).

8   The carburettor jet block can be removed after extracting the three screws which secure it to the throttle valve housing (Fig. 3.48).

9   Extract the accelerator pump piston from the jet block (Fig. 3.49).

10 The air correction jets, idling speed fuel jet and mixing tubes may now be unscrewed or shaken out of the jet block (Fig. 3.50).

11 Unscrew the main jets and valves noting carefully their location (Fig. 3.51).

12 The float can be removed after extracting the holder/pivot pin (Fig. 3.52).

13 Unscrew and remove the float needle valve and its sealing ring (Fig. 3.53).

14 Remove the float housing vent valve.

15 The float housing and throttle valve housing can be dismantled as necessary. If the valve plates must be dismantled, grind off the peened ends of the screws which retain the plates to the throttle spindles before extracting the screws. Use new screws on reassembly (Fig. 3.54).

16 Clean and examine all components for wear or damage. Blow jets and valves through with air from a tyre pump only, never probe them with wire or their calibration will be upset.

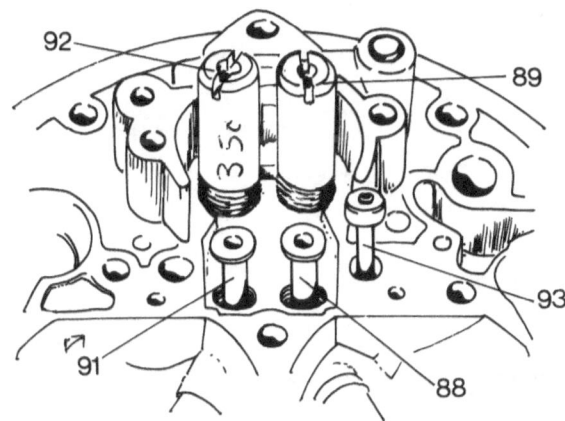

Fig. 3.50. Location of components in jet block (Sec. 22)

88   *Primary mixing tube*
89   *Primary air correction jet (N. America)*
91   *Secondary mixing tube*
92   *Secondary air correction nozzle (N. America)*
93   *Idling fuel jet*

Fig. 3.51. Location of components in jet block (Sec. 22)

87   *Primary main jet*
90   *Secondary main jet*
94   *Transition jet*
95   *Accelerator pump intake valve*
97   *Pump pressure valve*

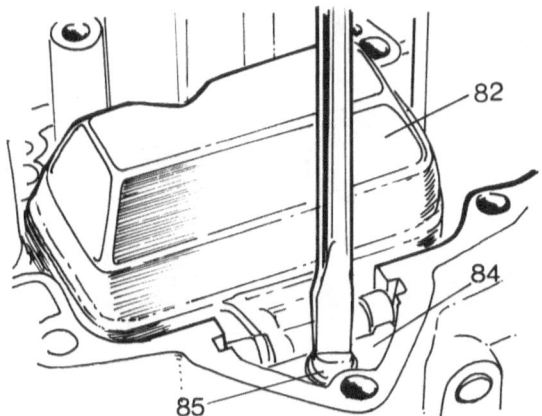

Fig. 3.52. Carburettor float details (Sec. 22)

82   *Float*
84   *Pivot pin retainer*
85   *Securing screw*

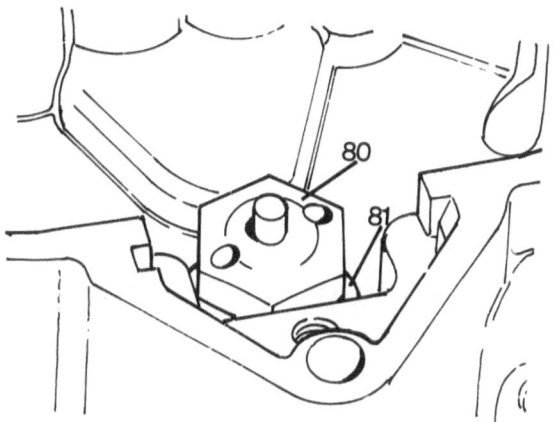

Fig. 3.53. Fuel inlet needle valve (Sec. 22)

80   *Valve assembly*
81   *Sealing washer*

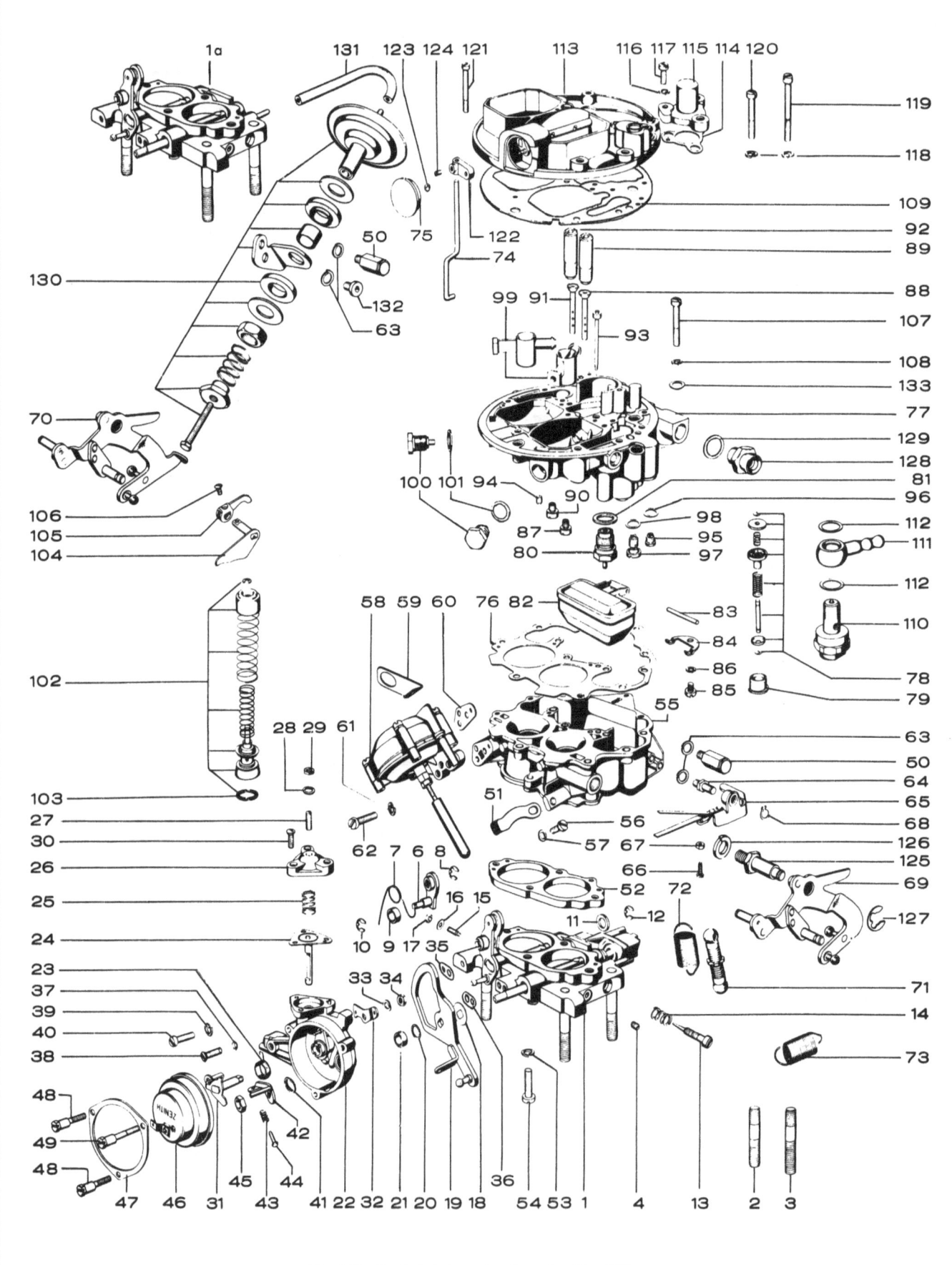

Fig. 3.54. Exploded view of carburettor (Sec. 22)

1   Throttle valve housing
     (manual transmission)
1a   Throttle valve housing
     (automatic transmission)
2   Studs
3   Studs
4   Grub screw
6   Lever
7   Spring
8   Lockwasher
9   Roller
10   Lockwasher
11   Plain washer
12   'E' clip
13   Idle speed mixture screw
14   Spring
15   Adjusting screw
16   Spring washer
18   Nut
19   Throttle lever
20   Lockwasher
21   Spacer
22   Automatic choke housing
23   Spring
24   Diaphragm
25   Spring
26   Diaphragm unit cover
27   Adjusting screw
28   Seal
29   Locknut
30   Cover screw
31   Actuating lever
32   Actuating arm
33   Lockwasher
34   Nut
35   Gaskets
36   Gaskets
37   Lockwasher
38   Countersunk head screw
39   Lockwasher
40   Securing screw
41   Lockwasher
42   Stop lever
43   Spring
44   Stop screw
45   Nut
46   Automatic choke housing
     cover
47   Nut
48   Screws
49   Screws
50   Pillar bolt
51   Link plate
52   Insulator
53   Lockwasher
54   Screw
55   Float housing
56   Screw
57   Lockwasher
58   Secondary throttle vacuum
     capsule
59   Cable clip
60   Gasket
61   Lockwasher
62   Screw
63   Lockwasher
64   Pivot pin
65   Lever
66   Screw
67   Nut
68   Circlip
69   Actuating lever
70   Actuating lever
71   Pushrod
72   Return spring
73   Return spring
74   Connecting rod
75   Closure cap
76   Gasket
77   Jet block
78   Vent valve
79   Bush
80   Fuel inlet needle valve
81   Sealing washer
82   Float

83   Pivot pin
84   Pivot pin holder
85   Screw
86   Lockwasher
87   Primary main jet
88   Primary mixing tube
89   Primary air correction jet
90   Secondary main jet
91   Secondary main jet
92   Secondary air correction jet
93   Idling speed jet
94   Transition jet
95   Pump valve
96   Sealing washer
97   Pressure valve
98   Sealing ring
99   Pre-atomizer
100 Lock bolt
101 Sealing ring
102 Accelerator pump
103 Spring ring
104 Pump lever
105 Arm
106 Screw
107 Screw
108 Lockwasher
109 Gasket
110 Fuel return valve
111 Banjo union
112 Sealing washers
113 Top cover
114 Gasket
115 Pump cover
116 Lockwasher
117 Screw
118 Lockwasher
119 Screw
120 Screw
121 Screw
122 Arm
123 Washer
124 Screw
125 Pivot stud
126 Lockwasher
127 'E' clip
128 Union
129 Sealing washer
130 Throttle closure damper
     vacuum unit
131 Vacuum pipe
132 Screw

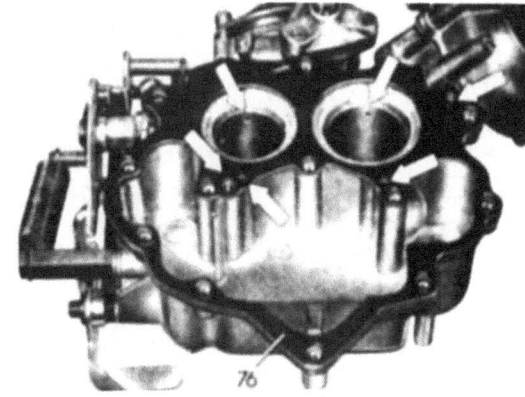

Fig. 3.55. Venturi bleed holes for secondary vacuum diaphragm (Sec. 22)

17 Obtain a repair kit which will contain all the necessary gaskets and other renewable items.

18 Reassembly is a reversal of dismantling but the following checks and adjustments must be carried out as the work proceeds.

Float level

19 Invert the jet block (with the float attached) so that the float arm is resting on the fuel inlet needle valve. Measure the distance between what is the bottom of the float when in its normal 'in car' attitude and the surface of the jet block below the float (no gasket fitted). The distance should be between 0.827 and 0.906 in (21.0 and 23.0 mm). If incorrect, change the washer which is located under the fuel inlet needle valve housing for one of a different thickness. The washers are of copper and are available in four different thicknesses - 0.020, 0.039, 0.059 and 0.079 in (0.5, 1.0, 1.5 and 2.0 mm). Use only one sealing washer and tighten the fuel inlet needle housing securely as any leakage at the washer will of course cause fuel to bypass the needle valve and cause flooding.

Accelerator pump

20 Check the leather seal on the pump piston. If it is hard or cracked, renew it and manipulate the new one with the fingers to make it pliable before fitting it.

Secondary vacuum diaphragm

21 Push the vacuum diaphragm/rod assembly upwards and then keep the venturi bleed holes covered with the fingers. Release the diaphram rod. If the diaphragm is leakproof, it should not move (Fig. 3.55).

23 Fuel injection system - description

The system used on cars covered by this manual is the Bosch mechanical type.

Fuel from the rear mounted fuel tank is drawn out by an electric fuel pump and pumped to the injection pump which is mounted on the left-hand side of the cylinder block.

Fuel is metered mechanically through injection tubes and nozzles to the combustion chambers.

The injection pump is driven by the auxiliary shaft of the engine.

The necessary filters, valves and vacuum and electrical switching and control devices are incorporated in the system.

As the major components of the system are very sensitive and the use of special instruments and gauges is required to adjust them, it is recommended that only the work described in this Chapter is carried out. Leave any other operations to your Mercedes-Benz dealer or Bosch service agent.

Refer also to Section 13 for control linkage adjustment.

Most fuel injection engines are already equipped with a mechanically driven revolution counter. Where this is not so, an electrical tachometer should be available for connection in accordance with the maker's instructions. It will be needed to carry out the adjustments described in the following Sections.

24 Fuel injection system - idle speed adjustment

1   Make sure that the ignition system is correctly adjusted and timed. Remove the air cleaner.

2   Run the engine to its normal operating temperature.

3   Press the throttle valve lever firmly against the idle speed stop screw (3) shown in Fig. 3.25. The throttle valve plate should be felt to stick slightly but not to bind. If necessary, adjust by turning the stop screw.

4   Check that the throttle linkage levers on the injection pump and on the venturi control unit rest against the idle speed stops.

5   An exhaust gas analyser should be obtained. This is essential for use on cars equipped with a full exhaust emission control system.

6   Alternatively, on cars without exhaust emission control, the use of a vacuum gauge will suffice.

7   If an exhaust gas analyser is available, connect it in accordance with the maker's instructions and check the CO level, which should be between 3.5 and 4.5%. Any adjustment required can be made by turning the idle speed adjusting screw (7) on the injection pump (Fig. 3.56). Turn the screw clockwise to enrich the mixture and anti-clockwise to weaken it. Note that the screw can only be adjusted with the engine OFF, therefore any alteration to this screw will necessitate stopping and re-starting the engine several times while after each movement of the screw through one notch the result is checked on the testing instrument. The screw must first be depressed against its spring and turned slightly in either direction until it is felt to engage in the slot of the head of the screw which is located behind it. Turn the screw one notch before re-checking the CO level with a maximum alteration in either direction of three notches (photo).

8   Once the CO level is correct, check the idle speed and readjust if necessary with the idle speed air screw shown in the photograph. If a rev counter is not fitted to the engine, connect a tachometer in accordance with the maker's instructions.

9   If the air screw has to be altered then the CO level must once again be checked and the idle speed screw re-adjusted if necessary.

10 If only a vacuum gauge is available, connect it to the connector provided on the venturi control unit.

11 Unscrew the idle air adjusting screw very slowly until the vacuum

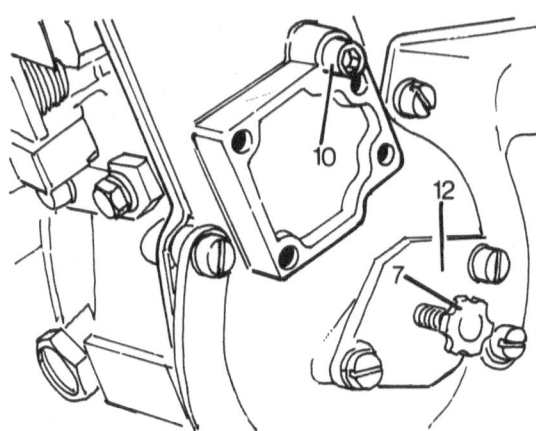

Fig. 3.56. Fuel injection pump adjusting screws (Sec. 24)

7   Idle speed adjusting screw
10 Locking screw - full load adjustment
12 Cover on partial load adjustment screws

24.7 Rear view of fuel injection pump

24.8A Idle speed air screw on fuel injection intake manifold

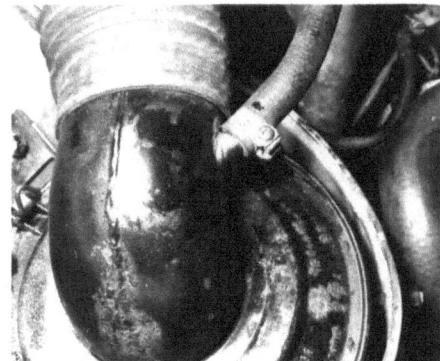

24.8B Clean air source for idle speed air screw (fuel injection)

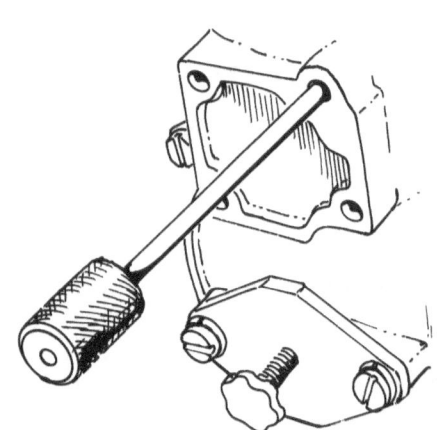

Fig. 3.57. Adjusting full load screw on fuel injection pump (Sec. 24)

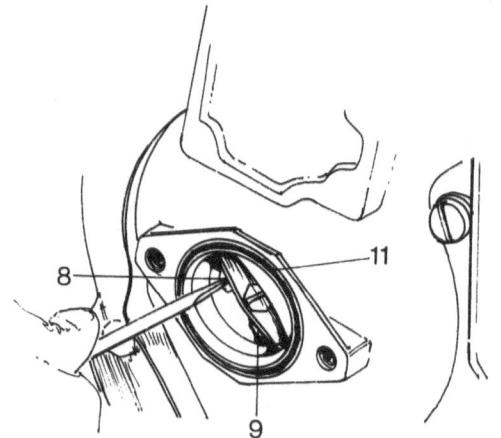

Fig. 3.58. Adjusting lower range partial load screw (8) on fuel injection pump (Sec. 24)

9   Upper range partial load screw   11   Sealing ring

reading on the gauge drops away and then turn the screw in until the vacuum pressure increases and finally drops off once more. From this last position, unscrew the idle air screw until maximum vacuum reading is obtained.

12 Now check the idle speed, if it is too high this means that the mixture is too rich. If the speed is too low then the mixture is weak. Adjust as necessary using the idle speed screw on the rear end of the injection pump. Repeat the adjustment previously describing using the idle air screw and vacuum gauge.

13 The idling adjustment operations just described should be adequate in cases where the fuel injection components have not been previously incorrectly set or tampered with. It is as well to know the location of the other adjustment screws however, but unless the necessary experience is available or you have an 'ear' for tuning, leave their adjustment to your dealer.

14 To adjust the full load point, remove the plug from the regulator cover and turn the screw one notch clockwise (weaker) or anti-clockwise (richer) (Fig. 3.57).

15 To adjust the lower partial load range, remove the diamond shaped flange from the rear of the injection pump. Turn the black screws together, two notches at a time clockwise (weaker) or anti-clockwise (richer). On no account touch the (white) upper partial load range screws (Fig. 3.58).

25 Fuel injection system - constant speed adjustment

1 Certain engines are fitted with a lifting solenoid which keeps the engine speed steady at progressively greater throttle openings. The device is used only in conjunction with automatic transmission (photo).

2 Start the engine, bring to normal operating temperature and engage 'DRIVE' or switch on the air conditioning system (where fitted).

3 Set the adjusting nut on the solenoid operating rod so that the engine idling speed is about 700 rpm (Fig. 3.59).

4 On later models, the solenoid to linkage relationship is different. Set the operating rod so that when it is pressed fully into the solenoid, there is a clearance between the end of the rod and the linkage of between 0.0039 and 0.0079 in (0.1 and 0.2 mm) (Fig. 3.60).

26 Fuel injection system - venturi vacuum governor adjustment

1 With the engine at idling speed and the transmission in 'N' or neutral, check the position of the adjusting screw (10). It should be just making contact with the clamp bolt (8) (Fig. 3.61).

2 Now engage 'DRIVE' and check whether there is a clearance 'B'

25.1 Constant speed solenoid on intake manifold of fuel injection engine

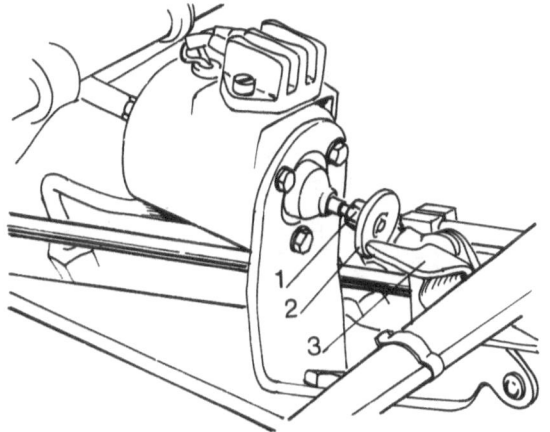

Fig. 3.59. Fuel injection constant speed solenoid (early models) (Sec. 25)

| 1 | Locknut | 2 | Adjuster | 3 | Actuating lever |

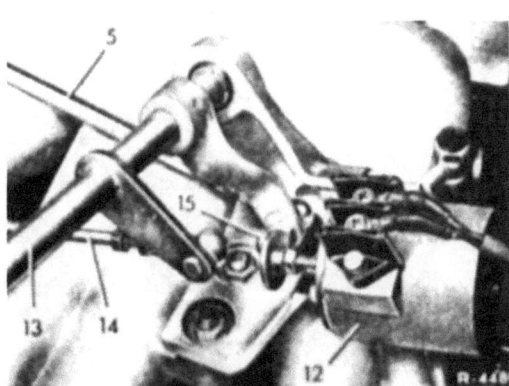

Fig. 3.60. Fuel injection constant speed solenoid (later models) (Sec. 25)

5	Threaded rod	14	Pull rod
12	Solenoid	15	Bolt
13	Regulating shaft		

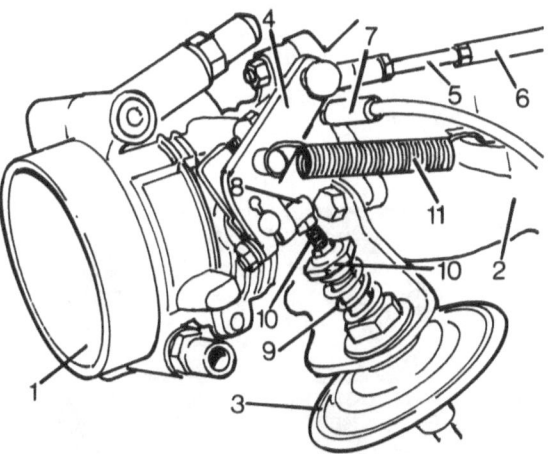

Fig. 3.61. Fuel injection system venturi control unit vacuum governor (Sec. 26)

1	Venturi control unit	7	Vacuum connection
2	Intake manifold	8	Pinch bolt
3	Vacuum unit	9	Spring
4	Throttle valve	10	Adjusting screw
5	Threaded rod	11	Return spring
6	Outer rod	12	Adjusting nut

as shown in Fig. 3.62 of between 0.039 and 0.059 in (1.0 and 1.5 mm). If adjustment is required to achieve this, alter the position of nut (12) (Fig. 3.61).
3   Re-check position of adjusting screw (10).

27 Fuel injection system - testing warm running device

1   Check (with the engine cold) that the fast idle speed is between 1000 and 1200 rev/min.
2   Run the engine slowly but progressively to its normal operating temperature.
3   With the engine running, unscrew the injection pump air filter (15). If, as a result of this, the engine speed increases, the air cleaner is clogged and must be renewed (Fig. 3.63).
4   The heat sensor should switch off at a coolant temperature of between 149°F (65°F) and 158°F (70°C) and this will be indicated by the cessation of suction at the injection pump air cleaner attachment collar. On later North American versions, the heat sensor switches off at a temperature of between 122°F (50°C) and 131°F (55°C).

5   Any adjustment required to bring the switching point within the specified range can be made by inserting or removing washers at the control valve housing mating face (Fig. 3.64).

28 Fuel injection system - testing fuel mixture

1   This work will normally only be required if the engine stalls when cold, or gases are blown back into the intake pipe or the engine oil is being diluted with fuel.
2   Have the engine cold and disconnect the regulating rod from the venturi control unit.
3   Disconnect the distributor vacuum hose from its connection and plug the connector.
4   Extract the grub screw from the venturi control unit, screw in a nipple and attach the vacuum hose to the nipple (Fig. 3.65).
5   Start the engine and observe the rev-counter, at the same time opening the throttle valve lever slowly until maximum speed is obtained. This increase in speed should be from 300 to 400 rpm above idling speed level. If the throttle valve is opened too far, the speed

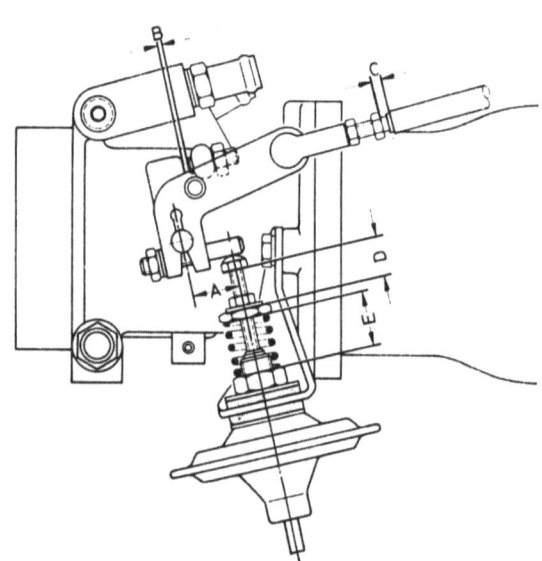

Fig. 3.62. Venturi control unit vacuum governor adjustment diagram (Sec. 26)

A   0.650 to 0.689 in (16.5 to 17.5 mm)
B   0.039 to 0.059 in (1.0 to 1.5 mm) with gear engaged
C   Free movement
D   0.571 to 0.610 in (14.5 to 15.5 mm)
E   0.768 in (19.5 mm)

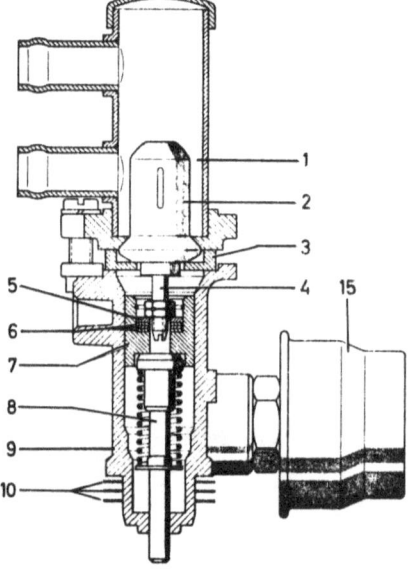

Fig. 3.64. Control valve/heat sensor unit on fuel injection pump (Sec. 27)

1   Housing   7   Control valve
2   Heat sensor   8   Guide rod
3   Guide ring   9   Control valve housing
4   Thrust rod   10   Compensating washers
5   Washer   15   Air filter
6   Compensating washers

Fig. 3.63. Fuel injection pump air filter (15) (Sec. 27)

Fig. 3.65. Test connection (13) on fuel injection venturi unit (Sec. 28)

will drop.

6 If the speed increase is below specification, switch off the engine and add compensating washers to the warm running device valve housing mounting face. If the speed increase is above specification, remove some washers.

29 Fuel injection pump - removal and refitting

1 Disconnect the battery earth lead.
2 Drain the cooling system.
3 From the injection pump, disconnect the coolant hoses, the supplementary air intake hose and the fuel lines and hoses. Do not twist the pipes when unscrewing the unions of the latter (Fig. 3.66) (photos).
4 Disconnect the oil line from the injection pump and the oil line connecting the oil filter and cooler.
5 Disengage the control rod and disconnect the solenoid lead (photo).
6 Unscrew and remove the pump mounting bolts and the socket - headed screws and withdraw the pump in a rearward direction.
7 Detach the coupling sleeve (photo).
8 If a new pump is to be fitted, make sure that it is supplied complete with a splined drive pinion. If not, have the supplier remove and refit the old one as a special wrench and puller are required to do the job.
9 Before fitting a new pump, remove the diamond shaped sealing flange from the rear of the pump and pour in 0.4 Imp pint (0.5 US pint, 0.25 litre) of engine oil.
10 Refit the sealing flange and the bracket.
11 Check the control rack rod for ease of movement. To do this either remove the control rack end cap and screw an M5 bolt into the rod to check the movement or in the case of a rack rod having no threads, push the rack rod to the rear and if it does not return by itself, push it forward again by applying pressure to the full load screw. (Fig. 3.67).
12 If the rack is still hard to move, try turning the splined drive pinion at the same time as the rack rod is pushed back and forth.
13 With the injection pump ready for refitting, turn the crankshaft until the TDC mark on the damper/pulley is opposite the pointer

on the front of the engine. Make sure that No. 1 piston is on its compression stroke either by removing the spark plug and feeling the compression being generated or by checking that the rotor arm of the distributor is pointing towards No. 1 HT lead contact in the distributor cap.
14 Continue turning the crankshaft until the timing pointer is opposite the 20° ATDC mark on the crankshaft damper scale (photo).
15 Rotate the splined drive pinion of the fuel injection pump until

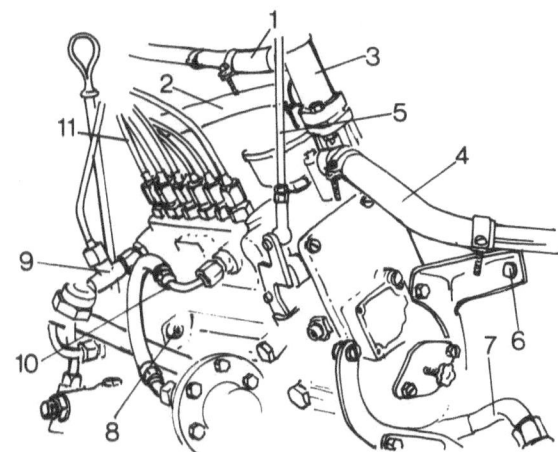

Fig. 3.66. Fuel injection pump attachments (Sec. 29)

1 Coolant hoses
2 Coolant hoses
3 Coolant heat sensor
4 Supplementary air intake hose
5 Control rod
6 Mounting bracket bolts
7 Oil line
8 Socket headed mouting screws
9 Fuel inlet pipe
10 Fuel return pipe
11 Fuel injection lines

29.3A Side view of fuel injection pump

29.3B Using two spanners to disconnect a fuel line

29.3C Disconnecting fuel inlet pipe from filter (fuel injection)

29.3D Layout of pipes and hoses adjacent to fuel injection pump

29.5 Solenoid at rear end of fuel injection pump

29.7 Fuel injection pump splined coupling sleeve

its alignment mark (master spline) is opposite the mark on the pump flange (Fig. 3.68).

16 Engage the coupling and fit the pump, using a new flange gasket each side of the insulator.

17 Connect the fuel hoses, the coolant hoses and the supplementary air hose and the injection lines.

18 Refill the cooling system.

19 Connect the oil lines to pump, filter and cooler.

20 Reconnect the battery.

21 As the fuel injection lines will be empty, actuate the starting valve at the intake pipe by earthing terminal 'W' of the thermal time switch

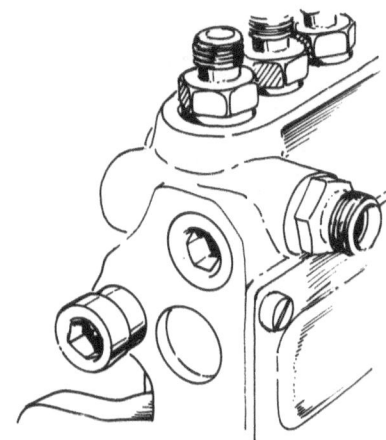

Fig. 3.67. Pushing fuel injection pump rack rod to test ease of movement (Sec. 29)

and operating the starter motor until the engine fires.

22 Run the engine to its normal operating temperature and carry out the checks and adjustments described in Sections 24 to 28.

30 Fuel injection valves - removal and refitting

1 The removal of an injection valve is simply a matter of unscrewing and removing them having first disconnected the fuel pipes at their unions (photo).

2 When refitting, always use new sealing rings and tighten the securing bolts to a torque wrench setting of 25 lb f ft (35 Nm) (photo).

31 Fuel injection pump - overhaul

1 The operations should be limited to those described in this Section, otherwise, leave further dismantling to your Mercedes-Benz or Bosch dealer.

2 To remove the heat sensor assembly, clean away all external dirt and unscrew and remove the bolts, housing (1) and sensor (2) (Fig. 3.64).

3 Check the control guide pin (8) for ease of operation.

4 Do not extract the thrust pin (4) but rotate it to check that it is moving easily.

5 When reassembling the new components, seal the sensor with the recommended sealant and then before fitting the assembly make sure that the housing (1) and the guide ring (3) are correctly aligned.

6 Tighten the securing bolts evenly.

7 To remove a ball pressure valve, clean away any external dirt and unscrew the associated fuel pressure line and pipe unions.

8 A suitable extractor must now be obtained (Service tool MB 000 589 623300 or Bosch EF 8117A) to extract the pressure valve (Fig. 3.69).

9 With the valve removed, switch on the ignition for a few seconds

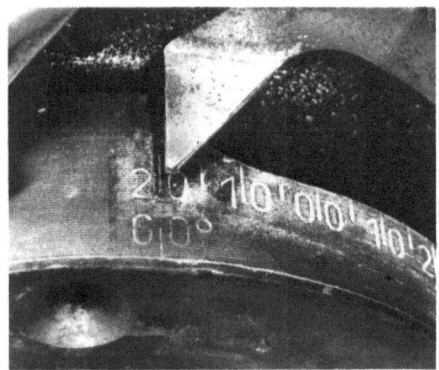

29.14 Timing set for 20° ATDC for fuel injection pump installation

30.1 Fuel injection valve

30.2 Fuel injection valve with seal

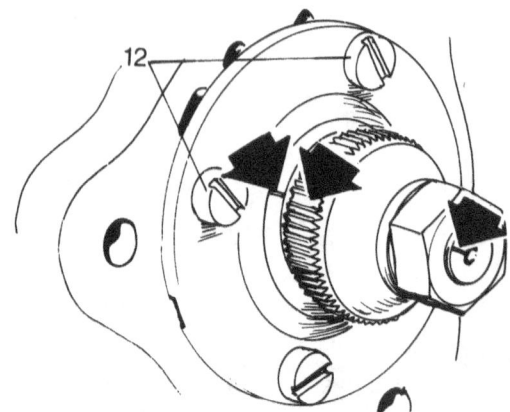

Fig. 3.68. Fuel injection pump drive pinion and flange alignment marks (Sec. 29)

12 Securing screws

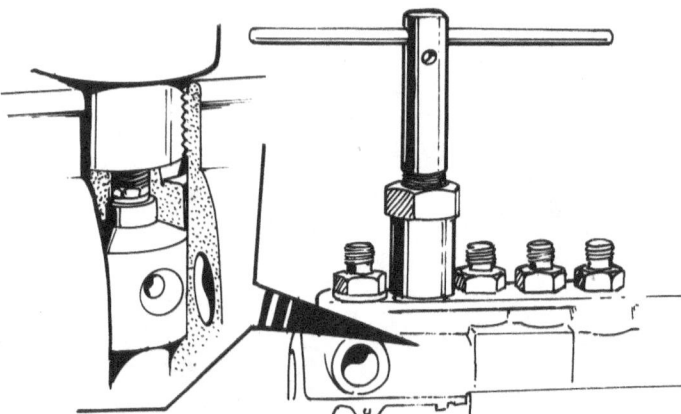

Fig. 3.69. Extracting a fuel injection pump pressure valve (Sec. 31)

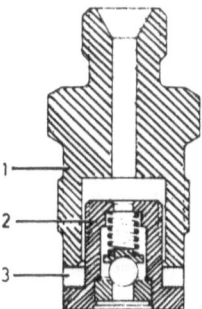

1 Union connection
2 Pressure valve
3 Sealing ring

Fig. 3.70. Sectional view of fuel injection pump pressure valve (Sec. 31)

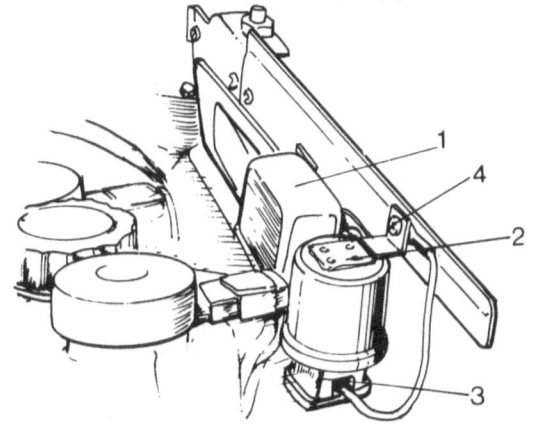

Fig. 3,71. Fuel injection system starting valve relay (1) Time switch (2) Connector plug (3) and securing screw (4) (Sec. 32)

to flush out the suction chamber of the injection pump.

10 A new sealing ring must always be fitted when the original or a new valve is being fitted. If a new pressure valve is being fitted, make sure that it carries the same calibration code as the other five valves.

11 When fitting the pressure valve and its pipe union connection, proceed exactly as described in the following in order to ensure a perfect seal. Tighten the pipe connection to a torque of 29 lb f ft (40 Nm), loosen and retighten again to the same torque, loosen and finally tighten to 25 lb f ft (35 Nm) (Fig. 3.70).

32 Fuel injection system - starting valve modifications

1 On later cars, a one-second time switch is fitted to actuate the electric starting valve on the intake pipe for a period of one second even when the engine cooling water temperature is above 95°F (35°C). This arrangement improves the engine warm-up characteristics.

2 Earlier cars may be modified in the following way.

3 Working within the engine compartment, move the relay (1) to provide space to mount the time switch (Part No. 001545 1624). (Fig. 3.71).

4 Remove the coupling from the main cable harness on the relay (1) and insert the connectors of the supplementary harness (Part No. 108 540 1009).

5 Refit the coupling (3) and fasten the earth cable under the time switch mounting screw.

6 Test the fitting by observing whether the starting valve on the intake pipe operates for one second at the specified coolant level when the ignition is switched on.

33 Emission control - general description

The type of system used depends generally upon the date of production and destination of the car.

All cars have a Crankcase Ventilation System and later models also have a Fuel Evaporative Control System (refer to Section 11).

An Exhaust Emission Control System was introduced in 1968 and has become progressively more complex (particularly on North American models) during succeeding years.

In addition to any emission control system which may be fitted, modifications have been carried out to the fuel and ignition systems to further reduce the emission of noxious fumes and it is important that the timing of these systems is to the highest standard, also, that the engine is in first class mechanical condition without undue wear.

34 Crankcase ventilation system - description and maintenance

1 Gases which accumulate in the crankcase and are the result of engine oil fumes or blow-by gases which have passed the piston rings are vented into the intake manifold where they are burned during the normal engine combustion cycle.

2 On carburettor engines, the gases are routed either through a moisture separator located in the air cleaner, or a by-pass nozzle, according to the vacuum pressure in the manifold (Fig. 3.72).

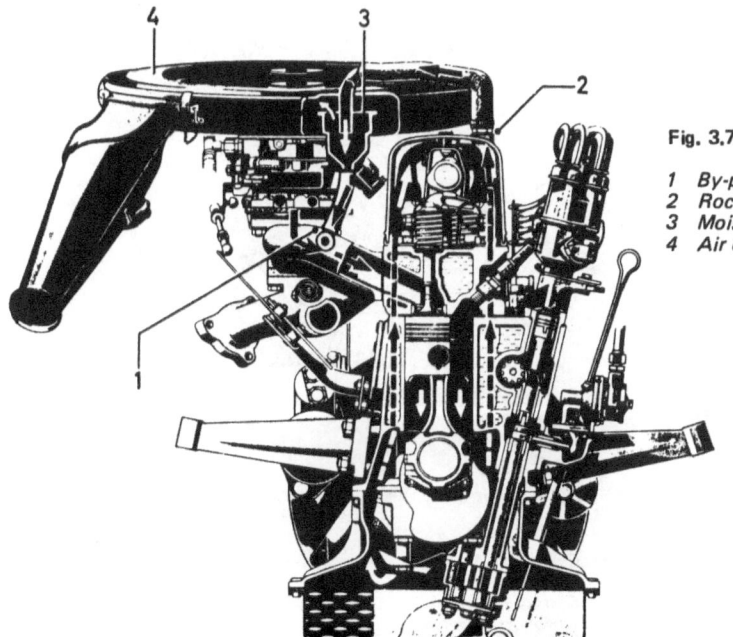

Fig. 3.72. Crankcase ventilation system on carburettor engine (Sec. 34)

1 By-pass
2 Rocker cover connection
3 Moisture separator
4 Air cleaner

3 *On carburettor engines built for North America,* a flame trap is incorporated in the hose which runs between the rocker cover and the air cleaner (Fig. 3.73).

4 *On fuel injection engines,* the crankcase ventilation system is similar to that just described except that the gases are directed into the venturi control unit just ahead of the throttle valve. Any tendency for the moisture in the gases to freeze in cold weather is overcome by the warmth of the coolant - heated venturi control unit (Fig. 3.74).

5 . Maintenance consists of checking the security of the connecting hoses and unions and cleaning the moisture separator and flame trap in paraffin and drying them at the specified intervals.

35 Exhaust emission control (1968 - 69) - description, maintenance and testing

Carburettor engines

1 *An after burner system* is fitted to carburettor engines. Essentially this is a method of injecting air close to the exhaust valves in order to dilute the proportion of carbon monoxide and unburned hydrocarbon

in the exhaust gases (Fig. 3.75).

2 A belt driven air pump provides the air pressure required and the circuit incorporates a non-return valve and air overflow (by-pass) valve to prevent reverse flow and over rich mixture during certain engine conditions.

3 At the specified intervals, check the security and condition of the connecting hoses. Check the tension of the drivebelt which should have a deflection of ½ in (12.7 mm) at the centre of its longest run between two pulleys. If necessary, move the alternator on its mountings to adjust it.

4 To check the operation of the air pump and the air pump pressure relief valve, have the engine idling and then remove the hose from the outlet nozzle on the air pump. Feel if air is coming out of the nozzle to prove that the pump is functioning.

5 Now cover the nozzle of the pump with the hand and hold it there until the air pressure relief valve blows off to prove that the valve is operating correctly.

6 To check the functioning of the non-return valve, detach the hose from it at the side furthest from the air pump and verify that no exhaust gas is emitted from the valve.

7 ,To check the functioning of the air overflow valve, disconnect the hose from the side of the valve furthest from the air pump. At idling speed no air should be felt to be drawn into the valve.

8 Increase the engine speed momentarily and then let the engine return to idling when air should be felt to be drawn into the valve for one second.

9 If any of the valves do not operate correctly then they should be renewed. To renew the air pressure relief valve, remove the air pump and use an extractor to draw out the valve. Drive the new valve into position (interference fit) using a hammer and an insulator on the valve. Before fitting the valve, remove the pressure adjuster and refit it again later.

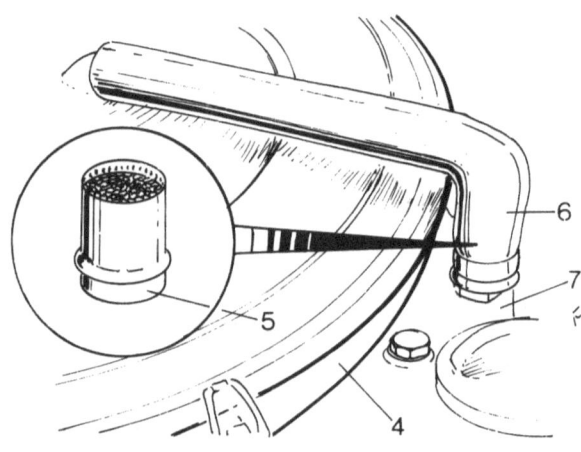

Fig. 3.73. Location of crankcase ventilation system flame trap (Sec. 34)

4 *Air cleaner*	6 *Hose*
5 *Flame trap*	7 *Rocker cover*

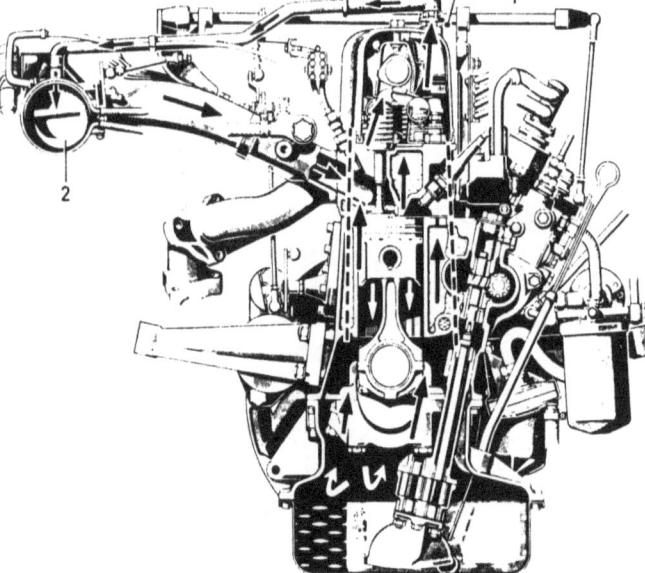

Fig. 3.74. Crankcase ventilation system on fuel injection engines (Sec. 34)

1 *Rocker cover connection*	2 *Venturi control*

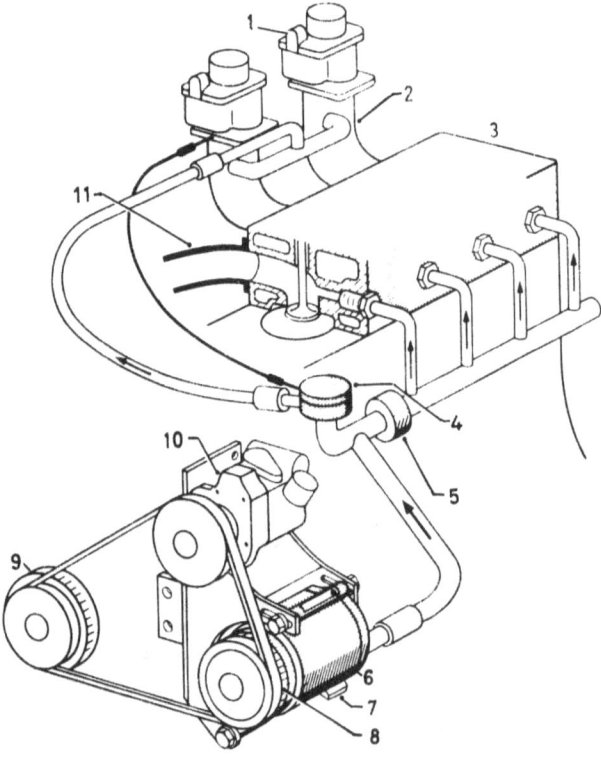

Fig. 3.75. Layout of exhaust emission control afterburner systems (Sec. 35)

1 *Carburettors*	7 *Pressure relief valve*
2 *Intake manifold*	8 *Air intake*
3 *Cylinder head*	9 *Crankshaft pulley*
4 *Air overflow valve*	10 *Power steering pump*
5 *Non-return valve*	11 *Exhaust line*
6 *Air pump*	

Fuel injection engines with automatic transmission
10 The emission control devices on these engines comprise modifications to the fuel injection pump and venturi control unit.
11 The fuel injection pump is fitted with a fuel cut-off solenoid which is controlled by various switches to monitor engine and transmission characteristics under all engine conditions, particularly downhill driving with the accelerator released (Fig. 3.76).
12 Maintenance consists of occasionally checking the leads and connections.
13 Testing of individual components can be carried out in the following way after having first connected a test lamp between the terminal of the fuel cut-off solenoid and a good earth. Have the leads long enough to be able to locate the test bulb inside the car.
14 Drive the car on the road with 4th speed selected until the transmission upshifts to 3rd or 4th speed. Maintain minimum throttle and the test lamp should illuminate at about 1100 rpm.
15 If the lamp does not come on at the specified speed, the micro-switch on the regulating shaft must be adjusted. To do this, pull the connector plug on the two-way contact relay and connect the test lamp to terminals 86 and 87a. (Fig. 3.77).

16 Move the speed selector lever to 2, 3, 4 or R and adjust the position of the micro-switch by means of its adjusting screw so that the test lamp will go out just before the throttle valve starts moving, which the regulating linkage has actuated.
17 To test the fluid pressure switch which is located on the automatic transmission casing, again connect the test lamp between the terminal of the fuel cut-off solenoid and a good earth. Drive the car with the speed selector lever in 3 and with the transmission upshifted to 3rd speed. At an engine speed of at least 1500 rpm move the selector lever to 2 and release the accelerator pedal; the test lamp should go out.
18 To test the speed switch, switch on the ignition, disconnect the connector plug on the switch and connect a test lamp between terminal 1, the black cable and a good earth. Start the engine and increase the engine speed to 1100 rpm, when the test lamp should light up.
19 Failure of any of the switches to operate correctly will necessitate their renewal.

Fuel injection system with manual transmission
20 The purpose of this system is similar to that described in paragraphs 10 and 11 for cars with automatic transmission but the switches used differ and their testing should be carried out as follows.
21 Connect a test lamp between the live terminal of the fuel cut-off solenoid of the fuel injection pump and a good earth.
22 Switch on the ignition, engage 3rd gear and 4th gear without touching the clutch or accelerator pedals. The test lamp should illuminate as these gear positions are selected (Fig. 3.78).
23 Place the gearshift lever in neutral, 1st, and 2nd gear positions, also reverse. As each position is selected so the test bulb should go out. These tests prove that the switch on the transmission cover or the steering column (steering column gearshift) is satisfactory. Do not touch the clutch or accelerator pedals during this test (Fig. 3.79).
24 Depress the clutch pedal and engage 3rd gear, and then 4th gear. Do not touch the accelerator pedal. The test lamp should go out if the clutch pedal switch is satisfactory.
25 Engage 3rd, or 4th, gear without the use of the clutch pedal. Depress the accelerator pedal when the test lamp should go out if the regulating shaft micro-switch is satisfactory.

---

36 Exhaust emission control (1969 - 70) - description and testing

Fuel injection with automatic transmission (new type)
1 With the introduction of a new automatic transmission unit in May 1969, the emission control system described in the relevant paragraphs of the preceding Section was modified by making the fuel cut-off solenoid valve also dependent upon the temperature of the engine coolant.
2 Below a coolant temperature of 62.6°F (17°C) the system is

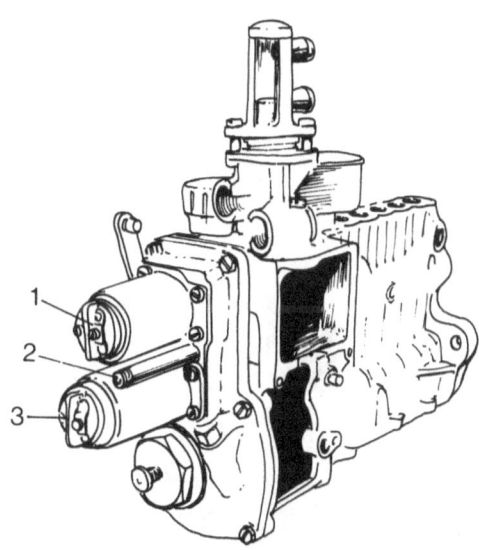

Fig. 3.76. Fuel injection pump fitted with starter solenoid (1) and Fuel cut off solenoid (3). Guide tube to full load adjusting screw (2)

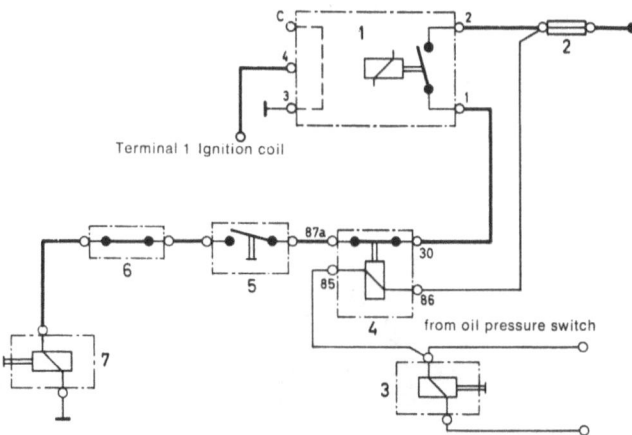

Fig. 3.77. Exhaust emission control test circuit (fuel injection and automatic transmission 1968-69) (Sec. 35)

1 Speed switch	5 Starter inhibitor/reverse
2 Fuse	lamp switch
3 Solenoid	6 Micro switch on
4 Relay	regulating shaft
	7 Fuel cut-off solenoid

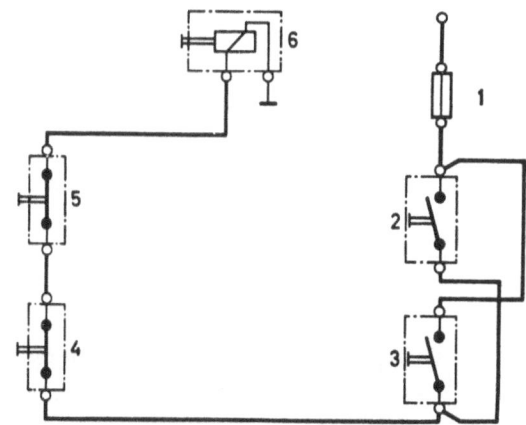

Fig. 3.78. Exhaust emission control test circuit (fuel injection and manual transmission 1968 - 69) with floor gearshift (Sec. 35)

1 Fuse	4 Clutch pedal switch
2 Transmission switch (3rd gear)	5 Micro switch on
3 Transmission switch (4th gear)	regulating shaft
	6 Fuel cut-off solenoid on
	injection pump

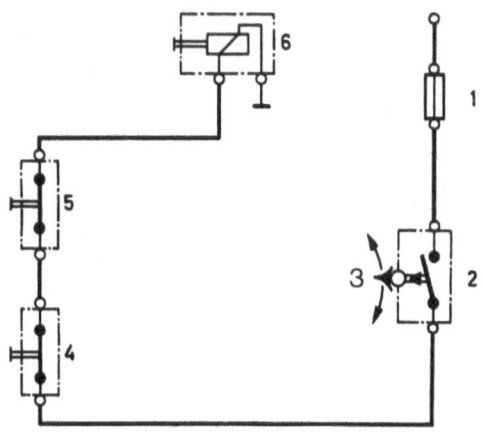

Fig. 3.79. Exhaust emission control test circuit (fuel injection
and manual transmission 1968 - 69) with steering column
gearshift (Sec. 35)

1 Fuse
2 Steering column switch
3 3rd and 4th gear switches
4 Clutch pedal switch
5 Micro switch on
   regulating shaft
6 Fuel cut-off solenoid on
   injection pump

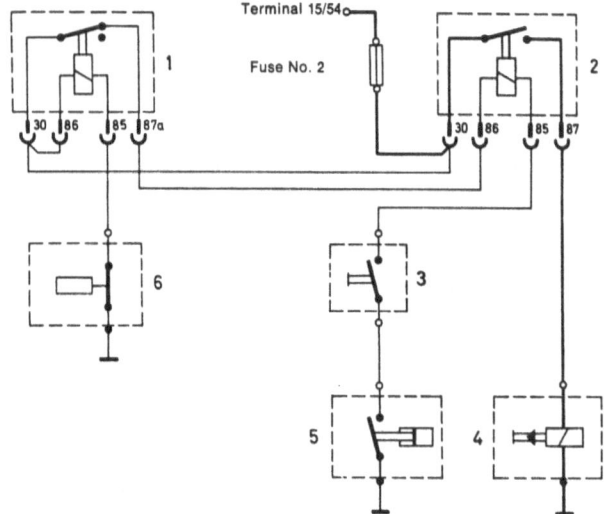

Fig. 3.80. Exhaust emission control test circuit (1969 - 70, fuel
injection and automatic transmission) (Sec. 36)

1 Relay (1)
2 Relay (2)
3 Micro switch
4 Fuel cut-off solenoid
5 Fluid pressure switch on
   transmission
6 Coolant temperature switch

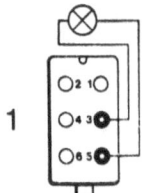

Fig. 3.81. Test lamp connected
between terminals of relay (1)
harness plug for testing coolant
temperature switch (Sec. 36)

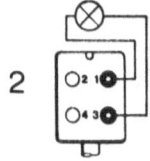

Fig. 3.82. Test lamp connected
between terminals of relay (2)
harness plug for testing
adjustment of regulating
shaft micro switch (Sec. 36)

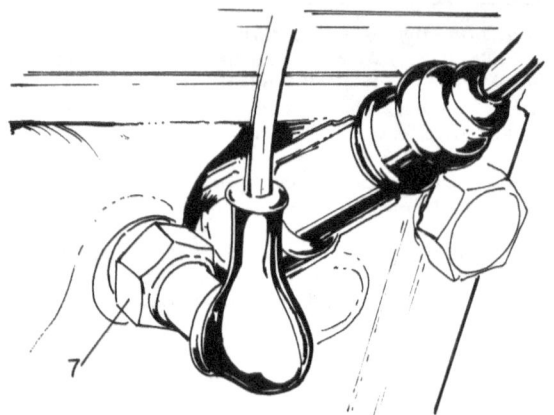

Fig. 3.83. Location of emission control 62.3°F (17°C) coolant
temperature switch (7) (Sec. 37)

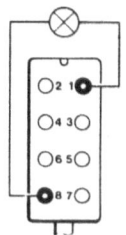

Fig. 3.84. Test lamp connected
between terminals of relay harness
plug for checking coolant
temperature switch (62.3°F - 17°C)
(Sec. 37)

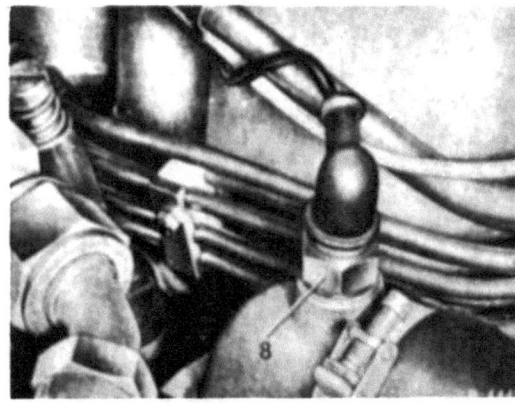

Fig. 3.85. Location of emission control 212°F (100°C) coolant
temperature switch (8) (Sec. 37)

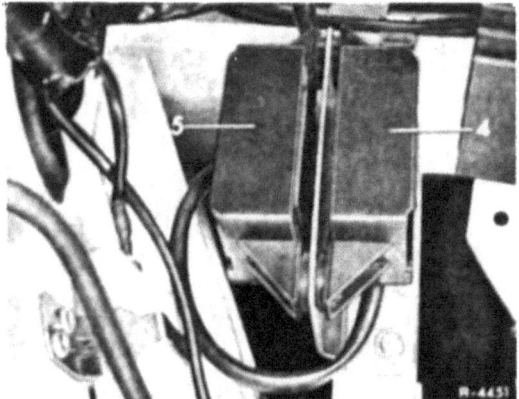

Fig. 3.86. Location of speed relay (4) and relay box (5) (Sec. 37)

inoperative. The temperature is monitored by a temperature switch screwed into the side of the cylinder block just above the oil filter.

3   To test the operation of the complete system, have the engine at normal operating temperature and connect a test lamp between the live terminal of the fuel cut-off solenoid and a good earth. Drive the car on the road at speeds up to 31 mph (50 kmh) when the test lamp lamp should remain extinguished. Release the accelerator pedal when under deceleration conditions, if the system is operating satisfactorily, the test lamp should come on at speeds above 22 mph (35 kmh) and go out at speeds below this (Fig. 3.80).

4   The individual switches of the system may be tested in the following way.

5   Pull the electrical connector plug from the relay which is located between the left-hand side of the radiator and the side of the engine compartment.

6   Connect the test lamp between contacts 3 and 5 of the relay connector plug (1). The test lamp should light up at a coolant temperature of below 62.3°F (17°C). This proves that the temperature sender switch is not faulty (Fig. 3.81).

7   Now test the micro-switch on the regulating shaft of the accelerator linkage. Connect the terminal on the transmission oil pressure switch to earth. Pull the four-contact connector plugs from the relay (2) and connect a test lamp to contact 1 (red/black) and 3 (brown/white). The test lamp should be on once the ignition is switched on and should go out if the accelerator linkage is actuated. If necessary, the micro-switch can be adjusted using the screw provided so that the test lamp will go out just before the throttle valve moves when the regulating linkage is actuated (Fig. 3.82).

8   To test the fluid pressure switch on the automatic transmission, again pull the connector plug from the relay (2) and connect the test lamp between contacts 30 and 85. Drive the car progressively up to a speed of 25 mph (40 kmh) and then release the accelerator pedal and let the car lose speed. At a speed of between 19 and 22 mph (30 and 35 kmh) the test lamp should come on.

9   The failure of any of the foregoing tests will mean that the appropriate switch must be renewed.

37 Exhaust emission control (1970 - 71) - description and testing

Carburettor engines

1   The emission control system used on these engines comprises a dual vacuum diaphragm distributor which depends upon the engine speed and temperature for its advance and retard angles.

2   The following tests can be made where the operation of the system is suspect.

3   Connect a tachometer to the ignition distributor, start the engine and increase its speed to 2500 rpm.

4   Release the accelerator and observe the vacuum diaphragm capsule on the carburettor. The adjusting screw on the capsule should be in contact with the actuating lever at speeds above 1800 rpm. At lower speeds, the screw should be clear of the lever.

5   Now connect a stroboscope (timing light) to the engine in accordance with the manufacturer's instructions. Start the engine and increase its speed. At engine speeds above 2400 rpm, the vacuum should advance the distributor setting and at speeds below 2200 rpm, it should retard it as observed with the stroboscope.

6   The 62.3°F (17°C) temperature switch can be tested by disconnecting the connector plug from the relay box and connecting a test lamp to contacts 1 and 8 of the plug. Switch on the ignition when the test lamp should light up only if the coolant temperature is below 62.3°F (17°C) (Figs. 3.83 and 3.84).

7   The 212°F (100°C) temperature switch can be tested by connecting the test lamp between contacts 6 and 8 of the relay connector plug. The lamp should light up at temperatures above 212°F (100°C) (Fig. 3.85).

8   The speed relay must only be tested using a voltmeter and not a test lamp, as the latter may damage the electronic content of the relay. The speed relay has two switches which actuate at different switch points: (i) between 1800 and 2000 rpm, at opening of throttle valve and (ii) between 2200 and 2400 rpm (Fig. 3.86).

9   To test the lower range switch point, pull the plug from the two-way valve (10) and connect a voltmeter between the contacts of the plug.

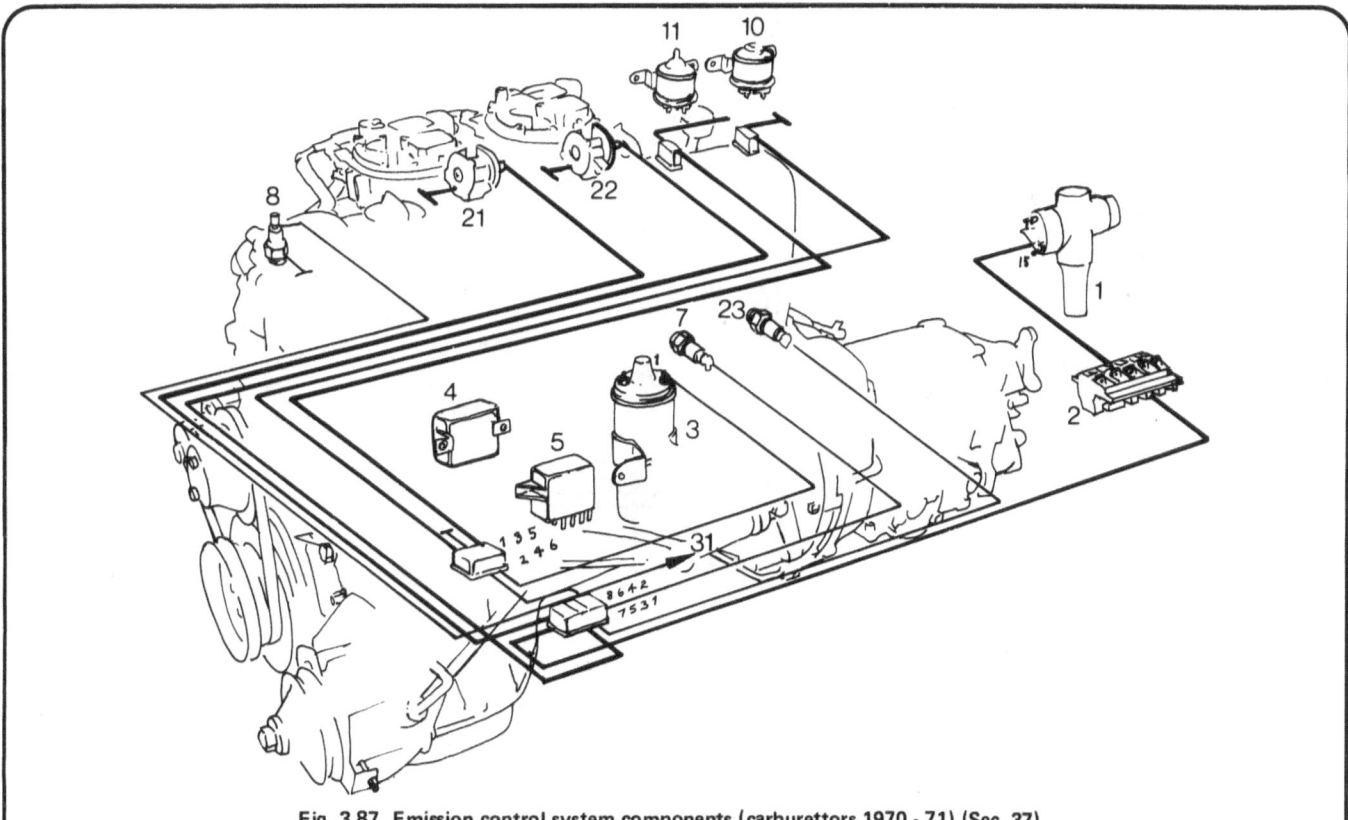

Fig. 3.87. Emission control system components (carburettors 1970 - 71) (Sec. 37)

1 Ignition switch	5 Relay box	10 Two-way valve	23 Coolant temperature switch
2 Fuses	7 Coolant low temperature switch	11 Three-way valve	(149°F - 65°C)
3 Ignition coil	8 Coolant high temperature	21 Automatic choke housing	31 To relay for air conditioning
4 Speed relay	switch	22 Automatic choke housing	supplementary fan

Start the engine and increase its speed. At engine speeds above 2000 rpm the voltmeter should read 13 volts and at speeds under 1800 rpm, no reading should be seen (Fig. 3.88).

10 Now pull the connector plug from the three-way valve and connect the voltmeter as previously described. Start the engine and increase the speed. Above engine speeds of 2400 rpm, the voltmeter should show no reading, and below 2200 rpm about 13 volts.

11 Any deviation from the foregoing test results will necessitate renewal of the component concerned.

12 On engines built from 1971 on for operation in North America, each carburettor is fitted with a solenoid fuel cut-off valve. The valve is screwed into the throttle valve housing and is energized when the ignition is switched on and de-energized when the ignition is switched off. The power circuit is fused.

13 To test these idle fuel cut-off valves, switch on the ignition and disconnect and then reconnect each of the leads to the valves in turn. Each valve should be distinctly heard to open with a click as the lead is reconnected.

14 Failure of one of these valves will give the same effect as a clogged idle fuel nozzle and so it must be renewed immediately.

Fuel injection with automatic transmission (280 SE/8 models)

15 The arrangement is similar to that just described in this Section for cars with carburettor engines except that some of the monitoring and sensoring controls differ (Fig. 3.89).

16 To test the fuel cut-off solenoid which fitted to the injection pump, connect a test lamp between the live terminal of the solenoid and a good earth. Make sure that the engine coolant temperature is above 62.3°F (17°C).

17 Drive the car on the road with speed selector position 4 engaged at about 31 mph (50 kmh) the test lamp should not come on. Release the accelerator pedal and let the car decelerate. The test lamp should come on at between 19 and 22 mph (30 and 35 kmh).

18 Connect a stroboscope and a tachometer to the engine in accordance with the maker's instructions. Start the engine and increase speed. By reference to the ignition timing marks, the moment of advance will be observed at about 2400 rpm.

19 To check the operation of the 62.3°F (17°C) coolant temperature switch, pull the connector plug from the relay box (5) and connect a test lamp between terminals 6 and 8 of the plug. Switch on the ignition when the test lamp should come on only if the coolant temperature is below 62.3°F (17°C) (Figs. 3.90, 91 and 92).

20 To test the idle throttle switch on the venturi control unit, connect the terminal of the fluid pressure switch on the automatic transmission to a good earth. Pull the coupling from the relay box and connect the test lamp between contacts 8 and 1 of the plug. Switch on the ignition and as the accelerator linkage is actuated so the test lamp

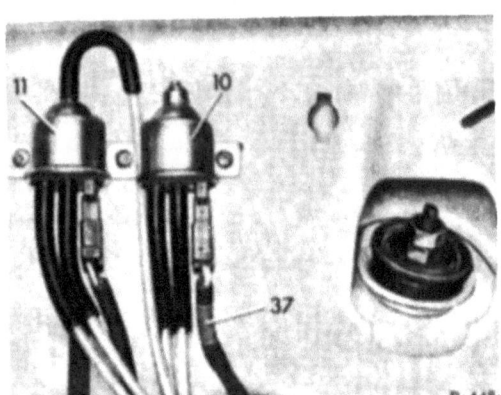

Fig. 3.88. Emission control system two-way valve (10), three-way valve (11) grey identifying tape (37) (Sec. 37)

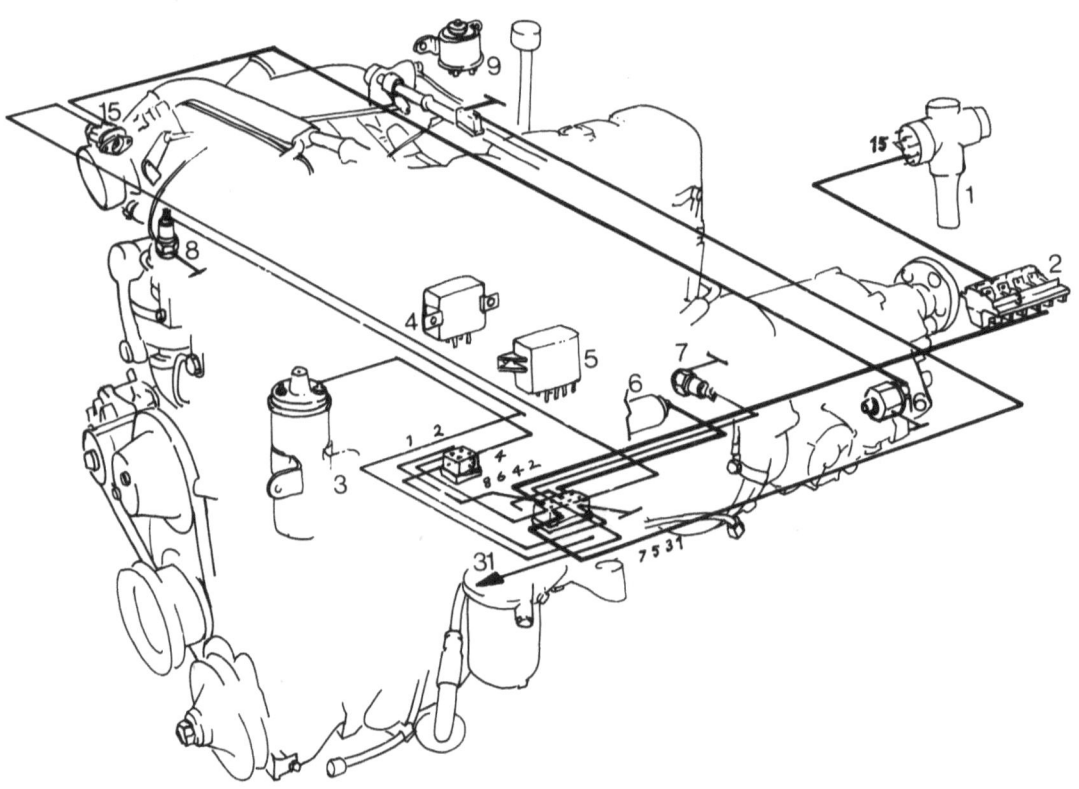

Fig. 3.89. Emission control system components (280 SE/8 models 1970 - 71 with automatic transmission (Sec. 37)

1 Ignition switch	5 Relay box	8 Coolant high temperature switch	15 Idle throttle switch
2 Fusebox	6 Fuel cut-off solenoid		16 Fluid pressure switch
3 Ignition coil	7 Coolant low temperature switch	9 Two-way valve	31 To relay for supplementary fan (air conditioning)
4 Speed relay			

Fig. 3.90. Coolant low temperature switch (7) and fuel cut-off solenoid (6) (Sec. 37)

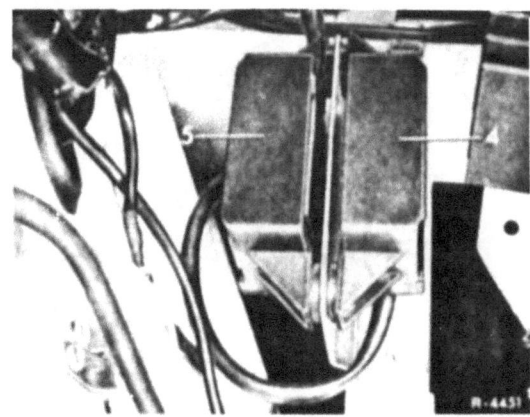

Fig. 3.91. Location of relay box (5) and speed relay (4) (Sec. 37)

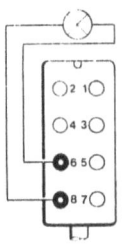

Fig. 3.92. Relay box connector plug contacts for testing coolant low temperature switch (Sec. 37)

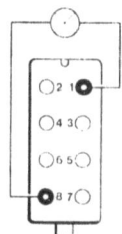

Fig. 3.94. Relay box connector plug contacts for testing fluid pressure switch (Sec. 37)

Fig. 3.93. Location of fluid pressure switch on automatic transmission (Sec. 37)

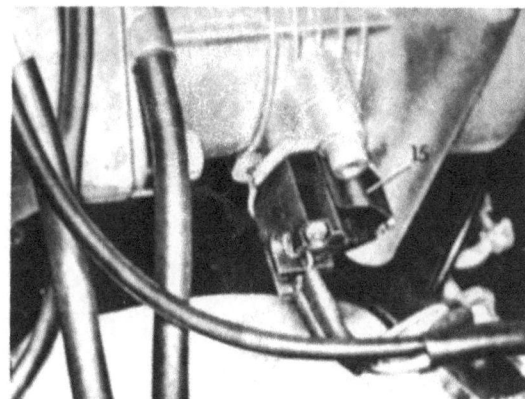

Fig. 3.95. Location of idle throttle switch on venturi control unit (Sec. 37)

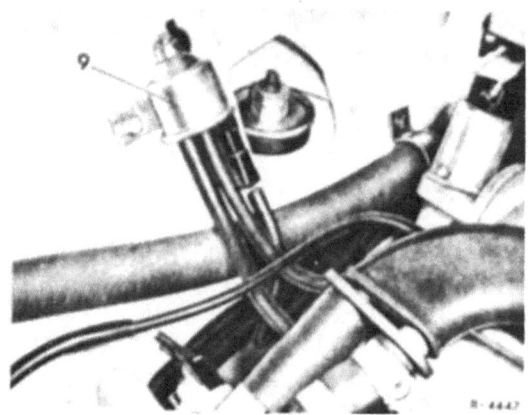

Fig. 3.96. Location of two-way valve (9) (Sec. 37)

should go out. Remake the original fluid pressure switch connection at the transmission (Fig. 3.93 and 3.94).

21 To test the fluid pressure switch on the automatic transmission casing, bridge the terminals of the idle throttle switch on the venturi control unit. Pull the connector plug from the relay box and connect the test lamp to contacts 8 and 1 of the plug. Drive the car on the road with speed selector in No. 4 position at about 31 mph (50 kmh) when the test lamp should be on. Release the accelerator and let the car decelerate when the test lamp should go out at betwen 19 and 22mph (30 and 35 kph) (Fig. 3.95) .

22 To test the speed relay, use only a voltmeter. Pull the connector plug from the two-way valve (9) and connect the voltmeter between the contacts of the plug. Start the engine and increase speed. Above 2400 rpm, the voltmeter should read 13 volts while below 2200 rpm, it should show no reading (Fig. 3.96).

23 To test the 212°F (100°C) temperature switch, pull the connector plug from the relay box and connect the test lamp between terminals 5 and 8 of the plug. If the coolant temperature is above 212°F (100°C) the test lamp should illuminate (figs. 3.97 and 3.98).

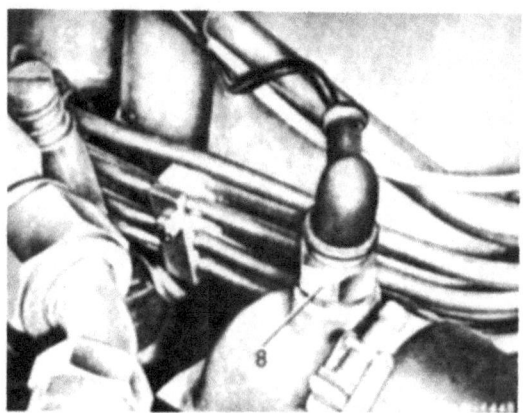

Fig. 3.97. Location of coolant high temperature switch (8) (Sec. 37)

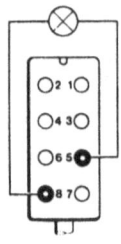

Fig. 3.98. Relay box connector plug contacts for testing coolant high temperature switch (Sec. 37)

Fuel injection with automatic transmission (280 SL/8 models)

24 The emission control system used on these cars is very similar to that described for 280 SE/8 models in paragraphs 15 to 23 of this Section but note the differences in the layout (Fig. 3.99).

25 Test the individual switches of the system as described in the following paragraphs keeping strictly to the sequence given.

26 Coolant temperature switch (above 62.3°F - 17°C) is located and should be tested just as described in paragraph 19 of this Section.

27 To test the idle throttle switch on the venturi control unit, refer to paragraph 20 of this Section.

28 To test the starter inhibitor switch, pull the connector plug from the speed relay (4) and connect the test lamp between contact 6 of the plug and a good earth. The test lamp should come on when the speed selector lever is moved to 2, 3, 4 and R with the ignition switched on. (Figs. 3.100, 101 and 102).

29 To test the speed relay, use only a voltmeter, not the test lamp which might damage its electronic components. To test the lower range switch point (1250 to 1450 rpm), bridge the terminals on the idle throttle switch on the venturi control unit. Start the engine and then withdraw the connector plug from the starter inhibitor switch. Bridge contacts 5 and 6 of the plug (Fig. 3.103).

30 Pull the connector plug from the current relay (29) (Fig. 3.101) and connect a voltmeter between contact 4 of the plug and a good earth. Increase the engine speed. When the engine speed is about 1450 rpm, the voltmeter should indicate 13 volts. Below 1250 rpm the voltmeter should show no reading (Fig. 3.104).

31 To test the higher range switch point, pull the connector plug from the two-way valve (9) (Fig. 3.101). Connect a voltmeter between the two contacts of the plug, start the engine and increase the engine speed. Above about 2400 rpm the voltmeter should indicate 13 volts, below 2200 rpm it should show no reading.

32 To test the fluid pressure on the automatic transmission, pull the connector plug from the relay box (5) (Fig. 3.101) and connect a test lamp between contacts 8 and 1 of the plug. Drive the car with the speed selector lever in position 4 at about 25 mph (40 kmh) then

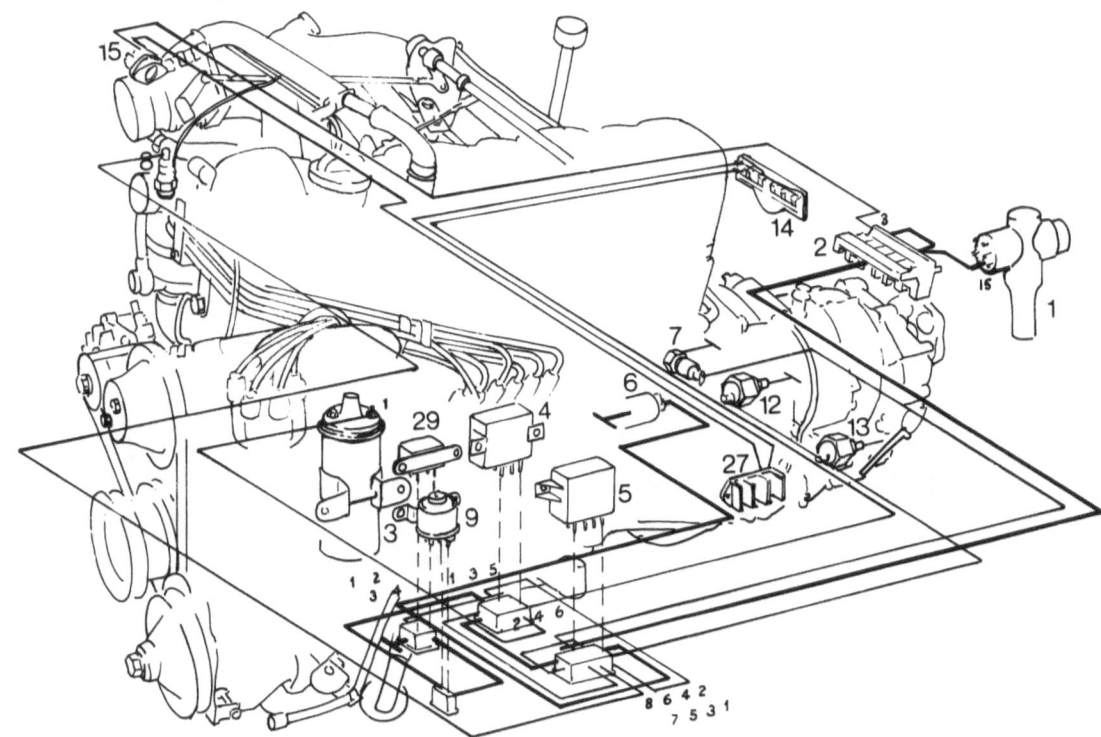

Fig. 3.99. Emission control system components (280 SL/8 models 1970 - 71) (Sec. 37)

1 Ignition switch	6 Fuel cut-off solenoid	12 Fluid pressure switches in transmission	15 Idle throttle switch
2 Fuse box	7 Coolant low temperature switch		27 Cable connector
3 Ignition coil	8 Coolant high temperature switch	13 Fluid pressure switch in transmission	29 Current relay
4 Speed switch	9 Two-way valve	14 Starter inhibitor and reversing lamp switch	
5 Relay box			

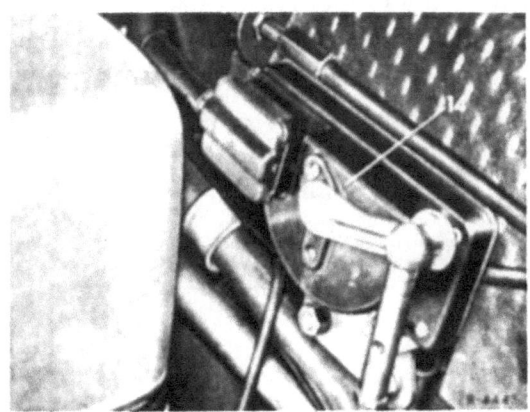

Fig. 3.100. Location of starter inhibitor and reversing lamp switch (14) (Sec. 37)

Fig. 3.101. Location of speed relay (4) relay box (5) two-way valve (9) and current relay (29) (Sec. 37)

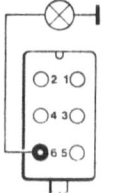

Fig. 3.102. Speed relay connector plug contacts for testing starter interlock switch (Sec. 37)

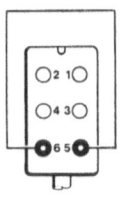

Fig. 3.103. Starter inhibitor connector plug contacts for testing speed relay (Sec. 37)

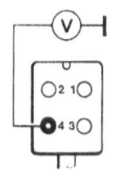

Fig. 3.104. Current relay connector plug contacts for testing speed relay (Sec. 37)

Fig. 3.105. Automatic transmission fluid pressure switch (12) (Sec. 37)

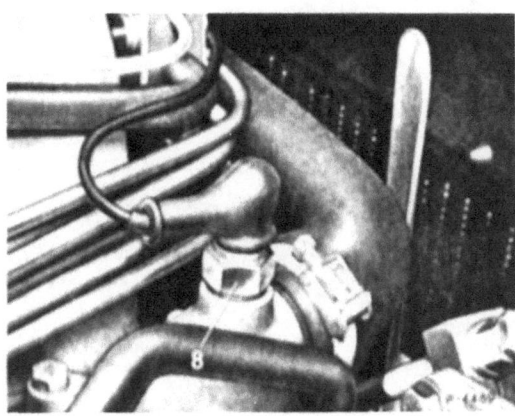

Fig. 3.107. Location of coolant high temperature switch (8) (Sec. 37)

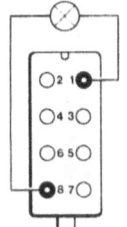

Fig. 3.106. Relay box connector plug contacts for testing transmission switch (Sec. 37)

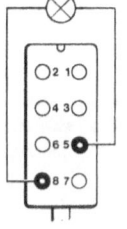

Fig. 3.108. Relay box connector plug contacts for testing high temperature coolant switch (Sec. 37)

release the accelerator. As the car slows down and downshifts to 2nd speed at about 11 mph (18 kmh) the test lamp should come on. (Figs. 3.105 and 106).
33 To test the 212°F (100°C) temperature switch, pull the connector plug from the relay box (5) (Fig. 3.101) and connect a test lamp between contacts 5 and 8 of the plug. Switch on the ignition when the test lamp should come on only if the engine coolant is above 212°F (100°C) (Figs. 3.107 and 108).

Fuel injection with manual transmission

34 The emission control systems are similar to those described in this Section for cars with automatic transmission but the following differences in testing procedures for some components should be noted. (Figs. 3.109 and 112).

35 To test the throttle switch (see Figs. 3.95) the clutch switch and the gearshift switch, carry out the following operations. It should be noted that the gearshift switch is connected in series with the clutch switch and on 280 SL/8 models, has two gearshift switches connected in parallel (Figs. 3.110, 111, 113 and 114).

36 Withdraw the connector plug from the relay box (5) (Fig. 3.101) and connect a test lamp between contacts 8 and 1 of the plug. Switch

on the ignition when the test lamp should light up when 3rd and 4th gears are selected. Do not depress the accelerator or clutch pedals during these tests (Figs. 3.115).

37 Now depress first the accelerator pedal and then the clutch in turn, on each occasion selecting first of all 2nd gear and then 1st gear. The test lamp should go out on each occasion.

38 If any of the foregoing tests do not prove satisfactory, first check the switch adjustments and observe whether the switches have moved on their mountings. The gearshift switches must be adjusted so that they are closed when 3rd and 4th gears are selected. Check the security of the connecting plugs and leads and the circuit fuses and if these are in order then the faulty switch or relay must be renewed.

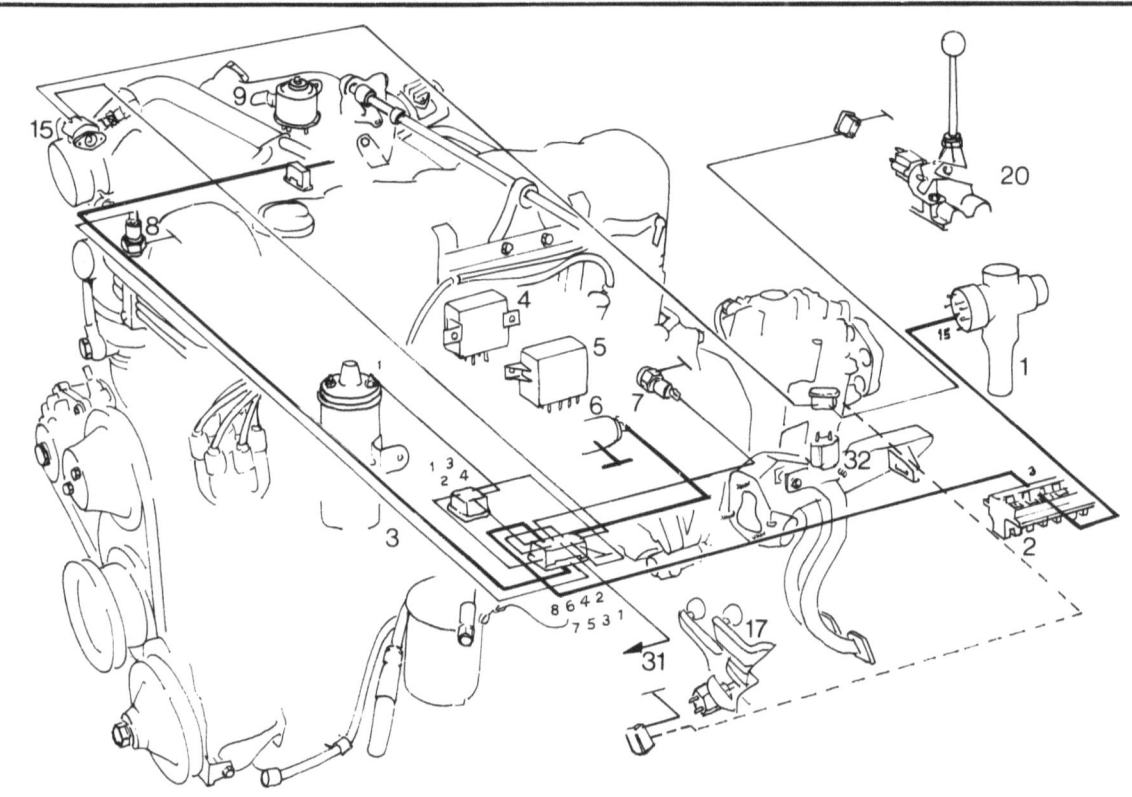

Fig. 3.109. Emission control system components (1970 - 71 model 280 SE/8 with manual transmission) (Sec. 37)

1	Ignition switch	6	Fuel cut-off solenoid	9	Two-way valve
2	Fusebox	7	Coolant low temperature switch	15	Idle throttle switch
3	Ignition coil	8	Coolant high temperature	17	Gearshift switch (steering column)
4	Speed relay		switch		
5	Relay box				

20	Gearshift switch (floor-mounted)
31	To relay for supplementary fan (air conditioning)
32	Clutch switch

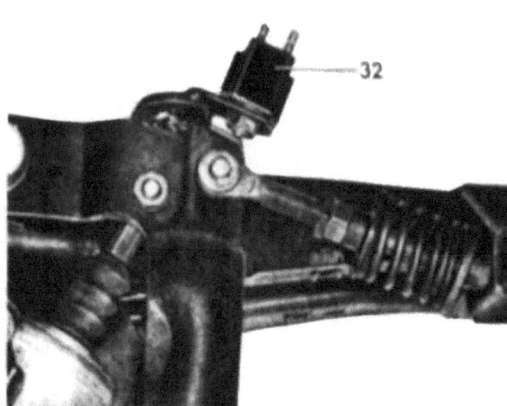

Fig. 3.110. Clutch switch (32) (Sec. 37)

Fig. 3.111. Location of floor-mounted gearshift switch (20) (Sec. 37)

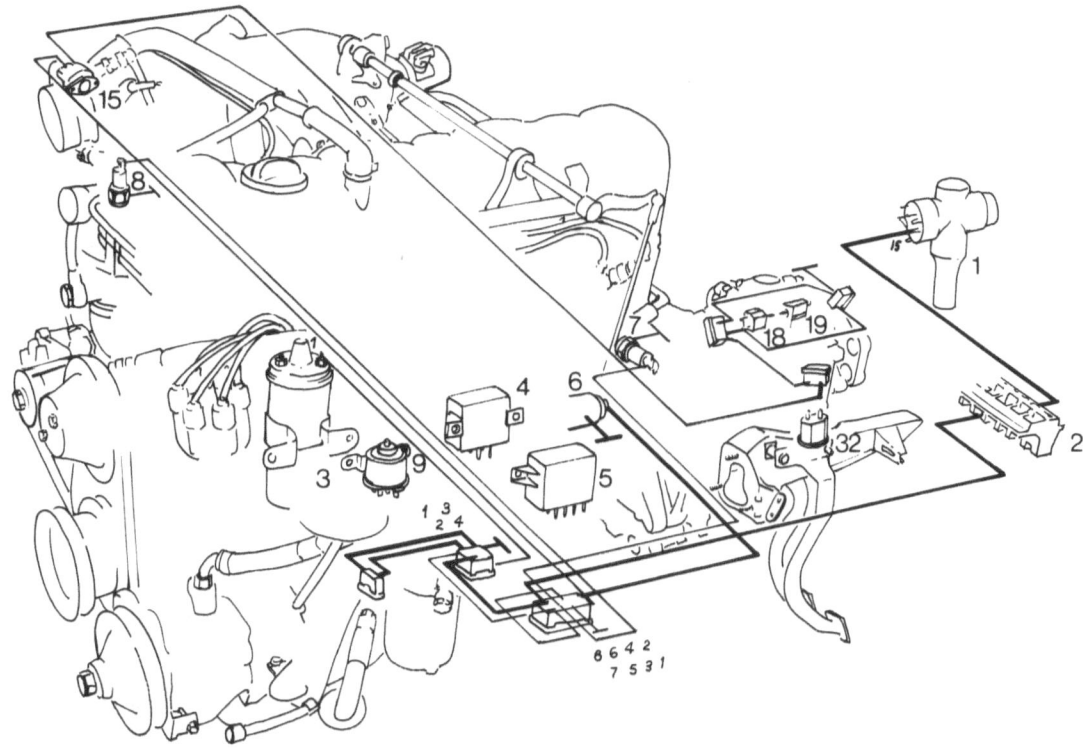

Fig. 3.112. Emission control system components (1970 - 71 model 280 SL/8 with manual transmission) (Sec. 37)

1	Ignition switch	5	Relay box
2	Fusebox	6	Fuel cut-off solenoid
3	Ignition coil	7	Coolant low temperature switch
4	Speed relay	8	Coolant high temperature switch
		9	Two-way valve
		15	Idle throttle switch
		18	Gearshift (3rd gear switch)
		19	Gearshift (4th gear switch)
		32	Clutch switch

Fig. 3.113. Location of steering column mounted gearshift switch (17) (Sec. 37)

Fig. 3.114. Location of 3rd gear (18) and 4th gear (19) switches on model 280 SL/8 (Sec. 37)

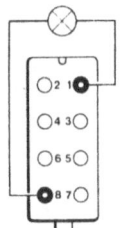

Fig. 3.115. Relay box contacts in connector plug for testing throttle switch (Sec. 37)

38 Exhaust emission control (1972) - description and testing

1 The emission control system was modified from the 1971 layout by the re-design of the injection pump drive pinion, the alteration of the distributor timing characteristics and the installation of a valve to admit extra air into the intake pipe during periods of deceleration.

2 The ignition timing is retarded when the engine oil temperature is above 62.3°F (17°C), the coolant temperature below 212°F (100°C) and the engine speed does not exceed 2500 rpm.

3 The ignition retard is not implemented when the temperature and speed levels are above those just specified or when driving in 4th speed.

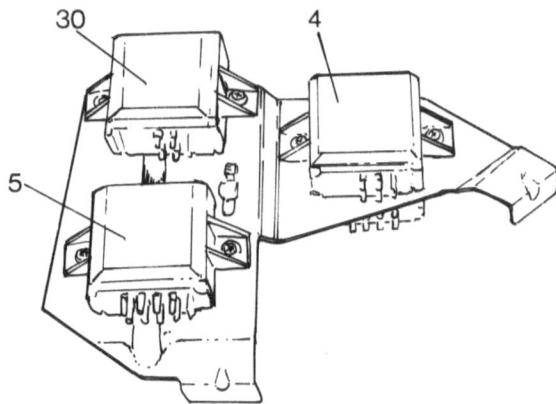

Fig. 3.115A. Location of relays (1972 emission control system) (Sec. 38)

4   Speed relay   30   4 to 8 second delay switch
5   Relay box   for fuel cut-off solenoid

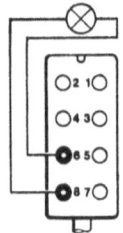

Fig. 3.116. Relay box contacts in connector plug for testing oil temperature switch (Sec. 38)

Fig. 3.117. Two-way valve (9) and deceleration valve (20) (Sec. 38)

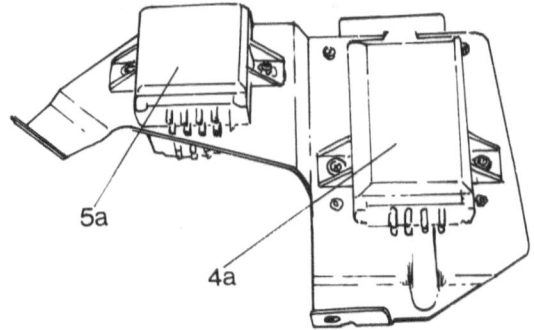

Fig. 3.118. Location of speed relay (2200/2500 rpm and 2600/2900 rpm (4a) and relay box (5a) (Sec. 38)

4 In order to dilute the exhaust gas emitted during deceleration, extra air is admitted to the engine when its speed exceeds 2900 rpm. At lower engine speeds, the control linkage is adjusted by a solenoid. As an aid to avoid stalling, the idle speed is increased by the action of a double acting solenoid as soon as the speed drops to a pre-determined level with a gear engaged. The purpose of individual components of the system is explained in the following paragraphs:

a) *Speed relay, opens at engine speeds above 1000 rpm, closes below 600 rpm. Actuates solenoid of anti-stall device by increasing throttle opening by about 180 rpm.*

b) *Delay switch, actuated for 4 to 8 seconds after ignition switched off to keep fuel cut-off solenoid energized.*

c) *Speed relay, implements and cancels retard at pre-determined speeds, also actuates deceleration valve and anti-stall solenoid.*

d) *Fuel cut-off solenoid sets injection pump rack to zero delivery (see b).*

e) *Engine oil temperature switch actuates two-way valve for ignition retard period.*

f) *Temperature switch (62.3°F - 17°C) mounted in the air conditioner receiver hydrator of 280 SE models, actuates the auxiliary fan.*

g) *Temperature switch (212°F - 100°C) actuates two-way valve and air conditioner auxiliary fan.*

h) *Two way valve, at pre-set oil and coolant temperature and engine speeds in 4th gear actuates vacuum unit to remove retard condition.*

j) *Deceleration valve, does not operate until engine oil temperature is above 62.3°F (17°C). Opens when accelerator pedal released in three lower speeds at engine speed above 2900 rpm. Operates in 4th speed irrespective of engine speed.*

k) *Anti-stall control solenoid (refer to a).*

l) *Idle switch, closed while accelerator pedal released, affects earth connection from 4th gear fluid pressure switch to relay.*

m) *Fluid pressure switch (4th gear) actuates deceleration and two-way valves which in turn remove retard condition.*

n) *Fluid pressure switch (1st, 2nd and 3rd gear) actuates solenoid of anti-stall device at engine speeds below 2600 rpm, and deceleration valve at speeds over 2900 rpm.*

p) *Auxiliary fan relays, mounted adjacent to brake booster used in conjunction with independent operation of air conditioning auxiliary fan from exhaust emission control system.*

5 To check that the ignition timing is being retarded correctly by the oil temperature switch and relay, use a stroboscope and observe if the timing marks are showing at least 10° retard from TDC with the engine idling at 800 rpm with the oil temperature above 62.3°F (17°C) and the coolant temperature below 212°F (100°C). If the ignition is not so retarded under these conditions, check the temperature switch and relay in the following way.

6 To check the oil temperature switch, pull the connector plug from the relay box (5) (Fig. 3.115A), and connect a test lamp between contacts 6 and 8 of the plug. With the ignition switched on, the lamp should come on only when the oil temperature level is below 62.3°F (17°C) (Fig. 3.116).

7 To check the low range speed switch, use only a voltmeter and not a test lamp. Disconnect the connector plug from the two-way valve (9) and connect a voltmeter between the two contacts of the plug. Start the engine and increase the engine speed. When the speed exceeds 2500 rpm, the voltmeter should indicate 13 volts. When the speed drops below 2000 rpm, the voltmeter should show no reading (Fig. 3. 117).

8 To check the two-way valve, refit the plug and increase the engine speed. At about 2500 rpm, the valve can be felt to vibrate by the movement of its piston.

9 To test the relay, pull out the connector plug from the 212°F (100°C) coolant temperature switch. Earth the plug when the retarded effect of the ignition should be removed and the auxiliary fan (air conditioning) will switch on at the same time. If the retard is not removed, renew the relay (Figs. 3.118 and 119).

10 To test the 212°F (100°C) temperature switch, pull out the connector plug from the relay box and connect a test lamp between contacts 5 and 8 of the plug (Fig. 3.120).

11 To check the operation of the idle switch on the venturi control unit see Fig. 3.95, pull the connector plug from the relay box and connect a test lamp between contacts 1 and 8. When the throttle

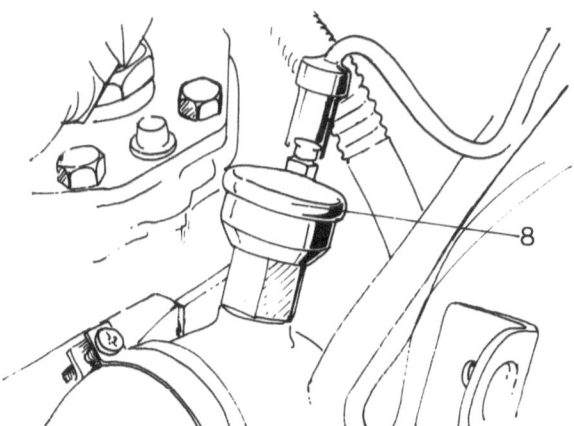

Fig. 3.119. Location of coolant high temperature switch (Sec. 38)

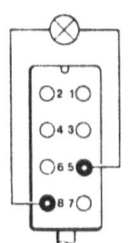

Fig. 3.120. Relay box connector plug contacts for testing coolant high temperature switch (Sec. 38)

Fig. 3.121. Location of transmission fluid pressure switch (1st, 2nd and 3rd speeds) (Sec. 38)

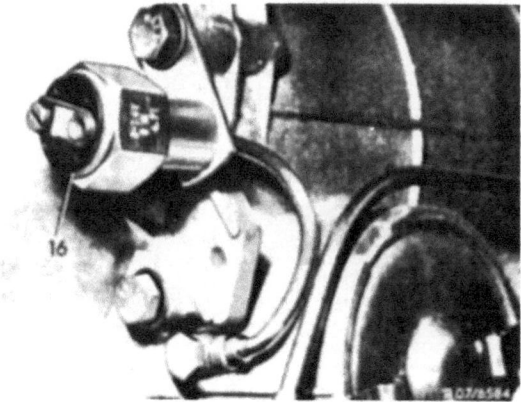

Fig. 3.122. Location of transmission fluid pressure switch (4th gear) (16) (Sec. 38)

control linkage is actuated, the test lamp should go out.

12 To test the fluid pressure switches on the transmission, commence by testing the 1st, 2nd, 3rd gear switch and pull the connector plug from the relay box and again connect a test lamp between plug contacts 1 and 8. Make sure that the handbrake is fully applied and then move the speed selector lever through all positions, the test lamp should come on only in positions L - S and D. To test the 4th gear pressure switch, disconnect the electrical lead from it and connect the lead to earth. Start the engine and check the ignition timing using a stroboscope. If the ignition timing marks are not retarded the switch must be renewed. If the marks are in the retarded position, then the relay box (5a)(Fig. 3.118) is faulty and must be renewed (Figs. 3.121 and 122).

13 To check the higher range speed switch, use only a voltmeter and not a test lamp. Pull the connector plug from the relay box (5a - Fig. 118). Connect the voltmeter between contact 4 of the plug and earth. start the engine and increase its speed. At engine speeds below 2600 rpm, the voltmeter should indicate 13 volts. At engine speeds above 2900 rpm the voltmeter should show no reading.

14 To check the idle speed stabilization which is controlled by the speed relay, connect a test lamp to the terminals of the solenoid switch (see Fig. 3.60). Switch on the air conditioner (where fitted) and turn the power steering to full lock (engine running). At minimum engine speed, the test lamp should come on and the core of the solenoid extend. At engine speeds exceeding 1000 rpm, the test lamp should go out and the solenoid switch retract. If the solenoid does not energize, check the speed relay (4) (Fig. 3.115A).

39 Manifolds and exhaust system

1   The intake and exhaust manifolds on all engines are mounted on the right-hand side. The technique for removal of the manifolds differs according to the fuel system used. Remove the air cleaner from the engine.

Carburettor engines

2   Disconnect the throttle linkage, fuel pipes and the automatic choke electrical lead from the carburettors, also disconnect the distributor vacuum pipe.

3   Disconnect the exhaust downpipes from the exhaust manifolds.

4   Unscrew and remove the manifold attaching bolts and nuts and withdraw the manifold assembly complete with carburettors.

Fuel injection engines

5   Drain the cooling system then disconnect the switch housing from the extreme front of the intake manifold (photo).

6   Disconnect the electrical lead and union nut from the start valve on the manifold which is located just ahead of the brake master cylinder (photo).

7   Unbolt and remove the constant speed (anti-stall) solenoid from the inner branch of the intake manifold.

8   Disconnect the fume extraction hose and the coolant hose from the front end of the intake housing (photo).

9   Disconnect the distributor vacuum hose.

10 Disconnect the securing clips and withdraw the intake manifold shield towards the front of the engine (photos).

11 On cars equipped with automatic transmission, disconnect the vacuum pipe from the banjo type union at the rear of the intake manifold. On all cars disconnect the coolant pipe union rest to the banjo union (photo).

12 Disconnect the accelerator linkage by unbolting the transverse regulating rod from the engine rocker cover and the intake manifold.

13 Disconnect the exhaust downpipes and pull them downwards out of their manifold sockets. Release the exhaust pipe lower bracket if necessary (photo).

14 Unscrew and remove all the manifold bolts and withdraw the intake and exhaust manifolds an inch or two from the cylinder head. The intake manifold can now be removed separately followed by the exhaust manifold.

15 The refitting of the manifolds is carried out by reversing the removal operations. Make sure that all mating flanges are quite clean and free from pieces of old gasket and always use new gaskets when refitting.

16 The exhaust system is similar on all models and comprises a front and rear (main) silencer and the connecting pipes. The system is

88

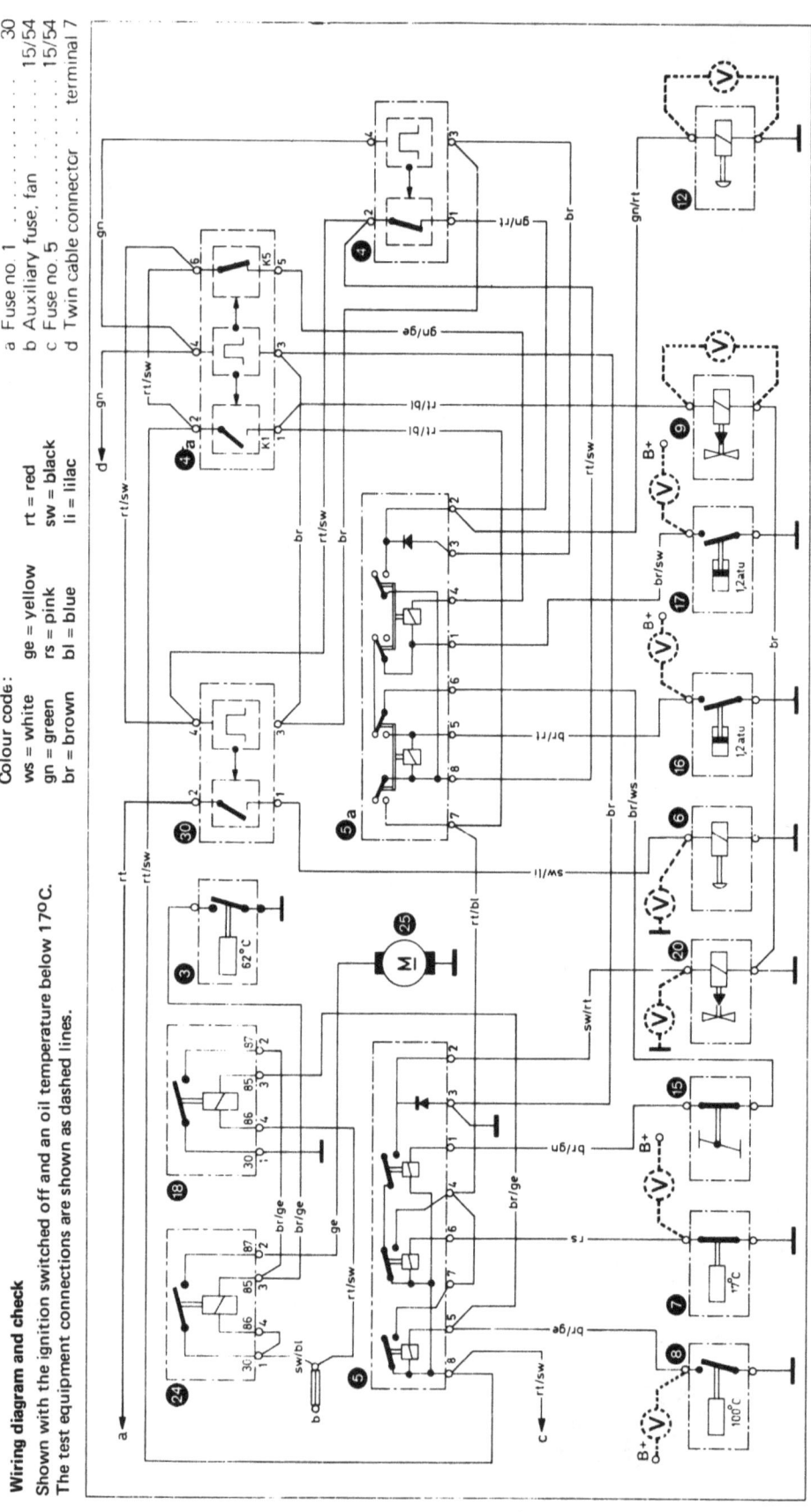

Wiring diagram and check

Shown with the ignition switched off and an oil temperature below 17°C.

The test equipment connections are shown as dashed lines.

Colour code:
ws = white	rs = pink	rt = red
gn = green	rs = pink	sw = black
br = brown	bl = blue	li = lilac
	ge = yellow	

a Fuse no. 1 30
b Auxiliary fuse, fan 15/54
c Fuse no. 5 .... 15/54
d Twin cable connector ... terminal 7

Fig. 3.123. Wiring diagram and test circuits for 1972 280 SE model emission control (Sec. 38)

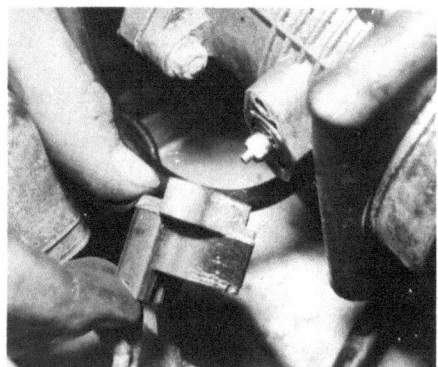

39.5 Switch housing at front end of air intake housing (fuel injection)

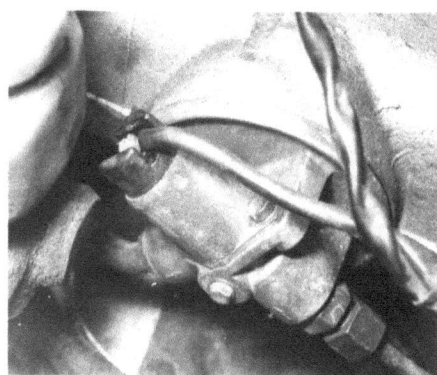

39.6 Start valve on intake manifold of fuel injection system

39.8 Crankcase vent hose and coolant pipe connections to front of fuel injection air intake housing

39.10A Intake manifold shield securing clips (fuel injection engine)

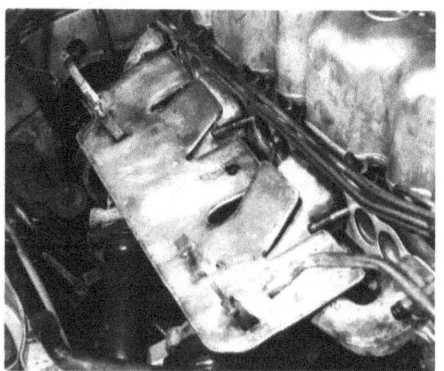

39.10B Intake manifold shield in position (manifold removed for clarity)

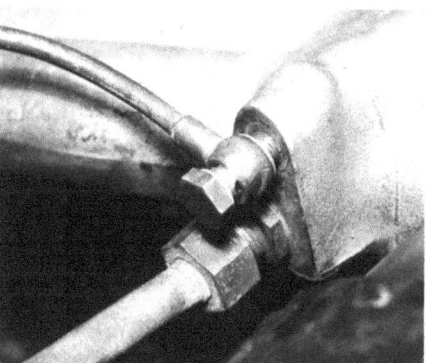

39.11 Vacuum pipe (auto trans) and coolant pipe connections at rear end of fuel injection engine intake manifold

39.13 An exhaust downpipe connection to manifold

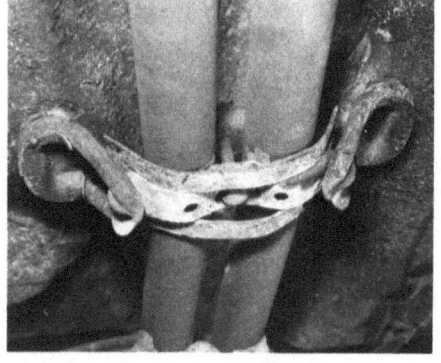

39.16 Exhaust system flexible mountings

suspended on rubber rings attached to mounting hooks (photo).

17 Examination of the exhaust pipe and silencers at regular intervals is worthwhile as small defects may be repairable when, if left they will almost certainly require renewal of one of the sections of the system. Also, any leaks, apart from the noise factor, may cause poisonous exhaust gases to get inside the car which can be unpleasant, to say the least, even in mild concentrations. Prolonged inhalation could cause sickness and giddiness.

18 As the sleeve connections and clamps are usually very difficult to separate it is quicker and easier in the long run to remove the complete system from the car when renewing a section. It can be expensive if another section is damaged when trying to separate a bad section from it.

19 To remove the system, jack-up the car at front and rear and then disconnect the front downpipes from the exhaust manifold.

20 Disconnect all the flexible mountings and withdraw the complete system from below and to the rear of the vehicle.

21 Cut away the bad section, taking care not to damage the good sections which are to be retained.

22 File off any burrs at the ends of the new sections of pipe and smear them with grease. Slip the clamps over the pipes and connect the sockets but do not tighten the clamps at this stage.

23 Push the complete system under the vehicle and jack it up so that the front pipes can be bolted to the manifold and the rear tail pipe mounting connected.

24 Now turn the silencer sections to obtain their correct attitudes so that they will not touch or knock against any adjacent parts when the system is deflected to one side or the other.

25 Tighten the clamp bolts and connect the suspension rubber rings of the system.

See overleaf for 'Fault diagnosis'.

40 Fault diagnosis

Symptom	Reason/s
Carburettors	
Difficult cold start	Defective bi-metallic spring in automatic choke or circuit fuse blown. Disconnected lead to automatic choke. Incorrect fast idle setting. Choke valve plate sticking in open position.
Engine stops almost immediately after cold start	Incorrect choke adjustment giving mixture too weak or too rich. Defective diaphragm in automatic choke vacuum capsule.
Engine stalls when cold and clutch depressed	Fast idle speed too low. Incorrect choke valve plate gap. Vacuum regulator incorrectly adjusted.
Rough idling	Automatic choke fuse blown. Choke valve plate sticking. Idling fuel nozzle or air jet clogged. Idling speed duct or by-pass clogged. Leaking fuel float. Incorrect float level. Damaged mixture adjusting screw. Leak in carburettor or intake manifold gaskets. Leak in distributor vacuum pipe.
Idling speed climbs above specified setting	Throttle lever does not return fully to stop. Float chamber vent valves sticking. Vacuum regulator requires adjustment.
Poor transition from Stage 1 to Stage 2	Fuel injection nozzle clogged in carburettor throat. Leaking accelerator pump valve. Fuel injection nozzle requires alignment.
Difficult hot start	Float chamber vent valves require adjustment. Float chamber vent valves require cleaning.
Excessive fuel consumption	Worn or loose fuel inlet needle valve. Incorrect float adjustment. Accelerator pump stroke incorrect. Fuel injection nozzle in carburettor throat requires alignment. Choke valve plates not fully open. Automatic choke heater coil not functioning correctly.
Fuel injection system	
Difficult cold start	Injection pump control rod binding. Defective fuel cut-off solenoid. Defective starting valve. Defective starting valve relay. Defective thermostatic time switch. Ball pressure valves leaking.
Engine stalls after cold start	Warm up device supplementary air filter clogged. Supplementary air valve sticking. Starting valve leaking. Injection pump control rack rod binding.
Difficult hot start	Clogged fuel filter. Injection pump by-pass valve leaking. Fuel pump feed pressure too low. Injection pump ball pressure valves leaking. Control rack rod leaking. Fuel evaporating due to engine heat (rectify by modifying starting valve see Section 32).
Rough idling	Throttle valve in venturi control unit not closing. Injection pump regulating arm not contacting idle speed stop. Starting valve leaking. Warm-up system will not switch off. Air leak in intake assembly.
Misfiring	Lack of fuel generally. Clogged fuel filter.

Symptom	Reason/s
Poor pick-up	Throttle control linkage requires adjustment. Injection pump requires adjustment under load to meet specified CO levels.
Engine surges on overrun	Vacuum connection for distributor in venturi control unit choked or inner opening of vacuum connection masked by throttle valve plate. Clear by filing chamfer or countersinking inner opening of vacuum connection.

Emission control

Symptom	Reason/s
Oil fume seepage from engine	Crankcase ventilation system connections loose or hoses split. Choked flame trap. Defective rocker cover gasket.
Fuel odour evident	Split or disconnected lines in system. Defective fuel filler cap.
Fume emission from exhaust pipe above acceptable level	**After burner system** Slack or broken air pump drivebelt. Faulty air pump pressure valve. Faulty non-return valve. Split or disconnected hoses in system. **Ignition retard system** Refer to the testing procedures described in Sections 35 to 38 and renew faulty components.

Note: The efficiency of the fume emission control system is also dependent upon the correct setting and adjustment of all other engine components. These include the ignition, cooling and lubrication systems, the valve clearances and the condition generally of the engine. Refer to the appropriate Sections and Chapters of this manual for servicing procedures.

Chapter 4 Ignition system

Contents

Specifications

System type ... ... 12V, negative earth, battery coil and mechanical contact breaker type distributor.

Firing order ... ... 1 - 5 - 3 - 6 - 2 - 4

Distributor

Basic points gap ... ... 0.012 in (0.3 mm)
Dwell angle ... ... 39 to 41°
Rotational direction ... ... Clockwise

Car model	Production year	Engine type	Static Ignition setting	DYNAMIC TIMING USING STROBOSCOPE				
				At idling speed	At 1500 rpm	At 3000 rpm	At 4500 rpm	Range of Vacuum advance
230/8 Sedan	1968-69	M180	TDC	TDC * **	19 to 28° BTDC *	29 to 35° BTDC *	37° BTDC *	7 to 13° advance
250/8 Sedan	1968-70	M114	TDC	TDC * **	19 to 28° BTDC *	29 to 35° BTDC ‘	37° BTDC *	7 to 13° advance
250 SE Saloon	1968-70	M114	3° BTDC	0 to 2° ATDC * **	13 to 20° BTDC *	30° BTDC *	30° BTDC *	11 to 17° advance
250SL Coupe	1968-70	M114	4° BTDC	6° BTDC * **	15 to 19° BTDC *	30° BTDC *	30° BTDC *	11 to 17° advance
250CE Coupe	1968-70	M114	4° BTDC	4° BTDC * **	12 to 19° BTDC *	30° BTDC *	30° BTDC *	7 to 13° advance
250/8 Sedan	1971-72	M130V	TDC	TDC ***	19 to 28° BTDC *	29 to 35° BTDC *	37° BTDC *	7 to 13° advance
250C Coupe	1970-72	M130V	8° BTDC	4° ATDC ***	12 to 19° BTDC *	30° BTDC *	30° BTDC *	7 to 13° advance
280S/8 Sedan	1968/71	M130V	2° BTDC	4 to 12° BTDC *	18 to 25° BTDC *	23 to 30° BTDC *	42 to 48° BTDC *	7 to 13° advance Standard compression
			4° BTDC	6 to 15° BTDC **	12 to 19° BTDC *	24 to 31° BTDC *	44 to 50° BTDC **	7 to 13° advance Low compression
			TDC	3° BTDC to 3° ATDC *	15 to 25° BTDC *	24 to 32° BTDC *	43 to 51° BTDC **	6 to 14° advance N. America emission cont. 68/69
			6° BTDC	4° ATDC **	1 to 9° BTDC **	31 to 39° BTDC **	41 to 49° BTDC **	9 to 15° retard 7 to 13° advance N. America emission cont. 70/71
280SL Coupe	1968/71	M130	8° BTDC	2 to 4° ATDC **	12 to 19° BTDC *	30° BTDC *	—	8 to 14° retard at idle
280SE/8 all models	1968/72	M130E	8° BTDC	2 to 4° ATDC **	12 to 19° BTDC *	30° BTDC *	—	8 to 14° retard at idle. Standard compression
			8° BTDC	2 to 4° ATDC **	12 to 19° BTDC *	30° BTDC *	—	8 to 14° retard at idle. Low compression
			10° BTDC	8° ATDC **	0 to 5° BTDC **	25 to 30° BTDC **	—	17 to 23° retard. N. America emission cont. 70/71
			14° BTDC	6° ATDC **	1° BTDC to 3° ATDC **	36 to 44° BTDC **	—	17 to 23° retard N. America emission cont. 1972

Car model	Production year	Engine type	Static Ignition setting	DYNAMIC TIMING USING STROBOSCOPE				
				At idling speed	At 1500 rpm	At 3000 rpm	At 4500 rpm	Range of Vacuum advance
280SEL/8 Sedan	1968/71	M130E	8° BTDC	2 to 4° ATDC **	12 to 19° BTDC *	30° BTDC *	–	8 to 14° retard at idle
			10° BTDC	8° ATDC **	0 to 5° BTDC **	25 to 30° BTDC **	–	17 to 23° retard at idle. N. America emission cont. 70/71
280SL/8 Roadster	1968/71	M130E	8° BTDC	2 to 4° ATDC **	12 to 19° BTDC *	30° BTDC *	–	8 to 14° retard at idle
			10° BTDC	8° ATDC **	0 to 5° BTDC **	25 to 30° BTDC **	–	17 to 23° retard. N. America emission cont. 70/71

Vacuum hose disconnected   **Vacuum hose connected*

Note: *In view of the continuing changes to ignition timing recommendations during the course of production of the cars covered by this manual and to the many versions of emission control systems installed, it is emphasised that the information given on the foregoing chart must be confirmed if possible by reference to the individual car sticker or decal.*

Spark plugs

M114 engine	... ...	Bosch WG250T28 or equivalent
M130 engine	... ...	Bosch W200T27 (standard) or equivalent or Bosch W225T28 (high speed) or equivalent
M180 engine	... ...	Bosch WG215T28 or equivalent or Bosch WG 235T28 or equivalent or Bosch W200T27 or equivalent

Original equipment spark plug types listed may have been recently superseded in the light of operating experience. Consult dealer plug recommendation chart for latest information.

Spark plug gap
M130 engine ...	... ...	0.028 to 0.032 in (0.7 to 0.8 mm)
M130 engine with resistor type plugs	... ... , ...	0.035 to 0.039 in (0.9 to 1.0 mm)
All other engines	... ...	0.020 in (0.5 mm)

Torque wrench settings

	lb f ft	Nm
Spark plugs	22	30

1 General description

In order that the engine can run correctly it is necessary for an electrical spark to ignite the fuel/air mixture in the combustion chamber at exactly the right moment in relation to engine speed and load. The ignition system is based on feeding low tension (LT) voltage from the battery to the coil where it is converted to high tension (HT) voltage. The high tension voltage is powerful enough to jump the spark plug gap in the cylinders many times a second under high compression pressures, providing that the system is in good condition and that all adjustments are correct.

The ignition system is divided into two circuits: the low tension circuit and the high tension circuit.

The low tension (sometimes known as the primary) circuit consists of the battery lead to the control box, lead to the ignition switch, lead from the ignition switch to the low tension or primary coil windings (terminal +), and the lead from the low tension coil windings (coil terminal –) to the contact breaker points and condenser in the distributor.

The high tension circuit consists of the high tension or secondary coil windings, the heavy ignition lead from the centre of the coil to the centre of the distributor cap, the rotor arm, and the spark plug leads and spark plugs.

The system functions in the following manner. Low tension voltage is changed in the coil into high tension voltage by the opening and closing of the contact breaker points in the low tension circuit. High tension voltage is then fed via the carbon brush in the centre of the distributor cap to the rotor arm of the distributor cap, and each time it comes in line with one of the metal segments in the cap, which are connected to the spark plug leads, the opening and closing of the contact breaker points caused the high tension voltage to build up, jump the gap from the rotor arm to the appropriate metal segment and so via the spark plug lead to the spark plug, where it finally jumps the spark plug gap before going to earth.

The distributor is of mechanical contact breaker type and is driven by a short shaft which is geared to the engine auxiliary shaft.

The ignition is advanced and retarded automatically, to ensure the spark occurs at just the right instant for the particular load at the prevailing engine speed.

The ignition advance is controlled both mechanically and by a vacuum operated system. The mechanical governor mechanism comprises two weights, which move out from the distributor shaft, and so advance the spark. The weights are held in position by two light springs and it is the tension of the springs which is largely responsible for correct spark advancement.

The vacuum control consists of a diaphragm, one side of which is connected via a small bore tube to the carburettor or fuel injection throttle housing and the other side to the contact breaker plate. Depression in the inlet manifold, which varies with engine speed and throttle opening, causes the diaphragm to move, so moving the contact breaker plate, and advancing or retarding the spark. A fine degree of control is achieved by a spring in the vacuum assembly.

Cars which are equipped with certain emission control systems to reduce the emission of noxious exhaust gases incorporate devices to vary the engine advance and retard settings according to engine conditions quite independently of the distributor mechanism and reference should be made to Chapter 3.

2 Distributor - maintenance

1 Routine maintenance consists of keeping the distributor cap clean and free from oil and checking the security of the HT leads in their sockets in the cap.
2 Periodically, prise both the cap securing spring clips and lift the cap from the distributor body. Wipe out the cap with a non-fluffy rag.
3 Pull off the rotor arm and then check that the contact breaker points are free from oil by gently prising them apart. If they are oily, clean them with a piece of cloth wrapped round a feeler blade which is soaked in fuel or methylated spirit.

4   When examining the points, if they are obviously severely burnt or corroded, then they must be renewed. If they are in good condition with only slight erosion, their renewal can wait until the specified mileage as shown in 'Routine Maintenance'. Once correctly set, the contact breaker points should not be adjusted between normal renewal times.

5   On some earlier type distributors, a small felt pad is located in the recess in the top of the distributor shaft. This pad should have two or three drops of engine oil applied to it. As from 1970, do not apply oil to the pad.

6   On some distributors, a small oil cup is located on the side of the body. Turn this to expose the oil hole and inject a few drops of oil.

7   Before refitting the rotor arm, apply just a smear of high melting point grease to the high points of the distributor cam.

3 Contact breaker points - renewal

1   The points of the contact breaker assembly should not be dressed or ground flat in an attempt to remove pitting or 'craters' but at the specified service intervals, renew them complete.

2   To do this, prise back the distributor cap clips and remove the cap.

3   Pull off the rotor arm.

4   On some distributors, a dust excluding shield is fitted. Where this is so, remove it to give access to the contact breaker points.

5   Unscrew and remove the contact breaker securing screws (4 and 11) and remove the bracket (9) (Fig. 4.1).

6   Loosen the nuts on the low tension (LT) terminal on the side of the distributor body and extract the cable lug (7).

7   Extract the circlip from the contact breaker arm pivot and remove the contact breaker.

8   Fitting the new breaker assembly is a reversal of removal but observe the following points:

   a) Wipe the faces of the new points free from protective grease.
   b) Apply a smear of high melting point grease to the rubbing cam and to the high points of the distributor shaft cam.

9   Make sure that the two contact points are in exact face alignment otherwise carefully bend them as necessary.

10 Do not fully tighten the screw which secures the contact breaker arm but only enough to permit the arm to move stiffly.

11 With a socket applied to the crankshaft pulley bolt, turn the crankshaft and observe the rotation of the distributor shaft until the rubbing cam of the movable contact arm is on one of the high points of the cam.

12 Insert a screwdriver between the slot in the contact breaker arm and the two raised lugs on the distributor baseplate and twist the blade of the screwdriver to open or close the points until a feeler blade (0.012 in - 0.3 mm) can be slid between them.

13 Without altering the position of the points, tighten the securing screw and remove the blade.

14 This setting is only to enable the engine to be started. The points dwell angle must then be checked as described in the next Section.

15 Refit the dust cover (if fitted), the rotor arm and the cap.

4 Dwell angle - checking

1   For optimum engine performance, the dwell angle must be checked. The dwell angle is the number of degrees through which the distributor cam turns during the period between the instant of closure and opening of the contact breaker points. It can only be checked using a dwell meter.

2   Connect the dwell meter in accordance with the maker's instructions which is usually between the negative terminal of the ignition coil and a good earth.

3   Have the engine at normal operating temperature and idling at specified rpm for the type of engine and transmission (see Specifications, Chapter 3).

4   If the reading on the dwell meter is not within the angle specified in the Specifications at the beginning of this Chapter, then the engine will have to be switched off and the points gap adjusted.

5   If the indicated angle is too large, increase the points gap. If the angle is too small, reduce the points gap. Recheck the dwell angle.

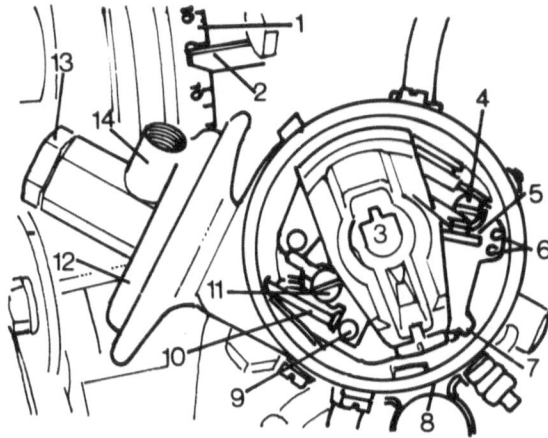

Fig. 4.1. View of distributor with cap removed (Secs. 3 and 6)

   1   Timing scale on crankshaft pulley/damper
   2   Timing pointer
   3   Rotor arm
   4   Contact breaker point securing screw
   5   Adjustment slot
   6   Baseplate adjustment lugs
   7   Contact breaker arm lead
   8   Distributor body rim mark (No. 1 piston at TDC on compression stroke)
   9   Pull rod anchor plate
   10 Adjustable vacuum pull rod
   11 Securing screw
   12 Vacuum advance unit
   13 Plug
   14 Vacuum line connection

5 Condenser (capacitor) - testing, removal and refitting

1   The condenser ensures that with the contact breaker points open, the sparking between them is not excessive, as this would cause severe pitting. The condenser is fitted in parallel and its failure will automatically cause failure of the ignition system as the points will be prevented from interrupting the low tension circuit.

2   Testing for an unserviceable condenser may be effected by switching on the ignition and separating the contact points by hand. If this action is accompanied by a blue flash then condenser failure is indicated. Difficult starting, missing of the engine after several miles running or badly pitted points are other indications of a faulty condenser.

3   The surest test is by substitution of a new unit.

4   To remove the condenser, unscrew its retaining screw and detach its lead from the LT terminal on the distributor body. Refitting is a reversal of removal.

6 Distributor - removal and refitting

1   Before removing the distributor, the following work should be carried out. This will make the job of refitting much easier.

2   Turn the crankshaft pulley bolt with a socket until the appropriate static timing mark (see Specifications) is opposite to the pointer on the front cover of the engine. To check that No. 1 piston is on its compression stroke, remove the distributor cap and observe the position of the contact end of the rotor arm. This should be in alignment with

6.9 Distributor rotor arm in alignment and distributor ready for installing

6.11A Distributor driveshaft being installed

6.11B Method of installing driveshaft spring into housing

No. 1 HT lead contact in the distributor cap (see Fig. 4.1).

3 Mark the rim of the distributor body at the point which is central to the contact end of the rotor arm. On some distributors, a mark is already made on the rim during production.

4 Release the distributor clamp and withdraw the distributor, having first disconnected the vacuum hose.

5 If the engine crankshaft or distributor driveshaft are not disturbed while the distributor is out of the engine, it can be fitted simply by turning the rotor arm to the alignment mark made on the rim. This will ensure that the large and small segments of the distributor shaft and driveshaft are in alignment.

6 If the engine has been dismantled or the distributor driveshaft has been removed while the distributor is out of the engine, then proceed as follows.

7 Turn the crankshaft until No. 1 piston is rising on its compression stroke. This can be ascertained by either removing No. 1 spark plug and placing a finger over the hole to feel the compression being generated as the crankshaft is turned or by removing the rocker cover and checking that the valves of No. 1 cylinder are both closed.

8 Continue turning the crankshaft until the appropriate static ignition timing mark on the crankshaft pulley/damper is opposite the pointer on the front of the engine.

9 Now hold the distributor over its recess in the engine with the rotor arm pointing at, or in alignment with, the No. 1 spark plug HT lead contact in the distributor cap and the vacuum unit pointing forwards and inwards at about 45° to the centre line of the engine (photo).

10 The large and small segments on the end of the distributor drive-shaft (which can be seen by looking down into the distributor recess in the distributor housing) should now be in a position to receive the mating segments of the distributor shaft without having to turn the rotor arm in either direction.

11 Where this is not so (or if the distributor driveshaft has been removed) the distributor driveshaft must be extracted and turned so that when it is pushed into its recess, the segments will be in alignment. This is not quite so easy as it would seem as the distributor driveshaft will turn as its gear meshes with the one on the auxiliary driveshaft of the engine. Allow for this by turning the distributor driveshaft segment dividing slot about 40 degrees out of alignment in an anti-clockwise direction before fitting it. Note the small coil spring in the centre of the distributor housing. Use a piece of wire to install it (photos).

12 Push the distributor into its recess so that the drive segments engage fully and then turn the distributor body until the contact points are just about to open. Tighten the clamp bolt.

13 Fit the distributor cap and clips.

14 The ignition must now be timed precisely using a stroboscope as described in Section 8.

7 Distributor - overhaul

1 It is seldom that the distributor requires dismantling to renew a broken or worn individual component. The unit usually wears gradually until after a high mileage it is economically sound to renew it with a new or factory reconditioned unit (Fig. 4.2).

2 Where the individual spare parts are available however, and complete dismantling is to be attempted, carry out the following operations.

3 Remove the distributor from the engine, lift off the cap and

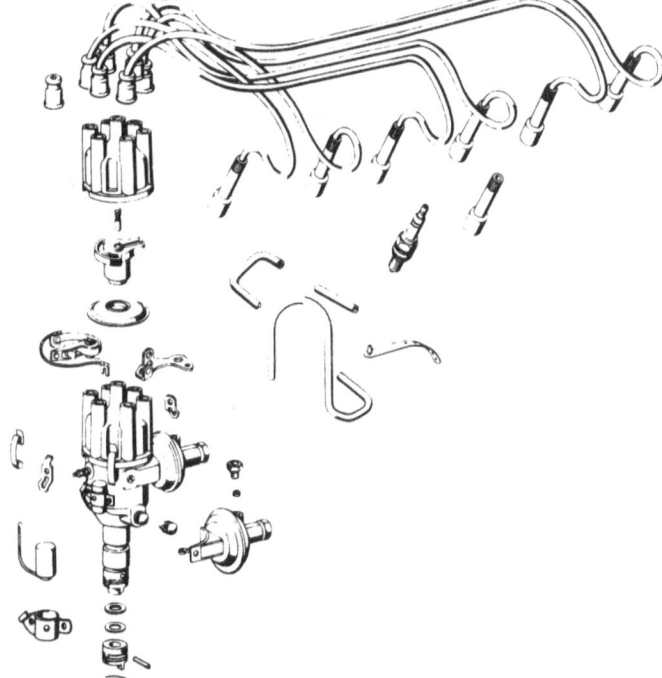

Fig. 4.2. Distributor components (Sec. 7)

remove the rotor and contact assembly as previously described.

4 Extract the circlip or angle bracket which secures the end of the vacuum unit pull rod to the distributor baseplate.

5 Unscrew and remove the vacuum unit retaining screws and lift the unit from the distributor body.

6 Extract the baseplate securing screws and remove the baseplate.

7 If the distributor shaft and counterweights are to be removed, mark the relative position of all components in relation to the shaft, particularly the location of the small and large segments of the shaft drive coupling.

8 Drive out the pin from the drive coupling at the base of the shaft and note the number and position of the thrust washers for exact refitting.

9 If the bushes are worn in the distributor body, it is better to renew the complete assembly.

10 Reassembly is a reversal of dismantling but use a new pin in the drive coupling at the base of the shaft.

8 Ignition timing

1 Prior to checking the ignition timing, the dwell angle must be correctly adjusted (see Section 4).

2 A stroboscope will be required to time the ignition, the use of a

simple timing light (test bulb) is not suitable for these engines.
3   Refer to the Specifications and mark the timing scale on the crankshaft pulley/damper at the appropriate graduation on the scale according to engine type with quick drying white paint. Also paint the tip of
the pointer on the front of the engine. Two designs of scale and pointer
are in use. The single scale is quite straightforward. While standing in
front of the engine, the graduations to the right of the O (TDC) mark
are BTDC (Before Top Dead Centre) while those to the left are
ATDC (After Top Dead Centre) (Fig. 4.3). The double scale is rather
more complicated and you must first establish which type of pointer
is fitted. If the earlier type pointer is fitted, then the scale nearer the
front edge of the pulley should be used in conjunction with it. If the
pointer is triangular in shape, then the scale which is on the rear edge
of the pulley (nearer to the engine front face) must be used. With
both these scales, the graduations to the right of O (TDC) are BTDC
and to the left, ATDC when viewed from the front of the car.
(Fig. 4.4). With all three scales, the increments between digits are
10 degrees with a dividing 5 degrees line.
4   Connect the stroboscope to the engine in accordance with the
maker's instructions and disconnect the vacuum pipe from the distributor only where expressly stated in the Specifications.
5   On model 280S/8 cars equipped with full exhaust emission control,
the distributor has a double vacuum diaphragm unit. With this kind of
distributor, before carrying out the ignition timing, pull off the lead
from the 212°F (100°C) coolant temperature switch (see Chapter 3)
which is located in the thermostat housing. This is to prevent the
vacuum characteristic of the distributor changing over from retard to
advance while carrying out the ignition timing operations (Fig. 4.5).
6   Start the engine and run it at one of the speeds which is specified
for timing adjustment according to engine type, again by reference to
the Specifications at the beginning of this Chapter. The two higher
timing speeds are considered dangerous and should only be used if the
distributor advance is suspect.
7   Point the light from the stroboscope at the timing marks on the
front of the engine when the pointer and the graduation line on the
damper will appear stationary and if the timing is correct, they will be
in alignment.
8   If the marks are not in alignment, release the distributor clamp and
turn the distributor one way or the other until they are.
9   Tighten the distributor clamp, switch off the ignition, remove the
stroboscope and remake any vacuum connections which were
disconnected.

9   Checking distributor vacuum advance range

1   To do this, run the engine first with the distributor vacuum pipe
connected and then without, at the speed levels shown in the Specifications according to engine type and car model.
2   Again using the stroboscope, observe the movement of the graduation scale on the crankshaft pulley damper in relation to the pointer
on the front face of the engine.
3   If the advance range indicated is outside that specified, switch off
the engine and adjust the effective length of the vacuum control unit
pull rod, on the distributor, by releasing its stop nut and turning it in
or out. Check the advance range characteristic after adjustment.

10   Coil polarity and testing

1   High tension current should be negative at the spark plug terminals.
If the HT current is positive at the spark plug terminals then the LT
leads to the coil primary terminals have been incorrectly connected. A
wrong connection can cause as much as 60% loss of spark efficiency
and can cause rough idling and misfiring at speed.
2   With a negative earth electrical system, the LT lead from the
distributor connects with the negative (primary) terminal on the coil.
3   The simplest way to test a coil is by substitution.
4   Maintenance consists of occasionally checking the connecting lead
attachment and wiping any dirt or grease from the insulated end of the
coil (photo).

11   Spark plugs and high tension leads

1   The correct functioning of the spark plugs is vital for the correct

Fig. 4.3. Single type timing scale and pointer (Sec. 8)

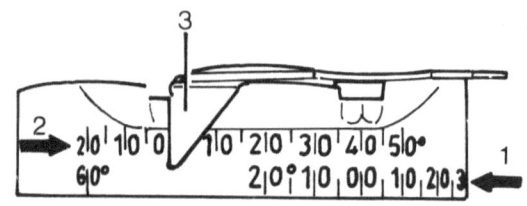

Fig. 4.4. Dual type timing scale and pointer (Sec. 8)

    1   Scale for earlier type pointer
    2   Scale for triangular type pointer
    3   Triangular type pointer

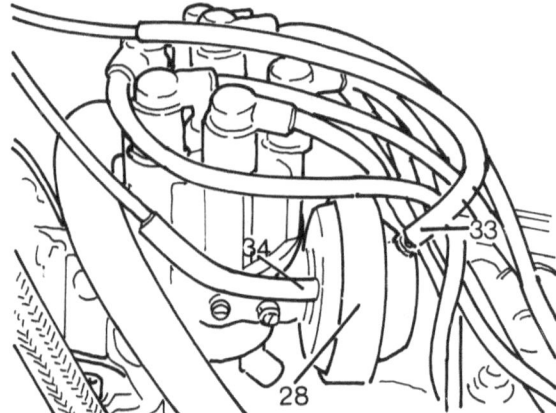

Fig. 4.5. Distributor with dual compartment vacuum diaphragm
unit (Sec. 8)

28 Vacuum unit   33 Advance connection   34 Retard connection

running and efficiency of the engine. The plugs fitted as standard are
listed on the Specifications page.
2   At intervals of 3,000 miles (4,800 km) the plugs should be removed,
examined and cleaned. If worn excessively, renew the plugs at 12,000
miles (19,600 km). The condition of the spark plug will also tell much
about the overall condition of the engine.
If the insulator nose of the spark plug is clean and white, with no
deposits, this is indicative of a weak mixture, or too hot a plug. (A hot
plug transfers heat away from the electrode slowly - a cold plug
transfers it away quickly) (see illustrations on next page).
4   If the top and insulator nose is covered with hard black looking
deposits, then this is indicative that the mixture is too rich. Should the
plug be black and oily, then it is likely that the engine is fairly worn,
as well as the mixture being too rich.
5   If the insulator nose is covered with light tan to greyish brown
deposits, then the mixture is correct and it is likely that the engine is
in good condition.
6   If there are any traces of long brown tapering stains on the outside
of the white portion of the plug, then the plug will have to be renewed,

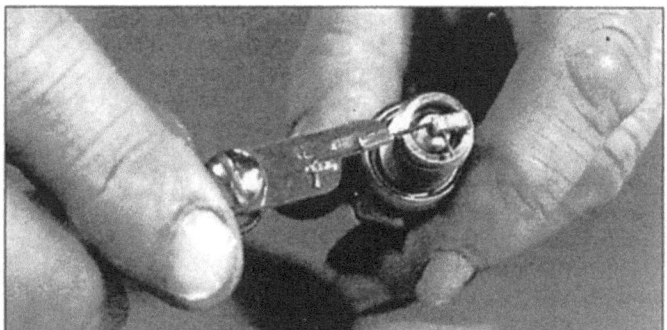

Electrode gap check - use a wire type gauge for best results

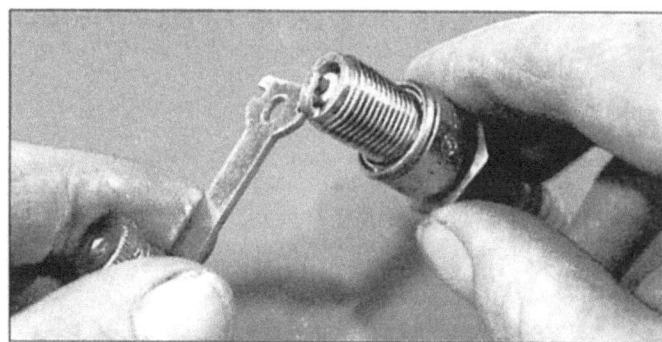

Electrode gap adjustment - bend the side electrode using the correct tool

Normal condition - A brown, tan or grey firing end indicates that the engine is in good condition and that the plug type is correct

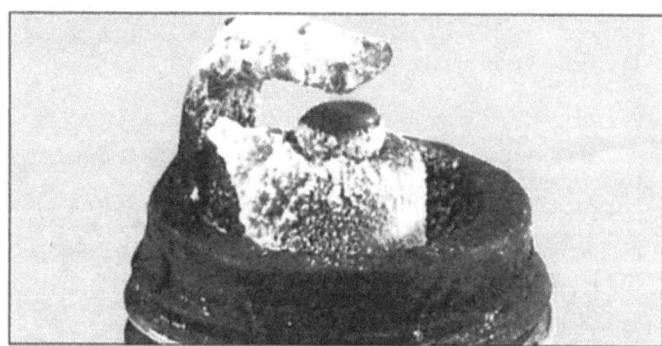

Ash deposits - Light brown deposits encrusted on the electrodes and insulator, leading to misfire and hesitation. Caused by excessive amounts of oil in the combustion chamber or poor quality fuel/oil

Carbon fouling - Dry, black sooty deposits leading to misfire and weak spark. Caused by an over-rich fuel/air mixture, faulty choke operation or blocked air filter

Oil fouling - Wet oily deposits leading to misfire and weak spark. Caused by oil leakage past piston rings or valve guides (4-stroke engine), or excess lubricant (2-stroke engine)

Overheating - A blistered white insulator and glazed electrodes. Caused by ignition system fault, incorrect fuel, or cooling system fault

Worn plug - Worn electrodes will cause poor starting in damp or cold weather and will also waste fuel

10.4 Location of ignition coil

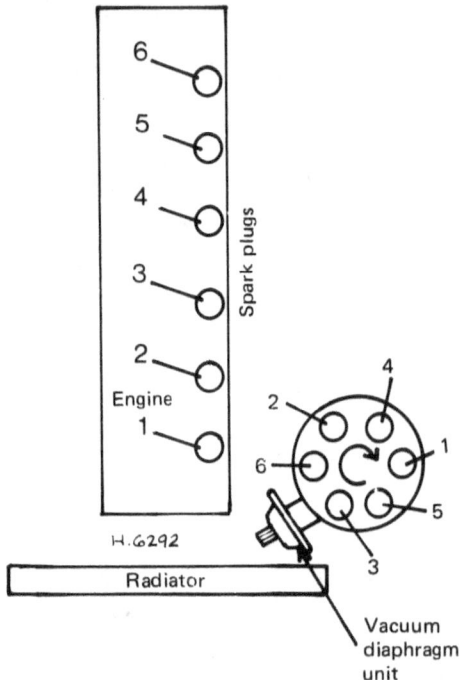

H.6292

Radiator

Vacuum
diaphragm
unit

Fig. 4.6. Spark plug lead connecting diagram (Sec. 11)

as this shows that there is a faulty joint between the plug body and the insulator, and compression is being allowed to leak away.

7   Plugs should be cleaned by a sand blasting machine, which will free them from carbon more thoroughly than cleaning by hand. The machine will also test the condition of the plugs under compression. Any plug that fails to spark at the recommended pressure should be renewed.

8   The spark plug gap is of considerable importance, as, if it is too large or too small the size of the spark and its efficiency will be seriously impaired. The spark plug gap should be set to 0.020 in (0.5 mm) for the best results.

9   To set it, measure the gap with a feeler gauge, and then bend open, or close, the outer plug electrode until the correct gap is achieved. The centre electrode should never be bent as this may crack the insulation and cause plug failure, if nothing worse.

10 When refitting the plugs, remember to connect the leads from the distributor in the correct firing order (Fig. 4.6) number 1 cylinder being the one nearest the crankshaft pulley.

11 The plug leads require no attention other than being kept clean and wiped over regularly.

---

12 Fault diagnosis - ignition system

Engine fails to start

1   If the engine fails to start and the car was running normally when it was last used, first check there is fuel in the fuel tank. If the engine turns over normally on the starter motor and the battery is evidently well charged, then the fault may be in either the high or low tension circuits. First check the HT circuit. **Note:** If the battery is known to be fully charged, the ignition light comes on, and the starter motor fails to turn the engine **check the tightness of the leads on the battery terminal** and also the secureness of the earth lead to its **connection to the body.** It is quite common for the leads to have worked loose, even if they look and feel secure. If one of the battery terminal posts gets very hot when trying to work the starter motor this is a sure indication of a faulty connection to that terminal.

2   One of the commonest reasons for bad starting is wet or damp spark plug leads and distributor. Remove the distributor cap, if condensation is visible internally, dry the cap with a rag and also wipe over the leads. Refit the cap.

3   If the engine still fails to start, check that current is reaching the plugs by disconnecting each plug lead in turn at the spark plug end, and hold the end of the cable about 3/16 inch (4.8 mm) away from the cylinder block. Spin the engine on the starter motor.

4   Sparking between the end of the cable and the block should be fairly strong with a regular blue spark. (Hold the lead with rubber to avoid electric shocks). If current is reaching the plugs, then remove them and clean and regap them. The engine should now start.

5   If there is no spark at the plug leads, take off the HT lead from the centre of the distributor cap and hold it to the block as before. Spin

the engine on the starter once more. A rapid succession of blue sparks between the end of the lead and the block indicate that the coil is in order and that the distributor cap is cracked, the rotor arm faulty, or the carbon brush in the top of the distributor cap is not making good contact with the spring on the rotor arm. Possibly the points are in bad condition. Clean and reset them as described in this Chapter.

6   If there are no sparks from the end of the lead from the coil, check the connections at the coil end of the lead. If it is in order start checking the low tension circuit.

7   Use a 12v voltmeter or a 12v bulb and two lengths of wire. With the ignition switched on and the points open, test between the low tension wire to the coil (it is marked +) and earth. No reading indicates a break in the supply from the ignition switch. Check the connections at the switch to see if any are loose. Refit them and the engine should run. A reading shows a faulty coil or condenser, or broken lead between the coil and the distributor.

8   Take the condenser wire off the points assembly and with the points open, test between the moving points and earth. If there now is a reading, then the fault is in the condenser. Fit a new one and the fault is cleared.

9   With no reading from the moving point to earth take a reading between earth and the (—) terminal of the coil. A reading here shows a broken wire which will need to be renewed between the coil and distributor. No reading confirms that the coil has failed and must be renewed, after which the engine will run once more. Remember to refit the condenser wire to the points assembly. For these tests it is sufficient to separate the points with a piece of dry paper while testing with the points open.

Engine misfires

10 If the engine misfires regularly, run it at a fast idling speed. Pull off each of the plug caps in turn and listen to the note of the engine. Hold the plug cap in a dry cloth or with a rubber glove as additional protection against a shock from the HT supply.

11 No difference in engine running will be noticed when the lead from the defective circuit is removed. Removing the lead from one of the good cylinders will accentuate the misfire.

12 Remove the plug lead from the end of the defective plug and hold it about 3/16th inch (4.8 mm) away from the block. Restart the engine. If the sparking is fairly strong and regular the fault must lie in the spark plug.

13 The plug may be loose, the insulation may be cracked, or the points may have burnt away giving too wide a gap for the spark to jump. Worse still, one of the points may have broken off. Either renew the plug, or clean it, reset the gap, and then test it.

14 If there is no spark at the end of the plug lead, or if it is weak and intermittent, check the ignition lead from the distributor to the plug. If the insulation is cracked or perished, renew the lead. Check the connections at the distributor cap.

15 If there is still no spark, examine the distributor cap carefully for tracking. This can be recognised by a very thin black line running between two or more electrodes or between an electrode and some other part of the distributor. These lines are paths which now conduct electricity across the cap thus letting it run to earth. The only answer is a new distributor cap.

16 Apart from the ignition timing being incorrect, other causes of misfiring have already been dealt with under the Section dealing with the failure of the engine to start. To recap - these are that:

   a) *the coil may be faulty giving an intermittent misfire;*
   b) *there may be a damaged wire or loose connection in the low tension circuit;*
   c) *the condenser may be short circuiting;*
   d) *there may be a mechanical fault in the distributor (broken driving spindle or contact breaker spring).*

17 If the ignition timing is too far retarded, it should be noted that the engine will tend to overheat, and there will be a quite noticeable drop in power. If the engine is overheating and the power is down and the ignition timing is correct, then the carburettor should be checked, as it is likely that this is where the fault lies.

Chapter 5 Clutch

Contents

Specifications

Type	Single dry plate, diapnragm spring, ball release bearing, hydraulic actuation
Pedal free movement	0.04 in (1.0 mm)

Torque wrench settings		lb f ft	Nm
Clutch bellhousing bolts to engine	... ...	36	50
Clutch pressure plate cover bolts	... ...	25	35
Clutch slave cylinder bolts	... ...	22	30
Clutch master cylinder bolts	... ...	26	36

1 General description

A hydraulically-operated diaphragm spring, single dry plate clutch is used on all models (Figs. 5.1, 5.2, 5.3 and 5.4).

The design of the clutch assembly, however, differs between the car models, the transmission fitted and the date of production. May 1969 was the date of a major change in clutch component design on

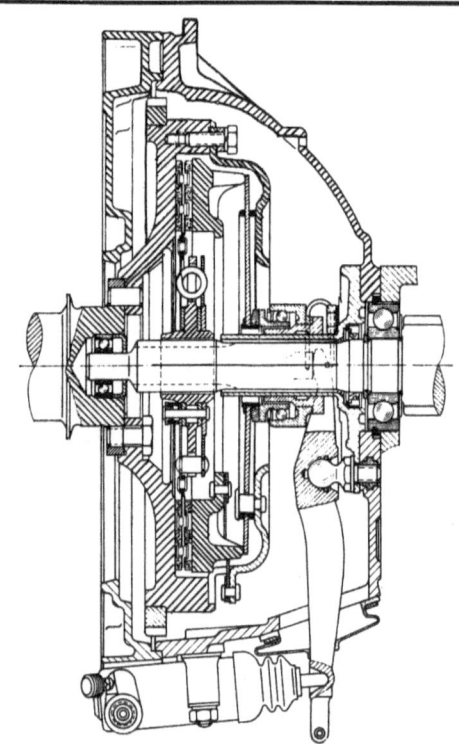

Fig. 5.1. Sectional view of typical early type clutch assembly

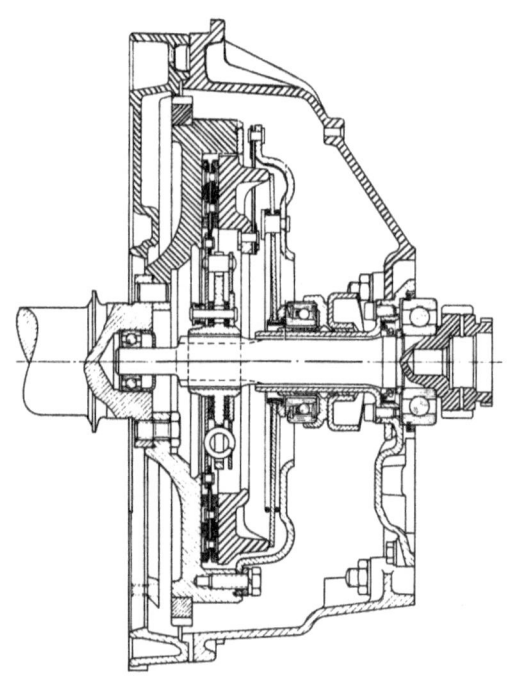

Fig. 5.2. Sectional view of typical later type clutch assembly

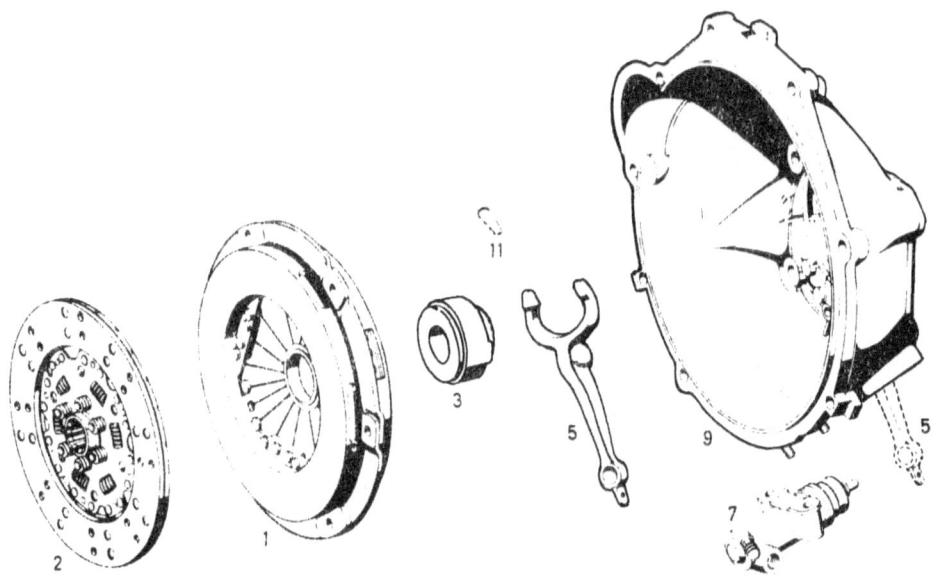

Fig. 5.3. Typical components of early type of clutch (for Key see Fig. 5.4).

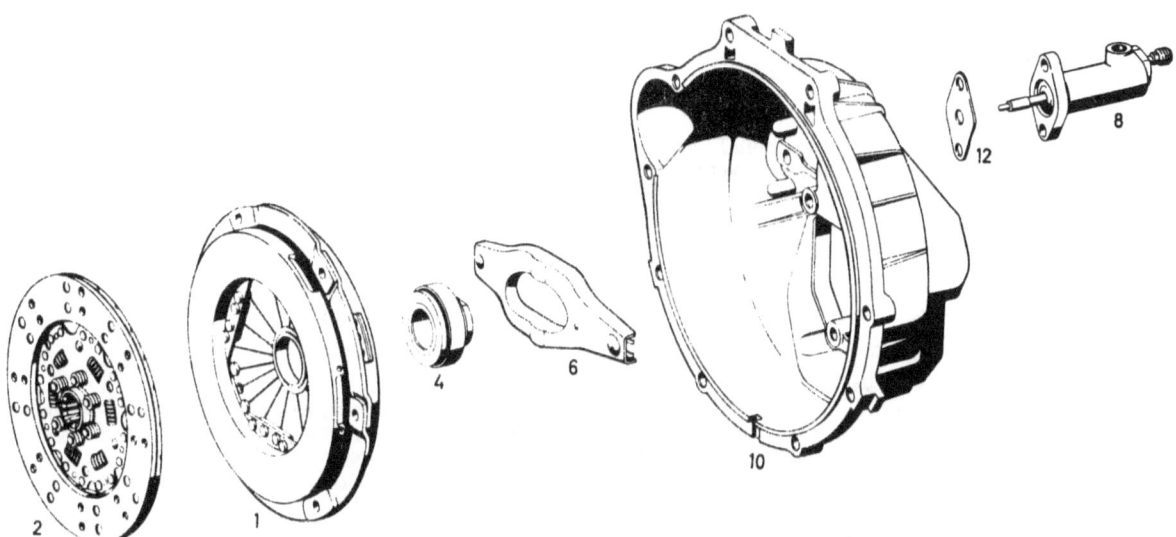

Fig. 5.4. Typical components of later type of clutch

1	Pressure plate assembly with	4	Release bearing	8	Slave cylinders	12 Shim
	diaphragm spring	5	Release lever	9	Bellhousing	
2	Driven plate	6	Release lever	10	Bellhousing	
3	Release bearing	7	Slave cylinder	11	Release bearing clip	

all models except SL/8 versions for which the original clutch continued to be fitted. It is very important therefore when renewing clutch components to quote the exact details of the car to the storeman.

Major components comprise a pressure plate and cover assembly, diaphragm spring and a driven plate (friction disc) which incorporates torsion coil springs to cushion rotational shock when the drive is taken up.

The clutch release bearing is of the sealed ball type and clutch actuation is hydraulic.

Depressing the clutch pedal moves the piston in the master cylinder forwards, so forcing hydraulic fluid through the clutch hydraulic pipe to the slave cylinder.

The piston in the slave cylinder moves forward on the entry of the fluid and actuates the clutch release arm by means of a short pushrod.

The release arm pushes the release bearing forwards to bear against the release plate, so moving the centre of the diaphragm spring inwards. The spring is sandwiched between two annular rings which act as fulcrum points. As the centre of the spring is pushed in, the outside of the spring is pushed out, so moving the pressure plate backwards and

disengaging the pressure plate from the clutch disc. When the clutch pedal is released the diaphragm spring forces the pressure plate into contact with the high friction linings on the clutch disc and at the same time pushes the clutch disc a fraction of an inch forwards on its splines so engaging the clutch disc with the flywheel. The clutch disc is now firmly sandwiched between the pressure plate and the flywheel so the drive is taken up.

The only two maintenance operations required are to maintain the pedal adjustment and to keep the fluid in the hydraulic system topped up as described in the following two Sections.

2   Clutch hydraulic system - topping up

1   At the intervals specified in 'Routine Maintenance' remove the cap from the clutch fluid reservoir and top up to the full mark if necessary (Fig. 5.5).
2   Continual need for topping up indicates a leak in the system which must be rectified immediately.

Fig. 5.5. Clutch fluid reservoir (arrowed) (Sec. 2)

3   It is recommended that the fluid is renewed every year by bleeding as described in Section 6. This is to ensure that corrosion does not affect the internal components of the hydraulic system as the fluid has a tendency to absorb moisture from the atmosphere over a period of time.

4   Keep hydraulic fluid away from paintwork; it acts as a paint stripper!

---

3   Clutch pedal free movement - adjustment

1   It is essential for correct operation of the clutch release bearing that the specified free movement is maintained between the end of the master cylinder piston and the end of the operating rod. This clearance cannot be measured directly but can be regarded as correct if an appropriate free movement is maintained at the clutch pedal pad as follows (Fig. 5.6).

2   Check that the upper end of the clutch pedal rests against its rubber back stop when it is fully released. If it does not, release the locknut on the coil type return spring and turn the adjusting nut until it does. Under normal circumstances, the overall length of the spring measured between the outer faces of the end retaining washers should be 1.59 in (40.5 mm).

3   With the pedal in its fully released position depress the pedal with the fingers and feel the point at which resistance occurs. This should be felt when the pedal has moved downwards through 0.04 in (1.0 mm).

4   If adjustment is required, release the nut on the eccentric adjuster bolt (20) which connects the push-rod to the pedal and turn the bolt to increase or decrease the free movement as required.

5   Recheck the free movement and then tighten the eccentric bolt without disturbing the setting.

---

4   Master cylinder - removal, overhaul and refitting

1   Syphon the hydraulic fluid from the clutch fluid reservoir which is located within the engine compartment.

2   Release the bleed screw on the clutch slave cylinder and repeatedly depress the clutch pedal until the fluid in the system is completely ejected.

3   Disconnect the fluid pipes from the master cylinder body and then unbolt the cylinder from its mounting bracket. Withdraw the master cylinder, leaving the operating push-rod attached to the pedal.

4   Clean away all external dirt.

5   It is recommended that the master cylinder is renewed complete but if internal components are available, carry out the following operations.

6   Remove the dust excluding bellows, extract the circlip and withdraw the internal piston/seal assembly.

7   Examine the surfaces of cylinder bore and piston. If they are scored or show signs of 'bright' wear areas, then the complete master cylinder should be renewed.

8   If the piston and cylinder bore appear to be in good condition, discard the old seals and obtain a repair kit which will contain new seals and other renewable items.

9   Reassembly is a reversal of dismantling but dip the seals in clean

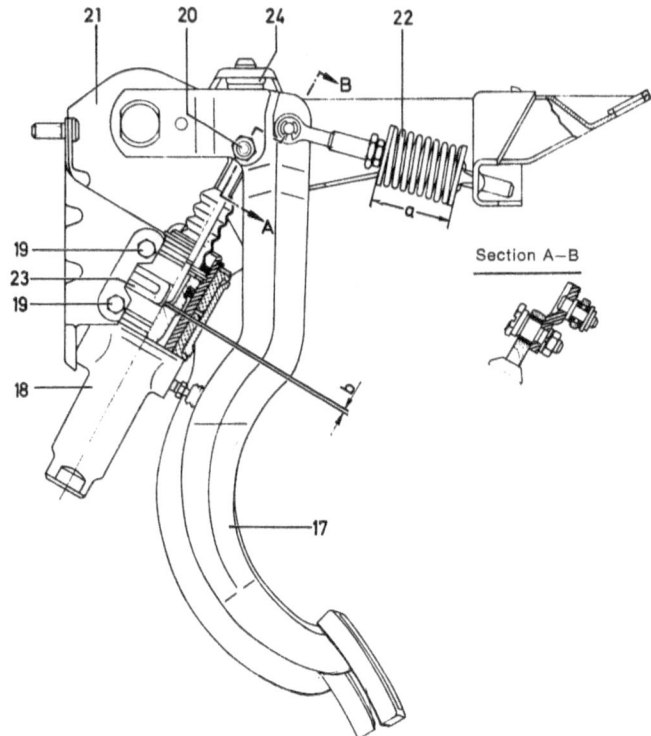

Fig. 5.6. Clutch pedal setting diagram (Sec. 3)

17 Pedal arm
18 Master cylinder
19 Master cylinder mounting bolt
20 Eccentric pivot bolt
For (a) and (b) see text.

21 Pedal mounting bracket
22 Coil return spring
23 Plate
24 Rebound stop

hydraulic fluid first and manipulate the seals into position using the fingers only. Make sure that the lips of the seals are facing the correct way as originally fitted.

10 Refit the master cylinder to its mounting and connect the fluid lines. The push-rod can simply be pushed into contact with the piston after inserting it through the dust excluding bellows.

11 Bleed the hydraulic system as described in Section 6 and check the adjustment of the pedal free movement (Section 3).

---

5   Slave cylinder - removal, overhaul and refitting

1   Working under the car, disconnect the fluid line from the slave cylinder and quickly cap the end of the pipe to prevent loss of fluid.

2   Disconnect the return spring from the end of the clutch release lever.

3   Unbolt and remove the clutch slave cylinder from the clutch bellhousing.

4   Clean away any external dirt, remove the dust excluding rubber bellows and the internal piston assembly.

5   Examine the condition of the piston and cylinder bore surfaces. If they are scored or show 'bright' wear areas then the slave cylinder should be renewed complete (Figs. 5.7 and 5.8).

6   If the piston and cylinder bore are in good condition, discard the seals and obtain a repair kit which will contain new ones and also any other renewable items.

7   Manipulate the new seals into position using the fingers only. Take care to ensure that the lips of the seals are facing the same way as originally fitted. Dip the internal components in clean hydraulic fluid before reassembling them.

8   Refit the slave cylinder and bleed the hydraulic system as described in Section 6.

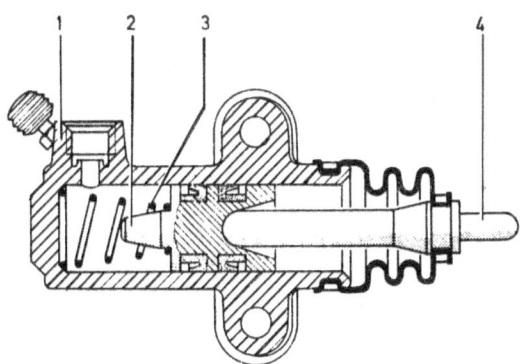

Fig. 5.7. Sectional view of older type clutch slave cylinder (Sec. 5)

1 Body   3 Spring
2 Piston   4 Pushrod

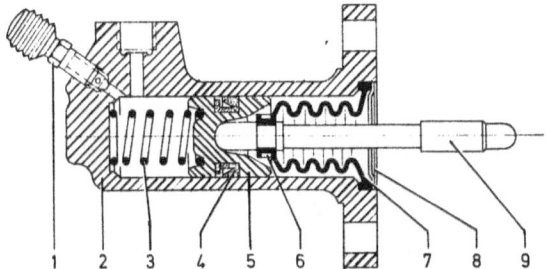

Fig. 5.8. Sectional view of later type clutch slave cylinder (Sec. 5)

1 Bleed nipple   6 Clip
2 Body   7 Rubber boot
3 Spring   8 Circlip
4 Seal   9 Pushrod
5 Piston

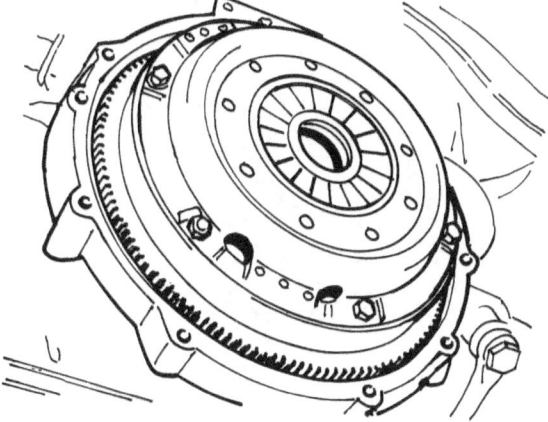

Fig. 5.9. Clutch mechanism bolted to flywheel (Sec. 7)

6 Clutch hydraulic system - bleeding

1 The need for bleeding the cylinders and fluid lines arises when air gets into them. Air gets in whenever a joint or seal leaks, or parts have to be dismantled. Bleeding is simply the process of venting the air out again.
2 Make sure that the clutch fluid reservoir is full.
3 If the clutch master cylinder has been removed and refitted, attach a bleed tube to the nipple on the master cylinder body and submerge the other end of the tube in a jar containing some clean hydraulic fluid.

4 Open the bleed nipple about ½ a turn and depress the clutch pedal fully to the end of its stroke. Release the foot and allow the pedal to return under the action of its return spring only. Repeat this procedure until no more air bubbles can be seen leaving the end of the tube in the jar.
5 Tighten the master cylinder bleed nipple while the pedal is held in the fully depressed state.
6 Remove the bleed tube and attach it to the bleed nipple on the slave cylinder.
7 Top up the fluid reservoir and then commence bleeding the system again exactly as described in the preceding paragraphs after having opened the slave cylinder bleed nipple. When no more air is seen to leave the end of the tube in the jar, tighten the nipple on the slave cylinder while the clutch pedal is held fully depressed.
8 Top up the fluid reservoir.
9 Always use clean fresh fluid for topping up which has been stored in an airtight container and has remained unshaken for the previous 24 hours. Discard the old fluid which has been bled from the system or use it only for bleed jar purposes.
10 During the bleeding operations, always keep the fluid reservoir topped up and always ensure that the end of the bleed tube is kept submerged in the jar.

7 Clutch - removal

1 One of two methods may be used to gain access to the clutch. Either remove the engine as described in Chapter 1 and unbolt the clutch mechanism from the flywheel or remove the transmission leaving the engine in the car as described in Chapter 6.
2 Method 2 should normally be adopted unless the engine requires a major overhaul at the same time.
3 The bolts which secure the clutch pressure plate cover should be unscrewed one turn at a time in a diametrically opposite sequence until the tension of the diaphragm spring is relieved and the clutch can be removed from the flywheel. As the cover is withdrawn, be prepared to catch the driven plate as it drops from its location between the pressure plate and the flywheel (Fig. 5.9).

8 Clutch - inspection and renovation

1 Due to the slow-wearing qualities of the clutch, it is not easy to decide when to go to the trouble of removing the gearbox in order to check the wear on the friction lining. The only positive indication that something needs doing is when it starts to slip or when squealing noises on engagement indicate that the friction lining has worn down to the rivets. In such instances it can only be hoped that the friction surfaces on the flywheel and pressure plate have not been badly worn or scored.
   A clutch will wear according to the way in which it is used. Much intentional slipping of the clutch while driving - rather that the correct selection of gears - will accelerate wear. It is best to assume, however, that the friction disc will need renewal every 50,000 miles (80,000 km) at least. The maintenance history of the car is obviously very useful in such cases.
2 Examine the surfaces of the pressure plate and flywheel for signs of scoring. If this is only light it may be left, but if very deep the pressure plate unit will have to be renewed. If the flywheel is deeply scored or has small surface cracks caused by overheating it should be taken off and advice sought from an engineering firm. Providing it may be machined completely across the face the overall balance of engine and flywheel should not be too severely upset. If renewal of the flywheel is necessary the new one will have to be balanced to match the original, see Section 20 of Chapter 1.
3 The friction plate lining surfaces should be at least 1/32 in (0.8 mm) above the rivets, otherwise the disc is not worth putting back. If the lining material shows signs of breaking up or has black areas where oil contamination has occurred it should also be renewed. If facilities are readily available for obtaining and fitting new friction pads to the existing disc this may be done but the saving is relatively small compared with obtaining a complete new disc assembly which ensures that the shock absorbing springs and the splined hub are renewed also. The same applies to the pressure plate assembly which cannot be readily dismantled and put back together without specialised riveting tools and balancing equipment. An allowance is usually given for exchange units.

9 Clutch release bearing - renewal

1   The sealed, ball bearing type release bearing, although designed for long life, is worth renewing at the same time as the other clutch components are being renewed or serviced.
2   Deterioration of the release bearing should be suspected when there are signs of grease leakage or the unit is noisy when spun with the fingers.
3   Remove the rubber dust excluder which surrounds the withdrawal lever at the bellhousing aperture on earlier cars (Fig. 5.10).
4   Disconnect the spring clips which hold the release bearing to the release lever, pull the lever away from the bearing and withdraw the bearing.
5   On earlier cars, the release bearing and its mounting hub can be separated by using an extractor and the new bearing pressed into position.
6   On later cars, no separate hub is used and the complete bearing assembly must be renewed (Figs. 5.11 and 5.12).
7   Refitting is a reversal of removal but apply just a smear of high melting point grease to the inside of the bearing hub or sleeve sliding surface.

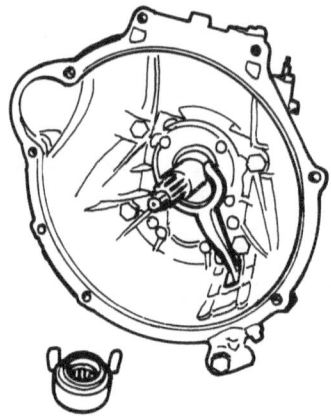

Fig. 5.10. Earlier type clutch release components (Sec. 9)

10 Clutch - refitting

1   Clean the face of the flywheel and the pressure plate.
2   Apply a little high melting point grease to the bearing in the centre of the flywheel. Apply grease also to the splines of the input shaft.
3   Locate the driven plate against the flywheel so that its larger projecting boss is to the rear.
4   Position the pressure plate assembly on the flywheel so that the positioning dowels engage.
5   Screw in each of the pressure plate bolts finger tight and then centralise the driven plate. This is accomplished by passing an old input shaft or stepped dowel rod through the splined hub of the driven plate and engaging it in the spigot bearing in the centre of the flywheel. By moving the shaft or rod in the appropriate directions, the position will be established where the centralising tool can be withdrawn without any side pressure from the driven plate, proving that the driven plate is centralised.
6   Without disturbing the setting of the driven plate, tighten the pressure plate bolts, a turn at a time, in a diametrically opposite sequence to the specified torque wrench setting.
7   Refit the gearbox to the engine (Chapter 6) when, if the driven plate has been correctly centralised, the input shaft of the gearbox will pass easily through the splined hub of the driven plate to engage with the spigot bearing in the centre of the flywheel. Do not allow the weight of the gearbox to hang upon the input shaft while it is passing through the clutch mechanism or damage to the clutch components may result.

Fig. 5.11. Removing later type clutch release bearing (Sec. 9)

1   Bearing   2   Release lever (rocker)

11 Clutch pedal - removal and refitting

1   The clutch and brake pedals operate on a common pivot shaft and they should be removed as an assembly.
2   Remove the cover from underneath the instrument panel.
3   Disconnect any electrical connector plugs which are obstructing access. On 280 SL/8 models, the rev. counter will have to be removed.
4   Disconnect the plugs from the brake stop lamp switch and the handbrake warning lamp.
5   On models which have a pull-out handbrake lever, disconnect the support bracket for the handbrake lever from the mounting bracket of the pedal assembly.
6   Disconnect the hydraulic lines from the clutch master cylinder. Take care not to let the escaping fluid damage the car interior trim but catch it in a suitable container.
7   Disconnect the master cylinder push-rod from the brake pedal on all cars except Model 280 SL/8.
8   Unscrew the bolt (9) which secures the pedal assembly to the bottom of the instrument panel and remove its nut from the rear. On 280 SL/8 models the nut can be removed through the hole vacated by the rev. counter (Fig. 5.13).
9   Unscrew and remove the nuts (7) which hold the pedal assembly

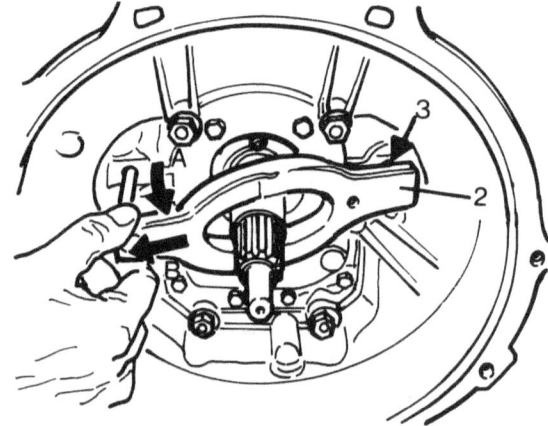

Fig. 5.12. Removing later type release lever (2) (Sec. 9)

A to B   Direction of pressure required to disengage end of release lever from ball stud (3)

to the engine compartment rear bulkhead. These nuts also retain the brake servo unit.
10 Pull the pedal assembly rearwards and downwards and remove it from under the instrument panel. Take care not to disturb the brake master cylinder/booster while its nuts and mounting bolts (7) are removed. Wire it up to prevent strain on the hydraulic lines (Fig. 5.14).
11 The pedal assembly may now be dismantled as necessary to renew bushes and other components by unbolting the clutch master cylinder,

disconnecting the springs and the pivot shaft (Fig. 5.15).

12 Reassembly and refitting are reversals of removal and dismantling, but apply grease to the pivot shaft and set the clutch pedal free movement as described in Section 3 of this Chapter and the brake pedal travel as described in Chapter 9.

13 Bleed the clutch hydraulic system (Section 6).

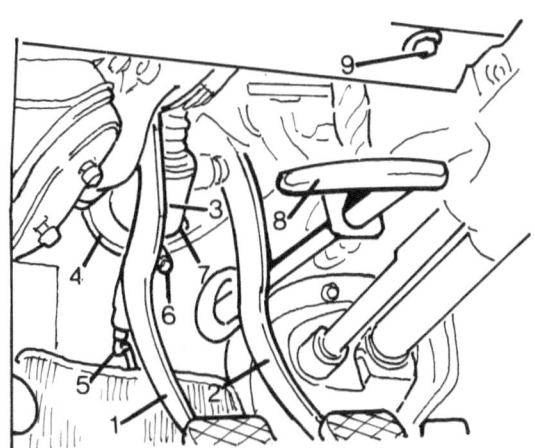

Fig. 5.13. Foot pedal attachment details (Sec. 11)

1 Clutch pedal
2 Brake pedal
3 Clutch master cylinder
4 Fluid line
5 Fluid line
6 Master cylinder bleed screw

7 Securing nuts (pedal bracket and brake servo)
8 Handbrake lever
9 Securing bolt (pedal bracket to instrument panel)

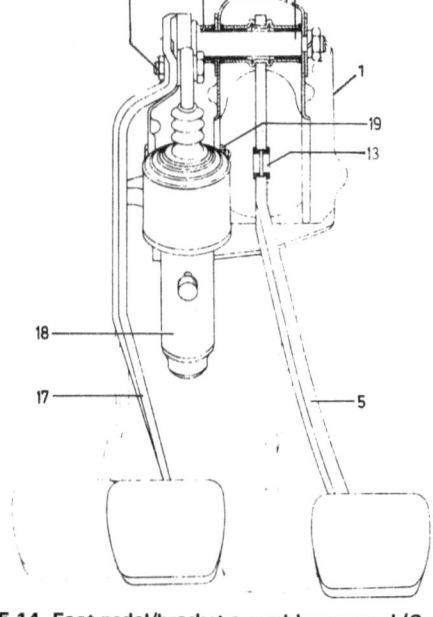

Fig. 5.14. Foot pedal/bracket assembly removed (Sec. 11)

1   Mounting bracket
5   Brake pedal
13 Flanged bushes
15 Pivot bolt
16 Bush

17 Clutch pedal
18 Clutch master cylinder
19 Master cylinder mounting bolt
20 Eccentric adjusting bolt

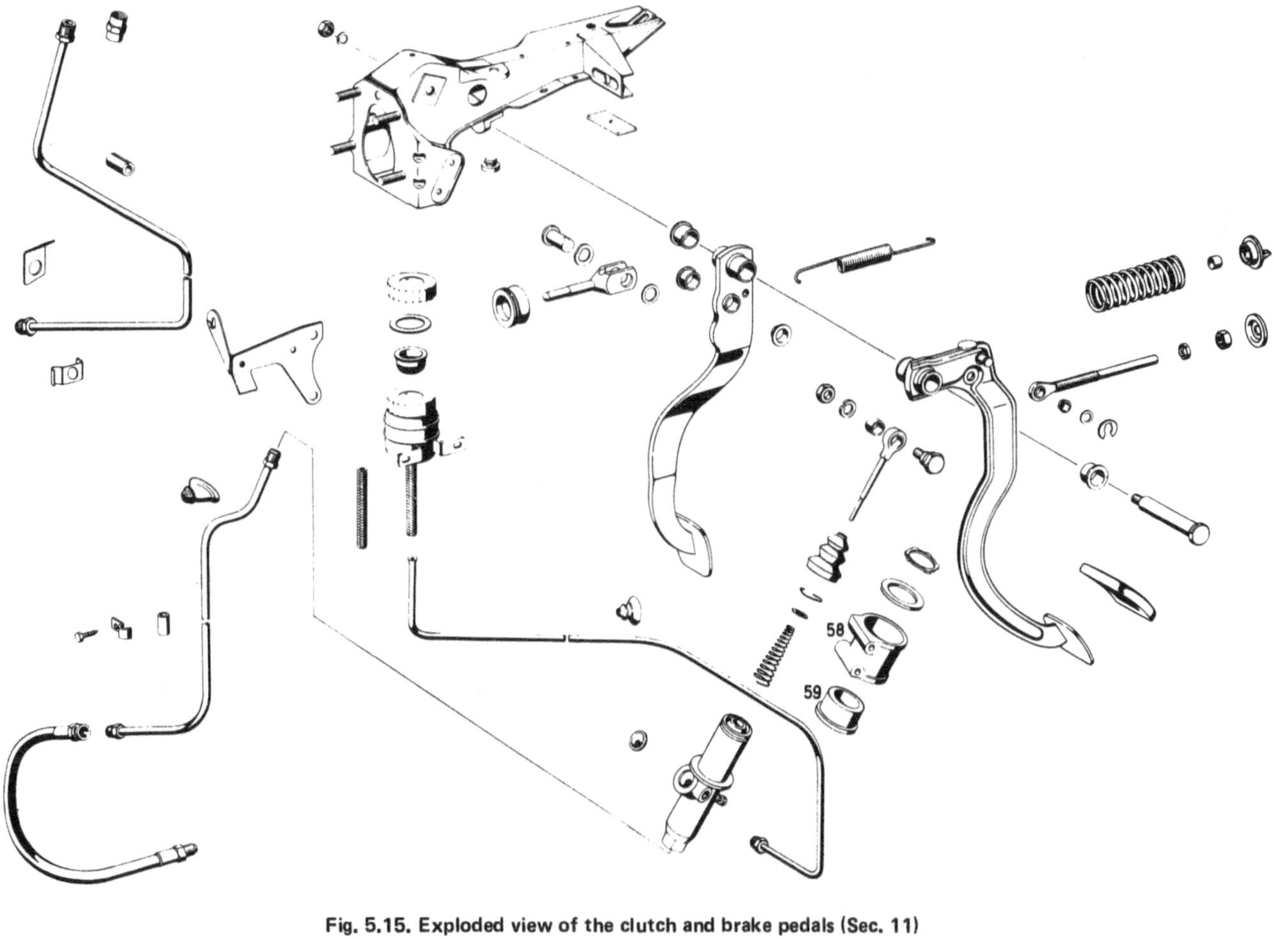

Fig. 5.15. Exploded view of the clutch and brake pedals (Sec. 11)

12 Fault diagnosis - clutch

Symptom	Reason/s
Judder when taking up drive	Engine or gearbox mountings loose. Badly worn friction surfaces or contaminated with oil. Worn splines on gearbox input shaft or driven plate hub. Worn input shaft bearing in flywheel.
Clutch spin (failure to disengage) so that gears cannot be meshed	Incorrect release bearing to diaphragm spring due to rust. May occur after vehicle standing idle for long period. Damaged or misaligned pressure plate assembly. Fault in hydraulic system.
Clutch slip (increase in engine speed does not result in increase in vehicle road speed - particularly on gradients)	Incorrect release bearing to diaphragm spring finger clearance caused by incorrect pedal adjustment. Friction surfaces worn out or oil contaminated.
Noise evident on depressing clutch pedal	Dry, worn or damaged release bearing. Insufficient pedal free-travel. Weak or broken pedal return spring. Weak or broken clutch release lever return spring. Excessive play between driven plate hub splines and input shaft splines.
Noise evident as clutch pedal released	Distorted driven plate. Broken or weak driven plate cushion coil springs. Insufficient pedal free travel. Weak or broken clutch pedal return spring. Weak or broken release lever return spring. Distorted or worn input shaft. Release bearing loose on retainer hub (early models).

Chapter 6 Transmission

Contents

Specifications

Part A - manual transmission

| Transmission type ... ... | Four or five forward speeds (synchromesh) and reverse |

Application

Transmission type	Car model
G76/18 (4 speed) and G76/18/5 (5 speed)	230/8, 250/8, 250SE, 250SL, 250CE, 250C
G72 (to 1969) 4 speed	280SL 250S/8
G76/27 (4 speed) and G76/27/5 (5 speed)	250S/8, 250SL, 280SE/8, 280SL
G72 (to 1969 4 speed and ZF S520 (5 speed)	280SL/8

Ratios

G72

1st	4.05 : 1
2nd	2.23 : 1
3rd	1.40 : 1
4th	1.00 : 1
Reverse	3.58 : 1

G76/18

1st	3.90 : 1
2nd	2.30 : 1
3rd	1.41 : 1
4th	1.00 : 1
Reverse	3.70 : 1

G76/18/5

1st	3.90 : 1
2nd	2.30 : 1
3rd	1.41 : 1
4th	1.00 : 1
5th	0.872 : 1
Reverse	3.70 : 1

G76/27

1st	3.96 : 1
2nd	2.34 : 1
3rd	1.43 : 1
4th ... ...•	1.00 : 1
Reverse	3.72 : 1

Ratios

G76/27/5

1st	3.96 : 1
2nd	2.34 : 1
3rd	1.43 : 1
4th	1.00 : 1
5th	0.875 : 1
Reverse	3.72 : 1

ZF S520

1st	3.92 : 1
2nd	2.215 : 1
3rd	1.418 : 1
4th	1 : 1
5th	0.848 : 1
Reverse	3.49 : 1

Fluid capacities

	Imp pints	US pints	Litres
G72	3.2	3.8	1.4
G76/18	5.1	6.1	1.6
G76/27			
4 speed	5.3	6.3	1.8
5 speed	7.5	9.0	2.5
ZF S520	3.5	4.2	1.1

Torque wrench settings

	lb f ft	Nm
Output flange nut	108	150
Drain and filler plug	43	60
Side cover bolts	11	15
Front cover bolts	11	15
Rear cover bolts (large)	32	45
Rear cover bolts (small)	11	15
Countershaft front and rear nuts	108	150
Mainshaft front nut	58	80
Clutch bellhousing to engine bolts	36	50

Part B - automatic transmission

Transmission type ... ...   Mercedes-Benz 4 speed with torque converter and four speed planetary geartrain

Application

Transmission type	Car model
K4C 025	230/8, 250/8, 250SE, 250SL, 250CE, 250C, The following to 1969 - 280S/8, 280SL, 280SE/8, 280SEL/8, 280SL/8
K4A 025	All 1969 on - 280S/8, 280SL, 280SE/8, 280SEL/8, 280SL/8

Ratios

	Type K4C 025	Type K4A 025
1st	3.98 : 1	3.98 : 1
2nd	2.39 : 1	2.52 : 1
3rd	1.46 : 1	1.58 : 1
4th	1.00 : 1	1.00 : 1
Reverse	5.47 : 1	4.15 : 1

Fluid capacity

	Imp pints	US pints	Litres
Drain and refill with change of filter	6.6	7.9	3.75
Filling new unit	9.5	11.4	5.3

Torque wrench settings

	lb f ft	Nm
Drive plate to torque converter bolts	25	35
Output flange nut	87	120
Oil pan bolts	5	7
Torque converter housing to engine bolts	36	50

Part A - manual transmission

1   General description

The cars covered by this manual have a four speed transmission fitted as standard with an optional five speed version.

The transmission has been subject to minor modifications over the years of production but this has not affected the operations described in this Chapter. The individual components cannot, however, be interchanged between the different versions.

All forward speeds have synchromesh and the gearshift may be of the floor-mounted or steering column type, with a side or top mounted selector cover.

2 Maintenance

1   This consists of checking the fluid level by removing the combined level/filler plug on the side of the transmission casing. Top up if necessary, noting that only specified **automatic transmission fluid** should be used in this manual gearbox (Fig. 6.1).
2   At the specified intervals, drain the lubricant when it is warm after a run and refill with fresh fluid.
3   Keep the outside of the casing clean and occasionally check the security of the nuts and bolts.

3 Steering column gear shift (type G76/18 transmission) adjustment

1   Disconnect the balljointed rods from the levers at the base of the steering column.
2   Align the levers by passing a rod through the holes provided in them (Fig. 6.2).
3   Shift the transmission to neutral by moving the levers on the side of the transmission.
4   Now measure the position of the levers as shown in Fig. 6.3, using the point of reference on the transmission casing. The dimensions should be in accordance with the following table. Release the pinch bolts on the levers if necessary and alter their setting to achieve these dimensions.

		Left-hand drive	Right-hand drive
A	1st - 2nd speed	5.98 in (152.0 mm)	6.54 in (166.0 mm)
B	3rd - 4th speed	3.19 in (81.0 mm)	3.54 in (90.0 mm)
C	Reverse	1.02 in (26.0 mm)	1.18 in (30.0 mm)

5   Adjust the lengths of the ball jointed rods by releasing the locknuts

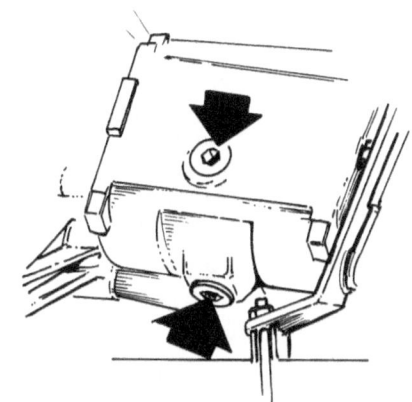

Fig. 6.1. Filler and drain plugs on manual transmission (Sec. 2)

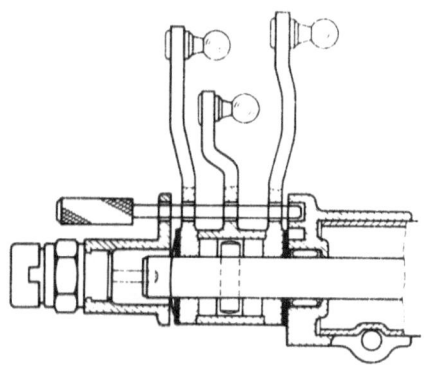

Fig. 6.2. Alignment of gearshift levers at base of steering column (type G76/18 manual transmission) (Sec. 3)

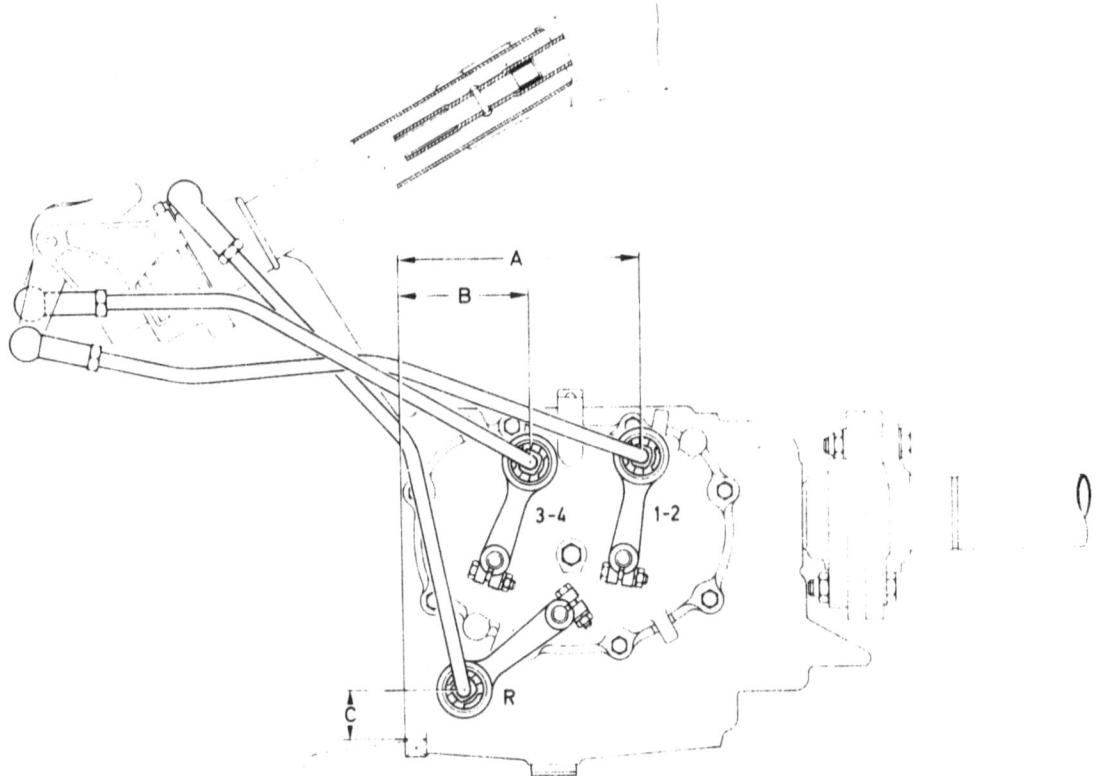

Fig. 6.3. Shift lever setting on type G76/18 manual transmission. For dimensions see table in text (Sec. 3)

and screwing the balljoints in or out. The rods should connect directly to the ball pins without any tendency to deflect the levers on the transmission casing.

4 Steering column gearshift (type G76/27 transmission) - adjustment

1 Prise the ball jointed rods from the levers at the base of the steering column.
2 Align the levers by passing a rod through the holes provided in them.
3 Set the selector levers on the side of the transmission to the neutral position and then measure their positions as shown in the diagram. If

necessary, release the pinch bolts and re-position the levers to achieve these dimensions (Fig. 6.4).
4 Now adjust the lengths of the connecting rods so that they will fit onto the ballpins without any tendency to deflect the levers on the transmission from their set position. A type of sliding pinch bolt is used to vary the length of the connecting rods (Fig. 6.5).

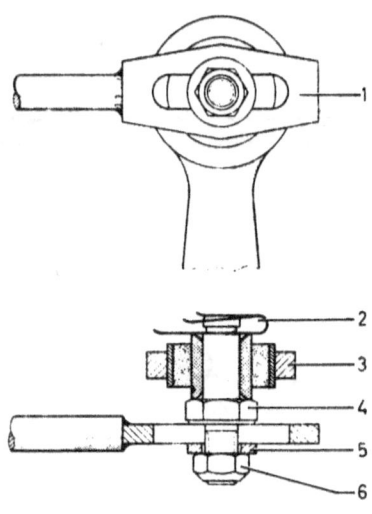

Fig. 6.5. Steering column gearshift connecting rod sliding pinch bolt (Sec. 4)

1 Connecting rod	4 Bolt
2 Locking spring clip	5 Shim
3 Shift lever on transmission	6 Locknut

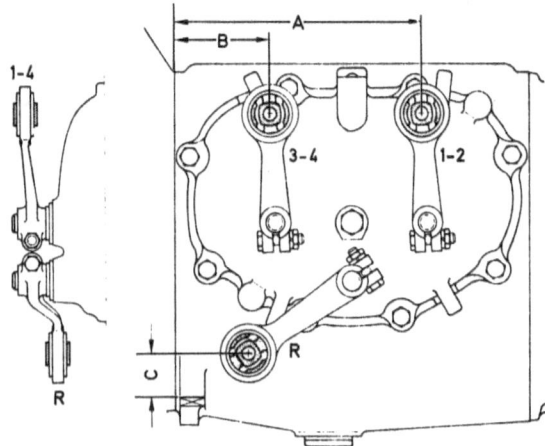

Fig. 6.4. Shift lever setting on type G76/27 manual transmission (Sec. 4)

A = 6.22 in (158 mm); B = 2.28 in (58 mm); C = 1.02 in (26 mm)

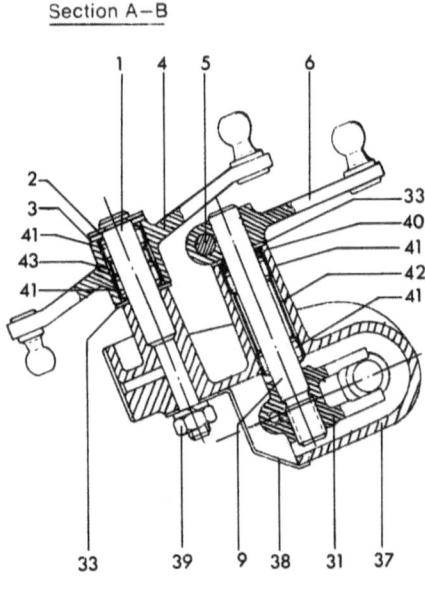

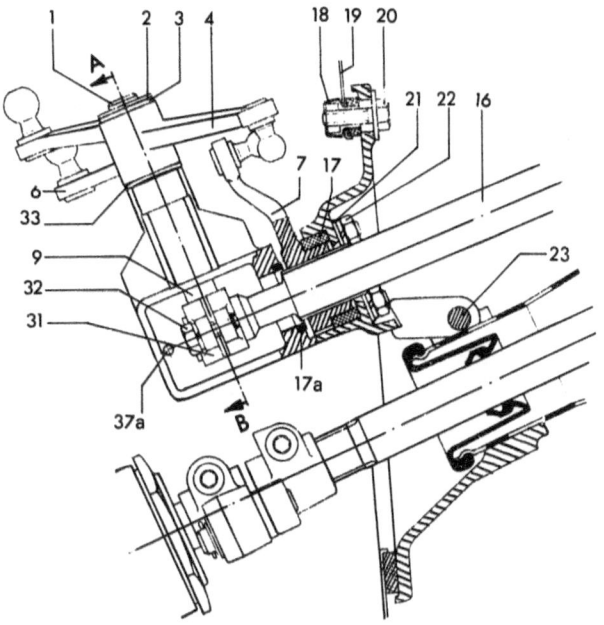

Fig. 6.6. Steering column gearshift control levers (type G72 manual transmission) (Sec. 5)

1	Pivot	9	Shaft	21	Washer
2	Circlip	16	Selector tube	22	Nut
3	Washer	17	Anti-friction bush	31	Lever
4	Intermediate lever	17a	Spacer	32	Pinch bolt
5	Clamp screw	18	Captive nut	33	Circlip
6	Selector lever	19	Bulkhead	37	Body
7	Shift tube lever	20	Bolt	37a	Drain hole

38	Cover
39	Nut
40	Seal
41	Needle bearing
42	Spacer
43	Spacer

5 Steering column gearshift (type G72 transmission) - adjustment

1 Check that the gearshift control lever springs back automatically to its end location after being pulled against reverse gear stop.
2 Move the gearshift control lever to neutral and then slacken the clamp screw (5) on the lever (6) (Fig. 6.6).
3 Pull the lever towards the front of the car and also pull the intermediate lever (4) so that fourth gear is engaged.
4 Remove the flexible cover from around the steering column shift control lever and have an assistant pull the shift control upwards until there is a clearance between the lever and the cut-out in the steering column of about 0.08 in (2.0 mm).
5 Tighten the clamp screw (5) while at the same time pushing on the lever to slightly pre-load the spring plate (33).
6 Check all gear positions with the clutch depressed and observe whether the gearshift control matches the positions shown in the diagram (Fig. 6.7).

6 Floor mounted gearshift (type G76/18 and G76/27 transmission) - adjustment

1 Working under the car, remove the spring locking clips and disconnect the shift rods from the levers at the base of the gearshift control (Fig. 6.8).
2 Align the three levers by inserting a suitable rod into the holes provided in them.
3 Move the transmission to the neutral position and then check the setting of the levers on the side of the transmission casing. These should be in accordance with the following table. If necessary, release the pinch bolts and move the position of the levers to achieve them (Fig. 6.9).

		G76/18 transmission	G76/27 and G76/27A transmission
A	1st - 2nd speed	5.98 in (152.0 mm)	6.61 in (168.0 mm)
B	3rd - 4th speed	2.76 in (70.0 mm)	2.44 in (62.0 mm)
C	Reverse	4.37 in (111.0 mm)	4.72 in (120.0 mm)

4 Now adjust the lengths of the connecting rods so that they will fit onto the gearshift control rod levers without any tendency to deflect the levers from their set positions.
5 Remove the temporary alignment pin and fit the spring locking clips.

7 Floor mounted gearshift (type G72 transmission) - adjustment

1 Position the shaft (1) against reverse speed stop and then engage 2nd speed by pushing the shaft inwards (Fig. 6.10).
2 Move the shift lever (16) into the 1st/2nd mode.

3 Push the tube (4) into the splines of the fork head (2). Make sure that the tube has entered at least by 0.59 in (15.0 mm).
4 Tighten the pinch bolt (3).
5 Shift through all the gear positions.
6 If any knocking occurs against the shift lever bearing (12) when engaging a gear position, the two rods (8) must be adjusted. To do this, remove the shift rods from the top of the transmission cover and rotate the end pieces (7) until the shift rod bolts in the shift lever bearing (12) are in the centre of the cover plate (14). Adjust the two end pieces equally.

8 Floor mounted gearshift (type G76-27/5 five speed transmission) - adjustment

1 Working under the car withdraw the dust excluder and remove the spring locking clips and disconnect the shift rods from the levers at the base of the gearshift control (Fig. 6.11).
2 Align the three levers by inserting a suitable rod into the holes provided in them. Do this while pushing the gearshift control lever fully to the right in neutral and then towards 5th speed.
3 Move the transmission to the neutral position and then check the setting of the levers on the side of the transmission casing. These should be in accordance with the diagram. If not, release the pinch bolts and reposition the levers (Fig. 6.12).
4 Release the bolts (3) and move the stop plate (1) in relation to the stop finger (2) to take up the setting shown in the diagram (Fig. 6.13).
5 Retighten the bolts.
6 Adjust the lengths of the shift rods to connect smoothly without having any tendency to deflect the levers from their set positions.
7 Refit the dust cover and check all gear positions with the clutch depressed.

9 Transmission - removal and refitting

1 Unless the car can be located over an inspection pit, raise the rear sufficiently high to permit the clutch bellhousing of the transmission to pass below the bodyframe and suspension as the transmission is withdrawn to the rear.
2 Disconnect the lead from the battery negative terminal.
3 Drain the fluid from the transmission.
4 Disconnect the shift rods from the transmission. Note how the locking spring clips are disengaged (Fig. 6.14).
5 Disconnect the speedometer drive cable from the transmission, the reversing lamp switch leads and the transmission to bodyframe earth strap.
6 Unbolt the clutch slave cylinder and tie it up out of the way. Where a rigid line is connected to the slave cylinder, disconnect the line and plug or cap the open pipes.

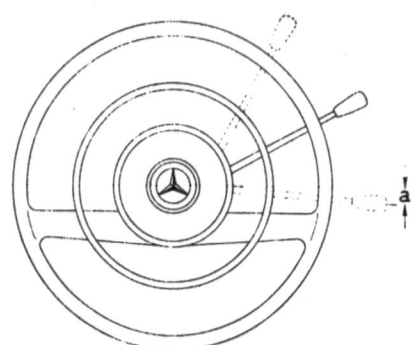

Fig. 6.7. Steering column gearshift positions (Sec. 5)

(a) Control lever from horizontal when in 2nd or 4th gear about 0.59 in (15 mm)

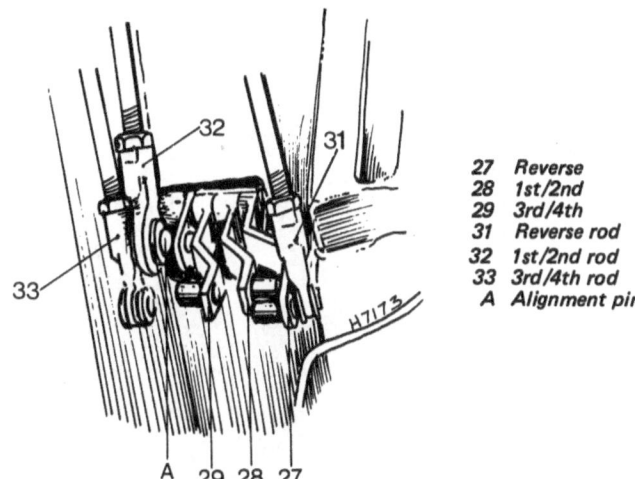

27	Reverse
28	1st/2nd
29	3rd/4th
31	Reverse rod
32	1st/2nd rod
33	3rd/4th rod
A	Alignment pin

Fig. 6.8. Levers at base of floor-mounted control (type G76/18 and G76/27 transmission) (Sec. 6)

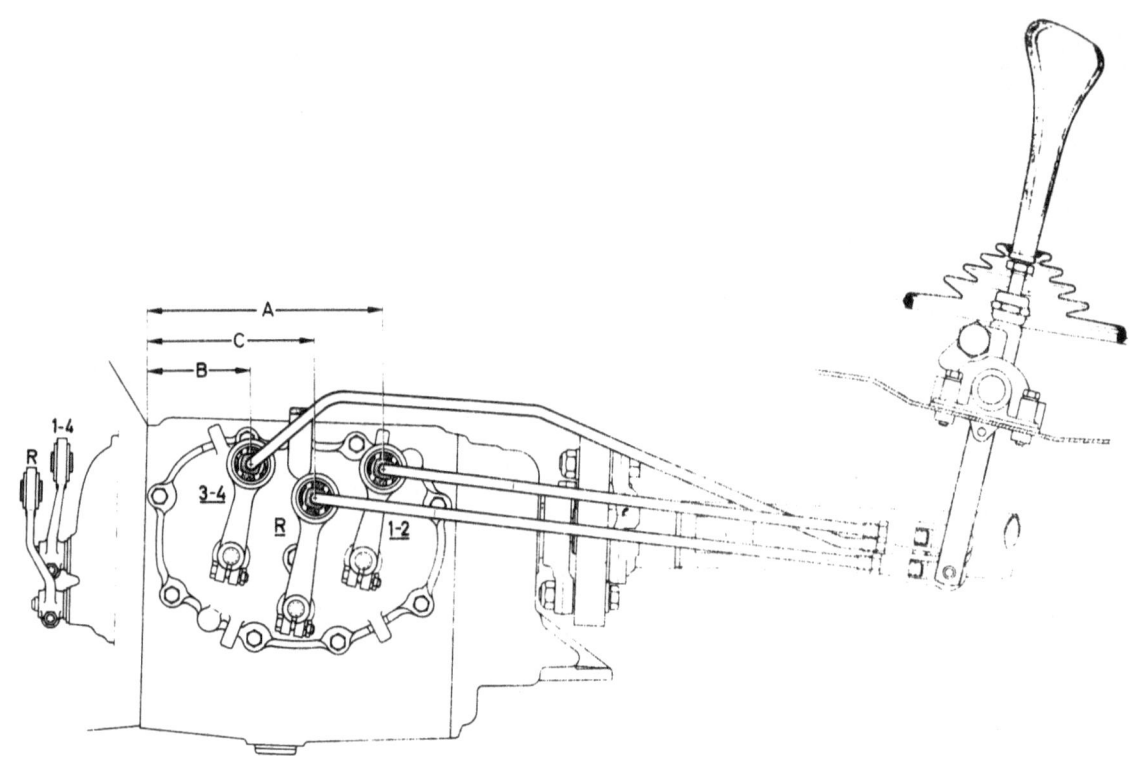

Fig. 6.9. Shift lever setting on type G76/18 and G76/27 manual transmission (Sec. 6)

For dimensions see table in text.

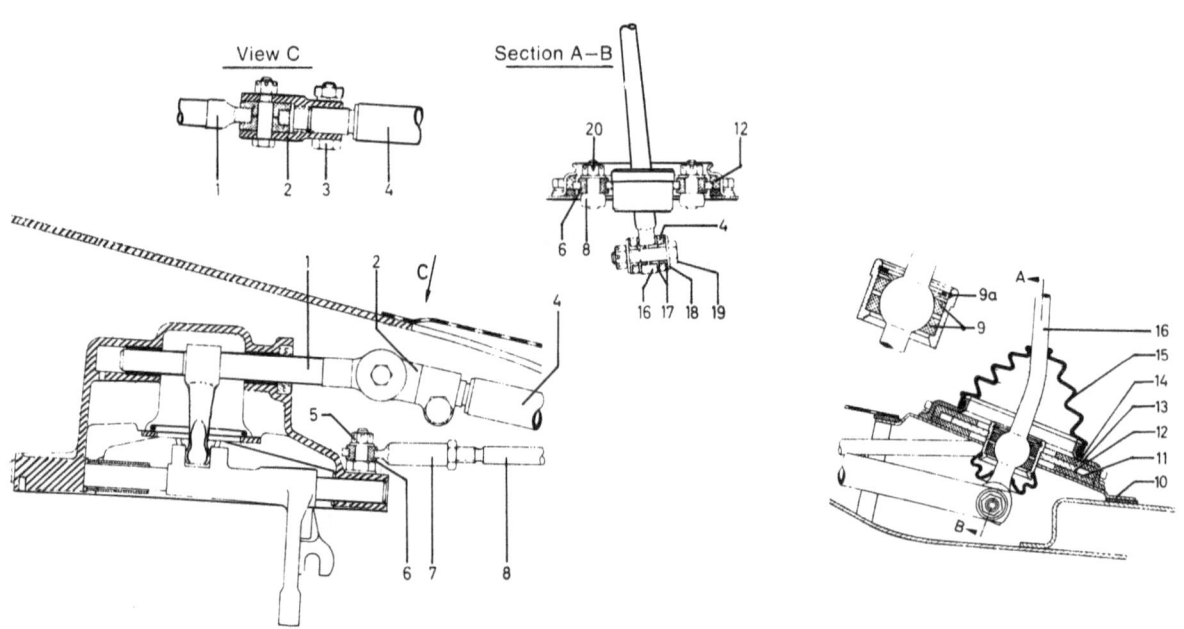

Fig. 6.10. Selector remote control on G72 manual transmission (Sec. 7)

1	Remote control rod	6	Bush	10	Transmission tunnel	15	Sleeve
2	Coupling	7	End fitting	11	Cap	16	Gearshift lever
3	Pinch bolt	8	Rod	12	Bearing	17	Bush
4	Shift tube	9	Anti-friction socket	13	Cap	18	Washer
5	Castellated nut	9a	Circlip	14	Cover plate	19	Bolt
						20	Castellated nut

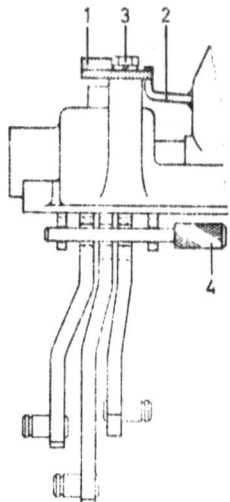

Fig. 6.11. Levers at base of floor-mounted control (type 76/27/5 manual transmission) (Sec. 8)

1   Stop plate   3   Bolt
2   Stop finger   4   Alignment pin

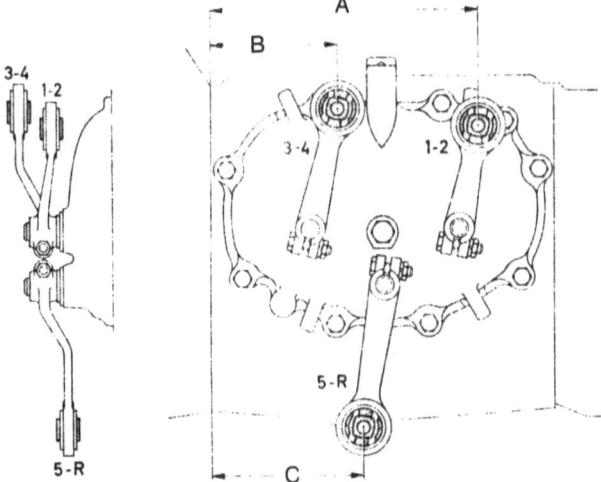

Fig. 6.12. Shift lever setting on type 76/25/5 manual transmission (Sec. 8)

A = 6.61 in (168 mm); B = 3.19 in (81 mm); C = 3.74 in (95 mm)

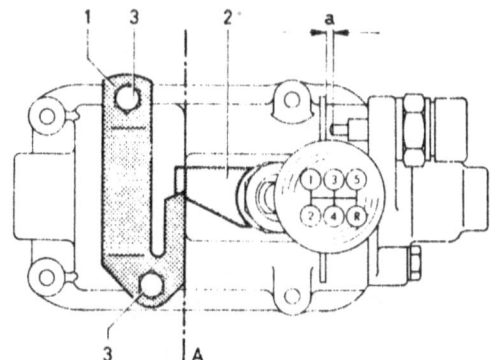

Fig. 6.13. Stop plate setting on type 76/27/5 floor mounted control (Sec. 8)

1   Stop plate   2   Stop finger   3   Bolt

A = alignment of stop plate and finger
a = clearance between reverse lamp switch plunger 0.059 in (1.5 mm)

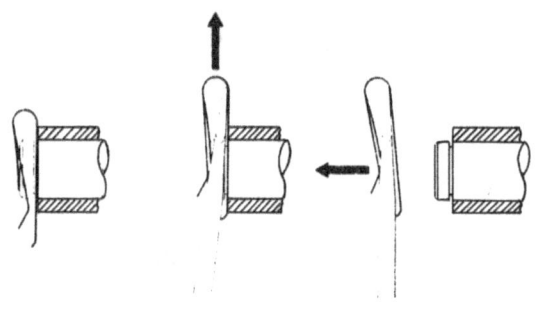

Fig. 6.14. Method of releasing a locking spring clip used to secure control rods to levers (Sec. 9)

Fig. 6.15. Propeller shaft disconnected at front end and supported on block of wood on crossmember (17). Note block above exhaust pipes (Sec. 9)

7   Release the nuts at the sliding section of the propeller shaft (refer to Chapter 7).

8   Extract the mounting bolts from the propeller shaft centre bearing.

9   Disconnect the propeller shaft front flange from the flange on the transmission output shaft. Push the propeller shaft upwards and support it on a block of wood (Fig. 6.15).

10 Unscrew the bolt which connects the transmission rear mounting to the crossmember.

11 Locate a jack, preferably of trolley type under the transmission and then unbolt and remove the mounting crossmember. Use a piece of wood to insulate the oil pan of the transmission. Place a second jack under the engine sump.

12 Disconnect and remove the exhaust pipe support bracket from the transmission.

13 Disconnect the exhaust downpipes from the exhaust manifolds and then use a block of wood to keep them depressed downwards and to one side out of the way of the transmission.

14 Use a socket attached to several extension bars to unscrew and remove the bellhousing to engine bolts.

15 Use the same number of extension bars to unscrew the starter motor mounting bolts but an Allen key will be required to unscrew the socket headed type bolts.

16 With the help of assistants, withdraw the transmission rearwards and downwards at the same time as the jacks are lowered. Do not let the weight of the transmission rest upon the input shaft while the latter is engaged in the splined hub of the clutch driven plate. The transmission should be turned as it is withdrawn to prevent the starter housing dome catching on the transmission tunnel (Fig. 6.16).

Note: On some models, a large plate is bolted to the floor pan as a rear mounting support instead of a crossmember. This should be

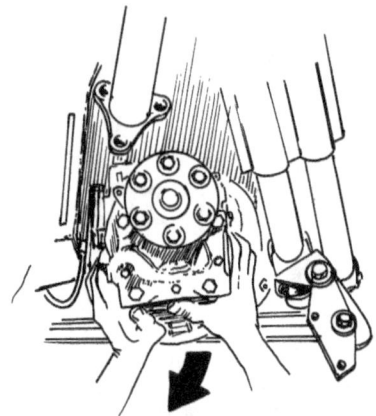

Fig. 6.16. Withdrawing the manual gearbox (Sec. 9)

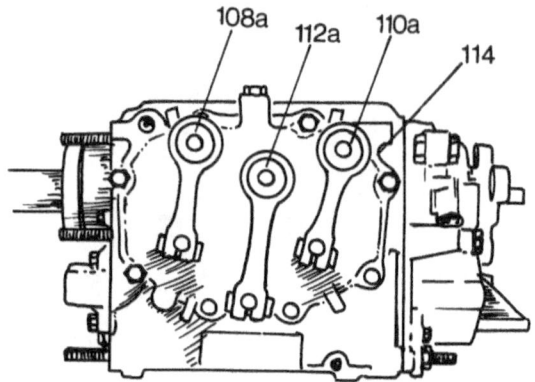

Fig. 6.17. Shift lever identification (Sec. 10)

108a 3rd/4th   110a 1st/2nd   112a Reverse   114 Cover

removed instead. On other models, disconnection of the handbrake cable at the equaliser is required to prevent it obstructing the transmission during removal.

17 Refitting is a reversal of removal but make sure that the clutch driven plate has been centralised before attempting to refit the transmission (see Chapter 5).

18 Check the gearshift adjustment as described earlier in this Chapter.

19 Bleed the clutch hydraulic circuit (if disconnected).

20 Fill the transmission with the correct quantity and type of fluid.

21 Reconnect the battery and transmission earth leads.

10 Transmission - dismantling into major assemblies

1 The following operations apply to all types of manual (G76) transmission although the design of individual components may vary slightly between one version and another.

2 If the transmission is to be changed for a new or reconditioned unit, then the clutch bellhousing must be removed from the old unit for refitting to the new one.

3 The type G72 transmission is different in that it has a top mounted selector mechanism instead of being side mounted as is the case with G76 transmissions (Figs. 6.18 and 6.19).

4 Clean any dirt and grease from the outside of the transmission casing once it has been removed from the car.

5 Remove the clutch release mechanism from within the clutch housing and then unbolt and remove the clutch bellhousing from the transmission casing.

6 From the side of the transmission, release the pinch bolt and remove the reverse shift lever (112a) (Fig. 6.17).

7 Prise out the circlip (121) and extract the washer (120) (Fig. 6.20).

8 Unscrew and remove all the cover bolts. Any that are masked by

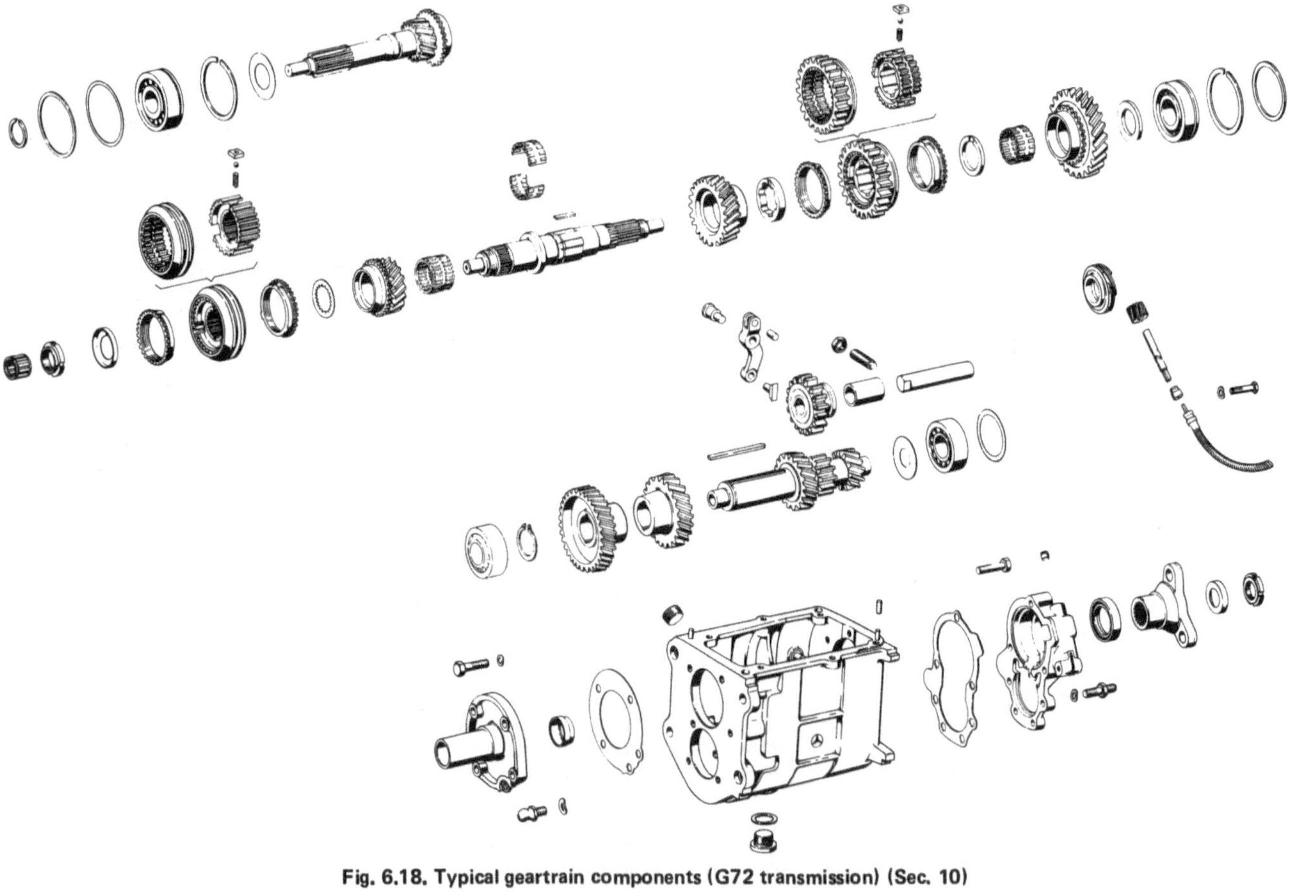

Fig. 6.18. Typical geartrain components (G72 transmission) (Sec. 10)

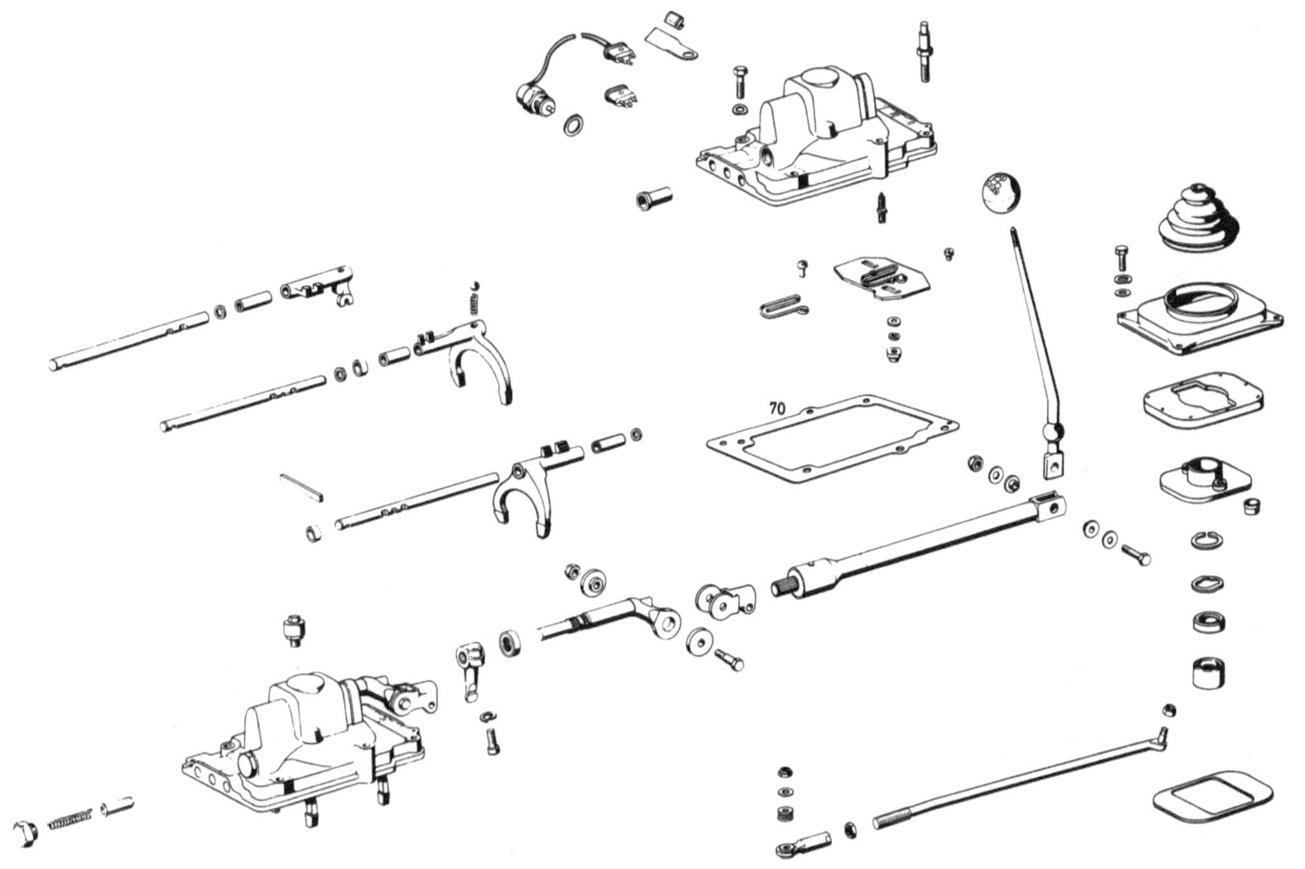

Fig. 6.19. Typical selector components (top mounted shift cover) - G72 transmission (Sec. 10)

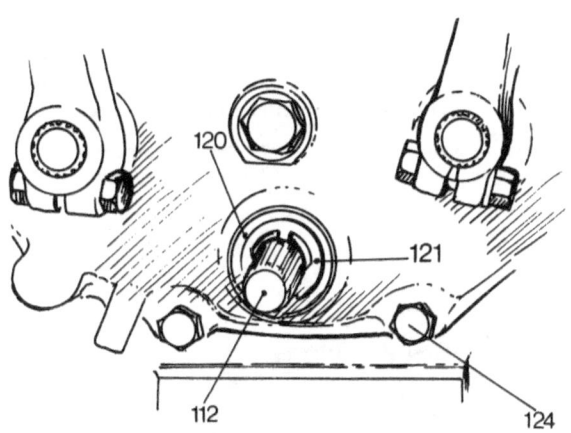

Fig. 6.20. Reverse shift lever removed (Sec. 10)

| 112 | Reverse gear shift shaft | 121 | Circlip |
| 120 | Thrust washer | 124 | Cover bolt |

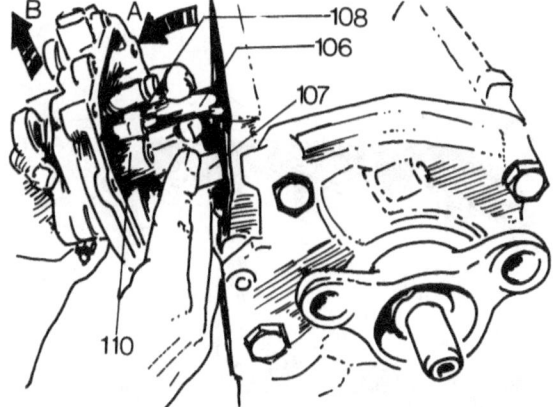

Fig. 6.21. Removing the side cover assembly (Sec. 10)

106	3rd/4th fork	110	1st/2nd rocker
107	1st/2nd fork	A - B	Removal direction
108	3rd/4th rocker		

the remaining shift levers can be made accessible if the shift levers are moved aside.

9   Tap the cover carefully outwards off its positioning dowels while simultaneously tapping the end of the reverse speed shaft (112) inwards with a plastic faced hammer.

10 As soon as the fingers can be inserted behind the cover, disconnect the shift forks from the rockers and then tilt the cover's upper edge and withdraw it outwards and upwards. Remove the paper gasket (Fig. 6.21).

11 Unbolt and remove the cover from the front of the transmission casing (Fig. 6.22).

12 Retain the compensating washers (Fig. 6.23).

13 Unscrew and remove the ring nut which secures the output flange. Remove the flange with a suitable puller.

14 Unbolt the rear cover from the transmission and remove it (Fig. 6.24).

15 Withdraw the speedometer worm drive gear from the rear end of the mainshaft.

16 Withdraw the reverse gear from the mainshaft (Fig. 6.25).

17 Hold the reverse idler gear in position and withdraw the reverse idler shaft.

18 Unscrew and remove the nut from the rear end of the countershaft. To hold the mainshaft still while unscrewing the nut, temporarily refit the output flange and lock it with a rod or hold it with a large wrench.

19 Prise off the countershaft reverse gear using a screwdriver.

20 Remove the shift forks from the grooves in the sleeves of the synchroniser units (Fig. 6.26).

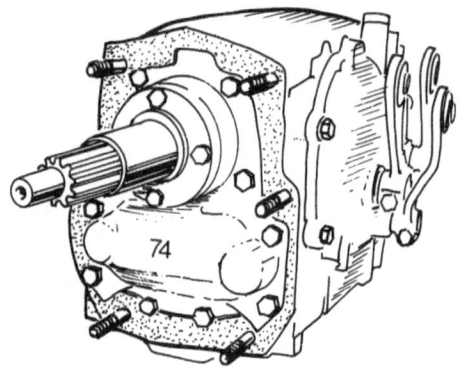

Fig. 6.22. Transmission front cover (74) (Sec. 10)

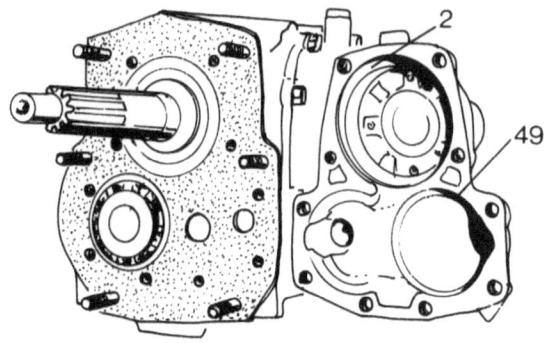

Fig. 6.23. Location of spacer (compensating) washers in transmission front cover (Sec. 10)

2   Washer for input shaft   49   Washer for countershaft

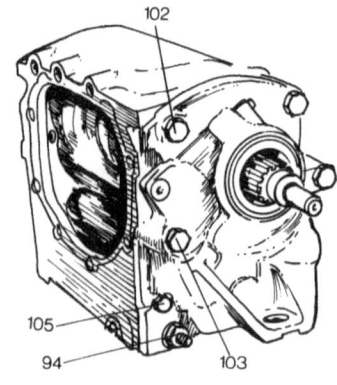

Fig. 6.24. Transmission rear cover (Sec. 10)

94 Stud   103 Bolt
102 Bolt   105 Bolt

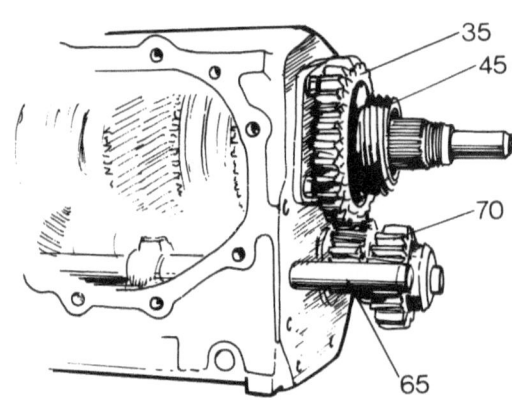

Fig. 6.25. Location of components after removal of rear cover (Sec. 10)

35   Mainshaft reverse gear   65   Selector rod for reverse gear
45   Speedometer drive gear   70   Reverse idler gear

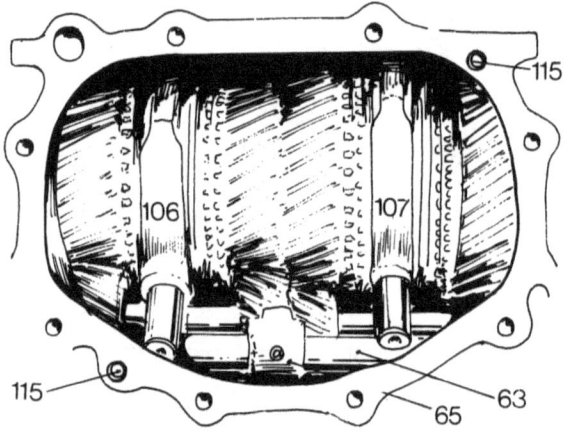

Fig. 6.26. Shift fork identification (Sec. 10)

63   Reverse selector rod   107   1st/2nd shift fork
65   Reverse selector dog   115   Locating dowel
106 3rd/4th shift fork

21 Drive out the tension pin which holds the selector dog (63) to the reverse selector shaft and then push the dog as far forward as possible (Fig. 6.27).
22 Pull the reverse selector rod from the transmission and remove the dog.
23 Lock two gears together by moving one of the synchro. units and then from the front face of the casing unscrew and remove the countershaft bearing ring nut using a 'C' spanner or similar tool.

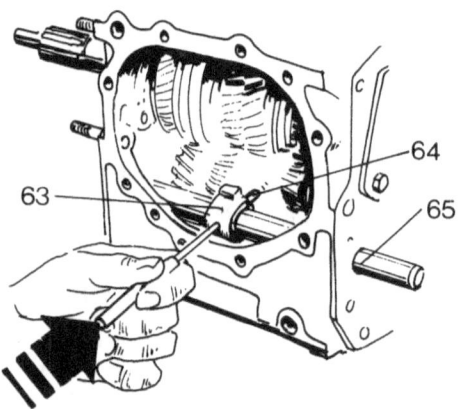

Fig. 6.27. Removing reverse selector dog roll pin (Sec. 10)

63   Reverse dog   65   Reverse selector rod
64   Roll pin

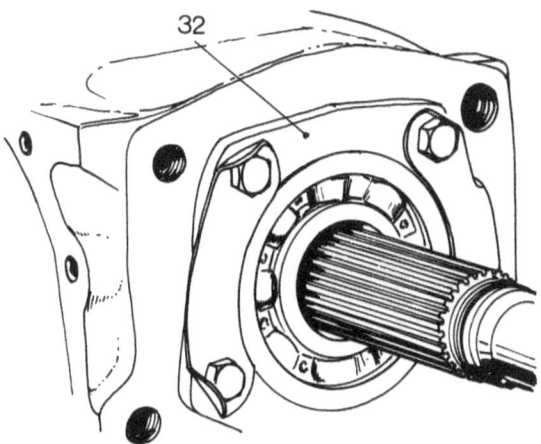

Fig. 6.28. Mainshaft rear bearing retainer plate (32) (Sec. 10)

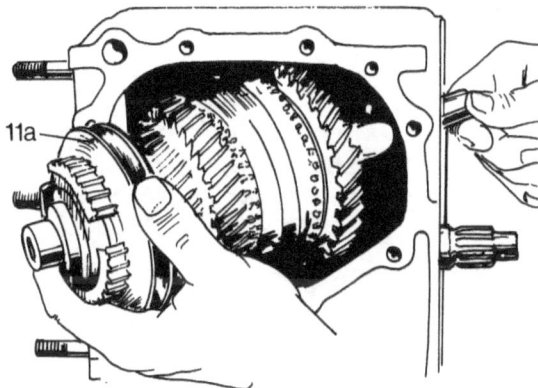

Fig. 6.29. Removing the mainshaft assembly (Sec. 10)

11a   3rd/4th synchro sleeve

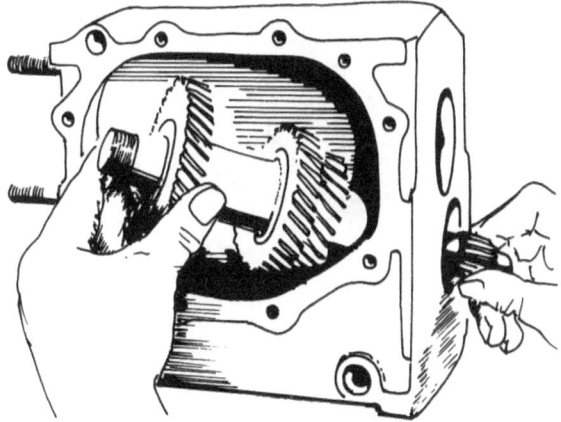

Fig. 6.30. Removing the countershaft assembly (Sec. 10)

24 Unscrew and remove the retaining plate from the rear face of the casing (Fig. 6.28).
25 Withdraw the front and rear bearings from the countershaft.
26 Withdraw the mainshaft rear bearing.
27 Lift the rear end of the mainshaft, taking care not to displace the 1st gear from its needle bearings and then pull the input shaft out of the front of the transmission. Take care to retain the 4th gear synchro ring and the needle bearings (input shaft to mainshaft).
28 Move the 3rd/4th synchro sleeve into 3rd speed position, push the mainshaft assembly towards the rear and then incline its front end upwards and remove it forward (Fig. 6.29).
29 Remove the countershaft assembly in a similar way (Fig. 6.30).

30 Examine all the components for wear or damage, particularly the gear teeth, bearings, selector components and the synchro unit sleeve grooves.
31 If there has been a history of noisy gear changing, renew the synchro unit concerned.

11 Mainshaft - dismantling and reassembly

1   With the mainshaft removed from the transmission casing, temporarily refit the output flange to its rear end and then grip the flange in a vice so that the shaft is held vertically.
2   Unscrew and remove the ring nut on the front of the mainshaft using a 'C' spanner or another suitable tool (Fig. 6.31).
3   Remove the 3rd/4th synchro unit from the front of the mainshaft (Fig. 6.32).
4   Remove the thrust washer (3) (Fig. 6.33).
5   Remove the 3rd speed gear (14) and the needle roller cage (15) (Fig. 6.34).
6   Remove the mainshaft from the vice and from its rear end pull off the thrust washer (28) (Fig. 6.35).
7   Remove the 1st speed gear (27) and the needle roller cage (26) (Fig. 6.36).
8   Remove the 1st gear needle bearing inner race from the mainshaft.
9   Remove the thrust washer (24) and the 1st/2nd synchro ring and synchro unit (Figs. 6.37 and 6.38).
10 Remove the thrust washer (20) (Fig. 6.39).
11 Remove the 2nd speed gear (19) the synchro ring (21) and the needle roller cage (18) (Fig. 6.40).
12 If the synchroniser units are suspect, check them for wear by first

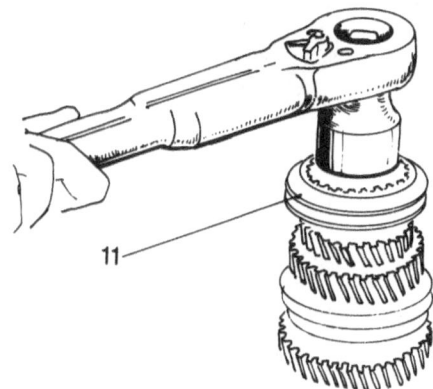

Fig. 6.31. Unscrewing nut from front of mainshaft (Sec. 11)

11 3rd/4th synchro unit

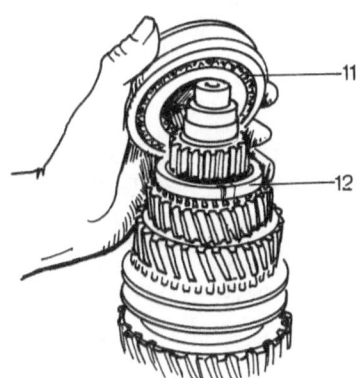

Fig. 6.32. Removing 3rd/4th synchro from front of mainshaft (Sec. 11)

11 Synchro unit   12 Synchro ring

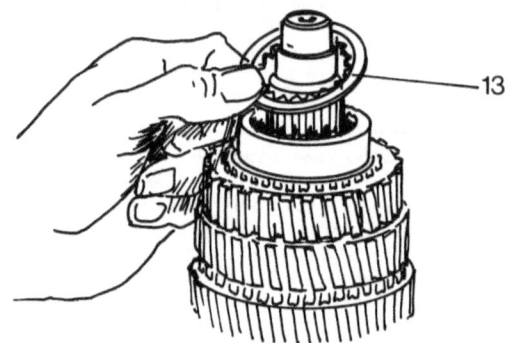

Fig. 6.33. Removing brass thrust washer (13) from mainshaft (Sec. 11)

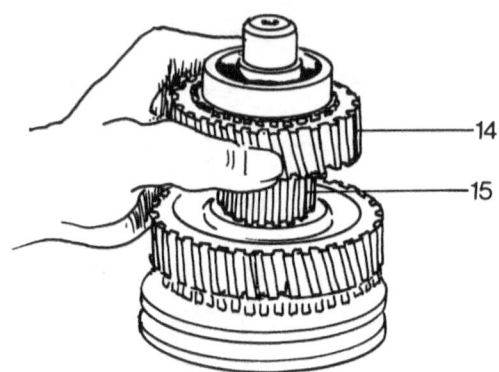

Fig. 6.34. Removing 3rd speed gear (14) and needle roller cage (15) from mainshaft (Sec. 11)

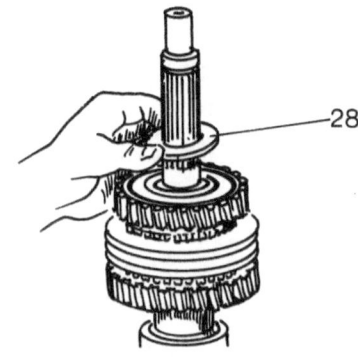

Fig. 6.35. Removing 1st gear thrust washer (28) from mainshaft (Sec. 11)

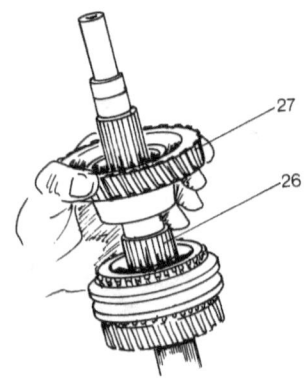

Fig. 6.36. Removing 1st speed gear (27) and needle roller cage (26) from mainshaft (Sec. 11)

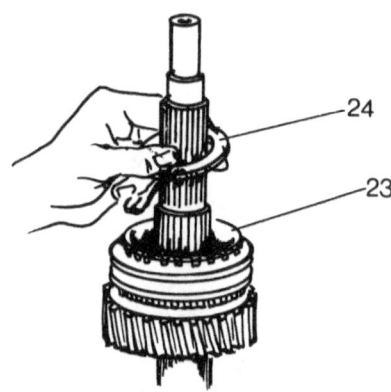

Fig. 6.37. Removing 1st/2nd synchro unit thrust washer (24) and 1st speed synchro ring (23) from mainshaft (Sec. 11)

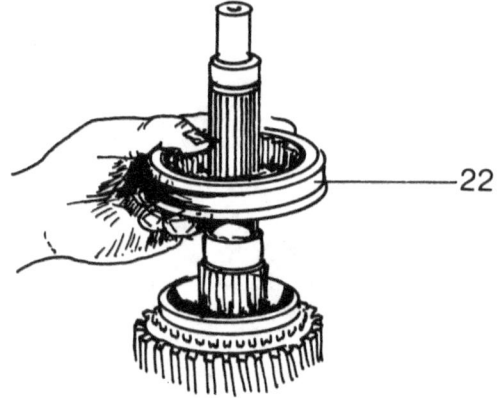

Fig. 6.38. Removing 1st/2nd synchro unit (22) from mainshaft (Sec. 11)

pressing the synchro ring onto its respective gear cone and then use a feeler blade to determine the clearance between the two sets of teeth as shown. If the clearance exceeds 0.020 in (0.5 mm) renew the synchro ring (Fig. 6.41).

13 If the synchro unit is to be dismantled to renew worn components, first inspect the unit to see whether it incorporates coil or circular type springs.

14 *To dismantle a coil spring type synchro unit,* wrap a cloth round it and then press the hub out of the sleeve. As the hub is ejected so the keys, balls and springs will be displaced.

15 Renew the components as necessary and then reassemble them by inserting the springs and keys into the hub and, while holding the keys depressed, partially insert the hub into the sleeve. Locate one ball at a time and when all three are fitted, push the hub fully home. Fit the hubs into the sleeves in accordance with the diagrams. Note that the 1st/2nd synchro keys have a chamfer on one corner. Make sure that the chamfer is towards the 2nd gear wheel (Figs. 6.42, 6.43, 6.44, 6.45 and 6.46).

16 *To dismantle a circular spring type synchro unit,* push the hub from the sleeve and extract the keys and springs (Fig. 6.47).

17 Renew components as necessary and then reassemble them so that the hub to sleeve relationship is in accordance with the transmission

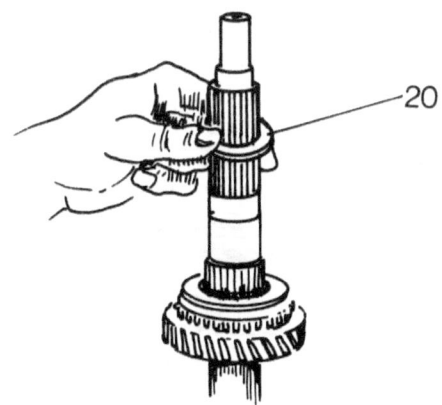

Fig. 6.39. Removing 2nd speed thrust washer (20) from mainshaft (Sec. 11)

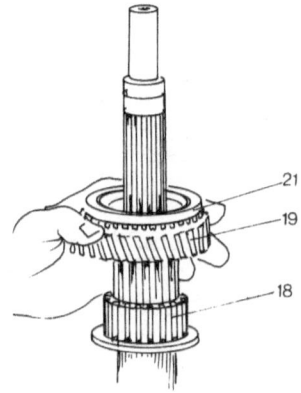

Fig. 6.40. Removing synchro ring (21), 2nd speed gear (19) and needle roller cage (18) (Sec. 11)

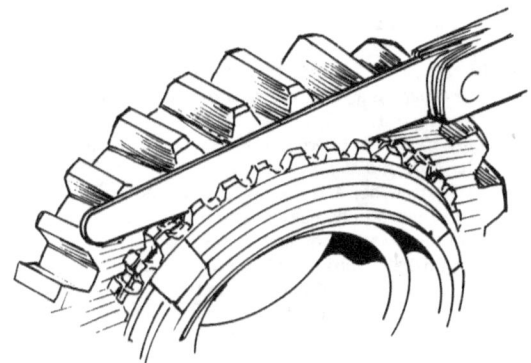

Fig. 6.41. Checking a synchro ring for wear (Sec. 11)

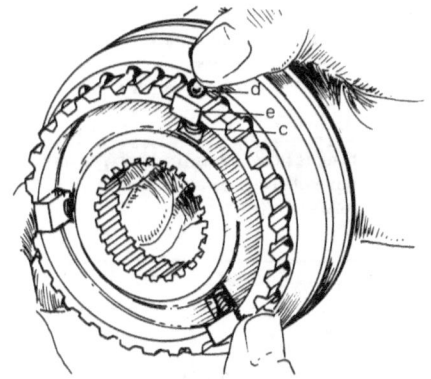

Fig. 6.42. Assembling a coil spring type synchro unit (Sec. 11)
c = spring   d = ball   e = key

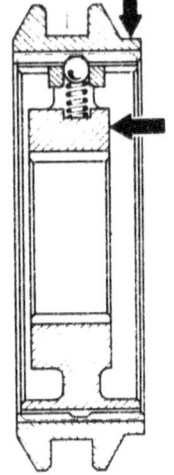

Fig.6.43. Synchro unit for 1st/2nd speed on type G76/18 transmissions. 1 - 2 indicates direction of fitting towards gears (Sec. 11)

Fig. 6.44. Synchro unit for 1st/2nd speeds on type G76/27 transmission. 1 - 2 indicates direction of fitting towards gears (Sec. 11)

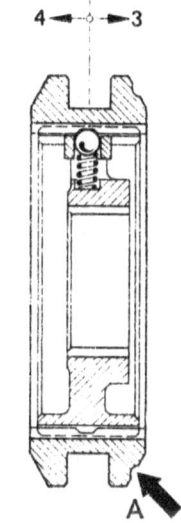

Fig. 6.45. Synchro unit for 3rd/4th speed. 3 - 4 indicates direction of fitting towards gears (Sec. 11)

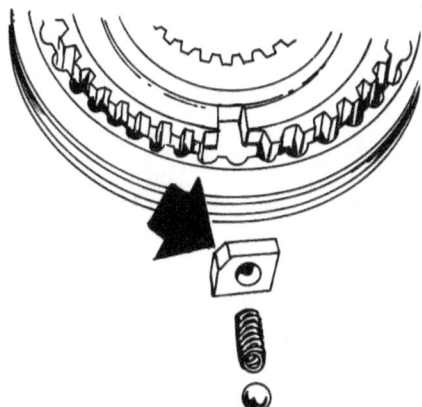

Fig. 6.46. Chamfer on key in synchro unit (coil spring type) (Sec. 11)

model and gear speed as shown in the diagrams (Figs. 6.48 and 6.49).

18 Make sure that the circular spring right angular ends do not engage in the same key and that they do in fact run in opposite directions on each side of the hub (Fig. 6.50).

19 With all components, renewed and clean, reassemble the mainshaft. Commence by securing the front end of the mainshaft in a vice which has been fitted with protection jaws.

20 To the rear end of the mainshaft fit the needle roller cage, the 2nd gear with the synchro ring and the thrust washer.

21 Fit the 1st/2nd synchro unit to the mainshaft making sure that the flange on its sleeve is towards the rear of the shaft.

22 Fit the synchro ring and the thrust washer.

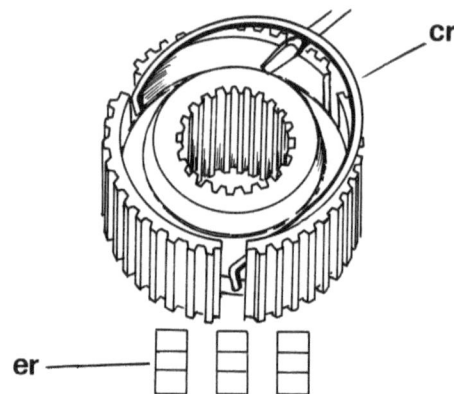

Fig. 6.47. Circular spring type synchro hub (Sec. 11)

cr Spring   er Key

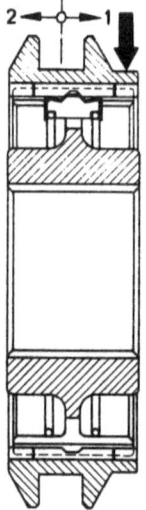 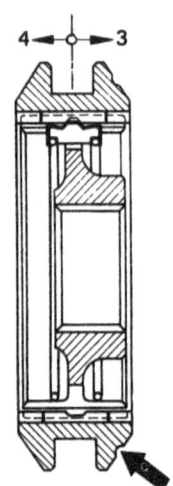

Fig. 6.48. Circular spring type synchro unit (1st/2nd speed). 1 - 2 indicates direction of fitting towards gears (Sec. 11)

Fig. 6.49. Circular spring type synchro unit (3rd/4th speed) (Sec. 11). 3 - 4 indicates direction of fitting towards gears

Fig. 6.50. Engagement of ends of circular springs in synchro hub (Sec. 11)

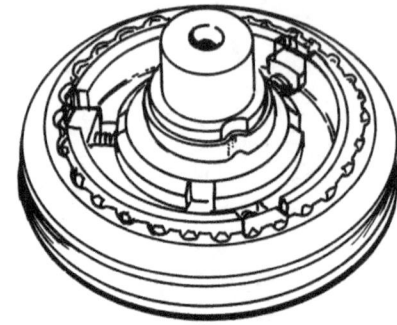

Fig. 6.51. Mainshaft front nut (ring type) (Sec. 11)

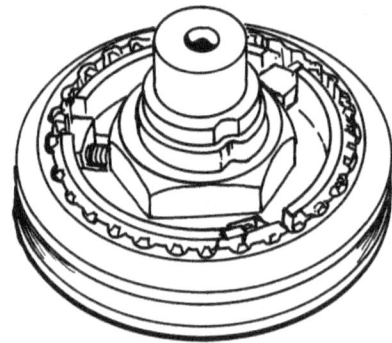

Fig. 6.52. Mainshaft front nut (hexagon nut) (Sec. 11)

23 Heat the inner bush of the 1st gear and tap it into position on the mainshaft.

24 Fit the needle roller cage and the 1st speed gear.

25 Fit the thrust washer up against the face of the 1st gear and then fit and tighten the ring nut.

26 Turn the mainshaft upside down and to the front end of the shaft fit the needle roller cage and the 3rd gear.

27 Fit the brass thrust washer and the 3rd speed synchro ring.

28 Fit the 3rd/4th synchro unit making sure that the side with the machined recess on the sleeve is towards the 3rd gear.

29 Screw on the mainshaft front nut. Temporarily fit the output flange so that it can be secured in a vice while the nut is tightened to the specified torque wrench setting. Stake the nut or lockplate according to the type used (Figs. 6.51 and 6.52).

30 The mainshaft assembly is now ready for refitting as described in Section 13.

12 Countershaft - dismantling and reassembly

1   Support the 3rd gear on the shaft and press the countershaft from it (Fig. 6.53).

2   Extract the Woodruff key.

3   No further dismantling is possible as the shaft, complete with the 1st and 2nd gear, is renewable only as an assembly (Fig. 6.54).

4   Reassembly is a reversal of dismantling.

13 Transmission - reassembly

1   With the casing on the bench, lower the countershaft assembly into position.

2   Move the synchro sleeve for the 3rd/4th speeds into its 3rd gear position and then lower the mainshaft into the gear casing keeping it at an inclined angle and inserting it from front to rear. Make sure that

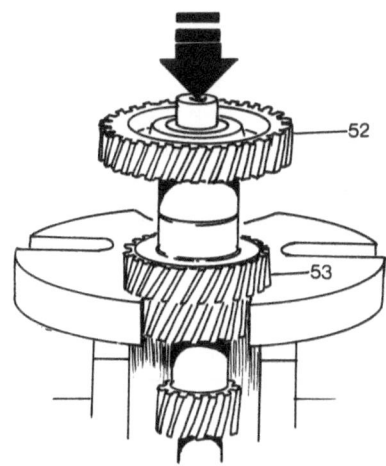

Fig. 6.53. Pressing countershaft from gear (Sec. 12)

52   Constant mesh gear   53   Countershaft 3rd speed

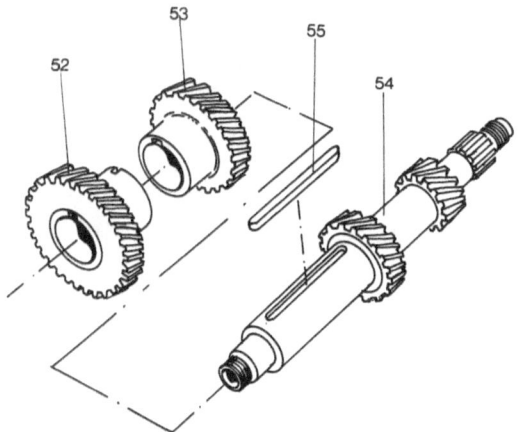

Fig. 6.54. Countergear components (Sec. 12)

52   Constant speed gear   54   1st/2nd speed gears
53   Countershaft 3rd speed   55   Key

Fig. 6.55. Countershaft front bearing and ring nut (Sec. 13)

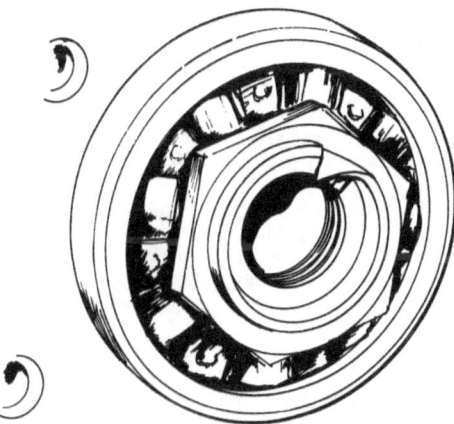

Fig. 6.56. Countershaft front bearing and alternative hexagon nut
(Sec. 13)

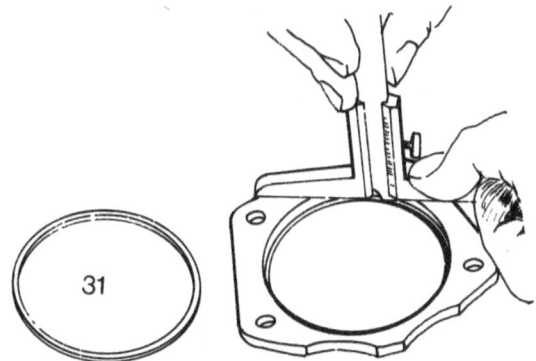

Fig. 6.57. Measuring mainshaft rear bearing retainer plate recess
(Sec. 13)

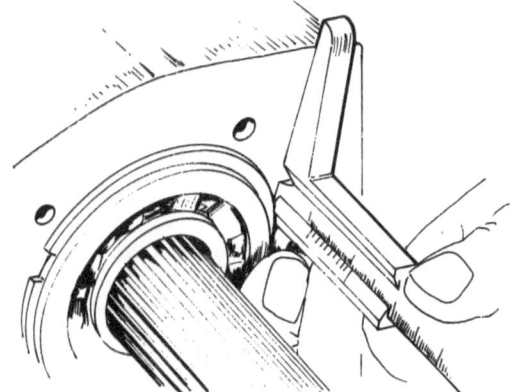

Fig. 6.58. Measuring mainshaft rear bearing circlip thickness (Sec. 13)

1st gear does not slide off its needle bearing cage during this operation.
3   Fit the needle roller cage into the recess in the input shaft and fit the 4th gear synchro ring to the shaft. If the bearing was removed, refit it now.
4   Fit the input shaft through the front of the casing and then connect the mainshaft to it.
5   Fit the rear bearing to the end of the mainshaft. Tap the bearing into position while maintaining pressure on the front end of the input shaft.
6   Lift the countershaft slightly and fit the front and rear bearings to it.
7   Lock up the gear train by engaging two gears at once and then

tighten the ring nut on the front end of the countershaft to the specified torque wrench setting, and lock it in position. On later versions, a hexagon nut is used (Figs. 6.55 and 6.56).
8   At this stage, spacing washers must now be selected to provide the mainshaft with the minimum endfloat. To do this, measure the depth of the recess in the rear bearing retainer plate and then the thickness of the rear bearing outer track circlip. Subtract one dimension from the other and then obtain a spacer washer which equals in thickness the dimensions just calculated. A remaining endfloat not exceeding 0.0020 in (0.05 mm) is acceptable (Figs. 6.57 and 6.58).
9   Bolt on the retainer plate with the selected spacer washer and bend down the tabs of the lock plates.

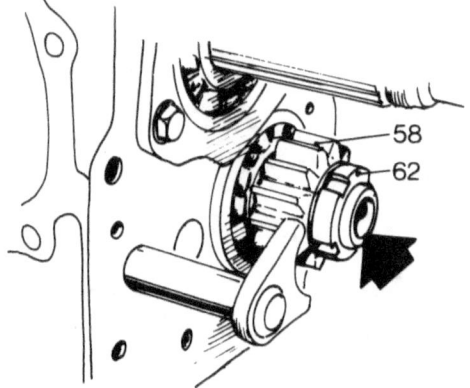

Fig. 6.59. Countershaft rear nut (62) and reverse gear (58) (Sec. 13)

10 Fit the reverse gear to the countershaft, screw on and tighten the nut. Hold the mainshaft still when tightening the nut to torque by temporarily installing the output flange. Fit the mainshaft reverse gear and speedometer drive gear and then the reverse idle shaft and gear (Fig. 6.59).
11 Bolt on the rear cover, fit the output flange and tighten the securing nut to the specified torque wrench setting.
12 Select a spacing washer to provide the input shaft with the minimum endfloat. This is carried out in exactly the same way as described in paragraph 8.
13 Bolt on the transmission front cover complete with the selected spacer washer. Remember to use a new seal and gasket.
14 Place a new paper gasket on the side cover flange of the transmission casing.
15 Fit the reverse selector rod and dog. Pin the dog to the rod. Fit the shift forks to the synchro sleeve grooves.
16 Set the rod/dog exactly centrally and then offer the side cover into position. Make sure that the reverse speed selector lever engages with the dog on the selector rod and the two shift forks engage in the rockers.
17 Tighten the side cover bolts evenly in a diametrically opposite sequence.
18 Fit the thrust washer and circlip to the reverse selector shaft stub and then fit the reverse shift lever referring to the appropriate adjustment diagram in Sections 3 to 8 as applicable.
19 Check the selection of all gear positions and then fill with transmission fluid.
20 Bolt on the clutch bellhousing and then fit the clutch release mechanism.

14 Five speed transmission

1   The operations described in this Chapter apply generally to the five speed transmission as well as four speed versions.
2   Due to the location of the 5th speed (Overdrive) gear at the rear of the mainshaft, the transmission is longer by reason of the extension housing and heavier because of the additional components.
3   Keep this in mind when preparing equipment for removal of the transmission.

15 Fault diagnosis - manual transmission

Part B - automatic transmission

16 General description

The automatic transmission is a four speed unit of Mercedes-Benz manufacture.
It comprises a torque converter in series with a four speed planetary gear train.
Due to the complexities of the unit, operations should be limited to those described in this Chapter (Fig. 6.60).
Always observe absolute cleanliness when carrying out work on the automatic transmission as dirt entering the hydraulic system and valve block will cause faulty operation.

17 Fluid level - checking and topping up

1   Check the fluid level after a run when the transmission fluid will be at operating temperature.
2   Position the car on a level surface, selector lever in 'P', handbrake fully on and engine idling. The engine should have been idling for a minimum of two minutes.
3   Withdraw the automatic transmission dipstick, wipe it clean, re-insert it, withdraw it and read off the fluid level.
4   If the level is between the upper and lower marks the fluid level is correct. If necessary, top it up to the specified level with the recommended fluid.
5   As a guide to the topping up requirement, the distance between the low and high marks on the dipstick represents ¾ Imp pt (9/10 US pt, 0.3 litre) of fluid.

18 Fluid and filter - renewal

1   At the specified mileage intervals (or earlier, on cars subject to particularly arduous conditions) the transmission fluid should be drained and the filter renewed.
2   Have the fluid at the normal operating temperature but with the engine switched off.
3   Place a container under the car and then disconnect the fluid filler pipe from the transmission oil pan. Let the fluid drain out, taking care as it will be very hot.
4   Now turn the crankshaft until the drain plug on the torque converter becomes visible through the cut-out in the grille at the base of the converter housing.
5   Unscrew the drain plug and let the fluid run into the container. On some units a cut-out is not made in the grille, in which case unbolt the grille complete (photo).
6   Unbolt and remove the oil pan (photo).
7   Drain out the remaining fluid from the oil pan and wipe it out with a non-fluffy rag.
8   The filter is attached to the underside of the transmission and may be of a rectangular or circular type depending upon the transmission model (Figs. 6.61 and 6.62).
9   The circular type of filter is retained by a single bolt while the rectangular type has several securing bolts.
10 Refitting is a reversal of removal but make sure that the seals on

Symptom	Reason/s
Weak or ineffective synchromesh	Synchronising cones worn, split or damaged. Baulk ring synchromesh keys worn or damaged.
Jumps out of gear	Gearbox coupling dogs badly worn. Selector fork rod groove badly worn in synchro. sleeve.
Excessive noise	Incorrect grade of oil in gearbox or oil level too low. Ball or needle roller bearings worn or damaged. Gear teeth excessively worn or damaged. Mainshaft or countershaft washers too thin allowing excessive end play.
Excessive difficulty in engaging gear	Clutch pedal adjustment incorrect (see Chapter 5).

18.5 Air intake grille at base of torque converter housing

18.6 Oil pan removal

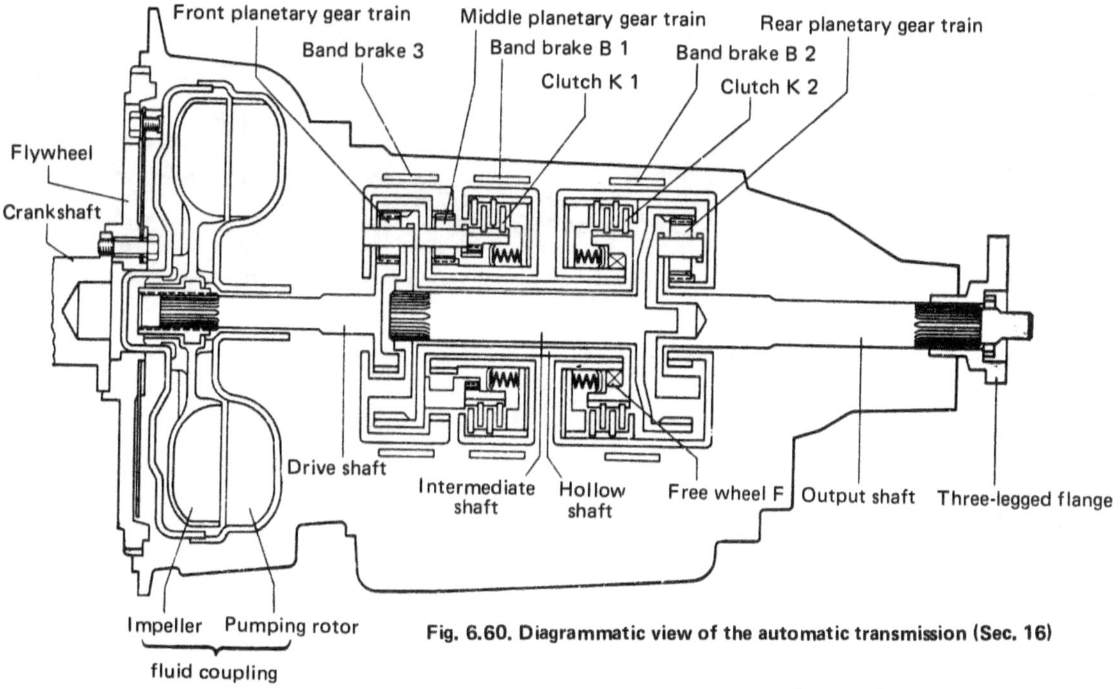

Front planetary gear train   Middle planetary gear train   Rear planetary gear train
Band brake 3   Band brake B 1   Band brake B 2
Clutch K 1   Clutch K 2

Flywheel

Crankshaft

Drive shaft

Intermediate shaft   Hollow shaft   Free wheel F   Output shaft   Three-legged flange

Impeller   Pumping rotor

fluid coupling

Fig. 6.60. Diagrammatic view of the automatic transmission (Sec. 16)

Fig. 6.61. Automatic transmission filter (oil pan removed) (Sec. 18)

3 Torque converter drain plug   7 Filter element
5 Cooler pipe   8 Filter securing screw
6 Cooler pipe

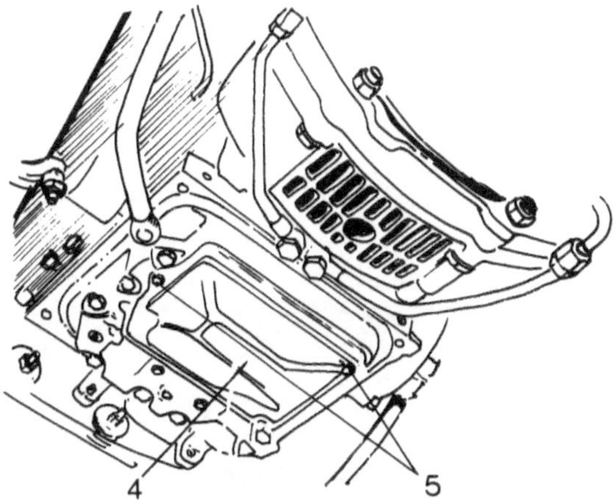

Fig. 6.62. Alternative type rectangular fluid filter (Sec. 18)

4 Filter element   5 Securing bolts

the filler pipe union and the torque converter drain plug are in good condition. On some cars, the filter incorporates a semi-circular baffle on its lower face. This is designed to prevent fluid surge at low oil level conditions or during rapid acceleration. Make sure that the open end of the baffle faces the rear of the transmission (photos).

11 Fill the transmission with 5.3 Imp pints (6.3 US pints, 3 litres) of fresh automatic transmission fluid. Start the engine and let it idle in 'P' and slowly pour in a further 1.3 Imp pints (1.6 US pints, 0.75 litres) of fluid.

12 After the first run on the road, check the fluid level again when hot.

19 Speed selector linkage - adjustment

1 *On cars with type K4C 025 transmission and steering column shift,* loosen the locknut on the balljoint (2) and disconnect the selector rod (1) from the selector lever (3) (Fig. 6.63).

2 Set the lever (7) on the transmission to 'N' and also the steering wheel control. Adjust the length of the selector rod by unscrewing the

balljoint so that it can be fitted to the ball stud on the intermediate lever without any tendency to deflect the levers from their previously set positions. Tighten the locknut.

3 *On cars with type K4C 025 transmission and floor shift,* disconnect selector rod (5) from the lever on the side of the transmission (Fig. 6.64).

4 Move the transmission lever and the shift control to 'N'.

5 Release the locknut on the selector rod and adjust the length of the rod until it can be fitted directly to the transmission selector lever without any tendency to deflect it from its 'N' setting. Tighten the locknut. Adjust the speed range indicator if necessary by turning the knurled nut on the cable (Fig. 6.65).

6 *On cars with type K4A 025 transmission and steering column shift,* disconnect the selector rod (7) and loosen the locknut on the balljoint (Fig. 6.66).

7 Set the selector lever on the transmission and the control on the steering column to 'N'. Adjust the length of the selector rod by turning the balljoint so that the rod can be reconnected to the intermediate lever without any tendency to deflect the lever from its previously set position.

8 Now adjust the short balljointed rod (2) if necessary, so that the

18.10A Filter removed

18.10B Filter baffle and securing screw

18.10C Filter locating lug

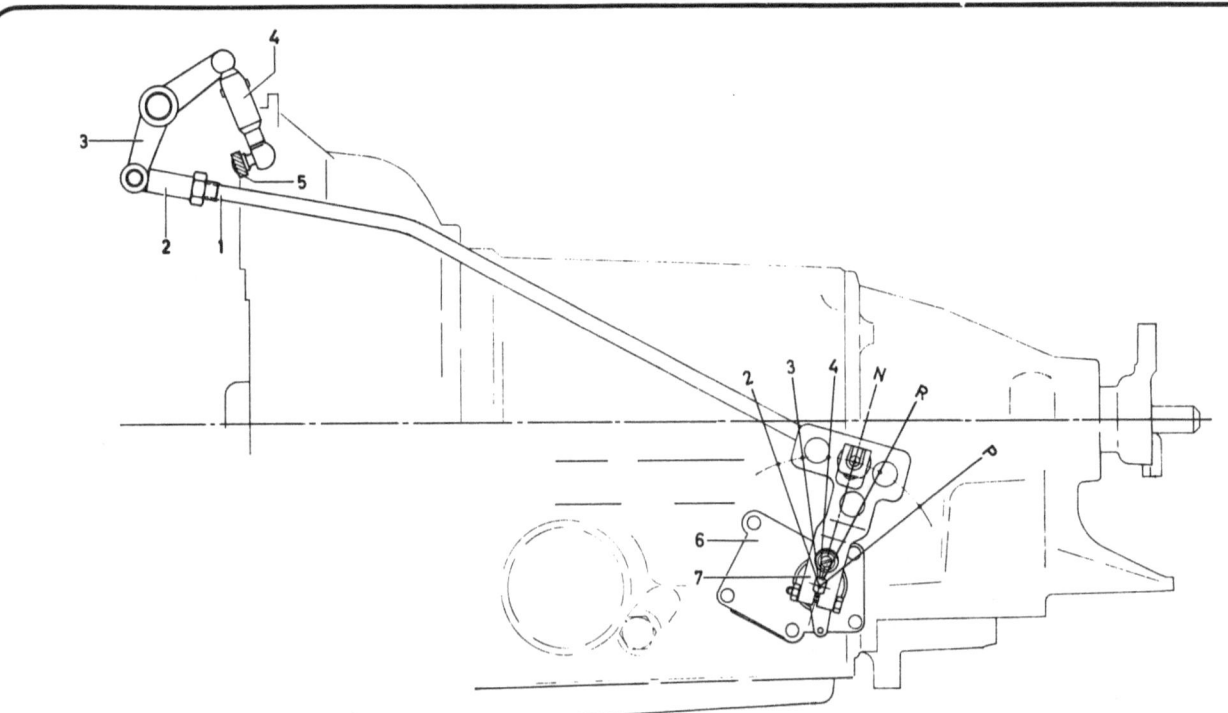

Fig. 6.63. Speed selector linkage (type K4C 025 - steering column shift (Sec. 19)

| 1 | Selector rod | 3 | Intermediate lever | 5 | Ball stud | 7 | Speed range selector |
| 2 | Balljoint socket | 4 | Spring-loaded connecting piece | 6 | Starter inhibitor and reversing lamp switch | | lever |

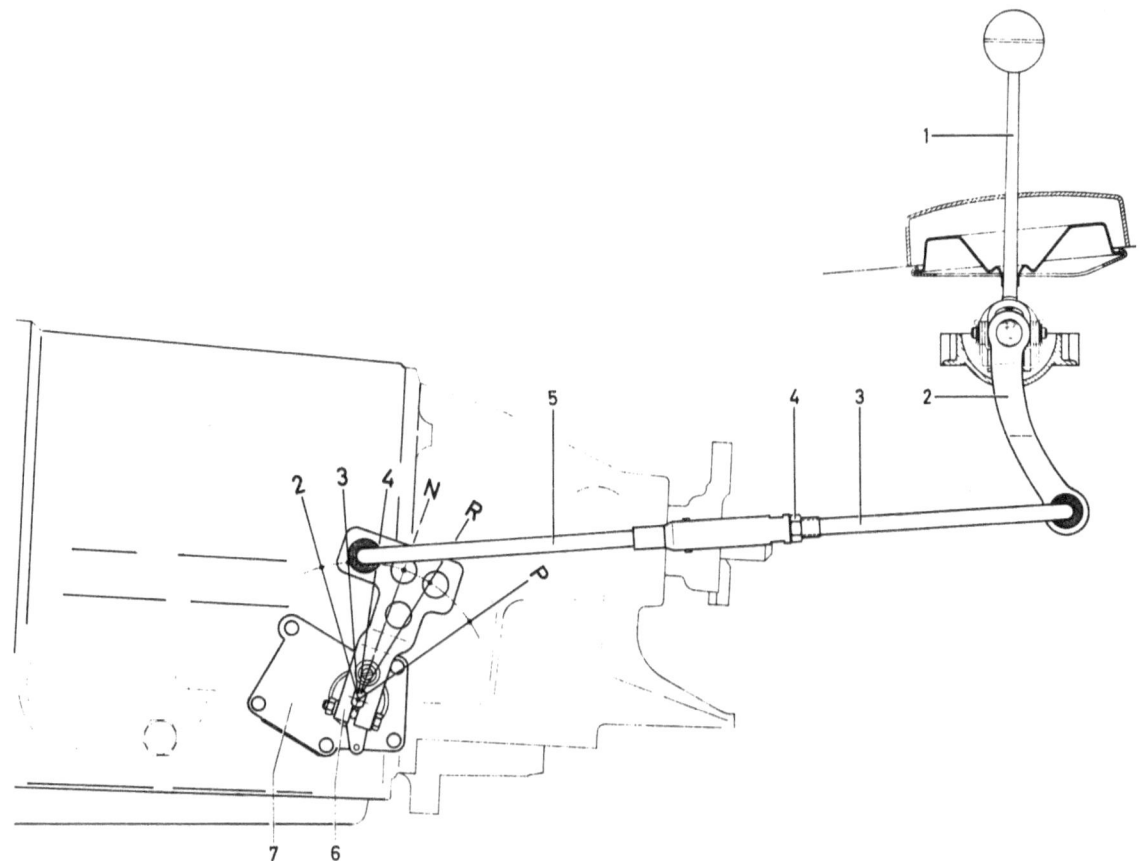

Fig. 6.64. Speed selector linkage (type K4C 025 - floor shift) (Sec. 19)

1   Hand control lever   5   Selector rod
2   Lower shift lever   6   Range selector lever
3   Selector rod   7   Starter inhibitor switch
4   Locknut

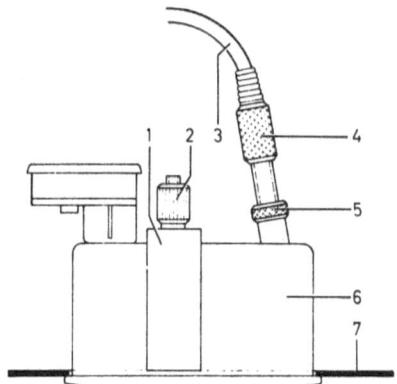

Fig. 6.65. Speed range indicator adjustment (Sec. 19)

1   Clamp bracket   5   Locknut
2   Clamp nut   6   Housing
3   Control cable   7   Instrument panel
4   Knurled nut

lever on the starter inhibitor switch is located exactly between the two lines marked on the switch.

9   *On cars with type K4A 025 transmission and floor shift,* disconnect and remove the selector rod (4) from the two levers (2 and 5). Set the speed range selector lever (6) and the hand control (1) to 'N' (Fig. 6.67).

10 Loosen the pinch bolts on the supplementary lever and move the supplementary lever on the range selector lever until the alignment mark on the upper lever is centralised with the middle of the lower lever. Tighten the pinch bolts (Fig. 6.67).

11 Adjust the length of the selector rod (4) until it can be connected to both levers (2 and 5) without any tendency to deflect them from their previously set positions.

12 Now set the switch cable (by moving the two outer conduit locknuts) so that the arm on the starter inhibitor/reverse lamp switch is between the two marks on the switch body.

20 Starter inhibitor/reverse lamp switch (K4C 025 transmission) - adjustment

1   Disconnect the selector rod and then move the speed range lever on the side of the transmission to 'N'. Check that the pinch bolt (6) is tight (Fig. 6.68).

2   Loosen the screw (3) and insert a pin (5) through the lever (5) into the hole in the transmission shift cover. Without moving the position of the lever, tighten the screw (3).

3   Set the hand control in 'N' and reconnect the selector rod. Check operation of switch in 'P' and 'N' for ability to start and in 'R' for reverse light operation.

21 Kickdown switch - adjustment

1   On type K4C 025 transmission, with the accelerator pedal depressed so that it rests against the kickdown switch, there should be a clearance of between 0.12 and 0.16 in (3.0 and 4.0 mm) between the throttle valve lever and the full load stop on the venturi control unit (fuel injection) or throttle valve stop (crburettors).

2   When the pedal is pushed beyond this point, the throttle valve lever

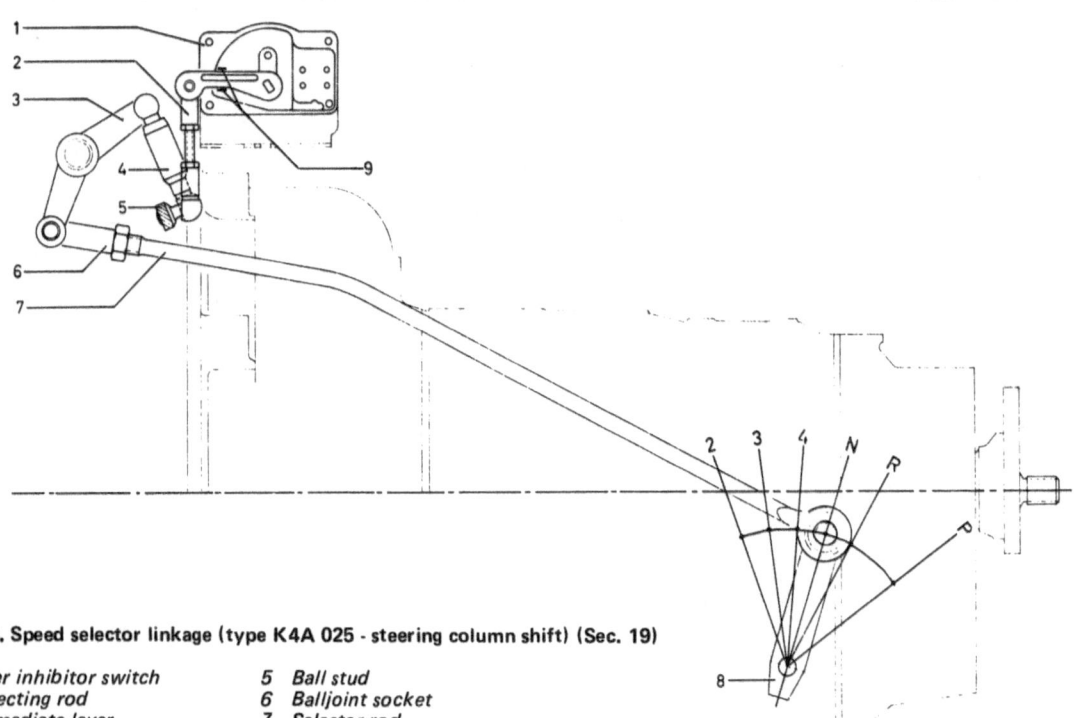

Fig. 6.66. Speed selector linkage (type K4A 025 - steering column shift) (Sec. 19)

1 Starter inhibitor switch
2 Connecting rod
3 Intermediate lever
4 Spring loaded connecting piece

5 Ball stud
6 Balljoint socket
7 Selector rod
8 Speed range selector lever

Fig. 6.67. Speed selector linkage (type K4A 025 - floor shift) (Sec. 19)
Inset - close up of supplementary lever (5) range selector lever (6)
(a) alignment marks

1 Hand control
2 Lower shift lever
3 Link eye
4 Selector rod
5 Supplementary lever

6 Speed range selector lever
7 Control cable
8 Outer conduit threaded stop
9 Starter inhibitor/reverse lamp
   switch

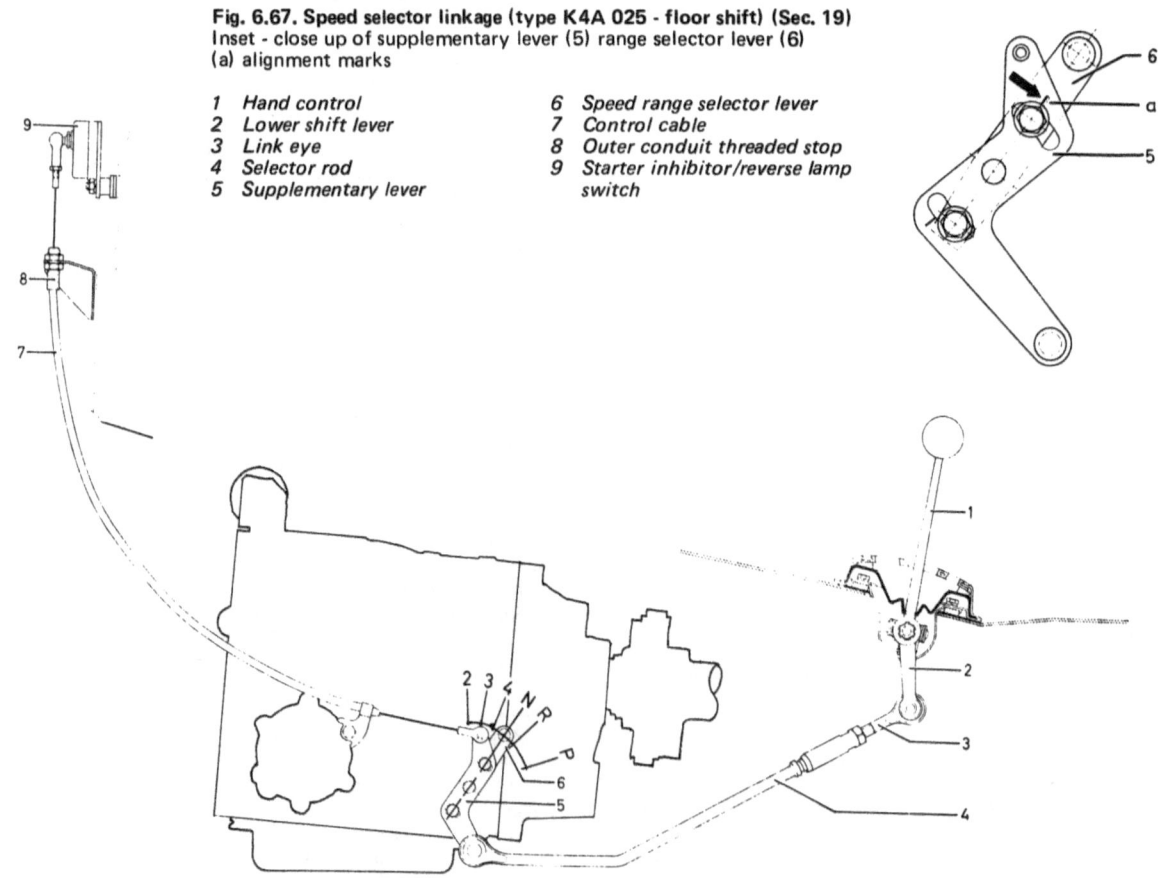

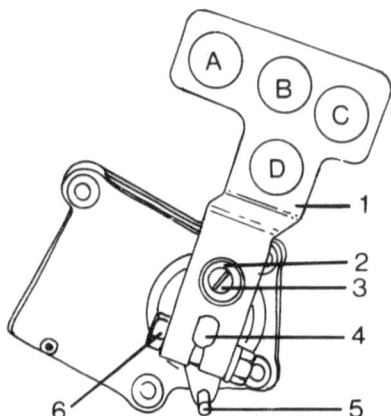

Fig. 6.68. Starter inhibitor/reverse lamp switch on K4C 025
transmission (Sec. 20)

1	Selector range lever	4	Shaft
2	Washer	5	Alignment pin
3	Adjusting screw	6	Pinch bolt

A Connecting hole for 230/8, 250/8, 280 S/8, 280 SE/8
B Connecting hole for lhd 230/8, 250/8
C Connecting hole for rhd 230/8, 250/8
D Connecting hole for lhd 280 S/8, 280 SE/8

should move against the full load stop.

3   Adjust if necessary, by releasing the pinch bolt on the clamp on the
return lever of the accelerator pedal rod to set the throttle lever
opening and then alter the position of the kickdown switch to
compensate.

4   Adjustment on type K4A 025 transmission is very similar except
that there should be a clearance of only 0.04 in (1.0 mm) between the
throttle lever and the full load stop when the pedal is resting against
the kickdown switch (Fig. 6.69).

22 Automatic transmission - removal and refitting

1   The automatic transmission can be removed leaving the engine in
position in the car, or together with the engine as described in Chapter
1, Section 6.

2   Removal of the transmission leaving the engine in the car is as
follows: Position the car over an inspection pit or jack up the rear of
the car sufficiently high to permit the torque converter housing to
pass under it towards the rear.

3   Disconnect the battery. Drain the transmission fluid (photos).

4   Disconnect the control cable from the lever on the starter
inhibitor/reverse lamp switch on the engine compartment rear
bulkhead (photo).

5   Disconnect the transmission cooler lines from the transmission and
plug the openings.

6   Disconnect the earth strap from the upper corner of the torque
converter housing or bodyshell (photo).

7   Disconnect the vacuum hose which runs between the transmission

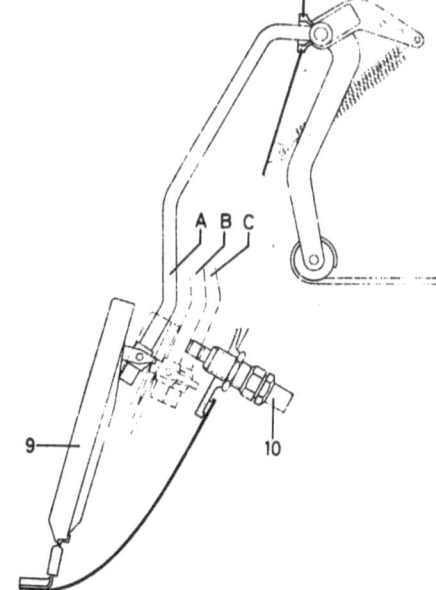

Fig. 6.69. Kickdown switch adjustment diagram (Sec. 20)

A	Idle speed	9	Accelerator pedal
B	Full throttle position	10	Kickdown switch
C	Kickdown		

and the intake manifold.

8   Working under the car, disconnect the speedometer drive cable
from the transmission.

9   Unbolt and remove the fluid filter/dipstick tube from the rearmost
manifold bolt (photo).

10 Disconnect the leads from the multi-terminal block on the left-
hand side of the transmission (photos).

11 Support the weight of the transmission on a jack and a block of
wood used as an insulator.

12 Remove the shield from above the exhaust pipes at the side of
the transmission.

13 Unbolt the transmission rear flexible mounting and crossmember
or support plate according to type (photos).

14 Disconnect the propeller shaft front flexible coupling by unbolting it from the transmission output flange, push the shaft upwards
and lock it with a piece of wood.

15 Disconnect the speed selector control rod from the lever on the
left-hand side of the transmission.

16 Disconnect the downshift cable from the transmission.

17 Unbolt and remove the cover plate from the lower front face of the
torque converter housing (photo).

18 The three pairs of bolts which secure the driveplate to the torque
converter must now be unscrewed. First mark the relative position of
the torque converter to the driveplate and starter ring gear using quick
drying paint.

22.3A Fluid filler pipe disconnected to drain
oil pan

22.3B Torque converter drain plug

22.4 Starter inhibitor/reverse lamp switch

22.6 Earth strap connection to body

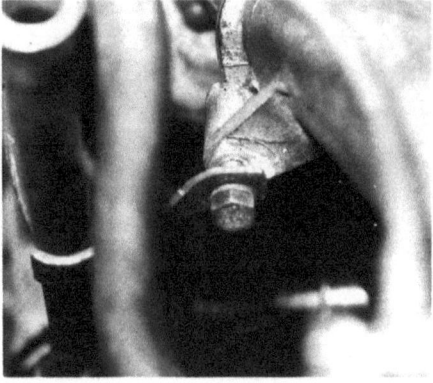
22.9 Fluid filler tube/dipstick attachment to intake manifold

22.10A Multi-terminal block cover on side of transmission

22.10B Multi-terminal block (cover removed)

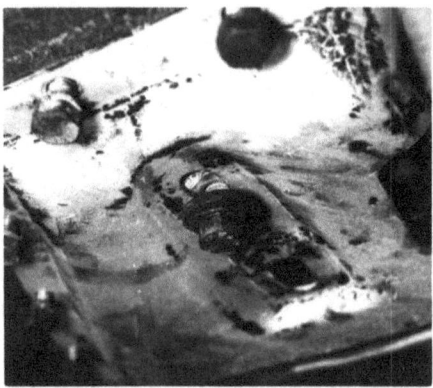
22.13A Transmission rear flexible mounting bolt and support plate

22.13B Rear support plate

22.13C Spacer located between flexible mounting and support plate

22.13D Transmission rear flexible mounting

22.17 Torque converter housing cover plate

22.19 Driveplate to torque converter bolts

22.23A Method of securing torque converter in position

22.23B View of torque converter

19 Now bring each pair of bolts into view by turning the crankshaft pulley bolt with a 28mm socket wrench and extension. Unscrew and remove the bolts (photo).

20 Unscrew and remove the bolts which secure the torque converter housing to the engine. The lower ones are readily accessible, but the upper ones can only be reached by using a socket wrench or a universally-jointed extension some two feet (0.6 m) in length and inserted through the propeller shaft centre bearing aperture in the floor pan.

21 The starter motor upper socket headed screw must be removed using a section cut from an Allen key and applying a 10 mm socket wrench attached to the universally-jointed extensions.

22 Using a second jack and a block of wood, support the weight of the engine under the sump.

23 Lower both jacks simultaneously until, with the help of assistants, the transmission can be withdrawn to the rear and from under the car. Try and keep the torque converter pressed to the rear during removal and once the transmission is out of the car bolt a small plate and block of wood to its front face as a means of keeping it fully engaged with the transmission fluid pump (photos).

24 Refitting is a reversal of removal. Fill the unit with the correct grade and quantity of fluid and then check the adjustments as described in Sections 19, 20 or 21 according to type (photo).

22.24 Right-hand side of the automatic transmission

23 Fault diagnosis - automatic transmission

Symptom	Reason/s
Starter will not operate	Incorrectly adjusted inhibitor switch.
Car moves during operation of starter	Incorrect selector linkage adjustment. Short circuit in starter inhibitor switch.
Thump on engaging drive	Idling speed too high.
Engine stops when engaging drive	Idling speed too low. Incorrect constant speed adjustment (fuel injection) or defective solenoid.
Excessive creep	Idling speed too high.
No kickdown	Kickdown switch out of adjustment. Accelerator pedal incorrectly adjusted. Accelerator pedal impeded by floor mat.
Noise or rattle from transmission while engine running	Low fluid level. Choked fluid filter.
Fluid seen to be black or smells of burning when checking level	Internal fault.
Smoke from exhaust (not due to engine wear)	Damaged modulating pressure transmitter diaphragm allowing fluid to enter intake manifold through vacuum line.

Chapter 7 Propeller shaft

Contents

Specifications

Type	Two section, tubular with intermediate (centre) bearing, needle roller and flexible universal joints

Torque wrench settings

	lb f ft	Nm
Intermediate bearing carrier bolts	15	21
Sliding sleeve nut	22 to 28	30 to 39
Flexible coupling plate self-locking nuts	30	41
Coupling flange bolts to rear axle drive pinion	32	44

1 General description

The propeller shaft used on all models is of a two-section tubular type (Figs. 7.1 and 7.2).

At its rear end the shaft is connected to the rear axle pinion coupling flange through the medium of a sealed universal joint or flexible coupling according to date of production of the car.

The propeller shaft is supported at its centre by an intermediate bearing which is attached to the floor pan of the car.

At the front end of the shaft, the connection to the output shaft of the transmission unit is by means of a flexible coupling.

2 Maintenance

1   The maintenance for all types of shaft consists mainly of inspection at the specified intervals. First check the condition of the flexible couplings for deterioration. Where a needle roller type rear universal joint is fitted, test for wear as described in Section 6. In the same way test the universal joint at the front end of the rear section of the propeller shaft.

2   Periodically, check the torque wrench setting of all propeller shaft connecting and mounting nuts and bolts.

3 Propeller shaft - removal and refitting

1   Place the car over an inspection pit or raise the rear and support it securely on axle stands.

2   Support the base of the transmission on a jack and unbolt and remove the rear mounting complete.

3   Using two large open-ended spanners, unscrew the sleeve nut (about two turns) which is located on the front section of the shaft.

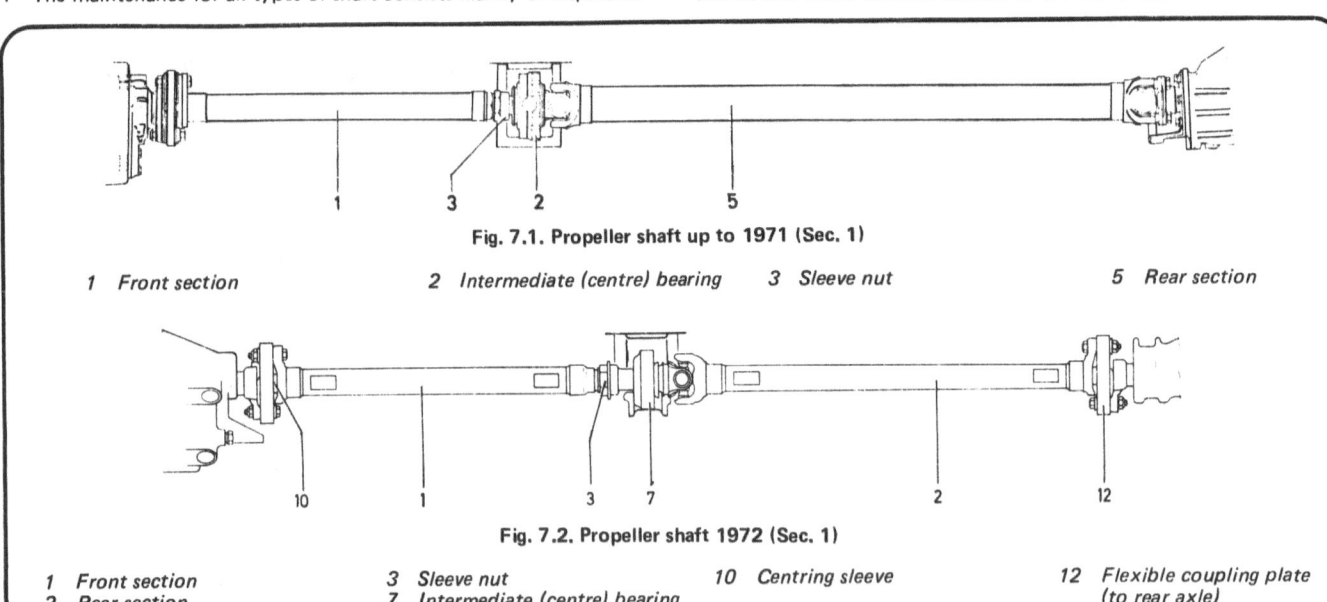

Fig. 7.1. Propeller shaft up to 1971 (Sec. 1)

1 *Front section*	2 *Intermediate (centre) bearing* 3 *Sleeve nut*	5 *Rear section*

Fig. 7.2. Propeller shaft 1972 (Sec. 1)

1 *Front section*	3 *Sleeve nut*	10 *Centring sleeve*	12 *Flexible coupling plate*
2 *Rear section*	7 *Intermediate (centre) bearing*		*(to rear axle)*

This will permit the shaft to be slightly compressed to simplify removal (Fig. 7.3).

4   Disconnect the front end of the propeller shaft from the output flange of the transmission unit. Do this by removing the bolts from the propeller shaft flange and not the transmission output flange.

5   Unscrew and remove the bolts which connect the intermediate bearing to the bodyframe.

6   Extract the bolts which connect the propeller shaft rear flange to the drive flange of the rear axle pinion.

7   Slightly compress the two sections of the shaft together so that the rear flange can be disconnected, and then withdraw the complete shaft assembly to the rear and remove it from the car. Take care while removing the shaft that the two sections are not separated at the sleeve nut.

8   To refit the propeller shaft, first fill the recesses in the centring sleeve of the connecting flange of the front section of the shaft with the specified grease (Fig. 7.4).

9   Pass the propeller shaft into position from the rear having previously ensured that the sleeve nut on the shaft is loose.

10 Connect the shaft to the transmission output flange.

11 Attach the intermediate bearing carrier to the bodyframe but only screw up the bolts finger tight.

12 Connect the propeller shaft rear flange to the rear axle drive pinion flange.

13 Refit the mounting to the rear of the transmission.

14 Remove the transmission jack and lower the car to the ground.

15 The car should now be pushed forward and backward two or three times and the body depressed on the suspension in order to position the intermediate bearing and the shaft length, which is able to increase or decrease its length by means of the slackened sleeve nut.

16 Tighten the propeller shaft sleeve nut to the specified torque wrench setting and then tighten the intermediate bearing carrier bolts.

4   Intermediate bearing - overhaul

1   Remove the propeller shaft as described in the preceding Section.

2   Mark the alignment of the front and rear sections of the propeller shaft by scribing lines on them.

3   With the sleeve nut already released for removal of the shaft, pull the two sections of the shaft apart (Fig. 7.5).

4   Remove the bearing carrier (3), the rubber mounting (4), the flexible sleeve (5), the circlip (11) and protective cap (8).

5   To renew the ball bearing (7) pull the bearing and housing (12) from the shaft with a suitable puller.

6   Once the bearing assembly is removed, extract the circlip (13) and press out the bearing.

7   Reassembly is a reversal of dismantling but it is essential that only a lubricant-sealed type of bearing is used for renewal purposes.

8   Apply a little grease to the splines of the sliding section of the shaft.

9   Refit the propeller shaft as described in Section 3.

5   Centring sleeve - renewal

1   If, on removal of the propeller shaft, the sealing lip on the centring sleeve is worn or damaged, this can be rectified without having to renew the complete shaft assembly.

2   Secure the centring sleeve in the jaws of a vice and drill a hole (0.39 in - 10.0 mm) in diameter at right angles through the sleeve. The hole should be located about 0.59 in (15.0 mm) from the end of the

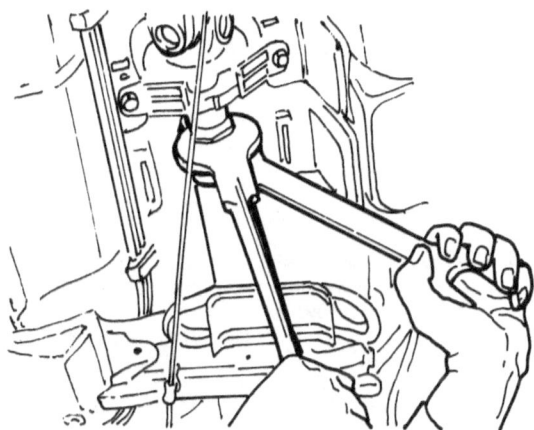

Fig. 7.3. Releasing propeller shaft sleeve nut (Sec. 3)

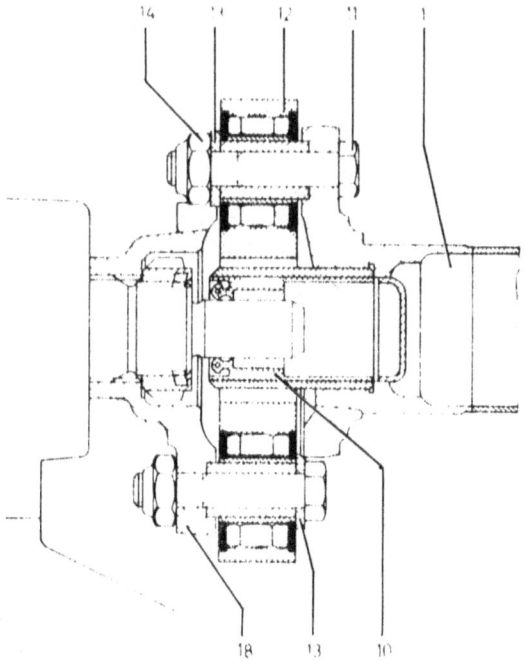

Fig. 7.4. Propeller shaft coupling to transmission output shaft (Sec. 3)

1 Propeller shaft	13 Washer
10 Centring sleeve	14 Self-locking nut
11 Bolt	18 Three-legged flange
12 Flexible coupling plate	

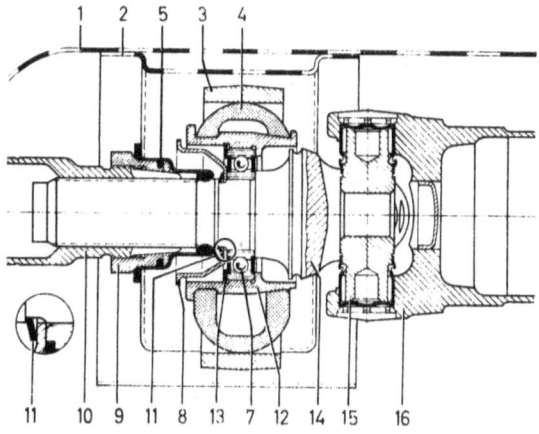

Fig. 7.5. Intermediate (centre) bearing sectional view (Sec. 4)

1 Bodyframe	10 Propeller shaft front
2 Propeller shaft tunnel	section
3 Bearing mounting bracket	11 Circlip
4 Flexible mounting	12 Bearing
5 Rubber sleeve	13 Circlip
7 Ball bearing	14 Yoke
8 Protective cap	15 Universal joint spider
9 Sleeve nut	16 Propeller shaft rear section

Fig. 7.6. Drilling hole in centring sleeve (8) (Sec. 5)

Fig. 7.7. Levering centring sleeve (8) from flange (Sec. 5)

sleeve (Fig. 7.6).

3   Now grip the propeller shaft behind the flange in the vice and using a suitable round bar and two levers, prise the centring sleeve from the shaft. On some early models, a closing cover is fitted and this must remain in the shaft (Fig. 7.7).

4   The new centring sleeve can be pressed into position and then a little high melting point grease applied to its cavity.

***

6   Universal joints - inspection and repair

1   Apart from the flexible coupling type of joint which is simply renewed by fitting a new flexible plate, needle type universal joints

7   Fault diagnosis - propeller shaft

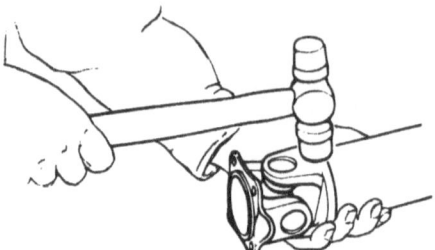

Fig. 7.8. Extracting universal joint bearing cups (Sec. 6)

are fitted to all models at the front of the rear section of the shaft and to some cars at the shaft to rear axle connection.

2   *On later cars,* the needle roller type universal joints are of staked type and in the event of wear occurring, the complete propeller shaft must be renewed.

3   *On earlier cars,* the joints incorporate circlips and they can be reconditioned by carrying out the operations described later in this Section.

4   To test a universal joint for wear, grip one of the yokes in each hand and try twisting them in opposite rotational directions. Carry out this test with the propeller shaft in a 'free' state with the handbrake released.

5   Now test for wear by gripping one section of the shaft while the adjacent section is pushed and pulled in the same direction as a line drawn through the two bearing cups of each spider trunnion in turn.

6   Any evidence of wear resulting from the foregoing tests must be put right by either repair or renewal of the joint.

7   To repair a universal joint on earlier cars, first clean away all external dirt from the joint.

8   Mark the positions of the yokes in relation to each other so that they can be refitted in their original positions to maintain the balance of the propeller shaft.

9   Extract the circlips with the aid of a screwdriver. If they are very tight, tap the end of the bearing race (within the periphery of the circlip) with a drift and hammer to relieve the pressure.

10 Once the circlips are removed, tap the universal joints at the yoke with a soft hammer and the bearings and race will come out of the housing and can be removed easily. If they are obstinate they can be gripped in a self-locking wrench for final removal (Fig. 7.8).

11 Once the bearings are removed from each opposite journal, the spiders can be disengaged.

12 Obtain a repair kit for each joint which will contain the spider, needle bearings and bearing cups.

13 Place the needles in each race and fill the race one-third full with grease prior to placing it over the trunnion, and tap each one home with a brass drift. Any grease exuding from the further bearing journal after three have been fitted should be removed before fitting the fourth race.

14 Refit the circlips ensuring they seat neatly in the retaining grooves.

Symptom	Reason/s
Vibration when car running on road	Out of balance shaft. Wear in splined sleeve. Loose flange bolts. Worn universal joints.

Chapter 8 Rear axle

Contents

Specifications

| Type ... ... | Hypoid, semi-floating with either:
(i) Enclosed axleshafts and axle casing pivoted at differential housing; or
(ii) Open axleshafts with differential unit mounted on sub-frame depending upon car model. 28SL/8 limited slip differential option. |

Ratios
With 4-speed manual or automatic transmission (K4A-025)	3.69 : 1 or 3.92 : 1
With 5-speed manual transmission or automatic transmission (K4C-025)...	3.92 : 1 or 4.08 : 1
Refer to rear axle plate for ratio details	

Oil capacity
Enclosed axleshaft type	4.4 Imp pts, 5.3 US pts, 2.5 litres
*Open axleshaft type	2.0 Imp pts, 2.4 US pts, 1.15 litres

Use special oil if limited slip differential fitted

Torque wrench settings

	lb f ft	Nm
Enclosed type axleshafts		
Differential suspension carrier upper mounting bolt	87	120
Differential suspension carrier mounting plate bolts to floor pan	32	45
Locating strut to bodyframe nuts	65	90
Locating strut bolts to differential housing	144	200
Front plate to differential housing bolts	25	35
Universal joint to side gear of differential	47	65
Left-hand axle tube to differential bolts	36	50
Differential carrier pivot bolt pinch bolt	87	120
Brake backplate bolts	18	25
Axleshaft bearing ring nut	144	200
Open type axleshafts		
Flexible mounting to differential end cover	94	130
Flexible mounting (rear) to floor pan	18	25
Front flexible mounting plate to floor pan	29	40
Front flexible mounting to differential carrier	87	120
Axleshaft to flange bolt	69	95
Differential end cover bolts	32	45

1 General description

All models have independent rear suspension and this is achieved in one of two ways according to the model.

On many 230, 250 and 280 Series cars, the rear axle is identified by the enclosed type of axleshafts. This type of axle casing is pivoted at the differential housing, movement being controlled by a heavy duty compensating spring or hydropneumatic strut.

On some 230 and 250 Series models, the differential unit is mounted on a sub frame and the drive is transmitted through open type axleshafts. The sub frame is bolted to the top of the differential unit and is attached to the floor pan with flexible mountings.

Repair and overhaul operations to the rear axle and differential unit should be limited to those described due to the need for very specialised tools, gauges and skill if more extensive work is undertaken.

Part A — Enclosed type shaft rear axle

2 Axleshafts - removal

1 *To remove the left-hand axleshaft,* jack up the car and support it securely on axlestands (Fig. 8.1).
2 Remove the roadwheel.
3 Remove the brake caliper and brake disc/drum as described in Chapter 9.
4 Remove the parking brake shoes (Chapter 9).
5 Unscrew the securing bolts and withdraw the brake backplate.
6 Attach a slide hammer to the axleshaft flange and withdraw the axleshaft from the axle casing.
7 *To remove the right-hand axleshaft,* proceed as described for the left-hand shaft but having attached the slide hammer, only extract the axleshaft until the axle bearing becomes visible.
8 Remove the slide hammer and then continue to pull out the axleshaft by hand until a firm resistance is felt. Now turn the axleshaft so that the circlip (4) makes a firm contact with the core of the sliding sleeve (2) (Fig. 8.2).
9 Jerk the axleshaft from the casing by giving it a sharp pull with the hand. Failure to observe this procedure or the use of excessive force may break the circlip and make removal of the shaft virtually impossible.

3 Axleshafts - dismantling and reassembly

1 With the axleshaft removed as described in the preceding Section, secure the axle flange in a suitable fixture. If some old bolts are temporarily inserted into the holes in the flange, the bolts can then be gripped in the jaws of a vice.
2 Bend down the tab of the locking plate and then using a drift or a 'C' spanner, unscrew the bearing ring type retaining nut and remove it.
3 Using a puller, extract the bearing from the axleshaft (Fig. 8.3).
4 Remove the brake backplate and the oil seal.
5 Commence reassembly by coating the outer edge of the oil seal with a jointing compound and pressing it into the brake backplate until it is flush.
6 Coat the oil seal lips with molybdenum disulphide grease and slide the brake backplate into position.

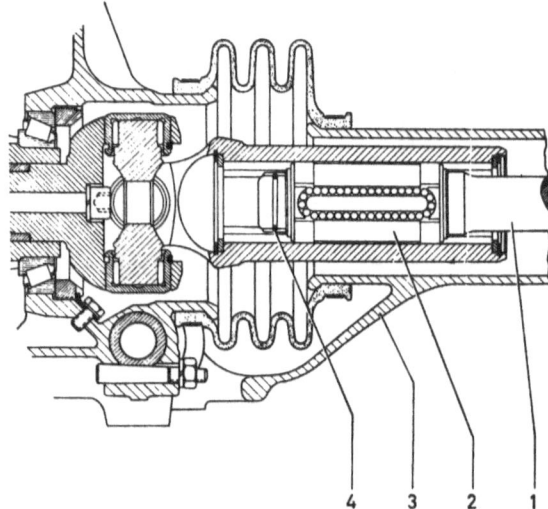

Fig. 8.2. Sectional view of right-hand axleshaft and joint (Sec. 2)

1 Axleshaft	3 Axle tube
2 Sliding sleeve	4 Circlip

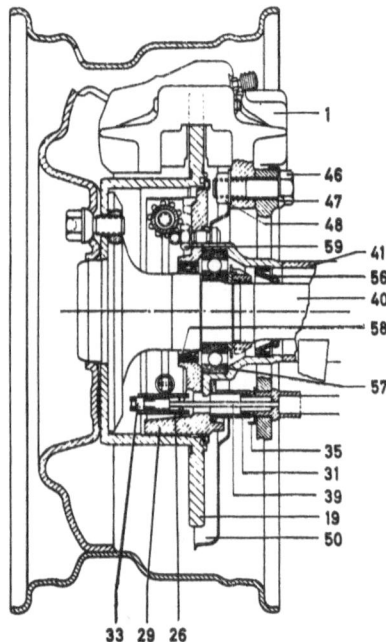

Fig. 8.1. Sectional view of left-hand rear hub (Sec. 2)

1 Caliper	41 Axle tube
19 Disc	46 Backplate bolt
26 Expander	47 Lockwasher
29 Brake backplate	48 Captive nut
31 Rubber sleeve	50 Cover plate
33 Cable pin	56 Sealing ring
35 Brake outer cable lock plate	57 Bearing
39 Brake inner cable	58 Oil seal
40 Axleshaft	59 Bolt

Fig. 8.3. Removing axleshaft bearing (Sec. 3)

7   Fit the new bearing, applying pressure only to the inner track of the bearing.

8   Fit the locking plate with its flange against the inner track of the bearing. Screw on the ring nut and tighten it to the specified torque wrench setting. Lock the nut by punching in the lockplate into a slot in the nut (Fig. 8.4).

9   Fit a new gasket to the brake backplate. Coat both sides of the gasket with jointing compound.

10   Renew the inner oil seal in the axle casing and then apply enough bearing grease around the slotted bearing nut to fill the cavity between the inner and outer seals when the axleshaft is fitted.

4   Axleshafts - refitting

1   *To refit the left-hand axleshaft,* pass it carefully into the axle casing without damaging the lips of the oil seal.

2   Bolt the brake backplate to the end flange of the axle casing.

3   Refit the parking brake shoes.

4   Refit the brake disc/drum and caliper.

5   Check rear axle oil level on completion of the work when the car is on the roadwheels.

6   *Before refitting the right-hand axleshaft,* the following preliminary work must be carried out.

7   Remove both rear roadsprings as described in Chapter 11.

8   Remove the compensating spring (see Section 5 this Chapter).

9   Unscrew and remove the rubber buffers from the left and right-hand bodyframe members (Fig. 8.5).

10   Apply grease to the circlip on the axleshaft and insert the shaft carefully into the axle casing, taking care not to damage the lips of the oil seal. Push the shaft in until resistance is felt.

11   Bolt the brake backplate to the flange on the axle casing.

12   Raise the left-hand axle by means of a jack until it contacts the body.

13   Now raise the right-hand axle casing by hand until it also contacts the body.

14   If this work has been properly carried out then the circlip on the right-hand axleshaft will now snap into position behind the sliding sleeve. Failure to remove the rubber buffers or to raise the axle casings fully will prevent the necessary angle being obtained to ensure engagement of the circlip.

15   Lower both axle casings and refit the rubber buffers.

16   Refit the brake shoes for the parking brake.

17   Refit the disc/drum assembly.

18   Refit the rear roadsprings and the compensating spring.

19   Check the oil in the rear axle after the car has been lowered onto its roadwheels.

5   Rear axle compensating spring or strut - removal and refitting

1   One of two types of device may be encountered, according to the car model. On some cars, a normal coil spring is fitted while on other vehicles, a hydropneumatic strut is used.

2   *To remove the standard type spring,* compress it with a spring compressor (Fig. 8.6).

3   Unscrew and remove the carrier at the right-hand end of the spring by unscrewing the securing bolts.

4   Detach the spring and the carrier.
   On 280 SL models, the shock absorber upper mountings should be disconnected and the body raised to allow the outer ends of the axle casing to drop slightly.

5   *To remove the hydropneumatic type of strut,* unscrew and remove both the socket headed screws (8) on the right-hand balljoint (Fig. 8.7).

6   Unscrew the nut (7), pull out the compensating strut and withdraw the bearing ring (5).

7   *When refitting the standard type coil spring,* use the original rubber mounting rings. If the suspension height is to be altered, rings of different thickness can be used (refer to Chapter 11) (photo).

8   *When refitting the hydropneumatic type strut,* first fit the bearing ring (5) into the rear axle housing so that it is flush.

9   A clamp will now be required similar to the one shown. Fit the clamp and compress the spring to reduce the overall length of the strut by about 1.0 in (25.4 mm) (Fig. 8.8).

10   Attach the right-hand balljoint with the socket headed screws.

11   Release and remove the clamp and slide the sealing washer onto the ballpin.

12   Connect the left-hand balljoint to the rear axle housing making sure that the washer (6) has its spherical washer outwards and use a new self-locking nut.

13   Turn the strut so that the two filler plugs face rearwards and attach the dust excluding bellows with the hose clips. The vent hole in the bellows should be at the bottom.

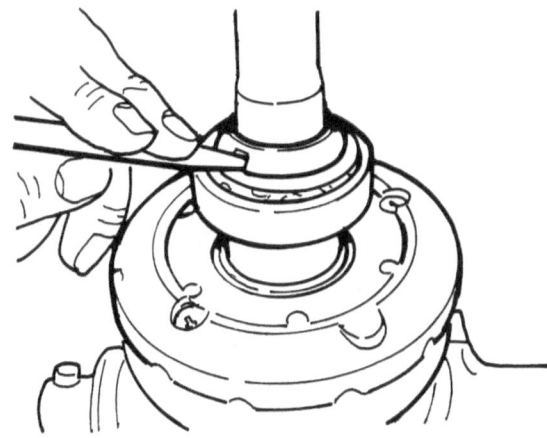

Fig. 8.4. Locking axleshaft bearing nut (Sec. 3)

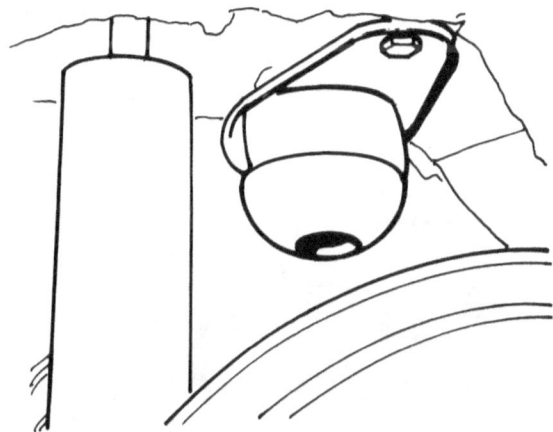

Fig. 8.5. Rubber buffers on bodyframe members (Sec. 4)

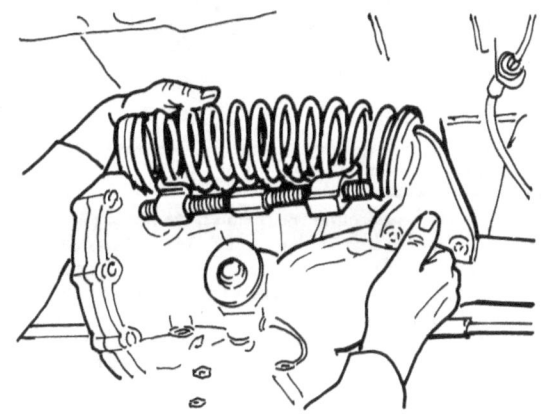

Fig. 8.6. Removing rear axle compensating spring (Sec. 5)

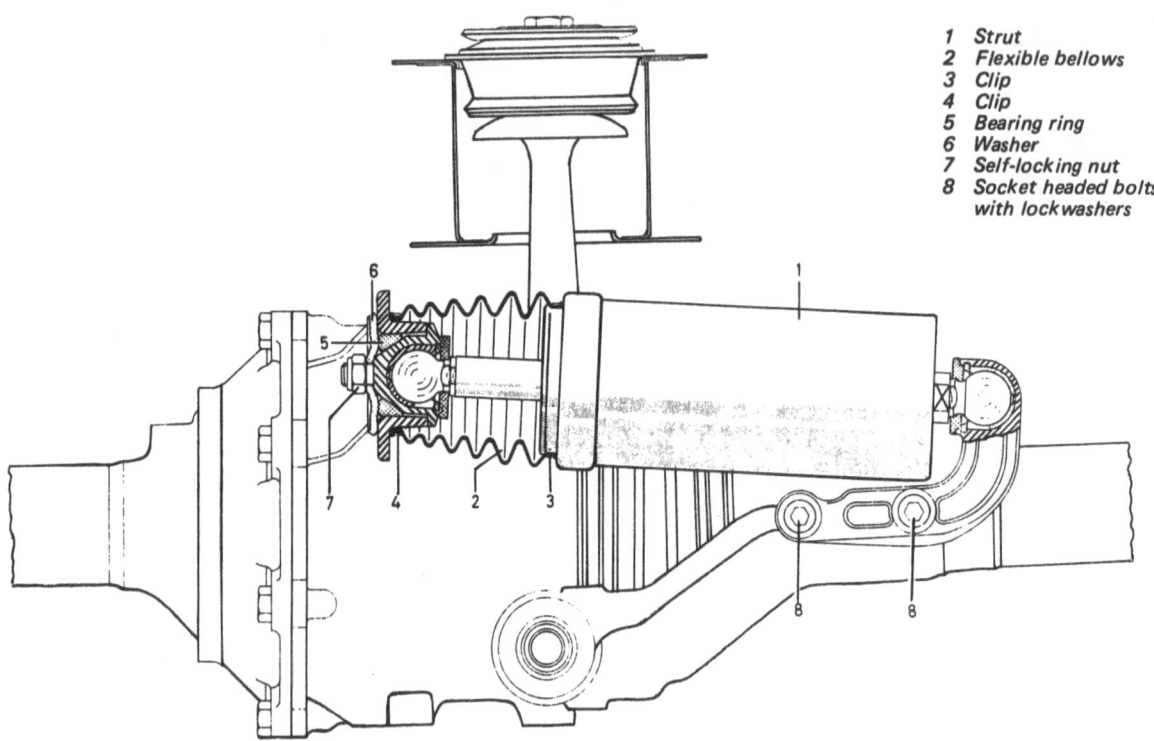

1 Strut
2 Flexible bellows
3 Clip
4 Clip
5 Bearing ring
6 Washer
7 Self-locking nut
8 Socket headed bolts
  with lockwashers

Fig. 8.7. Hydropneumatic type rear axle compensating strut (Sec. 5)

5.7 Axle compensating spring installed

6 Pinion oil seal - renewal

1   Oil leakage in the area around the pinion drive flange will almost certainly be due to a defective pinion oil seal. The seal can be renewed in the following way without having to remove the rear axle.

2   Disconnect the rear end of the propeller shaft from the drive pinion coupling flange.

3   Raise the rear of the car using jacks or stands placed under the axle tubes. The roadwheels should be off the ground and the handbrake fully released.

4   Now check the turning torque of the pinion. To do this, either use a suitable torque wrench or wind a length of cord round the pinion flange and attach it to a spring balance. Pull the spring balance and as soon as the pinion starts to turn, record the force indicated on the

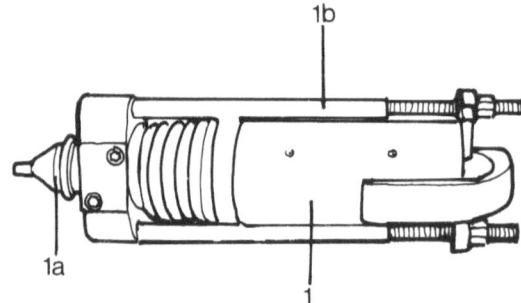

Fig. 8.8. Using a clamp to compress hydropneumatic strut (Sec. 5)

1 Strut   1a Balljoint   1b Clamp

spring balance scale. It is important that the brakes are not binding while carrying out this operation.

5   The pinion nut must now be unscrewed. To be able to do this, the coupling flange must be held quite still either by bolting a length of steel bar to two of the bolt holes in the coupling flange as shown, or by using a large adjustable wrench applied to the coupling itself. The slotted pinion nut can be unscrewed using a special wrench (tool no. 111589000700) or by the careful use of a drift and hammer. If the latter method is used, renew the nut (Figs. 8.9 and 8.10).

6   Once the nut is removed, withdraw the coupling and prise the oil seal from the pinion housing.

7   Coat the outer edge of the new oil seal with a jointing compound and tap it squarely into position.

8   Smear the oil seal lips with grease and fit the coupling flange.

9   Tighten the pinion nut very carefully until it just seats and then check the turning torque of the pinion as previously described. Tighten the nut an eighth of a turn at a time, rechecking the turning torque between each tightening, until the turning torque matches that recorded before dismantling.

10 Lock the nut securely with the lockplate (Fig. 8.11);

11 Reconnect the propeller shaft, lower the car and check the oil level in the axle, topping it up if necessary.

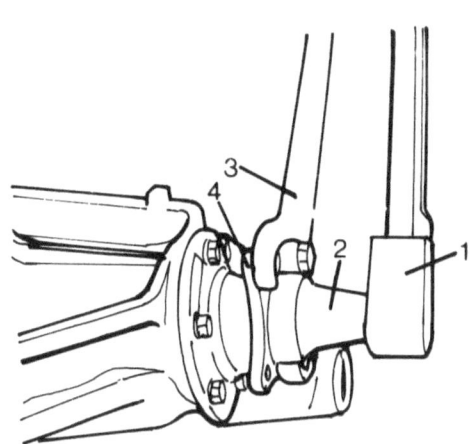

Fig. 8.9. Releasing pinion coupling nut (Sec. 6)

1	Wrench	3	Retaining lever
2	Special socket	4	Coupling flange

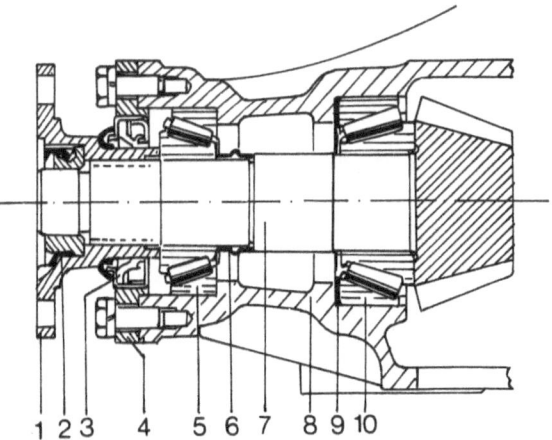

Fig. 8.10. Sectional view of rear axle pinion assembly (Sec. 6)

1	Coupling flange	6	Spacer
2	Nut	7	Pinion
3	Oil seal	8	Differential housing
4	Cover plate	9	Compensating washer
5	Tapered roller bearing	10	Tapered roller bearing

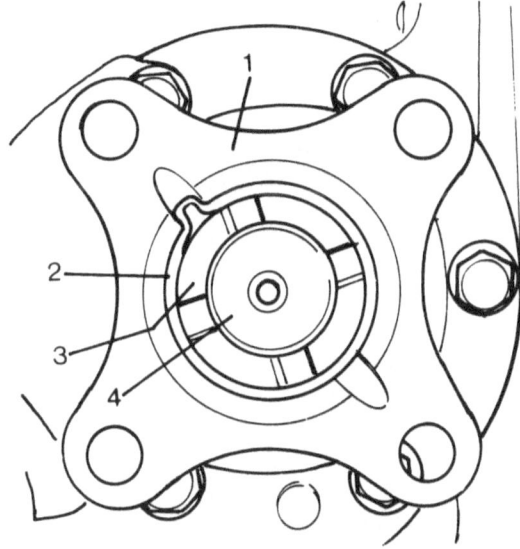

Fig. 8.11. Pinion coupling flange (1) Lockplate (2) Pinion nut (3)
Pinion (4) (Sec. 6)

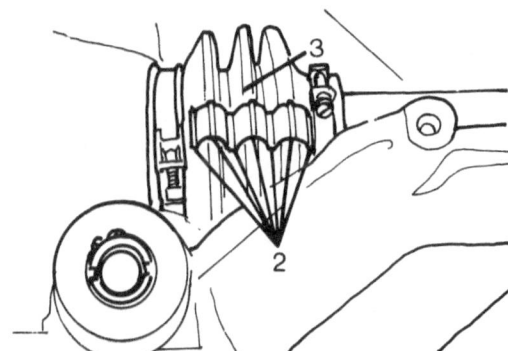

Fig. 8.12. Location of joining clips (2) on axleshaft joint bellows (3)
(Sec. 7)

7 Rear axle flexible bellows - renewal

1   The flexible bellows which are located at the inner end of the right-hand axle tube can be renewed with a special split type bellows to save having to remove and dismantle the complete axle.
2   Drain the oil from the axle.
3   Remove the compensating spring (see Section 5).
4   Clean away all external dirt from the axle casing.
5   Release the bellows clips and cut the bellows from the axle.
6   Adjust the height of the car with jacks and stands so that the axle tubes are horizontal.
7   Locate the new split type bellows so that the slit is towards the rear of the car.
8   The special joining clips supplied should be positioned one at each end of the bellows under the hose clips and the remaining seven at the point of each fold in the bellows. Bend the ends of the clips with a pair of pliers to secure them (Fig. 8.12).
9   Refit the hose clips. The left-hand clip screw should point downward and be turned by passing the screwdriver through the yoke end of the axle tube.
10 Refit the compensating spring and lower the car.
11 Refill the axle with oil.

8 Rear axle locating strut - removal and refitting

1   If the rubber bush in the axle housing is to be renewed only, then do not disturb the setting of the strut lock nuts.
2   Unscrew and remove the bolts (7) and (9) and withdraw the link (8).
3   Fit the new flexible bush and refit the link.
4   If the complete strut is to be removed for renewal of the flexible bushes at the body frame end, then after reassembly, the rear axle must be checked and centralised if necessary.
5   To do this, make up a rod which will engage on the centres of the rear axle link mountings on the body floor pan. From the centre of the rod and at right angles to it, a pointer should be arranged which should be in alignment with the centre of the large pivot bolt of the axle suspension carrier (11) (Figs. 8.13 and 8.14).
6   Where the pointer is not in alignment, adjust the strut by repositioning the nuts.
7   *On 280 SL/8 models,* the attachment of the locating strut to the body has a slightly different arrangement (as shown in Fig. 8.15).

9 Rear axle - removal and refitting

1   Raise the rear of the car and support the bodyframe on stands.
2   Using jacks, raise the axle tubes so that they are in the horizontal attitude.
3   Remove the roadwheels.
4   Disconnect the handbrake cables from the equaliser on the floor pan.

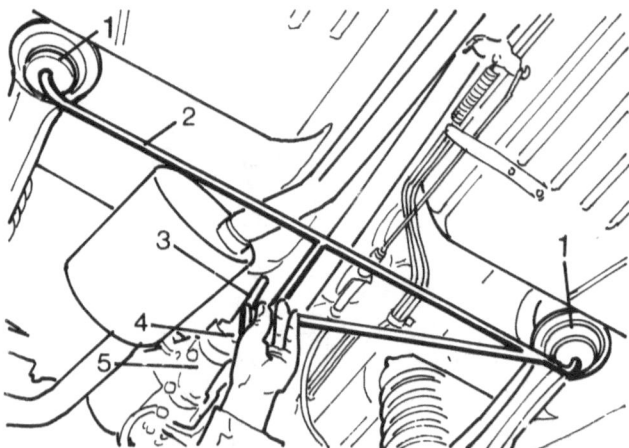

Fig. 8.13. Checking rear axle is centralised (Sec. 8)

1 Suspension link mounting	4 Pivot bolt of suspension
2 Measuring gauge	carrier
3 Gauge centre pin	5 Rear axle suspension carrier

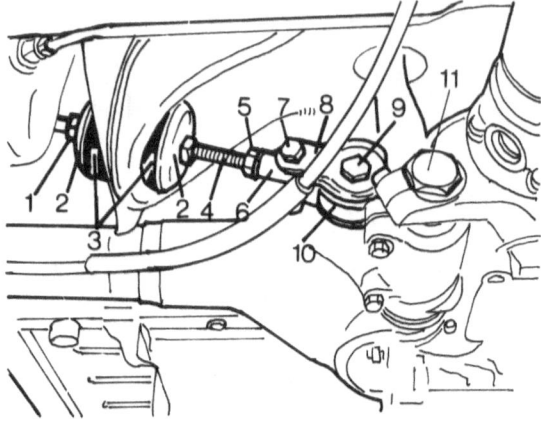

Fig. 8.14. Rear axle locating strut (Sec. 8)

1 Nut and locknut	7 Bolt
2 Cup	8 Inner link
3 Rubber cushion	9 Bolt
4 Strut	10 Bush
5 Locknut	11 Rear axle suspension carrier
6 Link	pivot bolt

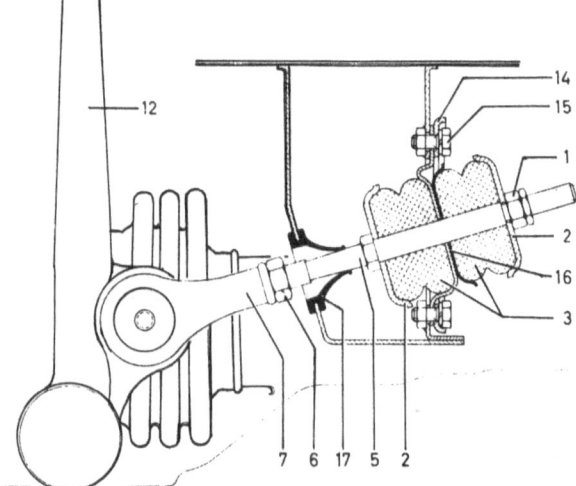

Fig. 8.15. Locating strut used on 280 SL/8 rear axles (Sec. 8)

1 Nut and locknut	12 Suspension carrier
2 Cup	14 Mounting plate
3 Rubber cushion	15 Bolt
5 Strut	16 Shims
6 Locknut	17 Grommet
7 Link	

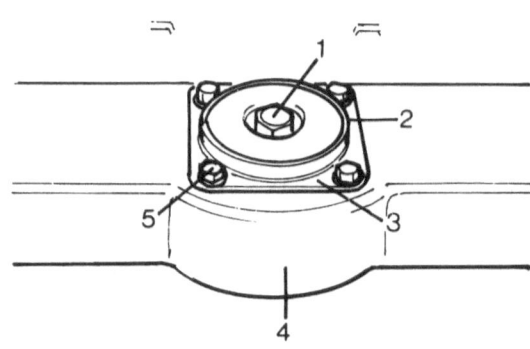

Fig. 8.16. Mounting for rear axle suspension carrier within luggage boot (Sec. 9)

1 Bolt	4 Crossmember
2 Clamp plate	5 Mounting attachment
3 Flexible mounting	screw

5   Loosen the propeller shaft centre bearing bolts but do not remove them. Release the propeller shaft sliding joint nut as described in Chapter 7.

6   Unscrew and remove the propeller shaft rear flange bolts from the rear axle pinion coupling flange. Push the propeller shaft slightly forward to disconnect it and then tie it to one side with a piece of wire.

7   Remove the compensating spring or strut as described earlier in this Chapter.

8   Remove the rear road springs as described in Chapter 11.

9   Disconnect the flexible brake hose from the rear axle and cap the open ends of the hose.

10 Disconnect the suspension links from the body floor pan as described in Chapter 11.

11 Disconnect and remove the rear axle locating strut as described in Section 8.

12 Disconnect the shock absorber lower mountings.

13 Support the centre of the rear axle on a trolley jack and adjust the axle tube jacks if necessary to keep them in their horizontal attitude.

14 Working inside the luggage compartment, unscrew the bolt which

retains the axle suspension carrier to its flexible mounting (Figs. 8.16 and 8.17).

15 Lower the axle assembly slightly and withdraw it from under the car. When removing the axle, do not allow the right-hand axle tube to drop otherwise the inner universal/sliding type joint may be damaged.

16 Before fitting the rear axle, first check the distance (a) shown in Fig. 8.17. This should be between 6.2 and 6.3 in (157.0 and 159.0 mm).

17 Adjust if necessary by releasing the two clamp bolts on the pivot mounting of the carrier.

18 Remove the rubber buffers from the bodyframe side members, see Fig. 8.5.

19 Locate the rear axle under the car and engage the end of the suspension carrier into the flexible mounting. Screw in the bolt and tighten it to the specified torque wrench setting.

20 Support the axle tubes and reconnect the shock absorber lower mountings.

21 Refit the locating strut.

22 Raise the left-hand axle tube until it comes up against the body-frame side member.

23 Raise the right-hand axle tube using the hands only until it comes up against the bodyframe side member, see Section 4, paragraph 14.

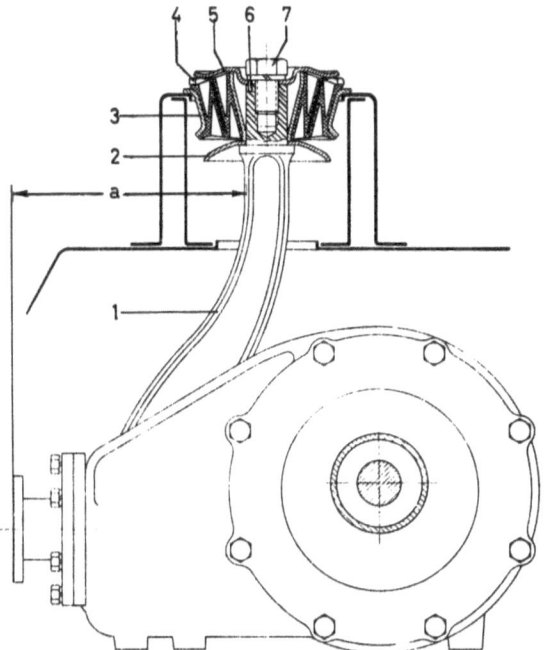

Fig. 8.17. Sectional view of mounting for rear axle suspension carrier
(Sec. 9)

1	Carrier	5	Upper clamp plate
2	Lower clamp plate	6	Locating pin
3	Flexible mounting	7	Centre bolt
4	Mounting attachment screw		

a   6.2 to 6.3 in (157 to 159 mm)

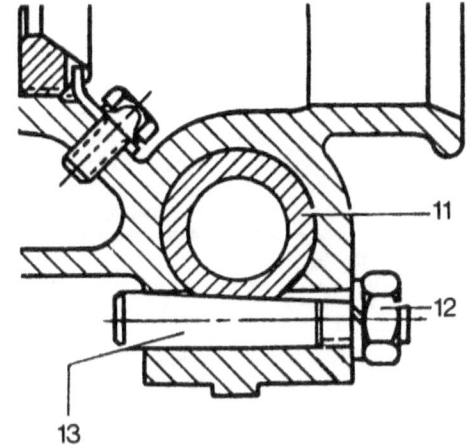

Fig. 8.18. Sectional view of rear axle suspension carrier pivot
tapered cotter bolt (Sec. 10)

11 Pivot bolt   12 Nut   13 Cotter pin

24 Now lower both axle tubes.
25 Refit the rubber buffers to the bodyframe side members.
26 Reconnect the suspension links to the body floor pan.
27 Connect the brake hoses.
28 Refit the rear road springs.
29 Refit the compensating spring or strut.
30 Reconnect the propeller shaft and then tighten the centre bearing bolts, finger tight only.
31 Lower the car to the ground and push it backwards and forwards several times. Now fully tighten the propeller shaft centre bearing mounting bolts and the propellor shaft sliding sleeve clamp nuts.
32 Fill the rear axle with oil.
33 Reconnect and adjust if necessary, the handbrake cables (see Chapter 9).
34 Check and adjust if necessary the locating strut setting to provide correct rear axle centralising (see Section 8). It is recommended that the car is driven for a short distance before carrying out this particular job in order to allow the suspension to settle.

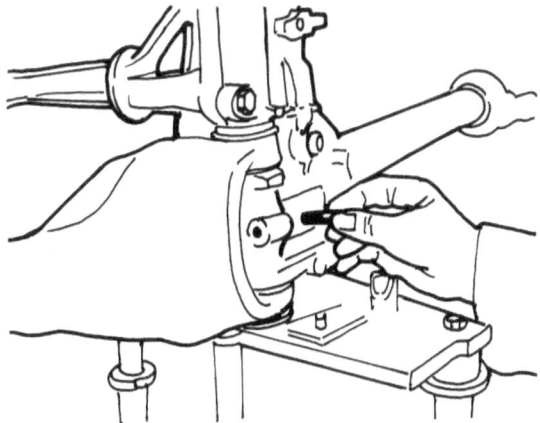

Fig. 8.19. Removing tapered cotter bolt (Sec. 10)

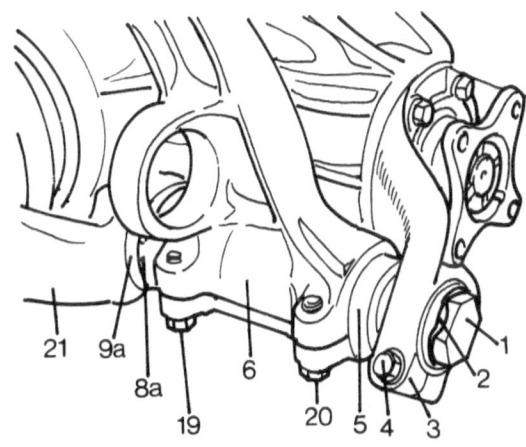

Fig. 8.20. Details of rear axle suspension carrier attachment to axle
(Sec. 10)

1	Pivot bolt	5	Flexible mounting
2	Lockplate	6	Carrier
3	Axle front cover plate and clamp	8a	Washer
		9a	Rubber ring
4	Pinch bolt	19	Bolt
		20	Bolt
		21	Right-hand axle tube

10 Right-hand axle tube and suspension carrier - removal and refitting

1   Remove the complete rear axle as described in the preceding Section. Withdraw the right-hand axleshaft as described in Section 2.
2   Unscrew and remove the nut (12) from the cotter bolt (13). Tap out the bolt taking care not to damage the threads (Figs. 8.18 and 8.19).
3   Bend down the tab of the lockplate (2) and unscrew the pivot bolt (1).
4   Release the pinch bolt (4) then, using a piece of tubing as a drift, knock out the pivot sleeve towards the rear. Release the bellow clips and withdraw the axle tube (Figs. 8.20 and 8.21).
5   Note the position of all the washers, spacers and sealing rings. Renew any worn components (Fig. 8.22).
6   Reassembly is a reversal of dismantling. Select compensating washers of suitable thickness which will allow the carrier to move freely.
7   Apply grease to the pivot sleeve before inserting it.
8   Do not fully tighten the carrier clamp screws until the dimension (a) has been set as shown in Fig. 8.17.
9   Refit the right-hand axleshaft (see Section 4).

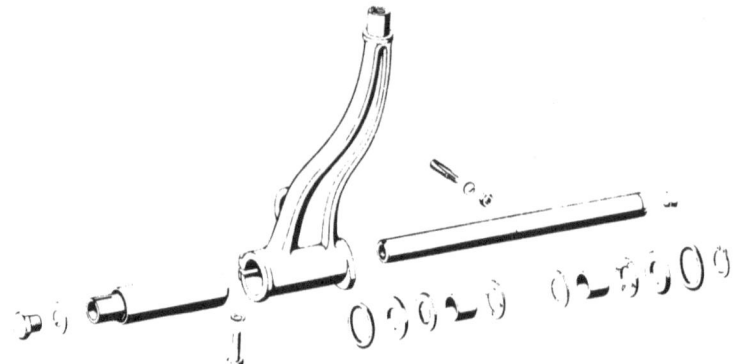

Fig. 8.21. Exploded view of rear axle suspension carrier (Sec. 10)

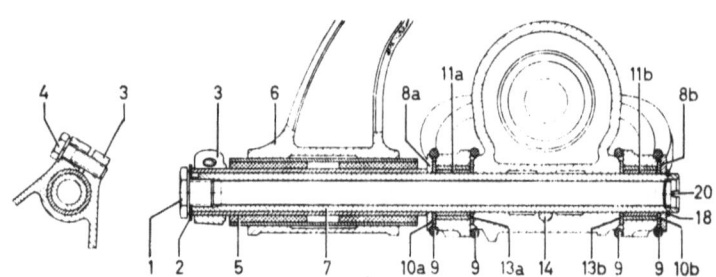

1　Pivot bolt
2　Lockplate
3　Axle front cover plate and clamp
4　Pinch bolt
5　Flexible mounting
6　Carrier
7　Pivot shaft
8a　Washer
8b　Washer
9　O-rings
10a　Washer
10b　Washer
11a　Sleeve
11b　Sleeve
13a　Compensating washer
13b　Compensating washer
14　Tapered cotter bolt
18　Circlip
20　Slot

Fig. 8.22. Sectional view of rear axle suspension carrier pivot (Sec. 10)

12 Differential unit - removal and refitting

1　As previously recommended, overhaul of the differential should be left to your dealer or a new or reconditioned unit obtained.
2　To prepare the differential for overhaul or exchange, remove the complete axle assembly from the car as described earlier in this Chapter. The subsequent operations are also fully described in earlier Sections.
3　Remove the axleshafts.
4　Remove the right-hand axle tube and the differential suspension carrier.
5　Remove the universal joint assembly.
6　Unbolt and remove the left-hand axle tube from the differential housing.

Part B – Open type shaft rear axle

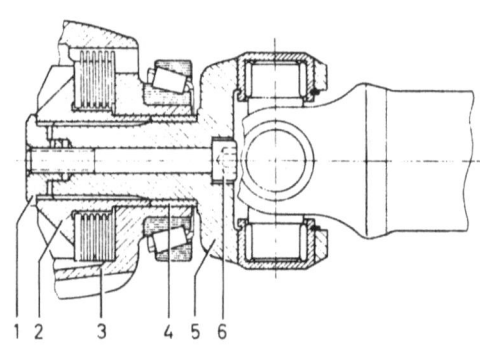

Fig. 8.23. Sectional view of axleshaft universal joint (Sec. 11)

1　Side gear nut
2　Side gear
3　Differential housing
4　Sleeve
5　Yoke
6　Centre securing bolt

11 Axleshaft universal joint - removal and refitting

1　Remove the rear axle assembly from the car.
2　Remove the axleshaft from the right-hand side.
3　Remove the right-hand axle tube.
4　Using a suitably long Allen key, unscrew and remove the socket headed screw which secures the yoke in position (Fig. 8.23).
5　The universal joint can now be withdrawn from the differential housing. If it is tight, use a suitable puller.
6　If the joint is worn or damaged it should be renewed as an assembly.
7　Before refitting the joint, clean the splines on the joint and the differential side gear with a suitable solvent and then lubricate them.
8　Tighten the joint socket screw to the specified torque wrench setting having first coated the threads with a thread locking compound.
9　Refit the axle tube and shaft and refit the rear axle assembly.

13 Axleshaft - removal and refitting

1　Drain the oil from the rear axle. Remove the roadwheel.
2　Unbolt the brake caliper and tie it up carefully to avoid strain on the flexible hose. There is no need to disconnect the hose (Fig. 8.24).
3　Apply the parking brake fully and unscrew the central hub nut. If the brake is not powerful enough to prevent the axleshaft turning as the nut is unscrewed, temporarily refit the roadwheel, lower the car to the ground and chock the wheel (Fig. 8.25).
4　A suitable puller should now be bolted to the hub using the roadwheel bolts, so that pressure can be applied to the end of the axleshaft to press it out of the hub. It is often easier to carry out this operation if the shock absorber is first disconnected and the suspension trailing arm lowered to its stop.
5　Support the differential housing on a jack, preferably of the trolley type.
6　Remove the rear flexible mounting from its attachment to both the body floor pan and the differential housing (Fig. 8.26).
7　Clean away external dirt and unbolt and remove the rear cover

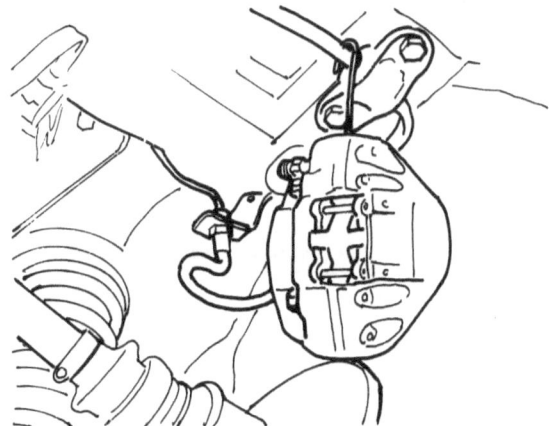

Fig. 8.24. Rear brake caliper removed and supported (Sec. 13)

Fig. 8.25. Unscrewing axleshaft to hub securing nut (Sec. 13)

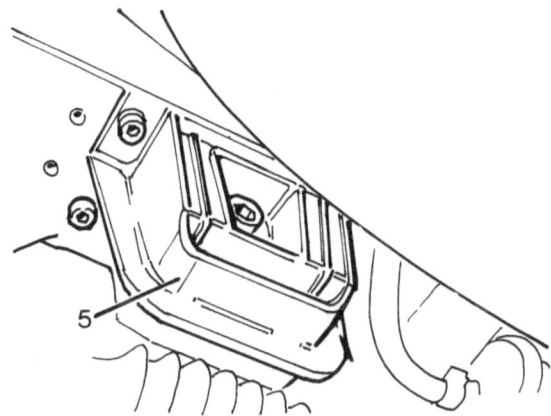

Fig. 8.26. Differential rear mounting (5) (Sec. 13)

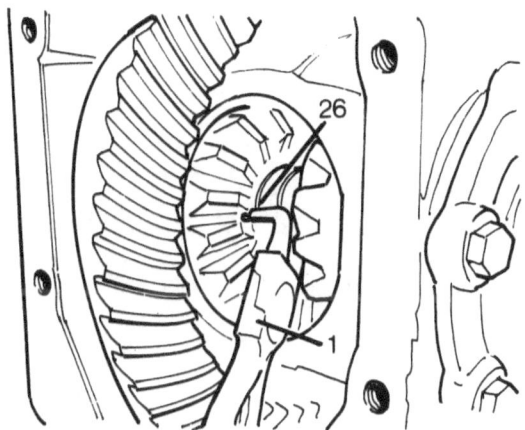

Fig. 8.27. Extracting circlip from differential unit (Sec. 13)

| 1 | Circlip pliers | 26 | Circlip |

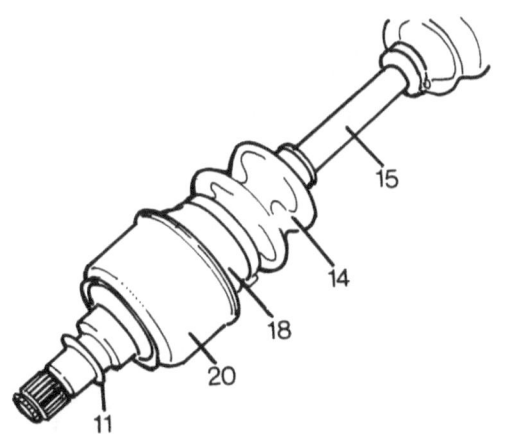

Fig. 8.28. Details of inner end of open type axleshaft (Sec. 13)

11	Spacer ring	18	Sleeve
14	Flexible bellows	20	Cover
15	Axleshaft		

Fig. 8.29. Axleshaft identification mark (Sec. 13)

from the differential housing.

8 Using a pair of pliers or a suitable hooked tool, extract the circlip from between the inner constant velocity joint and the differential side gear (Fig. 8.27).

9 Pull the axleshaft from the differential housing and recover the spacer ring (Fig. 8.28).

10 If both axleshafts are being removed at the same time, it is important that they are not mixed up. The letter 'L' or 'R' is stamped on the end face of the splined end of the shaft (Fig. 8.29).

11 Commence reassembly by fitting the spacer ring on the inner end of the shaft.

12 Locate the shaft in the differential and fit a new circlip. During the refitting operations, do not let the outer constant velocity joint drop at too acute an angle.

13 At this stage, check the endfloat between the inner joint and the differential housing. This should be almost imperceptible, otherwise,

change the circlip for one of a different thickness. The circlip selected must still be able to be turned in its groove (Fig. 8.30).

14 Compress the axleshaft lengthwise using hand pressure and locate its outer end in the hub assembly.

15 The threaded end of the shaft must now be drawn into the hub. In the absence of a special tool, use an old shaft nut and spacers of different thicknesses used in sequence to draw the shaft into position.

16 Screw on the axleshaft nut and tighten it to the specified torque wrench setting. If necessary, temporarily refit the roadwheel, lower the car to prevent the shaft turning while the nut is tightened.

17 Apply jointing compound and refit the differential end cover. Tighten the bolts to the specified torque wrench setting.

18 Raise the differential housing as necessary to be able to refit the flexible mounting to both the body floor pan and the differential housing.

19 Refit the brake caliper.

20 Refill the differential with oil.

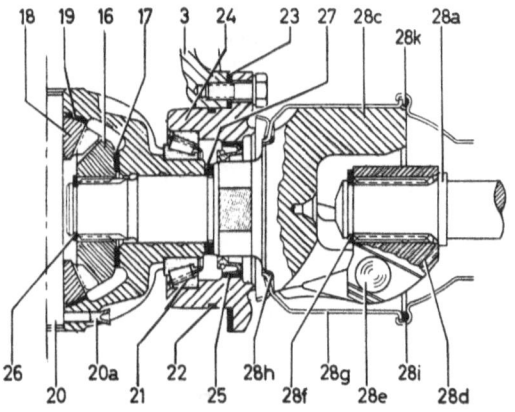

Fig. 8.30. Sectional view through inner joint of open type axleshaft (Sec. 13)

3	Differential housing	26	Circlip
16	Side gear	27	Spacer
17	Thrust washer	28a	Axleshaft
18	Pinion	28c	Yoke
19	Conical washer	28d	Spider
20	Pin	28e	Ball
20a	Clamp sleeve	28f	Circlip
21	Tapered roller bearing	28g	Cover
22	Sealing ring	28h	Sealing ring
23	Compensating washer	28i	Sleeve
24	Bearing cap	28k	Sealing ring
25	Oil seal		

14 Pinion oil seal - renewal

1   The operations are virtually identical with those described in Section 6 for rear axles with enclosed type shafts (Fig. 8.31).

2   Measure the turning torque before dismantling with the axleshafts in the horizontal attitude (Fig. 8.32).

15 Differential housing side oil seals - renewal

1   Remove the axleshaft as described in Section 14.

2   Clean away all dirt from the area of the bearing cap.

3   Prise the oil seal from the bearing cap using a large screwdriver as a lever (Fig. 8.33).

4   Before fitting a new seal note that the left-hand and right-hand seals are different. The left-hand seals are marked red and right-hand seals are marked green. Never interchange the seals as their oil return spirals are different.

5   Apply jointing compound to the periphery of the seal before driving it into position until it is flush.

6   Refit the axleshaft having first applied grease to the seal lips.

7   Check the rear axle oil level and top up if necessary.

16 Axleshaft flexible bellows - renewal

1   Remove the axleshaft as described in Section 13.

2   Remove the bellows securing clips and cut away the defective bellows from the inner joint (Fig. 8.34).

3   Disconnect the inner joint spider from the yoke and extract the six balls.

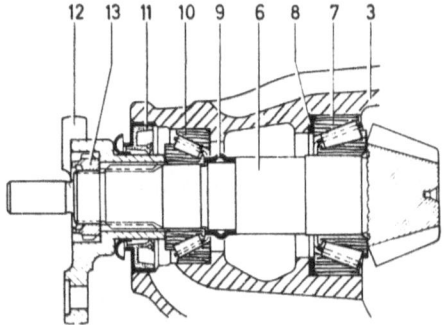

Fig. 8.31. Sectional view of rear axle pinion (Sec. 14)

3	Pinion housing	10	Tapered roller bearing
6	Drive pinion	11	Oil seal
7	Tapered roller bearing	12	Coupling flange
8	Compensating washer	13	Pinion nut
9	Spacer sleeve		

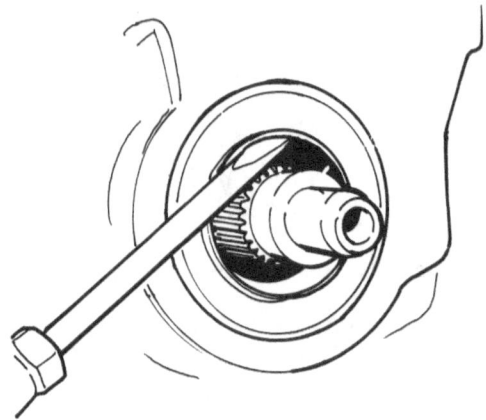

Fig. 8.32. Extracting pinion oil seal (Sec. 14)

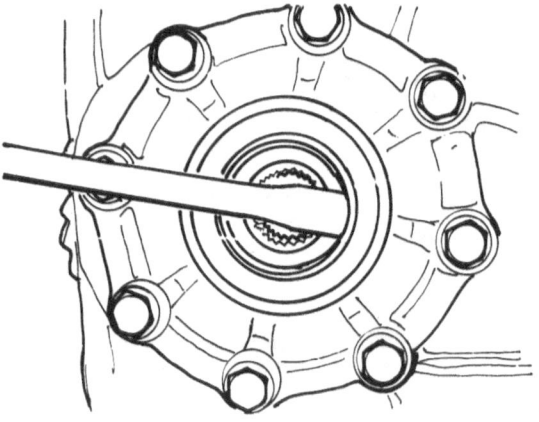

Fig. 8.33. Prising out a differential side oil seal (Sec. 15)

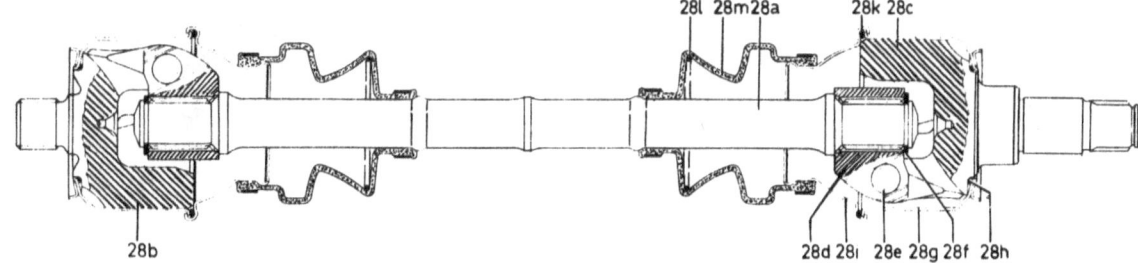

Fig. 8.34. Sectional view of complete open type axleshaft and joints (Sec. 16)

28a	Axleshaft	28d	Joint spider
28b	Outer joint yoke	28e	Ball
28c	Inner joint yoke	28f	Circlip

28g	Protective cover	28k	Sealing ring
28h	Sealing ring	28l	Clamp
28i	Sleeve	28m	Flexible bellows

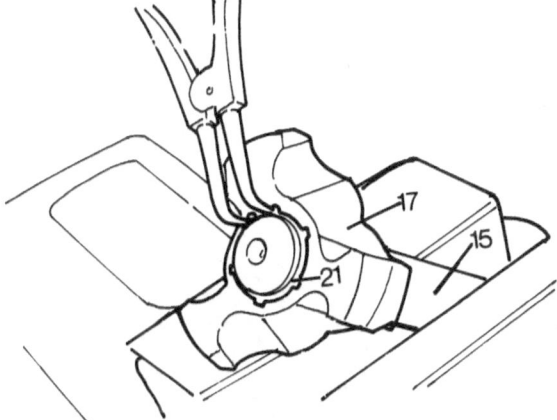

Fig. 8.35. Extracting inner joint circlip from end of axleshaft
(Sec. 16)

15 Axleshaft   17 Joint spider   21 Circlip

Fig. 8.37. Charging axleshaft joint with lubricant (Sec. 16)

4   Extract the circlip and press the inner joint spider from the axleshaft (Fig. 8.35).
5   If the flexible bellows on the outer joint are to be renewed, release the clips and pull the bellows off the inner end of the shaft.
6   Any wear or damage which is evident in the joint components must be rectified by renewal of the axleshaft complete.
7   Refitting the new bellows is a reversal of removal but observe the following points (Fig. 8.36).
8   If the outer joint is packed with grease, clean it away and refill with oil which is available in a metered quantity from your Mercedes dealer and should be substituted for the grease previously used.
9   The inner joint repair kit will contain the correct quantity of specified lubricant for injection into the joint before the bellows are sealed (Fig. 8.37).

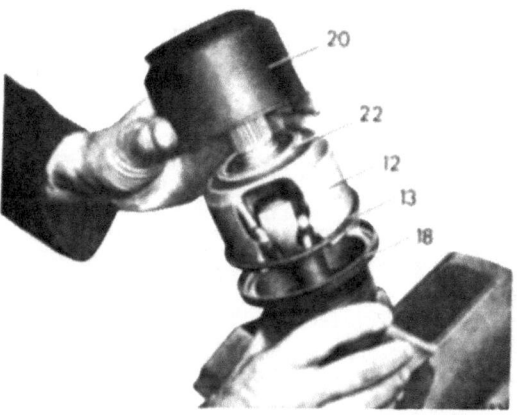

Fig. 8.36. Reassembling axleshaft joint (Sec. 16)

12	Yoke	20	Protective cover
13	Sealing ring	22	Seal
18	Support ring		

10 A beading or crimping tool should ideally be used to swage over the edge of the support ring but the careful use of a pair of pliers will offer a substitute.
11 Set the screws on the hose clips on the inner joint bellows in alignment with the screw heads pointing in the same direction.
12 Set the screws on the outer joint clips at 180° to each other.

17 Rear hub bearing - removal, refitting and adjustment

1   Support the car securely and then disconnect the outer end of the axleshaft as described in Section 13.
2   Tie the axleshaft with wire to the suspension so that it does not obstruct further work and is held in the horizontal attitude without straining the constant velocity joints.
3   Remove the caliper and the disc/drum assembly (see Chapter 9).
4   Remove the parking brake shoes (Chapter 9).
5   Make up a suitable plate with a lever which can be bolted to the axle flange (15) while the ring nut (8) is unscrewed on the inside face of the brake backplate. Use a 'C' spanner or drift to unscrew the nut (Fig. 8.38).
6   With the nut removed, prise out the oil seal assembly.
7   The axle flange should now be knocked out of the hub assembly by applying a suitable drift to the inner face of the brake backplate. Alternatively, a slide hammer may be used.
8   Remove the outer oil seal from the hub.
9   Draw or knock out the bearing outer tracks from the hub. Remove the bearing inner race from the axle flange.
10 Renew any worn components. If both rear hubs are being overhauled at the same time, take care not to mix up the axleshaft flanges. They are identified 'L' and 'R'.
11 Commence reassembly by fitting the new bearing inner race to the

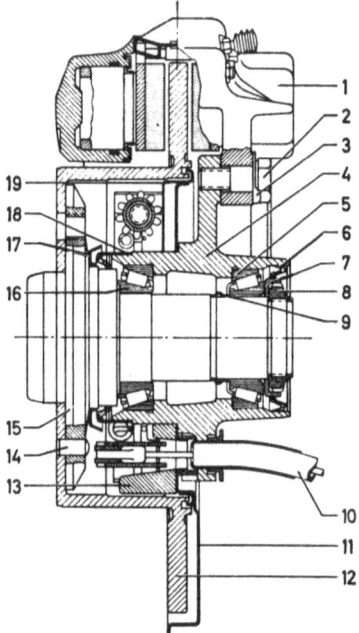

Fig. 8.38. Sectional view of a rear hub (Sec. 17)

1	Brake caliper	11	Shield
2	Bolt	12	Disc
3	Lockwasher	13	Reinforcement web
4	Hub	14	Dowel pin for drum
5	Inner tapered roller bearing		location
6	Inner oil seal	15	Axleshaft flange
7	Thrust washer	16	Outer tapered roller bearing
8	Ring nut	17	Dust deflector
9	Spacer	18	Outer oil seal
10	Handbrake outer cable	19	Backplate

axle flange. Use a piece of tubing of suitable diameter to do this (Fig. 8.39).

12 Fit the two bearing tracks to the hub.

13 Fit the outer oil seal to the hub so that it is up against the chamfer at the bottom of the hub.

14 Inject 1.75 oz (50.0 g) of multi-purpose grease into the space between the two bearing tracks in the hub.

15 Locate a new spacer sleeve in the axle flange and insert the flange into the hub.

16 To fit the flange inner tapered roller bearing first fill the space between the oil seal lips with grease and then press the bearing and seal in together.

17 Fit the seal thrust washer and screw on a new slotted nut.

18 Using the device described in paragraph 5, to hold the axle flange stationary, slowly tighten the ring nut until the endfloat is between 0.0016 and 0.0024 in (0.04 and 0.06 mm). Ideally a dial gauge should be used to check the endfloat but feeler blades can be used in conjunction with a straight edge. Do not overtighten the nut so that the endfloat disappears altogether as it is no good unscrewing the nut as the spacer will have been overcompressed and a new one will be required before carrying out the adjustment again.

19 When the adjustment is correct, lock the ring nut by staking at two points (Fig. 8.40).

20 Refit the axleshaft as described earlier in this Chapter.

21 Refit the parking brake shoes, the disc/drum and caliper and finally bleed the brakes all as described in Chapter 9.

---

18 Differential sub-frame flexible mountings - removal and refitting

Front mounting

1 Support the differential unit securely so that its weight is just taken without any tendency to raise the car itself.

2 Unbolt the supporting plate from the floor pan (Fig. 8.41).

3 Unscrew the centre bolt from the flexible mounting, insert a short

Fig. 8.39. Fitting bearing roller race to axle flange (Sec. 17)

1   Tubular drift   15   Flange   16   Tapered roller bearing

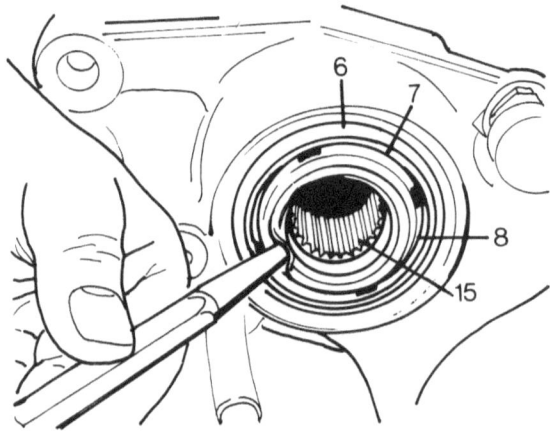

Fig. 8.40. Locking hub bearing ring nut (Sec. 17)

6   Seal   8   Ring nut
7   Thrust washer   15   Splines of axle flange

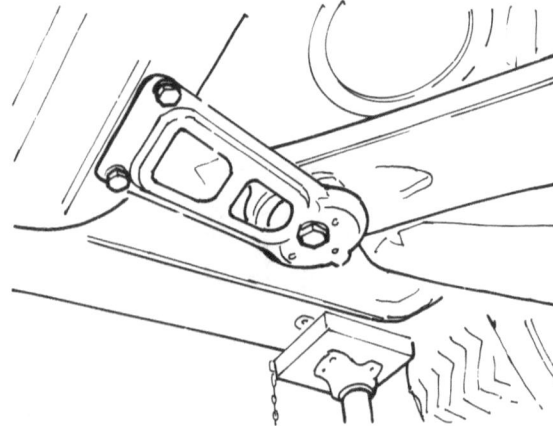

Fig. 8.41. Front mounting arrangement of differential carrier sub-frame to floor pan (one side shown) (Sec. 18)

rod into the bolt hole and, using a puller, extract the mounting from the differential sub-frame supporting member (Fig. 8.42).

4 Apply soapy water or brake fluid to the new mounting and draw it into position in the differential sub-frame supporting member using a bolt, washers and distance piece (Fig. 8.43).

5 Tighten the securing bolts to the specified torque wrench setting. Repeat the operations on the other front mounting.

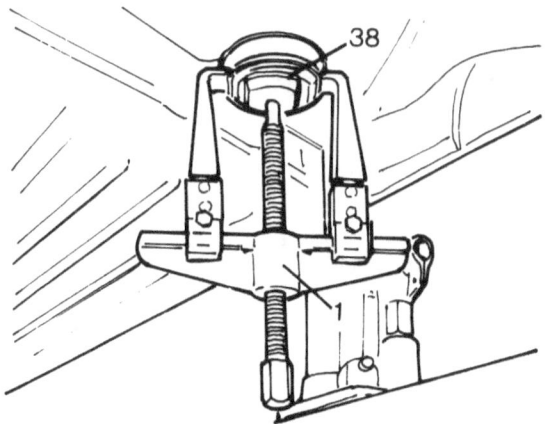

Fig. 8.42. Extracting differential sub-frame front mounting from support member (one side) (Sec. 18)

1   Puller   38   Flexible mounting

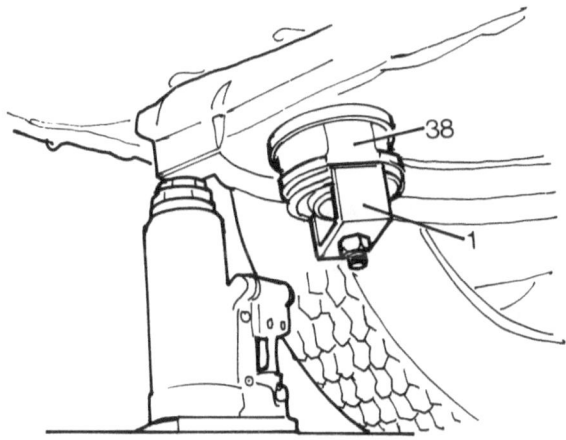

Fig. 8.43. Refitting differential sub-frame front mounting to support member (Sec. 18)

1   Fitting tool (bolt, washer, spacer)
38   Flexible mounting

Rear mounting

6   Renewal of the rear flexible mounting is simply a question of supporting the weight of the differential and unbolting the mounting from the differential end cover and from the floor pan.
7   Tighten the socket headed retaining screws to the specified torque wrench setting.

19 Differential unit complete with axleshafts - removal and refitting

1   Raise the rear end of the car and support the bodyframe on axle-stands and the differential unit on a trolley jack.
2   Disconnect both axleshafts from the hubs as described in Section 13, paragraphs 1 to 4.
3   Release the propeller shaft sliding joint and the two bolts which secure the centre bearing to the floor pan.
4   Disconnect the propeller shaft from the rear axle coupling flange by extracting the bolts and then pushing the shaft slightly forward.
5   Disconnect the differential unit rear flexible mounting and then unscrew the bolts which hold the top of the differential to the sub-frame.
6   Lower the jack carefully and withdraw the differential unit complete with axleshafts from underneath and to the rear of the car. Do not let the axleshafts or outer universal joints drop while the axle is being removed.

20 Rear axle assembly with hubs and suspension sub-frame - removal and refitting

1   Remove the exhaust system.
2   Disconnect the handbrake cables from the equaliser on the floor pan (Fig. 8.44).
3   Disconnect the rear end of the propeller shaft as described in paragraphs 3 and 4 of the preceding Section.
4   Remove the rear shock absorbers and the roadsprings as described in Chapter 11.
5   Disconnect the brake hydraulic hoses and cap them to prevent loss of fluid and entry of dirt.
6   Support the bodyframe securely in a rear end raised attitude on axlestands. Place a trolley jack under the differential and take the weight of the unit. Remove the roadwheels.
7   Disconnect the differential rear flexible mounting and the two sub-frame front flexible mountings from the floor pan.
8   Lower the trolley jack and withdraw the complete axle assembly for subsequent dismantling into individual components. Take care not to damage the brake backplate during removal by allowing the weight of the axleshafts and hubs to rest on their bottom edges.

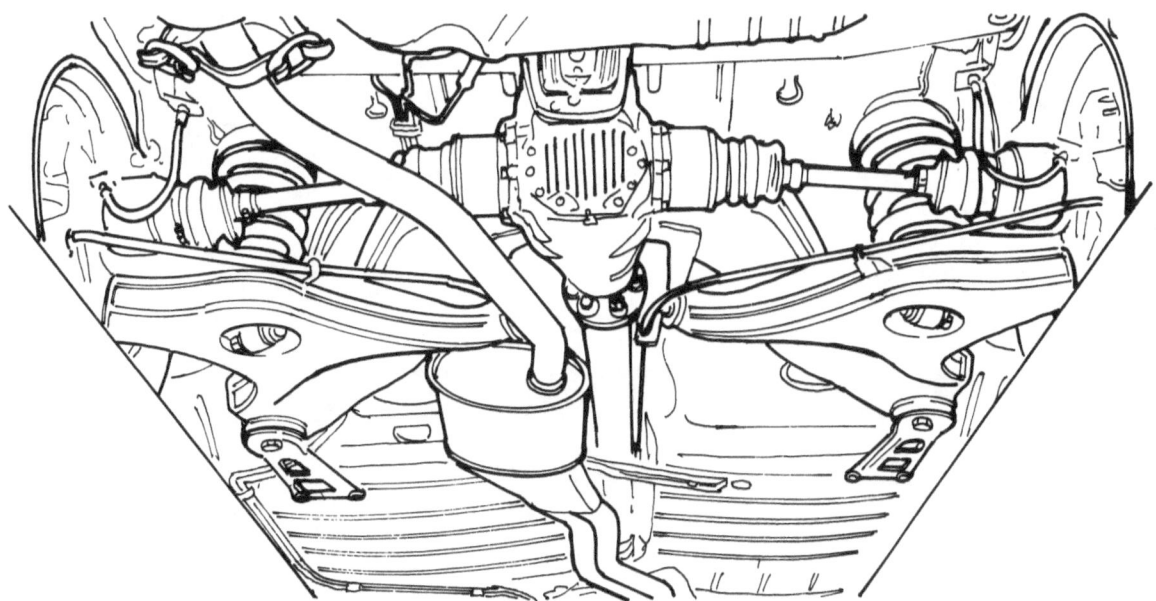

Fig. 8.44. View of open type shaft rear axle installed (Sec. 20)

21 Fault diagnosis

Symptom	Reason/s
Enclosed axleshafts	
Rumble or whine	Lack of oil in differential.
	Dry brake hold down bearing on axle tube.
	Axleshaft bearing dry or worn.
	Axle locating strut incorrectly adjusted.
	Axle locating strut flexible cushions hard or compressed.
	Worn shock absorber flexible bushes.
	Rear axle suspension carrier incorrectly positioned or flexible mountings perished.
	Suspension flexible bushes hard or worn.
'Clonk' on taking up drive or on overrun	Worn shaft or gear splines.
	Loose roadwheel bolts.
	Elongated roadwheel bolt holes.
	Worn or loose differential suspension carrier mountings or bushes.
Open driveshafts	
Rumble or whine	Worn constant velocity joints.
	Incorrect hub bearing endfloat.
	Dry or worn hub bearings.
	Loose axleshaft end nut.
	Faulty differential housing flexible mountings.
'Clonk' on taking up drive or on overrun	Loose roadwheel bolts.
	Elongated roadwheel bolt holes.
	Worn shaft splines.
	Worn constant velocity joints.
	Worn suspension sub-frame or arm flexible mountings.

Chapter 9 Braking system

Contents

Specifications

Type ... ...   Four wheel disc, dual circuit hydraulic with vacuum servo assistance. Handbrake, mechanical to auxiliary drums on rear wheels. Pressure regulator on rear hydraulic circuit

Make ... ...   ATE

Total braking area ... ...   39.8 in^2 (257.0 cm^2)

Master cylinder diameter (bore) ... ...   15/16 in (23.81 mm)

Caliper cylinder diameter (bore)
Front ... ...   2.24 in (57.0 mm)
Rear ... ...   1.38 or 1.65 in (35.0 or 42.0 mm depending upon model)

Brake servo unit ... ...   ATE 8 in or 9 in depending upon model

Minimum disc pad friction lining thickness ... ...   0.08 in (2.0 mm)

Disc diameter
Front ... ...   10.75 in (273.0 mm)
Rear ... ...   11.0 in (279.0 mm)

Disc thickness
Front ... ...   ½ in (12.6 mm)
Rear ... ...   0.39 in (10.0 mm)

Maximum refinishing cut on each side of front disc ... ...   0.020 in (0.5 mm)

Maximum refinishing cut on each side of rear disc ... ...   0.012 in (0.3 mm)

Parking brake drum internal diameter ... ...   6.30 in (160.0 mm)

Torque wrench settings

	lb f ft	Nm
Front disc to hub bolts	82	113
Caliper securing bolts	82	113
Master cylinder mounting nuts	15	21
Fluid line unions	12	16
Master cylinder stop bolt	6	8
Vacuum line union to servo unit	22	30

1 General description

All cars are equipped with four wheel disc brakes.

Actuation is by dual hydraulic circuit with vacuum servo (booster) assistance.

Some models are equipped with a rear wheel anti-locking pressure regulating valve. It is fitted in the hydraulic circuit to prevent the rear wheels locking ahead of the front ones during heavy brake application.

The handbrake operates through cables to shoes in drums which are an integral part of the brake disc.

The brake shoes are adjustable but the disc brakes are self-adjusting.

Always observe absolute cleanliness when overhauling the braking system. Use only hydraulic fluid or methylated spirit for cleaning and

do not spill fluid on the paintwork, it acts as an effective paint stripper. Always quote your car identification details when ordering
spare parts, as there are minor differences between the brake assemblies on the various models.

2   Disc pads - inspection and renewal

1   Jack-up the car and remove the roadwheel.
2   Prise out the cover plate and inspect the thickness of the friction material of the disc pads (photo).
3   If the material has worn down to 0.08 in (2.0 mm) or less, renew the pads as an axle set.
4   To remove the pads, drive out the retaining pins inwards using a punch and extract the anti-rattle spring (photos).
5   Grip the pin eye of the pad with a pair of pliers and withdraw it from the caliper (photo).
6   Remove the other pad in a similar way.
7   Brush out any dirt or dust from the aperture in the caliper, taking care not to inhale it (photo).
8   Take the opportunity to examine the disc for deep grooving or scoring. Light grooves are normal, (See Section 4).
9   If there is any evidence of oil on the pads or disc, it is probable that the hub oil seals have failed. Renew them as described in Chapter 11 before fitting the new pads.
10 In order to accommodate the new thicker pads, the caliper pistons must be depressed into their cylinders. Use a flat piece of wood or metal to do this, keeping it quite square to the piston contact face. As the piston is depressed, fluid will be displaced from the cylinder and this will cause the level to rise in the brake master cylinder reservoir.
11 To compensate for this, either syphon some fluid from the reservoir (a poultry baster or old hydrometer is useful for this) or open the caliper bleed nipple as the piston is depressed.
12 Fit the pads, the anti-rattle spring and the retaining pins. Clip the cover into position (photo).
13 Depress the footbrake hard, several times, to position the pads against the disc.

14 Repeat the operations on the opposite brake and then the rear ones.

3   Disc brake caliper - removal, overhaul and refitting

1   Jack-up the front of the car and remove the roadwheel.
2   Unscrew the brake line union on the caliper body, cap the end of the hydraulic pipe.
3   Unbolt the caliper from its mounting and withdraw it from the disc (photo).
4   Clean away external dirt and withdraw the disc pads.
5   With a screwdriver, prise the dust excluder and retaining ring from each piston.
6   Apply air pressure from a tyre pump to the fluid inlet union on the caliper, hold one piston depressed and eject the opposite one. Very low air pressure is required for this and a foot-operated tyre pump will do the job.
7   Hold a thick rubber pad against the open cylinder, apply air pressure again and eject the second piston. Mark the pistons and their respective cylinders so that they will not be interchanged. A piece of masking tape will be useful for this.
8   Examine the surfaces of the pistons and cylinders for scoring or 'bright' wear areas. If there is any evidence of these, renew the caliper complete. If the pistons are seized or rusted in their bores and cannot be ejected then again the caliper must be renewed complete.
9   If the piston and cylinder are in good condition, carefully pick out the seals from their cylinder grooves and discard them, then obtain a repair kit which will contain new ones and any other renewable items. It is very important to quote the code number on the caliper body when ordering spare parts.
10 Manipulate the new seals into position using the fingers only for this work. Use only clean hydraulic fluid or methylated spirit for cleaning or lubrication - nothing else!
11 Dip the piston seal assemblies into hydraulic fluid and fit them into their cylinders. Before depressing the pistons fully, turn them so that the recessed part of the piston to pad contact face is at the top at an angle as shown in Fig. 9.3a. This arrangement is to minimise disc pad

2.2 Disc pad shield

2.4A Removing a disc pad retaining pin

2.4B Disc pad anti-rattle spring

2.5 Removing a disc pad

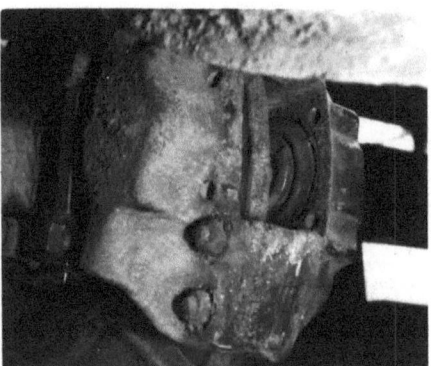
2.7 Caliper with disc pads removed

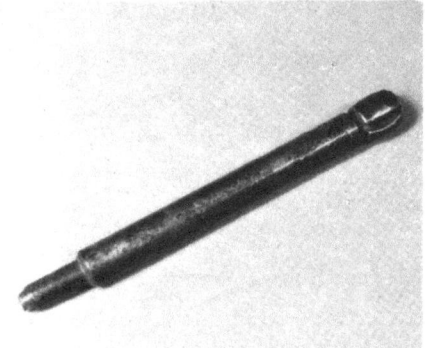
2.12 Detailed view of a disc pad retaining pin

Fig. 9.1. Front disc brake components (Sec. 3)

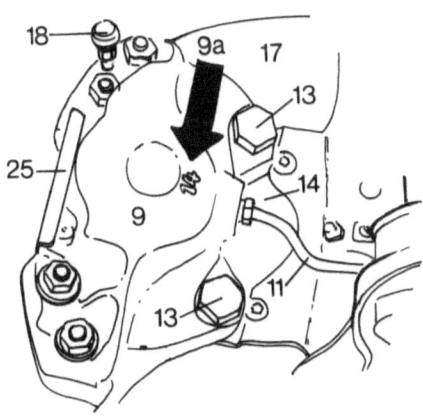

Fig. 9.2. Front caliper details (Sec. 3)

9	Caliper	14	Lockplate
9a	Identification code	17	Shield
11	Brake fluid line	18	Bleed nipple and dust cap
13	Mounting bolt	25	Disc pad cover plate

squeal.

12 Locate the dust excluder and the retaining ring and press the latter squarely into position without bending or deforming it.

13 The piston heat shields do not normally require removal from the piston but check that the raised part of the piston is at least 0.004 in (0.1 mm) above the surface of the heat shield. If necessary, press the heat shield further into the piston by means of a short bolt and nut located against a plate in the pad aperture of the caliper body. The heat shields for the inner and outer pistons are different and are not interchangeable (Fig. 9.4).

14 With the pistons fully depressed into their cylinder bores, refit the caliper and reconnect the fluid line.

15 Fit the disc pads as described in Section 2.

16 Bleed the hydraulic circuit as described in Section 8.

17 Fit the roadwheel and lower the jack.

18 During any work on a caliper unit never release the bolts which secure both halves of the caliper body together as they are specially tightened during manufacture.

4 Brake disc - inspection, removal and refitting

Front disc

1 Jack-up the front of the car and remove the roadwheel.

2 Disconnect the hydraulic line and cap the pipe.

3 Unbolt and remove the caliper.

3.3 Removing a disc brake caliper

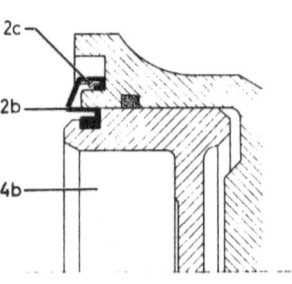

Fig. 9.3. Sectional view showing caliper dust excluder (26) retaining ring (2b) and piston (4b) (Sec. 3)

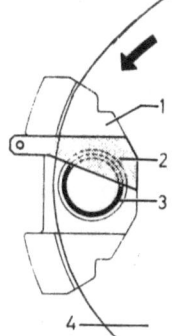

Fig. 9.3A. Caliper piston setting diagram (Sec. 3)

1	Caliper body	3	Piston
2	20° template	4	Brake disc

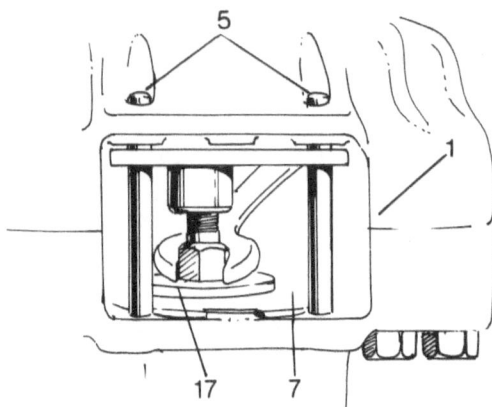

Fig. 9.4. Pressing a heat shield into a caliper piston recess (Sec. 3)

1 Caliper body	17 Nut, bolt and washer for
5 Pad securing pin	applying pressure to heat
7 Heat shield	shield

5.6 The tandem brake master cylinder

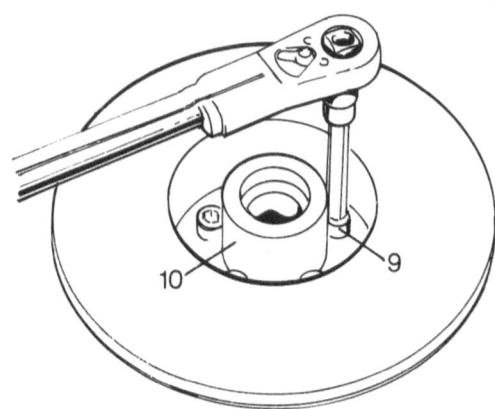

Fig. 9.5. Separating a front disc from hub (Sec. 4)

1   Disc   9   Socket headed bolt   10   Hub

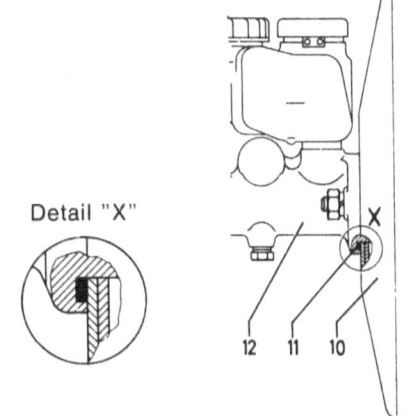

Fig. 9.6. Brake master cylinder mounting to servo unit (Sec. 5)

10   Servo unit   11   O-ring seal   12   Master cylinder

Detail "X"

4   Remove the hub/disc assembly as described in Chapter 11.
5   If the disc is to be removed and then refitted for further service, then mark its relative position to the hub before continuing.
6   Secure the hub and then unscrew the socket-headed bolts which hold the disc to the hub (Fig. 9.5).
7   If the disc is deeply grooved it may be refinished provided each side of the disc is not cut to a depth greater than 0.020 in (0.5 mm). If deep grooves cannot be removed by this treatment, then the disc will have to be renewed.

Rear disc
8   To remove the rear disc, jack-up the rear of the car and remove the roadwheel.
9   With the car safely chocked, fully release the handbrake, unbolt and remove the caliper.
10 On cars with enclosed axleshafts, if the rigid brake line clips are released from the axle casing, there will be enough play to enable the caliper to be moved aside without having to disconnect the fluid pipes.
11 On cars which have the open type axleshafts, unbolt the caliper and move it away from the disc as far as the flexible hydraulic hose will allow and then tie it to the bodyframe.
12 The disc/drum assembly is located on a positioning dowel. Tap off the assembly using a plastic faced hammer.
13 The disc may be refinished as described for the front disc, but do not go deeper than 0.012 in (0.3 mm) on either side of the disc. If grooves cannot be removed by this means, renew the complete disc/drum assembly.

14 Refit the disc/drum, the caliper and the roadwheel and lower the car to the ground.

5   Master cylinder - removal, overhaul and refitting

1   Fit a bleed tube to the bleed nipple on one of the front calipers.
2   Place the end of the tube in a container and then open the nipple one turn.
3   Depress the foot brake pedal repeatedly until the fluid from the master cylinder and the reservoir is completely ejected.
4   Close the front caliper bleed nipple and transfer the bleed tube and jar to one of the new nipples.
5   Open the nipple and repeat the fluid ejection operation as for the front hydraulic circuit.
6   Disconnect the connector plugs from the warning switches on the fluid reservoirs. To pull out the plugs, lift their retaining lugs with a small screwdriver (photo).
7   Disconnect both hydraulic lines from the master cylinder by unscrewing the connecting unions.
8   Cap or plug all fluid lines to prevent dirt entering.
9   Unscrew the nuts which hold the master cylinder to the front face of the vacuum servo unit (booster).
10 Withdraw the master cylinder and extract the flange O-ring seal. (Fig. 9.6).
11 Clean away all external dirt and prepare to dismantle.
12 Unless the fluid reservoirs are leaking there is no need to remove

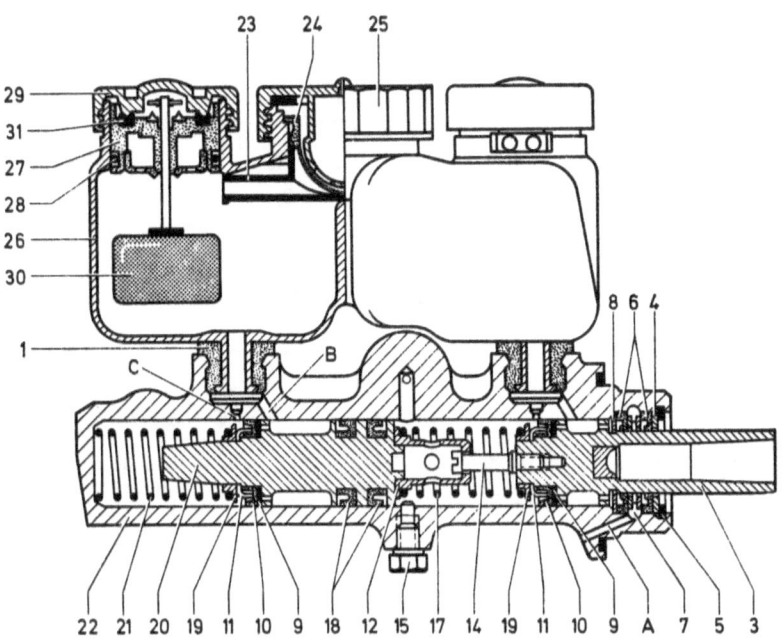

1	Reservoir sealing plug
3	Primary piston
4	Stop plate
5	Circlip
6	Seals
7	Intermediate ring
8	Thrust washer
9	Spacer
10	Primary sleeve
11	Support ring
12	Spring retainer
14	Connecting screw
15	Stop screw
17	Spring
18	Seals
19	Spring retainer
20	Secondary piston
21	Spring
22	Master cylinder body
23	Splash baffle
24	Strainer
25	Cap
26	Fluid reservoir
27	Contact for level warning switch
28	O-ring seal
29	Screw cap
30	Float
31	O-ring seal
A	Drain hole
B	Fluid entry
C	Equalising hole

Fig. 9.7. Sectional view of tandem master cylinder (Sec. 5)

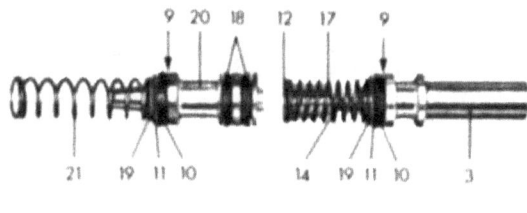

Fig. 9.9. Arrangement of master cylinder piston seals

3	Primary piston	17	Spring
9	Spacer	18	Secondary piston seals
10	Seal	19	Spring retaining seat
11	Support ring	20	Secondary piston
12	Spring retaining disc	21	Spring
14	Connecting disc		

a) Dip all components in clean hydraulic fluid before assembling and avoid any dirt contamination.
b) Use the fingers only to manipulate the new seals into position.
c) Make sure that the lips of the seals are facing exactly as shown in Fig. 9.9.
d) Install the piston assemblies using a twisting motion to avoid trapping the seal lip or bending it back.

22 To refit the master cylinder, locate a new 'O' ring at the mounting flange. This is important as a vacuum tight seal must be maintained between the master cylinder and the vacuum servo unit. Tighten the securing nuts to the correct torque wrench setting and reconnect the fluid lines.
23 Reconnect the warning switch plugs.
24 Fill the master cylinder reservoirs with clean hydraulic fluid which has been stored in an airtight container and has remained unshaken for the preceding 24 hours. **Make sure that the caliper bleed nipples are closed.**
25 Bleed the system as described in Section 8.

---

6 Pressure regulating valve

1   On some models, a pressure regulating valve is mounted on the floor pan just ahead of the rear axle.
2   Its function is to prevent the rear wheels locking ahead of the front wheels during heavy brake applications.

Fig. 9.8. Dismantling master cylinder primary piston

3	Primary piston	17	Spring
12	Spring retaining seat	19	Spring retaining disc
14	Connecting screw		

them from the master cylinder. If they must be removed, then pull the reservoirs sharply from their sealing plugs.
13 Depress the master cylinder piston slightly and then unscrew the stop screw (15) and remove it together with its seal (Fig. 9.7).
14 Continue to depress the piston slightly and extract the circlip (5).
15 Extract the primary piston assembly together with stop washer (4), seals (6), intermediate ring (7) and thrust washer (8).
16 Tap the end of the master cylinder on a piece of wood to eject the secondary piston assembly.
17 At this stage, examine the surfaces of the pistons and cylinder bores. If there is evidence of scoring or 'bright' wear areas, renew the master cylinder complete.
18 If these components appear to be in good condition continue dismantling by extracting the connecting screw (14) from the primary piston (3) (Fig. 9.8).
19 Remove the spring (17) disc (19) and supporting disc (12).
20 Clean all components in hydraulic fluid or methylated spirit, nothing else! Discard the seals and obtain a repair kit which will contain new seals and other renewable components.
21 Reassembly is a reversal of dismantling but observe the following points:

3   Testing of the valve cannot be carried out by the home mechanic but if the valve is suspected of being faulty, have it tested by your dealer.

4   The valve cannot be repaired and must be renewed complete where necessary.

5   Bleed the rear hydraulic circuit after the rear valve has been fitted.

7   Brake pipes and hoses

1   At the intervals recommended in 'Routine Maintenance' check the complete hydraulic system for fluid leakage at unions and joints.

2   Inspect the flexible hose for deterioration and chafing. Bend the hose almost double with the fingers and check for tiny cracks. If any are evident, renew the hoses.

3   Examine the rigid lines for abrasion at points where they run through holes in the bodyframe or where their securing clips are loose. If rust or corrosion is evident, the section of pipe must be renewed. Most garages can make up a new pipe if the old one is taken as a guide.

4   When renewing a flexible hose, disconnect it first at its union with the rigid line. Then disconnect it from its support bracket and finally unscrew it from the caliper body or connectors as the case may be. Never be tempted to try and unscrew a hose from the wrong end by twisting it round and round.

5   Having fitted a new hose, check that it does not rub against any part of the suspension or tyres. Turn the roadwheels from lock to lock to verify this. Where necessary, the lockplate at the flexible hose support bracket may be moved to give the hose a 'set' away from any adjacent components.

8   Hydraulic system - bleeding

1   Wherever any part of the hydraulic system has been dismantled, the system must be bled. Where only one circuit has been 'broken' then only that circuit need be bled. If the master cylinder has been removed then both circuits must be bled. Destroy the servo vacuum by repeated application of the pedal.

2   To bleed a brake circuit, fit a bleed tube to the nipple on one of the calipers. If the bleed tube does not incorporate a non-return valve then the help of an assistant will be required.

3   Place the open end of the valveless type bleed tube in a jar and submerge it under some hydraulic fluid. Tubes with a non-return valve should be located over a container to catch any ejected fluid.

4   Release the bleed nipple and unscrew it about half a turn.

5   Depress the footbrake pedal fully to the floor, then release it and allow it to return under the action of its return springs.

6   Repeat the operation until no more air bubbles are seen to emerge from the end of the tube under the fluid.

7   Tighten the bleed screw while the pedal is held fully depressed.

8   Repeat the bleeding operation on the other bleed screw of the circuit and then the other circuit if this too has to be bled.

9   It is vital that the fluid reservoirs on the master cylinder are kept topped up throughout the operations, otherwise air will only be drawn into the system once again if the level is allowed to drop so low that the fluid inlet ports of the master cylinder are exposed.

10 Always use clean fluid which has been stored in an airtight container and has remained unshaken for the preceding 24 hours.

11 If a bleed tube with a non-return valve is used, check the pedal travel every six bleed strokes, having tightened the bleed nipple. Any sponginess or excessive pedal travel will indicate the need for further bleeding.

12 Discard the expelled hydraulic fluid or retain it only for bleed-jar purposes.

9   Brake pedal - removal, refitting and adjustment

1   Removal and refitting of the brake pedal is described in Chapter 5 in conjunction with the clutch pedal.

2   *To adjust the brake pedal on all models except 280 SL/8,* turn the eccentric bolt (3a) until the notch on the bolt head points to the rear (Fig. 9.12).

3   The brake stop lamp switch should now have about 0.16 in (4.0 mm) of its contact button exposed. Alter the position of the switch if necessary to achieve this. Test the operation of the switch with the

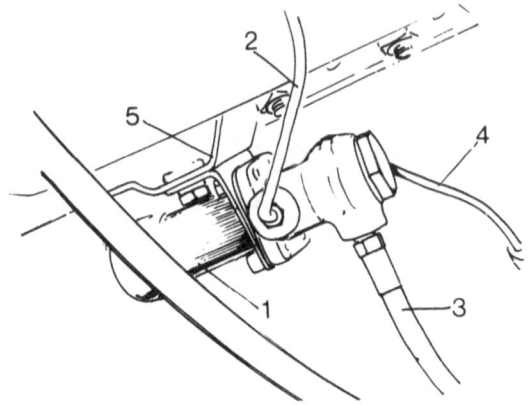

Fig. 9.10. Pressure regulating valve (Sec. 6)

1   *Regulating valve*
2   *Line from master cylinder*
3   *Hose to left-hand rear caliper*
4   *Hose to right-hand rear caliper*
5   *Valve support bracket*

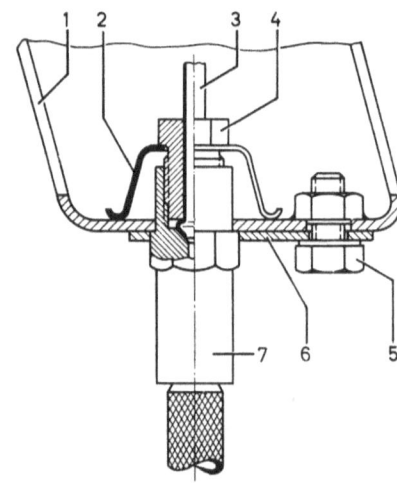

Fig. 9.11. Typical flexible hose connection to rigid fluid line (Sec. 7)

1   *Support bracket*
2   *Anti-rotation clip*
3   *Rigid brake line*
4   *Union*
5   *Bolt*
6   *Lockplate*
7   *Flexible hose end fitting*

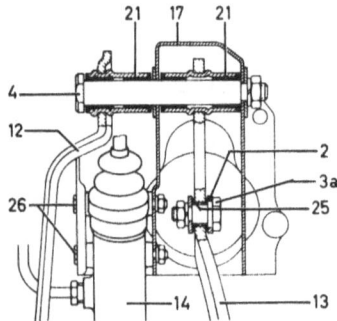

Fig. 9.12. Brake pedal arrangement except 280 SL/8 (Sec. 9)

2   *Pushrod to servo unit*
3a   *Eccentric adjuster bolt*
4   *Pivot bolt*
12   *Clutch pedal*
13   *Brake pedal*
14   *Clutch master cylinder*
17   *Mounting bracket*
21   *Bushes*
25   *Bush*
26   *Clutch master cylinder mounting bolts*

ignition on.

4 *To adjust the brake pedal on 280 SL/8 models,* turn the eccentric bolt (2) located on the top of the intermediate lever within the engine compartment until the notch on the bolt faces the rear of the car (Fig. 9.14).

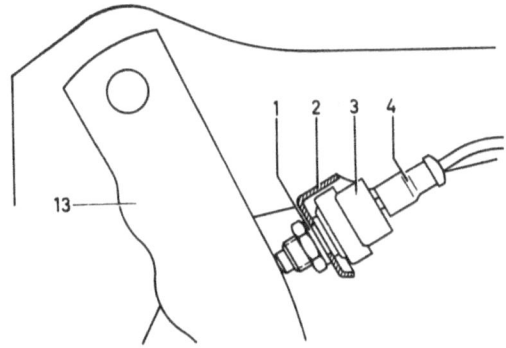

Fig. 9.13. Brake stop lamp switch (Sec. 9)

1	Nut	4	Connector plug
2	Switch mounting bracket	13	Brake pedal
3	Stop lamp switch		

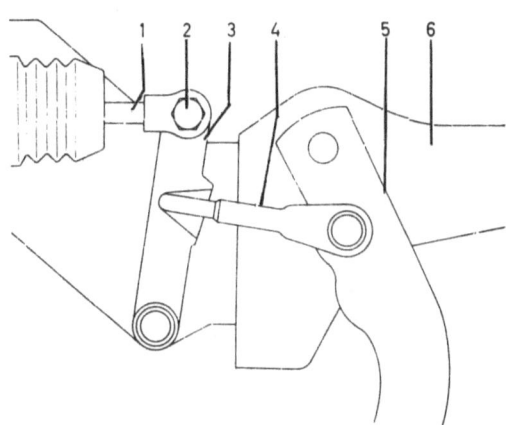

Fig. 9.14. Brake pushrod arrangement on 280 SL/8 models (Sec. 9)

1	Pushrod	4	Thrust rod
2	Eccentric adjuster bolt	5	Brake pedal
3	Intermediate lever	6	Pedal mounting bracket

10.5 Adjusting parking brake shoes

5 Adjustment of the brake stop lamp switch is similar to that described in paragraph 3 except that the hexagonal flange nut which locks the switch also serves as the brake pedal stop.

10 Handbrake - adjustment

1 Jack up the rear of the car so that the roadwheels are off the ground.
2 Fully release the handbrake.
3 Unscrew and remove one bolt from each of the rear roadwheels.
4 Turn the roadwheels until the star wheel brake adjuster is visible through the bolt hole. A torch will be necessary to see this.
5 Insert a screwdriver and turn the adjuster until the roadwheel can no longer be turned. Now back off the adjuster until the roadwheel is just free to rotate without binding (photo).
6 Repeat the adjustment on the opposite rear wheel.
7 Lower the car, remove the jacks and apply the handbrake.
8 With the brake shoes correctly adjusted, the handbrake control lever should be fully applied after it has been pulled over 5 or 6 notches of its ratchet. Where the lever travel is excessive adjust the cables by means of either the nut at the intermediate lever (except 280 SL/8) or the knurled adjuster set in the control lever (280 SL/8).
9 On some cars a pull-out type handbrake control is located under the instrument panel. Adjust this at the equaliser under the car.

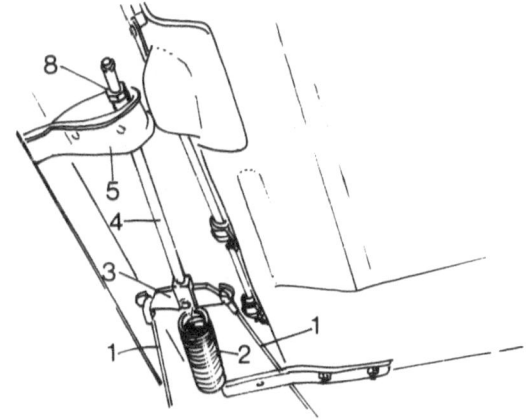

Fig. 9.15. Handbrake cables connected to equaliser (not 280 SL/8) (Sec. 10)

1	Rear cables	4	Rod
2	Return spring	5	Intermediate lever
3	Equaliser	8	Adjuster nut

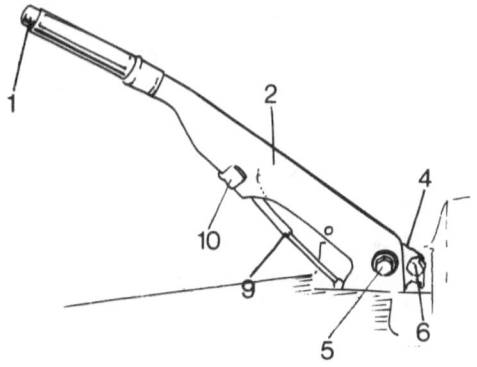

Fig. 9.16. Knurled adjuster on 280 SL/8 handbrake control (Sec. 10)

1	Push button	6	Mounting bolt
2	Control lever	9	Primary cable
4	Quadrant (ratchet)	10	Adjuster
5	Pivot bolt		

11 Parking brake shoes - inspection and renewal

1   Jack up the rear of the car, support it securely on axle stands and remove the roadwheel.
2   Release the brake line clips as necessary (enclosed type axleshafts) and unbolt and pull the caliper away just far enough to clear the disc. There is no need to disconnect the fluid line but do not bend or damage the pipe.
3   Make sure that the handbrake is fully released and then tap off the disc/drum assembly (photo).
4   If the linings have worn down to a thickness of 0.04 in (1.0 mm) or less, renew the shoes (photo). If the linings are in good condition, brush out any dirt, taking care not to inhale it, and refit the disc/drum. It is rarely that the shoes require renewal as the handbrake is usually

applied with the car stationary. The most common cause for shoe renewal is due to oil from a defective oil seal.
5   To remove the shoes, unhook the shoe lower return spring.
6   Turn the axle flange so that the larger hole is in alignment with one of the shoe steady springs.
7   Insert a suitable tool through the flange into the centre of the spring coils, turn the spring through 90° and withdraw it (Fig. 9.18).
8   Remove the shoe steady spring from the other shoe.
9   Prise both shoes apart against the action of the upper return spring and remove them.
10 Place the shoes on the bench and remove the upper return spring and the star wheel adjuster.
11 Detach the return spring at the equaliser under the car and unscrew the cable adjusting nut until the cables can be unhooked from the equaliser. On 280 SL/8 models, release the cable adjustment by means

Fig. 9.17. Rear brake components (Sec. 11)

11.3 Rear disc/drum removed from hub

11.4 Rear parking brake shoes

of the knurled adjuster screw incorporated in the handbrake control lever.

12 Disconnect the rear end of the handbrake cable by pushing out the pin (33) from the expander (26) (Fig. 9.19.).

13 Reassembly is a reversal of dismantling but set the star wheel adjuster to the fully retracted position and apply a smear of high melting point grease to all friction surfaces of the expander and brake backplate.

14 Assemble the upper ends of the shoes on the bench with the adjuster device and the return spring. Lower the assembly into position and engage the lower ends in the expander. Connect the lower return spring and fit the shoe steady springs, turning them through 90º to engage them.

15 Fit the disc/drum on its locating dowel (photo).

16 Refit the caliper.

17 Reconnect the handbrake cables and the roadwheel.

18 Adjust the shoes and the control lever and cables as described in Section 10.

19 Repeat the operations on the opposite rear brake.

20 Lower the car to the ground, refit the roadwheel bolts and check the tightness of all wheel bolts.

12 Vacuum servo unit (booster) - description and maintenance

1 A vacuum servo unit is fitted into the brake hydraulic circuit in series with the master cylinder, to provide assistance to the driver when the brake pedal is depressed. This reduces the effort required by the driver to operate the brakes under all braking conditions.

2 The unit operates by vacuum obtained from the induction manifold and comprises basically a booster diaphragm and non-return valve. The servo unit and hydraulic master cylinder are connected together so that the servo unit piston rod acts as the master cylinder pushrod. The driver's braking effort is transmitted through another pushrod to the servo piston and its built-in control system. The servo unit piston does not fit tightly into the cylinder, but has a strong diaphragm to keep its edges in constant contact with the cylinder wall, so assuming an airtight seal between the two parts. The forward chamber is held under vacuum conditions created in the inlet manifold of the engine and, during periods when the brake pedal is not in use, the controls open a passage to the rear chamber so placing it under vacuum conditions as well. When the brake pedal is depressed, the vacuum passage to the rear chamber is cut off and the chamber opened to atmospheric pressure. The

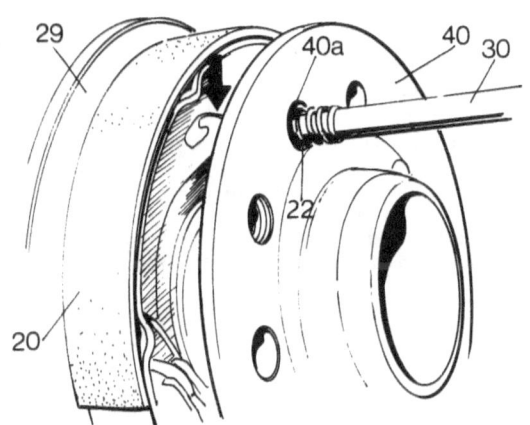

Fig. 9.18. Removing a brake shoe steady spring (Sec. 11)

20	Shoe	30	Spring removal tool
22	Steady spring	40	Axleshaft flange
29	Backplate	40a	Spring removal hole in flange

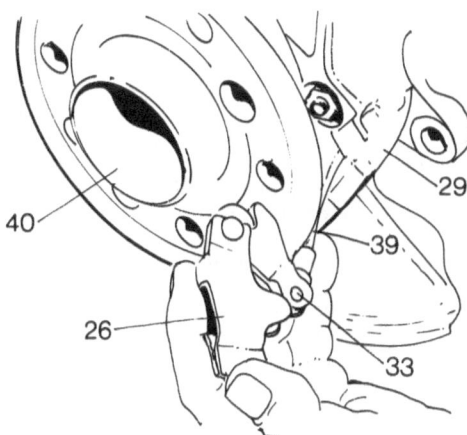

Fig. 9.19. Handbrake cable attachment to shoe expander (Sec. 11)

26	Expander	39	Handbrake cable
29	Brake mounting plate	40	Axleshaft
33	Clevis pin		

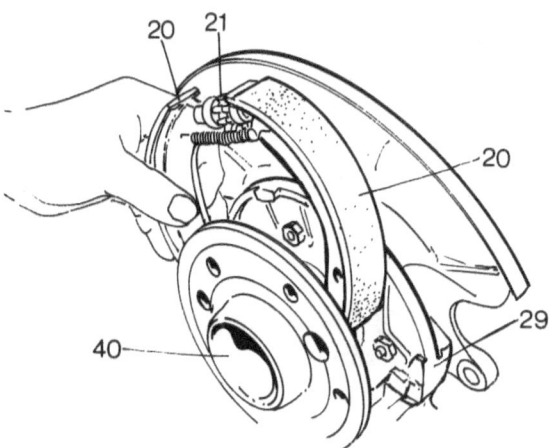

Fig. 9.20. Refitting handbrake shoes (Sec. 11)

20	Shoes	29	Brake mounting plate
21	Adjuster	40	Rear axleshaft

11.15 Rear brake drum alignment dowel

12.6 Vacuum servo (booster) hose to manifold and non-return valve

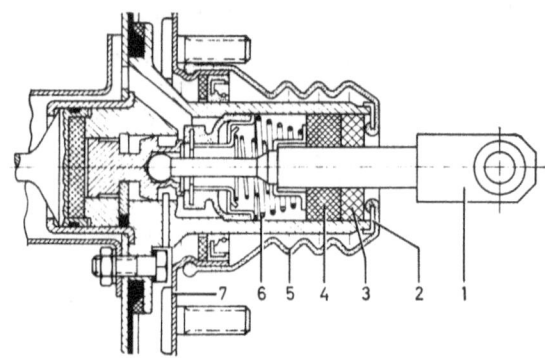

Fig. 9.21. Sectional view of brake servo pushrod housing (Sec. 12)

1	Pushrod	5	Dust excluding bellows
2	Retainer	6	Housing
3	Silencer	7	Servo unit rear shell
4	Filter		

consequent rush of air pushes the servo piston forward in the vacuum chamber and operates the main pushrod to the master cylinder.

3 The controls are designed so that assistance is given under all conditions and, when the brakes are not required, vacuum in the rear chamber is established when the brake pedal is released. All air from the atmosphere entering the rear chamber is passed through a small air filter.

4 Under normal operating conditions the vacuum servo unit is very reliable but when it becomes faulty or requires overhaul, it should be renewed complete rather than overhaul the original.

5 It is emphasised, that the servo unit assists in reducing the braking effort required at the foot pedal and in the event of its failure, the hydraulic braking system is in no way affected except that the need for higher pedal pressures will be noticed.

6 Periodically inspect the condition of the vacuum hose and clips. Renew the hose if it has deteriorated (photo).

7 At the specified mileage intervals, the booster air filter should be renewed. Access to this is obtained after removing the brake servo unit as described in Section 13.

8 Pull off the dust excluding bellows.

9 Remove the air silencer retainer by levering it out with two small screwdrivers.

10 Using a hooked piece of stout wire, pull out the air silencer pad and then the filter pad.

11 Fit the new filter and air silencer noting that the filter is twice as thick as the silencer and should be fitted first.

12 When the silencer has been fitted turn it so that the two inserts are at 90° to each other.

13 Fit the silencer retainer and dust excluder.

14 Refit the brake booster as described in the next Section.

13 Vacuum servo unit (booster) - removal and refitting

1 On cars with manual transmission, unscrew the clutch reservoir bracket from the servo unit and tie it to one side.

2 Empty the brake master cylinder fluid reservoir by syphoning. Disconnect the leads from the warning switches.

3 Disconnect the fluid outlet pipes from the master cylinder body, actuate the foot pedal and expel the fluid in the master cylinder into a container.

4 Cap or plug all fluid lines and openings.

5 Disconnect the vacuum hose from the servo unit.

6 On 280 SL/8 models, disconnect the brake push rod from the intermediate lever by extracting the eccentric adjuster bolt.

7 On all other models, disconnect the pushrod in a similar manner from the brake pedal.

8 On 280 SL/8 models unbolt the vacuum servo unit from its support within the engine compartment.

9 On all other models, remove the servo unit with its mounting flange by unscrewing two nuts within the engine compartment and one nut inside the car on the toe-board.

10 If the servo unit is to be renewed, unbolt the master cylinder from it. **Note: Take care not to knock the pushrod housing as it is made of a brittle plastic.**

11 Refitting the master cylinder to the servo unit must be made vacuum tight, therefore renew the O-ring flange seal.

12 Fit the servo unit and adjust the brake pedal as described in Section 9.

13 Connect the vacuum hose.

14 Connect the fluid lines and electrical plugs to the master cylinder.

15 Bleed the hydraulic system (both circuits) as described in Section 8.

14 Fault diagnosis - braking system

Symptom	Reason/s
Brake pedal spongy	Air in hydraulic system. Fault in master cylinder. Disc pads worn out. Overheated brake fluid due to excessive brake application.
Brakes binding	Fault in master cylinder. Swollen seals in system (due to use of incorrect fluid). Incorrect parking brake adjustment.
Poor retardation in spite of high pedal pressure	Pads contaminated with oil. Pads worn or burnt. Oily or grooved brake discs. No servo assistance due to leak in hose, faulty non-return valve or master cylinder mounting flange 'O'ring. Leak in one hydraulic circuit.
*Squealing brakes	Incorrect setting of recess in caliper piston. Pad too tight in caliper aperture.
Chatter or judder	Variable wear thickness of disc. Weak shock absorber on one side. Disc glazed with lining particles. (Clean with emery cloth).
Loss of fluid	Leak in circuit. Internal leak from master cylinder into vacuum servo unit.
Handbrake ineffective	Shoes contaminated with oil. Shoes require adjustment. Handbrake control lever or cables require adjustment.

Mild squealing is normal and varies with the weather conditions.

Chapter 10 Electrical system

Contents

Specifications

System type	12V negative earth with battery, alternator and pre-engaged starter

Battery capacity	55 Amp hour

Alternator

Type	
Standard	Bosch K1(RL) 14V 35 A 20
Heavy duty	Bosch K1(RL) 14V 55 A 20
Max. output	490 watts
Load current (amps) at alternator speed (rpm)	

Type	Stand	HD	Stand	HD
	10	10	1300	1200
	23	36	2000	2000
	35	55	6000	6000

Voltage regulator

Type	Bosch RS/ADN 1/14V with interference suppressor
Regulating voltage	13.9 to 14.8V
Load current	28 to 30 Amps
Type	Bosch RS/AD 1/14V without interference suppressor
Regulating voltage	13.9 to 14.8V

Starter motor

Type (up to August 1968)	Bosch EF 12V
Rating	0.8 HP
Idle test	35 to 45A at 12V at 6400 to 7900 rpm
Load test	165 to 200A at 9V at 1100 to 1450 rpm
Type (after August 1968)	Bosch GF 12V
Rating	1.4 HP
Idle test	50 to 70A at 12V at 9000 to 11000 rpm
Load test	290 to 330A at 9V at 1600 to 1800 rpm

Bulbs

Light unit	Wattage
Headlight	
Bulb type	45/40
Sealed beam	NA
Direction indicator	21
Front parking	4
Fog	35
Side marker (front)	4
Brake stop lamp	21

Bulbs

Light unit								Wattage
Side marker (rear)	...	...	...	...	...	...	...	5
Reversing lamp ...	...	...	...	...	...	...	...	15
Rear licence plate	...	...	...	...	...	...	...	5 (two)

All external bulbs are of bayonet fixing type with the exception of the rear licence plate which incorporates festoon type bulbs. Internal bulbs may be of festoon or capless type (warning and indicator).

1 General description

The electrical system is of 12 volt negative earth type and comprises a lead-acid battery (which is charged by a belt-driven alternator), a pre-engaged starter motor and a range of accessories.

A number of relays are incorporated in the system and all circuits are fused.

2 Battery - removal and refitting

1 The battery is located within the engine compartment on the left-hand side (photo).
2 To remove the battery first disconnect the lead from the negative (—) terminal followed by the positive (+) one.
3 Detach the battery holding down clamp bolts and lift the battery from its platform. Take care not to spill electrolyte on the bodywork or the paint will be damaged.
4 Refitting is a reversal of removal but make sure that the lead terminals and battery posts are clean and making a sound metal-to-metal contact. Finally smear the terminals with petroleum jelly as a protection against corrosion.

3 Battery - maintenance and inspection

1 Keep the top of the battery clean by wiping away dirt and moisture.
2 Remove the plugs or lid from the cells and check that the electrolyte level is just above the separator plates. If the level has fallen, add only distilled water until the electrolyte level is just above the separator plates.
3 As well as keeping the terminals clean and covered with petroleum jelly, the top of the battery, and especially the top of the cells, should be kept clean and dry. This helps prevent corrosion and ensures that the battery does not become partially discharged by leakage through dampness and dirt.
4 Once every three months, remove the battery and inspect the battery securing bolts, the battery clamp plate, tray and battery leads for corrosion (white fluffy deposits on the metal which are brittle to touch). If any corrosion is found, clean off the deposits with ammonia and paint over the clean metal with an anti-rust/anti-acid paint.
5 At the same time inspect the battery case for cracks. If a crack is found, clean and plug it with one of the proprietary compounds marketed for this purpose. If leakage through the crack has been excessive then it will be necessary to refill the appropriate cell with fresh electrolyte as detailed later. Cracks are frequently caused to the top of battery cases by pouring in distilled water in the middle of winter *after* instead of *before* a run. This gives the water no chance to mix with the electrolyte and so the former freezes and splits the battery case.
6 If topping up the battery becomes excessive and the case has been inspected for cracks that could cause leakage, but none are found, the battery is being over-charged and the voltage regulator which controls the output of the alternator must be at fault.
7 With the battery on the bench at the three monthly interval check, measure its specific gravity with a hydrometer to determine the state of charge and condition of the electrolyte. There should be very little variation between the different cells and if a variation in excess of 0.25 is present it will be due to either:

a) *Loss of electrolyte from the battery at some time caused by spillage or a leak, resulting in a drop in the specific gravity of electrolyte when the deficiency was refilled with distilled water instead of fresh electrolyte.*
b) *An internal short circuit caused by buckling of the plates or a similar malady pointing to the likelihood of total battery failure in the near future.*

2.1 The battery

8 The specific gravity of the electrolyte for fully charged conditions at the electrolyte temperature indicated, is listed in Table A. The specific gravity of a fully discharged battery at different temperatures of the electrolyte is given in Table B.

Table A

Specific Gravity - Battery Fully Charged

1.268 at 100°F or 38° electrolyte temperature
1.272 at 90°F or 32°C electrolyte temperature
1.276 at 80°F or 27°C electrolyte temperature
1.280 at 70°F or 21°C electrolyte temperature
1.284 at 60°F or 16°C electrolyte temperature
1.288 at 50°F or 10°C electrolyte temperature
1.292 at 40°F or 4°C electrolyte temperature
1.296 at 30°F or -1.5°C electrolyte temperature

Table B

Specific Gravity - Battery Fully Discharged

1.098 at 100°F or 38°C electrolyte temperature
1.102 at 90°F or 32°C electrolyte temperature
1.106 at 80°F or 27°C electrolyte temperature
1.110 at 70°F or 21°C electrolyte temperature
1.114 at 60°F or 16°C electrolyte temperature
1.118 at 50°F or 10°C electrolyte temperature
1.122 at 40°F or 4°C electrolyte temperature
1.126 at 30°F or -1.5°C electrolyte temperature

4 Battery - electrolyte replenishment

1 If the battery is in a fully charged state and one of the cells maintains a specific gravity reading which is 0.25 or more, lower than the others, and a check of each cell has been made with a voltage meter to check for short circuits (a four to seven second test should give a steady reading of between 1.2 to 1.8 volts), then it is likely that electrolyte has been lost from the cell with the low reading at some time.

2   Top up the cell with a solution of 1 part sulphuric acid to 2.5 parts of waters. If the cell is already fully topped up draw some electrolyte out of it with an hydrometer.

3   When mixing the sulphuric acid and water **never add water to sulphuric acid** - always pour the acid slowly onto the water in a glass container. **If water is added to sulphuric acid it will explode.**

4   Continue to top-up the cell with the freshly made electrolyte and then recharge the battery and check the hydrometer readings.

5   Battery - charging

1   In winter time when heavy demand is placed upon the battery, such as when starting from cold, and much electrical equipment is continually in use, it is a good idea to occasionally have the battery fully charged from an external source at the rate of 3.5 or 4 amps (see Section 7).

2   Continue to charge the battery at this rate until no further rise in specific gravity is noted over a four hour period.

3   Alternatively, a trickle charger at the rate of 1.5 amps can be safely used overnight.

4   Specially rapid 'boost' charges which are claimed to restore the power of the battery in 1 to 2 hours are most dangerous as they can cause serious damage to the battery plates.

6   Alternator - description and maintenance

1   Briefly, the alternator comprises a rotor and a stator. Current is generated in the coils of the stator as soon as the stator revolves. This current is 3-phase alternating which is then rectified by positive and negative diodes, and the level of voltage required to maintain the battery at a full rate of charge is controlled by a voltage regulator.

2   Maintenance consists of occasionally wiping away any dirt or oil which may have accumulated on the outside of the unit.

3   No lubrication is required as the bearings are grease sealed for life.

4   At the recommended intervals (see Routine Maintenance) check the drivebelt tension and adjust if necessary.

7   Alternator - special precautions

1   Take extreme care when making circuit connections to a car fitted with an alternator and observe the following:

When making connections to the alternator from a battery always match correct polarity.

Before using electric-arc welding equipment to repair any part of the vehicle, disconnect the connector from the alternator and disconnect the positive battery terminal.

Never start the car with a battery charger connected.

Always disconnect both battery leads before using a mains charger.

If boosting from another battery, always connect in parallel using heavy cable.

2   Never pull off a battery lead while the engine is running as a means of stopping it. If working under the bonnet and the engine must be stopped, pull the coil HT lead or LT lead from the distributor.

8   Alternator and voltage regulator - testing in car

1   To check for the cause of lack of charge to the battery, carry out the following test to verify operation of the regulator (Fig. 10.1).

2   Disconnect the lead from the battery negative terminal.

3   Connect a 0 to 16 V voltmeter between the B+ terminal on the alternator and the alternator body.

4   Disconnect the red cable from the B+ terminal and connect a 0 to 60A ammeter between the end of the cable and the terminal.

5   Reconnect the battery negative lead and then bridge the battery terminals with a 55A variable resistor.

6   Start the engine and run it at a constant speed of between 2000 and 3000 rpm.

7   Adjust the current on the load resistor to between 28 and 30A when the voltmeter should indicate between 13.9 and 14.8V. Any deviation

from these figures will require immediate attention to the voltage regulator by your dealer (photo).

8   To test the alternator output, switch on the load resistor, set the engine speed to 1300 rpm and at the same time increase the load current to 10A. The charge warning lamp should be out.

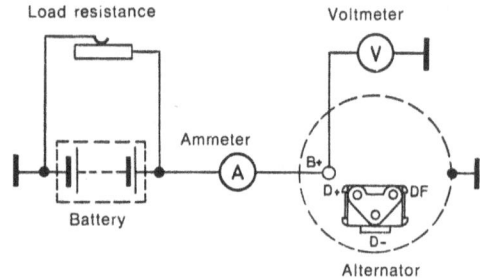

Fig. 10.1. Alternator test circuit (Sec. 8)

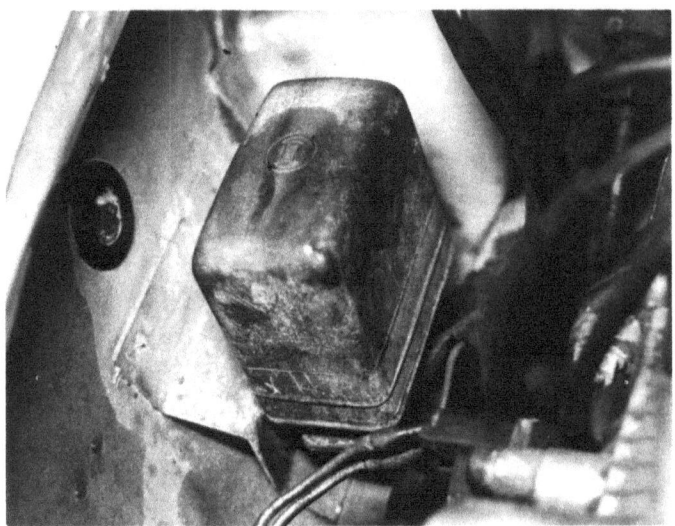

8.7 The voltage regulator in the charging circuit

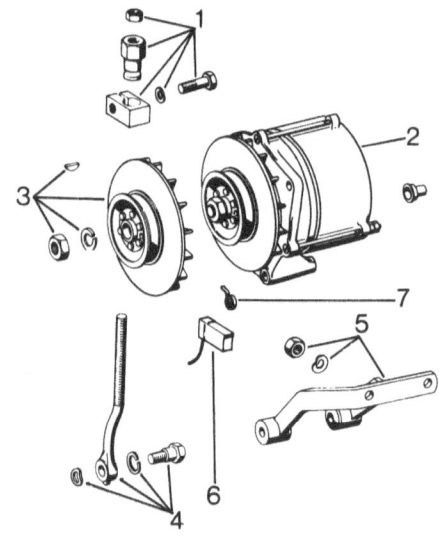

Fig. 10.2. Alternator components (Sec. 9)

1 Adjuster trunnion	*5 Mounting cradle*
2 Alternator	*6 Brush*
3 Pulley	*7 Brush spring*
4 Adjuster link	

9.2 Alternator adjuster link

9.3 Alternator terminal block

10.6 Starter motor

9   Repeat the test at 2000 and 6000 rpm, adjusting the load current to 23 and 35A respectively for alternator type K1(RL) 14V35A20 and 36 and 55A where alternator type K1 (RL) 14V55A20 is fitted.
10 Where a fault occurs in an alternator it is not recommended that it is dismantled but rather that it is overhauled by a Bosch agent or else a new unit is obtained.

9   Alternator - removal and refitting

1   Disconnect the lead from the battery negative (−) terminal.
2   Release the alternator mounting and adjustment link bolts and push the alternator in towards the engine so that the drivebelt can be slipped off its pulley (photo).
3   Disconnect the leads and connector plug from the rear end of the alternator (photo).
4   Extract the mounting bolts and lift the alternator from its bracket.
5   Refitting is a reversal of removal. Adjust the drivebelt so that with thumb pressure applied to the centre of the longest run of the belt, the deflection is ½ in (12.7 mm).

10 Starter motor - description, removal and refitting

1   A pre-engaged starter motor is fitted.
2   The method of engagement on the pre-engaged starter is that the drive pinion is brought into mesh with the starter ring gear before the main starter current is applied.
3   When the ignition is switched on, current flows from the battery to the solenoid which is mounted on the top of the starter motor body. The plunger in the solenoid moves inwards so causing a centrally pivoted lever to move in such a manner that the forked end pushes the drive pinion in to mesh with the starter ring gear. When the solenoid plunger reaches the end of its travel, it closes an internal contact and full starting current flows to the stator field coils. The armature is then able to rotate the crankshaft so starting the engine.
4   A special one way clutch is fitted to the starter drive pinion so that when the engine fires and starts to operate on its own, it does not drive the starter motor.
5   To remove the starter, first disconnect the lead from the battery negative terminal.
6   Disconnect the cables from the terminals of the solenoid (photo).
7   Unscrew and remove the bolts which secure the starter motor to the clutch bellhousing and remove the support bracket from the front end of the starter.
8   Withdraw the starter motor and remove it from the engine compartment. It will be found easier on some models to remove the starter if the front roadwheels are turned to full right lock.
9   Refitting is a reversal of removal.

11 Starter motor - overhaul

1   Failure of the starter motor to operate may be due to factors other than the motor itself. First check that the battery and solenoid terminal connections are tight and clean. Check that the battery is in a high state of charge.

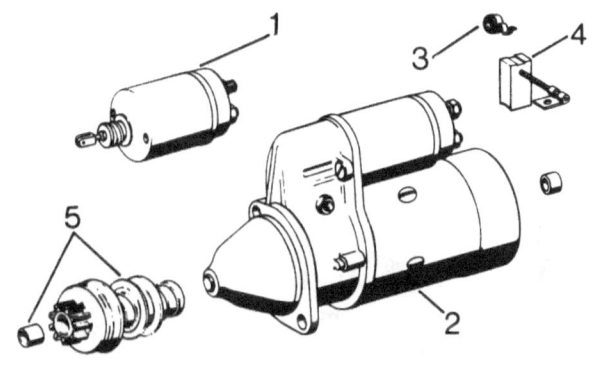

Fig. 10.3. Starter motor components (Sec. 11)

1   Solenoid
2   Motor complete
3   Brush spring
4   Brush
5   Starter drive pinion assembly

2   The starter motor usually has a very long life and it is normally economically sound to change it for a new or factory reconditioned unit when it fails. However, the brushes and commutator may be serviced but anything more extensive should be left to your Bosch agent.
3   To dismantle the starter motor, remove the end cap and examine the state of wear of the brushes (Fig. 10.3).
4   Disconnect the field coil cable from the terminal on the solenoids.
5   Unscrew and remove the nuts from the ends of the tie bolts and remove the drive bearing end frame from the armature housing.
6   Unbolt the solenoid bolts and withdraw the solenoid, unhooking it from the shift lever as it comes out.
7   The drive gear should be examined for wear or damaged teeth. Also inspect the overrunning clutch which should only be able to be turned clockwise when viewed from the pinion gear end.
8   Clean the commutator initially with a fuel soaked cloth. If the surfaces of the segments are burnt, they can be cleaned with glass paper, **not emery cloth** and the mica insulators then undercut to a depth of between 0.024 and 0.032 in (0.6 and 0.8 mm).
9   If the armature bushes are worn, leave renewal to your dealer.
10 Apply grease to the bushes and reassembly by reversing the dismantling operations.
11 If new brushes are being fitted, check that they slide easily in their holders and tighten the lead tag screws securely. Use a piece of wire to retain the brushes against their springs while the armature is pushed into the housing.
12 When the starter motor is reassembled energise the solenoid and check the clearance between the drive pinion face and its stop on the drive end housing. This should be between 0.04 and 0.16 in (1.0 and 4.0 mm). Adjust if necessary by releasing the locknut on the solenoid plunger and turning the core.

12 Fuses

1   The fuses which protect the various electrical circuits are located in a panel which is mounted either on the engine compartment rear bulkhead or under the instrument panel according to car model (Fig. 10.4). (photo).

2   The circuits protected and the relevant fuse capacity are listed on the fuse cover. The arrangement differs slightly between the models but a typical example is given at the end of this section.

3   The radio is protected by a separate 2A in-line fuse and there are supplementary fuses within the engine compartment for heated rear windows, sliding roof and electrically-operated windows (option on 250S).

Fuse No.	Amperage	Circuit Protected
1	8	Interior lights, headlamp flasher, hazard warning, luggage boot light.
2	25	Windscreen wipers, windscreen washer, horns, cigar lighter
3	8	Shift control light (auto-transmission)
4	8	Fuel pump
5	8	Direction indicators, stop lights, reversing lights, fuel reserve gauge, constant speed solenoid (auto-transmission)
6	25	Demister blower (when stationary) solenoid starting valve (280SL/8 only)
7	8	Right-hand tail light, right-hand front parking light, instrument lights
8	8	Left-hand tail light, left-hand front parking light, rear number plate light, fog lights.
9	8	Headlight right-hand main beam, main beam pilot warning light.
10	8	Headlight left-hand main beam
11	8	Headlight right-hand dipped beam
12	8	Headlight left-hand dipped beam

13 Relays

1   Certain relays may be incorporated in the electrical layout according to car model (photo).

2   A hazard warning/direction indicator flasher unit is located under the instrument panel.

3   On fuel injection models, a relay for the fuel pump is mounted on the side of the engine compartment (Fig. 10.5).

4   Relays are also fitted in conjunction with power operated windows, air conditioner supplementary fan and automatic radio aerial.

5   Always check the circuit fuse before inspecting the relay. If, however, the fault is traced to the relay, it will have to be renewed as a sealed unit.

6   Malfunction of a direction indicator flasher may be due to a poor lamp earth connection or a blown bulb.

12.1 Engine compartment fuse block

13.1 Engine compartment relays

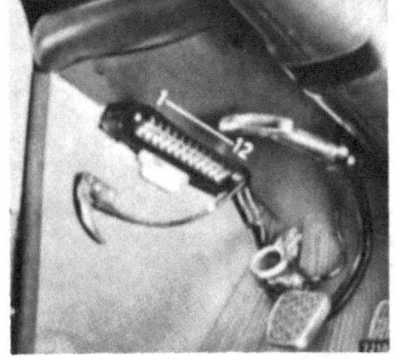

Fig. 10.4. Fuse block mounted under instrument panel (Sec. 12)

Fig. 10.5. Fuel injection engine (Sec. 13)

13   Fuel feed pump fuse box   14   Relay

Fig. 10.6. Headlight (bulb type) incorporating foglight (Sec. 14)

1 Securing screw	5 Vertical adjusting screw
2 Securing screw	6 Horizontal adjusting screw
3 Securing screw	7 Foglight adjusting screw
4 Securing screw	

Fig. 10.7. Rear view of bulb type headlamp unit incorporating foglight (Sec. 14)

8 Direction indicator	11	Foglight
9 Headlight bulb holder	12	Side marker
10 Parking light		

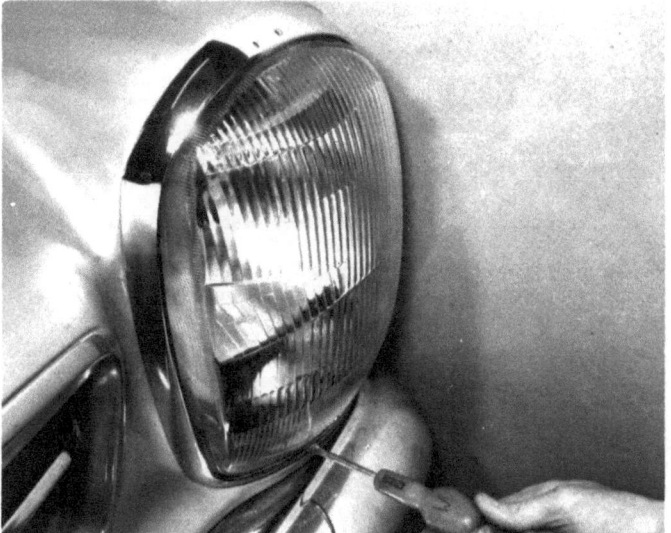

14.1 Extracting a headlamp rim screw

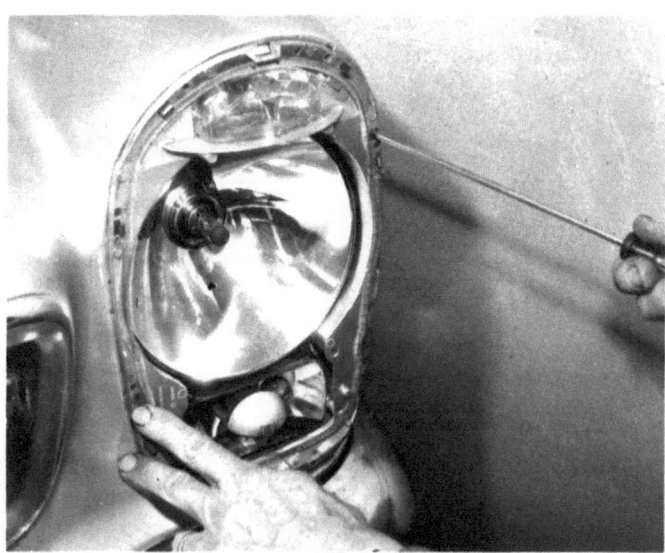

14.2 Extracting a headlamp body securing screw

14 Bulbs - renewal

Headlights (except N. America)
1   Extract the screw from the bottom of the headlight trim panel and remove the panel (Fig. 10.6) (photo).
2   Unscrew and remove the four lamp body securing screws. Do not confuse these with the headlamp adjusting screws (photo).
3   Pull the lamp body forward and remove the bulb holder from the rear of the headlamp.
4   Remove the bulb and fit the new one, taking care not to touch the new halogen type bulb with the fingers. If it is inadvertently touched, clean it with a cloth moistened in methylated spirit.

Headlights (N. America)
5   The headlights used on these cars are of twin sealed-beam type (Fig. 10.8).
6   To remove these lamps, extract the screw at the base of the head-lamp trim and withdraw it until the plugs can be disconnected from the direction indicator and parking lamps (Fig. 10.9).
7   Unscrew the headlamp mounting screws (not the adjusting screws), pull the lamp assembly forward and disconnect the plugs from the rear.
8   Disconnect the lamp unit from the frame and fit a new one. Some lamp units are mounted on spring-loaded screws and are removed by depressing and turning clockwise.

Fig. 10.8. Twin sealed-beam type headlights (Sec. 14)

1 Dipped light unit	4 Direction indicator light
2 Main beam unit	5 Side marker
3 Parking lamp (integral in headlight)	6 Foglight

9 This design of twin light unit is also used on cars not destined for N. America in which case, halogen type bulbs are used and access to the bulb sockets is obtained in exactly the same way as just described.

Front direction indicator and parking lights
10 Remove the headlights (in the case of bulb type units) and unscrew the smaller lamp unit from the rear of the headlamp assembly (photo).

Fig. 10.9. Twin type headlight unit (trim panel removed) (Sec. 14)

1 Dipped light unit	7 Mounting screws
2 Main beam unit	8 Vertical adjusting screw
3 Integral parking light	9 Horizontal adjusting screw
4 Direction indicator light	15 Mounting screw
5 Side marker	16 Retaining rim for lamp
6 Foglight	unit

11 With sealed-beam headlights, removal of the headlight trim will enable the direction indicator and parking lamp bulb holders to be unplugged from their sockets (paragraph 6, this Section).

Rear lamp cluster
12 The bulbs in the tail light, reversing light or stop light can be changed after releasing the two knurled nuts on the back of the cluster which are accessible within the luggage boot (photo).
13 Withdraw the lamp bulb holder assembly and renew the bulb as necessary (photo).

Rear number plate light
14 This lamp incorporates two bulbs which can be removed after the two screws which attach the lamp housing to the bumper have been extracted.

Luggage boot light
15 Access to this is gained by removing the small plate from the trim panel at the rear of the boot (photo).

Instrument panel courtesy light
16 Access to this bulb is obtained after first extracting the screws which hold the lower trim panel to the underside of the instrument panel (photo).

Instrument panel warning and indicator lights
17 In most cases, these bulbs can be reached if the cover panels are first removed from the underside of the instrument panel (Fig. 10.10).
18 Where difficulties are encountered, remove the instrument panel as described in Section 21.

Fog lights
Independently mounted type
19 Loosen the rim retaining screw which is located at the base of the lamp.
20 Pull the lens and rim from the lamp body.
21 Detach the retaining spring (3), remove the bulb(4) and disconnect

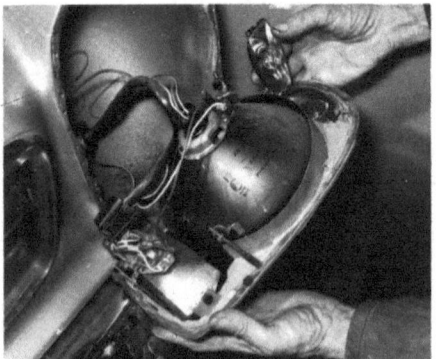

14.10 Headlamp unit removed showing parking and direction indicators

14.12 Rear light cluster

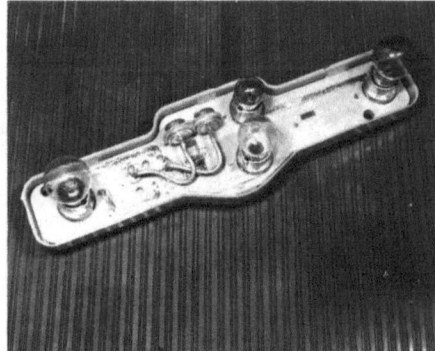

14.13 Rear light bulb holder

14.15 Luggage boot lid

14.16 Courtesy light

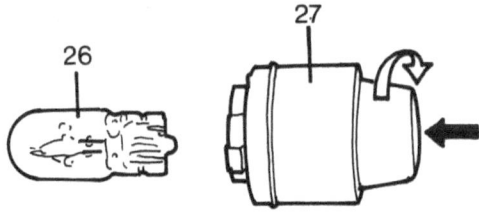

Fig. 10.10. Capless type indicator bulb (Sec. 14)

26 Bulb   27 Bulb holder

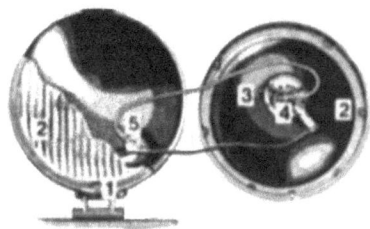

Fig. 10.11. Independently mounted type fog lamp (Sec. 14)

1 Screw   3 Spring clip   5 Plug
2 Lens   4 Bulb

17.1 One of the twin horns

the electrical plug (5) (Fig. 10.11).
22 Refitting the new bulb is a reversal of removal.

Integral type mounted in headlamp unit
23 Refer to Figs. 10.6 and 10.7 for bulb arrangement.

15 Headlights - adjustment

1   This is a job best left to a service station having the necessary beam
setting equipment.
2   In an emergency, the headlight main beams should be adjusted
using the adjusting screws provided so that the following conditions
are complied with.
3   With the car positioned square to and 16 ft (5.0 m) from a screen
and the headlight beams on main beam, the light pattern should not
project above a horizontal line drawn on the screen at a height
equivalent to the light centres on the car.
4   The brightest points of the light pattern should be in direct
alignment with the headlamps.

16 Steering column switches and ignition

1   The removal and refitting operations are described in Chapter 11 in
conjunction with the removal of the steering wheel and column.

17 Horns

1   The horns are mounted, one on each side of the car, below and
just to the rear of the radiator, adjacent to the front stabiliser bar
(photo).
2   Maintenance consists of keeping the connections secure on the
terminals.
3   The horns are adjusted during manufacture and they should not
normally require any attention.

18 Windscreen wiper blades and arms - removal and refitting

1   The wiper blades fitted as original equipment are removed by
first pulling the arm away from the screen until it locks and then
depressing the small clip so that the blade can be slid from the arm
(Fig. 10.12).
2   On some replacement type blades, two pinch screws are used
which grip the turned over end of the arm. Unscrew both of these to
release the blade (photo).
3   Refitting of both types is a reversal of removal.
4   To remove the wiper arm, unscrew the domed nut from the driving
spindle and remove it together with the spring washer.
5   Pull the arm from the splines of the driving spindle.
6   When refitting the arms, make sure that the wiper motor has been
switched off by means of the wiper control and that the splined
driving spindles are in the parked position.
7   Install the arms so that they are parallel to the bottom of the windscreen and make particularly sure that the left-hand arm (when
viewed from the car interior) is above the right-hand one.

19 Windscreen wiper motor and linkage - removal and refitting

1   Remove the panel from the underside of the instrument panel on
the left-hand side.
2   Reach up under the instrument panel and disconnect the balljoint
at the end of the main linkage rod from the ball stud on the motor
crank arm (Fig. 10.13).
3   Unscrew and remove the three motor mounting nuts.
4   Working within the engine compartment, disconnect the electrical
plug from the wiper motor and remove the motor from its mounting.
5   To remove the linkage and driving spindles, withdraw the wiper
arm/blade assemblies as previously describes.
6   From the splined ends of the driving spindles, unscrew and remove
the locknuts, washers and seals.
7   Working inside the car, disengage the balljoints from the driving
spindles or move the position of the linkage so that the screws, which
secure the driving spindles, can be removed (Fig. 10.14).
8   Removal of the fascia glove compartment will facilitate access to
the driving spindle screws.
9   Withdraw the driving spindles and linkage.
10 Avoid releasing the pinch bolt on the sliding section of the main
link strut as this will alter the arc of travel of the wiper arms and
necessitate readjustment on reassembly, which is a reversal of
dismantling and removal.

20 Windscreen washer system

1   The windscreen washer system comprises a fluid reservoir located
within the engine compartment, an electric pump and the necessary
control switch, jets and connecting pipes (photo).
2   Do not use plain water in the system as this can cause corrosion
and blockage of the jets. Use a recommended solvent in the water.
3   If a fault occurs, check the circuit fuse, the electrical connections
and the fluid pipe attachments.
4   A faulty pump will have to be renewed complete.

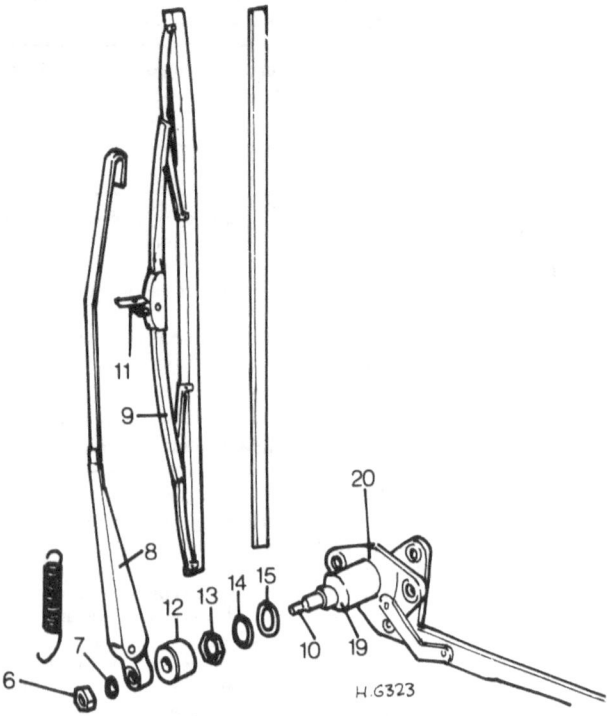

6   Domed nut
7   Spring washer
8   Wiper arm
9   Wiper blade
10 Driving spindle
11 Clip
12 Distance piece
13 Locknut
14 Washer
15 Seal
19 Grommet
20 Rubber seal

H.G323

Fig. 10.12. Typical windscreen wiper blade components (Sec. 18)

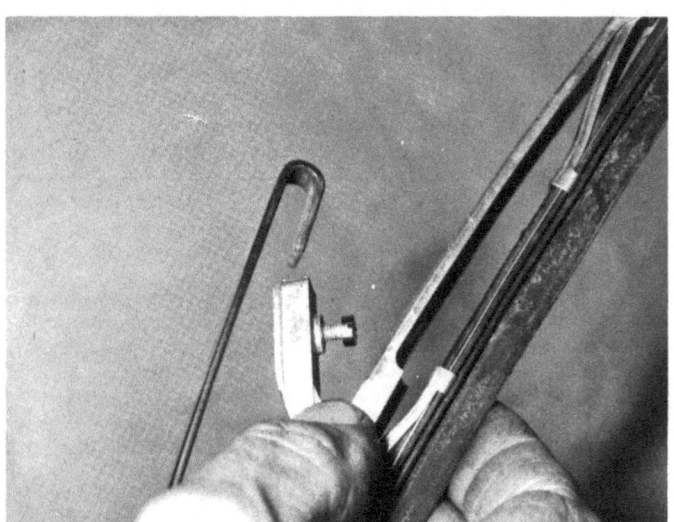

18.2 Wiper blade and arm

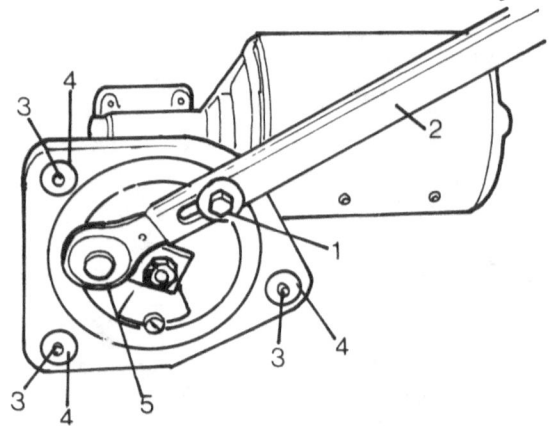

Fig. 10.13. Wiper motor connection to linkage (Sec. 19)

1   Pinch bolt   4   Flexible pads
2   Link rod   5   Crankarm balljoint
3   Mounting stud

21 Instruments - removal and refitting

1   *On cars equipped with a rev counter,* remove the cover panel from below the instrument panel, reach up and disconnect the drive cable to the rev. counter (Fig. 10.15).

2   Release the securing clips from the rear of the instrument and push it out of the panel (photos).

3   The hand can now be inserted through the hole vacated by the rev counter and the speedometer and other instruments removed in a similar manner. The instrument panel bulbs are also accessible.

4   Refitting is a reversal of removal but make sure that the rubber gaskets are evenly located under the bezels of the instruments.

5   *On cars without a rev counter,* remove the cover panel from the underside of the instrument panel.

6   If automatic transmission is fitted with a steering column shift, engage 'P' and disconnect the cable of the speed selector indicator on the steering column.

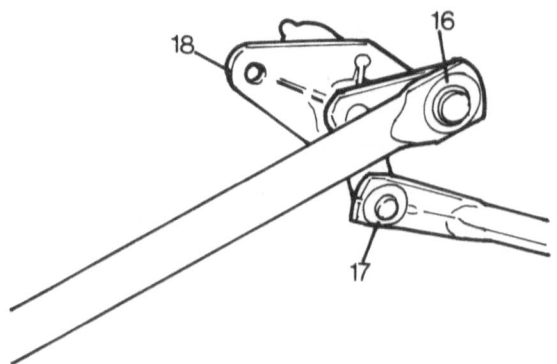

Fig. 10.14. Windscreen wiper linkage connection to driving spindle
(Sec. 19)

16 Balljoint   17 Balljoint   18 Mounting plate

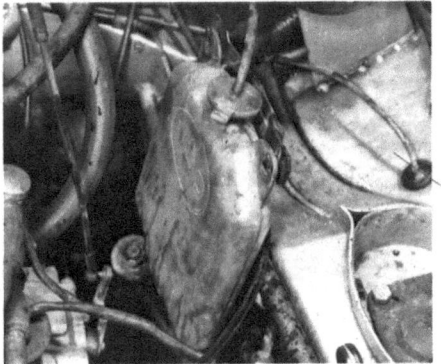

20.1 Windscreen washer fluid reservoir

21.2A Instrument removal

21.2B Instrument removal

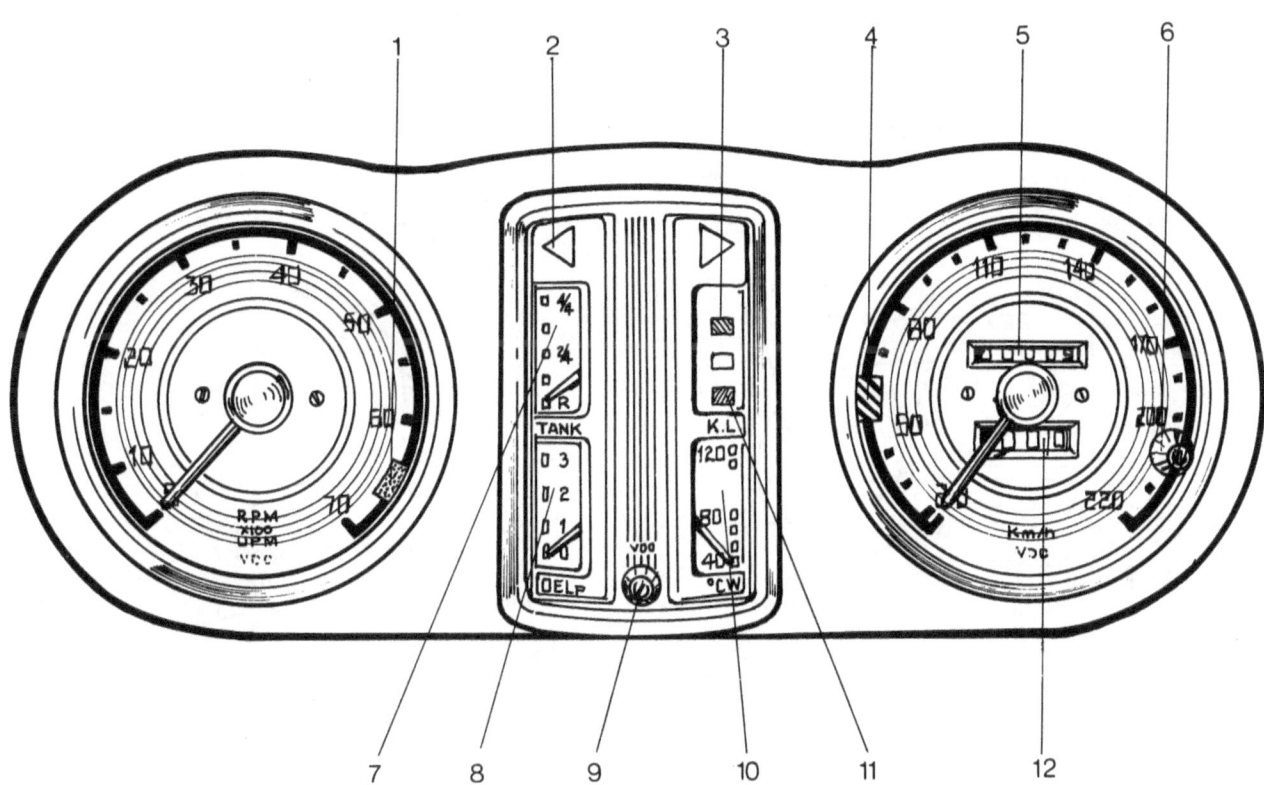

Fig. 10.15. Instrumentation on cars with revolution counter (Sec. 21)

1 Revolution counter	4 Speedometer	7 Fuel gauge	10 Coolant temperature gauge
2 Direction indicator light	5 Total mileage recorder	8 Oil pressure gauge	11 Headlight main beam warning light
3 Ignition warning light	6 Trip recorder reset button	9 Instrument lighting control	12 Trip mileage recorder

7 The instrument cluster may be held in position by one of two means and inspection will indicate the removal method (Fig. 10.16).

8 If a knurled nut is used, reach up and unscrew it and then pull the instrument panel far enough forward to be able to disconnect the speedometer drive cable. This is sufficient for the instrument bulbs to be renewed but for complete removal of the instrument panel, continue as follows (Fig. 10.17).

9 Disconnect the oil pressure line and all electrical connections.

10 On some models, a capillary type water temperature gauge is used and this must be disconnected at the cylinder head after first having drained the cooling system.

11 Withdraw the instrument cluster from the panel taking care not to damage the capillary tube or bulb as they pass through the hole in the engine compartment rear bulkhead.

12 On the other panels, no knurled nut is used to retain them but they are secured by a ribbed rubber strip located round the edge of the panel (Fig. 10.18).

13 To remove this type of panel, drain the cooling system and disconnect the capillary type water temperature tube from the cylinder head.

14 Push the instrument cluster a little way out of the panel and then disconnect the speedometer cable, the electrical connector plug and the oil pressure pipe.

15 Remove the instrument cluster and withdraw the capillary tube and bulb through the hole in the engine compartment rear bulkhead. Remove individual instruments from the panel as necessary by releasing their securing screws.

16 Refitting is the reversal of removal; remember to refill the cooling system.

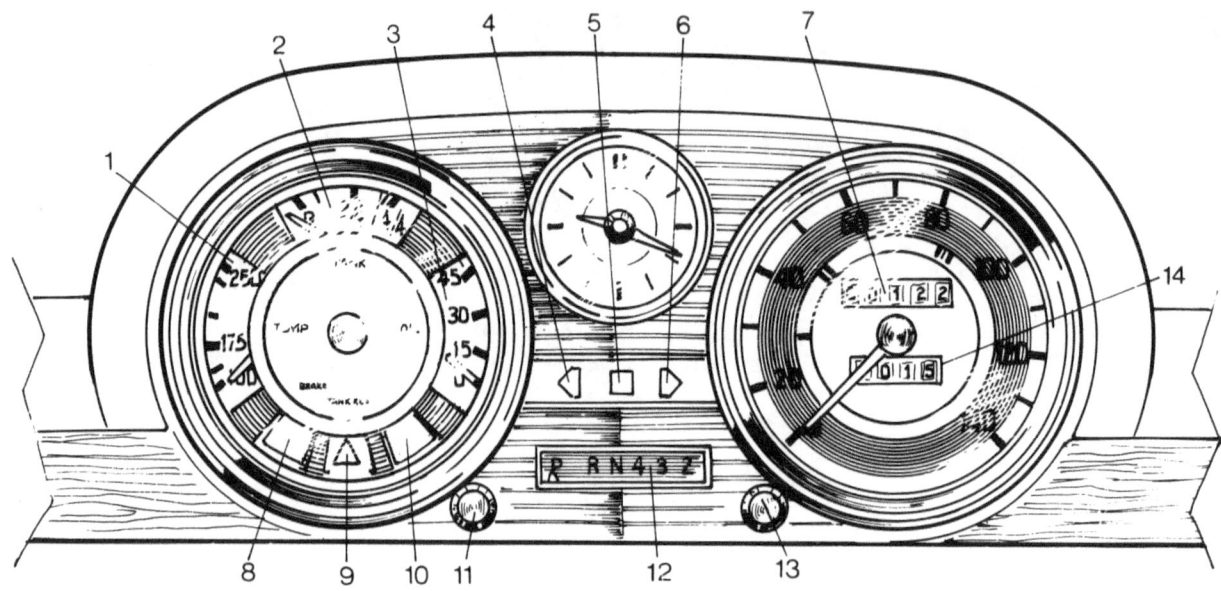

Fig. 10.16. Typical instrumentation on cars without a revolution counter (Sec. 21)

1 Coolant temperature gauge	5 Headlight main beam warning light	8 Brake warning light	12 Auto transmission selector position indicator
2 Fuel contents gauge	6 Direction indicator light	9 Fuel reserve warning light	13 Trip recorder reset button
3 Oil pressure gauge	7 Total mileage recorder	10 Ignition warning light	14 Trip mileage recorder
4 Direction indicator light		11 Instrument lighting control	

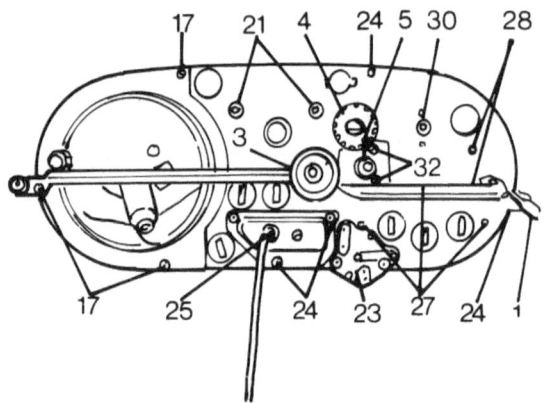

Fig. 10.17. Rear view of instrument panel (without rev counter)
(Sec. 21)

1 Water temperature capillary tube	25 Speed selector indicator adjuster screw
3 Knurled nut	27 Dial screws
4 Multi-plug connection	28 Coolant temperature gauge screws
5 Oil pressure line connection	30 Fuel gauge retaining nut
17 Speedometer retaining screws	32 Oil pressure gauge retaining screws
21 Clock securing screws	
23 Instrument lighting switch	
24 Plate screws	

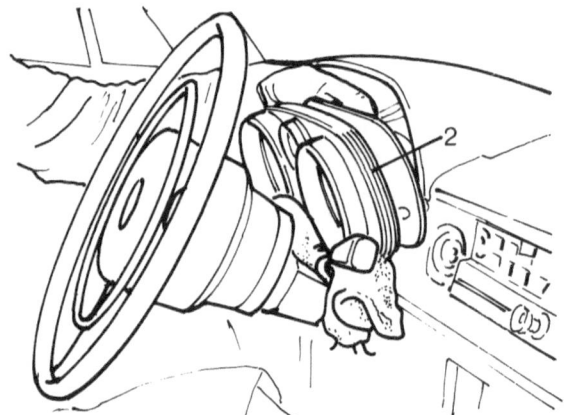

Fig. 10.18. Removing instrument cluster by easing out ribbed rubber strip (2) (Sec. 21)

---

22 Speedometer and rev counter cables - renewal

---

1 Access to and disconnection of the upper ends of these cables is described in the preceding Section.

2 The lower connection of the speedometer cable is to the transmission unit while the rev counter cable is joined to the auxiliary shaft housing on the left-hand side of the cylinder block.

3 If an inner cable has broken, it will probably be necessary to disconnect both ends of the outer cable (conduit) to extract the two sections.

4 Smear a little grease on the lower 2/3rds only of the inner cable before fitting it.

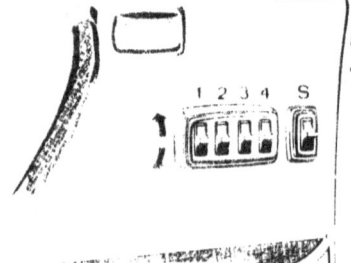

Fig. 10.19. Power-operated window regulator switches (Sec. 23)

1 to 4 Switches for individual windows
S   Safety switch

5 Make sure that the squared end of the inner cable projects sufficiently to engage positively with the gear socket in the instrument or drive pinion before screwing on the knurled type ring nut.

23 Electrically-operated window regulators

1 Power-operated door windows were a factory fitted option on some models covered by this manual.
2 Control switches are grouped together on the driver's door with an independent override switch under each window (Fig. 10.19).
3 The equipment is normally very reliable and in the event of a fault, first check the fuse and then the wiring and electrical connections within the door cavity for security and possible corrosion (Fig. 10.20).
4 If these are in order, have the relays checked which are located adjacent to the supplementary fuse box.

24 Seat belt warning system

1 Cars covered by this manual and destined for operation in North America are fitted with a simple type of seat belt warning system.
2 Basically, the system comprises a warning lamp and buzzer which

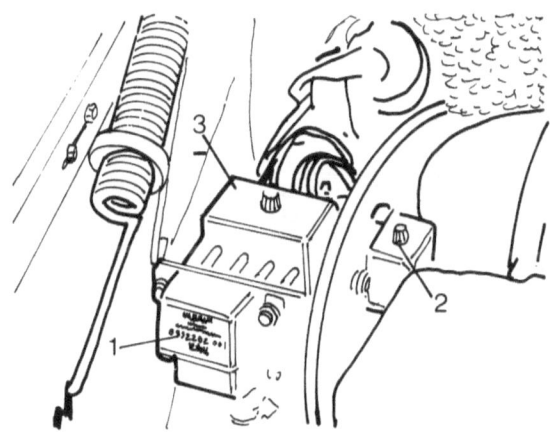

Fig. 10.20. Power-operated window electrical components (Sec. 23)

1   Make and break contact relay 3 Supplementary fuse box (4 x 25A)
2   Operating contact relay

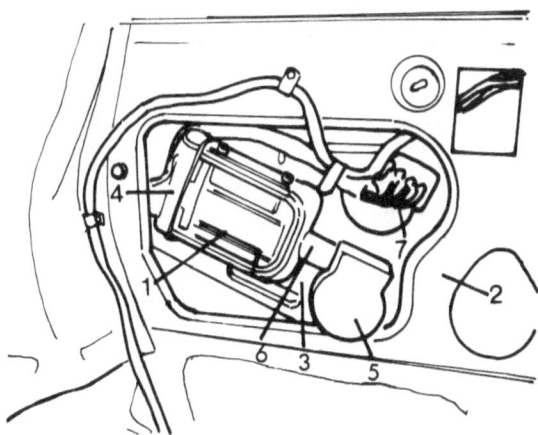

Fig. 10.21. Electric motor for power-operated window installed in door (Sec. 23)

1   Motor   5   Gearbox
2   Door panel   6   Driveshaft
3   Motor fixing bracket 7   Electrical connection
4   Motor connections

will be actuated if the ignition switch is turned to the 'ON' position while the transmission shift lever is in any position except neutral (manual transmission) or neutral and park (auto transmission) and the driver's seat belt is unfastened (Fig. 10.25).
3 If a passenger is occupying the front passenger seat, the warning light and buzzer will operate if that belt is unfastened even though the driver's seat belt is fastened.
4 Switches are located in the seat belt retractor units and a weight sensitive switch is fitted in the front passenger seat (Figs. 10.22 and 10.23).
5 If the car is equipped with air conditioning, the starter relay is wired up to ensure that the power to the air conditioning system is cut off when the starter motor is energised (Fig. 10.24).
6 The warning buzzer is located under the instrument panel (Fig. 10.26).

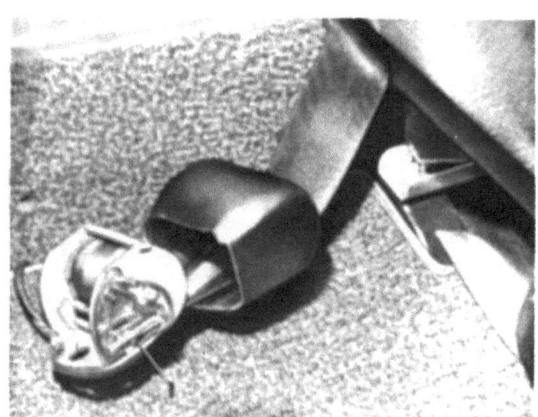

Fig. 10.22. Seat belt warning switch located in retractor (1) (Sec. 24)

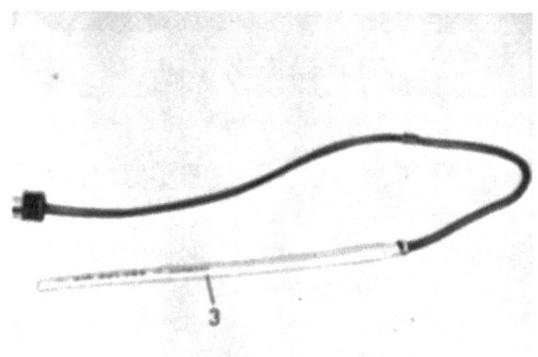

Fig. 10.23. Seat weight sensitive switch in passenger seat (3) (Sec. 24)

Fig. 10.24. Location of additional relays (Sec. 24)

13   Air conditioner/starter relay   14   Seat belt warning buzzer relay

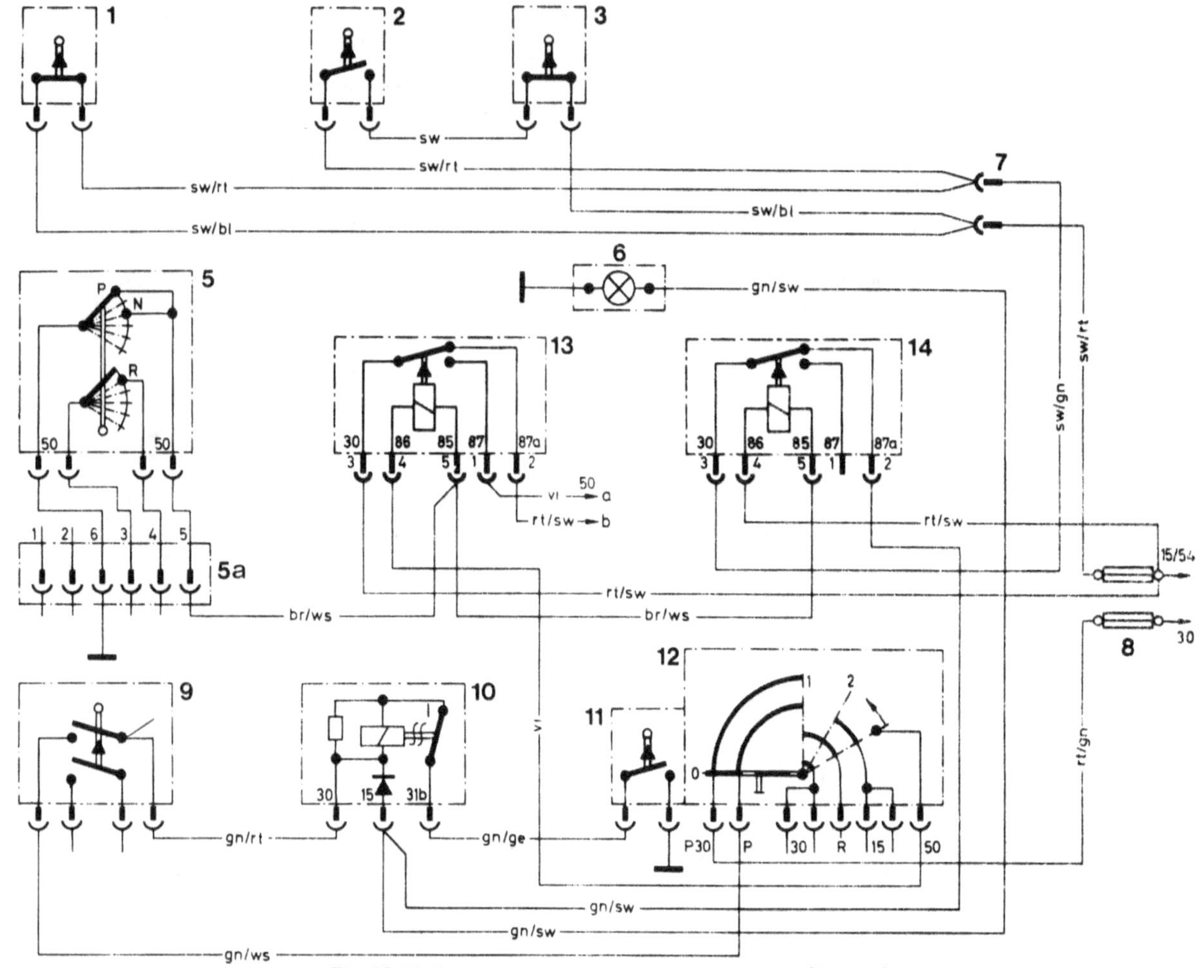

Fig. 10.25. Seat belt warning system circuit diagram (Sec. 24)

Fig. 10.26. Location of seat belt warning buzzer (10) (Sec. 24)

1 Seat belt retractor switch, driver seat
2 Seat sensor switch, passenger seat
3 Seat belt retractor switch, right side
5 Starter lock-out and back-up light switch
5a Connector
   1 & 2 = terminals for kick-down switch
   3 & 4 = terminals for back-up lights
   5 & 6 = terminals for starter lock-out switch
6 Warning light. Fasten Seat Belts
7 Terminals or 2-prong plug behind centre console
8 Fuses, main fuse box
9 Door contact switch, left side
10 Warning buzzer
11 Warning buzzer switch, ignition switch
12 Ignition switch
13 Relay, air conditioner/starter
14 Relay, warning buzzer

WIRE COLOUR CODE

bl	=	blue
br	=	brown
ge	=	yellow
gn	=	green
rt	=	red
sw	=	black
vi	=	violet
ws	=	white

a   to terminal 50 on starter
b   to fuse box, air conditioning

25 Fault diagnosis- electrical system

Symptom	Reason/s
Starter fails to turn engine	Battery discharged.
	Battery defective internally.
	Battery negative terminal loose or earth lead to body insecure.
	Loose or broken connections in starter motor.
	Starter motor switch or solenoid faulty.
	Starter motor brushes worn or sticking.
	Commutator worn, dirty or burnt.
	Starter motor armature faulty.
	Field coils earthed.

Symptom	Reason/s
Starter turns engine very slowly	Battery in discharged condition. Starter brushes badly worn, sticking or brush wires loose. Loose wires in starter motor circuit.
Starter spins but does not turn engine	Pinion or flywheel gear teeth broken or worn. Battery discharged.
Starter motor noisy or excessively rough engagement	Pinion or flywheel gear teeth broken or worn. Starter motor retaining bolts loose.
Battery will not hold charge for more than a few days	Battery defective internally. Electrolyte level too low or electrolyte too weak due to leakage. Plate separators no longer fully effective. Battery plates severely sulphated. Fan belt slipping. Battery terminal connections loose or corroded. Alternator not charging. Short in lighting circuit causing continual battery drain. Regular unit not working correctly.
Ignition light fails to go out, battery runs flat in a few days	Fan belt loose and slipping or broken. Alternator brushes worn, sticking, broken or dirty. Alternator brush springs weak or broken. Internal fault in alternator.

Failure of individual electrical equipment to function correctly is dealt with alphabetically, item-by-item, under the headings listed below

Horn

Horn operates all the time	Horn push either earthed or stuck down. Horn cable to horn push earthed.
Horn fails to operate	Blown fuse. Cable or cable connection loose, broken or disconnected. Horn has an internal fault.
Horn emits intermittent or unsatisfactory noise	Cable connections loose. Horn incorrectly adjusted.

Lights

Lights do not come on	If engine not running, battery discharged. Wire connections loose, disconnected or broken. Light switch shorting or otherwise faulty.
Lights come on but fade out	If engine not running battery discharged. Light bulb filament burnt out or bulbs or sealed beam units broken. Wire connections loose, disconnected or broken. Light switch shorting or otherwise faulty.
Lights give very poor illumination	Lamp glasses dirty. Lamps badly out of adjustment.
Lights work erratically - flashing on and off, especially over bumps	Battery terminals or earth connection loose. Lights not earthing properly. Contacts in light switch faulty.

Wipers

Wiper motor fails to work	Blown fuse. Wire connections loose, disconnected or broken. Brushes badly worn. Armature worn or faulty. Field coils faulty.
Wiper motor works very slowly and takes excessive current	Commutator dirty, greasy or burnt. Armature bearings dirty or unaligned. Armature badly worn or faulty.
Wiper motor works slowly and takes little current	Brushes badly worn. Commutator dirty, greasy or burnt. Armature badly worn or faulty.
Wiper motor works but wiper blades remain static	Wiper motor gearbox parts badly worn.

1	Right lighting unit
2	Left lighting unit
a	Upper beam
b	Lower beam
c	Flash signal
d	Parking light
e	Fog light
f	Clearance light
3	Instrument cluster
a	Left signal indicator
b	Right signal indicator
c	Fuel reserve warning light
d	Fuel level indicator
e	Electric clock
f	Control resistance for instrument lighting
g	Instrument lighting
h	Charging light
i	Upper beam control
k	Brake control
4	Two-tone horn mechanism
5	Blower switch (air intake)
6	Blower motor (air intake)
7	Stop light switch
8	Reversing light switch
9	Foot pump windshield washer
10	Wiper motor
11	Control switch for brake fluid
12	Control switch for parking brake
13	Flash signal mechanism
14	Horn ring
15	Combination switch
a	Flash signal switch
b	Flash approach signal switch
c	Hand dimmer
d	Windshield wiper switch
e	Wiper speed switch
16	Cigar lighter
17	Front left door contact
18	Reading light
19	Front right door contact
20	Roof-light switch (on model 250 only)
21	Rear roof light (on model 250 only)
22	Battery
23	Starter
24	Lead for optional extra (radio)
25	Automatic start mechanism on rear carburettor
26	Automatic start mechanism on front carburettor
27	Fuses
28	Rotary light switch
29	Ignition starter switch
30	Series resistance
31	Ignition coil
32	Spark plugs
33	Distributor
34	Sleeve union for tail light wiring harness
35	Fuel level indicator
36	Generator
37	Voltage regulator
38	Trunk compartment light
39	Right tail light
40	Left tail light
a	Flash signal
b	Tail light
c	Reversing light
d	Clearance light
e	Stop light
41	License plate light

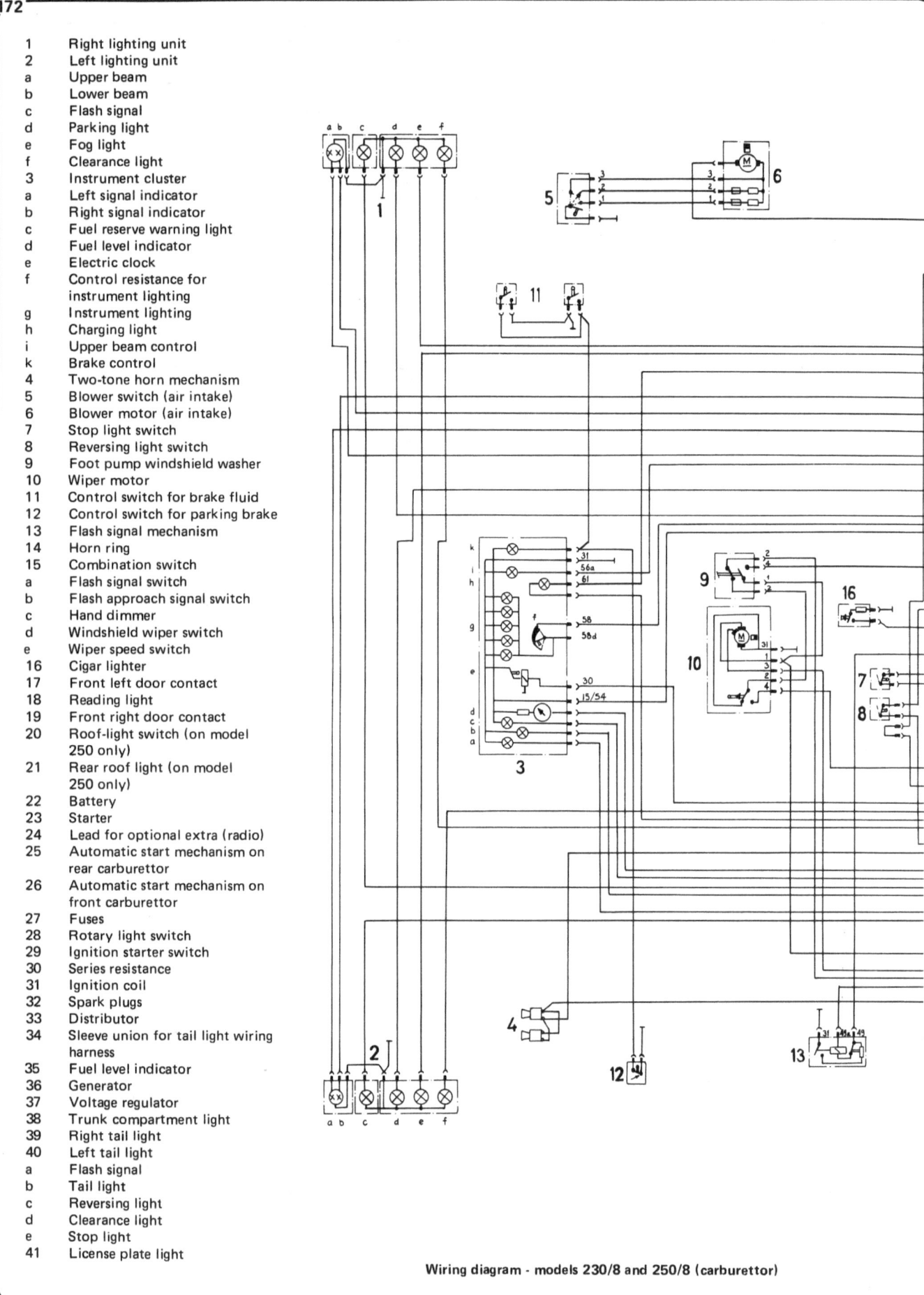

Wiring diagram - models 230/8 and 250/8 (carburettor)

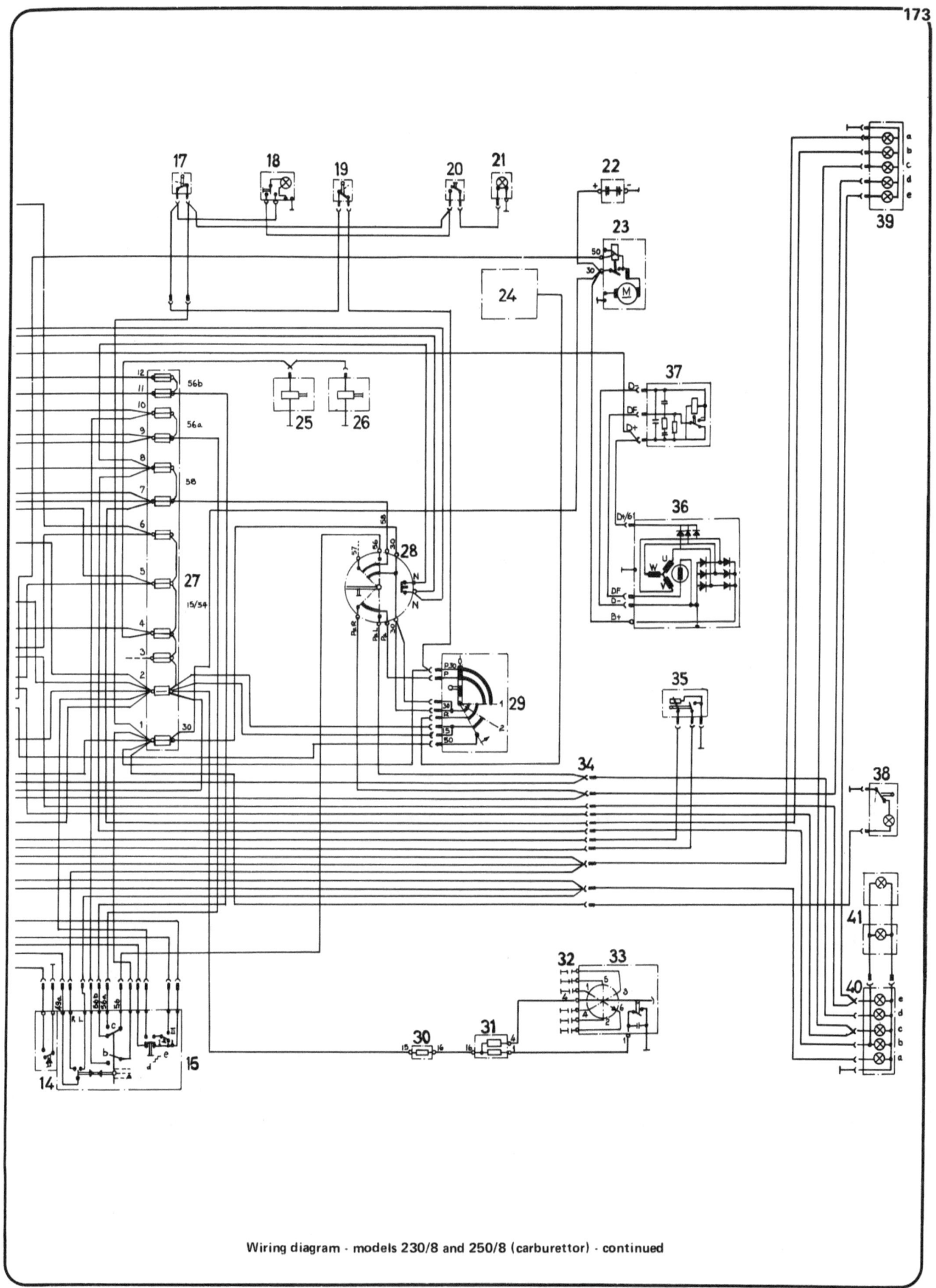

Wiring diagram - models 230/8 and 250/8 (carburettor) - continued

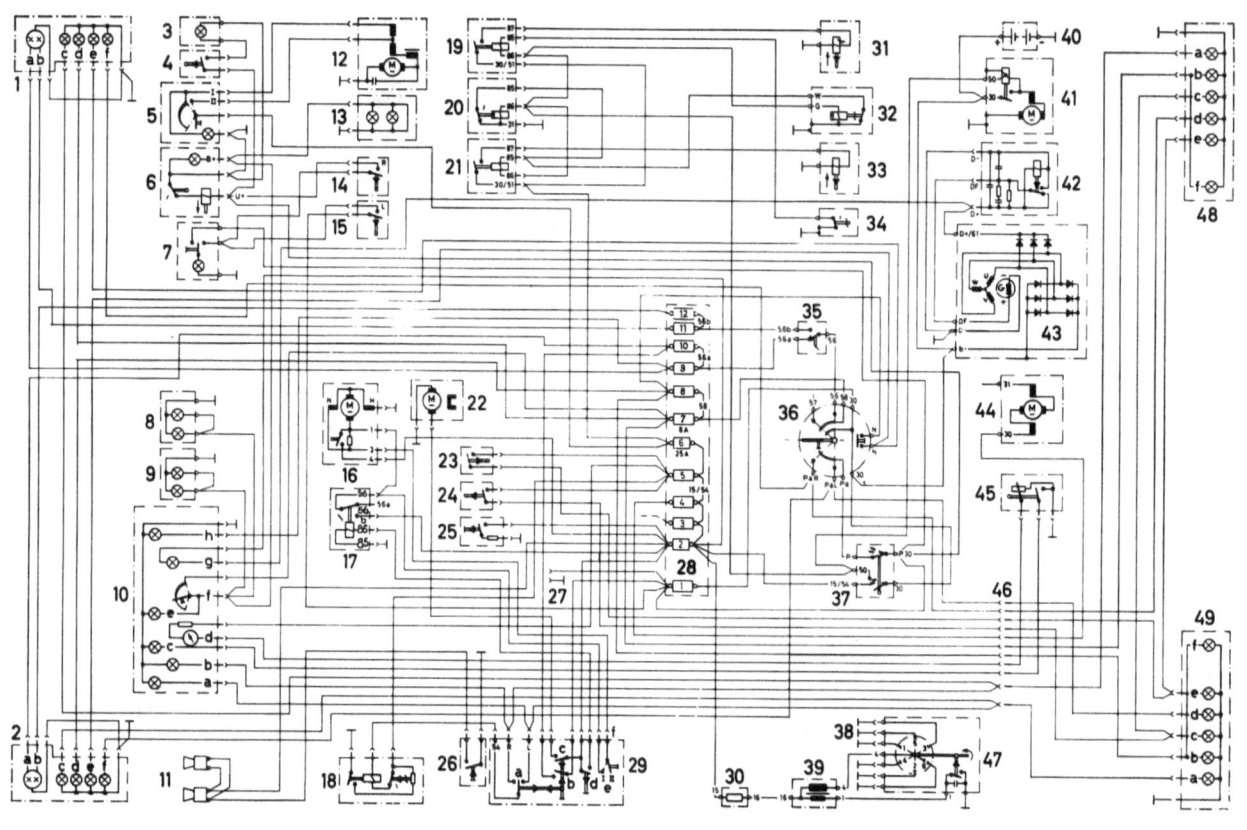

Wiring diagram - model 230 SL (fuel injection)

1	Lighting unit, right	12	Heater blower motor	31	Electromagnetic starter valve
2	Lighting unit, left	13	Illumination, heating control	32	Thermo time switch
a	High beam	14	Door contact switch, right	33	Solenoid for mixture control
b	Low beam	15	Door contact switch, left	34	Thermo switch
c	Direction signal light	16	Windshield wiper motor	35	Dimmer switch
d	Parking light	17	Relay for wiper motor	36	Rotary light switch
e	Fog light	18	Flasher unit	37	Ignition starter switch
f	Clearance light	19	Relay for electromagnetic starter valve	38	Spark plugs
3	Glove compartment and reading light	20	Time switch	39	Ignition coil
4	Switch for glove compartment light	21	Relay for mixture control solenoid	40	Battery
5	Heater blower switch	22	Windshield washer pump	41	Starter
6	Electric clock	23	Brake light switch	42	Voltage regulator
7	Courtesy light and switch	24	Back-up light switch	43	Generator
8	Speedometer light	25	Cigarette lighter	44	Fuel feed pump
9	Revolution counter light	26	Horn ring	45	Transmitter for fuel gauge
10	Instrument cluster	27	Socket	46	Plug connection tail light leads
a	Flasher control light, left	28	Fuses	47	Distributor
b	Flasher control light, right	29	Steering column switch	48	Tail light, right
c	Fuel reserve warning	a	Flasher switch	49	Tail light, left
d	Fuel level indicator	b	Headlight flash switch	a	Direction signal light
e	Instrument light	c	Windshield washer switch	b	Tail light
f	Regulating resistor for illumination	d	Windshield washer switch	c	Back-up light
g	Ignition warning light	e	Switch for wiper speed	d	Clearance light
h	High beam control light	f	Plug connection, steering column switch	e	Brake light
11	Dual tone horns	30	Series resistance	f	Identification light

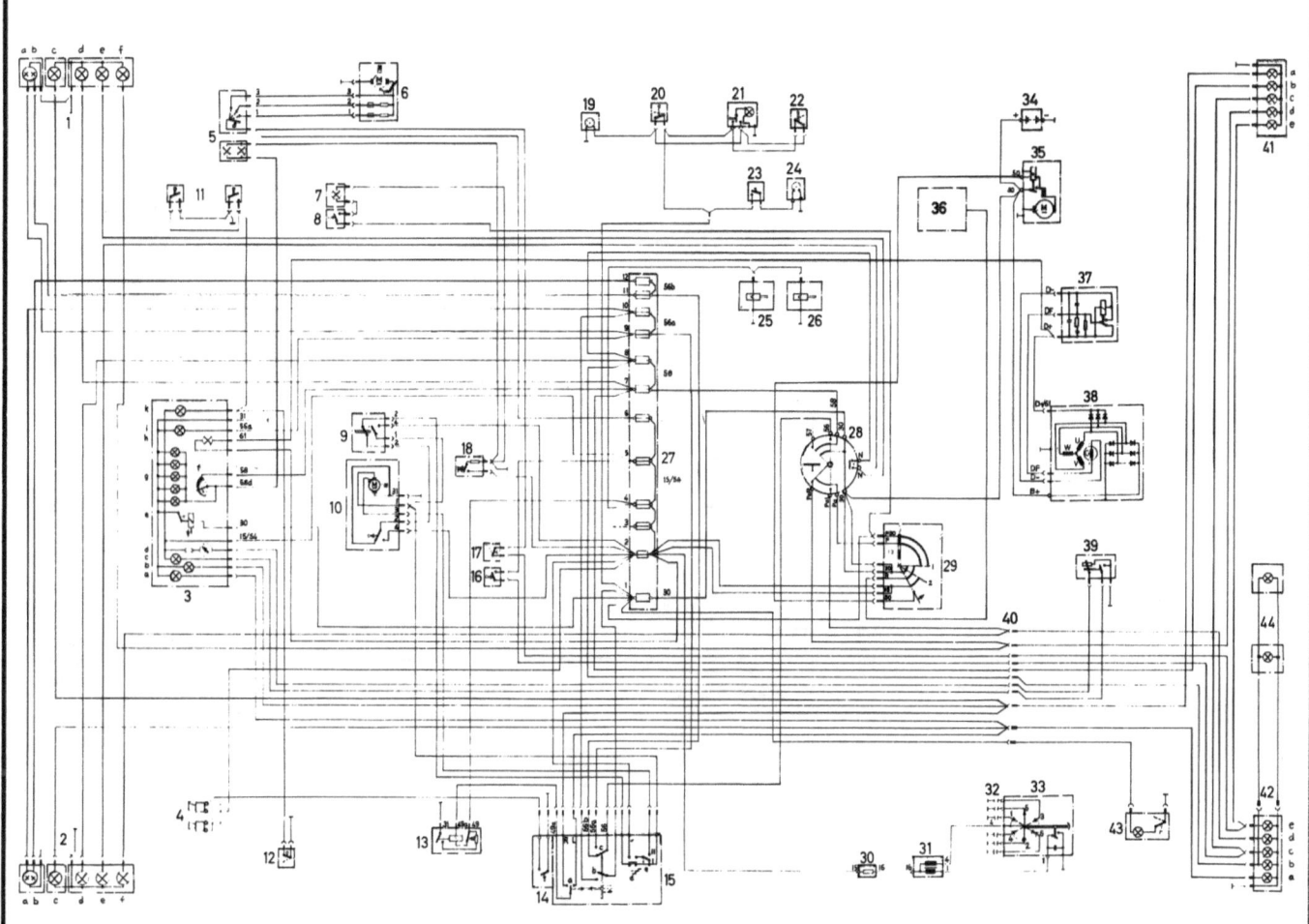

Wiring diagram - model 280S (carburettor)

1	Light assembly (right side)	11	Brake fluid level warning light control element	27	Fuses		
2	Light assembly (left side)	12	Parking brake warning light control element	28	Headlight switch		
a	High beam	13	Sending unit for turn signal light	29	Ignition starter switch		
b	Low beam	14	Horn ring	30	Series resistance		
c	Turn signal light	15	Combination switch	31	Ignition coil		
d	Parking light	a	Turn signal light switch	32	Spark plugs		
e	Fog light	b	Passing flasher switch	33	Distributor		
f	Side light	c	Headlight dimmer switch	34	Battery		
3	Instrument cluster	d	Windshield wiper switch	35	Starter		
a	Turn signal light indicator, left	e	Windshield wiper speed control switch	36	Power lead for optional equipment (radio)		
b	Turn signal light indicator, right	16	Back-up light switch	37	Voltage regulator		
c	Low fuel level warning light	17	Stop light switch	38	Alternator		
d	Fuel gauge	18	Cigar lighter	39	Fuel gauge sending unit		
e	Electric clock	19	Entrance light	40	Rear light unit wiring harness connecting plug		
f	Instrument lighting rheostat	20	Courtesy light switch, left front door	41	Rear light unit (right side)		
g	Instrument lighting	21	Reading light	42	Rear light unit (left side)		
h	Generator (alternator) charge warning light	22	Courtesy light switch, right front door	a	Turn signal light		
i	High beam indicator	23	Switch for dome light	b	Tail light		
k	Parking brake and brake fluid level warning light	24	Dome light, rear	c	Back-up light		
4	Dual horn system	25	Automatic choke, rear	d	Side light		
5	Heater blower switch	26	Automatic choke, front	e	Stop light		
6	Heater blower motor			43	Luggage boot		
7	Glove compartment light			44	Licence plate light		
8	Switch for glove compartment light						
9	Windshield washer foot pump						
10	Wiper motor						

1	Light assembly, left
a	Main beam
b	Dipped beam
c	Turn signal light
d	Parking light and side light
e	Fog light
2	Light assembly, right
a	Main beam
b	Dipped beam
c	Turn signal light
d	Parking light and side light
e	Fog light
3	Supplementary fan
4	Supplementary fan relay
5	Brake fluid control switch
6	Parking brake indicator light
7	Combined instrument
a	Turn signal indicator, left
b	Turn signal indicator, right
c	Fuel reserve warning light
d	Fuel gauge
e	Electric clock
f	Instrument lighting rheostat
g	Instrument lighting
h	Charging indicator light
i	Main beam indicator
k	Service and parking brake indicator light
8	Horn two-tone
9	Series resistor for blower motor
10	Blower motor (air intake)
11	Control unit, lighting (heating and ventilation)
12	Blower switch (air intake)
13	Wiper motor
14	Foot-operated windscreen washer pump
15	Glove compartment light switch
16	Glove compartment light
17	Thermostatic switch 212°F (100°C)
18	Solenoid valve on automatic transmission
19	Auxiliary fuse box for electric blower
20	Thermostatic switch, desiccator
21	Cigar lighter
22	Hazard warning flasher (electr.)
23	Horn ring
24	Combination switch
a	Turn signal switch
b	Headlight flasher switch
c	Hand dipper switch
d	Windscreen wiper switch
e	Windscreen wiper speed switch
25	Carburettor heater socket, rear
26	Exhaust emission control relay
27	Thermostatic switch 149°F (65°C)
28	Stop light switch
29	Fuses
30	Kickdown switch
31	Starter lock-out and reversing light switch
32	Carburettor heater socket, front
33	Blower switch (air conditioner)
34	Electro-magnetic coupling of air conditioner compressor
35	Air conditioner relay
36	Blower motor
37	Auxiliary fuse box for air conditioner
38	Temperature switch
39	Lighting turn switch
40	Starter/ignition switch

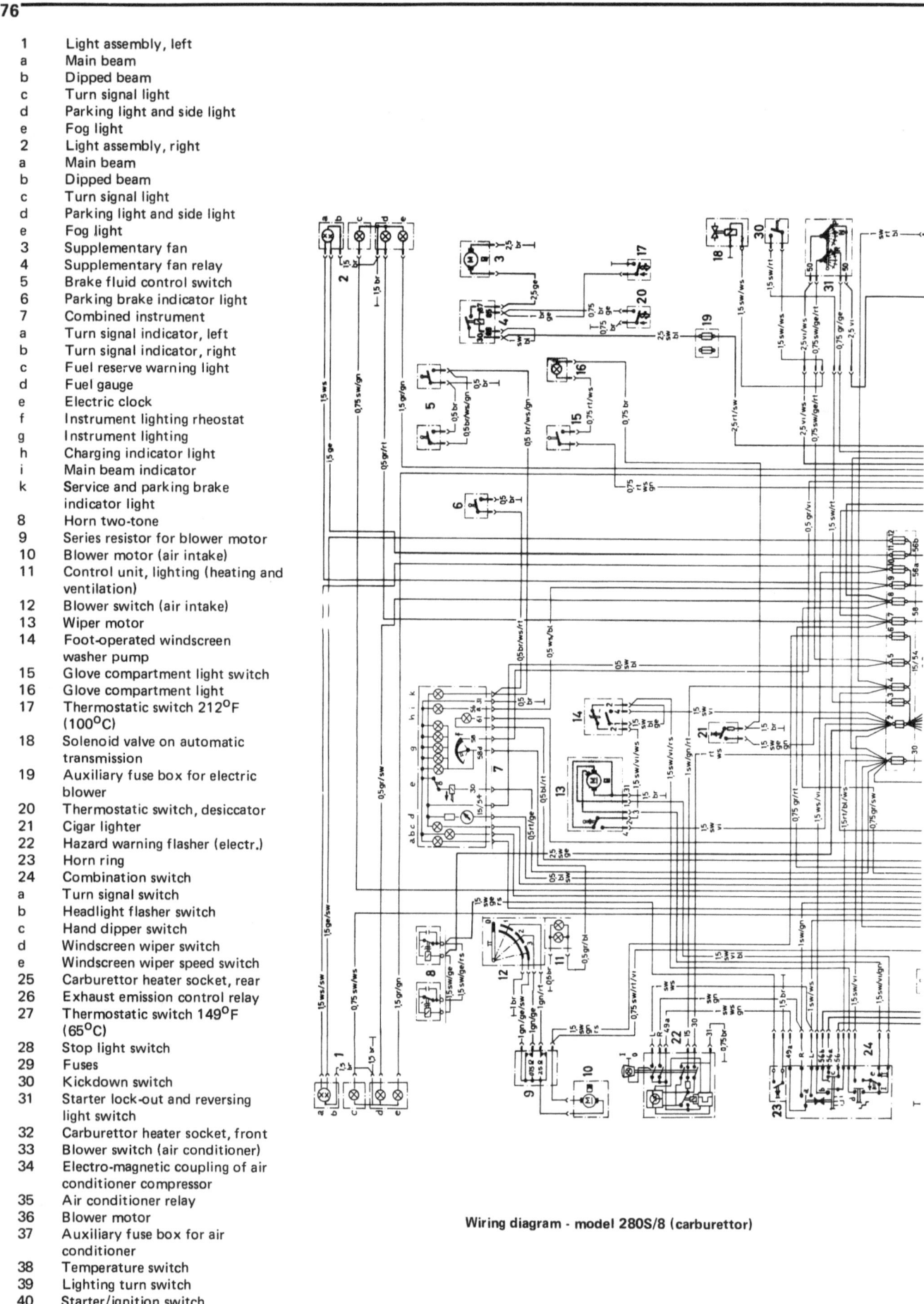

Wiring diagram - model 280S/8 (carburettor)

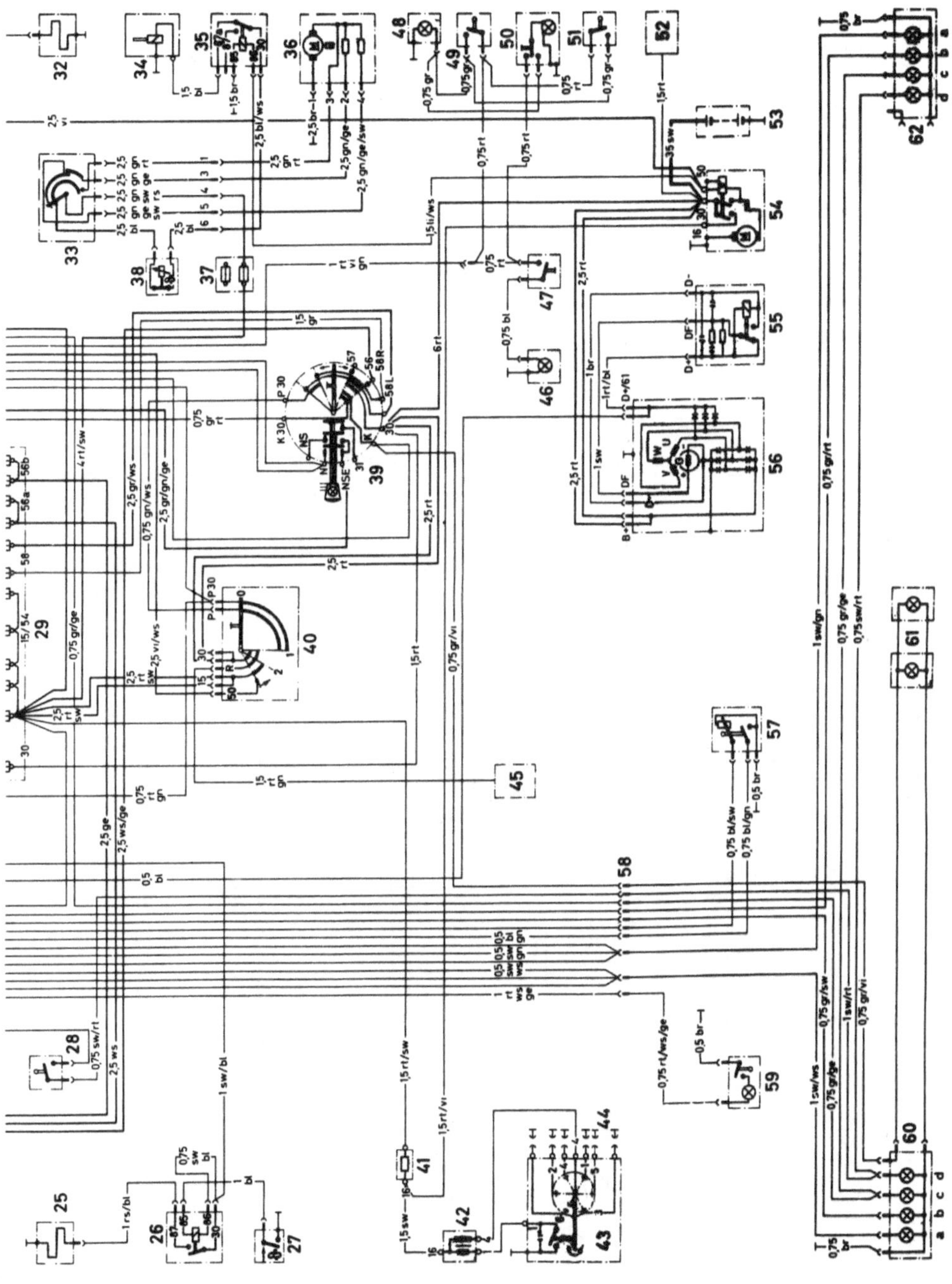

41	Series resistor
42	Ignition coil
43	Distributor
44	Spark plugs
45	Lead for optional extra (radio)
46	Rear roof light
47	Rear roof light switch
48	Courtesy light
49	Door contact switch (front left)
50	Front reading light
51	Door contact switch (front right)
52	Lead for optional extra (aerial)
53	Battery
54	Starter motor
55	Voltage regulator
56	Generator
57	Fuel gauge sending unit
58	Plug connection for tail light cable harness
59	Boot light
60	LH rear light unit
a	Turn signal light
b	Tail light and parking light
c	Reversing light
d	Stop light
61	License plate light
62	RH rear light unit
a	Turn signal light
b	Tail and parking light
c	Reversing light
d	Stop light

Wire colour code

ws	=	white
gn	=	green
br	=	brown
ge	=	yellow
gr	=	grey
rs	=	pink
bl	=	blue
rt	=	red
sw	=	black
el	=	ivory
nf	=	neutral
li	=	violet

Example:
Wire designation 1,5 gr/rt
Basic colour gr = grey
Identification colour rt = red
Cross section of wire 1,5 = 1.5 mm^2

Wiring diagram - model 280S/8 (carburettor) - continued

1	Lighting assembly, left
a	Main beam
b	Dipped beam
c	Turn signal light
d	Parking light and side light
e	Fog light
2	Lighting assembly, right
a	Main beam
b	Dipped beam
c	Turn signal light
d	Parking light and side light
e	Fog light
3	Electric fan (optional extra, air conditioning)
4	Relay for electric fan (optional extra, air conditioning)
5	Brake fluid control switch
6	Parking brake indicator light switch
7	Instrument cluster
a	Turn signal indicator, left
b	Turn signal indicator, right
c	Fuel reserve warning light
d	Fuel gauge
e	Electric clock
f	Rheostat for instrument lighting
g	Instrument lighting
h	Charging indicator light
i	Main beam indicator
k	Service and parking brake indicator light
8	Two-tone horn
9	Blower switch (control system)
10	Series resistor
11	Blower motor
12	Lighting for control system
13	Windscreen wiper motor
14	Foot-operated windscreen washer pump
15	Starter valve solenoid
16	Glove compartment light switch
17	Glove compartment light
18	Thermostatic switch for dehydrator (optional extra, air conditioning)
19	Thermostatic switch 212°F (100°C)
20	Solenoid valve for automatic transmission
21	Auxiliary fuse box (optional extra, air conditioning)
22	Thermostatic switch
23	Cigar lighter
24	Hazard warning flasher switch (electronic)
25	Horn ring
26	Combination switch
a	Turn signal switch
b	Headlight flasher switch
c	Hand-operated dipper switch
d	Windscreen wiper switch
e	Windscreen wiper speed switch
27	Brake light switch
28	Fuses
29	Kickdown switch
30	Starter lock-out and reversing light switch
31	Relay for starting valve
32	Idle speed increase solenoid (optional extra, air conditioning)
33	Blower switch (optional extra, air conditioning)
34	Temperature switch (optional extra, air conditioning)

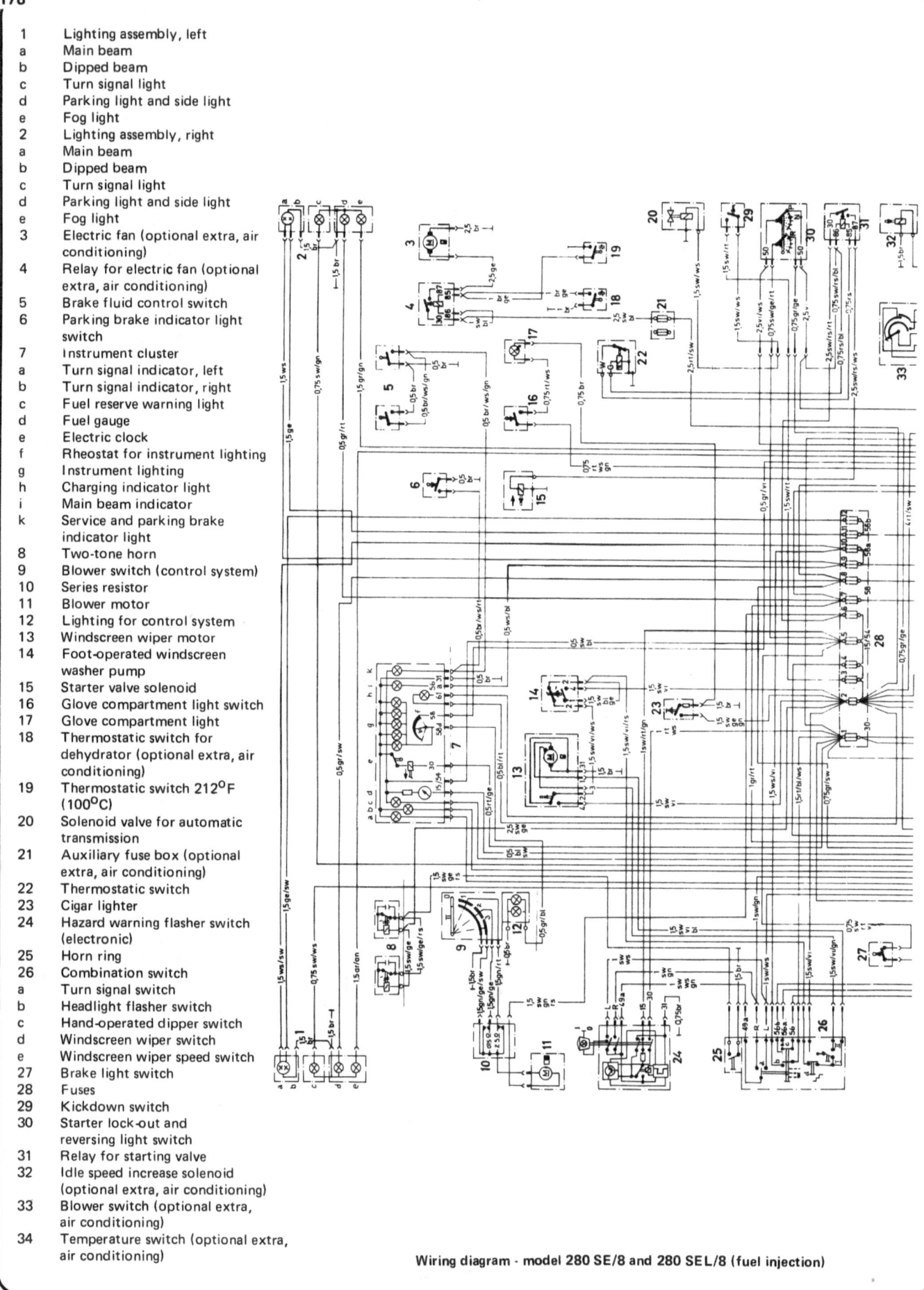

Wiring diagram - model 280 SE/8 and 280 SEL/8 (fuel injection)

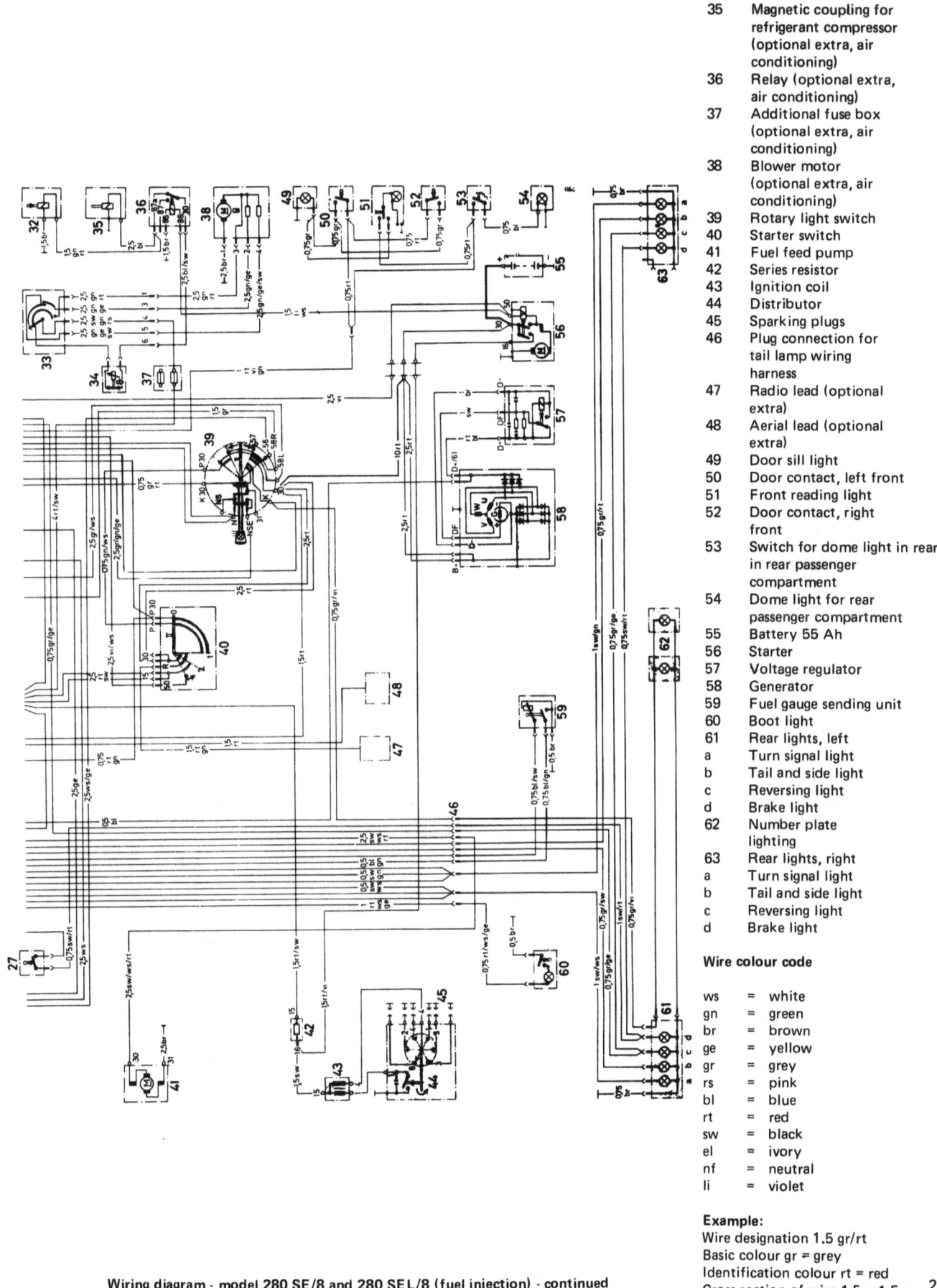

35 Magnetic coupling for refrigerant compressor (optional extra, air conditioning)
36 Relay (optional extra, air conditioning)
37 Additional fuse box (optional extra, air conditioning)
38 Blower motor (optional extra, air conditioning)
39 Rotary light switch
40 Starter switch
41 Fuel feed pump
42 Series resistor
43 Ignition coil
44 Distributor
45 Sparking plugs
46 Plug connection for tail lamp wiring harness
47 Radio lead (optional extra)
48 Aerial lead (optional extra)
49 Door sill light
50 Door contact, left front
51 Front reading light
52 Door contact, right front
53 Switch for dome light in rear in rear passenger compartment
54 Dome light for rear passenger compartment
55 Battery 55 Ah
56 Starter
57 Voltage regulator
58 Generator
59 Fuel gauge sending unit
60 Boot light
61 Rear lights, left
a Turn signal light
b Tail and side light
c Reversing light
d Brake light
62 Number plate lighting
63 Rear lights, right
a Turn signal light
b Tail and side light
c Reversing light
d Brake light

Wire colour code

ws = white
gn = green
br = brown
ge = yellow
gr = grey
rs = pink
bl = blue
rt = red
sw = black
el = ivory
nf = neutral
li = violet

Example:
Wire designation 1.5 gr/rt
Basic colour gr = grey
Identification colour rt = red
Cross section of wire 1.5 = 1.5 mm^2

Wiring diagram - model 280 SE/8 and 280 SEL/8 (fuel injection) - continued

1   Lighting unit, right
2   Lighting unit, left
a   High beam
b   Low beam
c   Blinker light
d   Parking light
e   Fog light
f   Side light
3   Glove compartment
     and reading light
4   Switch for glove
     compartment light
5   Heater blower switch
6   Electric clock
7   Entrance light and
     switch
8   Speedometer light
9   Revolution counter
     light
10   Instrument cluster
a   Blinker control light,
     left
b   Blinker control light,
     right
c   Fuel reserve warning
d   Fuel level indicator
e   Instrument light
f   Regulating resistor for
     lighting
g   Charging control light
h   High beam control light
i   Parking brake and
     brake fluid level
     warning light
11   Dual tone horns
12   Heater blower motor
13   Lighting, heating
     control
14   Door contact switch,
     right
15   Door contact switch,
     left
16   Windshield wiper
     motor
17   Relay for wiper motor
18   Direction signal
     transmitter
19   Luggage boot light
20   Relay for starter valve
21   Relay for rich mixture
22   Windshield washer
     pump
23   Brake light switch
24   Back-up light switch
25   Cigarette lighter
26   Horn ring
27   Socket
28   Fuses
29   Combination switch
a   Blinker switch
b   Headlight flasher
     switch
c   Windshield washer
     switch
d   Windshield wiper
     switch
e   Switch for wiper speed
f   Plug connection,
     steering column switch
30   Series resistance
31   Electromagnetic starter
     valve
32   Thermo time switch
33   Solenoid for rich
     mixture

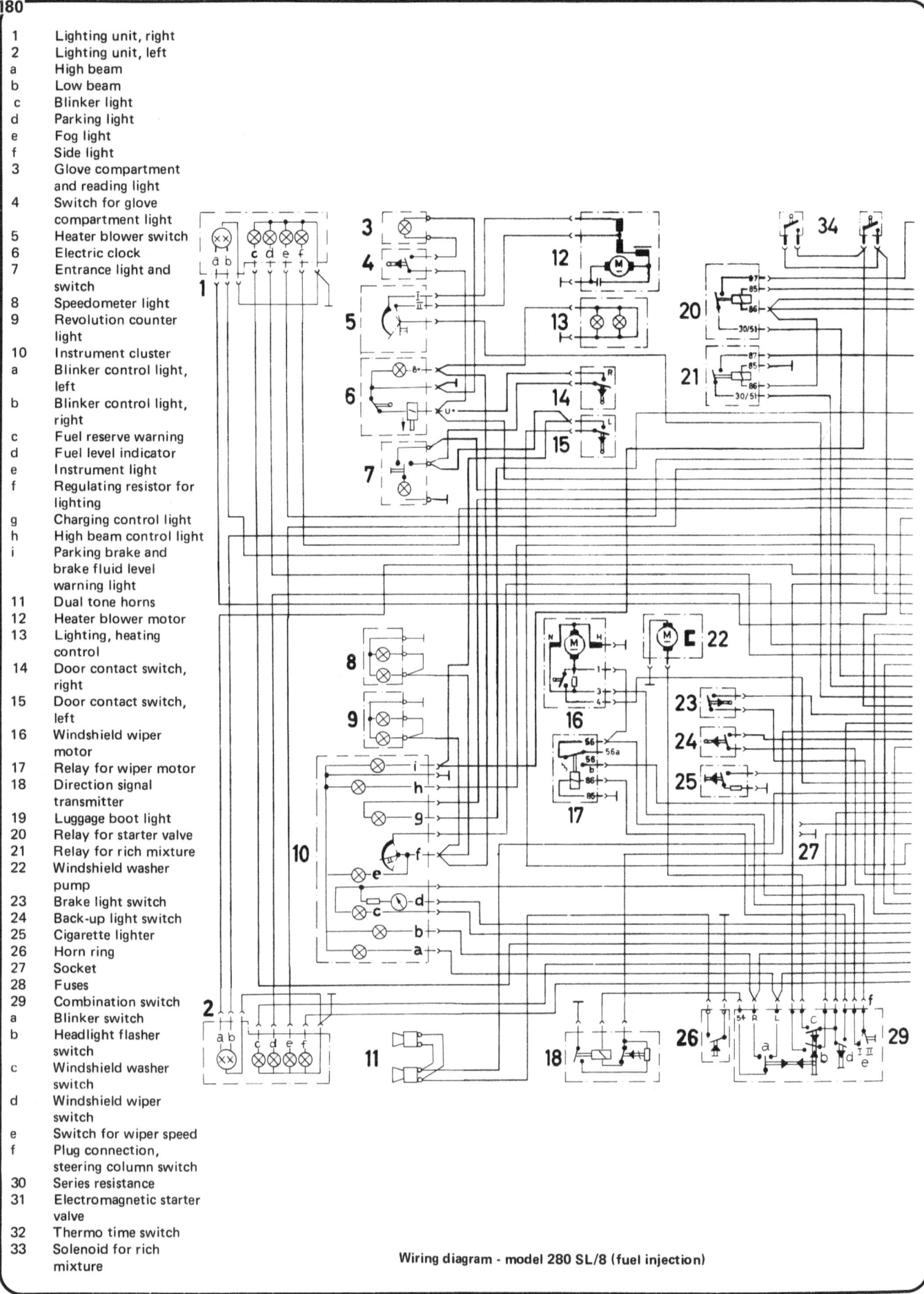

Wiring diagram - model 280 SL/8 (fuel injection)

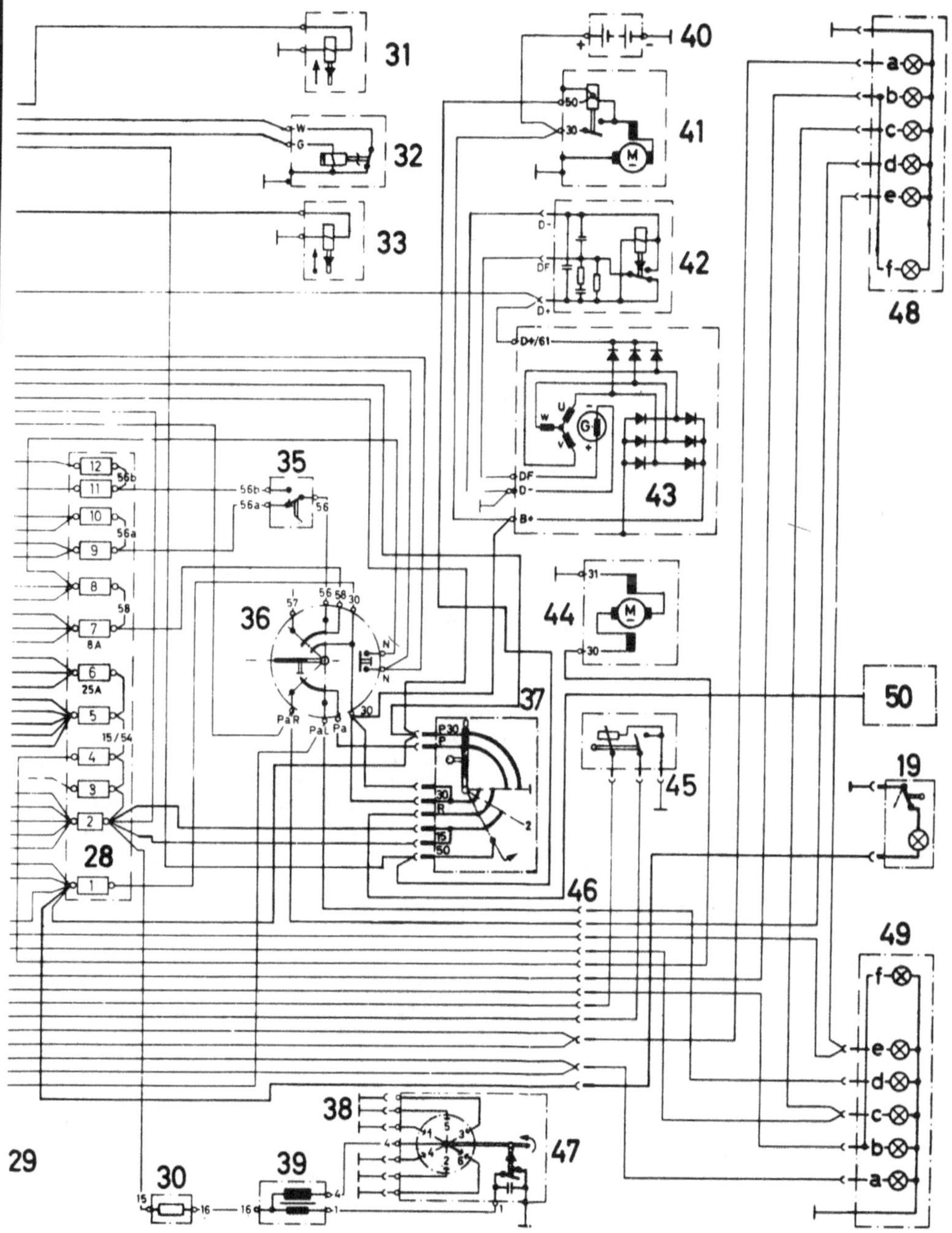

34	Brake fluid level warning light control element
35	Dimmer switch
36	Rotary light switch
37	Ignition starter switch
38	Spark plugs
39	Ignition coil
40	Battery
41	Starter
42	Voltage regulator
43	Generator
44	Fuel feed pump
45	Transmitter for fuel gauge
46	Plug connection tail light leads
47	Distributor
48	Tail light, right
49	Tail light, left
a	Flasher light
b	Tail light
c	Back-up light
d	Side light
e	Brake light
f	License plate light
50	Radio (optional)

Wiring colour code

bl	=	blue
br	=	brown
el	=	ivory
ge	=	yellow
gn	=	green
gr	=	grey
nf	=	natural
rs	=	pink
rt	=	red
sw	=	black
vi	=	violet
ws	=	white

Example:

Wire designation 1.5 gr/rt
Basic colour gr - grey
Identification colour rt = red
Wire cross section 1.5 = 1.5 mm^2

Wiring diagram - model 280 SL/8 (fuel injection) - continued

Chapter 11 Suspension and steering

Contents

Specifications

Front suspension
Type ... ...   Independent with coil springs, telescopic hydraulic shock absorbers and stabiliser bar

Rear suspension
Type ... ...   Independent with coil springs, telescopic hydraulic shock absorbers

Steering
Type ... ...   Recirculating ball with power option

Steering angles
Front wheels
Cars with king pin and bush type stub axle carriers:

Camber	$20'$ to $0^\circ 30'$ (280SL/8 $0^\circ 10'$ to $0^\circ 20'$)
Castor	
manual steering	$3^\circ 30' \pm 15'$
power steering	$4^\circ \pm 15'$
King pin inclination	$5^\circ 30'$
Toe-in	0.04 to 0.12 in (1.0 to 3.0 mm)
Track difference at 20° steering lock of inner wheel	$-0^\circ 30' \pm 40'$

Rear wheels
Camber	$0^\circ \pm 30'$
Toe in/out	0 to 0.08 in (0 to 2.0 mm) toe-in or toe-out

Front wheels

Cars with swivel balljoint type stub axle carriers:

Camber	0° 15'
Castor	2° 40' ± 20'
Toe-in	0.08 to 0.16 in (2.0 to 4.0 mm)
Track difference at 20° steering lock of inner wheel	0° 30' ± 40'

Rear wheels

Camber	Varies according to suspension lower arm height (− 2° 30' to + 3° 0')
Toe-in	Varies according to suspension lower arm height (0 to 0.20 in − 0 to 5.0 mm)

Turning circle ... ...   32.8 ft (10.0 mm)

Track

	Front	Rear
230/250 Series (except SL)	56.85 in (1444 mm)	56.69 in (1440 mm)
250/280 SL	58.43 in (1484 mm)	58.46 in (1485 mm)
280 Series (except SL)	58.35 in (1482 mm)	58.46 in (1485 mm)

Fluid capacity

Manual steering box	0.5 Imp pint (0.6 US pint/0.3 litre)
Power steering gear (including reservoir)	2.5 Imp pint (3.0 US pint/1.4 litre)

Roadwheels and tyres

Wheel size	6J x 14
* Tyre size	7.35 - 185 H 14 or 7.35 - 185 V 14 or 185 HR 14
* Tyre pressures (cold)	Front 29 lb/in² (2.04 kg/cm²)
	Rear 35 lb/in² (2.46 kg/cm²)

* Consult also car sticker for manufacturer's revised information

Torque wrench settings

Cars with king pin and bush type stub axle carrier and enclosed type axleshafts

	lb f ft	Nm
Front suspension		
Shock absorber lower mounting bolt	18	25
Crossmember flexible mounting bolt	72	100
Upper control arm pivot to crossmember bolts	72	100
Lower control arm pivot to crossmember bolts	94	130
Stabiliser bar leaf springs to bodyframe	87	120
Stabiliser bar flexible mounting clamps	18	25
Control arm threaded pivot bushes	130	180
King pin lower nut	65	90
Lateral positioning rod bolts	44	60
Lower control arm to stub axle carrier bolt	130	180
Upper control arm cam bolt	32	45
Rear suspension		
Shock absorber lower mounting bolt	32	45
Rear axle compensating spring right-hand carrier	87	120
Rear axle hydro-pneumatic strut left-hand balljoint	58	80
Rear axle hydro-pneumatic strut right-hand balljoint	87	120
Steering		
Steering box to bodyframe	43	60
Steering drop arm nut	144	200
Idler arm shaft self-locking nut	87	120
Track rod end and drag rod balljoint nuts	25	35
Steering coupling pinch bolts	18	25
Steering wheel to shaft nut	36	50
Steering wheel to hub (boss) nut	11	15
Roadwheels		
Roadwheel bolts	72	100

Cars with swivel balljoint type stub axle carriers and open type axleshafts
Torque wrench settings as foregoing except for:

	lb f ft	Nm
Lower control arm bearing cam bolts	87	120
Upper control arm bearing bolts	44	60
Front wheel bearing clamp pinch bolt	10	14
Steering arm to stub axle carrier bolts	58	80
Upper and lower control arm swivel balljoint nuts	58	80
Suspension rear link to rear axle carrier	87	120

1 General description

All models have four wheel independent suspension based upon hydraulic shock absorbers and coil springs, although the design of the suspension arms and joints differs slightly between the models.

A front stabiliser bar is fitted.

On cars which have enclosed rear axleshafts, the front steering swivels are of king pin and bush type.

On cars which have exposed rear axleshafts, the front steering axis consists of the upper and lower suspension arm outer balljoints.

The steering is of recirculating ball type with a collapsible type shaft and column. Power steering is available on certain models as an option or may have been included as standard specification on some others.

The roadwheels may be of pressed steel or light-alloy cast type with tyres of radial construction.

2 Maintenance and inspection

1 Regularly inspect the fluid level in the steering gear and the power steering reservoir as described in detail in Section 25.

2 Lubricate the suspension where grease nipples are provided. The steering balljoints are of grease-sealed type.

3 At the recommended intervals, check the condition of the suspension bushes, renewing them if they have deteriorated.

4 At the specified intervals, remove and test the shock absorbers as described later in this Chapter.

5 With the help of an assistant to rock the car or to push and pull adjacent components, observe the various suspension and steering assemblies to check for movement or slackness resulting from wear in the friction bearing surfaces of the parts. Renew as necessary.

6 Check the condition of the power steering flexible hoses and for fluid leaks.

7 At the intervals specified in 'Routine Maintenance' have all the steering and suspension angles checked by your dealer (see Section 41).

3 Shock absorbers - removal, testing and refitting

1 *To remove a front shock absorber,* work within the engine compartment and unscrew the upper mounting bolts. On some models it may be necessary to remove the radiator expansion tank to gain access to the right-hand mounting (Fig. 11.1).

2 Remove the rubber cushions and plate (Fig. 11. 2).

3 Disconnect the shock absorber lower mounting by unscrewing and removing the nuts from the lower face of the lower suspension arm (Fig. 11.3).

4 Compress the shock absorber and remove it.

5 *To remove a rear shock absorber,* work within the luggage boot and after pulling off the covering cap, disconnect the upper mounting (Figs. 11.4 and 11.5).

6 On some roadster versions, the upper mounting nuts are accessible within the hood storage locker while the hood is raised (Fig. 11.6).

7 Unscrew and remove the lower mounting pivot bolt and remove the shock absorber in a downward direction (Fig. 11.7) (photo).

8 With the shock absorber removed from the car, secure its lower mounting in a vice which has been fitted with protected jaws. Keep the shock absorber in a vertical attitude.

9 Fully extend and contract the unit ten or twelve times. Any lack of resistance in either direction or jerkiness of movement should be rectified by renewal of the shock absorber.

10 Renew any flexible bushes if they have worn or hardened.

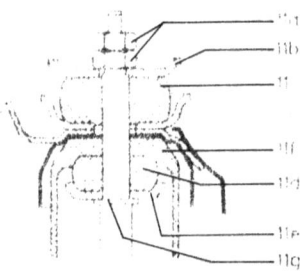

Fig. 11.2. Cutaway view of front shockabsorber upper mounting (Sec. 3)

11a *Nut and locknut*   11e *Cup washer*
11b *Washer*   11f *Shockabsorber protective*
11c *Rubber cushion*   *shield*
11d *Rubber cushion*   11g *Circlip*

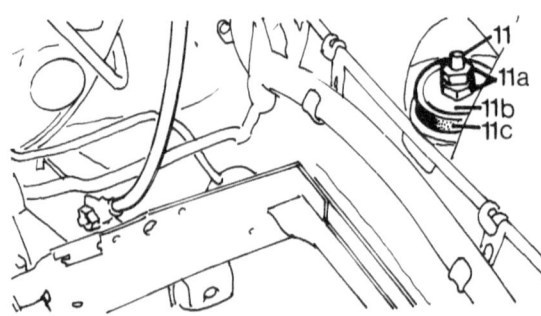

Fig. 11.1. Front shockabsorber upper mounting (Sec. 3)

11   *Shockabsorber*   11b *Washer*
11a *Nut and locknut*   11c *Rubber cushion*

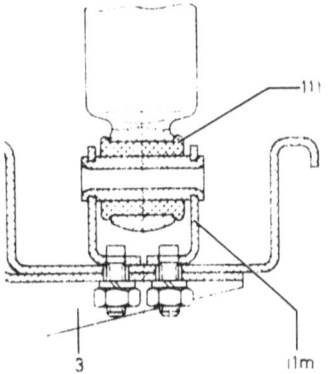

Fig. 11.3. Front shockabsorber lower mounting (Sec. 3)

3   *Suspension lower control arm*   11m   *Mounting plate*
11l *Rubber cushion*

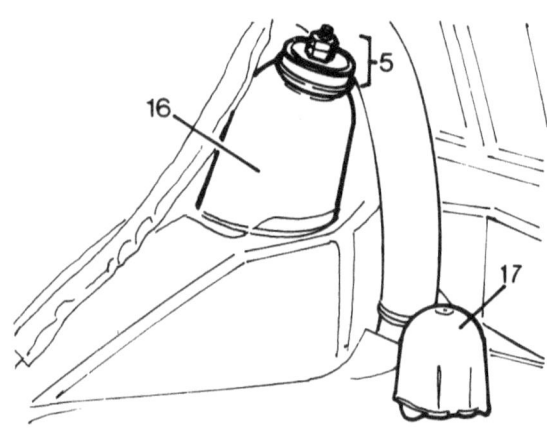

Fig. 11.4. Rear shockabsorber upper mounting (Sec. 3)

5   *Mounting cushions, plates*   17 *Cap (removed from top of*
    and nuts   *shockabsorber)*
16 *Domed cover*

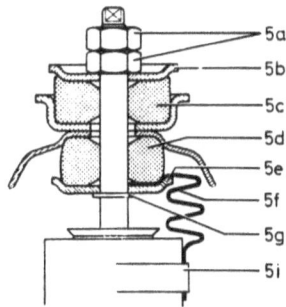

Fig. 11.5. Rear shockabsorber upper mounting (Sec. 3)

5a Nut and locknut   5e Washer
5b Washer   5f Dust excluding bellows
5c Rubber cushion   5g Circlip
5d Rubber cushion   5i Clamping band

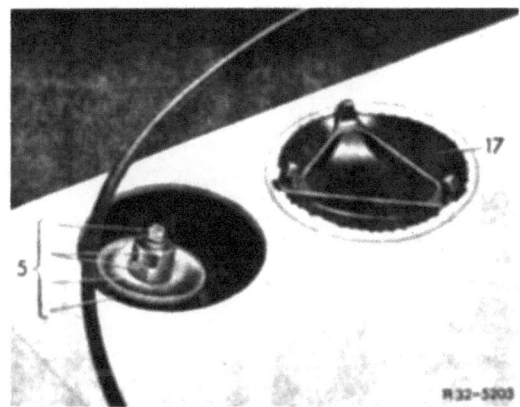

Fig. 11.6. Rear shockabsorber upper mounting on roadster version
(Sec. 3)

5 Mounting components   17 Cover plate

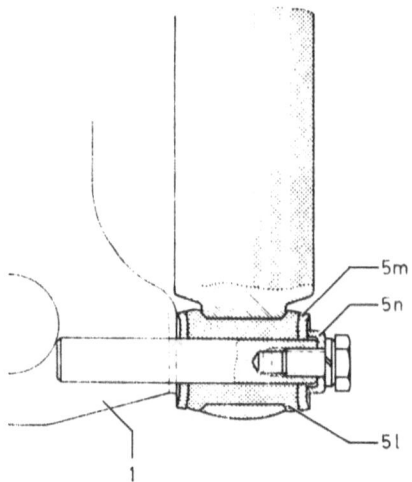

Fig. 11.7. Rear shockabsorber lower mounting (Sec. 3)

1   Axle tube   5m Washer
5l Flexible bush   5n Cup

11 Always renew a shock absorber if there is evidence of oil leakage
on the outside of the casing.
12 Refitting a shock absorber is a reversal of removal but make sure
that the mounting cushions and plates are refitted in their correct
sequence. Tighten the lower mounting bolt to the specified torque
wrench setting and tighten the upper nut (5G) so that no threads can
be seen above it. Tighten the upper mounting locknut. Note the
squared end at the top of the shock absorber piston rod to which a
spanner can be engaged to prevent the rod turning when the mounting
nuts are tightened or unscrewed.

3.7 Rear shock absorber lower mounting

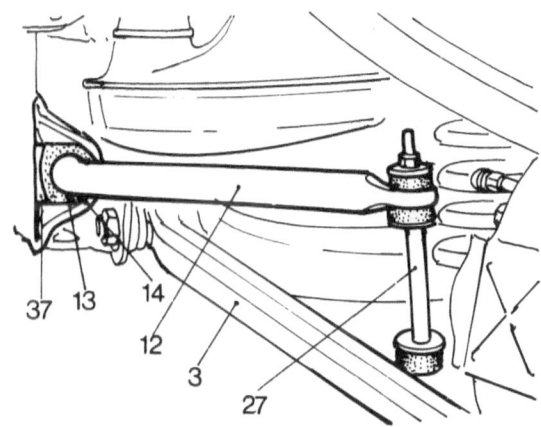

Fig. 11.8. Front stabiliser bar attachment (Sec. 4)

3   Suspension lower control   14 Clamp
    arm   27 Drop link
12 Stabiliser bar   37 Reinforcement plate
13 Flexible mounting

4   Front stabiliser bar - removal and refitting

1   Disconnect the drop links which attach each end of the stabiliser
bar to the front suspension lower control arms (Fig. 11.8).
2   Unscrew the nuts from the stabiliser bar flexible mounting brackets
and remove the brackets and the stabiliser bar.
3   Renew any rubber bushes which have worn or deteriorated and
refit the bar by reversing the removal operations.
4   When tightening the drop link nuts on earlier models which have a
locknut in addition to the securing nut, tighten the securing nut to the
specified torque wrench setting given in the 'Specifications'. When
tightening the single self-locking type nut on later models, tighten the
nut right up to the end of the threads on the link.

5   Front hubs - adjustment

1   Raise the front of the car, support it securely and remove the
roadwheel.
2   Lever or tap off the grease cap, also the radio interference contact
spring fitted to some later models.
3   Loosen the socket headed pinch bolt which is now exposed
(Fig. 11.9).

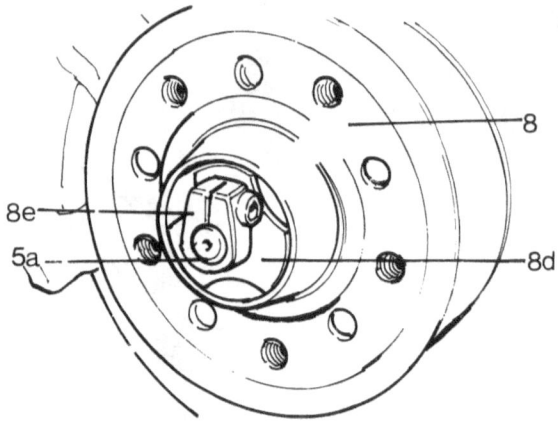

Fig. 11.9. Front hub details (Sec. 5)

5a Stub axle   8d Thrust washer
8   Hub assembly   8e Clamp nut

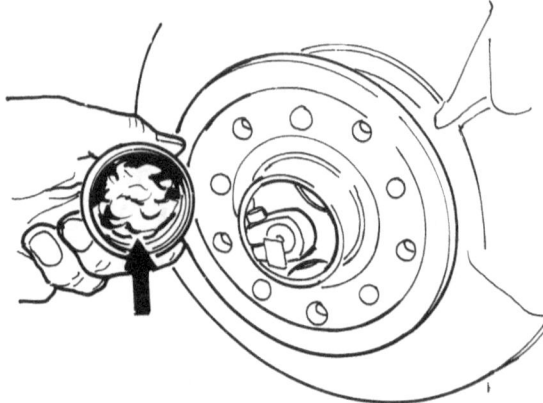

Fig. 11.10. Front hub grease cap. Note radio suppressor contact
spring on end of stub axle (Sec. 5)

4   Remove the disc pads as described in Chapter 9.
5   Turn the hub in the normal forward direction of rotation at the
same time tightening the clamp nut until the hub is stiff to turn. Back
off the clamp nut one third of a turn and then remove any tension by
tapping the end of the stub axle with a hammer.
6   If the adjustment has been correctly carried out, the hub should
have an endfloat of between 0.0004 and 0.0008 in (0.01 and 0.02 mm)
This should ideally be measured with a dial gauge but a reasonable
alternative is to try and turn the thrust washer which is located behind
the clamp nut with the fingers. If it can just be stiffly turned then
adjustment of the hub bearings is correct.
7   Tighten the clamp nut pinch bolt and refit the brake disc pads.
8   Refit the radio suppression spring and then half fill the cap with
grease and tap it onto the end of the hub (Fig. 11.10).
9   Fit the roadwheel.
10 Repeat the adjustment on the opposite front wheel and then lower
the car to the ground.

6 Front hubs - overhaul

1   Jack up the front of the car and remove the roadwheel.
2   Tap off the grease cap, remove the radio suppression spring contact.
3   Unscrew and remove the pinch bolt from the clamp nut.
4   Unscrew and remove the clamp nut and extract the thrust washer
(Fig. 11.11).
5   Withdraw the disc pads and the caliper as described in Chapter 9.
6   Withdraw the hub/disc assembly from the stub axle. If necessary, use
a suitable bolt-on type puller or a slide hammer attached to the roadwheel bolt holes.

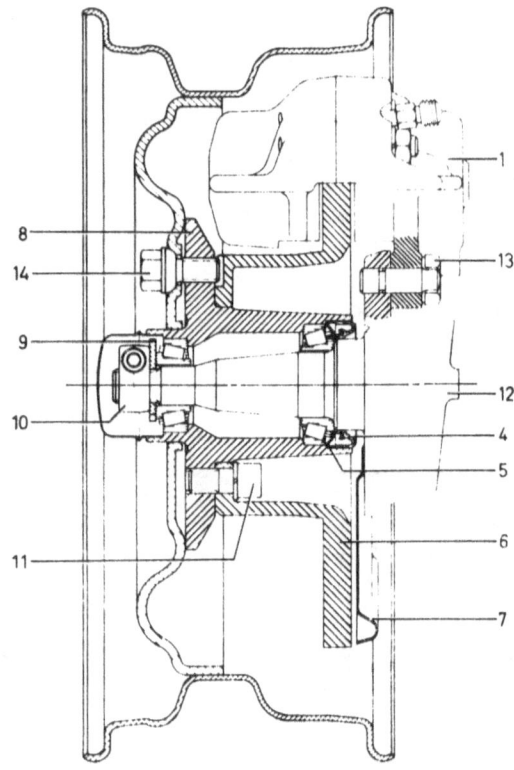

Fig. 11.11. Sectional view of front hub assembly (Sec. 6)

1 Brake caliper   9   Thrust washer
4 Oil seal   10 Clamp nut
5 Deflector   11 Socket headed screw
6 Brake disc   12 Stub axle carrier
7 Shield   13 Bolt
8 Hub   14 Roadwheel bolt

7   Examine the condition of the hub bearings. If they are noisy when
turned with the fingers or are grooved or chipped, prise out the oil
seal and discard it.
8   Extract the bearings and their tracks using a piece of tubing as a
drift.
9   Clean the inside of the hub free from old dirt and grease.
10 Drive the new bearing tracks into position, fit the tapered roller
bearings and tap in a new oil seal.
11 Fill the interior of the hub with 2 oz (57 g) of wheel bearing
grease. Do not exceed this amount. Smear the oil seal lips with the
same grease.
12 Fit the hub to the stub axle, fit the thrust washer and clamp nut
and then adjust the bearings as described in the preceding Section.
13 On completion of the work, bleed the front brake circuit.

7 Rear hubs - overhaul and adjustment

1   These operations are described in Chapter 8 in connection with the
rear axle.

8 Front road spring (king pin type stub axle) - removal and refitting

1   Jack up the car and support it securely under the bodyframe.
2   Disconnect the stabiliser bar end drop link from the control arm;
3   Unscrew and remove the two outer bolts of the four used for
securing the lower suspension arm inner pivot to the front crossmember.
4   Place a jack under the pivot and then unscrew and remove the two
inner securing bolts (Fig. 11.12).
5   Lower the jack very slowly until the coil type roadspring and its
flexible mounting can be withdrawn (Fig. 11.13).
6   Refitting is a reversal of removal. The spring must be refitted the
correct way up, however, as shown. The flexible mounting can be

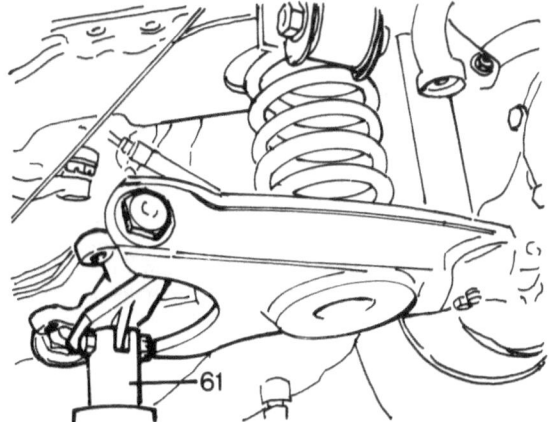

Fig. 11.12. Jacking up suspension lower control arm (kingpin type)
(Sec. 8)

61 Jack

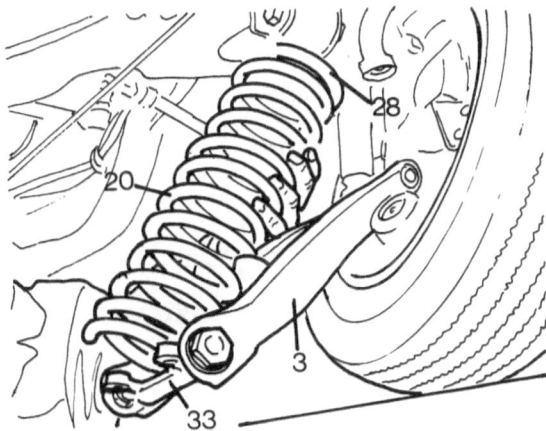

Fig. 11.13. Removing a front roadspring (kingpin type stub axle
carrier) (Sec. 8)

3   Lower control arm   28   Rubber insulator
20 Spring   33   Control arm pivot

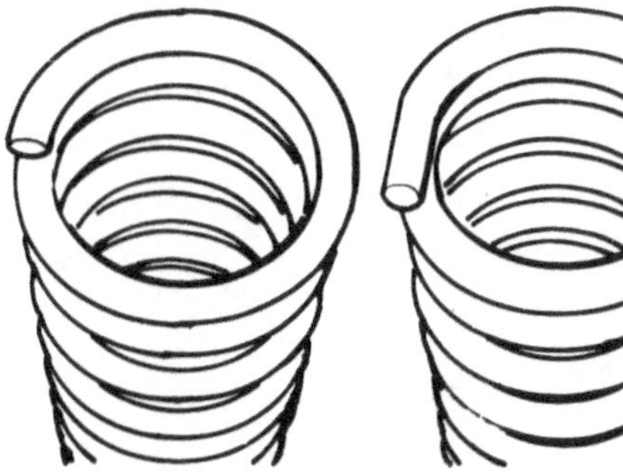

Fig. 11.14. Differences between top and bottom coils of front
roadspring (Sec. 8)

top   bottom

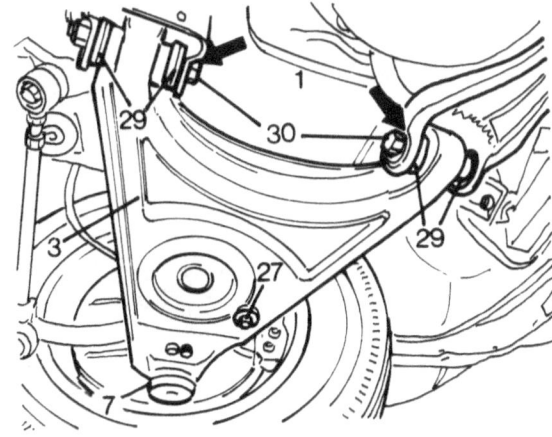

Fig. 11.15. Suspension lower control arm (balljoint swivel type)
(Sec. 9)

1   Crossmember   27   Stabiliser bar attachment
3   Control arm   29   Flexible bush
7   Lower swivel   30   Cam bolt

Fig. 11.16. Removing a front coil spring (balljoint swivel type stub
axle carrier) (Sec. 9)

1   Crossmember   11   Front shockabsorber
3   Lower control arm   12   Stabiliser bar
4   Upper control arm   29   Flexible bushes
10 Coil spring   31   Spring flexible insulator

or road surface conditions. If a change in the original specification is
being made, always change the opposite front spring and mounting for
ones of identical type.

9   Front road spring (balljoint swivel type stub axle) - removal and refitting

1   Jack up the front of the car and support it under the bodyframe.
Remove the roadwheel.
2   Disconnect the stabiliser bar drop link from the suspension lower
arm and disconnect the shock absorber lower mountings.
3   Mark the position of the cam bolts (30) in relation to the crossmember. Use a stroke of quick drying paint to do this or dot punch it
(Fig. 11.15).
4   Unscrew and remove the nuts from the cam bolts and then support
the suspension arm with a jack.
5   Carefully knock out the cam bolts without damaging their threads.
6   Lower the jack slowly and remove it.
7   Swivel the suspension member towards the front of the car and
then remove the road spring and the flexible mounting (Fig. 11.16).
8   To refit the spring, hold it so that its flat ground end is uppermost
and then place the flexible mounting on its top end.
9   Turn the suspension control arm as necessary in order to be able to
insert the spring and mounting and then turn the spring so that the

taped in position if necessary to facilitate refitment of the spring
(Fig. 11.14).
7   Note: *Make sure that the bolts which secure the suspension arm
inner pivot have their heads above the pivot.*
8   It is recommended that for replacement purposes, a coil spring and
flexible mounting of similar type to the original are always used. A
variety of spring lengths and flexible mounting thicknesses are available
if required to adjust the suspension characteristics for increased load

butt end of the lower coil is fully engaged in the indentation in the control arm (Fig. 11.17).

10 Turn the suspension arm to its normal position and then raise it with a jack until it is sufficiently aligned to enable the cam bolts to be inserted.

11 Fit the cam bolt nuts but do not fully tighten them at this stage. Turn the cam bolts so that the marks made before dismantling are in alignment.

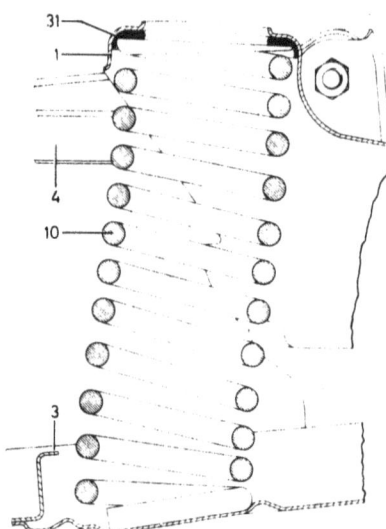

Fig. 11.17. Front spring mounting (swivel balljoint type stub axle carrier) (Sec. 9)

1 Crossmember	10 Spring
3 Lower control arm	31 Flexible insulator
4 Upper control arm	

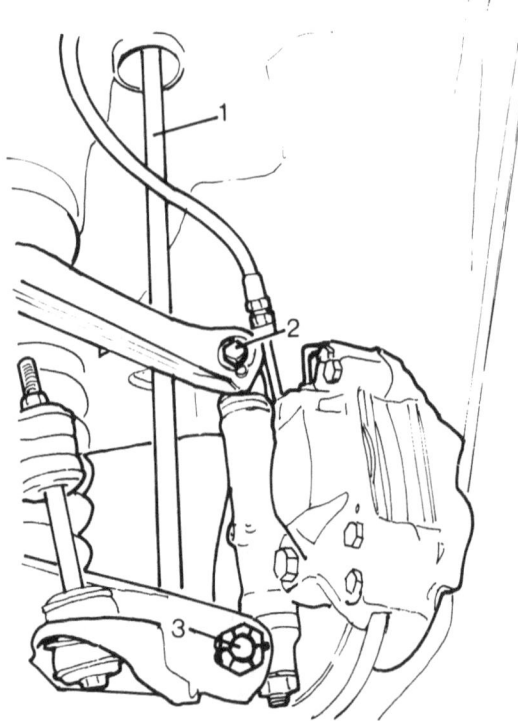

Fig. 11.18. Threaded support rod (1) used to hold lower control arm (kingpin type stub axle carrier) (Sec. 10)

2 Cam bolt	3 Lower bearing pivot

12 Refit the stabiliser bar and reconnect the shock absorber.

13 Refit the roadwheel.

14 Lower the car to the ground and then fully tighten the cam bolt nuts.

15 Although the cam bolts have been refitted in their original positions, it is recommended that the steering angles are checked by your dealer at the first opportunity (see Section 41).

10 Stub axle (king pin type) - removal, overhaul and refitting

1 Remove the disc caliper as described in Chapter 9.

2 Disconnect the brake hose and rigid line from the stub axle.

3 Using a suitable extractor, disconnect the track rod end balljoint from the steering arm of the stub axle assembly.

4 Remove the front shock absorber as described earlier in this Chapter.

5 Support the suspension lower arm on a jack or suspend it on a rod attached to the shock absorber upper mounting (Fig. 11.18).

6 Mark the position of the notch in the cam bolt (2) in relation to the castor adjusting disc and the disc and lockplate in relation to the suspension upper arm and then unscrew and remove the bolt.

7 Extract the split pin, unscrew the castellated nut and then unscrew the threaded bolt (3) from the base of the stub axle assembly.

8 Withdraw the stub axle complete with the hub/disc.

9 If the king pin bushes are to be renewed, first remove the hub/disc assembly as described in Section 6.

10 The hollow threaded bolt (8) can now be unscrewed from the top of the stub axle (Fig. 11.19).

11 Unscrew but do not remove the large nut from the bottom of the king pin, release the carrier (4) by giving the nut a sharp blow to loosen the king pin from its tapered seat. Pull off the carrier and compensating washer (5).

12 Withdraw the king pin and extract both thrust washers.

13 Remove the dust excluders.

14 Although worn king pin bushes can be removed with a suitable mandrel and new ones pressed in, it is recommended that this work is left to your dealer as the bushes have to be reamed after fitting.

15 Commence reassembly by fitting the dust excluders.

16 Fit the lower (6) of the two upper thrust washers so that the grease grooves face upwards (Fig. 11.20).

17 Fit the upper thrust washer.

18 Wipe the tapered seat of the carrier and the king pin free from grease, insert the king pin into the stub axle assembly and fit the carrier. Make sure that the cam bolt hole and the threaded bolt hole in the carrier are exactly parallel. Use two very long rods for this to accentuate any deviation.

19 Screw on the carrier nut, tap the top of the king pin and fully tighten the nut without disturbing the setting of the carrier to cam bolt hole relationship.

20 With the king pin bottom nut fully tightened, check the endfloat of the king pin. This should be approximately 0.020 in (0.5 mm). If no end play exists, change the compensating washer for a thinner one.

21 Screw the cam bolt hollow threaded sleeve in until both ends

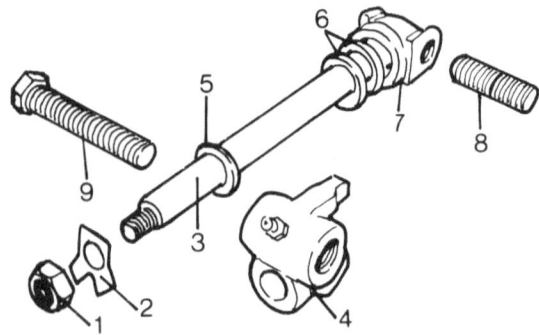

Fig. 11.19. Exploded view of kingpin and component parts

1 Nut	6 Thrust washer
2 Lockplate	7 Dust excluder
3 Kingpin	8 Threaded pivot bush
4 Lower bearing	9 Pivot bolt
5 Compensating washer	

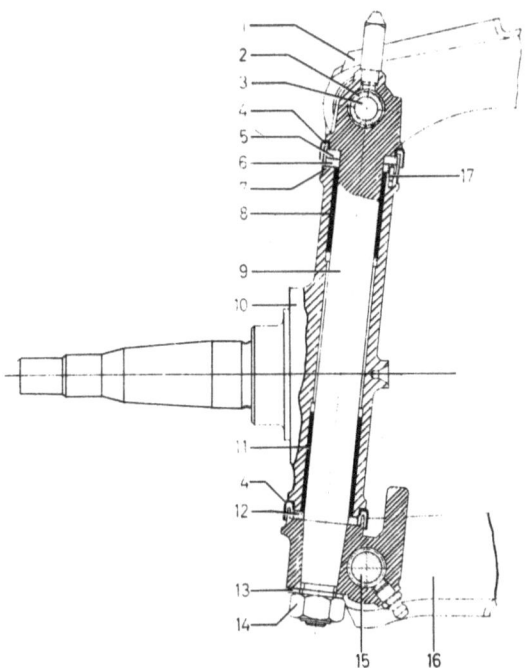

Fig. 11.20. Cutaway view of kingpin type stub axle carrier (Sec. 10)

1	Upper control arm	11	Lower bush
2	Threaded pivot bolt	12	Compensating washer
3	Cam bolt	13	Lockwasher
4	Dust excluder	14	Nut
5	Upper thrust washer	15	Bottom pivot/bearing
6	Second thrust washer		assembly
7	Dust excluding sleeve	16	Suspension lower control
8	Upper bush		arm
9	Kingpin	17	Pin
10	Stub axle carrier		

project equally. The grooved end of the sleeve should face the front of the car when fitted.

22 Refit the front hub.

23 Fit the assembly to the suspension lower control arm using new sealing rings and screwing in the threaded bolt at the base of the stub axle. Make sure that the head of the bolt is at the rear of the control arm (Fig. 11.21).

24 Connect the stub axle to the suspension upper control arm with the cam bolt. Make sure that the adjusting disc, bolt and lockplate are all in their original positions. Make sure that the lug of the adjusting disc (4) engages correctly in the groove of the bolt (3) (Fig. 11.22).

25 Raise the lower control arm, remove the temporary rod (if fitted) and fit the shock absorber.

26 Connect the track rod end balljoint to the steering arm of the stub axle.

27 Refit the caliper and brake lines.

28 Bleed the front hydraulic circuit.

29 Have the steering angles checked by your dealer at the earliest opportunity (see Section 41).

11 Front suspension control arms (king pin type stub axle) - removal and refitting

1 To remove either the upper or lower front suspension control arm, first remove the stub axle assembly as described in the preceding Section.

2 Disconnect the stabiliser bar from the lower control arm.

3 Carefully lower the jack which is supporting the lower control arm or if a threaded rod has been used to hold it up, release this. With the outer end of the control arm lowered, extract the coil spring.

4 Disconnect the bolts which hold the control arm pivot to the crossmember and remove the arm. Take careful note of any washers which are located between the pivot and the crossmember.

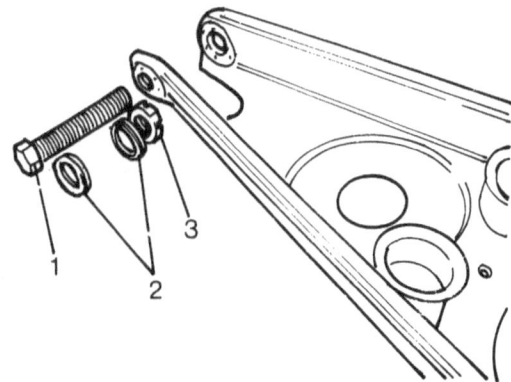

Fig. 11.21. Suspension lower control arm outer pivot bolt (1) seals (2) and castellated nut (3) (kingpin type stub axle carrier) (Sec. 10)

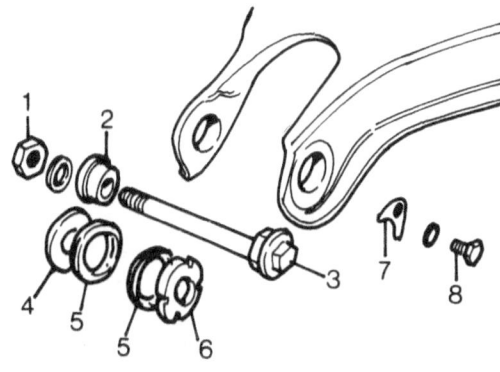

Fig. 11.22. Suspension upper control arm outer pivot details (Sec. 10)

1	Nut	5	Rubber seal
2	Cam (eccentric)	6	Castor adjusting disc
3	Cam bolt	7	Lock washer
4	Washer	8	Bolt

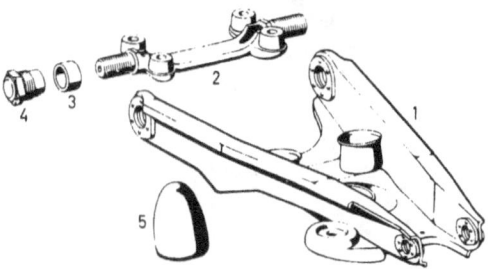

Fig. 11.23. Suspension lower control arm inner pivot details (kingpin type stub axle carrier) (Sec. 11)

1	Control arm	4	Threaded bush
2	Pivot	5	Rubber buffer
3	Flexible seals		

5 Removal of the upper control arm is similar except that only two bolts are used to retain the pivot.

6 Once a control arm is removed, it can be dismantled by unscrewing and removing the threaded bushes from both ends of the pivot, extracting the rubber seals and manoeuvring the pivot out of the arm (Figs. 11.23 and 11.24).

7 Renew worn components as necessary.

8 Commence reassembly by fitting new rubber sealing rings. Locate the pivot and screw in the threaded bushes. The bush at one end of the pivot has a different thread from the one at the other. The identification number 31, stamped on the control arm adjacent to a bush hole, signifies that the bush with a groove just in front of the threads should

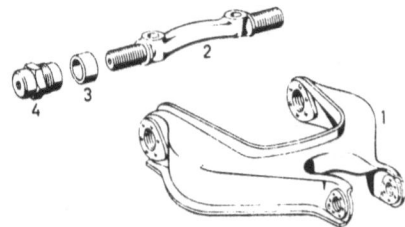

Fig. 11.24. Suspension upper control arm inner pivot details (kingpin type stub axle carrier) (Sec. 11)

1 *Control arm*   3 *Flexible bushes*
2 *Pivot*   4 *Threaded bush*

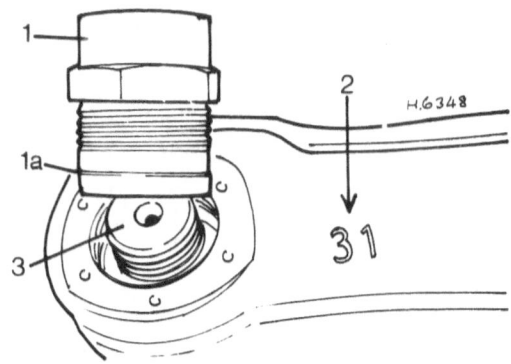

Fig. 11.25. Threaded bush identification number on front suspension upper control arm (kingpin type stub axle carrier) (Sec. 11)

1 *Bush*   2 *Identification number*
1a *Groove*   3 *Pivot bolt*

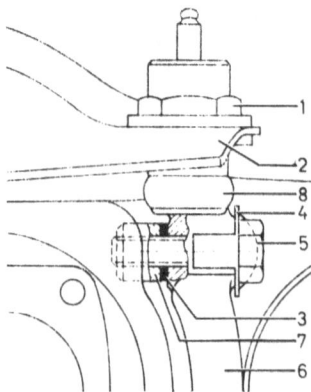

Fig. 11.26. Front suspension upper control arm attachment to crossmember (kingpin type stub axle carrier) (Sec. 11)

1 *Threaded bush*   5 *Bolt*
2 *Upper control arm*   6 *Pivot bolt*
3 *Washer*   7 *Crossmember*
4 *Lockwasher*   8 *Sealing ring*

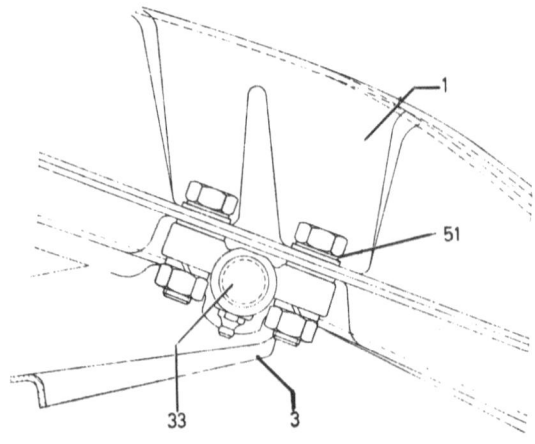

Fig. 11.27. Attachment of front suspension lower control arm to crossmember showing position of nuts (kingpin type stub axle carrier) (Sec. 11)

1 *Crossmember*   33 *Pivot bolt*
3 *Control arm*   51 *Washer*

camber has not been sufficient (see Section 41) (Fig. 11.26). A plain washer 0.08 in (2.0 mm) thick is located between the pivot and the crossmember. Never leave this out or the bolt may project and foul the road spring. This washer can, however, be transferred beneath the lockwasher under the bolt head where it will have the same effect of shortening the bolt (Fig. 11.27).

11 *The lower control arm* can be bolted in position with the road spring correctly located and then the stub axle assembly refitted as described in Section 10.

12 Reconnect the stabiliar bar and fit the shock absorber.

13 At the earliest opportunity, have the steering angles checked by your dealer (see Section 41).

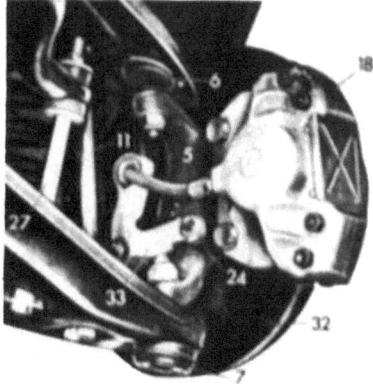

Fig. 11.28. Balljoint swivel type stub axle carrier (Sec. 12)

5 *Stub axle carrier*   24 *Steering arm*
6 *Upper swivel*   27 *Stabiliser bar drop link*
7 *Lower swivel*   32 *Shield*
11 *Shockabsorber*   33 *Brake flexible hose guide*
18 *Brake caliper*

be located at that point (Fig. 11.25).

9   Screw in both bushes an equal amount and then tighten them to the specified torque wrench setting. Check that the pivot turns smoothly without binding.

10 Bolt *the upper control arm* to the crossmember. Normally the washer (3) is only found where the normal eccentric adjustment for

12 Stub axle (balljoint swivel type) - removal and refitting

1   Jack up the front wheel by placing a jack under the suspension lower control arm. Place safety stands under the bodyframe but only so that they just make contact and do not raise the body.

2   **Note:** *On no account disconnect the shock absorber.*

3   Remove the roadwheel.

4   Unbolt the steering arm from the stub axle carrier (Fig. 11.28).

5   Disconnect the flexible brake hose from the rigid line. Plug the open ends. Remove the caliper (Chapter 9) (Fig. 11.29).

6   Unscrew the nuts from the taper pins of the upper and lower suspension arm swivel balljoints (Fig. 11.30).

7   A suitable balljoint separator will now be required to disconnect the swivels from the eyes of the stub axle carrier.

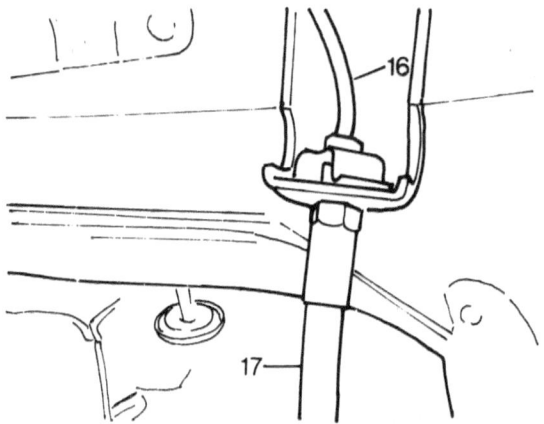

Fig. 11.29. Brake hose connection adjacent to front suspension
(Sec. 12)

16 Rigid line   17 Flexible hose

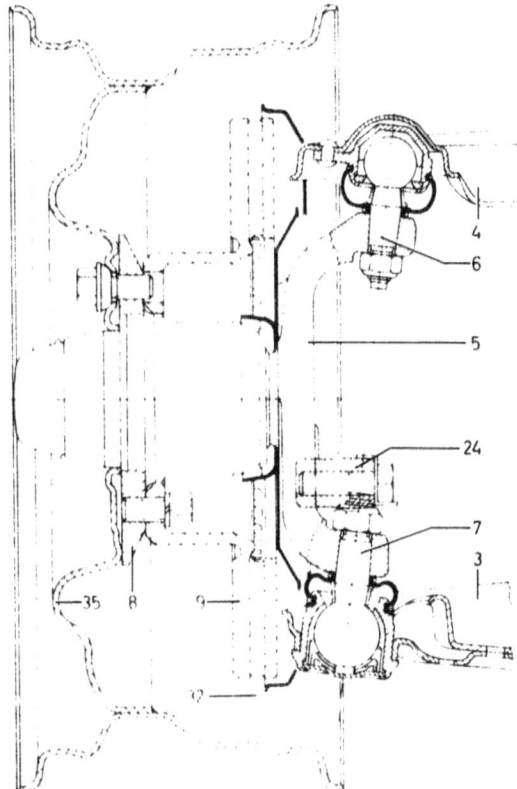

Fig. 11.30. View of front suspension stub axle carrier and swivel
balljoints (Sec. 12)

3	Lower control arm	8	Hub
4	Upper control arm	9	Disc
5	Stub axle carrier	24	Steering arm
6	Upper swivel	32	Shield
7	Lower swivel	35	Roadwheel

8   Remove the complete stub axle/hub assembly.
9   Refitting is a reversal of removal. Do not apply grease to the balljoint taper pins or eyes in the stub axle carrier. If the taper pin does
turn while the nut is being tightened, insert a forked wedge between
the nut and the eye of the stub axle carrier and apply as much leverage
as possible to press the eye onto the taper pin.
10 Bleed the brakes on completion and then have the steering angles
checked at the first opportunity.

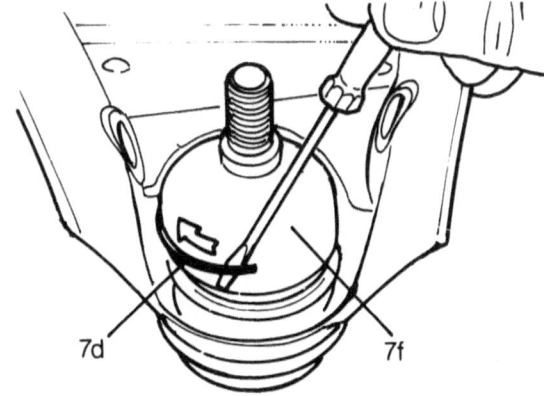

Fig. 11.31. Removing a swivel dust excluder retaining ring (Sec. 13)

7d Ring   7f Dust excluder

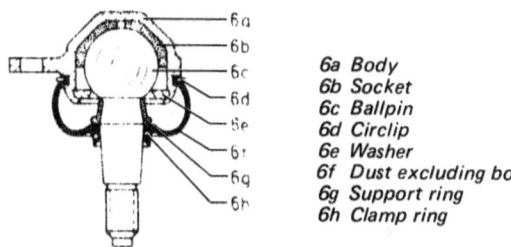

	7a Body
	7b Anti-friction shell
	7c Ballpin
	7d Circlip
	7e Sealing plate
	7f Dust excluding boot
	7g Support ring
	7h Clamp ring
	7i End socket

Fig. 11.32. Sectional view of lower swivel balljoint (Sec. 13)

	6a Body
	6b Socket
	6c Ballpin
	6d Circlip
	6e Washer
	6f Dust excluding boot
	6g Support ring
	6h Clamp ring

Fig. 11.33. Sectional view of upper swivel balljoint (Sec. 13)

13 Suspension balljoint dust excluders - renewal

1   If on inspection, any of the suspension swivel balljoint dust
excluders are seen to be split or damaged, then they must be renewed
immediately.
2   To do this, remove the stub axle carrier as described in the
preceding Section.
3   Using a small screwdriver, lever off the circlip and then pull off the
flexible dust excluder (Fig. 11.31).
4   Wiper away the old grease from the joint and pack it with fresh
lubricant.
5   Refit the new dust excluder having already fitted the clamping ring
and then fit the circlip (Figs. 11.32 and 11.33).
6   Refit the stub axle assembly.

14 Front suspension lower control arm (balljoint swivel type stub axle) - removal, overhaul and refitting

1   Disconnect the shock absorber lower mounting.
2   Jack up the car and unbolt the steering arm from the stub axle
carrier.
3   Disconnect the brake flexible hose from the rigid line. Plug the
lines.
4   Remove the coil spring as described in paragraphs 2 to 7 of
Section 9.
5   Disconnect the suspension lower swivel from the stub axle carrier

and remove the suspension lower arm.

6   If the swivel balljoint is worn, the joint can be pressed out of the control arm and a new one pressed in. The new joint must be kept straight during the fitting operation and unless suitable pressing facilities are available, leave the job to your dealer.

7   Check the suspension arm pivot flexible bushes. If these are worn, prise them out. Clean the bush recesses with emery cloth and press in new bushes. Apply some hydraulic fluid or rubber grease to ease their entry (Fig. 11.34).

8   Commence refitting by connecting the suspension swivel balljoint to the eye of the stub axle carrier.

9   Refit the front coil spring as described in Section 9 but do not fully tighten the cam bolts at this stage.

10 Bolt the steering arm to the stub axle carrier.

11 Reconnect the brake hose and bleed the hydraulic system, lower the car and fully tighten the cam bolts.

12 Take the earliest opportunity to have the steering angles checked by your dealer (see Section 41).

15 Front suspension upper control arm (balljoint swivel type stub axle) - removal, overhaul and refitting

1   Jack up the car under the suspension lower control arm. Use safety stands under the bodyframe but these should only just make contact and not support the weight of the car.

2   **Note:** *Do not disconnect the shock absorber.*

3   Unbolt the steering arm from the stub axle carrier.

4   Disconnect the flexible brake hose from the rigid line and plug the lines.

5   Unscrew and remove the nut from the taper pin of the upper swivel balljoint. Disconnect the balljoint from the eye of the stub axle carrier using a suitable balljoint separator.

6   Unbolt the pivot bolts of the upper control arm from the cross-member and remove the arm.

7   If the swivel balljoint is worn or damaged, it cannot be renewed on its own, but a complete new control arm will have to be obtained.

8   The flexible pivot bushes can be renewed if worn in a similar way to that described in paragraph 7 of Section 14.

9   Commence refitting by connecting the arm to the crossmember and pushing in the pivot bolts. Make sure that the nuts of the bolts are on the outside of the control arm.

10 Reconnect the swivel balljoint to the stub axle carrier.

11 Bolt the steering arm to the stub axle carrier.

12 Reconnect the brake hose and bleed the hydraulic circuit.

13 Have the steering angles checked at the earliest opportunity by your dealer.

16 Front axle/crossmember (king pin type stub axle) - removal and refitting

1   If a complete overhaul of the front suspension is required or its removal is needed due to collision damage, the withdrawal of the complete assembly will probably be as quick as removing individual components.

2   Raise the vehicle at the front and rear, allowing adequate clearance beneath, and then support the bodyframe side members on axle stands.

3   Remove the battery and the front roadwheels.

4   Support the weight of the engine on a hoist or by using a support bar and chain, located between the front panel upper cross strut, just ahead of the radiator and the engine compartment rear bulkhead.

5   Unscrew the centre bolts from the engine front mountings.

6   Disconnect the brake lines (left and right-hand) at the unions between the body and the crossmember. Plug or cap the open lines.

7   Disconnect the handbrake primary cable.

8   Using a suitable balljoint separator, disconnect the track rod end balljoints from the steering arms on the stub axle carriers.

9   Remove the front road springs (Section 8) making sure to mesh the position of the lower control arm cam bolts and washers.

10 Disconnect the stabiliser bar leaf spring support struts from the bodyframe (Fig. 11.35).

11 Support the crossmember on a trolley jack and then unscrew the bolts from each side of the engine compartment which secure the crossmember flexible mountings to the bodyframe. On 280SL models, a stop plate is secured under the mounting bolts (Figs. 11.36,

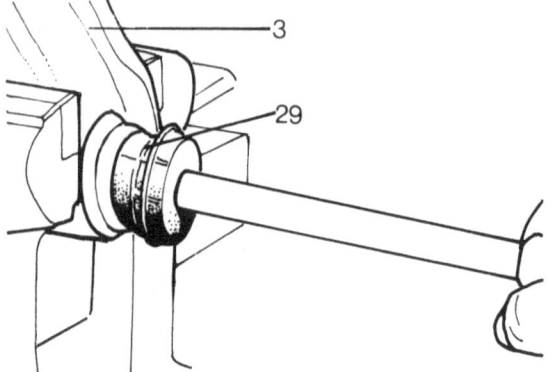

Fig. 11.34. Prising out a control arm flexible bush (Sec. 14)

3   *Control arm*   29   *Flexible bush*

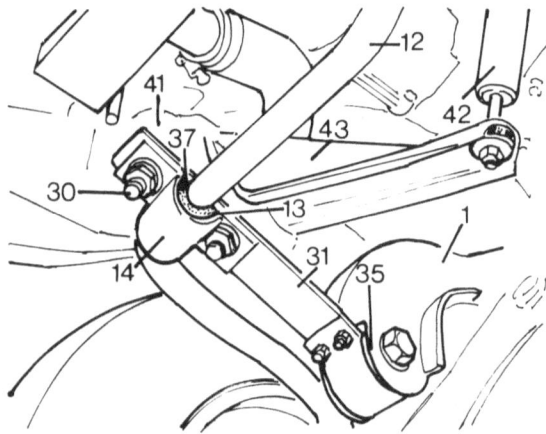

Fig. 11.35. Front suspension details (kingpin type stub axle carrier) (Sec. 16)

1	*Crossmember*	35	*Flexible bush*
12	*Stabiliser bar*	37	*Lockplate*
13	*Flexible mounting*	41	*Bracket*
14	*Clamp*	42	*Engine damper*
30	*Cam bolt*	43	*Mounting bracket for*
31	*Leaf spring*		*engine damper*

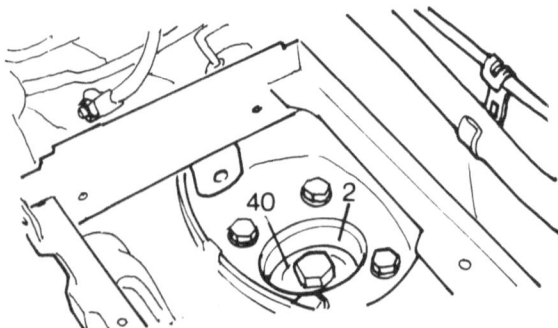

Fig. 11.36. Crossmember mounting bolts within engine compartment (kingpin type stub axle carrier) except 280 SL (Sec. 16)

2   *Flexible mounting*   40   *Stop plate*

11.37, 11.38 and 11.39).

12 Lower the trolley jack and withdraw the complete front axle assembly from beneath the car.

13 Refitting is a reversal of removal, but on completion, bleed the brake circuit and take the first opportunity to have the steering angles checked (see Section 41).

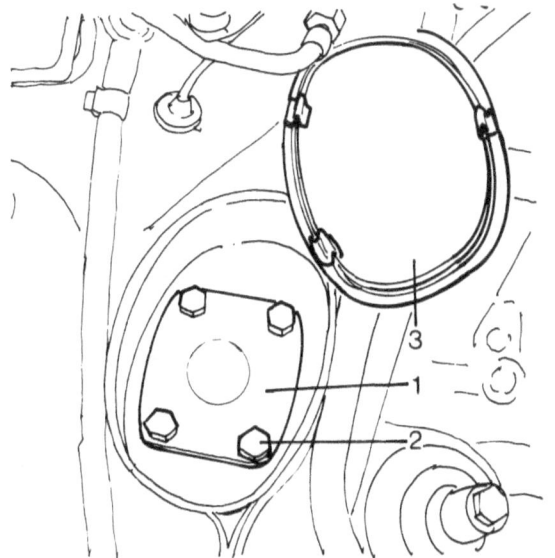

Fig. 11.37. Crossmember mounting bolts on 280 SL (Sec. 16)

1   Stop plate   2   Bolts   3   Cover

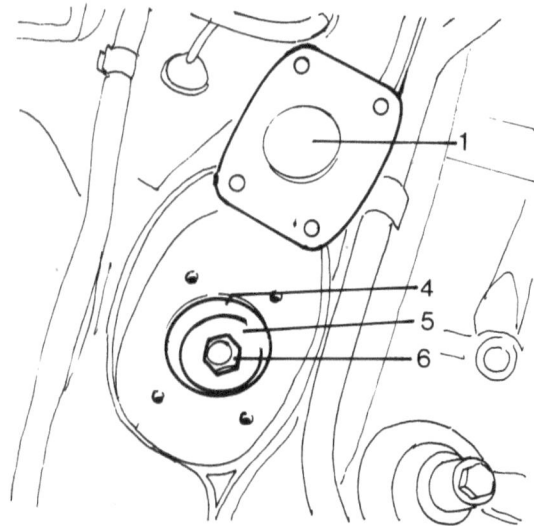

Fig. 11.38. Crossmember mounting stop plate removed (280 SL)
(Sec. 16)

1   Stop plate   5   Stop disc
4   Flexible mounting   6   Bolt

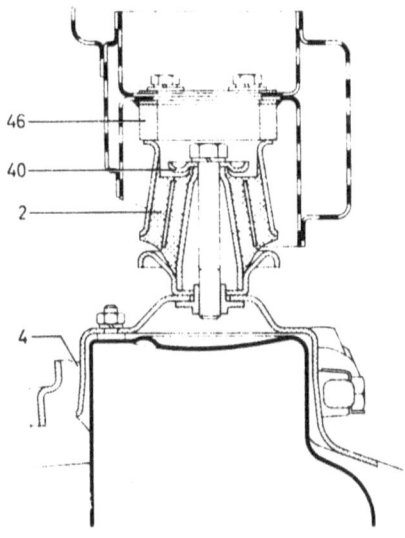

Fig. 11.39. Sectional view of crossmember mounting (Sec. 16)

2   Flexible mounting   40   Stop disc
4   Control arm   46   Cup

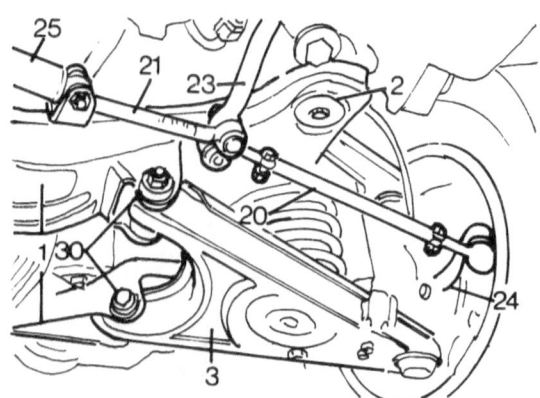

Fig. 11.40. One side of front suspension (swivel balljoint stub axle
carrier) viewed from the rear (Sec. 17)

1   Crossmember   23   Steering idler
2   Crossmember flexible mounting   24   Steering arm
3   Lower control arm   25   Steering damper
20 Trackrod   30   Cam bolts
21 Drag link

17 Front axle/crossmember (balljoint swivel type stub axle) - removal and refitting

1   Disconnect the front shock absorber lower mountings.
2   Jack up the car at the front and rear, allowing adequate clearance below to permit the withdrawal of the front axle assembly. Support the bodyframe side members on axle stands.
3   Remove the front roadwheels.
4   Remove the front shock absorbers.
5   Support the weight of the engine on a hoist or by using a support bar and chain located between the front panel upper cross strut just ahead of the radiator and the engine compartment rear bulkhead.
6   Unscrew the centre bolts from the engine front mountings.
7   Disconnect the two front flexible brakes hoses from the rigid lines. Plug or cap the open pipes.
8   Disconnect the two track rod end balljoints from the steering arms on the stub axle carrier using a suitable separator.
9   Remove the stabiliser bar.

10 On M180 type engines used in model 230/8 cars, disconnect the engine damper strut.
11 Remove the front road springs after referring to Section 9 and then re-attach the suspension lower arms again temporarily.
12 Support the crossmember with a trolley jack and then unscrew the four crossmember flexible mounting bolts. At this stage, the crossmember flexible mountings can be renewed if the trolley jack is lowered two inches (50.8 mm) (Figs. 11.40, 11.41 and 11.42).
13 To remove the complete axle/crossmember, lower the jack until the assembly can be withdrawn from beneath the car(Fig. 11.43).
14 Refitting is a reversal of removal, but on completion, bleed the hydraulic brake circuit and check the steering angles as soon as possible (see Section 41).

18 Rear road spring (enclosed axleshafts) - removal and refitting

1   Jack up the rear of the car and support the bodyframe side members on axle stands.

2   Place a jack under the centre of the suspension link arm and raise
the arm but not so much that the body starts to lift.
3   Do not disconnect the shock absorbers.
4   Unscrew the retaining nuts which secure the plate of the link arm
to the bodyframe floor (Fig. 11.44).
5   Slowly lower the jack and then withdraw the coil spring (Fig. 11.45).
6   Refitting is a reversal of removal, but renew the spring upper and

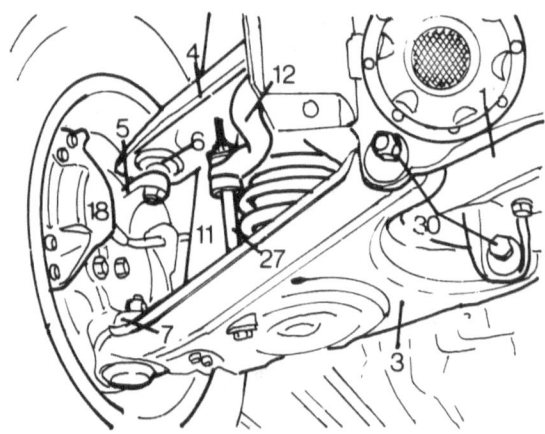

Fig. 11.41. One side of front suspension (swivel balljoint stub axle
carrier) viewed from the front (Sec. 17)

1	Crossmember	11	Shockabsorber
3	Lower control arm	12	Stabiliser bar
4	Upper control arm	18	Brake caliper
5	Stub axle carrier	27	Stabiliser drop link
6	Upper balljoint swivel	30	Cam bolt
7	Lower balljoint swivel		

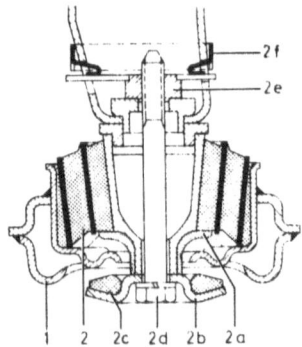

Fig. 11.42. Crossmember flexible mounting (swivel balljoint type
stub axle carrier) (Sec. 17)

1	Crossmember	2c	Buffer
2	Flexible mounting	2d	Bolt
2a	Buffer	2e	Nut
2b	Stop plate	2f	Nut lock

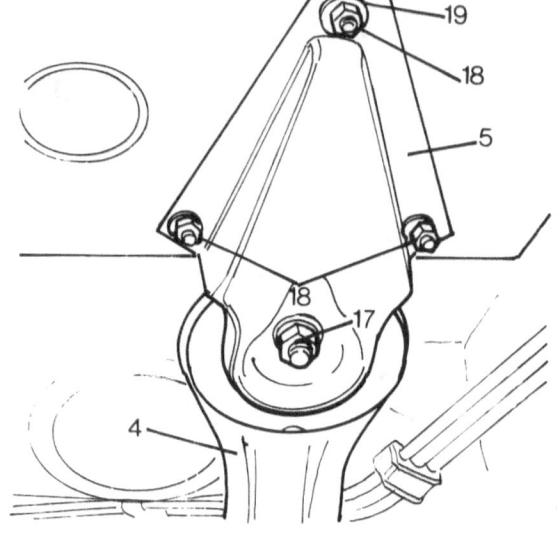

Fig. 11.44. Rear suspension link arm plate (enclosed type axleshafts)
(Sec. 18)

4	Link arm	18	Plate nuts
5	Plate	19	Washer
17	Nut		

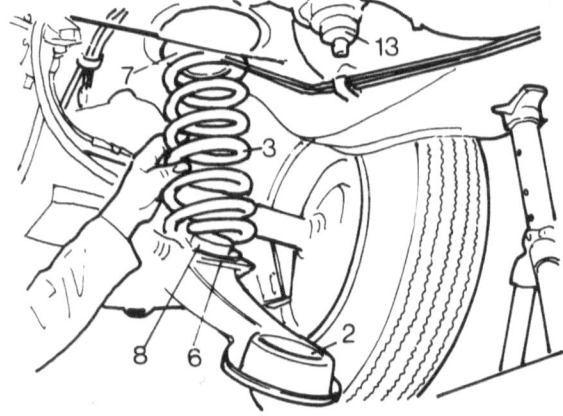

Fig. 11.45. Removing a rear road spring (enclosed type axleshafts)
(Sec. 18)

2	Suspension link	7	Spring flexible insulator
3	Spring	8	Spring flexible insulator
6	Spring seat	13	Suspension link mounting cone

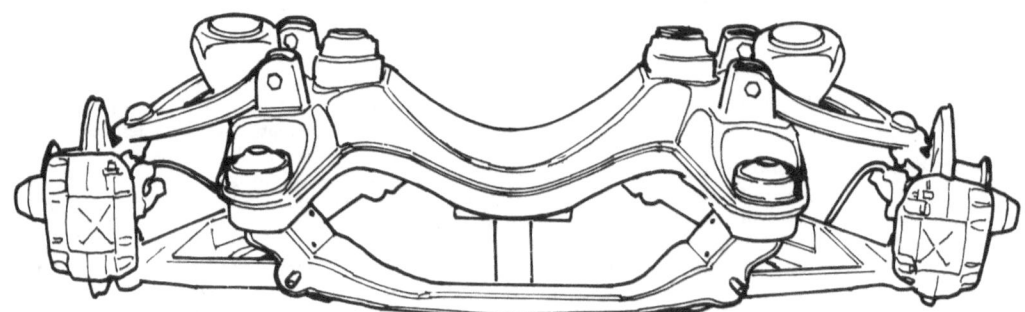

Fig. 11.43. Complete crossmember/axle assembly (swivel balljoint type stub axle) viewed from the front of the car (Sec. 17)

lower insulators if necessary and make sure that the lower end of the spring is correctly seated (Fig. 11.46) (photo).

---

19 Rear axle compensating spring (enclosed axleshafts) - removal and refitting

1   The operations are described in Chapter 8.

---

20 Rear suspension link arm (enclosed axleshafts) - removal, overhaul and refitting

1   Remove the rear coil spring as described in Section 18.

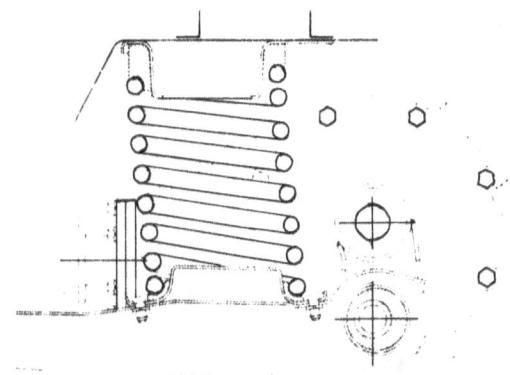

Fig. 11.46. Correctly installed rear road spring (enclosed type axleshaft) (Sec. 18)

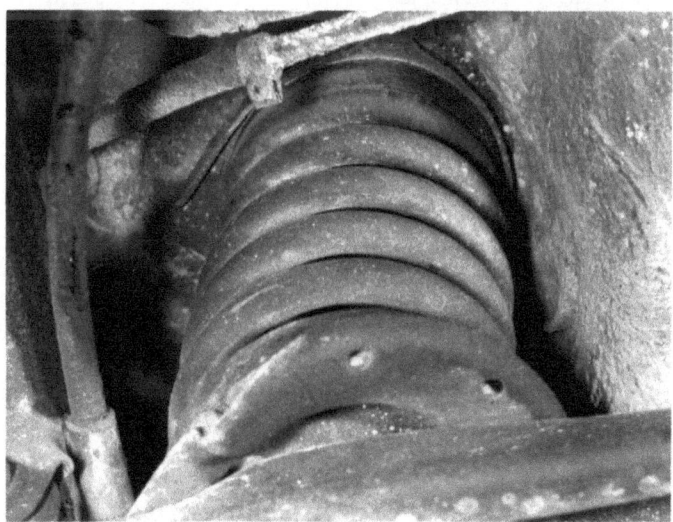

18.6 A rear coil spring in position

2   Disconnect the link arm from the rear axle by unscrewing the bolt from both sides of the flexible mounting. Retain the spacers (Fig. 11.47).

3   If the flexible bushes require renewal, compress the bush and prise out the circlip with a screwdriver. The flexible bushes are of the split type (Fig. 11.48).

4   If the flexible mounting between the link arm and the floor pan is compressed or has deteriorated, renew it (Fig. 11.49).

5   Refitting is a reversal of removal but tighten all nuts to the specified torque wrench setting.

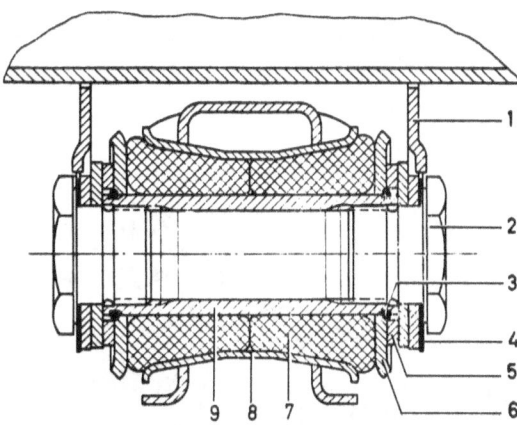

Fig. 11.47. Sectional view of rear suspension link to rear axle pivot (enclosed type axleshafts) (Sec. 20)

1 Axle bracket	6 Clamp plate
2 Pivot bolt	7 Flexible bush
3 Lockwasher	8 Suspension link
4 Lock	9 Threaded pivot
5 Spacer	

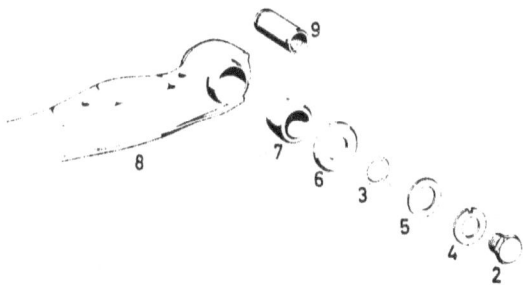

Fig. 11.48. Components (one side) of a rear suspension link to rear axle pivot (enclosed type axleshafts) (Sec. 20)

2 Pivot bolt	6 Clamp plate
3 Lockwasher	7 Flexible bush
4 Lockplate	8 Suspension link
5 Spacer	9 Threaded pivot

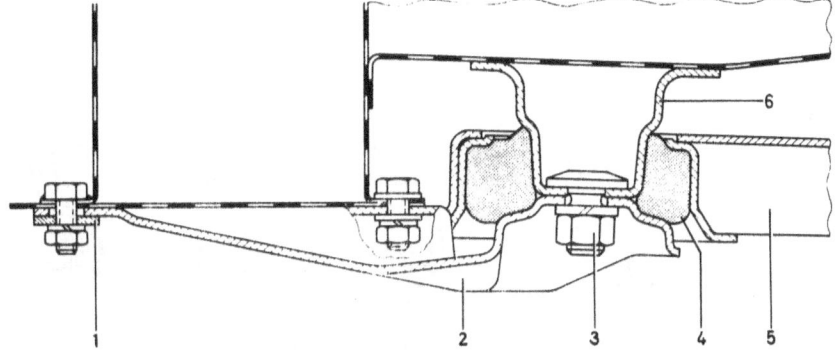

1   Washer
2   Plate
3   Bolt
4   Flexible mounting
5   Suspension link arm
6   Mounting cone

Fig. 11.49. Rear suspension link arm attachment to floor pan (Sec. 20)

21 Rear road spring (open axleshafts) - removal and refitting

1 Disconnect the rear shock absorber upper mounting first then the lower mounting and withdraw the shock absorber from the car.
2 Jack up the rear of the car and support it securely under the body-frame side members.
3 Fit compressors over five coils of the road spring which is to be removed and compress the spring.
4 Place a jack under the suspension control arm and raise the arm enough to be able to remove the roadwheel.
5 Lower the jack slowly and extract the road spring and rubber insulator (Fig. 11.50).
6 If the original spring is to be refitted there is no need to release the compressors. If it is to be renewed, unscrew the compressors very slowly.

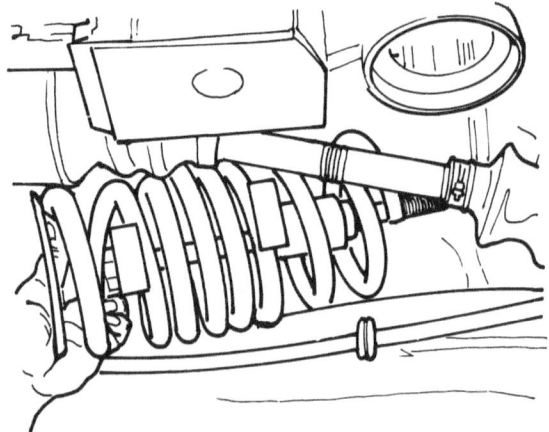

Fig. 11.50. Removing a rear road spring (open axleshafts) (Sec. 21)

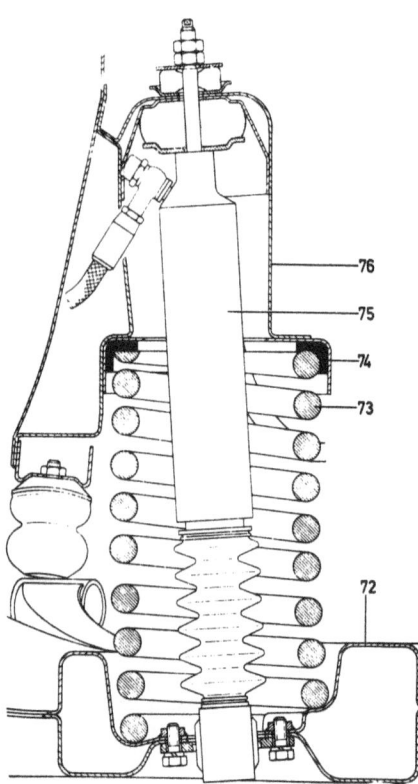

Fig. 11.51. Rear spring and shockabsorber installed (open axleshafts) (Sec. 21)

72 Suspension control arm   75 Shockabsorber
73 Rear spring   76 Mounting cone
74 Flexible mounting

7 Commence refitting by installing the spring (with compressors fitted) so that the ground end is uppermost.
8 Fit the rubber insulator and make sure that the bottom coil locates correctly in the suspension control arm.
9 Raise the suspension control arm into contact with the spring and then, holding the arm in this position on the jack, very carefully release the coil spring compressors, making sure that the spring is not displaced from its upper and lower seats.
10 Fit the roadwheel and lower the jack.
11 Fit the shock absorber by connecting the lower mounting first.
12 Check the rear suspension angles (see Section 41) (Fig. 11.51).

22 Rear suspension control arm (open axleshafts) - removal, overhaul and refitting

1 Remove the complete rear axle assembly as described in Chapter 8, Section 20.
2 Support the axle on blocks so that the suspension control arm can be lowered to its stop.
3 Unscrew and remove the nut from the end of the axleshaft.
4 Using a suitable extractor attached to the roadwheel bolt holes, press the axleshaft out of the hub flange.
5 Unscrew and remove the pivot bolts which hold the suspension control arm to the differential carrier sub-frame and remove the control arm.
6 If the flexible pivot bushes of the control arm are worn or damaged, they can be renewed by drawing the old ones out with a bolt, washers and tubular distance pieces. Draw the new bushes in using the same method (Fig. 11.52).
7 The renewal of the flexible mountings at the point of attachment of the differential carrier sub-frame to the body floor pan is described in Chapter 8, Section 18.
8 Refitting is a reversal of removal and tighten all nuts and bolts to the specified torque wrench settings.

23 Vehicle level - checking and adjustment on models with king pin type stub axles and enclosed rear axleshafts

1 After major overhaul or renewal of suspension components or after a very high mileage has been covered, when the road springs may have weakened, the following operations should be carried out.
2 Park the car on a flat surface with the front roadwheels in the straight ahead position, tyres correctly inflated and the car normally loaded (oil, water and fuel).
3 Measure the distance between the floor and the door sill (bottom edge of door) on both sides of the car (Fig. 11.53).
4 If the difference between the two sides does not exceed 0.39 in (10.0 mm) then the level adjustment can be regarded as correct and no further action need be taken.
5 If the difference between the two sides is greater however, then the control arm position on both sides of the front suspension must be checked and then the rear wheel camber measured.
6 To measure the control arm position, take the dimensions between

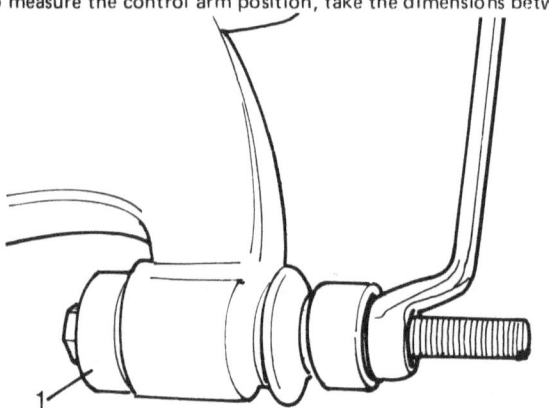

Fig. 11.52. Renewing a rear suspension control arm flexible bush (Sec. 22)

1 Distance piece

the centres of the suspension lower control arm inner and outer pivot bolts and the floor. Subtract one dimension from the other and record the figure remaining (a). This should normally be between 3.07 and 4.25 in (78 and 108 mm (Fig. 11.54).

7   Repeat the measuring operations on the other side of the front suspension.

8   To balance the two final figures, change the rubber spring insulator for one of different thickness. If one side has to be raised, change the insulator for a thicker one (0.08 in (2.0 mm) extra thickness will increase height (a) by 0.16 in (4.0 mm)). If one side has to be lowered, reduce the thickness of the insulator.

9   Rubber insulating rings are available from your dealer in a number of thicknesses.

10 Make sure that the rear axle is centralised as described in Chapter 8, Section 8.

11 The rear wheel camber should be checked. This is difficult without the correct instruments but as the camber should be $0^O \pm 30'$, a board with a plumb line hanging freely on it can be held against the rear wheel rims and a reasonably accurate reading obtained.

12 If the rear wheel camber must be altered, this can be done in one of the following ways:

   a) *Change the rear spring upper or lower rubber insulator. A difference of 0.24 in (6.0 mm) in thickness will alter the camber angle by 0° 30'.*
   b) *Fitting a washer 0.12 in (3.0 mm) thick on the left-hand balljoint of the rear axle hydropneumatic strut on cars so equipped, will alter the camber by 0° 30'.*
   c) *Moving coil spring lower seat to one of the other two alternative positions ('clicks') will alter the camber by 0° 10'.*

13 The front wheel steering angles should be checked as described in Section 41.

24 Vehicle level - checking and adjustment on models with swivel balljoint type stub axles and open rear axleshafts

1   The operations are similar to those described for the front suspension in the preceding Section, except that the outer point of measurement on the lower control arm is at the base of the swivel joint (Fig. 11.55).

2   The difference (a) between the two measurements should be (for cars with standard suspension) between 2.87 to 4.06 in (73 to 103 mm) and for cars with heavy duty suspension, 3.07 to 4.25 in (78 to 108 mm).

3   Any side to side difference can be altered by one of the following methods:

   a) *Changing the thickness of the spring rubber insulator by 0.20 in (5.0 mm) will alter the control arm dimension (a) by 0.35 in (9.0 mm).*
   b) *Change the spring for one of different colour code (blue instead of red and red instead of blue).*

4   It is important to note that on some models the spring rubber insulator is thicker on the road camber (kerb) side of the car according to whether the car has left-hand or right-hand drive steering. Bear this in mind before jumping to a conclusion that the insulator has been incorrectly fitted during production or by a previous owner.

5   Measuring the position of the rear suspension link arms on cars with open type axleshafts is very difficult, the measurements having to be taken from (i) the bottom edge of the outer axleshaft joint cover and (ii) the centre line of the suspension link pivot bearing. Subtract these dimensions when the difference (a) should be between 1.38 and 2.17 in (35 and 55 mm) for cars with standard suspension, and between 1.65 and 2.44 in (42 and 62 mm) for cars with heavy duty suspension (Fig. 11.56).

6   To alter the relative position of the suspension link arm, change the thickness of the rear spring insulator. An alteration in thickness of 0.20 in (5.0 mm) will change the position of the link arm by 0.28 in (7.0 mm).

25 Steering gear fluid level - checking and topping up

1   *To check the fluid level on manual type steering boxes, either turn*

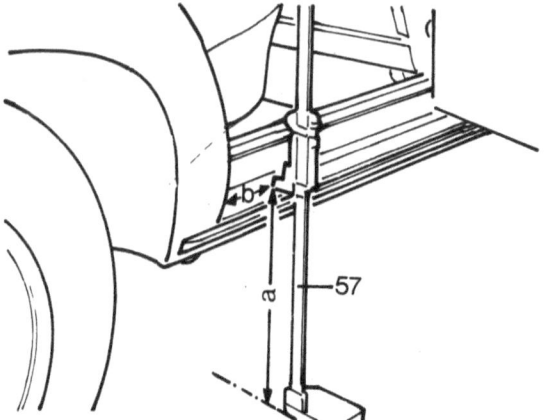

Fig. 11.53. Measuring vehicle height (Sec. 23)

57 Measuring gauge
(a) Height from floor
(b) Distance from front of wing 3.94 in (100 mm)

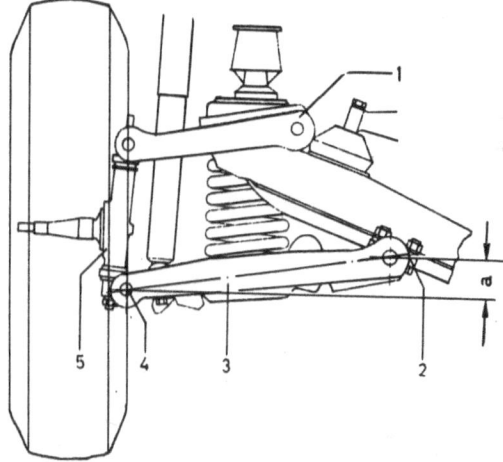

Fig. 11.54. Control arm measuring diagram (kingpin type stub axle carrier) (Sec. 23)

(a) Difference between control arm pivot bolts and floor
1   Upper control arm   4   Threaded pivot
2   Clamp bolt   5   Stub axle carrier
3   Lower control arm

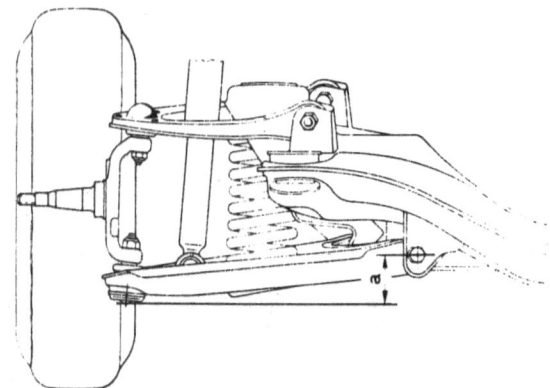

Fig. 11.55. Control arm measuring diagram (swivel balljoint type stub axle carrier)

(a) Difference between centre of inner pivot bolt and floor and lower face of bottom swivel balljoint and floor

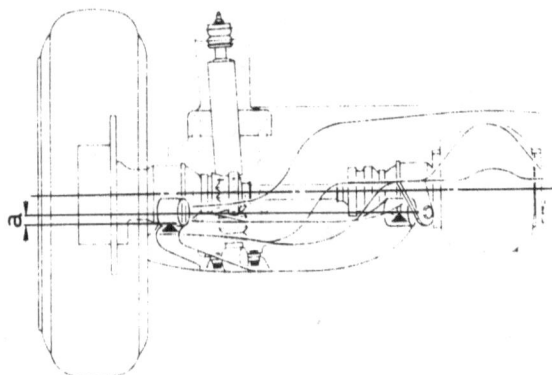

Fig. 11.56. Rear suspension link arm measuring diagram (open axleshafts) (Sec. 24)

(a) Difference between centre of pivot bearing and floor and lower face of outer axleshaft joint cover and floor

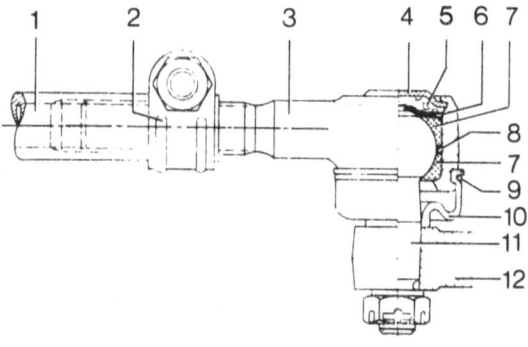

Fig. 11.58. A track rod end balljoint (Sec. 26)

1	Track rod	7	Anti-friction shell
2	Clamp	8	Ring
3	Track rod end (socket)	9	Boot retainer
4	Cover plate	10	Flexible boot
5	Internal spring	11	Ball pin
6	Thrust plate	12	Steering arm on stub axle carrier

the steering wheel to full left lock (LHD) or right lock (RHD).
2   Unscrew and remove the filler plug. The oil level should be approximately 1½ in (38.1 mm) below the filler neck.
3   *To check the fluid level on power steering fluid reservoirs,* have the engine idling and then remove the lid of the reservoir and observe whether the fluid is up to the 'FULL' mark. If it is not, top up with the specified fluid (Fig. 11.57).

26 Track rod end balljoints - renewal

1   If as a result of the checks described in Section 2, wear is observed in the track rod end balljoints, renew them in the following way.
2   Carefully count and record the number of threads which are exposed on the balljoint assembly at the outer ends of the track rods.
3   Unscrew and remove the nut from the balljoint taper pin and then, using a balljoint separator or a pair of forked wedges, separate the balljoint from the steering arm of the stub axle carrier (Fig. 11.59).
4   Release the clamp pinch bolt on the outer end of the track rod and unscrew and remove the track rod end balljoint assembly. Note that when facing in the normal direction of travel of the car the **left-hand** track rod end balljoint has a **left-hand** thread and the **right-hand** one has a **right-hand** thread.
5   Screw the new track rod end balljoint into its threaded track rod so that the same number of threads are exposed as was recorded for the original.
6   Make sure that all grease is cleaned from the balljoint taper pins and the eye of the steering arm and then connect the taper pin and tighten the nut. Insert a new split pin and bend over the ends.

Fig. 11.57. Power steering fluid reservoir. 'M' is full mark (Sec. 25)

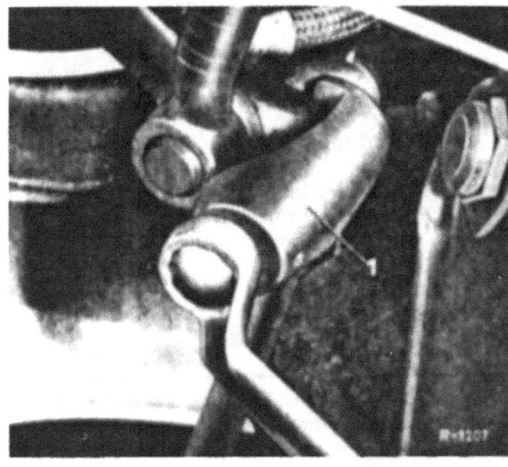

Fig. 11.59. Using a balljoint separator (1) to 'break' a joint (Sec. 26)

7   If one or both track rod end balljoints are renewed, always have the front wheel alignment (tracking) checked at the earliest opportunity.

27 Track rod and drag link - removal and refitting

1   Withdraw the split pins from the castellated nuts on the balljoint taper pins. Unscrew and remove the nuts.
2   Using a suitable separator or forked wedges, disconnect the balljoints from the steering arms of the stub axle carriers on the front hubs.
3   Again using a heavy duty puller, separate the balljoint from the bottom of the steering drop arm.
4   Now separate the balljoint from the steering idler arm. In order to provide room to engage the extractor, the strut (7) will have to be removed first (Fig. 11.60).
5   To remove the drag link, extract the split pins and then unscrew and remove the castellated nuts from the balljoints located one each end of the drag link.
6   Disconnect the steering linkage damper from its bodyframe anchorage (photo).
7   Disconnect the drag link balljoints with a balljoint separator and then remove the drag link complete with damper which can be withdrawn later if required.
8   Refitting is a reversal of removal but check the front wheel alignment at the earliest opportunity.

28 Steering drop arm - removal and refitting

1   The steering drop arm (Pitman arm) requires the use of a heavy duty puller to remove it and unless one is available, do not attempt makeshift methods as damage to the steering gear may result.
2   Using a balljoint separator, disconnect the track rod at the drag link from the steering drop arm (Fig. 11.61).
3   Extract the split pin from the castellated nut which holds the

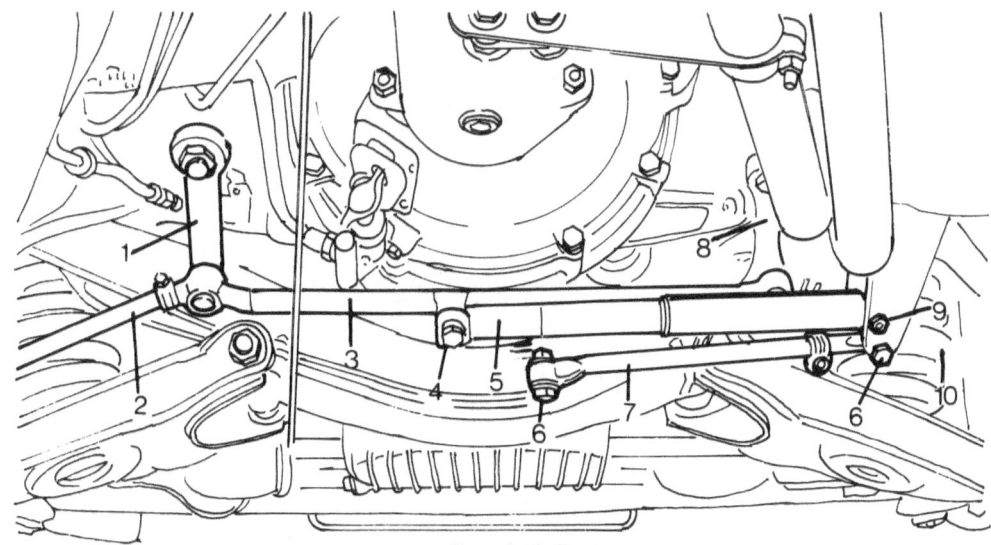

Fig. 11.60. Typical steering layout (Sec. 27)

1 Steering drop arm
2 Left-hand track rod
3 Drag link
4 Bolt
5 Steering damper
6 Anchor bolt
7 Lateral support strut
8 Steering idler arm
9 Bolt
10 Right-hand track rod

27.6 Steering damper

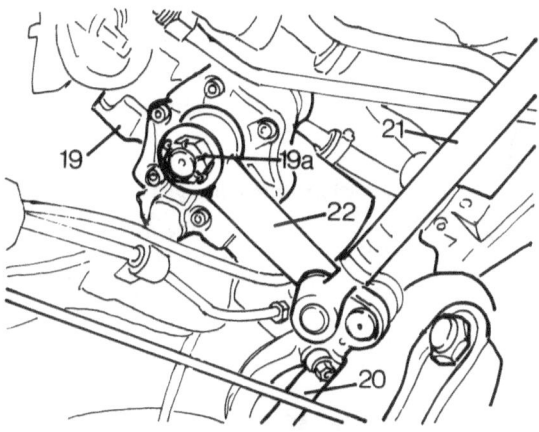

Fig. 11.61. Steering drop arm connections (Sec. 28)

19 Steering gear
19a Castellated nut
20 Track rod
21 Drag link
22 Drop arm

drop arm to the shaft of the steering gear and then unscrew and remove the nut.

4   Using the heavy duty puller, remove the drop arm from the shaft (Fig. 11.62).

5   Before refitting the drop arm, have the front roadwheels and the steering wheel centralised and fit the drop arm to the shaft making sure that the mating marks are in alignment (Fig. 11.63).

29 Steering idler - removal, overhaul and refitting

1   The method of attaching the steering idler arm to the idler assembly differs between the models. On some cars it is attached at the top of the assembly and on others at the bottom (Figs. 11.64 and 11.65) (photo).

2   Using a suitable balljoint separator, disconnect the track rod and the drag link balljoints from the idler arm.

3   Remove the protective shield (low mounted idler arm).

4   If the idler arm assembly is to be dismantled, unscrew and remove the self-locking nut and then withdraw the idler shaft and remove the various components according to type (Figs. 11.66 and 11.67).

5   Prise out and discard the rubber seals. The upper and lower flexible bushes should be knocked out carefully using a wooden or plastic rod.

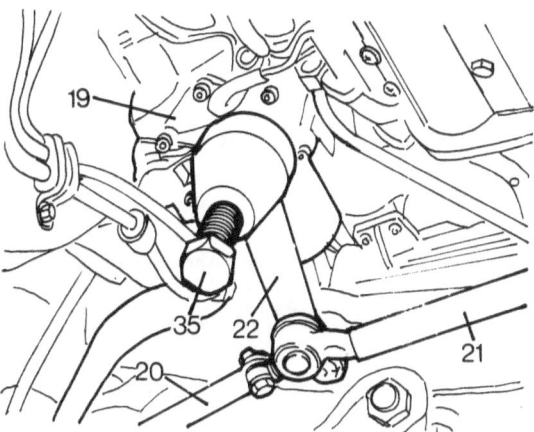

Fig. 11.62. Using a puller to remove the steering drop arm (Sec. 28)

19 Steering gearbox
20 Track rod
21 Drag link
22 Drop arm
35 Puller

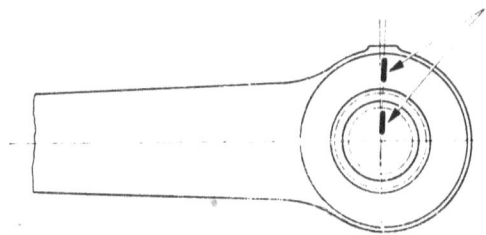

Fig. 11.63. Steering drop arm and sector shaft alignment marks
(Sec. 28)

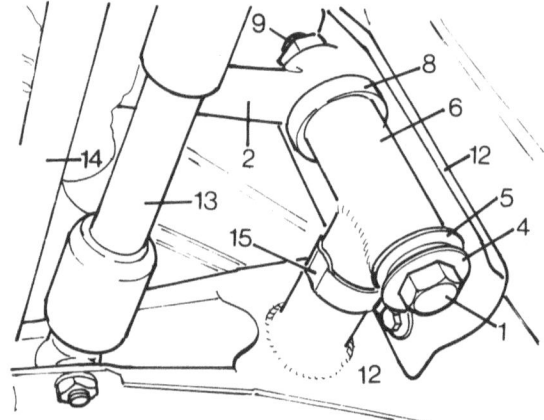

29.1 View of idler arm and lower control arm

Fig. 11.64. Steering idler with top mounted arm (Sec. 29)

1 Bolt	9 Self-locking nut
2 Idler arm	12 Shield
4 Seal	13 Steering damper
5 Flexible bush	14 Lateral support strut
6 Body	15 Clip
8 Dust excluder	

Fig. 11.65. Steering idler with bottom mounted arm (Sec. 29)

1 Bolt	6 Body
2 Idler arm	12 Shield
4 Seal	25 Steering damper

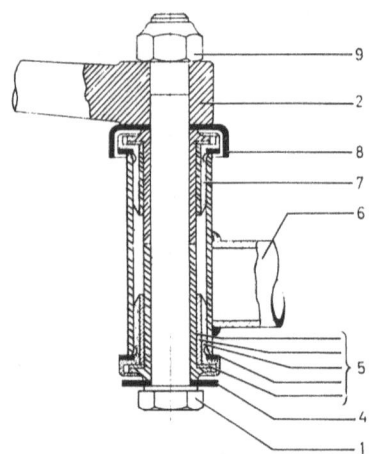

Fig. 11.66. Sectional view of steering idler with top mounted arm
(Sec. 29)

1 Bolt	6 Body
2 Idler arm	7 Upper flexible bush
4 Seal	8 Dust excluder
5 Flexible bush assembly	9 Nut

6   Apply rubber grease when reassembling and make sure that on
bottom-mounted idler arms, the cast part number is visible from below
(Fig. 11.68).
7   The remainder of the reassembly and refitting operations are
reversals of dismantling and removal. Tighten all nuts to the specified
torque wrench settings.

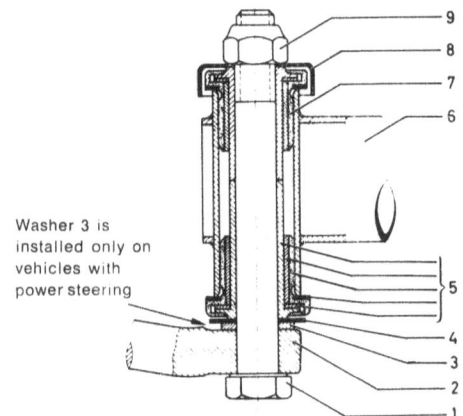

Washer 3 is
installed only on
vehicles with
power steering

Fig. 11.67. Sectional view of steering idler with bottom mounted arm
(Sec. 29)

1 Bolt	5 Lower flexible bush assembly
2 Idler arm	6 Body
3 Steel washer (power steering only)	7 Upper flexible bush
4 Seal	8 Dust excluder
	9 Self-locking nut

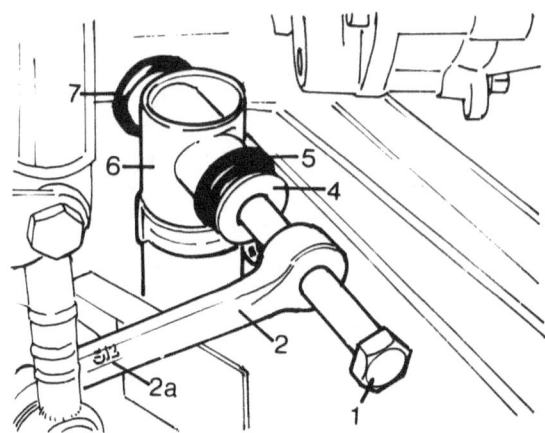

Fig. 11.68. Correctly installed bottom mounted type idler arm (Sec. 29)

1	Bolt	5	Lower flexible bush
2	Idler arm	6	Body
2a	Cast number	7	Upper flexible bush
4	Seal		

30 Steering lock/ignition switch - removal and refitting

1 The device is a three part assembly; the ignition and lock cylinder can be removed independently.
2 Remove the instruments as described in Chapter 10.
3 Disconnect the connector plug from the ignition switch.
4 Using a small screwdriver, remove the securing screws from the ignition switch and remove it (Figs. 11.69 and 11.70).
5 The method of removal of the lock cylinder depends upon the type of lock fitted. *On early models,* turn the ignition key to '1' and withdraw it. Lift the lock cover sleeve with a small screwdriver so that a hooked piece of wire can be used to pull the sleeve right out. Hold the switch bezel in position while doing this. Use the hooked wire between the lock cylinder and the bezel and, after depressing the lock-pin, pull the lock cylinder from the assembly (Fig. 11.71).
6 *On later models,* turn the key to '1'. It cannot be withdrawn in this position. Then, using a hooked piece of wire, pull the cover sleeve up to the edge of the key finger, hold, turn the key to 'O' and then withdraw the key complete with cover sleeve. Now insert the key by itself and turn to position '1', depress the lockpin and withdraw the lock cylinder.
7 To refit the earlier type lock cylinder, make sure that it is set to position '1' and then refit it so that the lockpin engages positively. Fit the cover sleeve.
8 To refit the later type lock cylinder, make sure that it is set to position '1' and refit it so that the lockpin engages positively. Insert the key and turn to 'O', then remove the key. Locate the cover sleeve, again insert the key, turn and push the cover sleeve into position while the key is held in position '1'.
9 To remove the steering column lock, disconnect the lead from the battery negative terminal.
10 Remove the instruments (Chapter 10).
11 Disconnect the connector plug from the ignition switch.
12 On early models, withdraw the ignition key while it is in position '1'. On later models, remove the key as described in paragraph 6 complete with the cover sleeve.
13 Remove the pinch bolt on the fastening clip (5) of the steering lock (Fig. 11.72).
14 On earlier models on which the ignition key was removable in position '1' now withdraw the cover sleeve of the lock.
15 *On North American cars,* disconnect the connector plug from the warning buzzer.
16 Using a rod 0.20 in (5.0 mm) diameter, depress the locking pin (7), rotate the lock and remove from its holder (8). It should be noted that the locking pin can only be depressed while the key slot is in the position '1'.

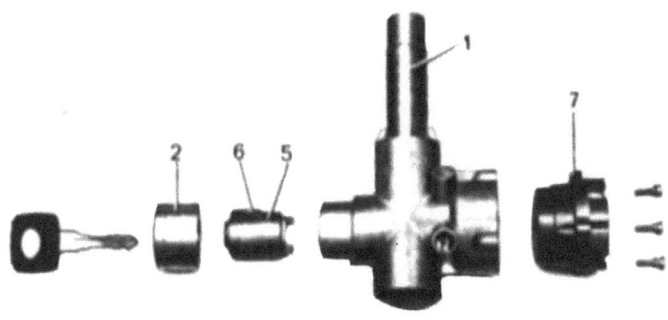

Fig. 11.69. Components of early type steering column lock (Sec. 30)

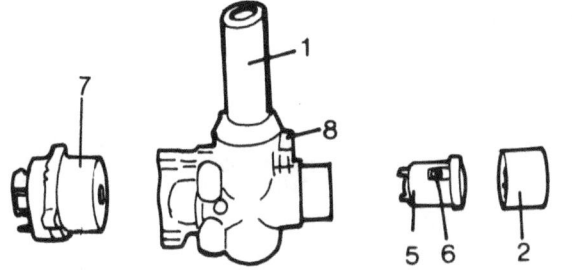

Fig. 11.70. Components of later type steering column lock (Sec. 30)

1	Steering lock	7	Ignition switch
2	Cover	8	Contact switch
5	Lock cylinder		(N. America only)
6	Locking pin		

1 Steering lock
2 Cover
5 Lock cylinder
6 Locking pin
7 Ignition switch

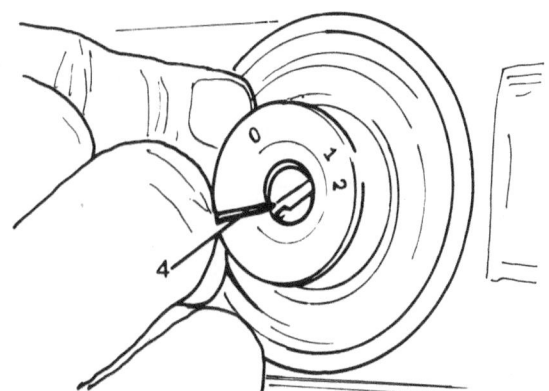

Fig. 11.71. Using a piece of wire (4) to extract ignition lock cover sleeve (Sec. 30)

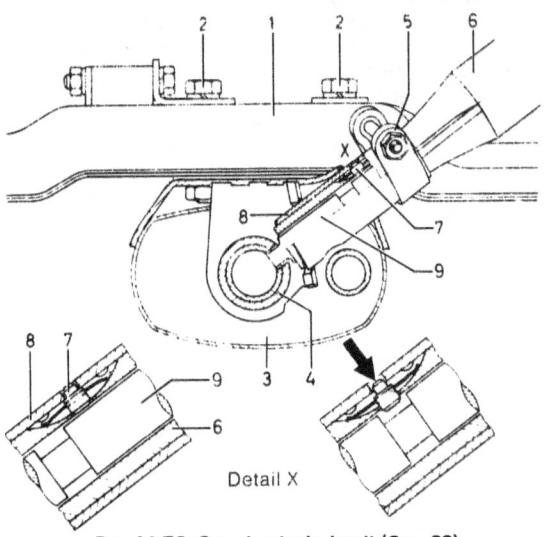

Fig. 11.72. Steering lock detail (Sec. 30)

1	Fascia crossmember	6	Steering lock
2	Bolt	7	Locking pin
3	Steering column	8	Steering lock socket
4	Steering shaft	9	Locking bolt
5	Clamp		

31 Steering wheel - removal and refitting

1   Carefully prise out the motif from the centre of the steering wheel. This will come away complete with the centre crash pad.

2   The steering wheel can be removed on its own by unscrewing the five nuts now exposed and disconnecting the horn wires as the wheel is withdraw, or by removal of the complete steering wheel and collapsible boss (Fig. 11.73).

3   To remove the latter, unscrew the nut from the end of the steering shaft.

4   The steering wheel, boss and horn ring and switch may be dismantled as necessary.

5   When refitting the steering wheel, set the roadwheels in the straight ahead position. This will ensure that the alignment mark on the end of

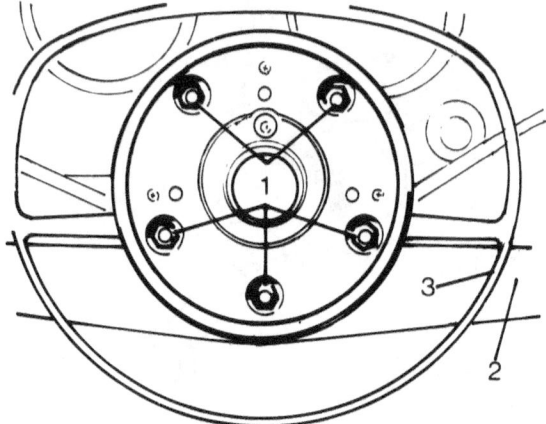

Fig. 11.73. Steering wheel to collapsible boss securing nuts (Sec. 31)

1   Nuts   2   Steering wheel   3   Horn ring

the steering shaft is vertical and at the top. Fit the steering wheel to the shaft so that the spokes are exactly horizontal.

6   The spring washer and nut should be taped to the socket wrench to facilitate their refitment. Tighten to the specified torque wrench setting.

7   If the steering wheel spokes take up the wrong attitude on the road, this may be due to one of the following factors:

a)   Incorrect front wheel alignment (tracking).
b)   One track rod longer than the other.
c)   Steering drop arm incorrectly fitted to steering shaft.

32 Steering shaft - removal and refitting

1   Unscrew and remove the upper pinch bolt from the flexible coupling just above the steering box.

2   Remove the steering wheel complete with boss as described in the preceding Section.

3   Remove the flexible cover from the combination switch from the upper steering column.

4   Unscrew the switch from the bearing body and withdraw it slightly.

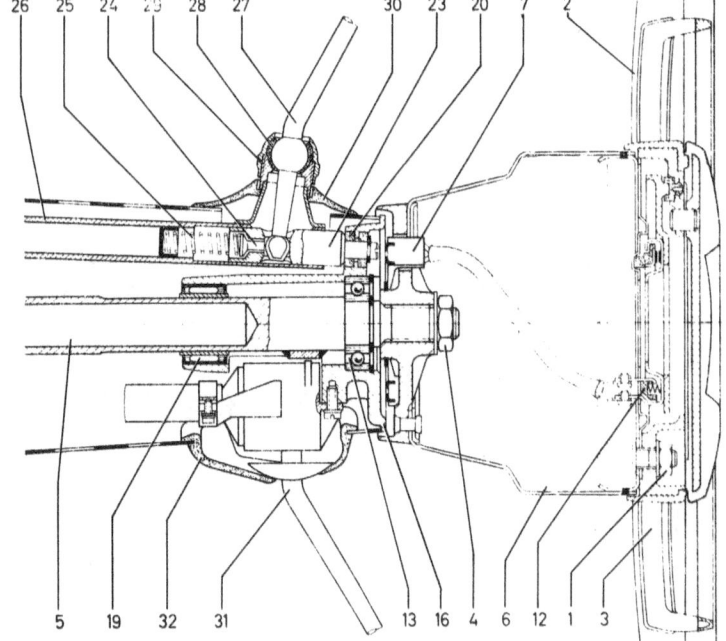

1   Wheel to boss retaining nut
2   Steering wheel
3   Horn ring
4   Boss retaining nut to shaft
5   Steering shaft
6   Collapsible boss
7   Slip ring and cable
12 Horn contact ring
13 Ball bearing
16 Bearing body
19 Needle bearing
20 Anti-friction ring
23 Guide pin
24 Pin
25 Spring
26 Shift tube (column gearshift)
27 Shift lever
28 Socket
29 Retainer cup
30 Flexible cover
31 Combination switch
32 Flexible cover

Fig. 11.74. Sectional view of upper end of steering column (Sec. 31)

5 Disconnect both the leads from the carbon brush on the combination switch (Fig. 11.75).
6 If the car is fitted with a steering column shift; remove the shift lever, turn the guide pin through 180° and remove the locking ring from the end of the pin (Fig. 11.76).
7 Unscrew and remove the socket headed screws (17) from the steering column and pull the steering shaft complete with bearing body (16) upwards.
8 Extract the circlip (15) which retains the radial ball bearing and use a plastic faced mallet to knock the shaft out of the bearing in a downward direction.
9 Renew any worn or damaged components. All steering shafts are of collapsible type and the shaft should be 'telescoped' to provide an overall length of 28.8 in (731.0 mm) for manual steering or 25.9 in (659.0 mm) for power steering on all cars except 280SL/8 on which it should be 25.9 in (659.0 mm) and 24.1 in (612.0 mm) respectively.
10 Use a plastic faced mallet to adjust the shaft.
11 Commence refitting by inserting the shaft/bearing into the column tube.
12 Check that the roadwheels are in the straight ahead attitude and that the resetting cam for the combination switch is in the centre of the recess in the column tube and that the notch on the steering shaft points upwards.
13 Engage the bottom end of the shaft in the splines of the flexible coupling without altering the effective length of the shaft through movement of its telescopic section. To avoid this, prise open the clamp on the flexible coupling using a screwdriver so that the shaft will enter easily.
14 On cars with a steering column shift, make sure that the control rod engages correctly as the shaft is fitted.
15 Screw in and tighten the socket headed column screws.
16 Insert the guide pin lock, turn the guide pin through 180° and fit the gearshift lever.
17 Using a suitable rod or drift, insert it into the appropriate hole (15a or 15b) in the steering column upper jacket. The rod should pass easily into the hole, otherwise, the effective length of the steering shaft will have to be adjusted (Fig. 11.77).
18 Fit the flexible coupling pinch bolt and tighten.
19 Fit the steering wheel.
20 Check the operation of the steering column lock.
21 Connect the leads to the brushes of the combination switch and fit the flexible cover to the steering column.

33 Steering column (complete) - removal and refitting

1 Set the roadwheels in the straight ahead attitude and then unscrew and remove the pinch bolt from the lower end of the flexible coupling at the bottom of the steering shaft.
2 On cars which have a steering column shift, disconnect the selector and shift rod on the bearing body at the top of the column and then remove the bearing body as described in the preceding Section.
3 Release the connector plug from the reversing light switch so that the cover plate at the base of the steering column can then be unbolted.
4 Remove the instrument cluster as described in Chapter 10.
5 Remove the steering column lock as described in Section 30.
6 On cars with steering column gearshift, remove the shift tube (Fig. 11.78).
7 Unscrew and remove the two bolts which attach the steering column to the crossmember under the fascia.
8 Withdraw the complete steering column assembly into the car interior.
9 The column can now be separated into component parts by withdrawing the shaft as described in Section 32.
10 Reassembly and refitting are reversals of dismantling and removal.

34 Steering column flexible coupling - removal and refitting

1 Unscrew and remove the upper of the two pinch bolts on the coupling.
2 Unbolt the steering box from the bodyframe side member and lower it slightly.
3 Unscrew and remove the coupling lower pinch bolt and pull the coupling from the splines of the steering worm.

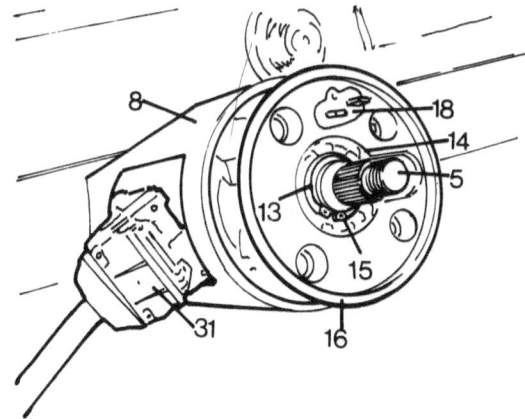

Fig. 11.75. Upper steering column details (Sec. 32)

5	Steering shaft	15	Circlip
8	Column	16	Bearing body
13	Bearing	18	Carbon brush
14	Circlip	31	Switch

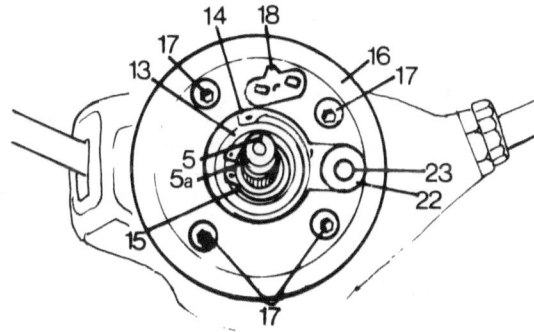

Fig. 11.76. Steering column shift connections (Sec. 32)

5	Steering shaft	16	Bearing body
5a	Alignment mark	17	Socket headed bolt
13	Ball bearing	18	Carbon brush
14	Circlip	22	Lockplate
15	Circlip	23	Guide pin

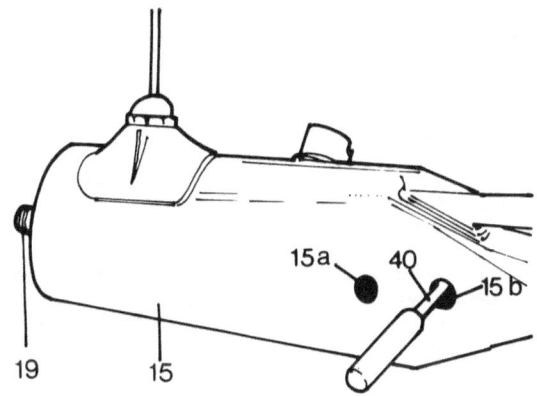

Fig. 11.77. Checking steering shaft length (Sec. 32)

15	Steering column	19	Steering shaft
15a	Inspection hole (power steering)	40	Guide tool
15b	Inspection hole (manual steering)		

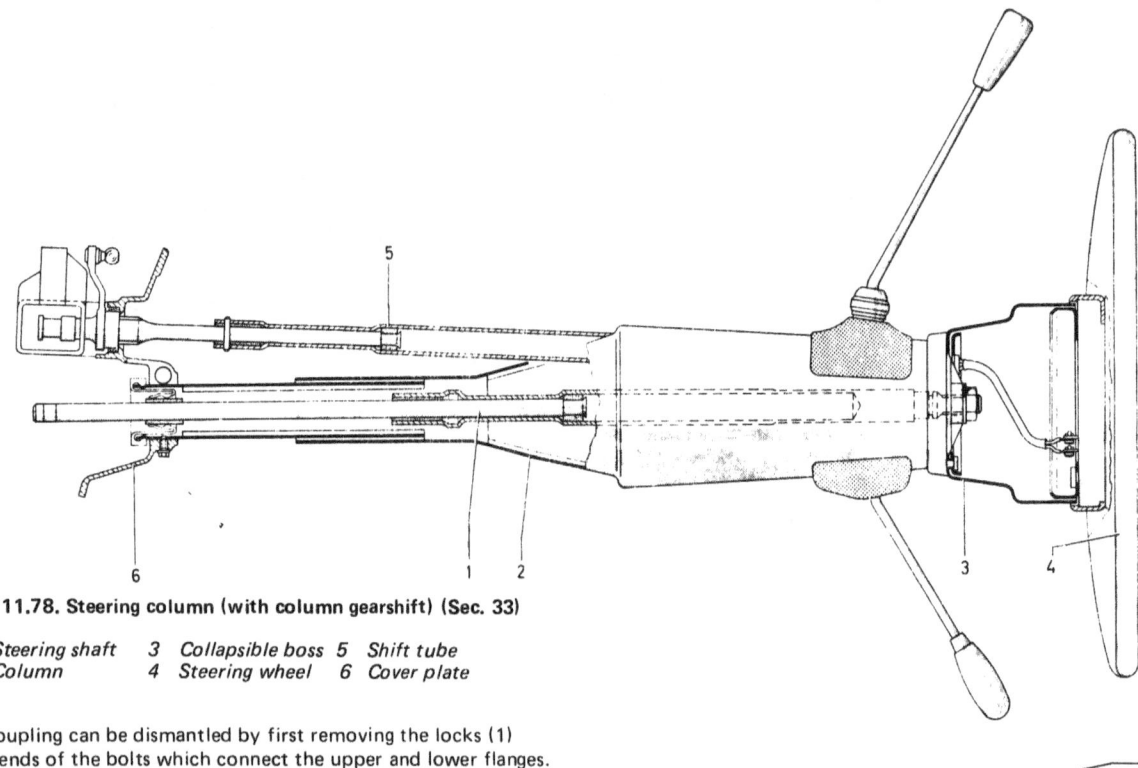

Fig. 11.78. Steering column (with column gearshift) (Sec. 33)

1 Steering shaft   3 Collapsible boss 5 Shift tube
2 Column   4 Steering wheel   6 Cover plate

4   The coupling can be dismantled by first removing the locks (1)
from the ends of the bolts which connect the upper and lower flanges.
Extract the steel and plastic washers and the bushes (Fig. 11.79).
5   Reassembly is a reversal of dismantling but compress the flanges
towards each other to contract the flexible bushes and permit fitting
of the locking clips to the ends of the flange connecting bolts.
6   Refit the coupling and the steering box and then tighten the
coupling pinch bolts.

35 Steering gear (manual) - removal

1   Set the roadwheels in the straight ahead position.
2   Unscrew and remove the lower pinch bolt from the flexible
coupling at the base of the steering column.
3   Disconnect the track rod and the drag link from the steering drop
arm (see Section 27).
4   Unscrew and remove the bolts which secure the steering gear to the
bodyframe side members.
5   Withdraw the steering box downwards after having slipped the
coupling off the splines of the steering shaft.

36 Steering gear (manual) - overhaul and adjustment

1   Even if the steering gear is to be adjusted and not overhauled, the
gear must first be removed from the car as just described. If adjustment
only is required, refer directly to paragraphs 26 and 33.
2   It is recommended that when general wear takes place in the
steering box, a new or factory reconditioned unit is obtained
rather than overhaul the original. However, if it is preferred to dismantle, proceed as follows but first check the availability of spares.
3   Clean away external dirt and then remove the coupling and the
drop arm.
4   Secure the steering box in the jaws of a vice, preferably bolting it
first to a support plate to avoid damage to the box itself.
5   Unscrew and remove the adjuster screw locknut (Fig. 11.80).
6   Unbolt and remove the top cover.
7   Wind the adjusting screw out of the cover as the latter is lifted and
remove the cover and its gasket.
8   Pull the steering shaft out of the steering box.
9   Extract the circlip (1) unscrew the ring nut (2) and then the
adjusting ring (5) and remove them. A pin wrench will be needed for
this job.
10 Remove the steering worm/nut/ball cage assembly.

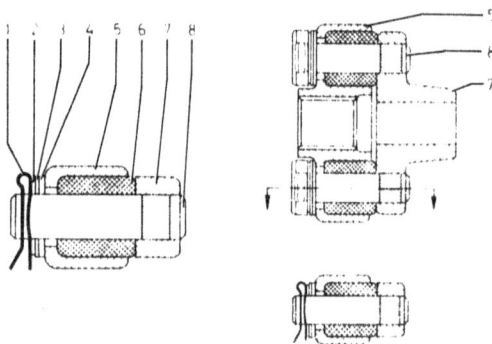

Fig. 11.79. Steering column flexible coupling (Sec. 34)

1 Locking clip   5 Lower flange
2 Plain washer   6 Flexible bush
3 Spring washer   7 Upper flange
4 Plastic washer   8 Bolt

11 Using a small puller, extract the outer bearing track from the
gearbox.
12 Remove the oil seal.
13 Extract the bearing inner races from the worm shaft. If the bearings
are to used again, tape the bearing together with its outer track; do
not mix them up.
14 Check for wear or damage in all the components. The worm/nut/
ball assembly can only be renewed as a complete unit.
15 Clean out the interior of the steering box and prepare for reassembly.
16 Commence reassembly by pressing the outer track of the lower
bearing (10) into the steering box.
17 Press the outer track of the upper bearing into the adjusting ring.
18 Heat the inner races of the bearings to 176°F (80°C) in hot oil and
fit them to the worm.
19 Locate the ball cage in the lower bearing outer track.
20 Fit the worm and nut.
21 Fit the new oil seal to the adjusting ring.
22 Fit the upper ball bearing cage to the worm.
23 Using a piece of thin plastic tubing fitted to the worm shaft as a
protection for the oil seal lips, push the adjusting ring into position and
then screw it in several turns.
24 Remove the temporary protection sleeve and tighten the adjusting
ring until the worm can just be turned, but stiffly.

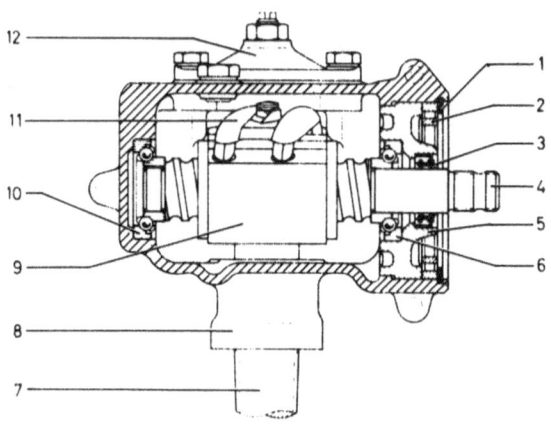
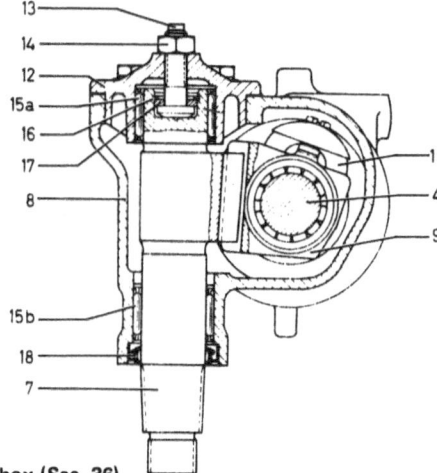

Fig. 11.80. Views of the steering box (Sec. 36)

1 Circlip	6 Ballrace	11 Ball guide	15b Lower needle bearing
2 Ring nut	7 Sector shaft	12 Top cover	16 Circlip
3 Seal	8 Gearcase	13 Adjuster screw	17 Spacer
4 Worm	9 Nut	14 Locknut	18 Seal
5 Adjusting ring	10 Ball race	15a Upper needle bearing	

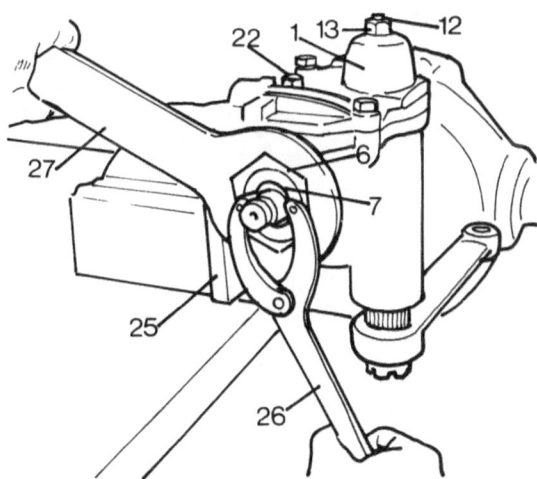

Fig. 11.81. Adjusting steering worm (Sec. 36)

1 Cover	22 Filler plug
6 Nut	25 Temporary support plate
7 Adjuster ring	26 Pin wrench
12 Adjuster screw	27 Ring nut spanner
13 Locknut	

25 Coat the threads of the ring nut with a thread locking compound and·screw the ring into the gearbox.
26 At this stage, adjust the steering worm. To do this, tighten the adjusting ring with the pin wrench until all endfloat just disappears and yet the worm turns easily. Without moving the position of the adjusting ring, fully tighten the ring nut (Fig. 11.81).
27 Fit the adjuster screw, spacer and locking ring into the recess in the end of the sector shaft. Any play between the adjuster screw head at the recess in the shaft should be eliminated by changing the spacer washer for a thicker one.
28 Fit the sector shaft into the steering box so that the centre tooth of the shaft engages in the centre gap of the worm nut.
29 Fit a new gasket to the flange of the steering box; fit the top cover by winding the adjuster screw through the cover. Fit and tighten the cover bolts.
30 Screw the locknut onto the adjuster screw but do not tighten it.
31 Slide a protective sleeve (or tape) over the splines on the exposed splines of the sector shaft and then fit the shaft oil seal using a piece of tubing as a drift.

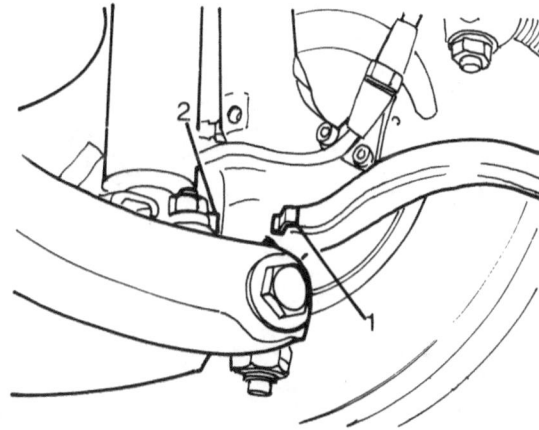

Fig. 11.82. Steering lock stops (Sec. 37)

1 Stop on steering arm   2 Stop on stub axle carrier

32 Fill the steering box with the correct quantity of the specified oil.
33 Now adjust the sector shaft endfloat. To do this, turn the steering to the centre position. This position can be determined by unscrewing the filler plug and observing that the centre point of the worm nut is directly under the plug hole. A dimple is made in the worm nut to indicate this.
34 Wind a cord round the splines of the sector shaft and attach it to a spring balance. Now check the force required to move the sector shaft off its central position. This should be between 12 and 16 lbs (5 and 7 kg) as shown on the spring balance. Turn the adjuster screw until the adjustment is correct and then tighten the locknut without altering the adjustment.
35 Refit the filler plug.

37 Steering gear (manual) - refitting

1   Set the steering gear to its centre position. To do this, remove the filler plug and observe the centre point of the worm nut. A dimple is made in the nut to indicate this.
2   Check that the roadwheels are in the straight ahead position and that the steering wheel is set with its spokes horizontal.
3   Offer the steering box into position and connect the coupling. Prise open the coupling clamps slightly in order to enable the splined steering and worm shaft to engage without force. If the steering shaft

is pressed in an upward direction then the collapsible section of the shaft may compress and have to be reset. If a pin is inserted into the appropriate hole in the steering column (see Fig. 11.77), this will prevent the shaft compressing.

4 Bolt the steering box to the bodyframe, tightening the bolts to the specified torque wrench setting.

5 Reconnect the track rod and the drag link to the drop arm.

6 Turn the steering to full left and then full right lock and check that the steering arms are in contact with the stops on the stub axle carrier in the full lock positions. Any discrepancy here may be due to unequal track rod lengths and incorrect front wheel alignment (tracking) (Fig. 11.82).

7 Check the steering box oil level and remove the guide pin (if used) from the steering column hole.

38 Power steering hydraulic pump - removal and refitting

1 Unscrew the wing nut from the top of the fluid reservoir on the pump, extract the spring and steady plate (photo).

2 Syphon out or draw off the fluid from the reservoir and extract the filter element (photo).

3 Disconnect the reservoir to pump hoses. Plug the openings.

4 Drain the cooling system (Chapter 2).

5 Remove the radiator.

6 Release the pump mounting bolts and then screw the nut on the adjuster link inwards so that the drivebelt becomes slack enough to be removed (photo).

7 Disconnect the hoses (at their unions on the pump) which run to the steering gearbox.

8 Unbolt and remove the pump completely from its mounting (Figs. 11.83 and 11.84).

9 It is not recommended that the pump is overhauled but if faulty, it should be renewed complete with a new or factory reconditioned unit.

10 The original pulley can be retained for fitting to the new pump and this can be removed with a puller after having unscrewed the securing nut.

11 Refitting is a reversal of removal. Tighten all bolts, nuts and unions to the specified torque wrench settings, tension the drivebelt to give a deflection of ½ in (12.7 mm) at the centre of the longest run of the belt.

12 Fill the system and bleed it as described in Section 40.

39 Power steering gear - removal and refitting

1 Syphon or draw off the fluid from the reservoir of the power steering hydraulic pump.

2 Unscrew the two fluid hoses from the steering box. Catch any oil which may be spilled and then plug all the openings.

3 Unscrew and remove the upper pinch bolt from the steering shaft flexible coupling.

4 The remaining operations are then as described for the manual steering gear in Section 35.

5 Refitting is a reversal of removal but bleed the system as described in the following Section.

40 Power steering system - bleeding

1 This operation is normally only required when some part of the

38.1 Power steering fluid reservoir

38.2 Power steering fluid reservoir filter

38.6 Power steering pump pulley and adjuster screw for drivebelt tension

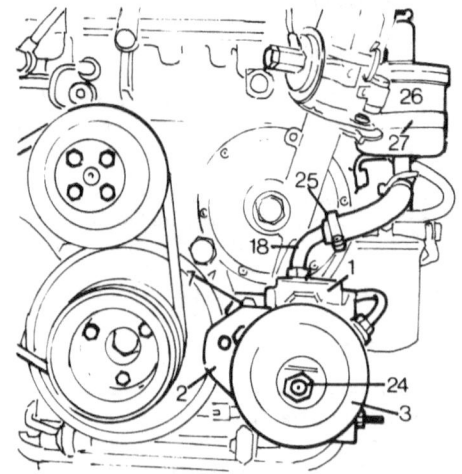

Fig. 11.83. Power steering pump (Sec. 38)

1	High pressure oil pump	24	Hex. nut
2	Carrier	25	Hose clip
3	Pulley	26	Supply tank
7	Hex. socket bolt	27	Fastening clip
18	Elbow		

Fig. 11.84. Power steering pump fixtures (Sec. 38)

1	High pressure oil pump	10	Pulley
5	Elbow	12	Carrier
7	Connecting hose	15	Clamping bolt
9	V-belt	16	Hex. nut

system has been disconnected or the fluid level in the reservoir has fallen so low that air has been drawn into the hydraulic circuit.

2   Remove the cover from the reservoir and fill to the correct level with the specified fluid.

3   Obtain a long piece of tubing which will fit tightly onto the bleed nipple on the steering box and permit the other end to be placed in the reservoir (Fig. 11.85) (photo).

4   Start the engine and run it at idling speed.

5   Open the bleed screw two full turns and keep it open until air bubbles cease to emerge from the end of the tube in the reservoir. Close the bleed nipple.

6   With the engine still idling, turn the steering to full left and right lock several times. It is best to raise the front of the car on a jack before doing this.

7   Centralise the steering and again open the bleed nipple and wait for any further air bubbles to escape.

8   Tighten the bleed nipple, remove tube and top up fluid reservoir.

9   Switch off the engine and lower the jack.

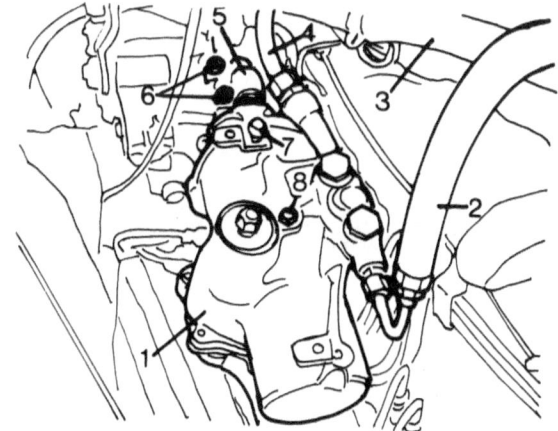

Fig. 11.85. Power steering gearbox (Sec. 40)

1	Gearbox	5	Steering flexible coupling
2	Hose	6	Bolt
3	Return hose	7	Bleed nipple
4	Elbow	8	Plug

41 Steering angles and front wheel alignment

1   Accurate front wheel alignment is essential for good steering and slow tyre wear. Before considering the steering angle, check that the tyres are correctly inflated, that the front wheels are not buckled, the hub bearings are not worn or incorrectly adjusted and that the steering linkage is in good order, without slackness or wear at the joints.

2   Wheel alignment consists of four factors:

Camber, is the angle at which the front wheels are set from the vertical when viewed from the front of the car. Positive camber is the amount (in degrees) that the wheels are tilted outwards at the top from the vertical.

Castor. is the angle between the steering axis and a vertical line when viewed from each side of the car. Positive castor is when the steering axis is inclined rearward.

Steering axis inclination is the angle, when viewed from the front of the car, between the vertical and an imaginary line drawn between the upper and lower suspension arm swivels (Fig. 11.86).

Front wheel tracking. This normally gives the front roadwheels a toe-in or toe-out.

3   Camber and castor angles can only be set if really accurate equipment is available and although this is beyond the scope of the home mechanic, it is useful to know how to adjust them.

4   *On cars with king pin type stub axle carriers,* the castor angle is altered by turning the cam bolts (30) which are located at the leaf springs on either side of the stabiliser bar. The engine mounting bolts and the transverse strut bolt should always be released before altering the cam bolts. After adjusting the two cam bolts uniformly any minor discrepancy can be equalised by turning the notched adjuster plate on the outer pivot of the upper control arm after first having slackened the pivot cam bolt (Fig. 11.87).

5   The camber angle is adjusted by slackening the nut on the cam bolt (1) and turning the bolt. Insufficient range of camber adjustment on these cars can be increased by removing or adding washers between the pivot (6) for the upper control arm and the crossmember (Figs. 11.88 and 11.89).

6   *On cars with swivel balljoint type stub axle carriers,* both the caster and camber angles are altered by turning the cam bolts on the inner pivots of the suspension lower control arms. The cam bolt nearer the front of the car mostly affects the castor angle while the rear one influences the camber angle (Fig. 11.90).

7   Front wheel alignment (tracking or toe-in) should also be checked on a tracking gauge at a service station, although it is possible to carry out a reasonably accurate check in the following way.

8   Set the roadwheels in the straight ahead position (steering gear centralised). Make sure that the car is standing on level ground with tyres correctly inflated.

9   If the track rods or ends have been removed and refitted, set their lengths equally so that the roadwheels are both still pointing in the straight ahead position. This can best be checked by laying a length of steel rod or wood along the side of the car. When it touches all four sidewalls of the front and rear tyres, then the front wheels will be approximately parallel with each other.

10 Obtain or make a tracking gauge. One may be easily made from tubing, cranked to clear the sump and bellhousing, having an adjustable nut and setscrew at one end.

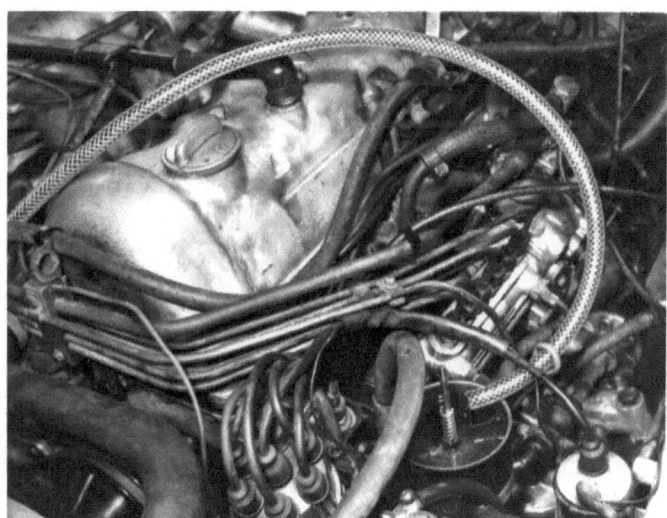

40.3 Bleeding the power steering systems

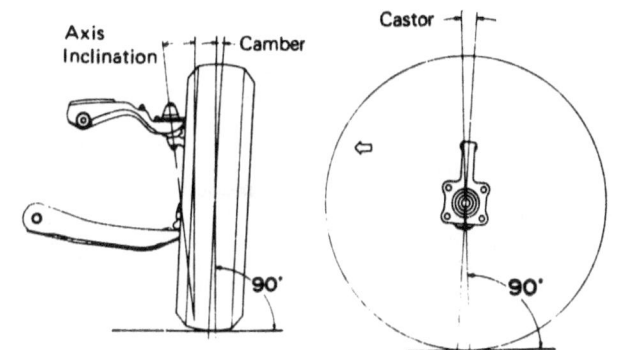

Fig. 11.86. Steering angle diagram (Sec. 41)

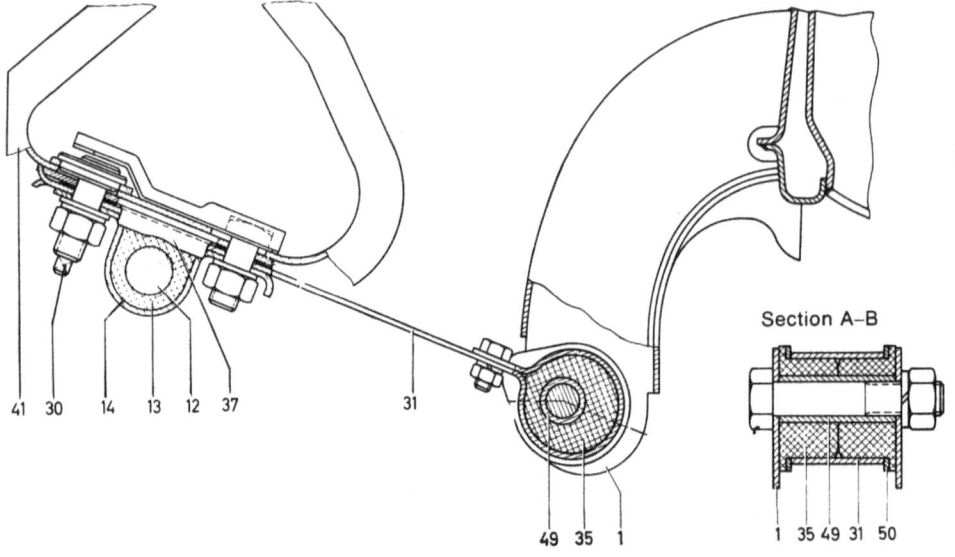

Fig. 11.87. Castor adjustment on cars with kingpin type stub axles (Sec. 41)

1   Crossmember
12 Stabiliser bar
13 Flexible mounting
14 Clamp
30 Cam bolt
31 Leaf spring
35 Flexible mounting
37 Lockwasher
41 Bracket
49 Spacer
50 Intermediate ring

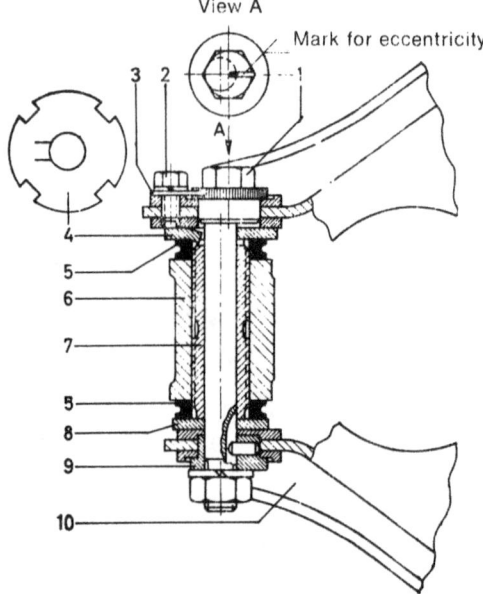

Fig. 11.88. Camber angle adjustment bolts (kingpin type stub axle carrier) (Sec. 41)

1   Cam bolt for camber   6   Kingpin upper pivot
    adjustment   7   Threaded pivot
2   Bolt   8   Washer
3   Lockwasher   9   Cam bush
4   Equaliser adjuster plate for 10 Front suspension upper
    castor   control arm
5   Sealing ring

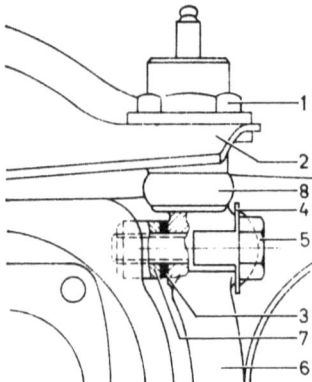

Fig. 11.89. Method of increasing camber angle (kingpin stub axle carrier) (Sec. 41)

1   Threaded pivot   5   Bolt
2   Upper control arm   6   Pivot member
3   Washer   7   Crossmember
4   Lockwasher   8   Seal

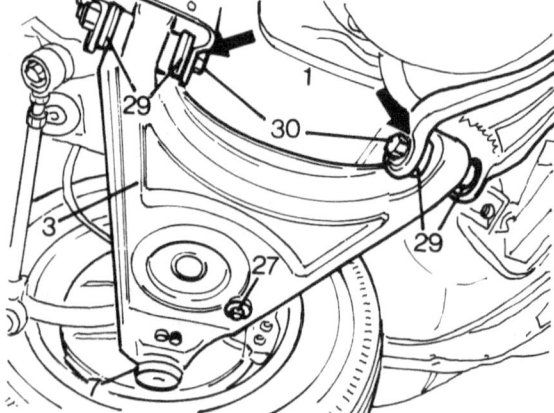

Fig. 11.90. Cam bolts for castor and camber adjustment on cars with swivel balljoint type stub axle carriers (Sec. 41)

1   Crossmember   27 Stabiliser bar link
3   Lower control arm   29 Flexible bush
                                30 Cam bolts

11 Using the gauge, measure the distance between the two inner wheel rims at hub height at the rear of the wheels.

12 Rotate the wheels (by pushing the car backwards or forwards) through 180° (half a turn) and again using the gauge, measure the distance at hub height between the two inner wheel rims at the front of the roadwheels.

13 This last dimension should be less than the first by the amount shown in the Specifications and represents the correct toe-in.

14 If the toe-in is incorrect, turn each track rod by an equal amount. Remember to turn the track rods in opposite directions as they have left and right-hand threads.

15 Recheck the toe-in. When correct, tighten the track rod clamp pinch bolts.

16 In addition to the front wheel steering angles and wheel alignment, remember that the setting of the rear wheels and centralising of the

rear axle also have an effect upon the steering and roadholding characteristics of the car. These factors are covered earlier in this Chapter and in Chapter 8.

42 Roadwheels and tyres

1 Whenever the roadwheels are removed it is a good idea to clean the insides of the wheel to remove accumulations of mud and in the case of the front ones, disc pad dust.
2 Check the condition of the wheels for rust and repaint if necessary.
3 Examine the wheel bolt holes. If these are tending to become elongated or the dished recesses in which the nuts seat have worn or become overcompressed, then the wheel will have to be renewed.
4 With a roadwheel removed, pick out any embedded flints from the tread and check for splits in the sidewalls or damage to the tyre carcass generally.

5 Where the depth of tread pattern is 1 mm or less, the tyre must be renewed.
6 Rotation of the roadwheels to even out wear is a worthwhile idea if the wheels have been balanced off the car. Include the spare wheel in the rotational pattern.
 With radial tyres it is recommended that the wheels are moved between front and rear on the same side of the car only.
7 If the wheels have been balanced on the car then they cannot be moved round the car as the balance of wheel, tyre and hub will be upset. In fact their exact bolt fitting positions must be marked before removing them from the hub.
8 It is recommended that wheels are re-balanced halfway through the life of the tyres to compensate for the loss of tread rubber due to wear.
9 Finally, always keep the tyres (including the spare) inflated to the recommended pressures and always refit the dust caps on the tyre valves. Tyre pressures are best checked first thing in the morning when the tyres are cold.

43 Fault diagnosis - steering and suspension

Before diagnosing faults from the following chart, check that any irregularities are not caused by:
1 *Binding brakes*
2 *Incorrect 'mix' of radial and crossply tyres*
3 *Incorrect tyre pressures*
4 *Misalignment of bodyframe*

Symptom	Reason/s
Steering wheel can be moved considerably before any sign of movement of the wheels is apparent	Wear in the steering linkage, gear and column coupling.
Vehicle difficult to steer in a consistent straight line - wandering	As above. Wheel alignment incorrect (indicated by excessive or uneven tyre wear). Front wheel hub bearings loose or worn. Worn suspension unit swivel joints or king pin bushes.
Steering stiff and heavy	Incorrect wheel alignment (indicated by excessive or uneven tyre wear). Excessive wear or seizure in one or more of the joints in the steering linkage or suspension unit balljoints or king pin bushes. Excessive wear in the steering gear unit.
Wheel wobble and vibration	Road wheels out of balance Road wheel buckled. Wheel alignment incorrect. Wear in the steering linkage, suspension unit bearings or control arm bushes. Broken front spring.
Excessive pitching and rolling on corners and during braking	Defective shock absorbers and/or broken spring.
Power steering Steering wheel knocks and jerks when turned	Slack drivebelt on pump.
Buzzing when turning steering wheel	Low fluid level.
Foam in fluid reservoir	Leak in system.
Steering hard to move immediately after quick turn of wheel	Air in system.
Steering hard to move when centred after turning	Tight sector shaft. Fault inside steering box.
Steering wheel hard to move when moving slowly during parking	Loose pump drive belt. Low fluid level. Fault in hydraulic pump Internal fault in steering gear.

Chapter 12 Bodywork and fittings

Contents

1 General description

The body and underframe are of the welded integral construction type. Mostly of steel, the various body types do incorporate some light alloy panels and castings.

The body styles include saloon, coupé and roadster versions and there is a wide variation in the design and complexity of the accessories fitted.

2 Maintenance - bodywork and underframe

1 The general condition of a car's bodywork is the one thing that significantly affects its value. Maintenance is easy but needs to be regular. Neglect, particularly after minor damage can lead quickly to further deterioration and costly repair bills. It is important also to keep watch on those parts of the car not immediately visible, for instance, the underframe, inside all the wheel arches and the lower part of the engine compartment.
2 The basic maintenance routine for the bodywork is washing - preferably with a lot of water, from a hose. This will remove all the loose solids which may have stuck to the car. It is important to flush these off in such a way as to prevent grit from scratching the finish.

The wheel arches and underframe need washing in the same way to remove any accumulated mud which will retain moisture and tend to encourage rust. Paradoxically enough, the best time to clean the underframe and wheel arches is in wet weather when the mud is thoroughly wet and soft. In very wet weather the underframe is usually cleaned of large accumulations automatically and this is a good time for inspection.
3 Periodically it is a good idea to have the whole of the underframe of the car steam cleaned, engine compartment included, so that a thorough inspection can be carried out to see what minor repairs and renovations are necessary. Steam cleaning is available at many garages and is necessary for removal of the accumulation of oily grime which sometimes is allowed to cake thick in certain areas near the engine, gearbox and back axle. If steam cleaning facilities are not available, there are one or two excellent grease solvents available which can be brush applied. The dirt can then be simply hosed off.
4 After washing paintwork, wipe off with a chamois leather to give an unspotted clear finish. A coat of clear protective wax polish will give added protection against chemical pollutants in the air. If the paintwork sheen has dulled or oxidised, use a cleaner/polisher combination to restore the brilliance of the shine. This requires a little effort, but is usually caused because regular washing has been neglected. Always

check that the door and ventilator opening drain holes and pipes are completely clear so that water can be drained out. Bright work should be treated the same way as paintwork. Windscreens and windows can be kept clear of the smeary film which often appears if a little ammonia is added to the water. If they are scratched, a good rub with a proprietary metal polish will often clear them. Never use any form of wax or other body or chromium polish on glass.

3 Maintenance - upholstery and carpets

1 Mats and carpets should be brushed or vacuum cleaned regularly to keep them free of grit. If they are badly stained remove them from the car for scrubbing or sponging and make quite sure they are dry before refitting. Seats and interior trim panels can be kept clean by a wipe over with a damp cloth. If they do become stained (which can be more apparent on light coloured upholstery) use a little liquid detergent and a soft nail brush to scour the grime out of the grain of the material. Do not forget to keep the head lining clean in the same way as the upholstery. When using liquid cleaners inside the car do not over-wet the surfaces being cleaned. Excessive damp could get into the seams and padded interior causing stains, offensive odours or even rot. If the inside of the car gets wet accidentally it is worthwhile taking some trouble to dry it out properly, particularly where carpets are involved. *Do not leave oil or electric heaters inside the car for this purpose.*

4 Minor body damage - repair

The photographic sequence on pages 214 and 215, illustrates the operations detailed in the following sub-Sections.

Repair of minor scratches in the car's bodywork

If the scratch is very superficial, and does not penetrate to the metal of the bodywork, repair is very simple. Lightly rub the area of the scratch with a paintwork renovator, or a very fine cutting paste, to remove loose paint from the scratch and to clear the surrounding bodywork of wax polish. Rinse the area with clean water.

Apply touch-up paint to the scratch using a thin paint brush, continue to apply thin layers of paint until the surface of the paint in the scratch is level with the surrounding paintwork. Allow the new paint at least two weeks to harden; then, blend it into the surrounding paintwork by rubbing the paintwork, in the scratch area, with a paintwork renovator, or a very fine cutting paste. Finally, apply wax polish.

An alternative to painting over the scratch is to use a paint patch.

Use the same preparation for the affected area; then simply pick a patch of a suitable size to cover the scratch completely. Hold the patch against the scratch and burnish its backing paper; the patch will adhere to the paintwork, freeing itself from the backing paper at the same time. Polish the affected area to blend the patch into the surrounding paintwork. Where the scratch has penetrated right through to the metal of the bodywork, causing the metal to rust, a different repair technique is required. Remove any loose rust from the bottom of the scratch with a penknife, then apply rust inhibiting paint to prevent the formation of rust in the future. Using a rubber or nylon applicator, fill the scratch with bodystopper paste. If required, this paste can be mixed with cellulose thinners to provide a very thin paste, which is an ideal way of filling narrow scratches. Before the stopper-paste in the scratch hardens, wrap a piece of smooth cotton rag around the top of a finger. Dip the finger in cellulose thinners and then quickly sweep it across the surface of the stopper-paste in the scratch; this will ensure that the surface of the stopper-paste is slightly hollowed. The scratch can now be painted over as described earlier in this Section.

Repair of dents in the car's bodywork

When deep denting of the car's bodywork has taken place, the first task is to pull the dent out, until the affected bodywork almost attains its original shape. There is little point in trying to restore the original shape completely, as the metal in the damaged area will have stretched on impact and cannot be reshaped fully to its original contour. It is better to bring the level of the dent up to a point which is about 1/8 inch (3 mm) below the level of the surrounding bodywork. In cases where the dent is very shallow anyway, it is not worth trying to pull it out at all. If the underside of the dent is accessible, it can be hammered out gently from behind, using a mallet with a wooden or plastic head. Whilst doing this, hold a suitable block of wood firmly against the impact from the hammer blows and thus prevent a large area of the bodywork from being 'belled-out'.

Should the dent be in a section of the bodywork which has a double skin or some other factor making it inaccessible from behind, a different technique is called for. Drill several holes through the metal inside the dent area - particularly in the deeper sections. Then screw long self-tapping screws into the holes just sufficiently for them to gain a good purchase in the metal. Now the dent can be pulled out by pulling on the protruding heads of the screws with a pair of pliers.

The next stage of the repair is the removal of the paint from the damaged area, and from an inch or so of the surrounding 'sound' bodywork. This is accomplished more easily by using a wire brush or abrasive pad on a power drill, although it can be done just as effectively by hand using sheets of abrasive paper. To complete the preparations for filling, score the surface of the bare metal with a screwdriver or the tang of a file, or alternatively, drill small holes in the affected area. This will provide a really good 'key' for the filler paste.

To complete the repair see the Section on filling and re-spraying.

Repair of rust holes or gashes in the car's bodywork

Remove all paint from the affected area and from an inch or so of the surrounding 'sound' bodywork, using an abrasive pad or a wire brush on a power drill. If these are not available a few sheets of abrasive paper will do the job just as effectively. With the paint removed you will be able to gauge the severity of the corrosion and therefore decide whether to renew the whole panel (if this is possible) or to repair the affected area. New body panels are not as expensive as most people think and it is often quicker and more satisfactory to fit a new panel than to attempt to repair large areas of corrosion.

Remove all fittings from the affected area except those which will act as a guide to the original shape of the damaged bodywork (headlamp shells etc.,). Then, using tin snips or a hacksaw blade, remove all loose metal and any other metal badly affected by corrosion. Hammer the edges of the hole inwards in order to create a slight depression for the filler paste.

Wire brush the affected area to remove the powdery rust from the surface of the remaining metal. Paint the affected area with rust inhibiting paint; if the back of the rusted area is accessible treat this also.

Before filling can take place it will be necessary to block the hole in some way. This can be achieved by the use of one of the following materials: Zinc gauze, Aluminium tape or Polyurethane foam.

Zinc gauze is probably the best material to use for a large hole. Cut a piece to the approximate size and shape of the hole to be filled, then position it in the hole so that its edges are below the level of the surrounding bodywork. It can be retained in position by several blobs of filler paste around its periphery.

Aluminium tape should be used for small or very narrow holes. Pull a piece off the roll and trim it to the approximate size and shape required, then pull off the backing paper (if used) and stick the tape over the hole; it can be overlapped if the thickness of one piece is insufficient. Burnish down the edges of the tape with the handle of a screwdriver or similar, to ensure that the tape is securely attached to the metal underneath.

Polyurethane foam is best used where the hole is situated in a section of bodywork of complex shape, backed by a small box section (eg. where the sill panel meets the rear wheel arch - most cars). The usual mixing procedure for this foam is as follows: Put equal amounts of fluid from each of the two cans provided in the kit, into one container. Stir until the mixture begins to thicken, then quickly pour this mixture into the hole, and hold a piece of cardboard over the larger apertures. Almost immediately the polyurethane will begin to expand, gushing out of any small holes left unblocked. When the foam hardens it can be cut back to just below the level of the surrounding bodywork with a hacksaw blade.

Bodywork repairs - filling and re-spraying

Before using this Section, see the Sections on dent, deep scratch, rust hole, and gash repairs.

Many types of bodyfiller are available, but generally speaking those proprietary kits which contain a tin of filler paste and a tube of resin hardener are best for this type of repair. A wide, flexible, plastic or nylon applicator will be found invaluable for imparting a smooth and well contoured finish to the surface of the filler.

Mix up a little filler on a clean piece of card or board - use the hardener sparingly (follow the maker's instructions on the packet) otherwise the filler will set very rapidly.

Using the applicator, apply the filler paste to the prepared area; draw the applicator across the surface of the filler to achieve the correct contour and to level the filler surface. As soon as a contour that approximates the correct one is achieved, stop working the paste - if you carry on too long the paste will become sticky and begin to 'pick-up' on the applicator. Continue to add thin layers of filler paste at twenty minute intervals until the level of the filler is just 'proud' of the surrounding bodywork.

Once the filler has hardened, excess can be removed using a metal plane or file. From then on, progressively finer grades of abrasive paper should be used, starting with a 40 grade production paper and finishing with 400 grade 'wet-or-dry' paper. Always wrap the abrasive paper around a flat rubber, cork, or wooden block - otherwise the surface of the filler will not be completely flat. During the smoothing of the filler surface the 'wet-or-dry' paper should be periodically rinsed in water. This will ensure that a very smooth finish is imparted to the filler at the final stage.

At this stage the 'dent' should be surrounded by a ring of bare metal, which in turn should be encircled by the finely 'feathered' edge of the good paintwork. Rinse the repair area with clean water, until all of the dust produced by the rubbing-down operation has gone.

Spray the whole repair area with a light coat of primer - this will show up any imperfections in the surface of the filler. Repair these imperfections with fresh filler paste or bodystopper, and once more smooth the surface with abrasive paper. If bodystopper is used, it can be mixed with cellulose thinners to form a really thin paste which is ideal for filling small holes. Repeat this spray and repair procedure until you are satisfied that the surface of the filler, and the feathered edge of the paintwork are perfect. Clean the repair area with clean water and allow to dry fully.

The repair area is now ready for spraying. Paint spraying must be carried out in a warm, dry, windless and dust free atmosphere. This condition can be created artificially if you have access to a large indoor working area, but if you are forced to work in the open, you will have to pick your day very carefully. If you are working indoors, dousing the floor in the work area with water will 'lay' the dust which would otherwise be in the atmosphere. If the repair area is confined to one body panel, mask off the surrounding panels; this will help to minimise the effects of slight mis-match in paint colour. Bodywork fittings (eg. chrome strips, door handles etc.,) will also need to be masked off. Use genuine masking tape and several thicknesses of newspaper for the masking operation.

Before commencing to spray, agitate the aerosol can thoroughly, then spray a test area (an old tin, or similar) until the technique is mastered. Cover the repair area with a thick coat of primer; the thickness should be built up using several thin layers of paint rather than one thick one. Using 400 grade 'wet-or-dry' paper, rub down the surface of the primer until it is really smooth. While doing this, the work area should be thoroughly doused with water, and the 'wet-or-dry' paper periodically rinsed in water. Allow to dry before spraying on more paint.

Spray on the top coat again building up the thickness by using several thin layers of paint. Start spraying in the centre of the repair area and then, using a circular motion, work outwards until the whole repair area and about 2 inches of the surrounding original paintwork is covered. Remove all masking material 10 to 15 minutes after spraying on the final coat of paint.

Allow the new paint at least 2 weeks to harden fully, then, using a paintwork renovator or a very fine cutting paste, blend the edges of the new paint into the existing paintwork. Finally, apply wax polish.

5 Major body damage - repair

Where serious damage has occurred or large areas need renewal due to neglect, it means certainly that completely new sections or panels will need welding in and this is best left to professionals. If the damage is due to impact it will also be necessary to completely check the alignment of the body shell structure. Due to the principle of construction the strength and shape of the whole can be affected by damage to a part. In such instances the services of a Mercedes-Benz agent with specialist checking jigs are essential. If a body is left misaligned it is first of all dangerous as the car will not handle properly and secondly uneven stresses will be imposed on the steering, engine and transmission, causing abnormal wear or complete failure. Tyre wear may also be excessive.

6 Maintenance - hinges and locks

1   Oil the hinges of the bonnet, boot and doors with a drop or two of light oil periodically. A good time is after the car has been washed.
2   Oil the bonnet release, the catch pivot pin and the safety catch pivot pin periodically.
3   Do not over lubricate door latches and strikers. Normally a little oil on the rotary cam spindle is sufficient.

7 Doors - tracing rattles and their rectification

1   Check first that the door is not loose at the hinges and that the latch is holding the door firmly in position. Check also that the door lines up with the aperture in the body.
2   If the hinges are loose or the door is out of alignment it will be necessary to reset the hinge positions, as described in Section 12.
3   If the latch is holding the door properly it should hold the door tightly when fully latched and the door should line up with the body. If it is out of alignment it needs adjustment. If loose, some part of the lock mechanism must be worn out and requires renewal.
4   Other rattles from the door would be caused by wear or looseness in the window winder, the glass channels and sill strips or the door buttons and interior latch release mechanism.

8 Windscreen and rear window glass - removal and refitting

1   Where the screen is to be removed intact and is of the laminated type then an assistant will be required. First release the rubber surround from the bodywork by running a blunt, small screwdriver around and under the rubber weatherstrip both inside and outside the car. This operation will break the adhesive of the sealer originally used. Take care not to damage the paintwork or catch the rubber surround with the screwdriver. Remove the windscreen wiper arms and interior mirror and place a protective cover on the bonnet.
2   Have your assistant push the inner lip of the rubber surround off the flange of the windscreen body aperture. Commence pushing the glass at one of the upper corners. Once the rubber surround starts to

peel off the flange, the screen may be forced gently outwards by careful hand pressure. The second person should support and remove the screen complete with rubber surround and bright trim as it comes out.
3   Remove the bright trim from the rubber surround.
4   Before fitting a windscreen, ensure that the rubber surround is completely free from old sealant and glass fragments, and has not hardened or cracked. Fit the rubber surround to the glass and apply a bead of suitable sealant between the glass outer edge and the rubber.
5   Cut a piece of strong cord greater in length than the periphery of the glass and insert it into the body flange locating channel of the rubber surround.
6   Apply a thin bead of sealant to the face of the rubber channel which will eventually mate with the body.
7   Offer the windscreen to the body aperture and pass the ends of the cord, previously fitted and located at bottom centre into the vehicle interior.
8   Press the windscreen into place, at the same time have an assistant pulling the cords to engage the lip of the rubber channel over the body flange.
9   Remove any excess sealant with a paraffin soaked rag and fit the bright trim.
10 Removal and installation of the rear window glass is carried out in an identical manner but (if fitted) disconnect the leads to the heating element in the glass.

Note: The following Sections describe typical operations and will not necessarily illustrate a particular model but generally the procedures apply to all cars with only detail differences in the components concerned.

9 Door interior trim panel - removal and refitting

1   Prise out the plastic insert from the window regulator handle, unscrew and remove the securing screw now exposed and pull off the handle (photo).
2   If a swivel type ventilator is fitted, prise out the cover plate from the centre of the control knob, unscrew and remove the securing screw and pull off the knob (Fig. 12.1).
3   Prise back the covering caps from both ends of the door pull to expose the securing screws and unscrew and remove the screws. Extract the armrest screws. On some models the door pull and armrest are one assembly (photos).
4   Extract the screws from the centre of the lock interior handle escutcheon plates. Remove the plates (photos).
5   Unscrew and remove the bright corner trim plates from the corners of the doors.
6   On rear doors, the ashtrays may require removal.
7   Depending upon the model, either lift the door interior trim panel

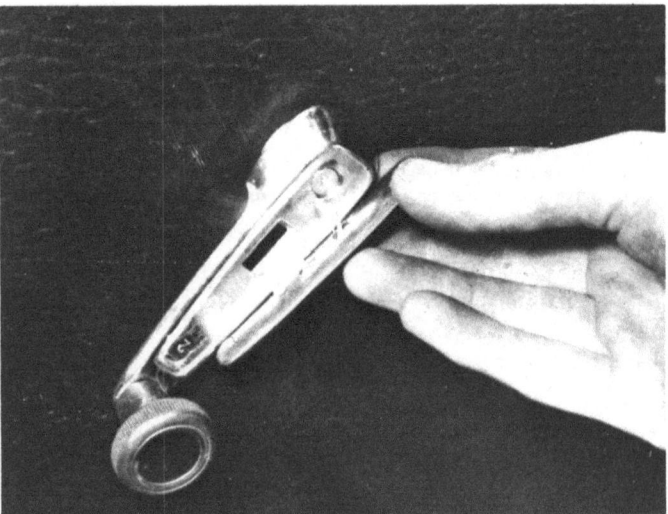

9.1 Prising out window regulator handle cover plate

directly from its lower support channel or use a wooden wedge inserted between the trim panel and the door frame to release the clips (photo).
8   The waterproof sheet may now be peeled away to give access to the door internal components.
9   Refitting is a reversal of removal.

10 Front door - dismantling and reassembly

1   With the door interior trim panel removed, extract the screws from the lower glass channel. Temporarily refit the regulator handle and wind up the window. Support the glass in the raised position using wooden props or obtain the help of a assistant.
2   Extract the screws which secure the window regulator mechanism

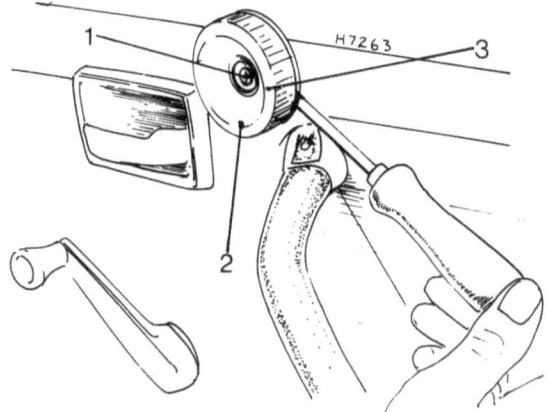

Fig. 12.1. Swivel ventilator control knob (Sec. 9)

1   Securing screw   2   Control knob   3   Cover plate recess

and withdraw the mechanism through the hole in the door interior panel (Fig. 12.2).
3   Extract the screws which secure the lower end of the glass guide channel. Pull the glass out of the guide and withdraw it downwards through the door aperture (photos).
4   The moulding can be prised out of its retaining clips using a wooden or plastic tool to prevent damage to the paintwork (Fig. 12.3).
5   The outer sealing strip can be removed in a similar way by prising off the retaining clips (Fig. 12.4).
6   The glass guide channel can be removed by first bending up the retaining plate on the two lower guide channels and then removing the rail.
7   If the car is equipped with electric windows, the motor can be removed from the door cavity (see Chapter 10) after disconnecting the leads and mountings.
8   The swivel ventilator lower pivot can be removed by first extracting the screw (1) from its lower pivot shaft. This is accessible through a hole in the door inner panel (Fig. 12.5).
9   Extract the two screws (2) and remove the pivot assembly downwards from the door cavity.
10 The swivel ventilator can be removed with or without its frame. To remove it without the frame, take out the moulding (paragraph 4) and the ventilator pivot (paragraphs 8 and 9). Turn the ventilator outwards at right angles to the car, press it hard in a downward direction and extract the top pivot pin.
11 To remove the ventilator complete with frame, extract the lower pivot (paragraphs 8 and 9) and pull away the window glass guide channel from around the swivel ventilator.
12 Extract the ventilator frame securing screws (3 and 4) (Figs. 12.6 and 7).
13 Pull the frame slightly towards the rear of the car and withdraw it at an angle (inclined outwards) from the door.
14 The door lock is removed by first disconnecting the remote control rod connecting spring (1) and then extracting the two screws from the remote control handle (Fig. 12.8) (photo).
15 Extract the screws (3) and (6) and withdraw the interior handle

9.3A Pull handle screws with end covers removed

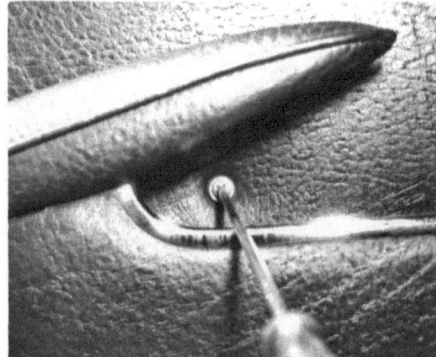
9.3B Extracting arm rest screw

9.4A Interior lock lever escutcheon plate screw

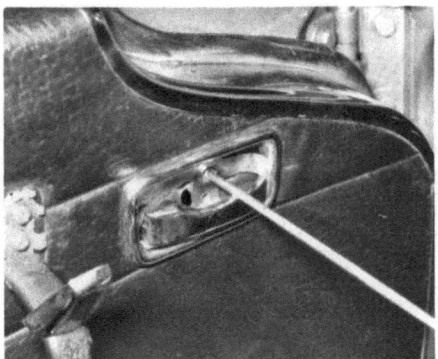
9.4B Interior remote control lock handle escutcheon plate screw

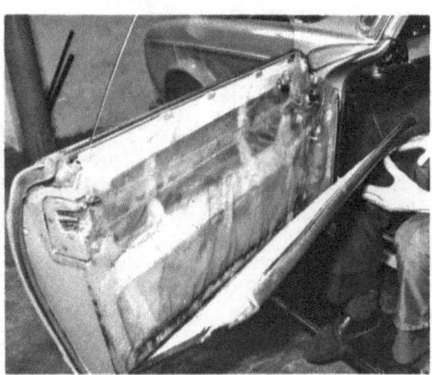
9.7 Removing door interior trim panel (280 SL)

This photographic sequence shows the steps taken to repair the dent and paintwork damage shown above. In general, the procedure for repairing a hole will be similar; where there are substantial differences, the procedure is clearly described and shown in a separate photograph.

First remove any trim around the dent, then hammer out the dent where access is possible. This will minimise filling. Here, after the large dent has been hammered out, the damaged area is being made slightly concave.

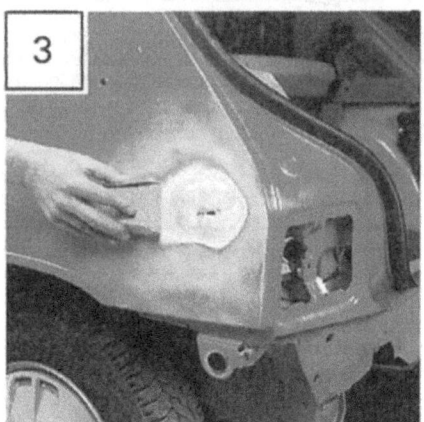

Next, remove all paint from the damaged area by rubbing with course abrasive paper or using a power drill fitted with a wire brush or abrasive pad. 'Feather' the edge of the boundary with good paintwork using a finer grade of abrasive paper.

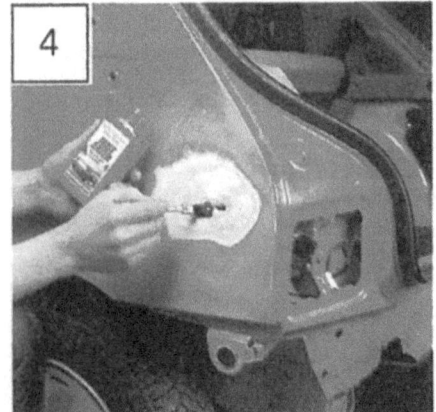

Where there are holes or other damage, the sheet metal should be cut away before proceeding further. The damaged area and any signs of rust should be treated with Turtle Wax Hi-Tech Rust Eater, which will also inhibit further rust formation.

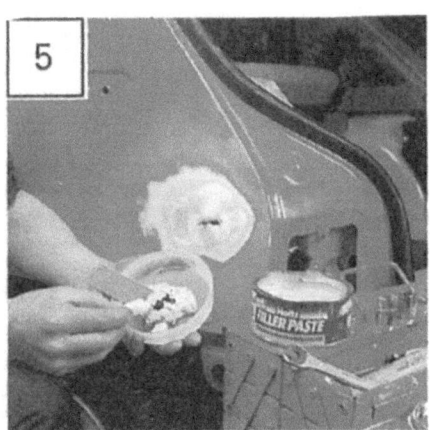

For a large dent or hole mix Holts Body Plus Resin and Hardener according to the manufacturer's instructions and apply around the edge of the repair. Press Glass Fibre Matting over the repair area and leave for 20-30 minutes to harden. Then ...

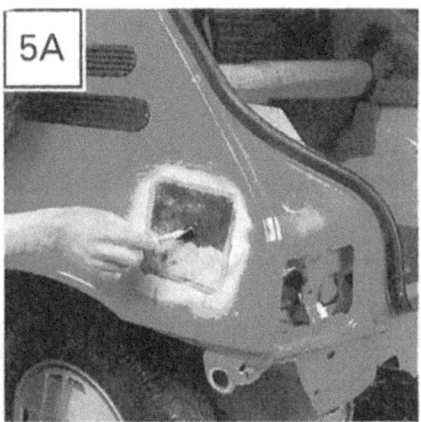

... brush more Holts Body Plus Resin and Hardener onto the matting and leave to harden. Repeat the sequence with two or three layers of matting, checking that the final layer is lower than the surrounding area. Apply Holts Body Plus Filler Paste as shown in Step 5B.

For a medium dent, mix Holts Body Plus Filler Paste and Hardener according to the manufacturer's instructions and apply it with a flexible applicator. Apply thin layers of filler at 20-minute intervals, until the filler surface is slightly proud of the surrounding bodywork.

For small dents and scratches use Holts No Mix Filler Paste straight from the tube. Apply it according to the instructions in thin layers, using the spatula provided. It will harden in minutes if applied outdoors and may then be used as its own knifing putting.

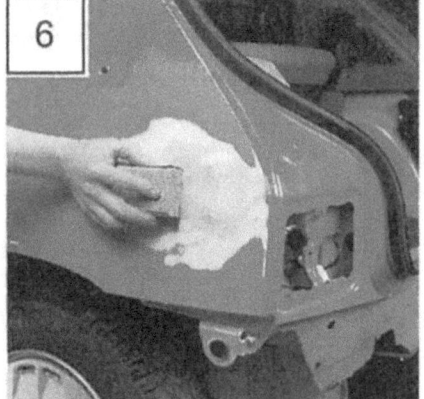

Use a plane or file for initial shaping. Then, using progressively finer grades of wet-and-dry paper, wrapped around a sanding block, and copious amounts of clean water, rub down the filler until glass smooth. 'Feather' the edges of adjoining paintwork.

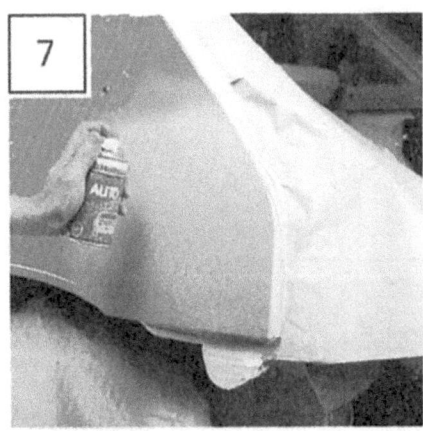

Protect adjoining areas before spraying the whole repair area and at least one inch of the surrounding sound paintwork with Holts Dupli-Color primer.

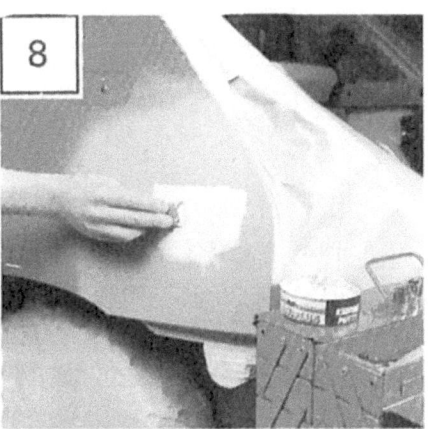

Fill any imperfections in the filler surface with a small amount of Holts Body Plus Knifing Putty. Using plenty of clean water, rub down the surface with a fine grade wet-and-dry paper - 400 grade is recommended - until it is really smooth.

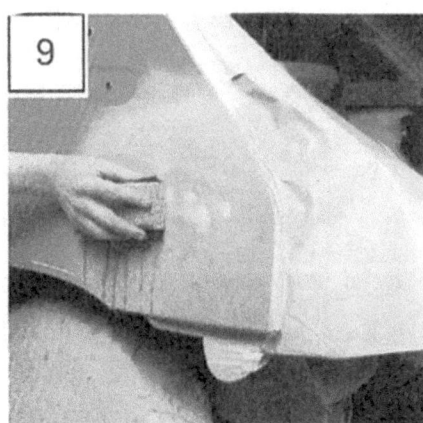

Carefully fill any remaining imperfections with knifing putty before applying the last coat of primer. Then rub down the surface with Holts Body Rubbing Compound to ensure a really smooth surface.

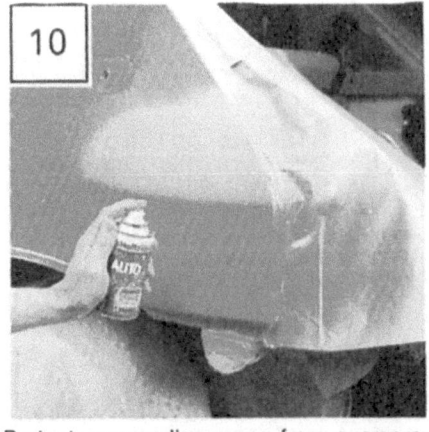

Protect surrounding areas from overspray before applying the topcoat in several thin layers. Agitate Holts Dupli-Color aerosol thoroughly. Start at the repair centre, spraying outwards with a side-to-side motion.

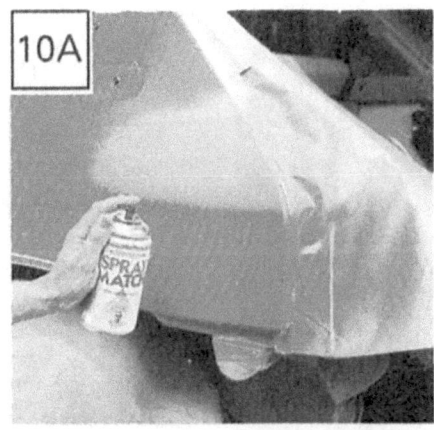

If the exact colour is not available off the shelf, local Holts Professional Spraymatch Centres will custom fill an aerosol to match perfectly.

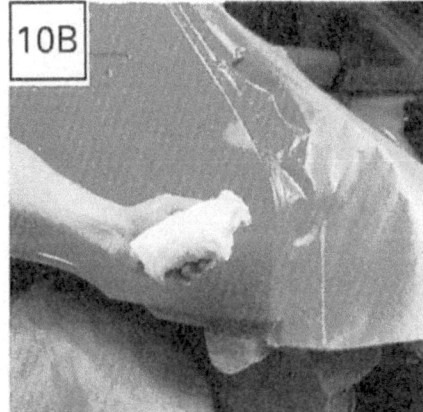

To identify whether a lacquer finish is required, rub a painted unrepaired part of the body with wax and a clean cloth.

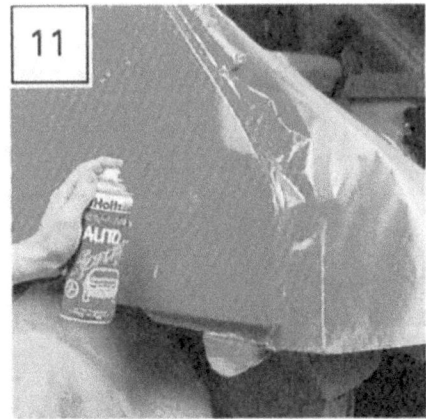

If no traces of paint appear on the cloth, spray Holts Dupli-Color clear lacquer over the repaired area to achieve the correct gloss level.

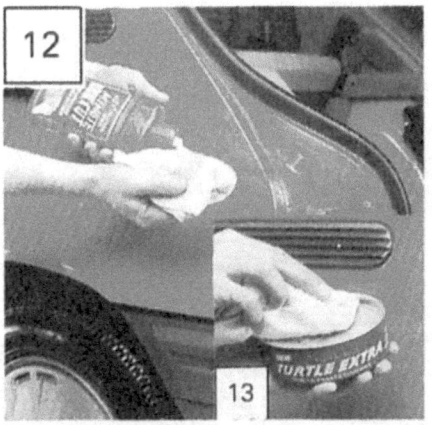

The paint will take about two weeks to harden fully. After this time it can be 'cut' with a mild cutting compound such as Turtle Wax Minute Cut prior to polishing with a final coating of Turtle Wax Extra.

When carrying out bodywork repairs, remember that the quality of the finished job is proportional to the time and effort expended.

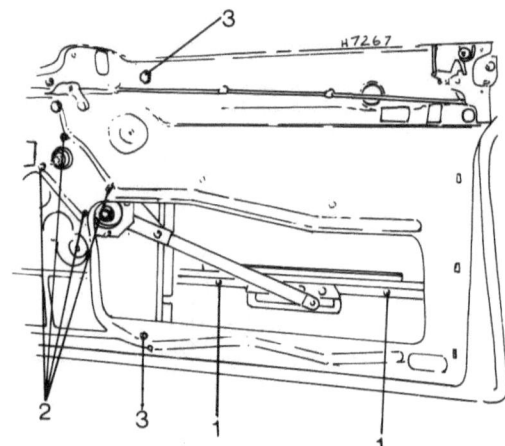

Fig. 12.2. Interior of front door (saloon) (Sec. 10)

1   Channel screw
2   Window regulator screws
3   Glass guide channel screw

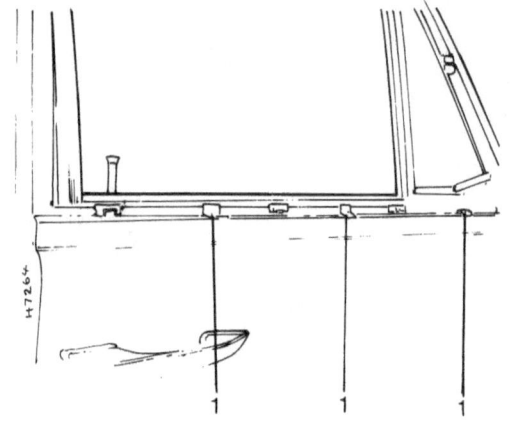

Fig. 12.3. Door moulding plastic pads (1) (Sec. 10)

10.3A Glass lower channel and adjustable stops (280 SL)

Fig. 12.4. Removing outer sealing strip (Sec. 10)

10.3B Glass lower channel and adjustable stops (280 SL)

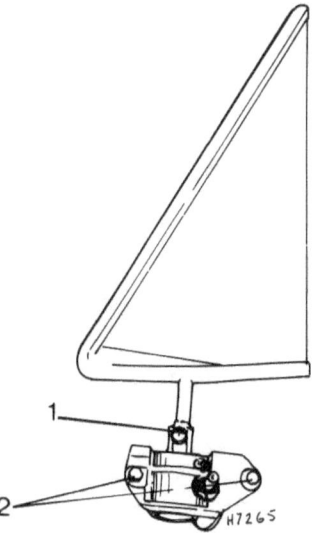

Fig. 12.5. Door swivel ventilator (Sec. 10)

1   Shaft screw
2   Pinch bolts

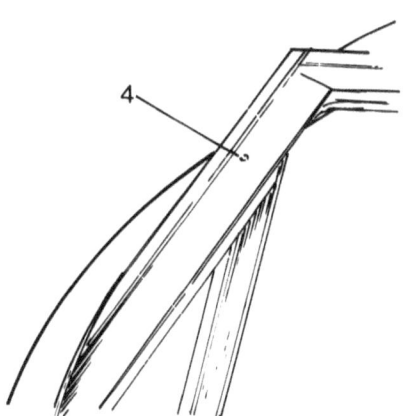

Fig. 12.6. Swivel ventilator upper screw (4) (Sec. 10)

10.14 Remote control lever detail

Fig. 12.7. Swivel ventilator lower screw (3) and corner cap (5)
(Sec. 10)

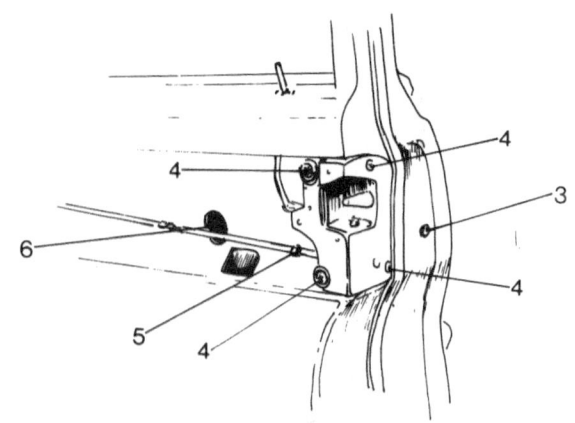

Fig. 12.9. Door handle screw (3) door lock screw (4) connecting
spring (5) aperture (6) (Sec. 10)

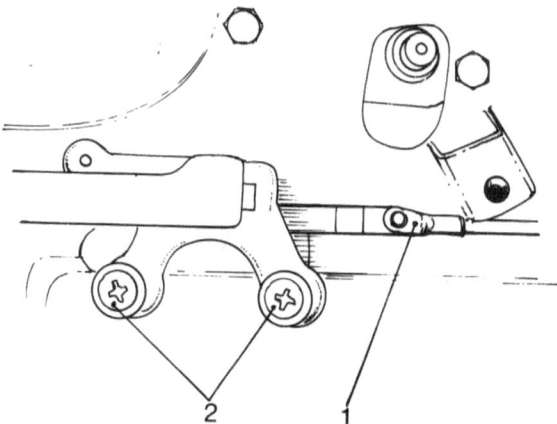

Fig. 12.8. Remote control lock handle screws (2) connecting spring
(1) (Sec. 10)

in a forward direction (Fig. 12.9) (photo).

16 Remove the lock assembly from the door frame edge after having
unscrewed and removed the fixing screws.

17 The screws which retain the door exterior handle are accessible
from within the door cavity.

18 Reassembly and refitting in all cases is a reversal of removal and
dismantling but note that a free movement should exist on the lock
remote control lever of 0.059 in (1.5 mm). Achieve this by moving the
position of the handle within the limits of its fixing screws.

10.15 Door lock and control rods

11 Rear door - dismantling and reassembly

1   The operations are similar to those just described for the front door with the following additions and variations.
2   Having first removed the interior trim panel, the fixed quarter window may be withdrawn in the following way. Wind down the door glass fully.
3   Pull away the glass guide channel (sliding window) from the proximity of the quarter light. Extract the screws (1) and (2) and remove the vertical bar (3) (Fig. 3.10).
4   The quarter window glass complete with rubber surround can now be withdrawn.
5   The main glass is removed from the door upwards having first turned it through 90° so that the channel on the edge of the glass is towards the door hinge side.
6   Refitting is a reversal of removal but make sure that the free movement of the door interior handle is 0.039 in (1.0 mm).

12 Door exterior mirror - adjustment and removal

1   If it is found that vibration is causing the exterior mirror to alter its setting, the mirror must be removed complete and the clamp screw tightened.
2   The glass can be renewed simply by prising it from the mirror head with a plastic or wooden lever.
3   To remove the mirror complete, push the small plastic lock (3) out of the mirror control handle (4) using a small screwdriver and withdraw the handle (Fig. 12.11).
4   Pull off the cover plate to expose the three mirror fixing screws. Extract the screws and remove the mirror.
5   Refitting is a reversal of removal.

13 Door check strap - removal and refitting

1   Remove the door interior trim panel as described in Section 9. Remove the waterproof sheet.
2   Disconnect the door check strap from the body pillar by extracting the pivot pin and plastic washers (Fig. 12.12).
3   Where the door check strap is to be removed completely, unscrew the anchor bolt (3) and screws (4).
4   Withdraw the check strap through the opening provided in the door panel.
5   Refitting is a reversal of removal but apply grease to the check straps and oil the pivots.
6   Note the alternative type door check used on SL models (photo).

14 Door - removal and refitting

1   Open the door to its fullest extent and support its lower edge on jacks or blocks covered with rags.
2   Disconnect the check strap from the body pillar.
3   If the car is fitted with electric windows, disconnect the electrical leads.
4   Mark the position of the hinge plates on the door frame edge and then unbolt and remove the hinge screws. Lift the door from the car.
5   Refitting is a reversal of removal and if the hinges are bolted back into their original positions, door alignment should be correct. If adjustment is required to lift or lower the door or to make the door panel flush with the body panels, slacken the hinge bolts and move the door as necessary. Check that the gap round the edge of the door is equal on both sides and at the top.
6   Adjustment of the striker plate on the body pillar will affect the door closure and also the flush apperance of the door edge with the body panel or pillar adjacent to it. The striker plate can be set by releasing the retaining screws so that it moves stiffly and then slamming the door shut. This will position the door closure point. Open the door carefully and fully tighten the screws. If necessary, shims can be removed or inserted behind the striker plate to ensure positive closure. Sometimes it is an advantage to adjust the door so that its locking edge is 0.039 in (1.0 mm) proud of the rear door panel or body panel to reduce wind noise.

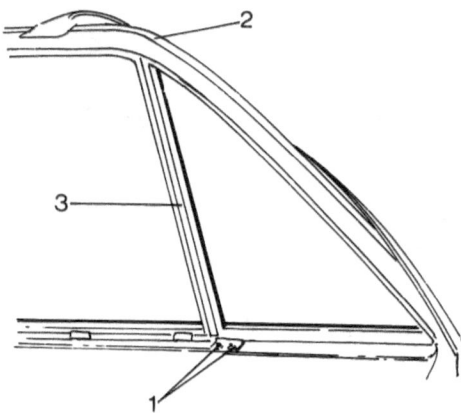

Fig. 12.10. Fixed quarter-light frame screws (Sec. 11)

1   Lower screws   3   Divider bar
2   Upper screws

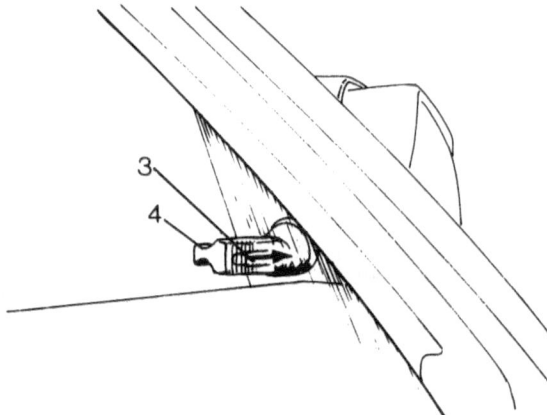

Fig. 12.11. Exterior mirror fixing detail (Sec. 12)

3   Locking piece
4   Handle

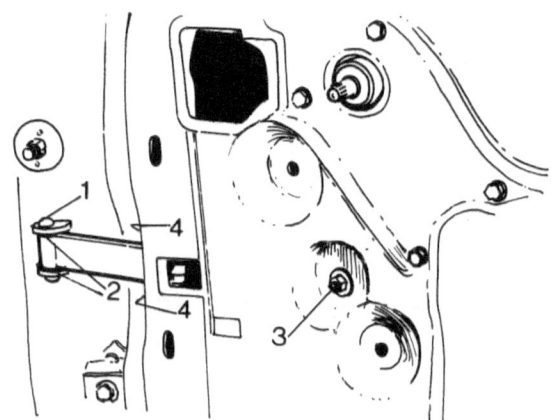

Fig. 12.12. Door check strap (Sec. 13)

1   Pivot pin
2   Plastic washers
3   Anchor nut
4   Check strap screws

13.16 Door check bar on 280 SL models

15.1 A bonnet hinge (280 SL model)

15.2 Anchor block for bonnet lid torsion rod. Note location of ignition coil ballast resistor below

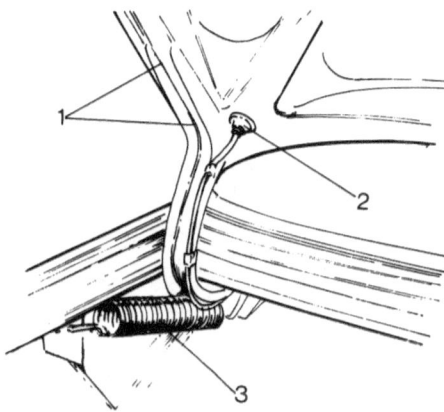
Fig. 12.13. Luggage boot lid hinge

1 Securing screws
2 Grommet
3 Counterbalance spring

Fig. 12.14. Fuel filler cap (Sec. 17)

1 Closure spring   2 Hinge screws

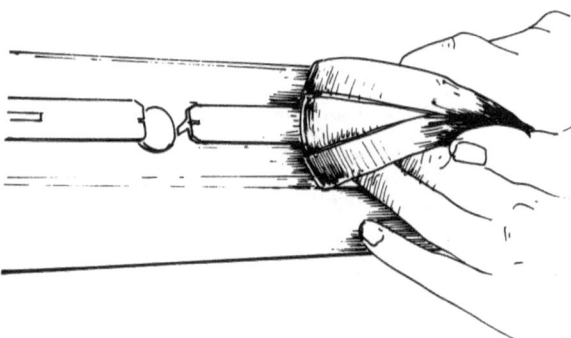
Fig. 12.15. Removing rubber insert from bumper bar (Sec. 18)

15 Bonnet - removal and refitting

1 Open the bonnet to its fullest extent and mark the position of the hinge plates on the underside of the lid (photo).
2 On some models including roadster versions, a spring type torque rod is used to hold the bonnet lid open. Disconnect this but take great care to place a pad between it and the lid or it will damage the paintwork as it is released (photo).
3 Have the help of an assistant to support the lid and then unscrew and remove the hinge bolts and lift the lid away.
4 Refitting is a reversal of removal; any adjustment can be made by moving the bonnet lid before fully tightening the hinge bolts.
Always keep the hinge pivots well lubricated especially on SL models as a seized hinge can tear away from the aluminium bonnet lid.

16 Luggage compartment lid - removal and refittings

1 Disconnect the lead from the boot light fitting . Withdraw the lead and grommet from the lid.
2 Place a thick pad on the rear window so that if the lid contacts the glass during removal, no damage will be caused.
3 Mark the position of the hinges on the underside of the lid and then with the help of an assistant unbolt the hinges from the lid and lift the lid from the car (Fig. 12.13).
4 The hinges themselves can be removed if necessary after first disconnecting the heavy counterbalance return springs with a lever.

17 Fuel filler flap - removal and refitting

1 Pull the flap half open and detach the spring by pulling in the direction of the arrow (Fig. 12.14).
2 Extract the two hinge screws and remove the flap.
3 Refitting is a reversal of removal.

18 Bumpers - removal and refitting

1 Steel type bumpers may be of several designs according to model. Some bumper bars are jointed at the centre and either half may be removed independently after unbolting the supporting bracket from the bodyframe.
2 Other bumper bars are of two section design split horizontally. The two sections can be disconnected once the rubber insert strip has been peeled away and the connecting screws extracted (Fig. 12.15).

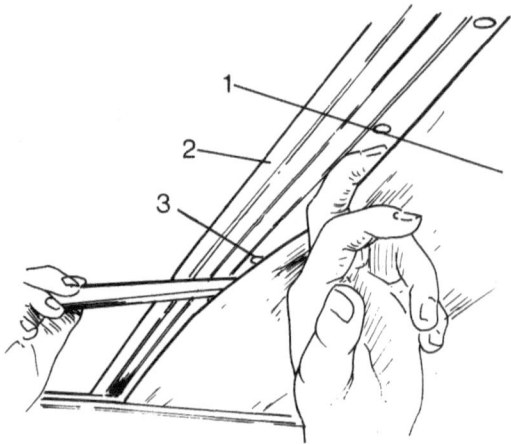

Fig. 12.16. Releasing sliding roof headlining (Sec. 20)

1   *Headlining*   2   *Panel*   3   *Headlining clip*

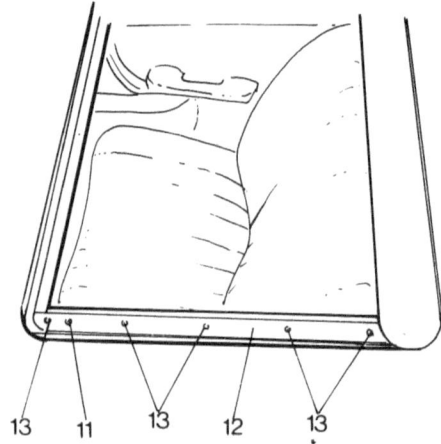

Fig. 12.17. Sliding roof adjusting and fixing screws (Sec. 20)

11 *Height adjusting screw (front)*
12 *Slide rail*
13 *Slide rail fixing screws*

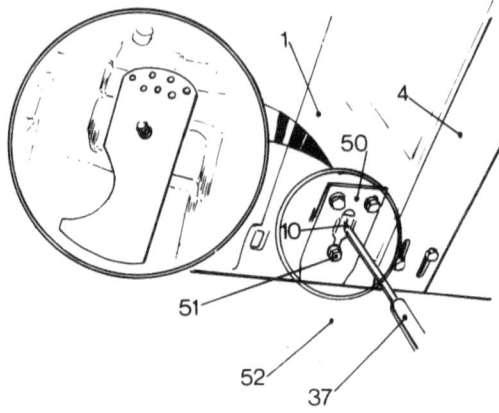

Fig. 12.18. Interior view of sliding roof mechanism (Sec. 20)

1 *Sliding roof panel*	37 *Screwdriver*
4 *Carriage*	50 *Lifting bracket*
10 *Height adjustment wedge shim*	51 *Nut*
	52 *Headlining*

19 Seat - removal and refitting

1   To remove a front seat, first disconnect the leads to the weight sensitive switch for the seat belt warning system (if fitted - N. America).
2   Push the seat as far back as possible.
3   Unscrew and remove the bolts from the front ends of the seat guide rails.
4   Push the seat fully forward and remove the bolts from the rear of the seat rails.
5   On bench type front seats, three guide rails are used and the seat, once unbolted, should be removed from the car through the door on the passenger side.
6   To remove the rear seat, lift the front edge of the rear seat cushion and remove it.
7   Unscrew the two nuts from the wheel arches in the rear passenger compartment then open the luggage boot lid and withdraw the bolts which belong to these nuts from within the luggage compartment.
8   The seat back can now be lifted out of the car.
9   Refitting is a reversal of removal.

20 Sliding roof - adjustment

1   To adjust the sliding roof, first open it about ¾ of its travel. Prise the sliding roof headlining off its clips and remove it in a forward direction (Fig. 12.16).
2   Adjust the sliding shoes of the roof panel so that the panel is in the exact centre of the roof aperture with the same gap on either side. Check for ease of opening and closing.
3   Open the sliding roof panel fully and release the screws (13) on the slide rails (Fig. 12.17).
4   Turn the adjuster screw (11) on both sides of the roof so that the front edge of the panel (when tested in the closed position) is 0.039 in (1.0 mm) below the level of the roof just ahead of it.
5   Tighten the slide rail screws.
6   Fully close the sliding panel and release the nut (51) on the lifting bracket (50). Now turn the wedge shim which is located under the lifting bracket until on testing the sliding roof in the fully closed position, the level of the panel is 0.039 in (1.0 mm) higher than the roof just to the rear of it (Fig. 12.18).
7   Tighten the fastening nut and refit the roof headlining.

21 Fascia panel - removal and refitting

1   Remove the steering wheel (Chapter 11).
2   Remove the centre console as described in Section 22 (Fig. 12.19).
3   Remove the interior rear view mirror and then extract the reveal mouldings from the edge of the windscreen and from the front pillars.
4   Remove the undercovers from the left and right-hand sides of the fascia panel.
5   Remove the instrument cluster as described in Chapter 10.
6   Disconnect the electrical leads from the panel switches.
7   Remove the knobs from the heater control levers.
8   Disconnect the air ducts from the heater housing (Fig. 12.20).
9   Remove the loudspeaker grille and insert the hand and disconnect the central air duct from the heater housing. Also detach the balljoint from the flap lever on the central air duct.
10 Prise the heater control lever escutcheon and then extract the two control lever assembly fixing screws which are exposed.
11 Disconnect the flexible duct which runs between the heater housing and the right-hand fascia air outlet.
12 Extract the fascia panel lower securing screws and then remove the three nuts from the top edge of the fascia panel. These nuts are located under the panel and are accessible by inserting the hand (i) through the loudspeaker aperture (ii) through the instrument cluster aperture (iii) reaching up under the fascia for the right-hand nut.
13 With the panel released, lift it slightly to disengage its locating pins, then raise it further on the passenger side and withdraw it from the car.
14 Refitting is a reversal of removal.

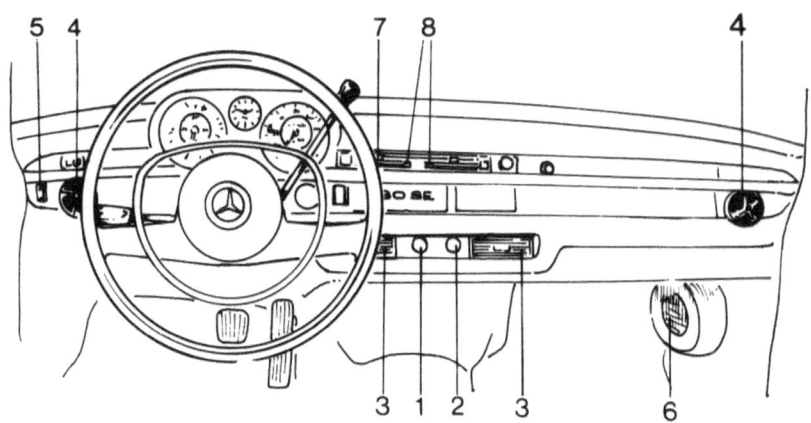

Fig. 12.19. Fascia panel (280 SE) (Sec. 21)

1 Temperature switch
2 Blower switch
3 Air outlet
4 Side air vents
5 Air vent lever
6 Blower for air conditioning system
7 Air volume control lever
8 Heater lever

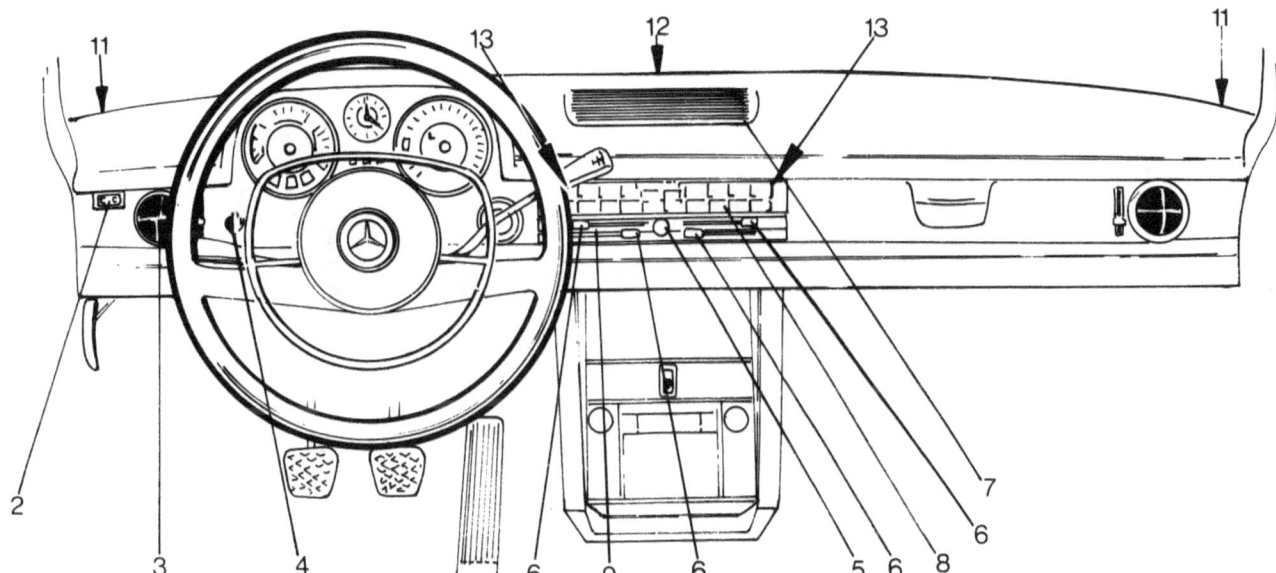

Fig. 12.20. Fascia panel (typical 230/250) (Sec. 21)

2 Rear interior light switch	5 Heater blower switch	9 Control lever escutcheon	12 Centre retaining nut
3 Left-hand side air vent	6 Heater control knobs	10 Right-hand air vent	13 Heater air outlet
4 Light switch	7 Loudspeaker grille	11 Fascia panel retaining nuts	retaining screw
	8 Heater air outlet		

22 Centre console - removal and refitting

1 To remove the upper section of the centre console, extract the screws from either side of it.
2 Pull the console upper section slightly forward so that the electrical connector plug can be disconnected and the console completely withdrawn.
3 To remove the lower section of the centre console, remove the floor mats from the front compartment.
4 Extract the securing screws from the console front brackets. If a bench type front seat is fitted, the seat will first have to be removed as described in Section 19.
5 Extract the screws from the rear end of the centre console and lift the console away.
6 Refitting is a reversal of removal.

23 Glove compartment - removal and refitting

1 Remove the glove compartment lid. To do this, extract the screws which attach the hinges to the lower side of the instrument panel.
2 Disconnect the lid check strap screw from the lid.
3 Remove the lid.
4 Using a small Allen key, press the pins from the securing clips (Figs. 12.21 and 12.22).
5 Lever out the clips (Fig. 12.23).

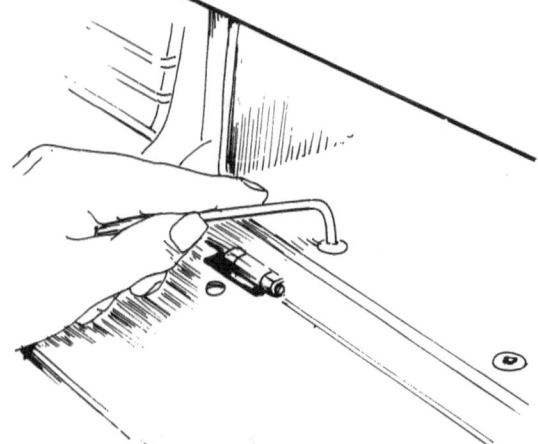

Fig. 12.21. Pressing out pins from glove compartment clip (Sec. 23)

6 Extract the two screws from the locking plate and remove the glove compartment.
7 Refitting is a reversal of removal but the pins should be just inserted in the clips before pushing the clips into position and then the pins should be pushed into the clips so that they are flush (Fig. 12.24).

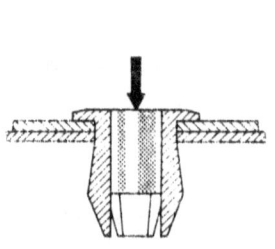

Fig. 12.22. Sectional view
of glove compartment
clip (installed) (Sec. 23)

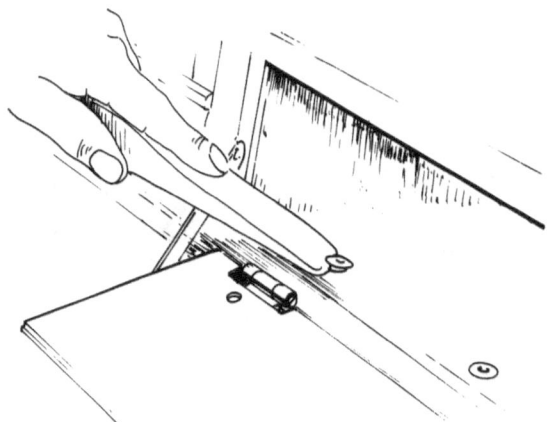

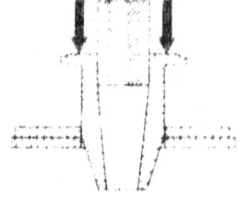

Fig. 12.24. Sectional view
of glove compartment
clip (about to be
installed) (Sec. 23)

Fig. 12.23. Prising out a glove compartment clip (Sec. 23)

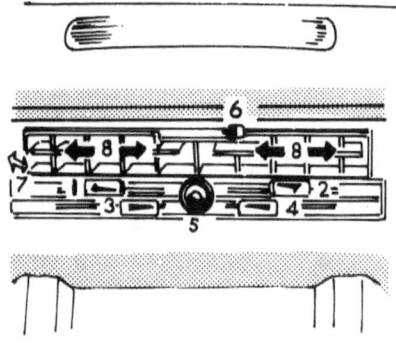

Fig. 12.25. Typical heater control panel (Sec. 24)

1   Demister for windscreen   5   Heater blower switch
2   Air to rear floor and driver   6   Extra cold air
3   Heater air vent (left)   7   Extra cold air
4   Heater right side   8   Extra cold air

Fig. 12.26. Heater air outlet for side window demisting (9) and
control lever (10) (Sec. 24)

24 Heater - description, removal and refitting

1   The heater operates from coolant supplied from the engine cooling system.
2   The heater hoses connect with the heater assembly at the engine compartment rear bulkhead.
3   The heater supplies fresh air at a temperature controlled by the setting of the control levers to the car interior and for demisting and defrosting purposes (Fig. 12.25).
4   A ball socket type fresh air outlet is also incorporated at either side of the fascia panel (Fig. 12.26).
5   The ram effect of the forward motion of the car is usually sufficient to provide the required volume of airflow but when the car is moving slowly or is stationary, a booster fan can be switched on.
6   Air is drawn into the heater assembly through an air intake grille just in front of the windscreen.
7   To remove the heater assembly, first drain the cooling system then disconnect the heater pipes at the engine compartment rear bulkhead.
8   Remove the centre console and fascia panel as described in earlier Sections of this Chapter.
9   Mark the position of the connecting control cables to the levers on the heater and disconnect them (Fig. 12.27).
10 Disconnect the leads from the heater blower motor.
11 Disconnect all ducting and then unbolt and remove the heater assembly.
12 Once removed, the heater matrix can be flushed with a cold water hose or reverse flushed if necessary to clear it. If the matrix is leaking, it is recommended that it is changed for a new or reconditioned unit rather than attempt to repair the old one.
13 A faulty blower motor may possibly be repaired if the brushes are worn or the commutator requires cleaning, otherwise renew it if more extensive repairs are required.

14 Refitting is a reversal of removal. Fill the cooling system on completion.

25 Air conditioning system - description

1   On cars so equipped, the air conditioning system supplies cooled and dehumidified recirculated air. The temperature is variable according to requirements by adjustable controls.
2   The major components of the system comprise a belt-driven compressor with electromagnetic clutch, a condenser and receiver and an evaportator (Fig. 12.28).
3   Due to the toxic nature of the refrigerant, no part of the air conditioning refrigeration circuit must be disconnected without first having the system discharged by your dealer or a refrigeration engineer.
4   The condenser and auxiliary electric fan are mounted just in front of the radiator and can normally be left in position while the radiator is removed from the engine compartment.
5   If the system is not to be disconnected then components such as the compressor can be unbolted and moved aside only as far as their flex-ible connecting hoses will allow. If repair or overhaul operations on adjacent components is still impeded, the system must be discharged before unscrewing any hose or pipe unions.
6   When reconnection of the system is complete, always have the circuit recharged professionally.

26 Air conditioning system - maintenance and precautions

1   Periodically check the security of hose and pipe unions and the condition of the flexible hoses.
2   Check the compressor drive belt tension. If it is not correct (½ in/ 12.7 mm deflection at centre point of longest run of the belt) adjust

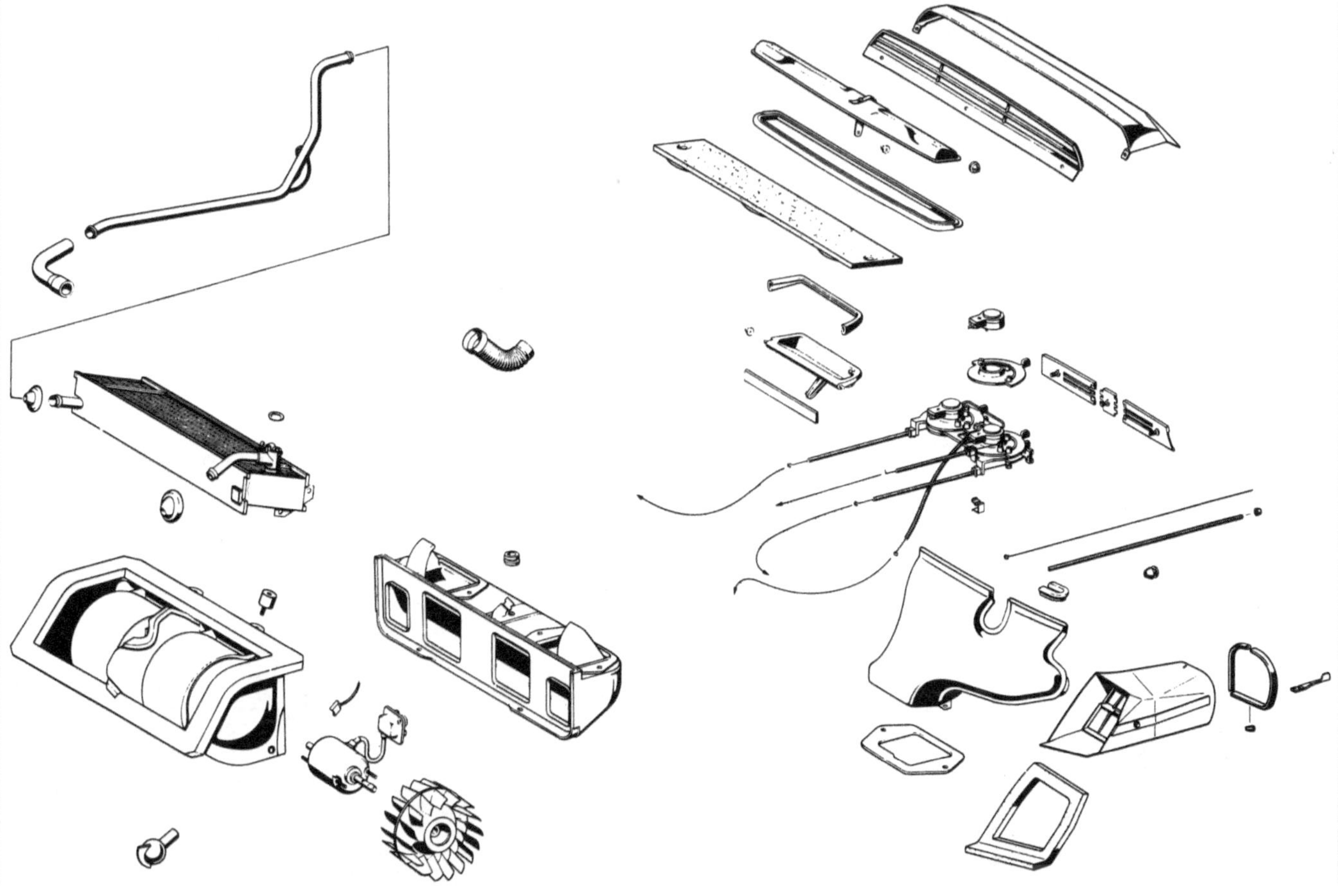

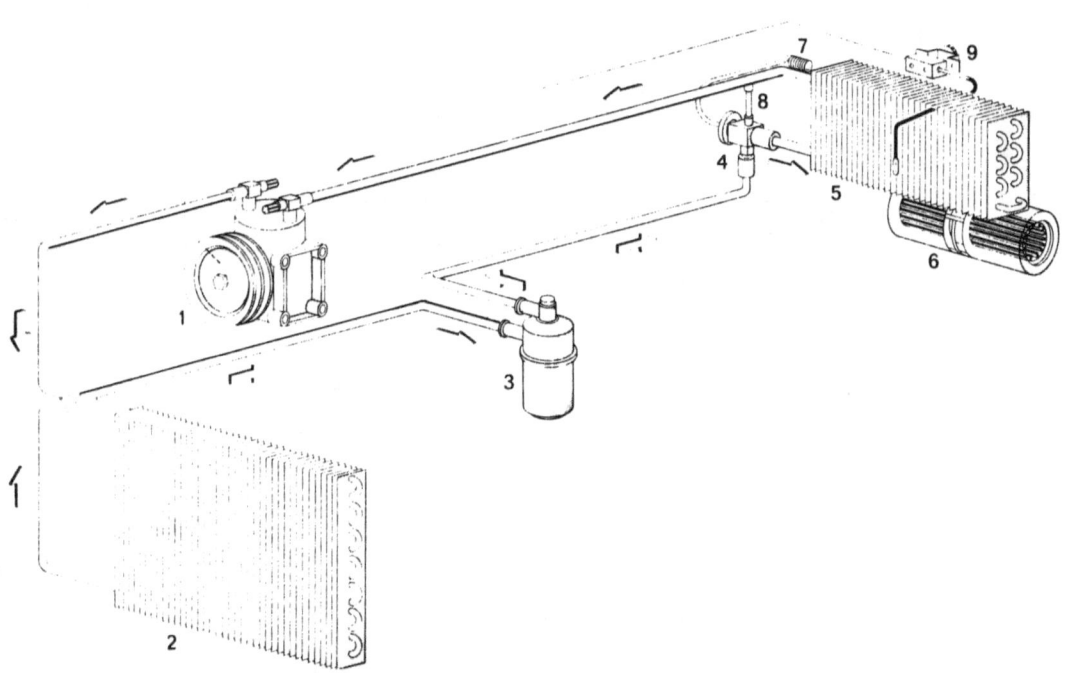

Fig. 12.27. Heater components (Sec. 24)

Fig. 12.28. Typical air conditioning layout (Sec. 25)

1	Compressor	3	Receiver with dehydrator	5	Evaporator	7	Capillary tube with
2	Condenser	4	Expansion valve	6	Blower		temperature sensor
						8	Compensating line
						9	Temperature switch

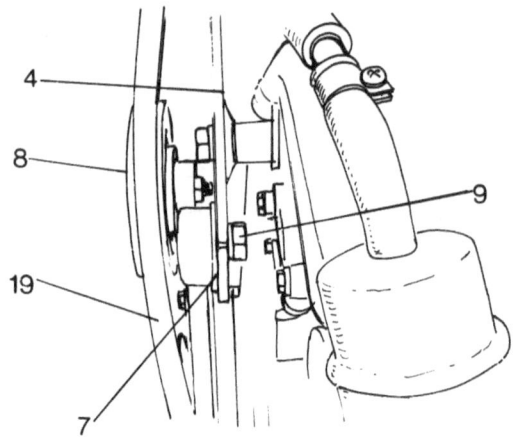

Fig. 12.29. Air conditioning system compressor and idler (Sec. 26)

4	Tensioning idler mounting bracket	8	Idler pulley
7	Washer	9	Bolt
		19	Drivebelt

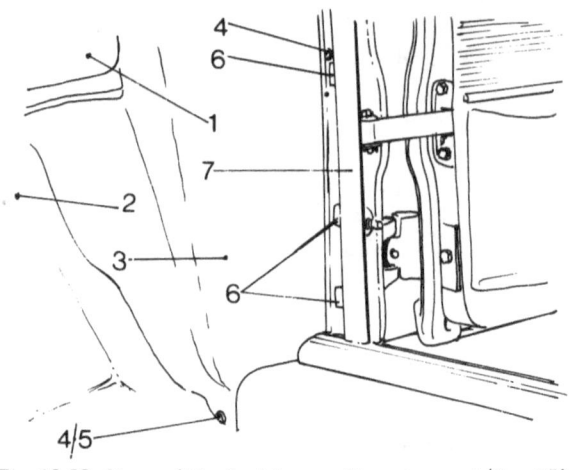

Fig. 12.32. Air conditioning blower with cover panel (Sec. 27)

1	Evaporator casing	5	Washer
2	Blower	6	Clip
3	Cover panel	7	Edge protective channel
4	Self-tapping screw		

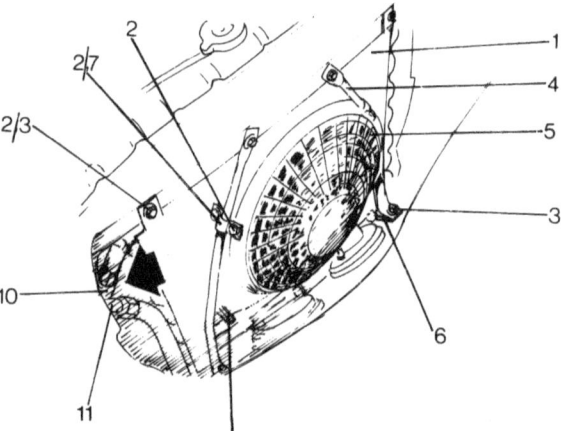

Fig. 12.30. Air conditioning condenser and electric fan (Sec. 27)

1	Condenser	8	Cable
2	Nut	10	Hose (compressor to condenser)
3	Self-tapping screw		
4	Strut	11	Hose (condenser to receiver dehydrator)
5	Fan and grille		
6	Bracket	12	Edge protective channel
7	Clip		

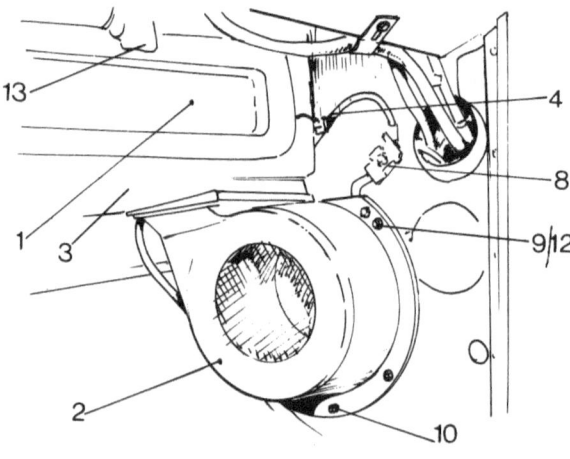

Fig. 12.33. Air conditioning blower fixing details (Sec. 27)

1	Evaporator	9	Self-tapping screw
2	Blower	10	Rubber washer
3	Condensation trap	12	Spacer
4	Spring	13	Coupling plug
8	Coupling plug		

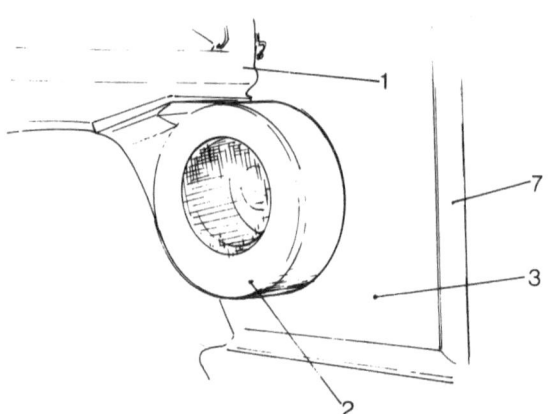

Fig. 12.31. Air conditioning blower without cover panel (Sec. 27)

1	Evaporator casing	3	Panel
2	Blower	7	Edge protective channel

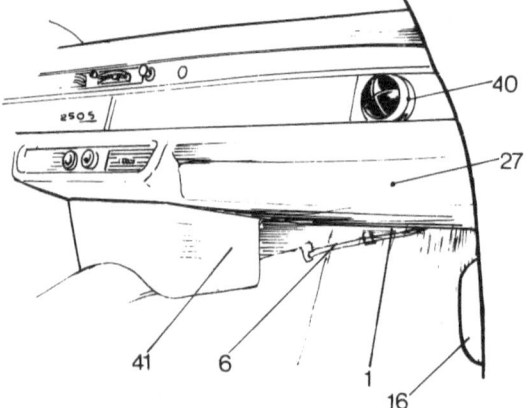

Fig. 12.34. Central tunnel box assembly on 250 S (Sec. 27)

1	Evaporator casing	27	Air duct
6	Hose	40	Side vent
16	Blower	41	Central box

it by moving the position of the idler pulley (Fig. 12.29).

3   During the winter months, run the air conditioning system for a few minutes once or twice per month. This will ensure continued lubrication of the compressor. Even in the winter during spells of wet or very humid weather, switching on the air conditioning system in addition to the heater will dehumidify the air inside the car and keep the windows from misting up.

4   In addition to the warning given in the preceding Section, never weld or solder near any part of the refrigeration circuit whether it has been discharged or not as an explosion may occur.

5   If refrigerant does come in contact with the skin, it should be treated in a similar way to frost bite.

27 Air conditioning system - removal and refitting of specified components

1   The following operations do not require disconnection of the refrigeration circuit and may be carried out by the home mechanic. **Note:** *Do not exceed the limits of the work described as it may be dangerous.*

2   *To remove the auxiliary fan* from the front of the condenser, first disconnect the battery and then disconnect the fan motor leads at the connector plug on the left-hand bodyframe side member within the engine compartment.

3   Release the wiring harness which runs to the fan motor so that the fan can then be unbolted (three clamps) from the support struts (Fig. 12.30).

4   *To remove the independently mounted blower* fitted to some models, disconnect the battery and move both front seats fully back.

5   Remove the edge protective strip (7) from the lower part of the front door pillar (Fig. 12.31).

6   Extract the side cover clips and the self-tapping screws and withdraw the cover panel (Fig. 12.32).

7   Extract the blower securing screws, lift the blower away and disconnect the leads at the coupling plug (Fig. 12.33).

8   *To remove the air duct,* first remove the blower as just described and then remove the central box assembly which joins the base of the

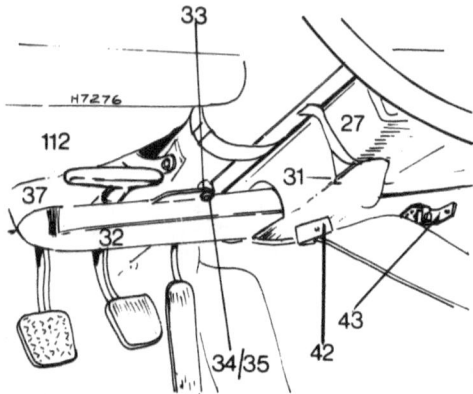

Fig. 12.35. Air conditioning air duct detail (Sec. 27)

27 *Air duct*	35 *Self-tapping screw*
31 *Air hose*	37 *Air hose*
32 *Connecting duct*	42 *Angle bracket*
33 *Spacer*	43 *Angle bracket*
34 *Washer*	112 *Cover*

fascia panel to the transmission tunnel (Fig. 12.34).

9   Remove the glove compartment as described in Section 23.

10 Remove the flexible strip from between the air duct and the evaporator case. Disconnect the multi-pin plug at the rear of the duct.

11 Remove the connecting duct (32) by extracting the sheet metal screw (35) and then disconnect the air hose which is located behind it (Fig. 12.35).

12 The air duct can now be removed from below the fascia panel after extracting its securing screws. The temperature sensor (7) which locates in the evaporator case will be withdrawn at the same time.

13 Refitting of all the components is a reversal of removal.

Safety first!

Professional motor mechanics are trained in safe working procedures. However enthusiastic you may be about getting on with the job in hand, do take the time to ensure that your safety is not put at risk. A moment's lack of attention can result in an accident, as can failure to observe certain elementary precautions.

There will always be new ways of having accidents, and the following points do not pretend to be a comprehensive list of all dangers; they are intended rather to make you aware of the risks and to encourage a safety-conscious approach to all work you carry out on your vehicle.

Essential DOs and DON'Ts

DON'T rely on a single jack when working underneath the vehicle. Always use reliable additional means of support, such as axle stands, securely placed under a part of the vehicle that you know will not give way.

DON'T attempt to loosen or tighten high-torque nuts (e.g. wheel hub nuts) while the vehicle is on a jack; it may be pulled off.

DON'T start the engine without first ascertaining that the transmission is in neutral (or 'Park' where applicable) and the parking brake applied.

DON'T suddenly remove the filler cap from a hot cooling system — cover it with a cloth and release the pressure gradually first, or you may get scalded by escaping coolant.

DON'T attempt to drain oil until you are sure it has cooled sufficiently to avoid scalding you.

DON'T grasp any part of the engine, exhaust or catalytic converter without first ascertaining that it is sufficiently cool to avoid burning you.

DON'T allow brake fluid or antifreeze to contact vehicle paintwork.

DON'T syphon toxic liquids such as fuel, brake fluid or antifreeze by mouth, or allow them to remain on your skin.

DON'T inhale dust — it may be injurious to health (see *Asbestos* below).

DON'T allow any spilt oil or grease to remain on the floor — wipe it up straight away, before someone slips on it.

DON'T use ill-fitting spanners or other tools which may slip and cause injury.

DON'T attempt to lift a heavy component which may be beyond your capability — get assistance.

DON'T rush to finish a job, or take unverified short cuts.

DON'T allow children or animals in or around an unattended vehicle.

DO wear eye protection when using power tools such as drill, sander, bench grinder etc, and when working under the vehicle.

DO use a barrier cream on your hands prior to undertaking dirty jobs — it will protect your skin from infection as well as making the dirt easier to remove afterwards; but make sure your hands aren't left slippery. Note that long-term contact with used engine oil can be a health hazard.

DO keep loose clothing (cuffs, tie etc) and long hair well out of the way of moving mechanical parts.

DO remove rings, wristwatch etc, before working on the vehicle — especially the electrical system.

DO ensure that any lifting tackle used has a safe working load rating adequate for the job.

DO keep your work area tidy — it is only too easy to fall over articles left lying around.

DO get someone to check periodically that all is well, when working alone on the vehicle.

DO carry out work in a logical sequence and check that everything is correctly assembled and tightened afterwards.

DO remember that your vehicle's safety affects that of yourself and others. If in doubt on any point, get specialist advice.

IF, in spite of following these precautions, you are unfortunate enough to injure yourself, seek medical attention as soon as possible.

Asbestos

Certain friction, insulating, sealing, and other products — such as brake linings, brake bands, clutch linings, torque converters, gaskets, etc — contain asbestos. *Extreme care must be taken to avoid inhalation of dust from such products since it is hazardous to health*. If in doubt, assume that they *do* contain asbestos.

Fire

Remember at all times that petrol (gasoline) is highly flammable. Never smoke, or have any kind of naked flame around, when working on the vehicle. But the risk does not end there — a spark caused by an electrical short-circuit, by two metal surfaces contacting each other, by careless use of tools, or even by static electricity built up in your body under certain conditions, can ignite petrol vapour, which in a confined space is highly explosive.

Always disconnect the battery earth (ground) terminal before working on any part of the fuel or electrical system, and never risk spilling fuel on to a hot engine or exhaust.

It is recommended that a fire extinguisher of a type suitable for fuel and electrical fires is kept handy in the garage or workplace at all times. Never try to extinguish a fuel or electrical fire with water.

Fumes

Certain fumes are highly toxic and can quickly cause unconsciousness and even death if inhaled to any extent. Petrol (gasoline) vapour comes into this category, as do the vapours from certain solvents such as trichloroethylene. Any draining or pouring of such volatile fluids should be done in a well ventilated area.

When using cleaning fluids and solvents, read the instructions carefully. Never use materials from unmarked containers — they may give off poisonous vapours.

Never run the engine of a motor vehicle in an enclosed space such as a garage. Exhaust fumes contain carbon monoxide which is extremely poisonous; if you need to run the engine, always do so in the open air or at least have the rear of the vehicle outside the workplace.

If you are fortunate enough to have the use of an inspection pit, never drain or pour petrol, and never run the engine, while the vehicle is standing over it; the fumes, being heavier than air, will concentrate in the pit with possibly lethal results.

The battery

Never cause a spark, or allow a naked light, near the vehicle's battery. It will normally be giving off a certain amount of hydrogen gas, which is highly explosive.

Always disconnect the battery earth (ground) terminal before working on the fuel or electrical systems.

If possible, loosen the filler plugs or cover when charging the battery from an external source. Do not charge at an excessive rate or the battery may burst.

Take care when topping up and when carrying the battery. The acid electrolyte, even when diluted, is very corrosive and should not be allowed to contact the eyes or skin.

If you ever need to prepare electrolyte yourself, always add the acid slowly to the water, and never the other way round. Protect against splashes by wearing rubber gloves and goggles.

When jump starting a car using a booster battery, for negative earth (ground) vehicles, connect the jump leads in the following sequence: First connect one jump lead between the positive (+) terminals of the two batteries. Then connect the other jump lead first to the negative (–) terminal of the booster battery, and then to a good earthing (ground) point on the vehicle to be started, at least 18 in (45 cm) from the battery if possible. Ensure that hands and jump leads are clear of any moving parts, and that the two vehicles do not touch. Disconnect the leads in the reverse order.

Mains electricity

When using an electric power tool, inspection light etc, which works from the mains, always ensure that the appliance is correctly connected to its plug and that, where necessary, it is properly earthed (grounded). Do not use such appliances in damp conditions and, again, beware of creating a spark or applying excessive heat in the vicinity of fuel or fuel vapour.

Ignition HT voltage

A severe electric shock can result from touching certain parts of the ignition system, such as the HT leads, when the engine is running or being cranked, particularly if components are damp or the insulation is defective. Where an electronic ignition system is fitted, the HT voltage is much higher and could prove fatal.

Conversion factors

Length (distance)

Inches (in)	X	25.4	= Millimetres (mm)	X	0.0394	= Inches (in)
Feet (ft)	X	0.305	= Metres (m)	X	3.281	= Feet (ft)
Miles	X	1.609	= Kilometres (km)	X	0.621	= Miles

Volume (capacity)

Cubic inches (cu in; in³)	X	16.387	= Cubic centimetres (cc; cm³)	X	0.061	= Cubic inches (cu in; in³)
Imperial pints (Imp pt)	X	0.568	= Litres (l)	X	1.76	= Imperial pints (Imp pt)
Imperial quarts (Imp qt)	X	1.137	= Litres (l)	X	0.88	= Imperial quarts (Imp qt)
Imperial quarts (Imp qt)	X	1.201	= US quarts (US qt)	X	0.833	= Imperial quarts (Imp qt)
US quarts (US qt)	X	0.946	= Litres (l)	X	1.057	= US quarts (US qt)
Imperial gallons (Imp gal)	X	4.546	= Litres (l)	X	0.22	= Imperial gallons (Imp gal)
Imperial gallons (Imp gal)	X	1.201	= US gallons (US gal)	X	0.833	= Imperial gallons (Imp gal)
US gallons (US gal)	X	3.785	= Litres (l)	X	0.264	= US gallons (US gal)

Mass (weight)

Ounces (oz)	X	28.35	= Grams (g)	X	0.035	= Ounces (oz)
Pounds (lb)	X	0.454	= Kilograms (kg)	X	2.205	= Pounds (lb)

Force

Ounces-force (ozf; oz)	X	0.278	= Newtons (N)	X	3.6	= Ounces-force (ozf; oz)
Pounds-force (lbf; lb)	X	4.448	= Newtons (N)	X	0.225	= Pounds-force (lbf; lb)
Newtons (N)	X	0.1	= Kilograms-force (kgf; kg)	X	9.81	= Newtons (N)

Pressure

Pounds-force per square inch (psi; lbf/in²; lb/in²)	X	0.070	= Kilograms-force per square centimetre (kgf/cm²; kg/cm²)	X	14.223	= Pounds-force per square inch (psi; lbf/in²; lb/in²)
Pounds-force per square inch (psi; lbf/in²; lb/in²)	X	0.068	= Atmospheres (atm)	X	14.696	= Pounds-force per square inch (psi; lbf/in²; lb/in²)
Pounds-force per square inch (psi; lbf/in²; lb/in²)	X	0.069	= Bars	X	14.5	= Pounds-force per square inch (psi; lbf/in²; lb/in²)
Pounds-force per square inch (psi; lbf/in²; lb/in²)	X	6.895	= Kilopascals (kPa)	X	0.145	= Pounds-force per square inch (psi; lbf/in²; lb/in²)
Kilopascals (kPa)	X	0.01	= Kilograms-force per square centimetre (kgf/cm²; kg/cm²)	X	98.1	= Kilopascals (kPa)
Millibar (mbar)	X	100	= Pascals (Pa)	X	0.01	= Millibar (mbar)
Millibar (mbar)	X	0.0145	= Pounds-force per square inch (psi; lbf/in², lb/in²)	X	68.947	= Millibar (mbar)
Millibar (mbar)	X	0.75	= Millimetres of mercury (mmHg)	X	1.333	= Millibar (mbar)
Millibar (mbar)	X	1.40	= Inches of water (inH₂O)	X	0.714	= Millibar (mbar)
Millimetres of mercury (mmHg)	X	1.868	= Inches of water (inH₂O)	X	0.535	= Millimetres of mercury (mmHg)
Inches of water (inH₂O)	X	27.68	= Pounds-force per square inch (psi, lbf/in², lb/in²)	X	0.036	= Inches of water (inH₂O)

Torque (moment of force)

Pounds-force inches (lbf in; lb in)	X	1.152	= Kilograms-force centimetre (kgf cm; kg cm)	X	0.868	= Pounds-force inches (lbf in; lb in)
Pounds-force inches (lbf in; lb in)	X	0.113	= Newton metres (Nm)	X	8.85	= Pounds-force inches (lbf in; lb in)
Pounds-force inches (lbf in; lb in)	X	0.083	= Pounds-force feet (lbf ft; lb ft)	X	12	= Pounds-force inches (lbf in; lb in)
Pounds-force feet (lbf ft; lb ft)	X	0.138	= Kilograms-force metres (kgf m; kg m)	X	7.233	= Pounds-force feet (lbf ft; lb ft)
Pounds-force feet (lbf ft; lb ft)	X	1.356	= Newton metres (Nm)	X	0.738	= Pounds-force feet (lbf ft; lb ft)
Newton metres (Nm)	X	0.102	= Kilograms-force metres (kgf m; kg m)	X	9.804	= Newton metres (Nm)

Power

Horsepower (hp)	X	745.7	= Watts (W)	X	0.0013	= Horsepower (hp)

Velocity (speed)

Miles per hour (miles/hr; mph)	X	1.609	= Kilometres per hour (km/hr; kph)	X	0.621	= Miles per hour (miles/hr; mph)

Fuel consumption*

Miles per gallon, Imperial (mpg)	X	0.354	= Kilometres per litre (km/l)	X	2.825	= Miles per gallon, Imperial (mpg)
Miles per gallon, US (mpg)	X	0.425	= Kilometres per litre (km/l)	X	2.352	= Miles per gallon, US (mpg)

Temperature

Degrees Fahrenheit = (°C x 1.8) + 32

Degrees Celsius (Degrees Centigrade; °C) = (°F - 32) x 0.56

*It is common practice to convert from miles per gallon (mpg) to litres/100 kilometres (l/100km), where mpg (Imperial) x l/100 km = 282 and mpg (US) x l/100 km = 235

Index

Zeitfracht Medien GmbH
Ferdinand-Jühlke-Straße 7
99095 Erfurt, Deutschland
produktsicherheit@kolibri360.de